Seventh Edition

W9-CCI-271

Language, Culture, and Communication

THE MEANING OF MESSAGES

Nancy Bonvillain
Bard College at Simon's Rock

PEARSON

Boston   Columbus   Indianapolis   New York   San Francisco   Upper Saddle River
Amsterdam   Cape   Town   Dubai   London   Madrid   Milan   Munich   Paris   Montréal   Toronto
Delhi   Mexico City   São Paulo   Sydney   Hong Kong   Seoul   Singapore   Taipei   Tokyo

Editorial Director: Craig Campanella
Editor in Chief: Ashley Dodge
Publisher: Nancy Roberts
Editorial Assistant: Molly White
Director of Marketing: Brandy Dawson
Executive Marketing Manager: Kelly May
Marketing Coordinator: Jessica Warren
Marketing Assistant: Paige Patunas
Production Manager: Meghan DeMaio
Creative Director: Jayne Conte
Cover Designer: Bruce Kenselaar
Cover Art: © Blend Images / Alamy
Project Coordination, Text Design, and Electronic Page Makeup: Kirubhagaran. P, Jouve India Pvt Ltd
Printer/Binder/Cover Printer: Courier Companies

Credits and acknowledgments borrowed from other sources and reproduced, with permission, in this textbook appear on the appropriate page within text.

Library of Congress Cataloging-in-Publication Data
Bonvillain, Nancy.
   Language, culture, and communication : the meaning of messages / Nancy Bonvillain.—7th ed.
     p. cm.
   Includes bibliographical references and index.
   ISBN 978-0-205-91764-8
   1. Language and culture.   2. Communication.   3. Linguistics.   I. Title.
   P35.B6 2013
   306.44—dc23

                                 2012041132

10 9 8 7 6 5 4 3 2 1—CRW—14 13

ISBN 10: 0-205-91764-X
ISBN 13: 978-0-205-91764-8

CONTENTS

PREFACE

This book presents a discussion of the multifaceted meanings and uses of language. It emphasizes the ways that language encapsulates speakers' meanings and intentions. It includes data from cultures and languages throughout the world in order to document both similarities and differences in human language.

NEW TO THIS EDITION

This seventh edition of *Language, Culture, and Communication* contains updated information throughout the chapters as well as several new sections and reworking of some material. New discussion of research in various topics are included, with particular attention to examples of language practices in African societies.

- Chapter 2 ("The Form of the Message"): streamlined to focus on significant examples of language structure.
- Chapter 6 ("Digital Communication and Signed Languages"): expanded discussion of online communication, especially of distance learning contexts.
- Chapter 10 ("Language and Gender"): new section on language and sexuality, including discursive practices of gay men and lesbians.
- Chapter 12 ("Bilingual Communities"): new introductory section on the cognitive benefits of bilingualism that explores cognitive research with bilingual infants and with elderly bilinguals. Also expanded discussions of language and development and of language revitalization strategies for endangered languages.

FORMAT OF THE BOOK

This book contains 13 chapters that together present surveys of the field of linguistic anthropology and the study of language and culture. In addition to discussing research that is basic to the discipline, it focuses on the analysis of discourses as central to communicative interactions, revealing how social relations are produced and continually reproduced through speech. The text also highlights the analysis of language ideologies, that is, the beliefs that people have about language structure itself, about language usage, and about appropriate norms for producing and evaluating speech. These concepts are introduced in Chapter 1 and then discussed throughout the book.

Chapter 2 presents some of the structural features of language that are basic to an understanding of what language is. Chapter 3 discusses current issues in linguistic relativity, cultural and cognitive categorization, and the uses of metaphor. The next two chapters (Chapters 4 and 5) describe situational aspects of communication, including structural and interactional features of conversation and the social meanings conveyed through speech encounters. Chapter 6 deals with digital communication, that is, telephones and the Internet in personal communication, chats, and online courses. It also contains material on signed languages, drawing upon data from several countries. Chapters 7 and 8 describe the processes of language acquisition, including the learning of structural properties of language and of communicative competence. Chapter 9 focuses on speakers' class and race as significant influences on speech style. In Chapter 10, we discuss the role of gender identities on one's choices of speaking. Chapter 11 focuses on language use, loyalty, and conflict in multilingual nations. Chapter 12 discusses multilingualism in communicative interactions, including both the micro level of individual choices and the national and international processes that affect local patterns of usage and meaning. The last chapter, Chapter 13, is devoted to analyzing inequalities of power in institutional encounters.

I express my thanks to Pearson's reviewers for their useful critique of the manuscript: Desire Baloubi, Shaw University; and Sean O'Neill, University of Oklahoma. I also thank my publisher, Nancy Roberts, for suggesting and encouraging this new edition. And I express my thanks to Dat Nguyen, a student at Bard College at Simon's Rock, for research help in locating sources. I also thank Jennifer Jacobson and Dan Vest of Ohlinger Publishing Services for an excellent and thorough job guiding the book's production.

Nancy Bonvillain

CHAPTER 1

Introduction

Language is an integral part of human behavior. It is the primary means of interaction between people. Speakers use language to convey their thoughts, feelings, intentions, and desires to others. Language links interlocutors in a dynamic, reflexive process. We learn about people through what they say and how they say it, we learn about ourselves through the ways that other people react to what we say, and we learn about our relationships with others through the give and take of communicative interactions.

Language is enriched by the different ways that people use it. These uses, and the meanings transmitted, are situational, social, and cultural. *Situational* meanings are conveyed through forms of language that occur or are excluded in various contexts. For example, in formal encounters, speakers pronounce sounds clearly, avoid slang or profanity, and employ elaborate grammatical constructions. *Social* meanings are signaled by linguistic alternatives chosen by different groups of people within a community. For example, women and men may pronounce sounds differently; workers in particular occupations employ special terminology or jargon; members of diverse social classes typically use more or less complex sentence patterns. Finally, *cultural* meanings are expressed both in the symbolic senses of words and by the ways that interlocutors evaluate communicative behavior.

When situational, social, and cultural factors are considered, the apparent variation in speaking actually becomes quite systematic. Consistent patterns of speech emerge in given situations, and consistent cultural norms are used to interpret communicative behavior.

Speaking is an action through which meaning is contextually created. Its complex functions are best studied ethnographically. An *ethnography of communication* (Hymes 1974) includes analysis of speech, situational contexts, and cultural norms used in evaluating talk. An ethnographic perspective that emphasizes the vital links between language and culture is important in the fields of linguistics, anthropology, and sociology. It enables linguists to appreciate the range of social and cultural meanings conveyed by words and grammatical constructions. It enables anthropologists and sociologists to appreciate the contribution that communication makes to all human activity. For social scientists to understand how people organize their lives, carry out work, practice religions, and the like, they need to be aware of how people talk to each other. Studying behavior within one's own or another culture is limited if it ignores a critical aspect of behavior—namely, speech—just as studying language is limited if it ignores the cultural contexts in which language is produced.

In subsequent chapters of this book, we will explore the many interconnections among language, culture, and communicative meaning. We will stress interactional, situational, and social functions of language as they take place and are actively created within cultural contexts. The notion of cultural models will be relevant to much of the ensuing discussion. A *cultural model* is a construction of reality that is created, shared, and transmitted by members of a group. It may not be explicitly stated by participants but it is, nevertheless, used to guide and evaluate behavior. For example, people in all cultures construct models expressing their views of the dimensions of the physical universe, the structure and functioning of their society, and proper ways for people to live and to treat each other. Because cultural models are shared and accepted, they are assumed by members to be natural, logical, necessary, and legitimate. As they become a background for behavior, they are not recognized as culturally constructed but rather are considered the natural order of life. According to Naomi Quinn and Dorothy Holland, "Largely tacit and unexamined, [cultural] models embed a view of 'what is' and 'what it means' that seems wholly natural—a matter of course. Alternative views are not even recognized, let alone considered" (1987:11). As we shall see, language and language use express, reinforce, and thus perpetuate underlying cultural models.

Although people within a given culture share many assumptions about the world, they are not a completely homogeneous group. People are differentiated on the basis of gender, age, and status in all societies. In addition, distinctions of class, race, and ethnicity are used to segment populations in most modern nations. All these factors contribute to diversity in communicative behavior and to disparities in evaluations given to the behavior of different groups of people. Interrelationships between social differentiation and communication are relevant to many topics pursued in subsequent chapters and will be discussed accordingly.

SPEECH COMMUNITIES

Talk takes place within a *speech community* consisting of people who, although heterogeneous, are united in numerous ways. Several researchers have taken pains to define such a community. Leonard Bloomfield described it as "a group of people who interact by means of speech" (1933:42). Bloomfield recognized that, in addition to speaking the same language, these people also agree about what is considered "proper" or "improper" uses of language (ibid.:155). Dell Hymes stressed the fact that members of a speech community are unified by norms about uses of language: "A speech community is defined as a community sharing knowledge of rules for the conduct and interpretation of speech. Such sharing comprises knowledge of at least one form of speech, and knowledge also of its patterns of use" (1974:51). And "a person who is a member of a speech community knows not only a language but also what to say...sharing of grammatical knowledge of a form of speech is not sufficient. There may be persons whose English I could grammatically identify, but whose messages escape me. I may be ignorant of what counts as a coherent sequence, request, statement requiring an answer, situation requiring a greeting, requisite or forbidden topic" (ibid.:49, 123).

In discussing speech communities, William Labov emphasized the social and evaluative norms shared by members: "A speech community cannot be conceived as a group of speakers who all use the same forms; it is best defined as a group who share the same norms in regard to language...who share a set of social attitudes toward language" (1972:158, 248). In Labov's view, norms are revealed by the ways that members of a community evaluate their own and others' speech.

Although the notion of speech community is useful in delineating a group of speakers, it is an abstraction in the sense that individuals do not interact with all other members. To focus on people who actually do interact, Lesley Milroy and James Milroy developed the concept of *speech network* (Milroy 1980; Milroy and Milroy 1978). People in a speech network have contact with each other on a regular basis, although the frequency of their interactions and the strength of their association vary. Thus, people in "dense networks" have daily, or at least frequent, contact. They are likely to be linked by more than one type of bond—that is, they may be related, live in the same neighborhood, and work together. In addition, all of their associates also know each other. People in "weak networks" have less regular contact and do not know all of each other's associates.

Dense networks exert pressure on members to conform because values are shared and individuals' behavior can be readily known. Because linguistic usage is one type of behavior that is monitored and regulated within dense networks, members tend to maintain speech norms with little variation (Milroy and Milroy 1992:13). In contrast, members of weak networks do not share values as consistently. And weak networks do not have mechanisms that can apply social sanction against nonconformists on an individual basis, although the society as a whole does exert pressures for conformity through the transmission of cultural models on both conscious and nonconscious levels.

The concept of speech network is useful because it focuses on actual speakers and explains the mechanisms of control that lead to establishing and maintaining group norms in small-scale, daily interactions. Speech is constantly, although nonconsciously, evaluated. Therefore, speakers are always vulnerable to the judgments of their peers.

Throughout this book, we frequently return to issues of language use and evaluation of talk within speech communities and networks because they reveal social and cultural beliefs about how society is structured and the ways that people are expected to act and interact.

Ethnolinguistics

Studies in language, culture, and communication are based on two different, but compatible, methodologies. One, an ethnographic or *ethnolinguistic* approach, employs anthropological techniques of gathering data from observations of people's daily lives and of attempting to understand behavior from the participants' point of view. Ethnolinguists try to extract communicative rules by observing the behaviors that do or do not occur in various contexts and the reactions of members of a community to each other's actions. They attempt to understand what one needs to know in order to function appropriately in a given culture—how to make requests, issue commands, and express opinions, for example.

Studying language use within speech communities from an ethnolinguistic approach includes analysis of contexts, norms of appropriateness, and knowledge of language and its uses. Analyses of these facets of communicative behavior reveal underlying cultural models and demonstrate the cognitive and conceptual bonds that unify people within their culture.

Ethnolinguists also use elicitation techniques for obtaining linguistic data. They work with individual native speakers to collect material dealing with specific categories of vocabulary or types of grammatical constructions.

Sociolinguistics

The second approach to studying communicative behavior is *sociolinguistic*. This method is concerned with discovering patterns of linguistic variation. Variation in language use is derived from differences in speech situations and from social distinctions within a community that are reflected in communicative performance. Although some speech differences are idiosyncratic, it is possible to study intracommunity variables by recording and analyzing the actual speech behavior of members of distinct sectors of a population.

A basic assumption in sociolinguistics is that two complementary processes operate in the dynamic connection between language and social factors. From one viewpoint, social differentiation among people is correlated with differences in their speech; from the other viewpoint, divergence in the way language is used is a gauge of social segmentation. Factors such as gender, age, class, region, race, ethnicity, and occupation frequently account for linguistic differences. Interrelationships between societal factors and language use are extremely complex for several reasons. First, sociolinguistic behavior is inherently variable; that is, each speaker uses the full range of options available in the community, such as alternatives of pronunciation, vocabulary, and sentence construction. However, options chosen in a particular instance of speech cannot be predicted. Sociolinguistic "rules" therefore are actually statements of probability rather than rules that can predict any single speech occurrence. Both individual and societal patterns are based on behavior exhibited over time and in diverse situations.

The second reason is that individuals are not isolates of sociological factors. A person is not simply female or male, child or adult, employer or worker. Rather, each person embodies an aggregate of factors, for example, a female adult worker with two children. Choices in speech style are motivated by many aspects of one's identity. Sociolinguistic studies consider the ways that specific attributes influence a speaker's selection in any given situation.

A third complication in sociolinguistic analysis is that of context itself. Components of speech contexts, such as setting, participants, topics, and goals, all influence speech. In some cultures, the styles of speech used in different contexts are sharply distinguished, whereas in others, linguistic styles are less differentiated. Even within a culture, some people are more sensitive than others to contextual cues and adjust their speech accordingly. Sensitivity to context may be related to social factors such as gender or class, or it may be related to an individual's participation in many different types of situations.

Because sociolinguistic patterns are discoverable on the basis of frequencies of usage, research methodologies emphasize interviews, experimental and situational observations, and quantitative analysis. Sociolinguists ideally collect large samples of ongoing communicative behavior and then try to isolate determining factors that result in linguistic variation.

Discourse

An additional, overarching approach to the study of language use centers on *discourse,* the connected stretches of speech that occur in informal as well as formal contexts. A focus on discourse allows for analyses of multiple interrelated layers of communication. Discourse analysis examines the speech that speakers produce and the complex arrays of meaning produced and interpreted from perspectives of form, content, and interactional dynamics. That is, we need to understand what speakers say, what they intend to mean, what they intend to do, and how their speech is interpreted by other participants in the conversation. We need to analyze the cultural contexts in which speech occurs, the norms of production and interpretation that give it meaning, and the ways that social processes affect what is done and what is not done in communicative interactions. A field referred to as critical discourse analysis adds to this study an emphasis on the sociopolitical relations of power that inform both the production and interpretation of discourse. Not all members of society and not all participants in a given interaction have equal rights to contribute or equal power to determine or influence specific features of the interaction.

Language Ideologies

Finally, we will consider topics that reflect anthropological and linguistic interest in *language ideologies*. These are ideologies, or beliefs, about language, about what constitutes a language, and about what is acceptable or appropriate language use. Every society has systems of beliefs about the world, including ideas about human beings, their abilities and rights, and the ways they interact with each other. These ideas are contextually created and serve specific social functions. As conditions change through historical processes, cultural beliefs change too—and so do the linguistic behaviors that reflect them.

Belief systems not only explain but also legitimate social orders and constructions of reality. Meaning is never divorced from the society that creates it. And once created, it becomes part of the consciousness of individuals. This consciousness is formed in a reflexive process, interacting with the view of reality that society constructs. This consciousness is formed in a reflexive process, interacting with the view of reality that society constructs. V.N. Volosinov believed that by the process of social interaction, organized groups create external and material signs that serve as a foundation for individual consciousness. Thus, consciousness can be defined as rooted in the sociological framework. The individual consciousness grows from and reflects a society's belief system as evidenced in cultural norms. (1973:12–13).

Belief systems, or ideologies, are transmitted through many social modes, such as religious rituals, moral and aesthetic values, political displays, and the like. And they are expressed in and through language. Words in themselves are neutral, but their use gives them social and symbolic content. Words and the beliefs they express form a coherent cultural system, or, as Volosinov stated, "a unity of the verbally constituted consciousness" (ibid.:15).

Linguists and anthropologists have increasingly focused on the ways that social power and control are reflected in language, language use, and language ideologies. Speech communities, whether small, homogeneous villages or large, heterogeneous state societies, develop ideologies about language and language use that are transmitted through communicative behavior and through the ways in which people talk about language and linguistic activities.

As Kathryn Woolard points out, "ideologies of language are not about language alone.... Through linkages [to identity, to aesthetics, to morality], they underpin not only linguistic form and use but also the very notion of the person and the social group, as well as such fundamental social institutions as religious ritual, child socialization, gender relations, the nation-state, schooling, and law" (1998:3). In various sections throughout the text, we will investigate the ways in which these notions of language ideology relate to cultural meanings and worldview; speakers' rights and obligations to co-participants; societal segmentation and issues of class, race, and gender; national language policies and attitudes; and institutional power and resistance.

Plan of the Book

We will review many studies of linguistic behavior that are based on a variety of methodological and analytic approaches. Each reveals a different aspect of the communicative process. Taken together, they allow us to understand the full range of interactional, social, and cultural meanings conveyed by talk.

Chapter 2 presents structural properties of language and nonverbal behavior, then analyses of cultural and social meanings, contexts, and uses of language. In Chapters 3 and 4, we focus on connections between language and cultural models. Rules of conversation and linguistic means for expressing politeness are discussed in Chapter 5. Chapter 6 discusses several specialized communicative practices, including those made possible by modern technologies (telephones and computers) and signing communication used by Deaf conversationalists. Topics related to acquisition of linguistic and communicative skills are treated in Chapters 7 and 8. The next two chapters present analyses of linguistic variation and societal segmentation: In Chapter 9 we discuss factors of class and race; in Chapter 10, gender differences in language and speech are considered, with data from numerous societies throughout the world. Chapters 11 and 12 present reviews of language and its functions in multilingual communities. Finally, in Chapter 13, we discuss the ways that talk is managed in several institutional settings.

The diversity of topics dealt with in this book is an indication of the breadth of the field of language, culture, and communication, and a demonstration of the importance of language in human behavior.

References

BLOOMFIELD, LEONARD. 1933. *Language*. New York: Holt, Rinehart & Winston.

HYMES, DELL. 1974. *Foundations of Socio-Linguistics*. Philadelphia: University of Pennsylvania Press.

LABOV, WILLIAM. 1972. *Sociolinguistic Patterns*. Philadelphia: University of Pennsylvania Press.

MILROY, LESLEY. 1980. *Language and Social Networks*. Oxford: Blackwell.

MILROY, LESLEY, AND JAMES MILROY. 1978. Belfast: Change and variation in an urban vernacular. In *Sociolinguistic Patterns in British English,* ed. P. Trudgill. London: Edward Arnold, pp. 19–36.

MILROY, LESLEY, AND JAMES MILROY. 1992. Social network and social class: Toward an integrated sociolinguistic model. *Language and Society* 21:1–26.

QUINN, NAOMI, AND DOROTHY HOLLAND. 1987. Culture and cognition. In *Cultural Models of Language and Thought,* ed. D. Holland and N. Quinn. New York: Cambridge University Press, pp. 3–40.

VOLOSINOV, VALENTIN NIKOLAEVICH. 1973 (1929). *Marxism and Philosophy of Language.* Cambridge, MA: Harvard University Press.

WOOLARD, KATHRYN. 1998. Language ideology as a field of inquiry. In *Language Ideologies: Practice and Theory,* ed. B. Schieffelin, K. Woolard, and P. Kroskrity. New York: Oxford University Press, pp. 3–47.

CHAPTER 2

The Form of the Message

Language is a communicative system consisting of formal units that are integrated through processes of combination. Components of sound, structure, and meaning are obviously interrelated and expressed simultaneously, but they can be separated for analytic purposes. In this chapter, we present descriptions of formal properties of language and introduce relevant concepts and terminology in the field of linguistics. We then discuss some aspects of nonverbal communication as they contribute to transmission of speakers' messages.

Structural linguistic topics are presented here as background for the following two chapters, which directly explore relationships among language, communication, and culture. Although the focus of this text is on cultural, social, and interactional functions of communication, it is important to understand what it is that people do when they speak.

PHONOLOGY: THE SOUNDS OF LANGUAGE

Phonology is the study of sound systems in language. It includes *phonetics,* the description of sounds occurring in a language, and *phonemics,* the analysis of the use of these sounds to differentiate meanings of words.

Phonetics

The first task of phonology is to describe how sounds are produced, or *articulated.* Human language is made possible by manipulation of the vocal apparatus, which consists of lungs, pharynx, larynx, glottis, vocal cords, nose, mouth, tongue, teeth, and lips (Figure 2.1).

Components of the vocal apparatus can be modified by speakers to produce sounds of different qualities. Several kinds of contrasts serve to distinguish sounds, and we discuss them in subsequent sections. (Note that examples given to illustrate linguistic structure are obtained from a number of sources, including Bonvillain 1973; Bonvillain n.d.; Cowan and Rakusan 1987; Finegan and Besnier 1989; Gleason 1955; Ladefoged 1982; and O'Grady, Dobrovolsky, and Aronoff 1989.)

FIGURE 2.1 The Vocal Apparatus. (Adapted from Wardhaugh 1977:33.)

I. Sounds are either voiced or voiceless, depending on activity of the vocal cords, a pair of small muscular bands in the throat. If the vocal cords are close together when air passes through, the cords vibrate and produce *voiced* sounds; if they are apart and stationary, resulting sounds are *voiceless.* Voiced/voiceless contrasts can be illustrated by *minimal pairs,* two words composed of sounds that are identical except for one feature of significant difference. The following list contains some voiceless/voiced consonant pairs in English (examples written in standard orthography):

Voiceless		*Voiced*	
p :	p̱it	f :	f̱an
	tap̱		grief̱
b :	ḇit	v :	̱van
	taḇ		grie̱ve
t :	ṯen	s :	s̱ap
	biṯ		hiss̱
d :	ḏen	z :	̱zap
	biḏ		hi̱s

All vowels in English are voiced. However, voiceless vowels occur in many other languages, including Japanese, Totonac (Mexico), and Chatino (Mexico). In Totonac, voiceless vowels always occur at the ends of words (voicelessness is indicated by a small circle [V̥] beneath a vowel):

/kuku̥/	"uncle"
/miki̥/	"snow"
/snapapḁ/	"white"

II. Sounds are either *oral* or *nasal*—the former produced by raising the velum to the back of the throat and expelling air only through the mouth (oral cavity), the latter by relaxing the velum and allowing air to pass through the nose. For instance, *m* and *n* are nasal consonants. All languages have some nasal consonants, and many have nasal vowels as well. The latter group includes French, Portuguese, Hindi (India), Tibetan, Yoruba (Nigeria), and Navajo (North America).

III. In addition to binary characteristics relevant for all sounds (voiced/voiceless, oral/nasal), each sound is produced by manipulating parts of the vocal apparatus. Figure 2.2 illustrates most consonants found in human language and classifies sounds according to two dimensions: place of articulation and manner of articulation. The first dimension, *place of articulation,* refers to where the sound is formed ("articulated") in the mouth; for example, *bilabial* sounds are formed with the help of two lips, and *apicoalveolar* sounds are made with the tip of the tongue (apico = apex) and the alveolar ridge. The second dimension, *manner of articulation,* refers to the degree of interference or modification made of the airstream as it passes through

Place of Articulation

Manner of Articulation		Bilabial	Labiodental	Apicodental	Apicoalveolar	Retroflex	Alveopalatal	Palatal	Dorsovelar	Uvular	Pharyngeal	Glottal
Stops												
Plain	vl.	p			t	ṭ	tʸ	k̯	k	q		ʔ
	vd.	b			d	ḍ̥	dʸ	g̯	g	G		
Aspirated	vl.	pʰ			tʰ				kʰ			
	vd.	bʰ			dʰ				gʰ			
Glottalized	vl.	p'			t'				k'			
Labialized	vl.	pᵂ			tᵂ				kᵂ			
	vd.	bᵂ			dᵂ				gᵂ			
Nasals	vl.	m̥			n̥		ñ̥		ŋ̊			
	vd.	m			n	ṇ	ñ		ŋ	N		
Affricates	vl.				c		č	ç				
	vd.						ǰ					
Fricatives	vl.	Φ	f	θ	s	ṣ	š		x		ħ	h
	vd.	β	v	ð	z		ž		ɣ		ʕ	
Liquids												
Laterals					l	ḷ	ł					
Central					r	ṛ						
Flaps					ř							
Trills					r̃					R		
Glides								y	w			

FIGURE 2.2   **Classification of Consonants.**

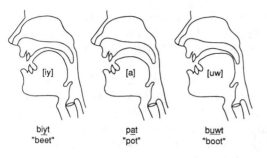

biyt   pat   buwt
"beet"   "pot"   "boot"

FIGURE 2.3 **Tongue Positions for Three English Vowels.** (Adapted from O'Grady et al. 1989:28.)

the oral cavity; for example, *stops* are produced by momentary complete blockage of air, and *fricatives* by narrowing the vocal channel and thus creating turbulence or friction in the airstream. Each difference in place and/or manner of articulation results in a difference in sound quality. Symbols in the chart in Figure 2.2 are written in phonetic transcription adapted from the International Phonetic Alphabet, a system of standardized notation applicable to all languages. (For a detailed discussion of phonetic notational systems, see Pullum and Ladusaw 1986.) In some cases, symbols in the chart correspond to English letters, but in others they do not. Note also, vd. = voiced, vl. = voiceless.

Vowels are produced with relatively greater openness of the vocal tract and relatively less interference with the airstream than is characteristic of consonants. Differences in vocalic quality are made by movement of the tongue and rounding or unrounding of the lips, resulting in changes in resonance. Additionally, voicing/unvoicing or oral/nasal contrasts are significant in many, but not all, languages. Figure 2.3 illustrates the physical manipulations involved in vowel production. Tongue positions are depicted for three English vowels: [iy], as in the word "b<u>ee</u>t," [a] as in "p<u>o</u>t," and [uw] as in "b<u>oo</u>t."

Common vocalic segments, represented by phonetic symbols, are classified in Figure 2.4 Dimensions of vowel production are positioned in the mouth from front to back and height from high to low. Lip-rounding (rd.) or unrounding (unrd.) is also significant.

Each language selects its phonetic inventory from among the possible human sounds. No language contains all sounds because requiring speakers to make too many or too fine articulatory distinctions is not feasible. Languages vary in the number of their sounds, ranging from as few as eight consonants in Hawaiian to as many as 96 in !Kung (spoken in Namibia). Some languages have only three vowels, although about half of all languages contain five vowels, and others, such as English and French, have more than a dozen. Following are representative English words illustrating some of the symbols in the consonant (Figure 2.2) and vowel (Figure 2.4) charts.

		Front		*Central*		*Back*	
		Unrd.	*Rd.*	*Unrd.*	*Rd.*	*Unrd.*	*Rd.*
High	Upper	i	ü	ɨ		w	u
	Lower	I	ʊ̈	ɨ			ʊ̈
Mid	Upper	e	ö	ə			o
	Lower	ɛ	æ	ʌ			ɔ
Low		æ		a		d	

FIGURE 2.4 **Classification of Vowels.**

1. *Oral stops* (complete closure or blockage of airstream):

Bilabial:	p :	pɪn	(pin)	Dorsovelar:	k :	kat	(cot)
	b :	bɪn	(bin)		g :	gat	(got)
Apicoalveolar:	t :	tɛfn	(ten)
	d :	dɛn	(den)

2. *Nasals* (velum is lowered to allow air to pass through the nose):

Bilabial: m: mʌt   (mutt)
Apicoalveolar: n :   nʌt   (nut)
Dorsovelar: ŋ :   hʌŋ   (hung)

3. *Affricates* (complete closure followed by narrow opening for air to pass through):

Palatal: č :   čɪn   (chin)
               ǰ :   ǰɪn   (gin)

4. *Fricatives* (narrowing and partial obstruction of vocal passage resulting in turbulence or friction):

Labiodental:	f :	fæn	(fan)	Palatal:	š :	šap	(shop)
	v :	væn	(van)		ž :	ruwž	(rouge)
Interdental:	θ :	θay	(thigh)	Glottal:	h :	hɛd	(head)
	ð :	ðay	(thy)
Apicoalveolar:	s :	sæp	(sap)
	z :	zæp	(zap)

5. *Liquids* (relatively less obstruction of airstream resulting in modification of air but no turbulence):

Lateral: l :   lɛd   (led)
Central: r :   rɛd   (red)

6. *Glides or semivowels* (little obstruction; intermediate between consonants and vowels):

Palatal: y :   yɛt   (yet)
Velar: w: wɛt   (wet)

7. *Vowels:* In English, some vowels are *monophthongs* produced in one place in the mouth; others are *diphthongs* or *glides,* involving movement of the sound from one position to another. Diphthongs are noted by a *y* or *w* following the vocalic symbol:

Front (all unrounded):   *Back (all rounded):*

iy :	biyt	(beet)		uw :	buwt	(boot)
ɪ :	bɪt	(bit)		ʊ :	bʊk	(book)
ey :	beyt	(bait)		ow :	bowt	(boat)
ɛ :	bɛt	(bet)		oy :	boy	(boy)
æ :	bæt	(bat)		ɔ :	bɔt	(bought)

Central (all unrounded):

ʌ :   bʌt   (but)
ay :   bayt (bite)
aw :   bawt (bout)

Phonemic Analysis

Every language organizes its phonetic inventory into a system of phonemes. A *phoneme* is a minimal unit of sound that functions to differentiate the meanings of words. It may have only one phonetic representation or it may contain two or more sounds, called *allophones,* that occur in predictable linguistic environments based on rules of allophonic patterning. For example, in English, each of the voiceless stops /p/, /t/, and /k/ has two allophones: One is *aspirated,* produced with a strong release of air; the other is *unaspirated.* Allophones for English voiceless stops are produced with aspiration when they occur at the beginning of a syllable, whereas they are unaspirated following /s/ in the same syllable. Aspirated and unaspirated allophones are illustrated in the following words:

/p/	aspirated:	[pʰɪn]	(pin)	/k/	aspirated:	[kʰɪn]	(kin)
	unaspirated:	[sp ⁼ ɪn]	(spin)		unaspirated:	[sk ⁼ ɪn]	(skin)
/t/	aspirated:	[tʰʌn]	(tun)				
	unaspirated:	[st ⁼ ʌn]	(stun)				

Native speakers of English are likely unaware of the fact that the *p*'s, *t*'s, and *k*'s in the words above have slightly different articulations. Speakers learn to make nonconscious allophonic distinctions in early stages of language acquisition. Because the rules are applied consistently thereafter, without exception, they become automatic patterns not requiring conscious thought.

Liquids and glides in English also have allophones that occur in accordance with conditioning rules. Voiceless counterparts of /l, r, w, y/ occur following voiceless stops /p, t, k/. In all other environments, liquids and glides are voiced. Compare the following contrasts (voicelessness is indicated by a small circle [C̥] beneath a consonant):

/r/	voiceless:	[tr̥ɪp]	(trip)
	voiced	[drɪp]	(drip)
/l/	voiceless:	[pl̥ayt]	(plight)
	voiced	[blayt]	(blight)
/w/	voiceless:	[tw̥ɪn]	(twin)
	voiced	[dwɪndl]	(dwindle)
/y/	voiceless:	[ky̥uwt]	(cute)
	voiced	[ar̥gyuw]	(argue)

Specific allophonic patterns are not universal but instead operate within each language according to its own rules. In some languages, the difference between aspirated and unaspirated stops is not allophonic, as in English, but phonemic. *Phonemic* contrasts signal differences in meanings of words. The following words in Korean constitute minimal pairs for plain /k/ and aspirated /kʰ/ and have separate meanings:

/keda/	"fold"
/kʰeda/	"dig out"

Similarly, Chinese contrasts /p/ and /pʰ/ (note that high pitch is indicated by a [V̄] above a vowel):

/pā/	"trumpet"	/pī/	"compare"
/pʰā/	"strip"	/pʰī/	"indigestion"

Finally, aspirated /tʰ/ and unaspirated /t/ are separate phonemes in Hindi (a language of India):

| /táli/ | "key" | /tórṇa/ | "pluck" |
| /tʰáli/ | "dish" | /tʰŌra/ | "little" |

Some sounds that are separate phonemes in English are allophones in other languages. As we have seen, English distinguishes between voiceless and voiced stops, p/b, t/d, k/g, but in the Mohawk language (spoken in New York State and in Ontario and Quebec, Canada), these sounds are allophones rather than phonemes. They occur in predictable environments. In Mohawk, voiceless stops are produced at the ends of words or preceding other consonants (except glides), whereas voiced stops occur preceding vowels or glides.

As evidence of the automatic, nonconscious nature of allophones, when Mohawk speakers use English, they frequently follow Mohawk allophonic patterns so that, for example, the English word "chicken" /cɪkɪn/ is pronounced [cɪgɪn]. This pronunciation is consistent with Mohawk rules requiring voiced stops preceding vowels. In fact, a "foreign accent" in any language consists, in part, of the application of native allophonic rules when speaking foreign languages.

Prosodic Features

In addition to consonants and vowels, sound systems use *prosodic,* or *suprasegmental,* features to alter and therefore contrast the sounds or rhythms of speech. Three prosodic features that often affect meaning are stress, pitch, and length.

STRESS.   The term *stress* or *accent* refers to the degree of emphasis placed on the syllables of words. In multisyllabic words, stress is not evenly distributed on all syllables. Rather, different syllables receive different degrees of stress. In some languages, stress rules are automatic. For example, in Czech, Finnish, and Hungarian, every word is accented on the first syllable; in French and Mayan (Mexico), words are accented on the final syllable; and in Polish, Swahili (Africa), and Samoan (Polynesia), the penultimate (next to last) syllable is always stressed. Stress placement in other languages is unpredictable; therefore, changes in stress can serve to differentiate meanings or functions of words. Note the following contrasts in some English words, where the difference in stress signals the difference between a noun and a verb: Nouns are stressed on the first syllable; verbs are stressed on the second syllable. (Note that slight differences in vowels when unstressed are not marked here.)

	Noun	*Verb*
present	prɛ́zɛnt	prɛzɛ́nt
object	ábjɛkt	abjɛ́kt
construct	kánstrʌkt	kanstrʌ́kt
implant	ímplænt	Implǽnt

PITCH.   *Pitch* or *tone* refers to the voice pitch accompanying a syllable's production. Variation in pitch results from changes in relative tension of the vocal cords. Pitch generally occurs with vowels, although some consonants (e.g., /l, r, m, n/) can function as syllable nuclei and carry tone. Many languages use pitch to distinguish meanings of words—for example, Asian languages, such as Chinese and Thai; African languages, including Yoruba, Zulu, and Luganda; Native American languages, such as Navajo (Southwest) and Sarcee (western Canada); and the European Latvian.

The following sets of Chinese words have separate meanings, each signaled by patterns of pitch:

high level:	mā	"mother"	fū	"skin"
high rising:	má	"hemp"	fú	"fortune"
low falling/rising:	mä	"horse"	fǔ	"axe"
falling:	mà	"scold"	fù	"woman"

In some languages, changes in tone function to signal different grammatical meanings. Compare verbs from Bini, a language spoken in Nigeria:

low pitch:	ìmà	"I show" (timeless)
high/low:	ímà	"I am showing" (continuous)
low/high:	ìmá	"I showed" (past)

Pitch is a feature of all languages on units of clauses and/or sentences. It is one of the components of intonation. In English, declarative statements and questions are characterized by contrastive pitch contours. Level or falling pitch appears at the ends of statements, whereas rising pitch terminates questions:

Statement: They came in.
Question: They came in?

LENGTH.   *Length* refers to continuation of a sound during its production. Some languages use length to differentiate meanings of words. Short and long vowel contrasts occur in Danish, Czech, Finnish, Arabic, Japanese, Korean, Cree (Canada), Yap (Pacific), and others. Here are some examples from Korean (long vowels are indicated by [V:] following a vowel):

/il/	"day"	/i:l/	"work"
/seda/	"to count"	/se:da/	"strong"
/pam/	"night"	/pa:m/	"chestnut"

Contrastive length for consonants is less common than for vowels, but it is found in several languages, including Turkish, Finnish, Hungarian, Luganda (Africa), and Arabic. In Luganda, the word /kúlà/ "grow up" contains a short /k/, whereas /kkúlà/ "treasure" has a long /k/.

Although not all languages use length to distinguish meanings, changes in the duration of sounds can serve as markers of emphasis or exaggeration. Lengthening a vowel in English can indicate exaggeration, as in "He is bi-i-i-ig!" This utterance implies greater size than would be conveyed by simply saying "he is big" (Lakoff and Johnson 1980:127–128).

MORPHOLOGY: THE STRUCTURE OF WORDS

Morphological Analysis

Morphology is the analysis of word structure. Words are composed of units of sound and meaning called *morphemes*. A word may contain one morpheme—{kæt} "cat"—or it may contain two or more morphemes:

cat-s   /kæt-s/

sing-ing   /sɪŋ-ɪŋ/

good-ness   /gʊd-nɛs/

un-happi-ly   /ʌn-hæpɪ-liy/

Morphemes can be added to words in cycles, producing longer and more complex sequences:

act

active (act-ive)

inactive (in-act-ive)

inactivity (in-act-iv-ity)

Some morphemes, called *roots* or *stems,* represent basic lexical or referential meanings of words (e.g., cat, sing, good, happy). They refer to or name objects, events, qualities, ideas, and the like. Other morphemes, called *affixes,* are attached to roots or stems (e.g., un-, -s, -ing, -ness, -ly). They express grammatical or relational meanings, such as number, tense, aspect, person, gender, or case. Affixes are of three varieties: *Prefixes* precede stems (*un-*happy), *suffixes* follow stems (happi-*ness*), and *infixes* appear within the stem itself.

The infix is absent from English but occurs elsewhere. Infixes are especially productive in Malayo-Polynesian languages, spoken in parts of Asia and the Pacific. Note the following words from Tagalog (a language of the Philippines):

1. stem: {-basa-} "read"

   with infix {-um-}:   /bumása   akó   naŋ   libró/
   read   ɪ   the   book
   "I read the book" (completed)

   with infix {-in-}:   /binása   aŋ   libró/
   was read   the book
   "the book was read"

2. stem: {-ka²(ɪn-} "eat"

   with infix {-um-}:   /kumá²(ɪn   akó/
   ate   I
   "I ate (it)"

   with infix {-in-}:   /kiná²ɪn   aŋ   mansánas/
   was eaten   the   apple
   "the apple was eaten"

In Bontoc, another Philippine language, an infix {-um-} denotes change from a noun or adjective into a verb of becoming:

| /fikas/ | "strong" | /fumikas/ | "he is becoming strong" |
| /fusul/ | "enemy" | /fumusul/ | "he is becoming an enemy" |

Morphemes may occur in one constant form, or they may have two or more shapes, called *allomorphs.* Allomorphs of each morpheme have the same meaning but vary in phonological form. They occur in predictable, conditioned environments. The English plural suffix {-s} has three allomorphs, accounted for by these rules:

{-s} →   /-iz/   following sibilants (/s, z, š, ž, č, ǰ/)
/-s/   following voiceless consonants (except sibilants)
/-z/   following voiced consonants (except sibilants); following all vowels

Application of this set of rules is illustrated in these examples:

klæs / klæsiz	(class / classes)
kæt / kæts	(cat / cats)
tʌb / tʌbz	(tub / tubs)
biy / biyz	(bee / bees)

The fit between form and meaning in construction of words is not always consistent. Irregularities or exceptions to morphological patterns sometimes occur. For instance, the rules given above for English plural marking account for the overwhelming majority of nouns, but unpredictable exceptions exist. Some plurals are signaled by vowel changes in stems:

/maws/mays	(mouse/mice)
fʊt/fiyt	(foot/feet)
wumɪn/wɪmɪn	(woman/women).

Three nouns take a restricted, nonproductive suffix, {-ɪn} (spelled "en"): child/children, ox/oxen, and the somewhat archaic brother/brethren. Additionally, a set of words having foreign sources retains the original plural markers—for example, datum/data (from Latin), phenomenon/phenomena (from Greek), cherub/cherubim (from Hebrew). A final class of nouns does not change at all, and therefore singular or plural meaning must be inferred entirely from context: deer, sheep, caribou.

Irregular forms must be learned for each individual case. Because it is much easier to learn a standard rule and apply it systematically than to memorize specific exceptions, languages limit the proliferation of irregularities. Preference for consistency accounts for children's tendency to overgeneralize morphological rules when acquiring language, as in mouse/mouses and foot/foots.

Morphological Typologies

Languages differ in their methods of creating words out of morphemes. Three types of languages will first be defined and then examples will be given.

Languages are often described as either isolating, agglutinating, or synthetic. *Isolating* languages (such as English or Chinese) allow comparatively few morphemes per word and have relatively simple methods of combining morphemes within words. *Agglutinating* languages have words containing many morphemes that are combined according to highly regular rules. *Synthetic* (or polysynthetic) languages also have words containing many morphemes, but their rules for combining morphemes may be quite complex. The form of morphemes is often altered considerably when morphemes are combined within words. A few examples from isolating, agglutinating, and polysynthetic languages are given below.

MANDARIN CHINESE (AN ISOLATING LANGUAGE).   In Mandarin Chinese, most words consist of only one morpheme. Lexical meanings are expressed by using separate words. Grammatical meanings are conveyed either by separate words, by the order of words within sentences, or simply by context.

1a.

wǒ	gāng	yào	gěi	ní	ná	yì	bēi	chá
I	just	want	for	you	bring	one	cup	tea

"I am about to bring you a cup of tea."

1b. Xià   yǔ
    down   rain
    "It was/is/will be raining."

SWAHILI (AN AGGLUTINATING LANGUAGE). Swahili permits many morphemes to combine within a word. These morphemes express different kinds of lexical and grammatical meanings. To translate a single Swahili word into English, several words and sentences are required. (Note abbreviations used in examples: PRES = present; PERF = perfect; FUT = future.)

2a. ni-na-pika "I hit" (I-PRES-hit)
     ni-na-wa-pika "I hit them" (I-PRES-them-hit)
     ni-li-wa-pika "I have hit them" (I-PERF-them-hit)
     ni-taka-pik-iwa "I will be hit" (I-FUT-hit-PAS)
     wu-taka-ni-pik-iz-wa "you(sg.) will cause me to be hit" (you-FUT-me-hit-CAUS-PAS)

MOHAWK (A POLYSYNTHETIC LANGUAGE). Mohawk combines many morphemes within a word. As in agglutinating languages such as Swahili, morphemes in Mohawk may express different kinds of lexical and grammatical meanings. However, rules for morpheme combination are not as regular as they are in agglutinating languages. When morphemes co-occur, they often undergo changes in their sounds. Also, a single morpheme may express multiple grammatical concepts so that the fit between form and function is more complex than in isolating or agglutinating languages.

Mohawk verbs can contain a large number of morphemes expressing various grammatical meanings. Prefixes denote person, number, negation, mood, location or direction, simultaneity of action, and so on. Several suffixes indicate different verbal aspects. A few illustrative examples follow. (Note that indicates a nasal vowel.)

3a. tehatkahtúnyũs
    "he looks all around"
    te - h- at -kaht- ũ   -nyũ   -s
    two-he-self-look-in state of-all around-doing
3b. yakon ʌ̃ yohlũkw hákye?
    "she's gathering up stones as she's coming along"
    yako-nʌ̃y-ohlũkw -   ʌ̃-   hákye   - ?
    she- stone-gather up-in state of-all the time-in state of

INUKTITUT (A POLYSYNTHETIC LANGUAGE OF ARCTIC CANADA). The following word in Inuktitut illustrates complexities of morpheme meaning and structure possible in polysynthetic languages:

4a. Qasuirrsarvigssarsingitluinarnarpuq
    "someone did not find a completely suitable resting place"
    qasu-irr-sar-vig-ssar-si-ngit-luinar-nar-puq

qasu	-irr	-sar	-vig	-ssar
tired	-not	-cause to be	-place	-for suitable
-si	-ngit	-luinar	-nar	-puq
-find	-not	-completely	-someone	-3rd sg. (he/she)

Grammatical Concepts

As mentioned, morphemes express lexical or grammatical meaning. Grammatical meaning includes concepts applying to nouns, verbs, modifiers, and so on. Some common concepts for nouns are case, number, and gender. *Case* refers to grammatical relationships between nouns (e.g., subject or object) or between nouns and verbs within larger constructional units such as clauses and sentences. Some languages, called *inflecting,* mark case with affixes. For instance, Russian nouns have inflectional suffixes to indicate cases. The paradigm below presents the inflection of a masculine noun {zavod-} "factory, plant." Feminine and neuter nouns select different sets of suffixes.

{zavod-} "factory"

Case	Singular	Plural
Nominative	zavod	zavod-i
Genitive	zavod-a	zavod-ov
Accusative	zavod	zavod-i
Dative	zavod-u	zavod-am
Locative	zavod-ɛ	zavod-ax
Instrumental	zavod-om	zavod-ami

Uses of these cases are illustrated in the following simple sentences:

Nominative:	zavód	bolšóy	
(subject)	factory	big	
	"the factory is big"		
Genitive:	to	kríša	zavód-a
(possessive)	this	roof	factory + genitive
	"this is the roof of the factory"		
Accusative:	aní	vídyeli	zavód
(direct object)	they	saw	factory (accusative)
	"they saw the factory"		
Dative:	aná	pisála	iván-u
(indirect object)	she	wrote	Ivan + dative
	"she wrote to Ivan"		
Locative:	na	zavód-ɛ	poryádok
	in	factory + locative	order
	"there is order in the factory"		
Instrumental:	ya	pisú	karandaš-óm
	I	write	pencil + instrumental
	"I write with a pencil"		

Different languages may express grammatical concepts in different ways. For instance, the notion of *number* has a variety of manifestations. Some languages do not indicate singular/ nonsingular differences; number is signaled solely by separate enumerators and/or by context. Sentences out of context, therefore, can be ambiguous. The noun in the following sentence, in Nancowry, a language spoken on the Nicobar Islands of India, can refer to one or many "pig(s)":

sák	nɔ́t	ʔin	ciʔʌy
Spear	pig	the	we
"We speared the pig(s)."			

In Indonesian, number is not overtly marked for subjects or objects. Whether nouns are definite (refer to a specific entity) or indefinite is likewise not marked. Therefore, nouns in sentences can have multiple possible senses:

harimau   makan   kambing
(the, a) tiger(s)   eat (ate, will eat)   (the, a) goat(s)

If context does not supply enough information to disambiguate meanings, separate specifying words can be added.

Other languages, such as English, make distinctions between singular and plural (two or more):

one cat; two or more cats.

And still other languages have markers for singular, dual (two), and plural (three or more), for example, Inuktitut (Arctic Canada):

/iglu/   "a house"
/iglu<u>k</u>/   "two houses"
/iglu<u>t</u>/   "three or more houses"

Many languages organize their nouns into separate classes that are overtly marked and differentiated. A common type of classification system is called *gender,* usually dividing nouns into masculine and feminine, or masculine, feminine, and neuter. European languages of the Romance, Slavic, and Germanic families (except English) have systems of this type. In Romance languages, gender is signaled by the form of definite articles that precede nouns, for example, French "*le* mur" (masculine, "the wall") and "*la* table" (feminine, "the table"). Slavic languages indicate gender by forms of case endings that are suffixed to nouns, for example, Russian /dom/"house" (masculine), /kriš<u>a</u>/ "roof" (feminine), /okn<u>o</u>/ "window" (neuter).

Some languages categorize nouns on the basis of complex kinds of meanings. For instance, Navajo noun classes are determined by shape and texture of objects. Navajo transitive verbs have different forms, depending on the class of noun that occurs as their direct objects according to the following characteristics, exemplified by the verb *to handle* (Young and Morgan 1987:251–263; note that nasal vowels are marked by a curve [V̨] beneath the vowel):

Class	*Examples*	*"handle"*
solid, roundish	nut, car, newborn baby	/ní'ą́/
slender, flexible	chain, feather, flower	/nílá/
slender, stiff	corn, fork, tree trunk	/nítą́/
flat, flexible	blanket, dollar bill, pillow	/níłtsooz/
mushy, viscous	mashed potatoes, mud, molasses	/nítłéé'/
noncompact	corn silk, shredded cabbage, moss	/níłjool/
in open vessel	broth, dirt in a shovel, stew	/ník ą́/
load, quantity	bundle, firewood, wool fleece	/níyį́/

Swati, a Bantu language of Africa, has more than a dozen noun classes based on various meanings, each class noted by a distinctive prefix on a noun. Some of these are given below:

Class	Prefix	Example	
persons	um(u)	um-fana	"boy"
body parts, fruit	li	li-dvolo	"knee"
instruments	s(i)	si-tja	"plate"
animals	in	in-ja	"dog"
abstract properties	bu	bu-bi	"evil"
locations	pha	pha-ndle	"outside"

Grammatical concepts relevant to verbs include *tense* (time of an event's occurrence), *aspect* (manner in which an event occurs), and *mode* (likelihood of an event's occurrence or speaker's attitude toward such an occurrence). Many languages also mark such categories as person, number, gender, and/or case relations by affixes within verbs. Examples from Mohawk illustrate some possibilities of mode and aspect (note: {-k-} "I"; {-yʌ́tho-} "plant"):

1. Modes (prefixes):
   a. Definite (definite present or past occurrence):
      {wa$^?$-}
      wa$^?$kyʌ́tho$^?$ "I planted (it)"
   b. Indefinite (probable or desired occurrence): {a-}
      wakũ$^?$ wéskwani$^?$ ne$^?$ akyʌ́tho$^?$
      I like   that   I plant
      "I like to plant"
   c. Future (definite occurrence in future): {ʌ́-}
      ʌ̃yʌ́tho$^?$ "I will plant"
2. Aspects (suffixes):
   a. Punctual (single event): {-$^?$}
      wa$^?$kyʌ́tho$^?$ "I planted (it)"
   b. Serial (repeated events): {-s}
      kyʌ́thos "I'm planting, I'm a planter"
   c. Perfective (states): {-ũ}
      kayʌ́thũ "it is planted"

SYNTAX: THE STRUCTURE OF SENTENCES

Most talk consists of multiword units, not single words spoken in isolation. Every language has rules of *syntax* that describe possibilities of co-occurrences and orders of constituents. Syntactic patterns are often used to express case relations between words. Note the following contrastive sentences in English:

The dog chased the cat.

The cat chased the dog.

Subject and direct object are indicated by the relative sequence of words. Subjects precede verbs; direct objects follow verbs. The words themselves do not undergo internal changes.

In the next two sentences, direct and indirect objects are also strictly ordered. Direct objects precede indirect ones when the preposition *to* is used; otherwise, indirect objects come first:

I sent a letter to Ruth.

I sent Ruth a letter.

A language like English, which signals case by word order, is fundamentally different from an inflecting language like Russian. In Russian, word order does not affect underlying case relations because, as we have seen, cases are marked by affixes attached to nouns. The following Russian sentences express the same referential meaning, translated as "the cat is chasing the dog" (*košk-a* = cat + nominative; *sobak-u* = dog + accusative; *presleduet* = is chasing):

Koška presleduet sobaku.

Sobaku presleduet koška.

Presleduet koška sobaku.

Presleduet sobaku koška.

Koška sobaku presleduet.

Sobaku koška presleduet.

Although changes in word order in inflecting languages do not alter the fundamental meaning of sentences, they signal other kinds of meanings or uses. They may mark focus or emphasis, relations between topics and comments, or stylistic preferences. In the set of Russian sentences, the first example best answers the question, "What is the cat chasing?" whereas the second is a response to "What is chasing the dog?" Each of the other sentences also has its contextual usage.

Isolating languages, such as Chinese, rely heavily on word order to convey grammatical meaning. In the following two sentences, word order alone expresses the difference between definite and indefinite nouns:

1a. huǒ   che   lái   le
     train   arrive   new-situation
     "The train has arrived."
1b. lái   huǒ   che   le
     arrive   train   new-situation
     "A train has arrived."

The next two sentences exemplify word orders that distinguish between active and passive meanings in Chinese:

2a. Zhū   laǒshī   pīyuè   lé   wǒdė   kaǒshì
     Zhu   professor mark   PAST   my   test
     "Professor Zhu marked my test."
2b. wǒdė   kaǒshì   beì   Zhū   laǒshī   pīyuè   lé
     my   test   by   Zhu   professor mark   PAST
     "My test was marked by Professor Zhu."

Most languages organize the three basic units of subject, object, and verb in one of three patterns. Unmarked sequences (simple, common constructions) are

Verb + Subject + Object (VSO)

Subject + Verb + Object (SVO)

Subject + Object + Verb (SOV)

The contrasting feature is essentially that of the relative placement of verbs either initially, medially, or finally. Subjects occur prior to objects. Only a few of the world's languages have unmarked word orders that place objects before subjects. Because subjects precede objects in the vast majority of languages, this pattern probably reflects human cognition. People perceive subjects as more salient than objects because they have the potential of agency, that is, an ability to initiate, control, direct, or affect actions and events. Objects are not doers but receivers of actions and are therefore less cognitively prominent. Significantly, cognitive prominence is reflected in linguistic structure.

Since Noam Chomsky revolutionized the field of linguistics with his publications in 1957 (*Syntactic Structures*) and 1965 (*Aspects of the Theory of Syntax*), linguists have attempted to describe and explain syntactic systems in terms of universal rather than language-specific patterns. A fundamental principle in linguistics is that words do not occur in sentences as random or isolated units but rather co-occur with others and form larger units called *phrases*. An important component of grammar is a set of "phrase structure" rules that describes the possible units internal to sentences. The most basic phrase structure rule states that a sentence (S) is composed of a Noun Phrase (NP) and a Verb Phrase (VP), shown by the notation:

S ⟶ NP   VP

Noun Phrases consist minimally of a Noun but may also contain Determiners (DET; e.g., *the, a, this, some*), Adjectival Phrases (ADJ), and/or Prepositional Phrases (PP). Verb Phrases must contain a Verb and may have Noun Phrases, Adverbial Phrases (ADV), and Prepositional Phrases as well. Sentences may also contain Auxiliaries (Aux; e.g., forms of *be, have, do, can, will*). As an example, the simple sentence "the dog chased the cat" can be described by the following rules:

S ⟶ NP	VP
NP ⟶ Det	Noun
VP ⟶ Verb	NP
NP ⟶ Det	Noun
[Det ⟶ the	
Noun ⟶ dog, cat	
Verb ⟶ chase(d)]	

Linguists also represent sentences by tree diagrams (or phrase markers) to depict constituents of phrases and their syntactic relations. The tree diagram for "the dog chased the cat" is

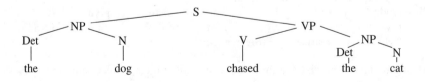

More complex sentences are represented by more elaborate tree diagrams, but they are all based on similar principles of grouping and relating constituents. Following is a tree diagram for the sentence "the good student will read a book in the library":

The purpose of grammar is to describe linguistic facts so that speakers can produce, or *generate,* rules accounting for all possible sentences in a particular language. A *generative grammar* should also block or constrain generation of impermissible constructions.

Chomsky introduced the distinction between *surface structure*—the surface appearance of sentences as they appear in actual speech—and *deep structure*—the underlying order of words as they are generated by basic phrase structure rules. Deep structure is transformed into surface structure by *transformations* that act on underlying components and, by stages, result in actual speech. The deep and surface structures of a sentence may be similar, as in the simple sentence illustrated earlier, "the dog chased the cat." However, many sentences require changes or transformations of the underlying order of components. For example, "Did the dog chase the cat?" is a question requiring several transformations. It begins with the string "INTERROGATIVE + the dog chase the cat." The interrogative transformation introduces an auxiliary "do," which is then shifted to the initial position. The auxiliary also attracts tense markers applicable to verbs, for example, "do" + Past "did."

Transformational rules can also account for nonoccurrence of segments in surface structure by *deletion,* eliminating redundancies that might otherwise be generated. When sentences are combined through a conjunction (*and*), redundant sequences are deleted:

The cats played in the yard and the dogs played in the yard.

The cats and dogs played in the yard.

Transformational grammar provides insights that enable linguists to decipher the origin of ambiguity in sentences. Consider one of Chomsky's well-known examples:

Flying planes can be dangerous.

This sentence is an ambiguous surface realization of two different deep structures, expressible as

1. To fly planes can be dangerous.
2. Planes—planes fly—can be dangerous.

The latter sentence exemplifies a process of *embedding,* which is common in English and many, but not all, languages. One sentence, "planes fly," is first embedded within the matrix "planes can be dangerous." It is then transformed into an adjective, "flying," eliminating the redundant "planes." Finally, "flying" is moved to its proper adjectival position preceding the head noun "planes." By these transformations, the deep structure "Planes—planes fly—can be dangerous" becomes the surface sentence "Flying planes can be dangerous." In the first underlying sentence, "To fly planes can be dangerous," the infinitive "to fly" is turned into a gerund, "flying," that remains in initial position preceding its direct object.

This example demonstrates the steps by which two different deep structures can eventually have the same surface appearance. Different transformational rules were applied, coincidentally achieving identical end results.

SEMANTICS: THE ANALYSIS OF MEANING

The function of language is to express the speaker's meaning. Although meaning is global in the sense that it is thought and experienced as a simultaneous whole, it must be encoded through language in segmented linear form. Morphemes have semantic content (meaning) and combine with one another to produce further meaning. And words are combined, in turn, in larger, multiword constructions, yielding additional meaning.

Semantic analysis, or the study of meaning, is complex because meaning includes many kinds of input. Words have referential senses, labeling persons, objects, events in the world, or in thought and imagination. Words also have cultural meanings, reflecting attitudes, values, or shared symbols (e.g., apple pie). Words and sentence constructions can have situational relevance, some used in formal contexts and others in informal situations (e.g., Please pass the salt/Gimme the salt). Words or constructions can be associated with different kinds of encounters; their selection, therefore, conveys interactional meaning (e.g., Dr. Jones/sweetheart). Finally, utterances can have affective meaning, indicating attitudes of speakers (e.g., John told me about his accomplishments/John boasted about his accomplishments). Here we will touch only briefly on some notions in semantic analysis; subsequent chapters will deal at length with issues of cultural, situational, and interactional meaning.

Influenced by advances in generative grammar, linguists attempt to discover universal principles in semantics. One approach is to specify meanings of words in terms of underlying semantic components. Once components are identified, linguists can determine the types of features that co-occur or are blocked from co-occurring. For instance, Chomsky's famous example of an unacceptable sentence, "Colorless green ideas sleep furiously," is rejected because of semantic inconsistencies even though it is grammatically well formed; that is, adjectives, noun, verb, and adverb are all placed in correct sequence. The problem with the sentence is that its semantic components cannot co-occur: "ideas" do not "sleep"; "ideas" are not "green"; something that is "green" cannot be "colorless." Syntactic rules alone do not provide adequate constraints; rather, restrictions are based on semantic rules, identifiable as co-occurrences of certain kinds of features with one another. Semantic features need not be overtly marked, but they are, nonetheless, significant attributes of words.

Nouns may contain the following *semantic features* (among others):

count/mass

specific/generic

potent/nonpotent

animate/inanimate

masculine/feminine

human/nonhuman

The presence of particular components can be discovered for any given noun. For example,

COW: count, potent, animate, feminine, nonhuman

Semantic features may be expressed through various linguistic forms. Some languages overtly mark features of animate/inanimate, mass/count, definite/indefinite, and so on, whereas others do not. In English, animate or inanimate nouns are not differentiated in their structure but are distinguished by their ability to occur as subjects of certain verbs. For example, only animate nouns can be subjects of *breathe, eat,* and *sleep.* The feature of count or mass is indicated by whether a noun can be enumerated or counted: "two cats" but not "two waters." And definite/indefinite distinctions are signaled by articles—for example, definite: "*the* cat came home"; indefinite: "*a* cat ran by the house."

Nouns in sentences fulfill several types of *semantic roles*. Common roles in transitive sentences can be illustrated for the sentence "Amy sent a letter from Paris to her friend in Iowa":

AGENT: performer of an action: Amy

PATIENT: entity affected by an action: a letter

SOURCE: starting point of an action: Paris

GOAL: end point of an action: her friend in Iowa

Other semantic roles occur as well:

experiencer (entity experiencing some action or state) *Ruth* likes classical music.

instrument (entity used to carry out an action) Ruth cut the cake with *a knife*.

Verbs can be semantically characterized as actions, processes, or states. Each type selects a particular semantic relation with accompanying nouns. Consider the following sentences (adapted from Chafe 1970:98):

ACTION: Jane ran.

PROCESS: The wood dried.

ACTION/PROCESS: Jane dried the wood.

STATE: The wood is dry.

Action verbs take *agent* nouns as grammatical subjects. In the first sentence, "Jane" acted as agent; she did something (she ran). By contrast, *process* verbs take *patient* subjects. In the second sentence, "the wood" did not do anything; rather, something happened to it. *Action/process* verbs (transitives), exemplified by the third sentence, require an agent subject who does something and a patient as object that has something done to it. Finally, *states,* as in the last example, select patient subjects. They depict inherent conditions or states of being. These distinctions among verbs reflect the importance of differentiating between surface grammatical subjects/objects and underlying semantic roles of agent/patient.

MANUAL LANGUAGE

The term *manual language* refers to a system of communication that employs hand movements to convey meanings. This complex system forms the basis of American Sign Language (ASL), used by Deaf people in the United States. ASL and sign languages developed and used by people in other countries are complete languages consisting of rules of phonology, morphology, and syntax. Several features of ASL are briefly described in this section.

Formation of Signs

ASL signs are composed of formally distinct features that co-occur in various combinations. Composition of signs, then, is analogous to phonological structure of oral languages. ASL employs four basic kinds of articulatory parameters in the production or articulation of signs: (1) hand configuration: how the hands are shaped; (2) place of articulation: where a sign is formed in relation to a signer's body; (3) movement of hands in space; and (4) orientation of hands in relation to the body.

HAND CONFIGURATION.   ASL signs are made from numerous configurations of the hand and fingers. These are illustrated in figure 2.5 demonstrating signs that are used in finger spelling the letters of the alphabet. Five of these are called "neutral" shapes: A, B, C, G, and O. Of all hand configurations, these five shapes occur most frequently in ASL words. These neutral shapes are employed in sign languages used in other countries as well. Friedman suggests that their frequency of occurrence in words and their universality are due to the fact that they are the "least complex shapes the hand can assume (in terms of muscular arrangement)" (ibid.:18).

FIGURE 2.5   **Hand Shapes in American Sign Language.** Learning American Sign Language by Tom Humphries and Carol Padden. Prentice Hall, 1992.

PLACE OF ARTICULATION.   Signs are formed, or articulated, in "signing space" consisting of the area in front of a signer's body extending from the top of the head to the waist and from side to side to the extent of arm's reach with elbow bent. The most frequently used space in ASL is located on or near a signer's face and head. Because ASL depends on visual channels for transmitting messages, it makes sense to produce signs in proximity to the face or head. In addition, Friedman suggests that this area is chosen for articulation because there are more distinct "landmarks" on the face than elsewhere on the body (ibid.:40). Such landmarks include forehead, eyes, nose, mouth, and cheeks.

Signs are formed with one or both hands. According to Klima and Bellugi, approximately 40 percent of ASL signs are made with only one hand, 35 percent with both hands moving actively, and 25 percent with one hand acting on the other as a base (1979:42). To produce signs, hands may assume different spatial relations to one another. For example, "establish" is formed with one hand above the other; "with" is made with one hand beside the other; "follow" is made with one hand behind the other; and "assistant" is formed with one hand below the other (ibid.:44).

MOVEMENT OF HANDS IN SPACE.   Hand movements in ASL are complex and involve the use of various dimensions of physical space and of changes in hand position. Direction of movement is a significant articulatory factor. Possibilities include movement along a vertical axis: upward, downward, and up and down; and movement along a horizontal-depth axis: rightward, leftward, and side to side.

Another distinctive feature is manner of movement of hands—that is, whether the hand moves in a straight, circular, or twisting path. Manner of hand movement also includes bending at the wrist or knuckles, wiggling the fingers, and opening or closing the hand.

ORIENTATION.   The last articulation parameter in ASL is the orientation of the palms of the hands in relation to a signer's body. Hands may be oriented with palms up or down, facing left or right, or directed toward or away from a signer. Orientation of the hands may involve contact between parts of the hand and other parts of a signer's body. Points of contact on the hand include fingertips, thumb tip, palm, side of the hand, and back of the hand.

Figure 2.6 illustrates the signs for 1st, 2nd, and 3rd persons. Note that plural persons are expressed by using the same hand configurations as singulars but they are accompanied by movement of the hands.

ASL Vocabulary and Grammar

The vocabulary of ASL consists of thousands of distinct signs. Most signs are completely arbitrary in the sense that their form has no inherent physical relationship to their meaning. Arbitrariness of form and meaning is therefore a linguistic trait shared by both oral and manual language. However, some ASL signs do have an "iconic" relationship to concepts that they express. That is, they convey meaning through direct physical depiction. For instance, reference to signer or addressee (i.e., "I," "you") is conveyed with the hand in a neutral shape pointed toward the signer's body ("I") or toward the addressee ("you"). Spatial relations of hands can also have iconic functions. Examples cited earlier demonstrate such a process; for example, "with" is signed with one hand beside the other, and "follow" is made with one hand behind the other.

Although a number of ASL signs do have some physical correspondence to their meanings, it is important to note that even these signs are conventionalized, stylized representations. Similar to words in oral language, they are "socially constituted" symbols (McNeill 1987:244).

I, me   **YOU**   **HE/SHE/IT, him/her**

WE, us   **THEY, them**   **YOU–plural**

FIGURE 2.6   ASL signs for first, second, and third persons. Learning American Sign Language by Tom Humphries and Carol Padden. Prentice Hall, 1992.

Words in ASL may contain a single sign or a combination of signs. Principles of word structure and word formation are thus similar in both ASL and oral language. Morphological rules apply in both systems. Just as morphemes can be combined in oral languages, manual morphemes can be combined within ASL words. Nouns, verbs, adjectives, and adverbs are often formed through compounding (Klima and Bellugi 1979:205):

Compound Sign	Meaning of Compound
sick + spread	epidemic
face + new	stranger
think + alike	to agree
wrong + happen	accidentally or by chance
sure + work	seriously

Grammatical meanings are conveyed in ASL through modifications of signs. For instance, to represent meanings of "intensification" of an activity (translated as "very," e.g., "very fast," "very slow"), a sign is produced with a short, rapid movement as contrasted with its neutral articulation.

EVERY-MORNING I GET-UP READ NEWSPAPER.
I get up every morning and read the newspaper.

FIGURE 2.7   I get up every morning and read the newspaper. Learning American Sign Language by Tom Humphries and Carol Padden. Prentice Hall, 1992.

The grammatical concept of tense is depicted in ASL as a vertical spatial plane running along the side of a signer's body. If a sign is made in this space immediately in front of a signer's body, present tense is conveyed; if a sign is made further in front, a verb has a future tense meaning; and if a sign is made in the side vertical area behind a signer's body, a verb is interpreted with reference to past tense (Friedman 1977:51–52).

Signs can be modified in their production in order to transmit aspectual meanings of verbs. Among the many aspects depicted in ASL are the following (ibid.:249, 257, 293–294):

1. *Continuative* (continuation of action or state)—"My brother's leg has pained him for a long time."
2. *Incessant* (frequent occurrence and duration of a trait or quality)—"My sister gets sick incessantly; it never stops."
3. *Predispositional* (tendency to have a trait or quality)—"That's his way; he is characteristically quiet."
4. *Allocative* (allocation or distribution of objects)—"He gave something to each of them."

In addition to articulatory and morphological rules, ASL contains syntactic rules as well. Most sentences follow Subject-Verb-Object (SVO) order, similar to the basic word order of oral English.

In sum, structural and functional characteristics of ASL demonstrate both its complexity and its adherence to standardized rules of lexical and grammatical formation. It is therefore a distinct, elaborate, and meaningful linguistic system that is used by a population in the United States estimated to number from 250,000 to 500,000 (Woodward 1991). Some communicative practices employed in signing by Deaf people will be further discussed in Chapter 6.

NONVERBAL COMMUNICATION

Nonverbal Actions

People convey meaning not only through spoken language, but also through gestures, facial expressions, body posture, and use of space. These aspects of communication are not merely embellishments to talk but are critical components of participants' messages. Nonverbal communication uses both kinesic and proxemic acts. The term *kinesics* refers to gesture, facial expression, eye contact, and body posture. *Proxemics* includes uses of touch and definitions of personal space.

Research in nonverbal behavior reveals both universal and culture-specific patterns. Because human bodies are constructed on a species-wide model, it follows that possible behavioral repertories are determined by the same fundamental constraints throughout the world. However, just as each language employs only some of the possible sounds that the human vocal apparatus can produce, each system of nonverbal communication selects only some possible human gestures, facial expressions, and so on. And nonverbal actions that "look the same" in different systems may have very different meanings because the meanings are culturally constructed and assigned. The meanings of gestures, expressions, and body postures do not flow from the actions themselves any more than the meanings of words flow from the particular sounds with which they are made.

Researchers in nonverbal communication generally emphasize one of two modes of interpretation. Although these interpretations are sometimes framed as opposites, they need not be incompatible. One school stresses biological/behaviorist features of nonverbal communication. Jolly (1972) states that certain gestures, body postures, and facial movements may have universal (or at least widespread) significance. In fact, some may be of primate origin. According to Jolly, humans and other primates appear to employ similar signals of enjoyment, distress, threat, and submissiveness. For example, observe the human and nonhuman primate expressions in the photographs in Figure 2.8 (Jolly 1972:156–165).

Some kinesic acts may have widespread functions. The two photographs in Figure 2.9 illustrate the eyebrow flash, which Eibl-Eibesfeldt describes as a "universal expressive pattern used during greeting at a distance" (1972:304ff). The set contains two pictures, one of a person with lowered eyebrows at the start of greeting and the second of the same person with maximally raised eyebrows.

Although biological/behaviorist interpretations of nonverbal actions are still common, more recently anthropologists studying nonverbal communication have argued that little, if any, actions are universal in their meaning. Instead, they stress the fact that all human behavior is culturally constructed and therefore all meaning is culturally assigned (Farnell 1995).

Some researchers have attempted to develop a system for notating gestures, expressions, and movements that could be used for comparative analyses of kinesic behavior in diverse cultures. Ray Birdwhistell's "kinesograms" (1970) are symbols specifying each possible expression, gesture, and change of position. Although planned as comparable to the International Phonetic Alphabet in its worldwide relevance, problems in its application arise because nonverbal communication is essentially fluid. Whereas sounds are segmentable into discrete units that can be represented by a single symbol (e.g., /p/, /o/), kinesic behavior is continual and multilayered. Therefore, it is difficult to decide where one segment ends and another begins. As an alternative, some researchers use notational systems based on *Labanotation,* a system originally introduced in the 1930s by Laban for recording dance movements (Farnell 1995).

Whatever the origin of nonverbal actions, all behaviors are learned as part of socialization within one's group. As Sheila Ramsey stated, "According to culturally prescribed codes, we use eye movement and contact to manage conversations and to regulate interactions; we follow rigid rules governing intra and inter personal touch, our bodies synchronously join in the rhythm of others in a group, and gestures modulate our speech. We must internalize all of this in order to become and remain fully functioning and socially appropriate members of any culture" (1979:111).

Some nonverbal actions have the status of so-called emblems: gestures that are understood by participants to express a specific meaning, often substituting for spoken words. Emblems in

FIGURE 2.8a Human Tense-Mouth Face. Heads of state are dominant males, often photographed making gestures of confident threat.

FIGURE 2.8b The Chimpanzee Open-Mouth Threat.

FIGURE 2.8c The human smile is a greeting gesture. It often grades into our laughter and play face. These girls enjoy playing together on a team, and it shows on their faces.

FIGURE 2.9a   French Eyebrow Flash. (From I. Eibl-Eibesfeldt, *Human Ethology*; New York: Aldine de Gruyter, 1989.)

FIGURE 2.9b   French Eyebrow Flash. (From I. Eibl-Eibesfeldt, *Human Ethology*; New York: Aldine de Gruyter, 1989.)

Euro-American societies include head nods to signal assent or shrugging the shoulders to convey uncertainty. Because emblems function within a particular interpretive system, similar actions may have different meanings in different cultures.

An important research question in nonverbal behavior concerns the relationship between gesture and spoken language. Young children's earliest gestures function for "pointing," that is, physically pointing to an object or person before they have acquired the words to label objects or events. This use of gesture compensates for the inability to express oneself verbally. However, after the age of 2 years, children's use of gesture changes dramatically, becoming more adultlike.

In an intriguing study of five bilingual children who were videotaped in conversations every 6 months from the age of 2 until 3½ years, Rachel Mayberry and Elena Nicoladis (2000) found that gestural development was correlated with the complexity of language structure acquired by the child. The children, all firstborn boys who were bilingual in English and French from birth, were observed in conversations separately with their mothers and fathers. Length of utterance was measured and plotted along with gestural use. One finding was that the frequency of gesture increased with age and linguistic development. That is, at 2 years of age, 81 percent of the children's gestures were made while speaking and by the age of 3½ years, 90 percent of gestures were made while speaking (Mayberry and Nicoladis 2000:194). This finding is consistent with adult patterns, in which adults use gestures in coordination with as much 80 percent to 90 percent of their words in spoken language (McNeill 1992).

Mayberry and Nicoladis further divided children's gestures into types, that is, iconic gestures, beats, and pointing, in order to understand their development and relationship to spoken language. In their definition, iconic gestures are actions that "depict some aspect of spatial images, actions, people, or objects," while beat gestures are "hand and arm movements that emphasize spoken words or mark the structure of discourse" (ibid.). The category term of *pointing* includes pointing, reaching, clapping, and waving. Analysis of the data revealed that, in the initial stages of language development, children's gestures were of the pointing type. However, once their utterances consisted of more than two words, they began to use iconic and beat gestures while speaking. An additional clue into the relationship between gesture type and spoken language was the fact that the children's use of gestures accompanying each of their two languages (English and French) was correlated with the complexity of their language abilities in each language (ibid.:195). For three of the children, their linguistic abilities developed unevenly in each of their two languages, and their use of gestures was consistent with the pattern expected by the preliminary analysis. For example, the two children whose English advanced more quickly than their French used iconic and beat gestures when speaking complex sentences in English but did not use these gestures when producing one-word or two-word utterances in French. The reverse pattern was shown by the child whose French advanced more quickly than his English, that is, he used iconic and beat gestures when speaking complex sentences in French but did not use these gestures when speaking simpler utterances in English. These findings make it clear that the use of gestures does not correlate with any specific language but rather with language development and complexity.

Cultural diversity in interpreting nonverbal behaviors can lead to misunderstandings between people of different ethnic backgrounds. Two sources of problems are possible. One is that an emblem or signal used by one participant is absent from the repertory of the other and therefore no meaning is conveyed. The other problem is more serious: Similar behaviors exist for both participants, but their meanings differ. When someone is confronted with an unfamiliar act, the person knows that she or he cannot properly decode the message intended by the sender, but when a nonverbal act is familiar in its form, an addressee decodes the message according to her or his own norms without realizing that the intended meaning is different. "Misled by the familiarity of the gesture, the decoder will most likely be unaware of this discrepancy, and consequently act according to [his/her] erroneous interpretation.... While a strange gesture will cause discommunication, the false decoding of familiar gestures will produce miscommunication, that is, misunderstanding" (Schneller 1988:155–156).

Misunderstanding between people of diverse ethnicities has been documented in Israel, a multicultural country (Schneller 1988). Even though most Israelis speak a common language (Hebrew), their diverse origins can lead to misinterpretation of nonverbal messages. In experimental situations, Israeli college students from 14 cultural backgrounds viewed videotaped gestures made by recent immigrants from Ethiopia. Of the 26 Ethiopian emblems demonstrated, 85 percent were recognized by the students. However, only 23 percent of the recognized gestures were correctly decoded; 7 percent were given "approximate" decodings; and 70 percent were misinterpreted (ibid.:158). Misunderstanding, then, is much more common than nonunderstanding.

Additional research by Raphael Schneller demonstrated that decoding of gestures commonly used by native-born Israelis was also problematic. In this experiment, Israelis from five different cultural backgrounds were shown videotapes of other Israelis and were asked to attribute meanings to the gestures. Of the nine emblems shown, 85 percent were recognized, although many were incorrectly decoded. Some emblems had high rates of correct decoding, but others had extremely low rates. Frequencies of misunderstanding varied, but some gestures were incorrectly interpreted by as much as 70 percent of respondents (ibid.:160–161).

These studies demonstrate the lack of congruence between participants' intended and received messages. When speech accompanies gestures, understanding is, of course, much more likely. Problems can still arise, though, because discrepancies between the perceived meanings of verbal and nonverbal behaviors result in confusion. And because nonverbal decoding usually occurs nonconsciously, people are unaware of the source of their confusion, potentially deepening their sense of discomfort with co-participants.

Although different meanings attributed to nonverbal behaviors by members of different groups can contribute to tense encounters, the discrepancies can also be a source of cultural humor. For example, the Western Apache of Arizona have developed joking routines that play, in part, on the intrusive, domineering communicative styles of Anglos (Basso 1979:48–55). In the routines, Apaches imitate numerous behaviors that Anglos typically perform but which Apaches consider offensive. These include making direct eye contact with or staring at interlocutors and touching another person while talking to them, stereotyped by the friendly backslap or hug.

Within a given society, patterns of nonverbal behavior often function to signal differences in status. Gestures, eye movements, smiles and other facial expressions, touching, and defining personal space are used in displays of status. In many cultures, a constellation of nonverbal behaviors appears to be consistent with high status or power. Dominant people tend to use broad gestures; look or even stare at others; maintain "serious," unsmiling faces; and inhabit wide areas of personal space. Conversely, in encounters between unequals, subordinates tend to use restricted, small gestures; avert their eyes when looked at; smile frequently; and allow their space to be encroached on even to the point of being touched. Whereas high-status people use expansive gestures and attempt to enlarge the appearance of their bodies, low-status individuals act to limit their body images by lowering their heads and keeping their legs together and their arms close to their bodies.

In some cultures, specific gestures can be used as general markers of politeness. Patterns of bowing in Japan and other Asian societies are intricate signs of respect and deference. Reciprocal bowing (both participants bow to the same degree) signals equality and mutual respect. Nonreciprocal bowing occurs when a subordinate person bows deeply to a high-status person who acknowledges the bow with a head-nod (Morsbach 1988:190–191).

Nonverbal behaviors reflecting gender inequalities have been well documented in Western societies, including the United States. The constellation of acts mentioned above associated with dominant people tends to be employed by men, whereas women tend to use nonverbal markers of subordination or deference. Women typically smile, avert their eyes when looked at, condense their bodies and gestures, avoid encroaching on others' space, and allow intrusions into their own space (Hall 1984; Henley 1977). Nancy Henley reported numerous studies demonstrating that in mixed-sex interactions, men touched women twice as often as women touched men; men initiated eye contact twice as often with women as women did with men; and women returned smiles of men nearly all the time, whereas men returned only two-thirds of the smiles given by women (1977:115, 164, 176).

The Meaning of Silence

Silence is an act of nonverbal communication that transmits many kinds of meaning dependent on cultural norms of interpretation. Our tendency to describe silence as an absence of speech reveals a particular cultural bias, implying that something is missing, but silence is a "something" with purpose and significance. Silent behavior occurs in all societies, although its message varies both between and within different groups. It conveys meaning, as does all communication, partly from the situational and interactional contexts of its use. Emphasizing the use of silence also focuses on the fact that silence does not simply exist but is actively created by participants.

In US society, silence is required of individuals or groups engaged in several types of encounters. Most tend to have a ceremonial or formalized character where participants have established roles and behave in predictable ways. Audiences at ceremonies, governmental or legal proceedings, and theatrical events are generally constrained from speech or are limited to making brief, formulaic responses.

Silence or paucity of speech also underscores status differences between individuals in various kinds of role relationships, including employer/employee, teacher/student, and adult/child. In encounters between unequals, disproportionate use of talk or silence reveals underlying social hierarchies. Individuals of higher status tend to talk more, whereas those of lower rank are expected to be silent or less talkative.

In US society, interpersonal silence is not well tolerated, especially between people who are not intimates. Greater familiarity leads to greater ability to refrain from speech. In the opinion of Ishii and Bruneau, "One function of speech is to avoid silence" (1988:313). This assessment offers a possible explanation of Western behaviors such as formulaic greetings, so-called small talk, and frequent question-and-answer sequences occurring in much daily conversation.

Because talk is preferred in interpersonal encounters, silence is often given negative interpretations. Feelings of hostility, disdain, disinterest, or anger are often attributed to silent participants. Despite these attitudes, silence is sometimes perceived as a mark of an individual's contemplative thought, respect for others, or desire to avoid conflict. Contrasting interpretations may be motivated by context or by social or personality attributes of participants.

In other cultures, as expected, the situational and interactional functions of silence are varied, although some cross-cultural similarities do pertain. Among the latter are status-related patterns in which people of lower status in unequal encounters tend to be more silent than those of higher rank.

Cultural variations, though, abound in terms of contexts where silence is expected. Among the Western Apache, silence is the norm in situations of ambiguity or uncertainty, such as encounters between strangers, initial courtship, times of mourning, greeting people who have been away for an extended period, and reactions to displays of anger (Basso 1972:71–79). These circumstances have a common theme: An individual is interacting with someone who is unpredictable either because he or she is unknown, not known well, has been absent for some time, or is in a distressed psychic state. When interacting with such people, one must take care to silently observe them in order to pick up clues and anticipate their likely behavior.

Among the Igbo of Nigeria, talk and social gregariousness are highly valued, so silence stands out as unusual behavior. It is mandated in ritual or ritualized situations. For example, 4 days after a death in a household, villagers show sympathy by entering the house, standing in silence in front of bereaved family members, sitting silently for a period, and again presenting themselves to mourners before departing (Nwoye 1985:186). Silence is the norm in other ritual endeavors, including sacrifices and consulting with ancestor spirits (ibid.:186–187). In these contexts, silence marks the occasion's solemnity and signals the detachment of participants from normal routines.

Silence is also employed by Igbos as a means of social control. Wrongdoers are punished by group silence. All villagers refuse to speak to the guilty party and his or her family (ibid.:188). In the traditional life of communal interdependence, wrongdoers quickly correct their behavior. Finally, Igbo silence can be used to demonstrate hostilities between people, especially by withholding greetings. Because greetings are signals of sociability, silence eloquently speaks of disharmony. Therefore, Igbos' refusal to greet or speak to each other is a clear manifestation of animosity or evil intentions. In Gregory Nwoye's words, "The Igbo expression of the English equivalent of 'not to be on speaking terms' is much more sinister than its English equivalent" (ibid.:190).

It is important, of course, to be wary of overgeneralizing or stereotyping any society. Not all members are equally silent or loquacious or adhere to interpretive norms to the same degree. Discrepancies always exist between ideals and actual practice.

Summary

In this chapter, we have explored various means by which co-participants produce messages. Transmission of meaning from one individual to another is the essence of communication. To accomplish this purpose, people employ verbal and nonverbal techniques.

Linguists have developed numerous descriptive and explanatory tools to analyze the structure of language. Talk is achieved through the interdependent components of sounds, words, sentences, and meanings. Although every language is unique, some universals can be specified, including the human range of phonetic inventories, recurring types of morphological and syntactic constructions, and underlying semantic relationships.

Nonverbal communication also consists of unique and common behaviors. Although some actions may occur in many societies, they are always given culturally specific interpretations. Silence is also a universal activity, but its display and contextual meaning are affected by cultural rules.

References

BASSO, KEITH. 1972. To give up on words: Silence in Western Apache culture. In *Language in Social Context,* ed. P. Giglioli. Harmondsworth, England: Penguin, pp. 67–86.

BASSO, KEITH. 1979. *Portraits of "The Whiteman."* New York: Cambridge University Press.

BIRDWHISTELL, RAY. 1970. *Kinesics and Context.* Philadelphia: University of Pennsylvania Press.

BONVILLAIN, NANCY. 1973. *A Grammar of Akwesasne Mohawk.* Mercury Series No. 8. Ottawa: National Museum of Canada.

BONVILLAIN, NANCY. n.d. Fieldnotes for Mohawk, Russian, Tagalog, Turkish.

CHAFE, WALLACE. 1970. *Meaning and the Structure of Language.* Chicago, IL: University of Chicago Press.

CHOMSKY, NOAM. 1957. *Syntactic Structures*. The Hague: Mouton.

CHOMSKY, NOAM. 1965. *Aspects of the Theory of Syntax*. Cambridge, MA: MIT Press.

COWAN, WILLIAM, AND JAKOMIRA RAKUSAN. 1987. *Source Book for Linguistics,* 2nd rev. ed. Philadelphia, PA: John Benjamins.

EIBL-EIBESFELDT, I. 1972. Similarities and differences between cultures in expressive movements. In *Nonverbal Communication,* ed. R. Hinde. New York: Cambridge University Press, pp. 297–312.

Eibl-Eibesfeldt, I. 1989. *Human Ethology;* New York: Aldine de Gruyter.

FARNELL, BRENDA. 1995. Movement and gesture. In *Encyclopedia of Cultural Anthropology,* ed. D. Levinson and M. Ember. New Haven, CT: Human Relations Area Files.

FINEGAN, EDWARD, AND NIKO BESNIER. 1989. *Language: Its Structure and Use*. New York: Harcourt Brace Jovanovich.

FRIEDMAN, LYNN. 1977. Formational properties of American Sign Language. In *On the Other Hand: New Perspectives on American Sign Language,* ed. L. Friedman. New York: Academic Press, pp. 13–56.

GLEASON, HENRY. 1955. *Workbook in Descriptive Linguistics*. New York: Holt, Rinehart & Winston.

HALL, JUDITH. 1984. *Nonverbal Sex Differences: Communication Accuracy and Expressive Style*. Baltimore, MD: Johns Hopkins University Press.

HENLEY, NANCY. 1977. *Body Politics: Power, Sex and Nonverbal Communication*. Englewood Cliffs, NJ: Prentice Hall.

ISHII, SATOSHI, AND TOM BRUNEAU. 1988. Silence and silences in cross-cultural perspective: Japan and the United States. In *Intercultural Communication,* ed. L. Samovar and R. Porter. Belmont, CA: Wadsworth, pp. 310–315.

JOLLY, ALISON. 1972. *The Evolution of Primate Behavior.* New York: Macmillan.

KLIMA, EDWARD, AND URSULA BELLUGI. 1979. *The Signs of Language*. Cambridge, MA: Harvard University Press.

LADEFOGED, PETER. 1982. *A Course in Phonetics,* 2nd ed. New York: Harcourt Brace Jovanovich.

LAKOFF, GEORGE, AND MARK JOHNSON. 1980. *Metaphors We Live By.* Chicago, IL: University of Chicago Press.

MAYBERRY, RACHEL, AND ELENA NICOLADIS. 2000. Gesture Reflects Language Development: Evidence from Bilingual Children. *Current Directions in Psychological Science* 9, no. 6:192–196.

MCNEILL, DAVID. 1987. *Psycholinguistics*. New York: Harper & Row.

MCNEILL, DAVID. 1992. *Hand and Mind*. Chicago, IL: University of Chicago Press.

MORSBACH, HELMUT. 1988. Nonverbal communication and hierarchical relationships: The case of bowing in Japan. In *Cross-cultural Perspectives in Nonverbal Communication,* ed. F. Poyatos. Lewiston, NY: CJ Hogrefe, pp. 189–199.

NWOYE, GREGORY. 1985. Eloquent silence among the Igbo of Nigeria. In *Perspectives on Silence,* ed. D. Tannen and M. Saville-Troike. Norwood, NJ: Ablex, pp. 185–191.

O'GRADY, WILLIAM, MICHAEL DOBROVOLSKY, AND MARK ARONOFF. 1989. *Contemporary Linguistics: An Introduction*. New York: St. Martin's Press.

PADDEN, CAROL, AND TOM HUMPHRIES. 1988. *Deaf in America, Voices from a Culture*. Cambridge, MA: Harvard University Press.

PULLUM, GEOFFREY, AND WILLIAM LADUSAW 1986. *Phonetic Symbol Guide*. Chicago, IL: University of Chicago Press.

RAMSEY, SHEILA. 1979. Nonverbal behavior: An intercultural perspective. In *Handbook of Intercultural Communication,* ed. M. Asante, E. Newmark, and C. Blake. Beverly Hills, CA: Sage, pp. 105–143.

SCHNELLER, RAPHAEL. 1988. The Israeli experience of cross-cultural misunderstanding: Insights and lessons. In *Cross-Cultural Perspectives in Nonverbal Communication,* ed. F. Poyatos. Lewiston, NY: CJ Hogrefe, pp. 153–171.

WARDHAUGH, RONALD. 1977. *Introduction to Linguistics*. New York: McGraw-Hill.

WOODWARD, JAMES. 1991. Personal communication. Gallaudet University, Washington, DC.

YOUNG, ROBERT, AND WILLIAM MORGAN. 1987. *The Navajo Language,* rev. ed. Albuquerque: University of New Mexico Press.

CHAPTER 3

Language and Cultural Meaning

Compare the different ways that speakers of English and Navajo express their intentions and actions (note that Navajo utterances have been translated into English):

ENGLISH SPEAKER:	I must go there.
NAVAJO SPEAKER:	It is only good that I shall go there.
ENGLISH SPEAKER:	I make the horse run.
NAVAJO SPEAKER:	The horse is running for me.

In their use of language, speakers of English and Navajo express different views of events and experiences. By framing their intentions or activities with contrasting words and grammatical forms, they show in these examples that they have different attitudes about people's rights and obligations. English speakers encode the rights of people to control other beings (people or animals) or to be controlled or compelled themselves. In contrast, Navajo speakers give all beings the ability to decide for themselves, without compulsion or control from others.

The words used by speakers of English and Navajo express and reflect attitudes about the world that come from their own cultures. Although the attitudes indicated by these examples are specific, the process of encoding values, ideas, and emotions in language is universal. Such culturally shared attitudes, or *cultural models,* are based on people's ideas about the world they live in. Cultural models are expressed in several ways, but language is key to their transmission. Cultural models may be stated overtly, as in proverbs such as "don't cry over spilt milk" or "the early bird catches the worm," and either direct one's actions and attitudes or provide explanations for one's circumstances. Beliefs about the world may also be conveyed through accepted myths and legends, whether religious or secular, for example, the depiction of events in the Garden of Eden or the story of George Washington and the cherry tree. Such accounts guide human thought and action by providing moral lessons for individual behavior. More frequently, however, cultural models are covertly expressed throughout daily communicative interaction. The words we use have many layers of meaning, including concrete reference to objects and events and metaphoric or symbolic significance. Taken together, cultural meanings and models form a unique worldview, providing both an understanding of the world as it is thought to be and a blueprint for the way one ought to behave. Reality is not absolute or abstract; it is lived within familiar contexts of social behavior and cultural meanings.

In this chapter, we examine some linguistic means used to express models of the physical and social universe, including ideas about the shape and content of the environment, the kinds of forces affecting humans, and the ways people are expected to interact. We also explore the role of language in helping to construct and reinforce these models. All these issues are addressed in the field of linguistic anthropology. Studies examine the *lexicon,* or vocabulary, of a language in order to discover direct and indirect meanings of words. Issues raised include the degree of specialization in various areas of meaning; the extent to which the words available in a language influence people's perceptions of their world; and the ways that words encode and transmit cultural, emotional, and symbolic meanings and values.

Researchers also seek to understand whether grammatical categories and structure affect speakers' worldviews. These studies raise questions concerning how the grammatical requirements of a language influence, direct, and reflect people's thought.

FOUNDATIONS OF LINGUISTIC ANTHROPOLOGY

The two most influential figures in the development of linguistic anthropology were Edward Sapir (1884–1939) and Benjamin Whorf (1897–1941). Both men studied the languages and cultures of several Native American peoples. Among Sapir's many interests and contributions to the field were his discussions of the importance of analyzing vocabulary in order to uncover the physical and social environment in which people live. According to Sapir, "The complete vocabulary of a language may indeed be looked upon as a complex inventory of all the ideas, interests and occupations that take up the attention of the community" (1949a:90–91). Sapir argued that all human experience is, to some extent, mediated through culture and language. Objects or forces in the physical environment become labeled in language only if they have cultural significance—that is, if they "take up the attention of the community." And once a language provides a word for an object or activity, that object or event becomes culturally significant. The relationship of vocabulary and cultural value is multidirectional. Speakers give names (words) to important entities and events in their physical and social worlds, and those entities and events, once named, become culturally and individually noticed and experienced. Through this interdependent process, unique cultural models are created and reinforced. As Sapir noted, "The worlds in which different societies live are distinct worlds, not merely the same world with different labels attached" (1949b:162).

Sapir's statement applies most concretely to geographic features, which can either be named in minute detail or glossed over with general terms. People name details when their survival depends directly on their environment. For example, in the language of Paiute people living in semidesert areas of Arizona, Utah, and Nevada, among the geographic terms translated by Sapir are the following: "divide, ledge, sand flat, semicircular valley, circular valley or hollow, spot of level ground in mountains surrounded by ridges, plain valley surrounded by mountains, plain, desert, knoll, plateau, canyon without water, canyon with creek, wash or gutter, gulch, slope of mountain or canyon wall receiving sunlight, shaded slope of mountain or canyon wall, rolling country intersected by several small hill-ridges" (1949a:91). The English language is able to express these numerous topographical features in a descriptive way, as shown by Sapir's translations, but it lacks separate words unique to each. The Paiute language labels each feature with a separate name and thereby gives it distinctive value. A motivating force behind the strategies of both English and Paiute is the relative interest and importance that speakers attribute to environmental conditions.

Vocabularies in different languages can therefore be compared and conclusions can be drawn about cultural attitudes from the degree of specialization within sectors of vocabulary.

One caution is worth noting concerning relationships between cultural interest and elaboration of vocabulary. Because cultures often change more rapidly than do languages, a "linguistic lag" can account for the fact that words or contrasts may reflect previous rather than current cultural interests. In time, as linguistic change catches up with cultural change, such words are likely to shift in meaning or to disappear.

Benjamin Whorf, who had been a student of Sapir, investigated whether grammatical structures provide frameworks for orienting speakers' thoughts and behaviors. He believed that the influence of language can be seen both through vocabulary and through more complex grammatical relations. For example, while Whorf was working for a fire insurance company, he noticed that fires were often caused by a person's inappropriate behavior motivated by labels given to objects. He found that workers occasionally threw matches and cigarette stubs into "empty" gasoline drums even though the drums contained combustible vapors and invisible traces of gasoline. Whorf concluded that the men's behavior resulted from their misinterpretation of the word "empty," which usually refers to "null and void, negative, inert" (1956b:135).

Whorf also wrote extensive analyses of the language spoken by Hopi people in Arizona, focusing on its distinctive underlying grammatical categories. One important issue raised through this research is the role that grammar plays in influencing the kinds of relations that speakers perceive in their world. In Hopi, there are three words translated as "that" in English. Each Hopi word signals a different relationship between clauses in a sentence (1956a:85). Compare the following:

1. I see that it is red.
2. I see that it is new.
3a. I hear that it is red.
3b. I hear that it is new.

In the first sentence, a speaker makes deductions based on direct sensory (in this case, visual) awareness. In the second sentence, a speaker makes inferences about "newness" based on evaluations of data (possibly including that "it" is shiny, clean, etc.). In sentences 3a and 3b, a speaker repeats or reports a fact provided by someone else, not directly experienced by the speaker herself. Comparing Hopi forms with English, we can conclude that because Hopis must choose among the various words, they are directed by grammatical requirements of their language to notice underlying causes of their knowledge of things (through direct senses, through inference, or through reported facts), whereas speakers of English need not pay attention to such differences. This does not mean that English speakers cannot become aware of different sources of knowledge; it simply means that they are not habitually led to making such distinctions.

In a comparison of Hopi and a language like English (which Whorf categorized as Standard Average European [SAE] to emphasize that European languages share basic grammatical characteristics), Whorf concluded that Hopi and English have different ways of conceptualizing time, number, and duration (1956b). He felt that these concepts are fundamental in creating a culture's metaphysics or view of the universe. According to Whorf, the Hopi language emphasizes continuity, cyclicity, and intensity in events, whereas SAE emphasizes the boundedness and objectification of entities. For example, English uses nouns to refer to phases in a cycle of time, such as "summer" or "morning." Hopi, though, treats phases as continuing events (or "eventings"). Words like "morning" are translated into Hopi as kinds of adverbs such as "while morning-phase is occurring" (ibid.:142–143). Contrasting the verb systems of English and Hopi, Whorf noted that English tenses divide time into three distinct units of past, present, and future, whereas Hopi verbs do not indicate the time of an event as such but instead focus on the manner or duration of an event. Whorf concluded that "concepts of 'time' and 'matter' are not given in substantially the same form by experience to all [people] but depend upon the nature of the language or languages through the use of which they have been developed" (ibid.:158).

The opinions of Sapir and Whorf on relationships among language, thought, and behavior have been the subject of research and debate. Several key variations of their ideas are advocated differently in various writings. One version is that some elements of language, for example, in vocabulary or grammatical systems, influence speakers' perceptions and can affect their attitudes and behavior. Another version suggests that language is ultimately directive in this process. The difference between the two versions seems to be the degree of control that language exerts. In fact, both Sapir and Whorf wavered in their statements on the issue of causal or directional relationship between language and thought. To quote Sapir,

> Human beings do not live in the objective world alone, nor alone in the world of social activity as ordinarily understood, but are very much at the mercy of the particular language which has become the medium of expression for their society. The fact of the matter is that the "real world" is to a large extent unconsciously built up on the language habits of the group. (1949b:162)

However, in the very next paragraph, Sapir stated that "we see and hear and otherwise experience very largely as we do because the language habits of our community predispose certain choices of interpretation" (ibid.). There is a difference between being "at the mercy" of one's language and being predisposed to "choices of interpretation," the latter implying options of thought.

In answer to one of Whorf's own questions about whether there are "traceable affinities between (a) cultural and behavioral norms and (b) large-scale linguistic patterns," Whorf answered that "there are connections but not correlations or diagnostic correspondences" (1956b:159). Discussing the historical development of the "network of language, culture and behavior," Whorf asked, "Which was first: the language patterns or the cultural norms?" And he answered: "In the main they have grown up together, constantly influencing each other. But in this partnership the nature of the language is the factor that limits free plasticity and rigidifies channels of development in the more autocratic way" (ibid.:156).

Sapir also discussed historical processes and asserted that "culture and language may be conceived of as in a constant state of interaction and definite association for a considerable lapse of time. This state of correlation, however, cannot continue indefinitely." Because cultures change more rapidly than do languages, "the forms of language will in course of time cease to symbolize those of culture" (1949b:102).

A review of the writings of Sapir and Whorf indicates that neither thought of the relationships among language, culture, and human thinking as rigid and mechanistic but rather as coexisting in fluid and dynamic interactions.

A Contemporary Comment

Working in an entirely different tradition, but overlapping historically with Sapir and Whorf, the Soviet linguist V. N. Volosinov expressed quite similar views about relationships of language, thought, and experience. Like the American researchers, Volosinov believed that language and speakers' perceptions of experience are intertwined. There exists an inner and external element in expression, a process by which the experiential is translated into a form where it embodies signs and obtains meaning. The inner element is the thought or idea that seeks expression to the external, to its "outward objectification." This external element requires that what is expressible be organized into a fixed medium or material. As the inner element is translated for delivery to the external it is transformed. Thus, compromises are made in order for the inner expression to be manifested outwardly. Volosinov stressed, "It is not experience that organizes expression, but the other way around...*expression organizes experience. Expression is what first gives experience its form and specificity of direction* [emphasis in original]." (1973: 84, 85). He stated:

Volosinov believed that an individual's thought is guided by possibilities offered by his or her language:

> It is a matter not so much of expression accommodating itself to our inner world but
> rather of our inner world accommodating itself to the potentialities of our expression,
> its possible routes and directions. (ibid.:91)

Finally, Volosinov stressed the social nature of inner personal experience: "The structure of experience is just as social as is the structure of its outward objectification. The degree to which an experience is perceptible, distinct and formulated is directly proportional to the degree to which it is socially oriented" (ibid.:87).

There are no indications that the American and Soviet scholars knew of each other's work, but their contemporaneous intellectual interests and conclusions were compatible.

Reexamination of Linguistic Relativity

Recent research has examined issues earlier introduced by Sapir and Whorf about the relationships among language, culture, and thought. To pursue these investigations, a comparative approach is vital. Comparison of lexical forms and grammatical structures from different languages allows researchers to disentangle the interrelated factors of language structure, cultural influences, and thought processes. In addition, some studies attempt to develop experimental designs focusing on memory and perception tasks that can lead to understanding how speakers of various languages use different cognitive resources to classify objects and events.

Studies in linguistic relativity also consider the functions and uses of language to investigate the full range of meanings produced when people speak. Using a comparative perspective in the analysis of discourse provides a framework for understanding the interrelationships of linguistic and cultural factors. Discourse analysis also contributes an emphasis on analyzing both the production and interpretation of speech in the context of use and evaluation. These studies move away from the analysis of context-free words and grammatical structures toward investigating language in use.

To examine the possible interplay of language and cognitive processes, John Lucy (1996) developed an analytic and experimental design studying the effects of grammatical requirements on memory and sorting tasks with speakers of English and Yucatec, a Mayan language spoken in Mexico. Lucy focused on two grammatical features distinguishing the two languages: marking for plural number and use of numerals that modify nouns. The first feature is that English requires an obligatory marker of plural number on the vast majority of its lexicon, including nouns referring to animate beings (humans and animals) and most inanimate objects. Plural marking does not occur with amorphous substances such as sugar, mud, water, and so on. In contrast, Yucatec allows for, but does not require, plural marking for only a very small number of nouns. Plural marking is more likely to occur with animate beings, but even with these, it is not obligatory.

Lucy devised experiments presenting pictures of scenes of Yucatec village life to speakers of Yucatec and English and asked them to perform a number of tasks requiring recalling and recognizing the pictures and sorting depicted objects as similar or different. The results indicated a strong effect of language structure on memory and classifying tasks. In remembering and sorting, speakers of English paid attention to number for animate beings and objects but ignored number for substances (ibid.:49). Speakers of Yucatec paid attention to number only for animate beings, ignoring number for everything else.

A second distinction between English and Yucatec concerns use of numerals. In English, count nouns are preceded directly by a numeral modifier (e.g., one dog, two cats). In contrast, Yucatec numerals are used in conjunction with a classifier that provides information about the shape, texture, or other material properties of the noun referent. For instance, the utterance translated from Yucatec as "one candle" is better understood as meaning "one long thin candle" (ibid.:50). As Lucy explains, the meaning of English nouns includes their form or unit, but the meaning of Yucatec nouns focuses on their substance rather than their form. So, for example, "one long thin candle" is better translated as "one long thin wax," with the cultural presupposition that wax occurring in a long thin shape is a candle. Note that English does use numeral classifiers with noncount nouns, for example, "a glass of water," providing information about the shape or unit in which the substance is contained.

To investigate the effect of numeral structure on cognition, Lucy provided speakers of English and Yucatec with sets of three test objects and asked the subjects to classify one of the objects as more like another (i.e., "Is item *X* more like *A* or more like *B*?"). Results of this experiment revealed that English speakers classified objects on the basis of shape, whereas Yucatec speakers classified objects on the basis of their material composition.

Both types of experiments confirm the strength of linguistic structuring and meaning in interaction with cultural patterning and cognitive processes. Further research with young speakers of English and Yucatec indicated that children younger than 7 years tended to classify objects as similar on the basis of shape rather than material, but that at about the age of 8 years, Yucatec children shifted to a preference for material as their basis for sorting objects (ibid.:51). Studies such as this suggest the significance of conducting future research that includes additional comparative and longitudinal data.

In a study investigating temporal concepts in English and Mandarin Chinese, Lera Boroditsky (2001) questioned whether speakers of languages that differ in the ways they talk about time also think about time differently. According to Boroditsky, concepts of time have both universal and language-specific features. From experience, time is "a phenomenon in which we, the observer, experience continuous unidirectional change that may be marked by appearance and disappearance of objects and events" (ibid.:4). But languages may vary in the way in which they develop metaphors and abstract conceptualizations of time. Many languages use metaphors derived from spatial concepts to express notions of time. For example, English talks about time in terms of horizontal space (e.g., "he took three steps *forward*" or "the dumpster is *behind* the store"). While speakers of Mandarin may also use horizontal front/back expressions for time, they also commonly use vertical or up/down metaphors when talking about the order of events, weeks, months, and so on. In these constructions, earlier events are expressed as "up" (or *shang* in Mandarin) while later events are "down" (or *xia* in Mandarin). For instance, /shang ge yue/ (up month) refers to "last (or previous) month" and /xia ge yue/ (down month) is used to indicate "next (or following) month" (ibid.:4–6).

To test whether the different metaphors for time in English and Mandarin have an effect on the ways speakers think about time, Boroditsky conducted several experiments with native speakers of English and Mandarin who were all students at Stanford University, completing the tests in English. Participants were given test questions after seeing primes depicting either horizontal or vertical spatial metaphors applied to time (see Figures 3.1a and b and 3.2a and b). The participants were asked to respond true or false to statements such as "March comes *before* April." They were also given questions of purely temporal constructions such as "March comes *earlier* than April." Their response times were noted as a measure of their comprehension of horizontal spatial metaphors. The results demonstrated that English and Mandarin speakers had faster response times for *before/ after* after horizontal primes than after vertical primes. However, English speakers answered purely temporal questions (earlier/later) faster after horizontal primes, while Mandarin speakers answered these questions faster after vertical primes.

Another experiment tested the effect of English learning on native Mandarin speakers' responses. Results showed that the older a person was when starting to learn English, the greater was the effect of Mandarin on one's thinking vertically about time. However, the length of exposure to English had no effect. Rather, age of acquisition was the significant factor.

According to Boroditsky, the results of these experiments demonstrated that "language shapes thought.... One's native language appears to exert a strong influence over how one thinks about abstract domains like time" (2001:18). In the absence of experiential data (through the senses of sight, sound, etc.), language may play a critical role in shaping the way that speakers conceptualize abstract notions like time.

Issues of language and perception can also be addressed by examining differences in conversational style favored by speakers of different languages. Much of the work of John Gumperz and his associates focuses on analyzing the role of what Gumperz calls "conversational

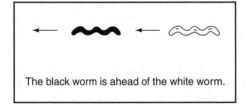

The black worm is ahead of the white worm.

FIGURE 3.1a   Example of a Horizontal Spatial Prime. (Boroditsky 2001)

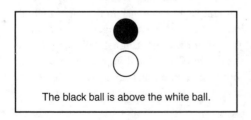

The black ball is above the white ball.

FIGURE 3.1b   Example of a Vertical Spatial Prime. (Boroditsky 2001)

The white fish will lose.

FIGURE 3.2a   Example of a Horizontal Spatial Prime. (Lera Boroditsky: "Does Language Shape Thought?: Mandarin and English Speakers' Conceptions of Time," 2001, *Cognitive Psychology,* vol. 43: 1–22.)

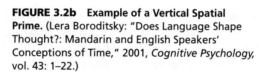

The white fish will lose.

FIGURE 3.2b   Example of a Vertical Spatial Prime. (Lera Boroditsky: "Does Language Shape Thought?: Mandarin and English Speakers' Conceptions of Time," 2001, *Cognitive Psychology,* vol. 43: 1–22.)

inference," defined as "the situated and presupposition-bound interpretive processes by which interlocutors assess what they perceive at any one point in a verbal encounter and on which they base their responses" (1996:375). That is, when people interact verbally with one another, they continually interpret and evaluate their co-participant's speech in order to ascertain not only its meaning but also its intention. On the basis of these interpretations, each speaker responds to what he or she perceives as the other person's meaning. However, when people learn second or third (or more) languages, they may learn to properly use the pronunciations, words, and grammatical patterns of their additional language, but they may unconsciously transfer the conversational inferences they learned with their native language into verbal encounters in which they speak a nonnative tongue. Therefore, they may misinterpret the meanings and intentions of their co-participants regardless of the fact that they may understand the literal meaning of the words spoken to them.

Communicative practices that are considered appropriate within a particular community foster feelings of identity and group membership. Among the kinds of practices that may signal group membership are features of intonation (pitch, rhythm, velocity), pausing, and stylistic and rhetorical choices. Because people rely on these patterns without consciously reflecting on their meaning, they are usually unaware that they are making a communicative choice but instead believe that their conversational practices are natural. Therefore, people are also not consciously aware of making particular interpretations and evaluations of other people's speaking styles, instead assuming that their reactions are natural as well.

People with different cultural backgrounds may assume that different styles of speaking are appropriate in particular settings, resulting in a kind of miscommunication. For example, research with South Asian immigrants in Great Britain reveals contrasting discourse norms both in production and interpretation. In the following extract from an interview between a native Pakistani applicant for admission to a paid training course (ibid.:390–391), the applicant and the

British interviewer misinterpret each other's communicative cues (/*/ indicates word said with strong stress):

INTERVIEWER (I):	[A]nd you put here that you want to apply for that course, because there are more jobs in the *trade.
APPLICANT (A):	Yeah.
I:	So perhaps you could explain *apart from that reason, *why else you want to apply for *electrical work.
A:	I think I like this job in my as a profession.
I:	And *why do you think you'll *like it?
A:	Why?
I:	Could you explain to me *why?
A:	I why do I like it? Well, I think is ah more job prospect!

In this encounter, the interviewer is using British norms by indirectly asking the applicant to expand on his interests and past experiences, but the applicant, unfamiliar with these norms, interprets the interviewer's words literally and simply rephrases his statements. Here we find a demonstration of people thinking differently about what is going on in their interaction. Each one misinterprets the other's contribution. And both find it difficult to move beyond their own interpretation, becoming increasingly annoyed and frustrated. They do not realize that their sense of what is happening is derived from their own culturally specific patterns of discourse production and interpretation. (See Chapter 12 for a more detailed discussion of interethnic miscommunication.)

LEXICAL AND CULTURAL CATEGORIES

Building on the pioneering foundations of the first half of the twentieth century, modern research-ers have broadened the exploration of topics in language and culture. Some study taxonomic systems in vocabulary and raise questions about possible universality of linguistic and cognitive processes. Other research investigates how cultural values and symbols are encoded in words or expressions and are then used by speakers to transmit emotional, attitudinal, and symbolic meanings.

Domains

Studies of categories and taxonomies in vocabulary often focus on analyses of semantic domains. A *semantic domain* is an aggregate of words, all sharing a core meaning, related to a specific topic—for example, kinship terms, body-part words, and colors. Words within a domain are united by similarities and contrasts. The words share certain features of meaning because they refer to the same type of object, person, or event, but each word contrasts with all others in the set and labels a distinctive entity. By discovering systematic principles of similarity and contrast in a given domain, we can make inferences about how speakers experience their world. The number of distinctions made within a domain reflects the degree of cultural interest, as shown, for instance, by comparing the English and Paiute topographical terms given earlier from Sapir's research.

Cultural focus can also be seen in distinctions made by English terms for animals. For certain animals, we note age and sex, whereas for others we ignore such factors. For instance, within the species of "horse," we have separate words for female and male adults (*mare* and *stallion*), for babies (*foal*), and for female and male preadults (*filly* and *colt*). Age and sex of cattle are similarly distinguished: *cow, bull, calf, heifer,* and *bullock*. Also, we have numerous words for different breeds of these animals. In contrast, we treat other animals in much more generalized ways, using only one term for all individuals—for example, *chipmunk, otter,* and *moose*. These differences in linguistic treatment obviously parallel, and are based on, our cultural interest in various kinds of animals because of our economy, eating habits, or other needs.

Cultural interest is not static; it changes over time as new items and practices are introduced. When innovations are adopted, words are required to label these new entities and activities. Speakers can either create new words or extend the semantic range of existing words to include new items. In some cases, innovations replace indigenous objects, resulting in changes in meanings or functions of native words. For instance, shifts have occurred in meanings of the word *čih* (now meaning "sheep") in a dialect of Tzeltal, spoken by native people in Mexico (Witkowski and Brown 1983:571). When sheep were introduced to the Tzeltal people by the Spanish in the sixteenth century, Tzeltal speakers applied their indigenous word for "deer," *čih,* to this new animal, adding a descriptor, "cotton," *tunim,* so that "sheep" were called *tunim čih* ("cotton deer"). Over the centuries, sheep have been incorporated into the Tzeltal economy while at the same time, deer have become of peripheral interest. Now the word *čih* is used exclusively for "sheep," whereas "deer" is labeled as *te'tikil čih,* literally "wild sheep." In this process, special marking for "sheep" has disappeared, emerging instead on "deer" in the modifier "wild."

In many languages of native North and South America, replacement of indigenous items and changes in cultural importance are reflected in marking older entities with attributes such as "native," "real," or other descriptive terms. When new items are introduced, speakers associate them with already existing entities and name them with indigenous words. Then, when older entities become eclipsed in importance by innovations, shifts occur in meanings so that the new item is the neutral term and the indigenous one receives modification. These processes can be seen in the following examples (ibid.:572–575):

1. Huastec (Mexico):
   precontact: *bičim*   "deer"
   contemporary: *bičim*   "horse"
                   tenek bičim   "deer"   (lit. native horse)
2. Biloxi (southeast United States):
   kcixka   "pig"
   kcixka yoka   "opossum"   (lit. swamp pig)
3. Comanche (US Plains):
   *kahn*I   "house"
   *nïmïkahn*I   "teepee"   (lit. Indian house)

Lexical Components

In some domains of vocabulary, cross-cultural comparisons uncover basic differences in the ways that people perceive their universe. For example, study of kinship terms (words used to name relatives) can reveal people's perceptions of their social relations. Americans generally use the following words for relatives: *grandmother, grandfather, mother, father, aunt, uncle, sister, brother, cousin, daughter, son, niece, nephew, granddaughter,* and *grandson.* By analyzing the kinds of contrasts made with these words, we can discover systematic components of meaning that are used to name relatives. First, we distinguish between generations: grandmother/mother/ daughter/granddaughter. Second, we note the sex of relatives: mother/father; sister/brother. Third, we distinguish between direct or lineal relatives and collateral relatives: mother/aunt; son/ nephew. These three sets of contrasts—that is, generation, sex of relative, and lineality—define the features of our kin that we consider meaningful. Another interesting aspect of English terminology is the reciprocity between alternate generations. The same combining form /grand-/ is used when skipping up one generation or downward: grandparent/grandchild.

The procedure used to determine significant contrasts is called *componential analysis* and was developed by Ward Goodenough in studies of American kinship (1956, 1965). Words in a domain are viewed as being composed of isolable "components" of meaning that co-occur in different combinations, for example, younger generation + female + lineal fi "daughter." Comparisons of distinctive components used in any system of terms allow linguists and anthropologists to understand better the *ethnosemantics,* or indigenous systems of meaning, of a culture and its members.

Underlying principles or components in the English system are not necessarily used in all languages. Other languages and therefore their speakers employ different sets of contrasts. In languages of Iroquoian peoples (indigenous inhabitants of present-day New York State and Ontario and Quebec, Canada), the following kinds of relatives are named (examples are from Seneca, one of the Iroquoian languages; Lounsbury 1964):

grandmother (and her sisters): *ʔakso:t*

grandfather (and his brothers): *hakso:t*

mother and mother's sister: *noʔyẽh*

father and father's brother: *haʔnih*

mother's brother: *hakhnoʔsẽh*

father's sister: *ake:hak*

older sister: *ahstiʔ*

younger sister: *kheʔkẽ:ʔ*

older brother: *hahtsiʔ*

younger brother: *heʔkẽ:ʔ*

cousin: *akya:ʔse:ʔ*

daughter: *khe:awak*

son: *he:awak*

niece: *khehsõʔneh* (female speaker); *kheyẽ:wõ:tẽʔ* (male speaker)

nephew: *hehsõʔneh* (female speaker); *heyẽ:wõ:tẽʔ* (male speaker)

granddaugther: *kheya:teʔ*

grandson: *heya:teʔ*

This system is organized around several key principles, some similar to English terminology and others that differ. Both systems use notions of generation and the sex of relative. However, Iroquoian speakers have separate terms for older and younger siblings (older sister/ younger sister and older brother/younger brother). A major contrasting feature between the two languages is their treatment of lineal and collateral relatives. In English, sisters of one's mother and father are lumped together with one term, "aunt," as are brothers of one's mother and father, "uncle." In the Iroquoian system, one's mother's sisters are called by the same word as one's own mother, whereas one's father's sister is named separately. Similarly, one's father's brother is called "father," whereas one's mother's brother is distinguished. This principle of associating mother and father with their same-sex sibling is carried logically through succeeding generations and results in merging some relatives who we would call "cousin" into categories of sister/brother:

> mother's sister's daughter = sister
>
> mother's sister's son = brother
>
> father's brother's daughter = sister
>
> father's brother's son = brother

The logic here is based on the fact that a child of one's mother or father is one's sibling; therefore, a child of anyone called "mother" or "father" is called "sister" or "brother."

Differences in kinship terminologies are not merely linguistic; they reflect societal attitudes toward one's relatives. Individuals called by each kin term are understood by speakers to stand in particular social relationships and to have certain rights and obligations vis-à-vis speakers. The meanings of words, then, reflect one's social universe.

Lexical Classifications

Research in vocabularies reveals that, in some domains, distinctions are clear and unequivocal, whereas in others, components and categories are more complex. In a domain such as kinship, people are easily differentiated from one another; for example, a person is either female or male, either younger or older than the speaker. But in other domains, items cannot be classified absolutely. In addition, speakers may disagree about whether to include or exclude particular items in any given category. And they need to know which aspects of an entity are critical in determining the category to which the entity belongs.

To classify words, speakers need to know the defining characteristics of each class. For example, in the United States, many people include a whale in the category of "fish" because whales live in the ocean and move by swimming, even though they are biologically mammals, giving birth to live young. The "mistake" of classifying a whale as a fish reveals that definitional criteria of category membership do not all have equal weight. Certain traits are considered by speakers to be more important than others. The most obvious facts about whales are that they look like fish, swim in the ocean, and do not come ashore (unlike seals and walrus, which do come ashore). Because whales share some key diagnostic criteria of the "fish" category, they can be thought of as "fishlike."

Category membership, then, is not always absolute but frequently involves questions of degree or "fuzziness." Fuzzy sets or categories are based on the idea that "instead of just being in the set or not, an individual is in the set to a certain degree" (Lakoff 1972:185). Fuzzy category membership is often signaled linguistically in English by use of *hedges,* "words whose meaning implicitly involves fuzziness," such as "sort of, loosely speaking, somewhat, essentially" (ibid.:195–196). In the case of whales, one can say

a. Strictly speaking, a whale is a mammal.
b. Loosely speaking, a whale is a fish.

In (a), a speaker focuses on primary diagnostic criteria of biological traits, whereas in (b), the speaker ignores these and instead focuses on secondary criteria of habitat and behavior. Both (a) and (b) are true statements, although

c. Strictly speaking, a whale is a fish.
d. Loosely speaking, a whale is a mammal.

are false.

Inherent fuzziness of hedges can also be shown by the falseness of either of the following:

a. Strictly speaking, a robin is a bird.
b. Loosely speaking, a robin is a bird.

Because a robin is unquestionably a bird, the sort of hedge that implies uncertainty cannot be used in this case because the entity is a typical example of its category.

Criteria used for classification are different in different languages. For example, some languages organize noun categories on the basis of gender (masculine/feminine/neuter) or animate/inanimate distinctions. Others employ semantic criteria of form or use (Swahili, Swati) or shape and texture (Navajo; see Chapter 2). However, labels used by linguists to refer to noun classes may be misleading because they may reflect Western thinking about attributes of referents rather than accurately capture indigenous worldviews. This point has been discussed by Mo Kaa (1976) in an analysis of Algonkian languages (spoken in eastern and central North America).

Linguists usually claim that Algonkian languages (Ojibwa, Cree, Blackfoot, Cheyenne) base noun classes on a distinction between animates and inanimates. Leonard Bloomfield's influential grammar of Algonkian noted the following members of the "animate" category: "all persons, animals, spirits, and large trees, and some other objects, such as tobacco, maize, apple, raspberry, calf of leg, stomach, spittle, feather, bird's tail, horn, kettle, pipe for smoking, snowshoe" (1946:94). Although this list may seem haphazard from a Euro-American sense of "animate" (to be "alive"), Kaa suggested that the problem is not with Algonkian inconsistencies but with the failure of Western terminology to express native meanings adequately.

Kaa offered an alternative statement of Algonkian "animate" that may be less concise but more attuned to the Algonkian people's perspective: "Animate" entities are "more spiritually relevant and personalized beings, things, and phenomena" (ibid.:92). This definition embodies several important aspects of the Algonkian worldview. First, it states criteria in relative rather than absolute terms, thus avoiding Western tendencies to think in polarities. Second, because the definition is relative, it recognizes that noun classifications are sensitive to contextual and individual variation, accounting for the fact that some nouns are categorized differently by different speakers. Third, it emphasizes the similarity among "beings, things, and phenomena" rather than their oppositions.

A conversation between an Ojibwa speaker and A. Irving Hallowell corroborated Kaa's description of Algonkian "animates." Hallowell was interested in discovering Ojibwa concepts of "personhood," understanding that "this category of being is by no means limited to *human* beings" (emphasis in original) (1960:22). Hallowell noted that "stones" are classed grammatically as "animates," so he asked an Ojibwa speaker: "Are *all* the stones we see about us here alive?" "No! But *some* are" was the reply (ibid.:26). In the Ojibwa worldview, stones have potential for motion and can occasionally take on other animate attributes. They are most apt to do so in religious contexts, especially related to rituals associated with *Midewiwin,* an Ojibwa ceremonial and curing society. Stones therefore can have agency and perform actions or, to quote Kaa again, they are "spiritually relevant and personalized."

Ethnoscience

Ethnoscience refers to systems of classification that people construct to organize knowledge of their universe. The term *ethnoscience* is derived from the Greek word *ethnos,* meaning "people" or "a division of people." Such systems are based on taxonomic hierarchies in which some entities are ordered hierarchically (e.g., a "spaniel" is a kind of "dog") and other entities are contrasted taxonomically (e.g., "dog" and "cat").

Studies of ethnoscientific domains in different cultures demonstrate the variety of underlying assumptions that can be used to group entities. Analysts of comparative data from many languages proposed the following universal taxonomy for living things (Berlin, Breedlove, and Raven 1974:25–27): Unique Beginner (most general and abstract term that subsumes all of the other categories, e.g., *plant, animal*); Life Forms (perhaps five or ten terms, each named by a separate, independent word, e.g., *tree, grass, bird, mammal*); Generics (many terms, usually named by separate words, e.g., *oak, pine, robin, blue jay, dog, horse*); Specifics (items within generic categories, often named by identifying modifiers, e.g., *blue spruce, white birch*); and Varietals (items within specific categories, e.g., *baby lima bean, butter lima bean*).

Grouping of items within a particular category is based on perceived similarities or shared parameters of meaning. Distinctions between categories are based on perceived contrasts. For example, the Digo, an indigenous people living in coastal regions of Kenya and Tanzania whose language belongs to the Bantu linguistic family, have a system of botanical terms that makes culturally relevant categories of form and function (Nicolle 2001). Most Digo consultants begin their taxonomy of plant terms with three "life form" labels: *linyasi* ("grass"); *mmea* ("plant"), and *muhi* ("tree"). Although they did not use a "unique beginner" term, they consider these three "life forms" as belonging to a related abstract category. While these life forms are distinct taxa, there may be some overlap in their application to particular specimens. For example, the term *mmea* ("plant") could be applied to any young plant, including a tree seedling, even though a mature tree would be in the category of *muhi* ("tree"). However, a tree seedling could also be considered *muhi*. The term *mmea,* then, may encompass any young member of the (unnamed) plant family (Nicolle 2001:38).

Digo speakers employ several contrastive parameters to distinguish specific botanical entities. Attention to these parameters allows speakers to decide whether something is a member of the category of *muhi* ("tree") or *mmea* ("plant"). The parameters include the entity's size and whether it is cultivated, where it is located, and whether it bears fruit. For instance, members of the category of *muhi* ("tree") are typically large (two meters or more in height), not cultivated, located in the bush outside villages, and may bear fruit that is edible. In contrast, members of the category of *mmea* ("plant") are small, cultivated in farms or gardens, and do not bear fruit. In addition to these parameters, the categories are distinguished on the basis of their uses. That is, *muhi* may be used for medicines but not for food (except for their edible fruits); *mmea* are used as foods or spices (Nicolle 2001:40).

Although there is general agreement about the distinctions among the life forms, speakers vary in the assignment of any particular exemplar to one or another category. Variations among speakers arise from the proportionate weight given to each of the parameters used to contrast category membership (Nicolle 2001:40). For instance, consultants disagreed about whether to place "cucumber tree" (*Averrhoa bilimbi*) among the *muhi* or *mmea*. The fact that "cucumber tree" is cultivated should place it among the *mmea,* but because of its size (usually more than two meters in height) and the fact that it bears edible fruit, it may be called *muhi*. In some cases, consultants did agree on the placement of potentially ambiguous exemplars. For example, "pigeon pea" (*Cajanus cajun*) is considered a member of the *mmea* group because it is one of the most important cultigens in Digo subsistence and economy, functioning in household consumption and commercial sale.

These characteristics outweigh other features that might lead it to be called *muhi*; that is. it may grow to more than two meters, it bears edible fruit, and its leaves are used as an eye medicine.

This analysis of Digo plant categories illustrates the important point that traits used to assign any particular entity to specific categories depends on speakers' consideration of various distinguishing features and the relevant weight given to each. It also illustrates the fact that there may be disagreements within communities about specific assignments and category membership.

Universal Processes: Color Terms

Rather than emphasizing linguistic and cultural differences in systems of categorization, many linguists are discovering universal principles of classification. Much attention has been given to the domain of color terminology. In a groundbreaking and influential study, *Basic Color Terms* (1969), Brent Berlin and Paul Kay presented a theory of universal color categories and their sequential development. In their study, Berlin and Kay collected color-term data from 98 languages by asking speakers to sort 329 color chips into categories that could not be subsumed within any other class. This testing procedure resulted in terms such as "red" but not "scarlet" or "maroon" because the latter two are recognized as "kinds of" red. On the basis of consultants' responses, Berlin and Kay postulated 11 basic color terms: *white, black, red, green, yellow, blue, brown, purple, pink, gray,* and *orange*. Not all languages contain all 11 terms. By examining the content of various color systems, Berlin and Kay proposed the following evolutionary sequence, which starts on the left and incrementally incorporates colors to the right.

$$\begin{array}{ccccc} \text{white} \rightarrow & \text{red} \rightarrow & \text{green} \rightarrow & \text{blue} \rightarrow & \text{brown} \rightarrow & \text{purple} \\ \text{black} & & \text{yellow} & & & \text{pink} \\ & & & & & \text{orange} \\ & & & & & \text{gray} \end{array}$$

Note that no language distinguishes less than two colors. A one-color system would actually be impossible because a classification scheme, by definition, must contain at least two members; that is, two items must be seen to contrast with each other. Berlin and Kay's sequence accounts for the instance when a language contains only two color terms: They are always "white" and "black." Additional terms are added in the order of development presented with examples in the following table:

Number of Terms	Color Terms	Language
Two	white, black	Jale (New Guinea), Ngombe (Africa)
Three	white, black, red	Arawak (Caribbean), Swahili (southern Africa)
Four	white, black, red, yellow	Ibo (Nigeria), Tongan (Polynesia)
Five	white, black, red, yellow, green	Tarascan (Mexico), !Kung (southern Africa)
Six	white, black, red, yellow, green, blue	Tamil (India), Mandarin (China)
Seven	white, black, red, yellow, green, blue, brown	Nez Percé (Montana), Javanese
Eight to eleven	white, black, red, yellow, green, blue, brown, purple and/or pink and/or orange and/or gray	English, Zuni (New Mexico), Dinka (Sudan), Tagalog (Philippines), among others

Source: Compiled from Berlin and Kay 1969:152–156.

Kay (1975) later revised the original sequence somewhat in order to account for the fact that certain languages—for example, Japanese, Inuktitut (Arctic Canada), Aguaruna (Peru)—encode a color of "green-blue" that may occur before labeling "yellow." Kay called this color category "GRUE" and placed it either preceding or following "yellow" in development. He noted that the category "GRUE" never splits separately into both "green" and "blue" before the naming of "yellow." The revised sequence, then, is given below:

		GRUE S yellow			purple
White	↗		↘	green	pink
→	red			and →	orange
Black	↘		↗	blue	gray
		yellow → GRUE			

A few languages seem to necessitate further minor modifications. For example, Russian does not have a word for a single color "blue" but rather distinguishes "dark blue" and "light blue." However, Berlin and Kay's sequence has essentially been substantiated.

Although there may be universal patterns in the development of systems of color-term classification, languages differ in the symbolic meanings embodied in color terms. Words for colors may be used to call forth emotional and ideological responses, for example, black for mourning, white for purity, and red for passion. But these meanings and uses vary cross-culturally.

Focal Meaning and Prototypes

Berlin and Kay's work in color systems has proven to be of great significance because it raised important questions concerning universal cognitive and linguistic processes. It also uncovered complexities in the organization of classes and in understanding how speakers make discriminations. These discoveries are not limited to color terms but have wider applicability in language.

The concept of focal meaning within classes has become relevant in ethnolinguistic studies. The *focal meaning* of a word is its central sense within the whole range of meanings that it has. A word's focal meaning refers to the "best example" or "most typical example" of possible meanings that it encompasses. For instance, in color terminology, each word covers a graded range of different hues along a continuum rather than a discrete and absolute quality, but each word also has a central meaning, a "best example." Speakers in a community agree on the focal meaning of a word, although they may well disagree about including or excluding peripheral cases in given categories. So, if asked to pick out the "best example" of "red," speakers agree on a color sometimes called "scarlet" or, colloquially, "fire-engine red." In their study, Kay and McDaniel found that focal meanings of basic color terms were substantially similar in all languages, suggesting a universal color system based on physical stimuli (Kay and McDaniel 1978).

The concept of prototypes can also be generally applied in semantic analyses. A *prototype* is an idealized, internalized conceptualization of an object, quality, or activity. Real-life objects and activities are measured against these internalized concepts and are named according to how well they approximate the ideal. As Charles Fillmore stated, a prototype approach to semantics "seeks to represent the meaning of a linguistic expression, not through a statement of the necessary and sufficient conditions for membership in a category...but rather through the analysis of instances (or near instances) of the category in terms of approximations to the prototype" (1982:32). For example, a category such as "bird" "is identified in terms of a fixed set of conditions, but the best examples are those that are close to an idealization of that category" (ibid.:33). Therefore, although a robin, penguin, and ostrich are all kinds of birds, speakers (in our culture) agree that "robin" is closest to the prototype or idealization or, as Fillmore said, "is somehow 'birdier' than the other two" (ibid.).

In classifying concrete objects, speakers may disagree about whether to place items in given categories because they disagree about whether the items approximate enough prototypical characteristics. For instance, "prototypical" or "best example" of "chair" in North American culture is an object with four legs, a seat, back, and two armrests. Although speakers generally include an object fitting such a description in the category "chair," they may disagree about whether to include objects lacking one or another defining property.

People categorize objects based on their use as well as on physical properties. In an experimental study, William Labov showed subjects drawings of cups and cuplike containers and asked them to provide names for these objects, such as cup, mug, bowl, dish, pitcher (1973:353–355). People were then asked to imagine the same series of objects containing coffee, mashed potatoes, or flowers. Respondents were most likely to label borderline or peripheral (i.e., untypical) objects as "cups" if they contained coffee and least likely to do so if they held flowers. Labov concluded that "language is essentially a categorical device" and that in order to understand it, processes of categorization must be studied "at work" (ibid.:368).

People and activities can also be evaluated with reference to prototypical constructs. In these cases, of course, speakers depend on cultural models consisting of expectations for and evaluations of behavior. A social category of this type, illustrated by the word *bachelor,* "is defined in terms of a set of conditions, but the best examples are those which are situated in a standard or prototype background setting" (Fillmore 1982:34). Although "bachelor" can be defined as an unmarried adult male, not all unmarried men would appropriately be called bachelors; a man living in a stable, conjugal relationship; a boy abandoned in a jungle and grown to maturity alone; a brain-damaged boy grown to adulthood in a coma; or the pope are examples (Quinn and Holland 1987:23). The point here is that categories like these cannot be defined abstractly; rather, they are appropriately understood only in the context of culturally shared expectations. This is what Fillmore termed a *background setting.*

Prototypes can also be used as guides in evaluating one's own or another's behavior. Because all communication occurs in cultural contexts, speakers' understanding of what is happening is often measured against prototypical constructs. Speech events, that is, instances of communicative interaction, form a domain that encompasses many kinds of genres, including conference, argument, negotiation, debate, lecture, confession, and apology. Participants evaluate ongoing behavior and form conclusions about what kind of interaction is taking place. Consensus among participants may or may not exist, depending on their perceptions of how the encounter conforms to a prototype model. Lack of consensus can also result when participants are motivated to define encounters in particular ways given their own goals and purposes—for example, people can disagree about whether they're having an argument.

These examples illustrate the importance of situating our understanding of the meaning of words and their usage in the context of culture.

Concepts of Space and Location

One of the universal sets of concepts that all people must have consists of notions of space, spatial relations, and location. These concepts are presumed by linguists and psychologists working in the field to be features of basic cognitive conceptual structure inherent in all human beings as part of our cognitive makeup (Jackendoff 1996; Levinson 1996). Developing and mastering concepts of space and location are critical to human life and are interrelated with visual and motor skills. People need to locate and manipulate objects and to be mobile within a spatial environment. While conceptual structure is universal, the way it is encoded in languages differs dramatically. These differences may be manifest in the lexicon and/or in syntax. Semantic features of words may encode specific reference to spatial concepts, and syntactic requirements may mandate the expression of certain kinds of spatial notions.

According to Jackendoff (1996:8–9), spatial representation must include the encoding of object shapes, dimensions, and variations and of the relations of objects and scenes. In addition, basic conceptual structure includes ideas of place or location and path or trajectory, as exemplified, for instance, in the following sentences: "The book is lying *on the table*" (place); "The arrow flew *through the air past my head*" (trajectory) (ibid.:9–10). Finally, conceptual structure contains notions of physical motion, enabling people to keep track of moving objects.

Languages have lexical and/or syntactic devices that allow speakers to describe spatial relations between objects and grounds. There seem to be two basic distinctions in emphases utilized by various languages. Some languages focus on systems that place objects in space by reference to intrinsic or object-internal orientations (e.g., "its back"), while others focus on contingent or reference-point relations (e.g., "at," "near," "here") (Lucy 1998:107). Languages also use techniques to coordinate these two types of concepts. These techniques emphasize either absolute systems of coordination, relative systems of coordination, or deictic systems of reference. Absolute systems describe a reference point and its placement within a presupposed orienting axis (e.g., a feature of local topography or cardinal directions), while relative systems extract intrinsic properties from the reference objects and project them over space (ibid.). Deictic or egocentric systems of spatial reference describe objects from the point of view of the speaker (e.g., noting an object's location to the left or right of the speaker) (Peterson et al. 1996).

While all languages have ways of indicating both intrinsic and contingent concepts and may utilize absolute, relative, and deictic systems, languages differ in their preference and frequency of usage. English emphasizes relativistic space, locating one object by reference to another object or spatial field. These relations are encoded in locative or directional prepositions (*at, near, away from, toward, in front of,* etc.). Other languages emphasize absolute space, locating objects in reference to absolute directions or topographical features. For example, the indigenous Australian language Guugu Yimithirr, spoken in North Queensland, specifies locations according to cardinal directions of east, west, north, and south. Therefore, an object is located as "to the north of," "to the south of," and so forth (Levinson 1996:180). To apply such a system correctly, speakers must constantly be aware of their absolute orientation in space. In experimental research, Guugu Yimithirr speakers were able to estimate locations within an average error of less than 14° (ibid.:181). And they remember spatial arrays in terms of their distribution relative to cardinal directions. In utilizing such a system, Guugu Yimithirr speakers have to access fundamentally different orientations to space and objects than do speakers of English.

Speakers of Tzeltal, a Mayan language of Mexico and Guatemala, employ a type of system of absolute spatialization, but one that differs from that of Guugu Yimithirr. In the Tzeltal language, a primary system of spatial reference is based on a fixed uphill/downhill inclined plane that roughly corresponds to the south/north axis of their landscape. This system is used for all referents regardless of whether they are located on inclined or flat surfaces. For example, two objects can be differentiated by referring to the northerly one as "downhill" of the other, even if both are on a flat surface (ibid.:181). A secondary system of spatial reference denotes objects that are in actual contact with others, but distinctions are made based on the kind of contact that they have. In addition, these two systems are supplemented by differentiation of objects according to nonlocational features such as shape, position of the figure, adhesion, and manner in which the position was obtained (ibid.:182). Finally, spatial reference is modified by a distinction between describing motion and describing location. Motion is encoded through a small set of motion verb roots, while location is encoded through a larger set of stative predicates with functions similar to English adjectives.

An additional significant contrast between Tzeltal and English is the way that each language distinguishes figures and grounds. English describes in great detail the nature of the ground while presupposing features of the figure, but Tzeltal focuses on details in the description of the figure while assuming the nature of the ground. For instance, to locate objects, English describes where to look, while Tzeltal describes what to look for (ibid.:185).

Intriguing questions remain concerning how these differences in lexical and syntactic patterning and in spatial and locational emphases are related to underlying cognitive structures in speakers of disparate languages. Summing up cross-cultural research in this field, Peterson and her associates observe, "It seems clear that different languages and/or cultures can utilize different cognitive skills to different degrees" (1996:570). Evidence from experimental research on problem solving and memory tasks supports the conclusion that speakers of languages that encode spatial relations differently have distinct perceptions about the way that objects relate to one another and to their environmental background. Therefore, it is not claimed that speakers of different languages have different underlying cognitive conceptual structures, but rather that particular cognitive structures may be more or less salient depending on the linguistic resources that speakers have to express basic notions. These linguistic resources are not absolutely constraining. Instead, they lead speakers into certain habitual ways of expressing concepts and therefore of thinking about underlying relationships.

Studies in children's acquisition of spatial concepts indicate that the way their language structures space and location influences their perceptual processes. As Melissa Bowerman (1996:386) notes, some form of spatial understanding predates mastering linguistic skills, but specific linguistic input has a very early (as early as 18 months) impact on children's perception. Although spatial knowledge is necessary to all humans, dividing space into categories and manipulating their meanings and relationships is learned linguistic behavior. Children build on basic prelinguistic knowledge as they acquire the words and syntactic patterns that their language requires to talk about spatial concepts. In morphologically analytic languages like English, separate words, often in the form of prepositions or postpositions, are used to describe relationships between objects or between an object and its ground, while in morphologically complex languages, nominal or verbal morphemes are used to express these relationships. Cross-linguistic research suggests that children acquire the means of expressing these notions in roughly the same order. First learned are concepts of containment or support, proximity, separation, surrounding, and order (ibid.:388). In English, such concepts are expressed through prepositions such as *in* (containment); *on* (support and contiguity); *under* (occlusion); *next to, beside,* and *between* (proximity), and *in front of* and *behind* (projective order). Of course, different languages may have words with similar translations in their lexicon, but these words may have ranges of meaning that do not translate exactly from one language to another. For instance, note the different concepts that the English word *in* expresses (Levinson 1996:187):

    a. The peaches are in the can. (enclosed)
    b. The peaches are in the bowl. (partially enclosed)
    c. The dog is in the yard. (bounded in two dimensions)
    d. The shuttle is in outer space. (unbounded)

Now examine some differences in how English, Finnish, Dutch, and Spanish treat some spatial relationship concepts, as illustrated in the diagrams in Figure 3.3 (Bowerman 1996:394).

Comparing English and Tzeltal, we find that while the English preposition *in* encodes containment of any object into any container, Tzeltal has numerous locative expressions depending

FIGURE 3.3   Classification of Three Static Spatial Situations in English, Finnish, Dutch, and Spanish. (Bowerman, M. 1996. Learning how to structure space for language: A cross linguistic perspective. In *Language and Space*, Bloom, P., et al., eds., pp. 385–436, MIT Press. *International Journal of American Linguistics*. Copyright © University of Chicago Press.)

on the distinct type of object and the distinct type of containment. For example, the following uses of the English *in* are differentiated in Tzeltal (Brown 1994):

a. A man is in a house. (be inside)
b. An apple is in a bowl. (in a bowl-shaped container)
c. Water is in a bottle. (in a taller-than-wide or cylindrical container)
d. An apple is in a bucket of water. (immersed in liquid)
e. A bag of coffee is in a pot. (inserted singly into a closely fitting container)
f. Pencils are in a cup. (long/thin objects inserted carefully into a bounded object)
g. A bull is in a corral. (inserted into container with a narrow opening)

Speakers of English can, of course, express the meanings that Tzeltal distinguishes, but they are not compelled by the requirements of their language to notice the contrasts in types of objects and types of containers that speakers of Tzeltal must be aware of every time they talk about containment. These facts raise critical questions about people's basic assumptions of similarities and differences among objects and their relationships. That is, English speakers may feel that certain spatial relationships are "the same" because they use the same words to describe them, whereas speakers of other languages may perceive other kinds of relationships as similar.

People tend to classify objects and events in their minds according to the resources available in their languages to express those objects and events. As Bowerman concludes, "A perceptual or action-based understanding of what is going on in given spatial situations is probably a necessary condition for learning to talk about space, but this knowledge alone does not buy children knowledge of how to *classify* space in their language" (1996:399). And finally, experimental observation comparing spatial descriptions elicited from American, Dutch, and Korean adults and children in three cohorts (2,0–2,5; 2,6–2,11; and 3,0–3,5) indicated that the languages spoken strongly influenced the way that people classified space and location (ibid.:410, 415). Although there were differences between the linguistic skills of children and adults, especially in some overgeneralizations and lack of refinement in children's descriptions, speakers of each language were more similar to each other than they were to their age cohorts who spoke other languages. Significantly, even the youngest children classified spatial actions in ways more similar to adults speaking their own language than to children of the same age who spoke different languages.

In sum, research concerning language and spatial concepts and their acquisition hints at both the role of prelinguistic cognitive concepts and of language in structuring and classifying those concepts. Although languages can express any given notion, the ease with which concepts are expressed and are retrievable varies with the linguistic resources available and required in any given language through which the concepts are classified and encoded.

CULTURAL PRESUPPOSITION

The vocabulary of a language is not merely an inventory of arbitrary labels referring to objects, entities, or events. Words also convey many kinds of cultural meanings that add to, transform, or manipulate basic senses of words. Research into these areas of meaning and usage includes investigation of cultural presuppositions, associational or extensional meanings, and uses of words to carry symbolic or ideological content.

The concept of *cultural presupposition* refers to the fact that participants in speech interactions come to encounters with an array of knowledge and understandings (models) of their culture as expressed and transmitted through language. The relevance of some of this shared knowledge is fairly obvious. For instance, if a speaker mentions the World Series, he or she assumes that listeners understand that the reference is to baseball, that teams compete throughout a season, and that winners of league competitions play each other for the championship. For conversation to run smoothly, much of what speakers say depends on their accurate assessment of hearers' knowledge. These presuppositions are collected by people during their lifetime of involvement in and learning through their experiences, that is, their enculturation. Because all human experiences are cultural, a tremendous amount of accumulated but unstated knowledge is continuously carried with us.

Other kinds of cultural presuppositions are more complex, and their incorporation into meanings of words is more subtle. For example, as shown in the four sentences that opened this chapter, English and Navajo express different concepts presupposing people's (and other animate beings') rights to individual autonomy (Young 1978). English has many terms expressing various types of coercion: *cause, force, oblige, make, compel, order, command, constrain, must, have to,* and *ought to.* In contrast, the Navajo language, spoken in New Mexico and Arizona, does not contain verbs of this sort. Rather than saying "I *must* go there" or "I *have to* go there," a Navajo speaker says *ákǫ́ǫ́ deeshááłgo t'éiyá yá? át'ééh* ("it is only good that I shall go there"). This construction "lacks the force of compelling necessity" (ibid.:168). Whereas English readily expresses the idea that a person has a right to impose her or his will on another animate being, Navajo again does not express direct compulsion, as seen in the contrasting sentences in English (I *make* the horse run) and Navajo (*łį́į́ shá yilghoł* ["the horse is running for me"]). The Navajo sentence "implies an action on the part of the horse that is essentially voluntary,...lacking the important overtone of coercive authority" (ibid.). These examples reflect the contrast in language ideologies as expressed through word choice and grammar, encapsulating differing views of speakers' rights in relation to others.

To use and interpret words appropriately, speakers make assumptions about each other's intentions, desires, or goals. For example, "joking" and "insulting" speech share certain important features; a speaker may "joke" or "insult" an addressee by pointing out the latter's mistakes, weaknesses, or inappropriate behavior. The difference between jokes and insults lies primarily in the speaker's perceived intent that she or he must make clear through choice of word, tone of voice, and/or facial expression. Interpretations of intent rely on cultural and social norms as well because appropriate topics or targets of joking are determined by culture. In some societies, people never joke with or tease their parents, whereas in other societies such behavior could be acceptable in certain contexts but not in others.

Cultural norms of communicative behavior also involve presuppositions. In our society, when two acquaintances meet, they may use greetings such as "Hi! How are you?" or "What's happening?" If speakers use the greeting "How are you?" do they actually want a substantive answer to this question? In casual encounters between acquaintances, a response that reveals personal problems or serious illness would be considered highly inappropriate. For participants to behave in an acceptable manner, they have to know the social purposes of particular words or utterances. In this example, speakers must know that an utterance that has been expressed in interrogative form is actually not intended as a question, that is, a request for information. Rather, it is a routinized request for a routinized response.

Words can also be used to convey symbolic meanings expressing cultural values and shared assumptions. For example, describing a group of people as "terrorists" expresses a strongly negative judgment against them. The power of language is not only that the values attached to words reveal the attitudes of speakers, but also that words are used to create compatible attitudes in hearers. Labeling someone as a terrorist is, in part, an attempt to influence hearers' opinions about this person because terrorism is an act that is socially condemned. In contrast, describing a person as a freedom fighter attempts to create a positive response.

Advertisers of products in our society (and presumably in many others as well) use an interrelated constellation of words and symbols that rely on and reinforce underlying cultural presuppositions. Advertisements often describe products as "new," "bigger," and "improved." These seemingly innocuous words reveal central themes of change and progress. An unstated assumption links concepts of newness and bigness with advances over items previously produced by both the same company and its competitors.

These are concepts implicit in commodity production, marketing, and consumerism. They are also interconnected with philosophical ideas of evolution. Life-forms are dynamic and ever-changing and lead naturally to better ("improved") versions. Change is conceived of as competitive based on analogies with biological processes—that is, organisms compete for econiches, resulting in "survival of the fittest." These ideas of change are so commonplace in our society that we take them to be *natural,* inherent in entities and processes themselves, rather than understanding that they are cultural constructs. Because change is "naturally" an advance, innovations are assumed to be desirable improvements. Advertisements that stress the diversity of products within a competitive environment have not created this imagery but exploit it. Repetitive exposure to such use of language reinforces overt and covert cultural and ideological messages implied and presupposed by the words. In this case, advertisements convey economic and philosophical presuppositions through word choice.

All language use has a manipulative aspect to it in the sense that speakers employ words in order to have an effect on hearers, such as to convey information, ask questions, or issue commands. But the words chosen are often not neutral in their connotations. They have associated senses that presuppose culturally shared symbolic meanings. Cultural symbols are transmitted through language and obtain their strength because speakers and hearers nonconsciously accept their indirectly expressed assumptions. The power of language to convey social messages is recognized, for instance, by many American women who object to being called "girl" or by African-American men who object to being called "boy."

Because of the covert symbolic aspect of language, it is difficult to understand the full range of meanings expressed by speakers in another culture. To gain insights into a people's worldview or system of values, it is necessary to ascertain the cultural symbols embedded in their words. This is one reason that translation from one language into another is never completely accurate. Words in isolation can be translated, but the full sense of those words in context cannot be conveyed easily or succinctly.

As difficult as it is to translate the meaning of words, it is an even more complex task to transfer the meanings conveyed by the structure and use of discourse from one language or culture to another. Discourse practices are taken for granted; these practices become part of a speaker's production and interpretation of speech without her or his conscious reflection on the presupposed meanings of particular choices. The practices become "naturalized," that is, thought of as natural rather than as culturally produced and evaluated. Differences in patterns of discourse include the kinds of meanings focused on, the way conversations or arguments are structured, the allocation of the right to speak, and a vast array of unstated assumptions about the world and about people's rights and powers.

EXTENDED AND TRANSFERRED MEANING

Metaphor and Metonymy

Cultural meanings are also expressed through complex processes of semantic extension and transfer. One such process is that of *metaphor.* Metaphors are based on unstated comparisons between entities or events that share certain features. The comparisons implicitly highlight similarities while ignoring contrasts. According to George Lakoff and Mark Johnson, "[T]he essence of metaphor is understanding and experiencing one kind of thing in terms of another" (1980:5). Analysis of recurring metaphors in a language reveals underlying concepts that help construct the reality or worldview of speakers. In a statement consistent with the writings of Sapir and Whorf, Lakoff and Johnson explain that "[c]ultural assumptions, values and attitudes are not a conceptual overlay that we may or may not place upon experience as we choose. It would be more correct to say that all experience is cultural...we experience our 'world' in such a way that our culture is already present in the very experience itself" (ibid.:57). They also argue that analyses of metaphor provide insights into cultural constructions of reality because "our ordinary conceptual system, in terms of which we both think and act, is fundamentally metaphorical in nature" (ibid.:3).

An example from their work that illustrates a frequent construct in English is the pervasive theme "Time is money" (ibid.:7–9). This concept is embedded in these statements:

> You don't use your time *profitably.*
>
> How do you *spend* your time these days?
>
> This gadget will *save* you hours.

These expressions are based on metaphors that treat intangible entities or qualities as though they were concrete objects. In our conceptual model, we conceive of time as a particular kind of object or commodity. "Time in our culture is a valuable commodity. It is a limited resource that we use to accomplish our goals.... Thus we understand and experience time as the kind of thing that can be spent, wasted, budgeted, invested wisely or poorly, saved or squandered" (ibid.:8).

Another recurring metaphorical construct discussed by Lakoff and Johnson is the opposition between "up" and "down." Activities or states viewed positively are expressed as "up"; those evaluated negatively are expressed as "down" (ibid.:15–17). The following list presents some of these comparisons:

	Up	*Down*
Emotions:	You're in *high* spirits.	He's feeling *low* today.
Consciousness:	Wake *up*!	She *sank* into a coma.
Health:	He's in *top* shape.	Her health is *declining*.
Control:	I'm *on top* of the situation.	He *fell* from power.
Status:	She'll *rise* to the top.	He's at the *bottom* of society.
Virtuousness:	He's *high*-minded.	I wouldn't *stoop* that low.

The English language characteristically employs lineal metaphors to describe many different kinds of events. Common expressions include *trace a relationship, follow a line of thought, set a course of action, follow the direction of an argument,* and *bridge a gap in conversation.* Certain ways of talking indicate that lineal order is positively valued in our society: *line up support for one's cause, set the record straight, keep someone in line, straighten up.* Contrasting expressions reveal cultural attitudes: *keeping to the straight and narrow* is virtuous, whereas *wandering from the path* is suspect. Similarly, in conversation, *getting straight to the point* is desirable in our society, but *talking around an issue* or *beating around the bush* indicates deception.

Another type of metaphoric construction common in English is the use of container images when depicting nonphysical entities or processes. This pattern is consistent with tendencies in English to make objects out of intangibles. Once a nonconcrete entity is transformed into an object, it can be contained, entered, left, held, or the like. Use of locative prepositions (prepositions that denote location, direction, or movement in regard to an object) often signals this type of metaphor: He's *out of* his mind; They're *in* love; I feel *under* the weather. In these expressions, subjects are depicted "as if" they were in some physical relation to a defined and contained space, for example, to be *in* love. Here, "love," an internal emotion, is transformed into a tangible object and then treated "as if" it were an objectified and tangible place on the model of actual physical space, such as "they're in the house."

Every language has characteristic conceptual metaphors that structure not only the language itself but also particular views of reality that speakers share and unconsciously assume. For example, in the Navajo language, the categorization of motion is a major focus of the verb system. Dozens of verbs denote specific aspects of movement and/or of objects affected by motion. Most important, many kinds of events are described with verbs having the theme of movement as their focal meaning. That is, Navajo uses metaphors of motion in "understanding and experiencing" the world. This pervasive metaphor is most clearly demonstrated by examining verbs with their Navajo meanings. In the act of dressing "one moves into clothing (*ʔéːh-háːh*)," to sing is "to move words out of an enclosed space (*ha-di-ʔàːh*)," and a youth is described as "one moves about newly (*ʔánˊɪː-nà-há*)." (Hoijer 1951:116–117)

A special type of metaphor occurring in many languages is *personification*—the process of attributing animate or human qualities to nonliving entities or events. Here are some examples from English:

> High prices are *eating up* my paycheck.
>
> Anxiety is *killing* him.
>
> The window *looks out* over the mountains.

These sentences are semantically inconsistent or anomalous in a literal sense, but they are transformed into culturally acceptable expressions through metaphor. In the last sentence, an inanimate object, window, is interpreted "as if" it were capable of an action, looking, which is inherently possible only for animate beings. In the other expressions, intangible processes are likewise treated as though they were concrete animate beings and therefore able to eat or kill.

Metonymy, another type of semantic transfer, is the substitution of one entity by another based on their shared occurrence in context rather than on the similarity of their attributes. It is a process of replacing one entity with another, not because one is treated "as if" it were another (metaphor), but because one is taken to "stand for" the other on the basis of some contextual relationship. Metonymic transfers highlight one aspect of an entity by decomposing the totality of the object or person and singling out one of its (or his or her) attributes. Associations between two entities may be of various kinds, including substitution of part of an object to represent the whole, the producer for the object produced, or the object used or owned by someone for the user/owner. Some examples from English are the following:

This business needs some new blood.

(part for whole: blood for person)

She likes to read Thomas Hardy.

(producer for product: author for books written by him)

Use of metonymy may stress a speaker's particular interest in an entity. Whereas metaphor adds to the meaning of words by increasing their semantic range through comparisons with other entities, metonymy narrows the semantic focus by highlighting only one aspect of an entity and ignoring its other attributes.

Metaphors of Kinship

In an analysis of extended and transferred meanings, each association of linguistic form and cultural content necessitates its own culturally based interpretation. However, certain domains tend to be extended metaphorically and/or metonymically in many languages. Kinship terminology is one such domain. *Kin terms* are frequently used to refer metaphorically to nonrelatives. In our society, in some families children call close friends of their parents by kin terms, usually *aunt* or *uncle*. For these families, it is considered impolite for a child to call an adult by her or his first name. But calling one's parents' close friend by a title and his or her last name, such as "Ms. Smith" or "Mr. Jones," appears highly formal and distant. The compromise of extending kin terms, such as "Aunt Susan" or "Uncle John," expresses informality and intimacy of a relationship without being rude. An adult is spoken about (or spoken to) "as if" she or he were a relative. For some speakers, the kin terms *brother* and *sister* are used in political, social, or religious contexts. Sisters and brothers are equals, share experiences of life, and owe each other reciprocal respect and support.

Another example of metaphoric extension of kin terms comes from the Navajo language. The morpheme for "mother" {-ma} is used to refer to the following entities: mother, the earth, agricultural fields, corn, sheep, and Changing Woman (a major Navajo deity) (Witherspoon 1975:15–16). These meanings are connected by a constellation of symbols of motherhood. In Navajo culture, the primary social and emotional bond is that between mother and child. Mother and child are linked through birth and nurturance. A mother gives life to her child and then continually safeguards that life with physical and emotional support.

The metaphor of motherhood is extended to the earth and agricultural fields because they share an essential attribute of mothers; they are fertile and bring forth life in the form of plants and foods. Metaphoric reference to corn and sheep is based on their economic importance to Navajos. Corn is their most important crop and forms the basis of traditional subsistence. Sheep are of great cultural significance, both as source of income and as measurement of personal wealth. For all these reasons, then, corn and sheep sustain Navajo people "as if" they were mothers. Finally, metaphoric use of *mother* to refer to the deity Changing Woman combines fertility and nurturing themes of motherhood. In Navajo myths, Changing Woman came into being at a time of chaos when people were not able to reproduce. The first puberty rite was conducted for her so that she could menstruate and become fertile. Afterward, she created the original Navajo clans from pieces of her skin. And she gave corn to the people, thus contributing to their daily sustenance. This myth expresses complex meanings linking Changing Woman's being, her fertility, and her actions to the birth and survival of Navajo people. Thus, she is a quintessential metaphor of motherhood.

Kinship terms (as well as other words) can be affected by multiple processes of semantic transfer, demonstrating the richness of language's creative possibilities. Meanings of the word *amma* (mother) in Kannada, a Dravidian language spoken by some 26 million people in India, are interconnected by complex processes of extension and transfer (Bean 1975). *Amma* has the focal meaning of "mother" but is extended through metaphor to refer to any adult woman and to goddesses. *Amma* is also used as a metonym in reference to smallpox. To appreciate the consistency of these meanings of *amma,* we need to understand the cultural implications of adulthood and the belief systems of Hindus.

According to Susan Bean, the word *amma* is extended to any adult woman, especially in polite speech, because in rural Indian society all adult women are assumed to be married and therefore are assumed to be mothers (ibid.:320–321). All women, therefore, are addressed "as if" they were mothers. The metaphor of "mother" is also extended to Hindu goddesses, who are either benevolent and nurturing or fierce and dangerous (ibid.:323–324). Benevolent goddesses are "like" one's mother; dangerous goddesses are spoken of "as if" they were mother in order to appease and placate them so that, by treating them respectfully, they will respond with kindness (like a mother). Finally, the word *amma* can be used in a metonymic transfer to refer to smallpox. The metonym results from a believed association between certain goddesses and smallpox (ibid.:324). Because the deities can cause and cure smallpox, they have become linguistically linked to the disease. The word *amma,* which was first extended through metaphor to "goddess," is then substituted through metonymy for "smallpox."

Metaphors of the Body

Another underlying metaphor found commonly in languages is the use of body-part terms to describe actions or states or to label inanimate objects. The latter process can entail personification, as in "leg of a table" or "arm of a chair." These items of furniture are depicted "as if" their physical structure were analogous to a human body. In English, we also use body-part imagery in more complex verbal expressions, such as:

Let's get to the *heart* of the matter.

She's willing to *face* her problem.

She *shoulders* many responsibilities.

The criminal *fingered* his accomplice.

Widespread use of corporeal metaphors probably results from the fact that human beings give central importance to their own bodies. We extend the imagery of body to inanimate objects and to descriptions of activities. It is a process of observing and experiencing the world through human eyes and, by analogy, with human form.

Many languages use body-part terms to describe activities or noncorporeal entities. In Zapotec, a language spoken in Oaxaca, Mexico, the human body provides the prototypical model for describing parts of any animate being or inanimate object (MacLaury 1989). The bodies of all animals are named from the perspective of human anatomy. For example, the front leg of a four-legged animal is called "hand" and the hind leg is called "foot." An animal is described "as if" it were a person walking on all fours (ibid.:121). In addition, human body-part names are extended metaphorically to describe inanimate objects by the following analogies:

top = head (*gìk*)

front = belly (*là?áyn*)

upper front = face (*lō*)

lower front = foot (*ye?e*)

back = back (*tîč*)

side = side (*ko?o*)

underneath = bottom, buttocks (*gìt*)

entrance, opening = mouth, lips (*ro?o*)

inside = stomach (*la?ayn*)

Note: The pitch markings on vowels follow these conventions: (´) extra high; (`) high; (¯) low; (unmarked) extra low; (ˆ) extra high-high.

Figures 3.4, 3.5, and 3.6 illustrate Zapotec human body-part terms and their analogous meanings related to various animate and inanimate entities. Figure 3.4 shows the words for human body parts, and Figure 3.5 shows their application to an animal. Body-part terms are applied to containers in Figure 3.6. The top of a box is called "head," front is "face," back is "back," inside is "stomach," and bottom is "foot."

Nearby indigenous languages belonging to the Mixtecan family also extend body-part terms, endowing them with many complex meanings (Hollenbach 1995). As in the semantic processes demonstrated in Zapotec, the words for "face" and "foot" are used for analogous parts of inanimate objects and for the space that "projects out from that part," or what Hollenbach calls "projecting space" (ibid.:171). Examples of "projecting space" for "face" include "the *front surface* of the house," "the *area in front* of the house"; examples for "foot" include "the *base* of the tree," "the *space near the foot* of the tree." In addition, words for "face" and "foot" are extended into temporal domains. That is, the spatial use of "face" to refer to "place (where)" has become the temporal "time (when)" and the spatial use of "foot" to refer to "bottom of" has become the temporal "beginning of" (ibid.:172).

The Mohawk language frequently uses the noun morpheme for "body," {-*ya?t*-}, in verbs with metaphoric meaning. Some examples are the following (Bonvillain 1989: 346–347):

I had a nightmare: it pressed, squeezed my body.
ũ-k-ya?t-ò:lalak-e?
DEF-I-body-press, squeeze-ASP
He judged it, weighed it: he cut the body in half.
wa?-t-ha-ya?t-ò:leht-e?
DEF-two-he-body-cut in half-ASP

Other metaphoric constructions in Mohawk employ specific body-part terms, such as (Bonvillain 1990):

You're crazy: Your brain is stirred, mixed.
te-se-nũ?wal-awɨ́:lye-?
two-you-brains-stir, mix-ASP

FIGURE 3.4   Zapotec Body-Part Terms.
(MacLaury, *International Journal of American Linguistics* 55 (1989) 122. Copyright © University of Chicago Press.)

I choked her: I broke her breath in two pieces.
  waʔ-khe-hǔl-yaʔk-eʔ
  DEF-I:her-breath-break in two-ASP
I take her advice: I stand up my inner ear to her.
  khey-at-ahǔhsa-t-eʔ
  I:her-self-inner ear-stand up-ASP

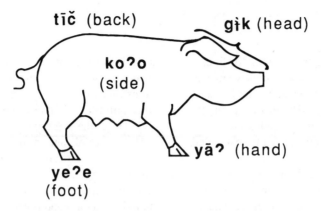

FIGURE 3.5 Zapotec Terms Applied to Animals. (MacLaury, *International Journal of American Linguistics* 55 (1989) 123. Copyright © University of Chicago Press.)

Human senses frequently provide the basis for metaphoric constructs. In English, the visual sense is particularly prone to such uses, as in "I see what you mean" or "that was an insightful remark"; or in a nice combination of visual, lineal, and bodily metaphors: "I can see where this argument is heading." The term *worldview* also derives from this same underlying sensory concept.

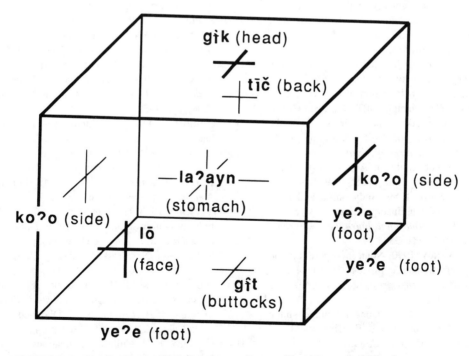

FIGURE 3.6 Zapotec Terms Applied to Boxes. (*International Journal of American Linguistics* by MacLaury. Copyright 1989 by UNIVERSITY OF CHICAGO PRESS-JOURNALS. Reproduced with permission of UNIVERSITY OF CHICAGO PRESS-JOURNALS in the format Textbook via Copyright Clearance Center.)

Summary

Cultural models provide frameworks for understanding the physical and social worlds we live in. These models are implicitly and explicitly transmitted through language. Therefore, linguistic analyses, particularly of words and expressions, reveal underlying assumptions, interests, and values.

Several different kinds of ethnolinguistic evidence contribute to an understanding of associations between language and cultural meaning. First, degrees of specialization and principles of classification within semantic domains indicate cultural interest and discrimination. Second, focal meanings of words and prototypes of categories demonstrate the ways that people make sense of the multitude of objects and events in their world. Third, the symbolic content of language, expressed in words and in metaphoric extensions, transmits and reinforces complex social and cultural messages. Finally, patterns of discourse in communicative interactions reflect cultural assumptions about appropriate use of language in context, about the rights and powers of participants, and about the meaning of communication itself.

References

BEAN, SUSAN. 1975. Referential and indexical meanings of *amma* in Kannada: Mother, woman, goddess, pox and help! *Journal of Anthropological Research* 31:313–330.

BERLIN, BRENT, AND PAUL KAY. 1969. *Basic Color Terms: Their Universality and Evolution.* Berkeley: University of California Press.

BERLIN, BRENT, DENNIS BEEDLOVE, AND PETER RAVEN. 1974. Principles of Tzeltal Plant Classification. New York: Academic Press.

BLOOMFIELD, LEONARD. 1946. Algonquian. In *Linguistic Structures of Native America,* ed. H. Hoijer. Publications in Anthropology No. 6. New York: Viking Fund, pp. 85–129.

BONVILLAIN, NANCY. 1989. Body, mind and idea: Semantics of noun incorporation in Akwesasne Mohawk. *International Journal of American Linguistics* 55:341–358.

BONVILLAIN, NANCY. 1990. Noun incorporation and metaphor: Semantic process in Akwesasne Mohawk. *Anthropological Linguistics* 32:173–194.

BORODITSKY, LERA. 2001. Does language shape thought? Mandarin and English speakers' conceptions of time. *Cognitive Psychology* 43:1–22.

BOWERMAN, MELISSA. 1996. Learning how to structure space for language: A crosslinguistic perspective. In *Language and Space,* ed. P. Bloom, M. Petersen, L. Nadel, and M. Garrett. Cambridge, MA: MIT Press, pp. 385–436.

BROWN, PENELOPE. 1994. The ins and ons of Tzeltal locative expressions: The semantics of static description of location. *Linguistics* 32:743–790.

FILLMORE, CHARLES. 1982. Towards a descriptive framework for spatial deixis. In *Speech, Place and Action,* ed. R. J. Jarvella and W. Klein. New York: Wiley, pp. 31–59.

GOODENOUGH, WARD. 1956. Componential analysis and the study of meaning. *Language* 32:195–216.

GOODENOUGH, WARD. 1965. Yankee kinship terminology: A problem in componential analysis. In *Formal Semantic Analysis,* ed. E. Hammel. *American Anthropologist* 67:259–287.

GUMPERZ, JOHN. 1996. The linguistic and cultural relativity of conversational inference. In *Rethinking Linguistic Relativity,* ed. J. Gumperz and S. Levinson. New York: Cambridge University Press, pp. 374–406.

HALLOWELL, A. IRVING. 1960. Ojibwa ontology, behavior and world view. In *Culture in History: Essays in Honor of Paul Radin,* ed. S. Diamond. New York: Columbia University Press, pp. 19–52.

HOIJER, HARRY. 1951. Cultural implications of some Navaho linguistic categories. *Language* 27:111–120.

HOLLENBACH, BARBARA. 1995. Semantic and syntactic extensions of body-part terms in Mixtecan.

International Journal of American Linguistics 61, no. 2:168–190.

JACKENDOFF, RAY. 1996. The architecture of the linguistic-spatial interface. In *Language and Space,* ed. P. Bloom, M. Petersen, L. Nadel, and M. Garrett. Cambridge, MA: MIT Press, 1–30.

KAA, MO. 1976. The logic of non-European linguistic categories. In *Universalism versus Relativism in Language and Thought: Proceedings of a Colloquium on the Sapir-Whorf Hypothesis,* ed. R. Pinxten. The Hague: Mouton, pp. 85–96.

KAY, PAUL. 1975. Synchronic variability and diachronic change in basic color terms. *Language in Society* 4:257–270.

KAY, PAUL, AND CHAD MCDANIEL. 1978. The linguistic significance of the meanings of basic color terms. *Language* 54:610–646.

LABOV, WILLIAM. 1973. The boundaries of words and their meanings. In *New Ways of Analyzing Variation in English,* ed. C. Bailey and R. Shuy. Washington, DC: Georgetown University Press, pp. 340–373.

LAKOFF, GEORGE. 1972. Hedges: A study in meaning criteria and the logic of fuzzy concepts. *Papers from the 8th Regional Meeting of the Chicago Linguistic Society.* Chicago, IL: Chicago Linguistic Society, pp. 183–228.

LAKOFF, GEORGE, AND MARK JOHNSON. 1980. *Metaphors We Live By.* Chicago, IL: University of Chicago Press.

LEVINSON, STEPHEN. 1996. Relativity in spatial conception and description. In *Rethinking Linguistic Relativity,* ed. J. Gumperz and S. Levinson. New York: Cambridge University Press, pp. 177–202.

LOUNSBURY, FLOYD. 1964. The structural analysis of kinship semantics. In *Proceedings of the IXth International Congress of Linguists,* ed. H. Lunt. The Hague: Mouton, pp. 1073–1093.

LUCY, JOHN. 1996. The scope of linguistic relativity: An analysis and review of empirical research. In *Rethinking Linguistic Relativity,* ed. J. Gumperz and S. Levinson. New York: Cambridge University Press, pp. 37–70.

LUCY, JOHN. 1998. Space in language and thought: Commentary and discussion. *Ethos* 26, no. 1:105–111.

MACLAURY, ROBERT. 1989. Zapotec body-part locatives: Prototypes and metaphoric extensions. *International Journal of American Linguistics* 55:119–154.

NICOLLE, STEVE. 2001. A comparative study of ethnobotanical taxonomies: Swahili and Digo. *SIL (Summer Institute of Linguistics), Notes on Anthropology,* vol. 5, pp. 33–43.

PETERSON, MARY, LYNN NADEL, PAUL BLOOM, AND MERRILL GARRETT. 1996. Space and language. In *Language and Space,* ed. P. Bloom, M. Petersen, L. Nadel, and M. Garrett. Cambridge, MA: MIT Press, pp. 553–577.

QUINN, NAOMI, AND DOROTHY HOLLAND. 1987. Culture and cognition. In *Cultural Models of Language and Thought,* ed. D. Holland and N. Quinn. New York: Cambridge University Press, pp. 3–40.

SAPIR, EDWARD. 1949a (1912). Language and environment. In *Selected Writings of Edward Sapir,* ed. D. Mandelbaum. Berkeley: University of California Press, pp. 89–103.

SAPIR, EDWARD. 1949b (1929). The status of linguistics as a science. In *Selected Writings of Edward Sapir,* ed. D. Mandelbaum. Berkeley: University of California Press, pp. 160–166.

VOLOSINOV, V. N. 1973 (1929). *Marxism and the Philosophy of Language.* Cambridge, MA: Harvard University Press.

WHORF, BENJAMIN. 1956a (1941). A linguistic consideration of thinking in primitive communities. In *Language, Thought and Reality,* ed. J. B. Carroll. Cambridge, MA: MIT Press, pp. 65–86.

WHORF, BENJAMIN. 1956b (1941). The relation of habitual thought and behavior to language. In *Language, Thought and Reality,* ed. J. B. Carroll. Cambridge, MA: MIT Press, pp. 134–159.

WITHERSPOON, GARY. 1975. *Navajo Kinship and Marriage.* Chicago, IL: University of Chicago Press.

WITKOWSKI, STANLEY, AND CECIL BROWN. 1983. Marking-reversals and cultural importance. *Language* 59:569–582.

YOUNG, ROBERT. 1978. English as a second language for Navajos. In *A Pluralistic Nation,* ed. M. Lourie and N. Conklin. Rowley, MA: Newbury House, pp. 162–172.

CHAPTER 4

Contextual Components: Outline of an Ethnography of Communication

"Would you be so kind as to pass the salt?"
"Gimme the salt!"

These sentences demonstrate a basic fact about language use: Alternative means can be used to achieve the same goal (in this case, obtaining salt). These sentences might be employed by different speakers and/or by the same speaker in different contexts. Variation in ways of speaking stems both from segmentation of the speech community into groups based on class, gender, race, and the like, and from differences in the contexts of speech events. In this chapter, we explore language use as it is influenced by the context of speech events (we will analyze factors of community segmentation in subsequent chapters). We examine various features of setting, participants, topics, and goals as they influence how people speak in any given encounter. We end the chapter with a discussion of some types of speech acts.

ETHNOGRAPHY OF COMMUNICATION

Speech behavior should be analyzed in its widest cultural and social context in order to discover culturally relevant features of variation. An *ethnography of communication* (Hymes 1974) includes descriptions of all explicit and implicit norms for communication, detailing aspects of verbal, nonverbal, and social parameters of interaction. To quote Dell Hymes: "The starting point is the ethnographic analysis of the communicative conduct of a community" (ibid.:9). Hymes lists several components of communication requiring description: (1) participants, minimally speaker and addressee; (2) code used by interlocutors; (3) channel (e.g., speaking, writing, nonverbal signals); (4) setting or context; (5) form or genre (e.g., conversation, folktale, chant, debate); and (6) topics and attitudes (ibid.:10).

In analyzing communicative events, primary consideration should be given to functions of speech. We need to recognize that there are many ways to achieve similar purposes, as in the two ways of requesting salt noted at the beginning of this chapter. We also need to recognize that any linguistic form may serve different functions. For example, the utterance "How are you?" can be a legitimate question if spoken by a close friend, or it may be a simple routine greeting.

All cultures provide rules for appropriate communicative interaction, defining behaviors that *should* occur, that *may* occur, and that *should not* occur in given contexts. These rules are learned through both formal and informal processes of socialization that begin in childhood. Children may be overtly instructed about how to act and what to say (or not to say) in particular places or to particular people—for example, "Say 'thank you' to the nice lady" or "Don't shout in the bus!" But children learn most rules of appropriate communicative behavior from their own observations of family members, peers, and even strangers in public places. Interactional norms are specific to each society and convey cultural messages of shared values and expectations. We use these guidelines to shape our own behavior and to evaluate the actions of others.

An ethnographic approach to analyzing communication stresses the cultural specificity of rules of communication and the totality of factors needing description. The most important aspects are settings, participants, topics, and goals. Each of these components can be studied separately, but it should be remembered that a speech event is an integrated occurrence and all of its components are interdependent. Relative primacy of any one factor depends on speakers' assessment of the entire situation and their judgment of likely outcomes. Certain behaviors tend to co-occur in given contexts and lead to an overall sense of consistency or coherence. In a focus on discourse, we can amend Hymes's call for an ethnography of communication to refer to an ethnography of discourse that emphasizes not only the text but the social aspects of interaction as well. Such an ethnography would include the cultural contexts in which texts are produced, the norms of interpretation, and the societal rules and roles that apply to both the production and interpretation of discourse.

For instance, speech actions in contexts designated as formal often take place in specified settings and among expected participants, and concern relatively fixed topics. A brief sketch of court proceedings in the United States provides a good example of the interconnectedness of factors:

1. *Setting:* Trials or hearings are communicative events that occur in particular settings, namely, courtrooms. The courtroom itself has a structural design with separate seating areas for various categories of participants that orient them in relation to one another.
2. *Participants:* Participants include judges, lawyers, defendants and plaintiffs, witnesses, jurors, spectators, and court officials. Each participant's behavior is conditioned by his or her role. The judge is singled out by her or his seating position in the front, usually on a raised platform, of the courtroom and by special attire. The judge clearly controls communicative behavior of the other participants, each of whom has certain obligations to speak or not to speak. In fact, failure to speak when so directed and failure to be silent otherwise are legally punishable offenses ("contempt of court"). Only judges, lawyers, and witnesses may speak publicly. Other participants (jurors, spectators, officers) must remain silent. Specific discourse patterns are expected of each type of participant. Lawyers may make introductory and concluding statements or ask questions. Witnesses answer questions. Judges have greater latitude in the kinds of speech appropriate for them; they can make statements, ask questions, issue commands, and make rulings.
3. *Topics:* Topics of discussion are rigidly defined. The communicative event is about "something," and all speech behavior must be relevant to that issue. Rights of participants

to introduce or change topics are narrowly limited, and permission must be asked of the judge (and granted) in order to incorporate extraneous speech. In lawyers' questioning of witnesses, it must be clear that questions are relevant to the central issue or are a logical development from it. Similarly, witnesses' answers must be germane to the topic. Judges have some flexibility in topic choice, but they, too, are limited by the overall focus.

4. *Goals:* Goals of participants vary according to their role in the proceeding. Speakers choose words, tone of voice, facial expression, gesture, and so on, to accomplish their purpose. For example, the judge must appear impartial, lawyers speak and act aggressively, defendants portray themselves as innocent, witnesses appear honest and reliable, and jurors remain silent but convey interest in the speech and behavior of others.

Although communicative events taking place in informal interactions are not as highly structured as are court proceedings, they, too, are constrained by cultural norms of roles, rights to speak, and ways of speaking. However, rules governing informal behavior are rarely objectified by participants and are not consciously stated or even recognized. We usually assume that behavior in these contexts is "natural," although it is in fact conditioned by our culture just as much as activities in formal settings.

The notion of an "ethnography of communication" is relevant also to analyzing informal communicative behavior. Underlying and unstated rules become evident by observing variation in actions and speaking styles. Reactions by individuals to ongoing behavior, showing either approval or disapproval, likewise indicate cultural norms. We generally become most aware of informal communicative norms when they are violated, that is, when someone speaks inappropriately. Then we can evaluate the "mistake" against our culturally shared models of appropriate behavior. Speakers' errors often come from misjudging the relative importance of given components within speech events—that is, misjudging the weight of settings, participants, topics, and goals in framing one's speech style, choice of words, and nonverbal cues.

SETTINGS

Settings of communicative events provide arenas for action, both in a physical and a social sense. They help define events as particular kinds of occasions invoking certain behaviors and restricting others. Settings for communication can be classified along a continuum of formality or informality.

After reviewing descriptions of formal events in many cultures, Judith Irvine suggested that the following four *aspects of formality* are universal: increased structuring, consistency of co-occurrence choices, emphasis on positional identities of participants, and emergence of a central situational focus (1979:776–779). Increased structuring of formal events is reflected in rules of etiquette that influence participants' attire and demeanor as well as their speech. Markers of formality may include features of pronunciation, intonation, facial expression, grammar, and vocabulary, with tendencies to use more prestigious or "correct" speech and to appear "serious." Rights of participants to speak may be curtailed or directed into certain kinds of exchanges and turn taking. Our example of courtroom proceedings demonstrates these principles of event structuring.

Participants in formal events tend to make stylistic choices that are highly consistent with the overall theme of "seriousness" appropriate to the occasion. People rarely make jokes, tease, or use expletives in highly formal situations, although they may be free to do so at other times.

Irvine's third aspect of formality refers to the social identities of participants. All people have multiple roles or identities: parent, friend, teacher, president of an organization. Formal situations define people by their "positional and public" rather than "personal" identities (ibid.:778). By invoking public roles, social distance rather than intimacy is stressed. An emphasis on positional identities is often reflected linguistically in forms of address. For instance, a married couple working together as doctors in a shared office are unlikely to address or refer to each other by first name in the presence of patients but instead use socially distancing forms such as Dr. Smith. They would be unlikely in this context to call each other "Honey" or to use any other term of endearment normally appropriate in their private interactions.

Formal situations tend to focus on specific issues and happenings. This aspect of events is typically reflected in constraints on topic choice and in restrictions on speakers' rights to change or introduce elements. For example, during religious ceremonies in our culture, speech is limited by participants' roles. Ceremonies are centered on particular rites, and most speech is highly predetermined, with few, if any, opportunities for shifts of focus. Even when delivering sermons or other individualized speech, speakers must keep within narrow guidelines of topic and topic relevance.

Norms for communicative behavior in informal settings are much more diffuse and flexible, although participants always assess speech and nonverbal actions according to cultural models of appropriateness. Structuring of informal situations is relatively loose. Speakers are able to select stylistic features of pronunciation, grammar, and vocabulary based on their individual habits and preferences rather than on dictates of the situation. Conversational patterns likewise are usually adaptable and spontaneous, given general cultural constraints. Topics also shift frequently within encounters and are dependent upon interlocutors' interests and goals.

Settings and the activities that occur in them may be bounded spatially and socially. Physical boundaries might include the kinds of buildings or spaces where a particular event typically takes place (e.g., a courthouse, a church, a school, a home, a kitchen, a playground, etc.). In conjunction with these physical spaces, people expect certain kinds of communicative interactions that are consistent and reliably predictable. Social boundaries might include specific participants and topics considered appropriate. But within any setting, communication does not just happen but rather needs to be negotiated and developed. Therefore, people learn how to begin and end particular kinds of interactions, each following normative patterns. For example, as members of a particular society, we share expectations about how court proceedings begin and end, how religious ceremonies begin and end, and how we can appropriately start a conversation and terminate one.

PARTICIPANTS

Participants in speech events include speakers, addressees, and audience. Individuals usually change roles during a given event. In two-party conversations, each person is alternatively speaker or addressee as she or he exchanges speaking turns. Only in the most formal occasions, such as religious ceremonies, public speeches, or lectures, does one person monopolize all (or nearly all) of the rights to speak. Even in these events, audiences have a communicative role to play by making appropriate responses to the speech of officiators.

People make choices about language use based on characteristics of other participants in a speech event. Such choices include many aspects of linguistic and nonverbal behavior:

1. *Pronunciation:* distinctiveness of articulation.
2. *Prosodic features of intonation:* velocity (speed of speaking), volume (loudness/softness).
3. *Syntax:* complexity or simplicity of word order, phrase construction, and so on.
4. *Choice of words.*
5. *Nonverbal cues:* facial expression, eye contact, touch, physical distancing.

Speakers determine, usually nonconsciously, which communicative features are most appropriate given the person(s) to whom they are speaking. If someone is a victim of a fender-bender episode, words chosen to describe the incident and the perpetrator will likely be different in recounting the event to one's friends or grandparents. Adult speech directed toward children typically consists of short, common words and simple sentence construction. And speaking to students in a lecture hall requires increases in loudness and decreases in speed compared to normal forms of speech.

In addition to these linguistic features, the choice of topic also depends on the speaker's awareness of cultural and individual expectations. Certain topics will be selected for discussion with some people, but not when conversing with others. In our society, it is considered highly inappropriate to talk about one's personal problems to a stranger or even to a casual acquaintance. Indeed, such topic selection would likely be evaluated as a symptom of a psychological disorder.

Finally, norms of conversational interaction are patterned in recognition of other participants in speech events. Dynamics such as turn taking, topic development, and signals of listenership are attuned to specific relationships between interlocutors. For instance, employers speaking with employees are more likely to take longer turns, to control topics, and to exert power through interruption than are workers when speaking to their employers.

Terms of Address

One of the most sensitive features of language in reflecting speakers' assessment of co-participants is the term of address chosen in a speech event. Terms of address include several linguistic types, all of which name, refer to, or address hearers. They may be personal names, titles, kinship terms, or personal pronouns that can be used separately or concomitantly.

In American English, the most frequently used address forms are First Name (FN) and Title + Last Name (TLN). There are three possible exchanges of these forms in two-party interactions: reciprocal FN (each participant calls the other by FN), reciprocal TLN, or nonreciprocal FN-TLN (one member uses TLN but receives FN; the other uses FN and receives TLN). Speakers select among the options, depending on the perceived relationship between themselves and their addressee. Speakers evaluate socially meaningful characteristics of individuals and then make judgments about their own status relative to that of the addressee. In general, reciprocal forms of address (mutual exchange of either FN or TLN) occur between status equals, and nonreciprocal forms are typical of unequal relationships. Reciprocal FN tends to indicate intimacy or casualness, that is, lack of social distance. Reciprocal TLN marks formality or politeness. Many societal factors influence speakers' decisions, including age, gender, class, and ethnicity.

In a complex multiethnic and multiclass society such as the United States, it is impossible to make generalizations that realistically apply to all people. However, in a well-known study of American address forms based on analysis of dialogue in American plays written from the 1930s through 1958 and of observations in business organizations located in Boston, Massachusetts, Roger Brown and Marguerite Ford (1961) found that reciprocal FN is the most common address form used by status equals. Reciprocal TLN is used between adults who have only recently become acquainted. Speakers shift from TLN to FN fairly quickly, especially if both speaker and addressee are young and/or of the same gender. In a historical note, characters in earlier American plays written between 1830 and 1911 allowed more time to elapse before switching to mutual FN than did those in modern plays (ibid.:377). Although plays are art forms and not actual life, they are reliable reflectors of social practice, and the difference portrayed in earlier and later works is undoubtedly an accurate indicator of changing social norms.

Use of nonreciprocal TLN-FN requires a complex assessment by speakers of their position vis-à-vis addressees. Brown and Ford found that occupational status and relative age were the most significant factors in choice of form. Occupation was especially critical, whether as an ongoing relationship (e.g., in an employer–employee dyad) or as a situational contact (e.g., waiter/customer). Status superiors use FN to subordinates but receive TLN in return. For instance, an employer calls workers John, Jane, and so on, but is addressed as Ms. Jones. Or a customer is addressed as Mr. Smith by an auto mechanic, who is called by his first name in turn.

Combining evidence from reciprocal and nonreciprocal usage, Brown and Ford concluded that the underlying meaning of FN is both "intimacy and condescension," whereas TLN marks "distance and deference" (ibid.:380). The specific social meaning of FN or TLN varies, depending on who is being addressed. FN indicates intimacy if spoken by a friend or relative but shows condescension if used by a superior to a subordinate in nonreciprocal exchanges.

As mentioned, other social factors can add complexity to the meanings of address forms. A study of address among Navajo women who relocated from the Navajo Nation in the Southwest to Los Angeles found different patterns of usage, depending on the ethnicity of the addressee (Fiske 1978). The women typically used TLN when conversing with Anglos, even of the same age as themselves, whereas they usually used FN to age equals. When talking to other Native Americans (but not to members of other "minority" ethnic or racial groups such as blacks, Hispanics, and Asians), TLN was used if the addressee was older than the speaker. This pattern parallels traditional Navajo extensions of kinship terms meaning "grandmother" and "grandfather" to unrelated elders (ibid.:81–82). Navajos' use of TLN can therefore have multiple meanings. First, it reflects recognition of the social and political powers of Anglos. Second, it indicates respect and deference when used for elder Native Americans, an attitude not accorded to members of other ethnic groups. Thus, in one context, to Anglos, TLN marks social distance, but in another, to elder Native Americans, it marks social solidarity.

American address is additionally complicated by possibilities of multiple usages to the same person, especially to intimates. We have several patterns of FN forms: full FN (Thomas), shortened FN (Tom), diminutive (Tommy). Nicknames and abbreviated or otherwise changed forms of LN are also possible. Many factors, especially age, gender, and personal relationship, influence speakers' choices. Children are usually addressed by shortened and/or diminutive names both by other children and by adults. Boys, especially, tend to "outgrow" diminutives when they reach later adolescence and make new acquaintances. Their relatives and childhood friends, however, typically continue to use them in address or reference. Many names for girls already contain the English diminutive /-y/ on the proper name itself (Amy, Nancy). Other girls' names undergo shortening and diminution in one step (Catherine/Cathy). In any case, diminutives for female names tend to continue as address forms much longer than for male names, indeed, often throughout life. Although address patterns directed toward the genders may differ, when used mutually between adults, diminutives signal intimacy and affection.

Pronouns

In most European languages (other than English), complexity of address is demonstrated in pronominal systems. Languages in the Romance, Slavic, and Germanic families have two pronouns for addressee (called second-person pronouns) in contrast to modern English, which has only one, *you.* European pronouns distinguish both number of hearers and relationship between participants. When talking to more than a single individual, a speaker must use the plural pronoun, referred to as the V form (from the French word *vous,* which has equivalents in all the other languages).

When talking to one person, speakers choose either the grammatically singular, referred to as the T form (from French *tu*), or the V form.

Choice of form is a sensitive indicator of personal relationships and societal values. In a now-classic study, Roger Brown and Alfred Gilman (1960) proposed that two semantic components operate in selecting pronouns: power and solidarity. When pronouns are exchanged reciprocally, solidarity between participants is stressed, whereas nonreciprocal usage reflects an unequal power relationship. That is, a superior uses T and receives V, whereas a subordinate uses V and receives T (ibid.:256–259). (Recall that the American naming address system was shown to function in parallel patterning.) Differences in power stem from various factors, including class, occupational hierarchies, age, and gender. For example, adults address children with T but receive V; employers address workers with T and receive V.

Brown and Gilman show that class distinctions affected the reciprocal use of V or T in former times. Members of upper classes exchanged V, and lower-class speakers addressed each other with T. Evidently this difference among equals within classes was based on emphasizing mutual solidarity. Because upper-class speakers were accustomed to receiving V from subordinates, they exchanged it among themselves. Likewise, lower-class speakers were regularly addressed with T.

Modern European pronominal systems have all shifted away from nonreciprocal usage. Brown and Gilman assert that "the reciprocal solidarity semantic has grown with social mobility and an equalitarian ideology.... The development of open societies with an equalitarian ideology acted against the nonreciprocal power semantic and in favor of solidarity. The larger social changes created a distaste for the face-to-face expression of differential power" (ibid.:264, 267). The result has been an increased preference for mutual exchange of T. The T pronoun has been chosen rather than V because the latter was formerly used by upper-class speakers among themselves and was the form given to them in nonreciprocal power relations. Therefore, V is associated symbolically with elite privilege, inconsistent with currently prevailing notions of equality (ibid.:265).

Pronominal use in modern English has resulted from a collapse of an older T/V system, that is, thee/thou and ye/you. In the seventeenth century, social norms were beginning to question the legitimacy of aristocratic power and privilege. One of the arenas of contestation was in language ideologies where "speaking plain" was promoted in opposition to ornate speech. In particular, Quakers dropped the formal and deferential ye/you in favor of the familiar, egalitarian thee/thou as a marker, in their belief system, of the social equality of all people before God. A situation of asymmetric usage therefore ensued because non-Quakers used the polite ye/you but received the familiar thee/thou. The use of the familiar pronouns became a symbol of Quaker social identity and therefore had to be avoided by non-Quakers. According to Michael Silverstein (1985), Quaker usage was both "subversive" and "insulting." Therefore, in a process of marginalizing Quakers, non-Quakers shunned the use of thee/thou because of its social and identity associations and insisted on the use of only ye/you for all contexts and participants. This usage won out by the end of the century. In Silverstein's analysis, ideologies about language and language users had a direct impact on the unfolding structure of the modern English language. As he concludes, "...a new system emerges, in which societal norms abandon T decisively as usage indexing speaker as Quaker and take up the invariant usage of Y" (ibid.:251). This analysis demonstrates the far-reaching effects of social attitudes about language and about specific language users on the structure of language itself.

Changes in social and linguistic norms for addressing interlocutors do not occur instantaneously; rather, they proceed through periods of transition and instability. Speakers are often uncertain and feel awkward when trying to adapt to new patterns, especially if they were socialized under previous conditions. For example, Christina Paulston's study (1976) of the shift in pronominal usage in Sweden from nonreciprocal forms to reciprocal T found that individuals may have personal difficulties adjusting to changing norms even while approving them.

Patterns of pronominal address in France, as well as attitudes of speakers toward pronominal usage, reveal the linguistic, social, and personal complexities that arise in social systems undergoing change. Although people in France report that usage has shifted toward a generalized use of *tu,* observation of actual speech shows considerable ambiguity and variation. Although the reciprocal use of *tu* has increased in the last 20 or 30 years, reciprocal *vous* as well as nonreciprocal uses also persist. Many French speakers view the generalized use of *tu* as a sign of social progress, greater social equality, and the decline of barriers of hierarchical relationships; others decry the loss of politeness and decency reflected in the use of *vous.* For example, a woman in her early fifties commented,

> I think we're going to a generalized use of *tu.* It's part of a general movement toward less ceremonial and more relaxed relations. I believe it's essentially a form of progress. The use of *tu* gives you a certain liberty that you don't have with *vous,* certain freedom to exchange things with others. (Morford 1997:11)

But as *tu* has become commonplace in interactions between people of different ages, genders, and status levels, some people believe that there has been a decline in the ability of the language to signal real intimacy. As one man, a senior executive in a large company, commented,

> At work, everyone calls each other *tu.* There is a negation of certain barriers, a refusal of authority.... This use of *tu* does not at all indicate true familiarity. And it doesn't really help people have better relations with others. I think there is more apparent proximity but fewer real relations, less true exchange and sharing of things, fewer relations that can admit the existence of conflict. (ibid.)

Some speakers prefer the reciprocal exchange of *vous* as a sign of respect, politeness, and social distance appropriate for speakers who do not know each other well. An initial exchange of *vous* also makes possible the affective significance of a switch to *tu* later in a relationship, signaling familiarity, affection, and intimacy. A middle-aged housewife who, along with her husband, hosts monthly discussion groups for students from their Catholic parish reported that she regularly greets the students with *tu:* "I do it intentionally. It's nicer, and it encourages them to say things that they would not say elsewhere" (ibid.:21). But others note that, in some job situations, it is strategically advantageous to use reciprocal *vous* because *tu* implies too much camaraderie that might make it difficult for status superiors to exert authority:

> Using *vous* keeps relations distant. It helps avoid confusion. It allows you to maintain a form of distance that is sometimes useful for both people. Saying *tu* in such a case makes for a mix of hierarchical and friendly relations. (ibid.:23)

Such a mix may lead to confusion, lack of efficiency in the workplace, and resentment when the affective meanings conveyed by *tu* are violated in the practical running of a workplace. These examples demonstrate that selection of a term of address is not a simple matter of making a choice between two options. Instead, language choice results from complex social and emotional processes of evaluating one's goals and relationships.

Patterns of address in the People's Republic of China have been transformed since the revolution of 1949, affecting pronominal usage and employment of various titles. The Chinese language marks second-person singular (addressee) by either *ni* or *nin* (Fang and Heng 1983: 502–503). Prior to the revolution, these pronouns were selected in similar fashion to the European *tu/vous*. The Chinese T pronoun, *ni,* expressed notions of familiarity and intimacy. It was employed reciprocally between friends, colleagues, and generational equals within the family, such as spouses and siblings. However, *ni* expressed differences in status when used nonreciprocally by employers or customers to clerks, workers, servants, and also to soldiers. The Chinese V pronoun, *nin,* marked the high status of addressees and was used in speaking to officials, landlords, and wealthy individuals. It was also employed to kin of ascending generations, such as parents and grandparents. Finally, *nin* was exchanged reciprocally between strangers as a marker of politeness and distance.

According to Fang and Heng, *nin* has been eliminated from colloquial speech altogether in modern China (ibid.:503). Evidently, the power semantic of inequality expressed by *nin* has led to its demise. In contrast, because *ni* encodes familiarity and solidarity, it has won out as the linguistic reflection of an altered social ideology.

In China, then, pronominal usage has shifted to reciprocal *ni* because it is recognized as a signal of egalitarian social relations. However, according to Blum (1997), Chinese speakers often avoid the use of pronouns altogether because of the very neutrality of the terms. People continue to favor linguistic markers of social distinctions, particularly to signal a hierarchical relationship between junior and senior. The reemergence of titles in addressing officials seems to have resulted from pressure from those elites who wish to have their status and power socially marked. In both cases, choice of address terms both expresses cultural models of people's rights and achieves specific goals in relation to officials who have power to grant requests.

Kinship Terms

Speakers can signal social meanings of intimacy, solidarity, or deference toward co-participants by extending kinship terms as address forms to nonkin. In Chapter 3, we saw examples of American children's use of *aunt* and *uncle* as addresses for friends of their parents and thus as markers of intimacy, and the extension of sibling terms with a solidarity semantic among members of political or religious groups. Many other cultures make much more productive use of kin terminology to demonstrate and manipulate status and attitudinal relations. Speakers can fictively apply kin terms to addressees in order to accomplish acts of either flattering and honoring, or insulting and denigrating.

Data on kin-term usage in China demonstrate subtleties in the negotiation of status and relations between co-participants. Speakers use kinship terms when addressing people senior to themselves, either within their own generation or in ascending generations. The most respectful term for addressing a man is *bóbö,* "elder paternal uncle," that is, father's brother, older than father (Hong 1985:207). This word incorporates deferential meanings associated with relative seniority (older than father) and patrilineal descent. Its use implies a combination of the exalted status of the addressee, worthy of extreme respect, and the concomitant humbling of the speaker. By using this kin term to a nonrelative, the speaker signals his or her attitude toward the addressee. Parents introducing their school-age child to a male friend of their own generation, co-participants nicely negotiate the propriety of address by starting with "Jiào Wáng bóbo" (literal translation: call Wang elder uncle) meaning "Say Hello to *bobo* Wang." The male friend, Wang, replies "Zěmme kéyǐ? Bù gǎndāng, bù gǎndāng." (literal translation: how can it be possible? not easy not easy) meaning "Oh, no, you do me too much honor." Wang then goes on to say "Jiào shūshū jiù xíng le." (literal translation: call younger uncle it's fine) meaning "Just call me younger uncle." (ibid.:207–208). (Note that literal translations and tone markers are added, supplied by Amy Cheng.)

In contrast (and revealing gender status), the kin term used for female nonrelatives is *ayi,* "mother's younger sister," unless the addressee is actually much older than the speaker (ibid.:208–209). This kin term does not connote as much social respect as the term used for men. Note also that *ayi* labels a relative on the mother's side, automatically conveying less prestige than the father's kin.

Whatever the term chosen, it is mandatory for the junior relative to address his or her senior by a kin term reflecting respect and implying social hierarchy. This linguistic practice is consistent with cultural models or prototypes of the valued relationship between "benevolent older kin who take care of the younger ones, who reciprocate with affection [and] later in life with care. Invocation of the kinship term calls up images of the prototype for speaker and hearer" (Blum 1997:372).

In Japanese, forms of address employed between spouses and words used to refer to one's spouse are reflections of unequal status within the family. Husbands typically address their wives by first name or by either of two second-person pronouns: *omae* and *kimi. Omae* is the pronoun generally used by status superiors to addressees of lower status; *kimi* is used to subordinates or intimates but not to superiors (Lee 1976:993). In contrast, if a wife addresses her husband by his first name, she adds the honorific suffix *san.* In addition, she employs the second-person pronoun *anata,* which is used by lower-status people to address higher-status addressees (ibid.:996–997).

In addition to distinctions in spousal address, Japanese patterns for referring to one's spouse indicate gender differentiation as well. For referring to his wife, a man has a number of options (ibid.:993–995):

kanai	(derived from *ka* "home, family, house" + *nai* "inside")
tuma	(also meaning "garnishing vegetable served with raw fish; side plank supporting the main part of a roof")
nyoboo	("assistant, secondary person")
uti no yatu	(derived from *uti* "my home" + *no* "of" + *yatu* "fellow")

According to Motoko Lee, these words and expressions connote a secondary person, restricted to the home or participating in a subsidiary capacity. *Uti no yatu* is an impolite or informal reference to a person of lower status.

Japanese wives can refer to husbands with the expression *uti no hito,* literally "person of my house." This phrase carries polite meaning, used by a lower-status speaker to label a superior. Wives also refer to their husbands as *shujin,* "master." Finally, Lee reported two humorous words used by women: *teishu,* "master of my house," and *yakoroku,* "my lodger." She stated that these words have sarcastic implications but did not specify the contexts of their use (ibid.:998).

Taken as a group, the differentiated pronouns, nouns, and expressions used by Japanese wives and husbands demonstrate gender inequality, directly symbolizing the subordinate status of women.

Honorifics

Honorifics are linguistic markers that signal respect toward an addressee. Honorific meanings can be expressed by a variety of linguistic forms, including nouns, pronouns, and verbs. Languages may also contain different levels of speaking to reflect degrees of respect. Honorifics and their usage are clear reflections of language ideologies. As Judith Irvine (1998) points out, "[E]xpressions of deference are incorporated into the language's grammatical rules...the deference payable by person A to person B is understood as an inherently communicated property of particular linguistic expressions, not just the contingent consequence of an expression's deployment in social life" (ibid.:52–53). That is, the honorific form itself becomes saturated with the meaning of respect or deference and is selected for use because it conveys this meaning. And its use is embedded within a cultural ideology of deference owed by some speakers to certain others.

The Nahuatl language, spoken in Mexico, has four distinct levels of direct address, marked by prefixes and suffixes in pronouns, personal names, titles, and yes or no responses to questions (Hill and Hill 1978:124–125). The four distinctions are as follows:

1. Intimacy or subordination (Level I).
2. Neutrality or distance (Level II).
3. Honor (Level III).
4. *Compadrazgo* relationship (Level IV).

Level I is used among intimates of similar age and status to signify closeness and solidarity. It is also employed by adults to children as a signal of the latter's subordination. Level II prefixes can be employed as neutral forms with strangers unless they are very young (Level I would be used) or very old (Level III would be used). Level II forms are not necessarily respectful; rather, they recognize social distance or "strangerness" (ibid.:130). However, they can convey respect if the speaker knows the addressee well; for example, they are used by younger speakers to their elder relatives. When occurring outside the personal address system, Level II prefixes on verbs in Nahuatl have the meaning of physical motion away from the speaker (ibid.:125). In a sense, Level II markers in address are metaphors of physical distance transferred to social relationships. Level III forms are used to address men and women of advanced age or exceptionally high status, such as village priests or officials. Level IV forms are restricted, occurring only between people in a *compadrazgo* relation, that is, parents and godparents or co-godparents of the same child.

In other languages, honorifics can signal the relative status of participants directly by marking the high status of an addressee or indirectly by lowering the speaker's status in relation to the addressee. The Japanese language contains both types of honorifics, as well as a third class expressing respect to the addressee by deferential marking of an entire utterance. To use the honorific system appropriately, Japanese speakers must be aware of relationships between themselves; their interlocutors; and the persons, entities, and activities spoken about.

One set of honorific affixes denotes the high status of addressees or referents. For example, in the following sentence, several honorifics are used, including a noun suffix *-san,* a noun prefix *o-,* and a verb suffix *-are-* (Yamanashi 1974:760–762). Note that honorifics are underlined in the examples:

1. yamada-<u>san</u> ga   musuko-<u>san</u> to   <u>o</u>-syokuzi o   tanosim-<u>are</u>-ta.
   yamada-HON   son-HON   HON-dinner enjoyed-HON
   "Yamada enjoyed dinner with his son."

In this sentence, the target of honor is Yamada, and therefore other people associated with him (his son) and entities and activities involving him (enjoying dinner) are all marked for respect.

A second set of affixes indirectly honors someone by humiliating the speaker or those associated with him or her. In the next example, "son," *gusoku,* contains a marker of humility because it refers to the speaker's son:

2. yamada-<u>san</u> ga   gusoku to   <u>o</u>-syokuzi o   tanosim-<u>are</u>-ta.
 yamada-HON   HUMIL-son   HON-dinner   enjoyed-HON
 "Yamada enjoyed dinner with (speaker's) son."

A third method of honorific marking includes the addition of the affixes -*masi*- and -*mas* to words within a sentence to "indicate speaker's polite attitude toward [his/her] interlocutor" (ibid.:762). These affixes can be added to any type of utterance, but they are particularly effective in issuing requests that are thereby mitigated, signaling deference to the addressee.

Appropriateness of honorific usage may depend on the semantic content of the statements. The utterance "His son helped Yamada" can be marked to honor Yamada (yamada-*san*) and also his son (musuko-*san*), but in the sentence "His son murdered Yamada," "son" would not be honored because of the nature of the act reported (ibid.:766).

In other societies, the use of honorific vocabulary and grammatical constructions by a lower-status person may have a manipulative effect in masking authority. For example, in a study of language and social rank in the Micronesian island of Pohnpei, Elizabeth Keating demonstrates the complexity of the pragmatic functions of honorific language. On Pohnpei, highest status is held by five chiefs, each the head of a territorial unit dividing the island. Chiefs' wives are the highest ranking women and indeed they rank higher than most men. Social status is enacted and validated in verbal and nonverbal features and communicative strategies. Status may be symbolized through speech of high-status people and through the ways that lower-status people talk to those of higher status. A lower-status person may use a combination of vocabulary and verb forms that simultaneously exalt the status of the addressee (exaltive) and lower the speaker's own status (humiliative) (1994:368). Relative status may also be demonstrated through the distribution of space and location within a setting.

An analysis of a specific interaction involving a high-status chief, his wife, and his adopted daughter demonstrates the interplay among these various features. The three principal interactants, in addition to several additional lower-status people, were present and about to take seats on the porch of the chief's house. This is a delicate matter because position on the porch reflects and communicates social standing in a highly structured manner. The chief was sitting toward the back of the porch, symbolizing higher status, while his wife sat somewhat in front of him, a violation of the usual norm that the chief and his wife should be seated at the same level. The daughter, a person lower in status than the chief and his wife, first used self-lowering, humiliative forms to inquire where she should sit. She then addressed the chief's wife employing exaltive pronouns with directives aimed at repositioning the chieftess. Finally, she used gestures to direct the chief himself to change his location. When the chief and chieftess responded, they did not employ honorifics in their speech but rather used ordinary style because, according to Pohnpeian etiquette, high-status people have no need to mark their own status through their speech. In fact, in this interaction, the chief's utterances contained hedges and markers of hesitation and deference.

This specific interaction demonstrates the ways that status can be represented and communicated through language and nonverbal behaviors. In addition, it is significant that hierarchical relationships are enacted through the words and actions of a lower-status person. Differentiation of high and low status then appears to be instigated by someone of lower status rather than by the holders of high status. While in this instance Pohnpeian etiquette seems to confer authority on the lower-status daughter, granting her rights to orchestrate the structured placement of individuals in a setting, it can also be seen to mask real power. The speech of the lower-status daughter is replete with exaltive pronouns and verb forms when she addresses higher-status people. And the chief and chieftess respond with ordinary speech that in effect communicates the message that others must defer to them.

All the diverse systems discussed here, including American names; European and Chinese pronouns; Chinese kin terms; and Nahuatl, Japanese, and Pohnpeian honorifics, demonstrate the complexities of the interdependence of language and social knowledge. To speak appropriately, members of each culture must evaluate various characteristics of co-participants before deciding on proper linguistic form. People may want to show intimacy or respect, but they need to know how to do so without making errors that insult addressees or exaggerate expressions of sentiment.

TOPICS AND GOALS

In addition to setting and participants, another component of speech events that is sensitive to overall context is the topic of conversation or discussion. People choose topics based on combinations of personal interest and sensitivity to preferences of co-participants, all within boundaries set by cultural norms. Violation of accepted rules for topic selection can result in mild social disapproval or in feelings of embarrassment, anger, or distress by addressees. Formal contexts such as ceremonies, lectures, or governmental proceedings tend to predetermine a specific range of topics. Informal interactions are less constraining, but cultural values are relevant to choice of topic, too. For instance, in our society, discussion of bodily functions during meals is generally countered with such admonitions as "Don't talk about it at the dinner table!" or "I don't want to hear about that while I'm eating."

A speaker's compliance with the wishes of others or the speaker's persistence in pursuing a topic of her or his own preference reveals issues concerning a speaker's goals in conversation. People have both individual and communal goals. They seek to express personal interests and engage co-participants in ego-centered topics, but, as social beings, they want to minimize potential conflict with others and to appear agreeable, cooperative, and polite. Politeness is achieved, in part, by acting in accordance with culturally approved ways of speaking.

The goals of speakers can be expressed by a variety of linguistic forms, sensitive to contextual evaluation. Recall the two sentences that began this chapter: "Would you be so kind as to pass the salt?" and "Gimme the salt!" In both cases, the speaker wants to obtain salt but uses alternative ways of conveying this intent. It is easy to imagine contexts in which a speaker would choose each option—the first perhaps at a formal holiday dinner and the second at a casual picnic on the beach. The sentences are characterized by the use of different words—one containing polite, mitigating words such as *be so kind* and *pass* and the other containing the colloquial *gimme*. Also note that the two sentences are of different linguistic types: The first is an interrogative (question), whereas the second is an imperative (command). The form and force of the sentences differ, but their underlying intent is the same, namely, to get the hearer to perform a specific act for the speaker's benefit. Imperatives express this directly; interrogatives do so indirectly.

The linguistic form of an utterance does not have an automatic correlation with particular goals; rather, its interpretation is necessarily contextual. Interrogatives are generally either "requests for information" or "requests for confirmation." In the first instance, speakers ask questions when they want hearers to provide information known to the latter but unknown by the former. In the second, speakers ask hearers to confirm or deny propositions (yes or no questions). The question "Would you be so kind as to pass the salt?" is framed as a "request for confirmation," but clearly the speaker does not want a yes or no response. It is evident that both this sentence and the imperative "Gimme the salt!" are "requests for action." Speakers choose linguistic form depending on personal stylistic preferences and assessment of settings and co-participants.

Alternative ways of phrasing the same goal can also covertly involve different assumptions about individuals' rights, obligations, and accepted norms of interaction. Rules of politeness often lead speakers to express judgments of other people's actions indirectly. Rather than telling someone who is late for an appointment "I always have to wait for you" or "I'm angry at you for making me wait," we can say, "I was beginning to worry that something happened to you."

Adults frequently convey implicit messages in their attempts to control a child's behavior. The following list offers possible ways of phrasing caregivers' admonitions (each containing a different social message) (Halliday 1973:65):

1. That was so out of line. (behavior disapproved on moral grounds)
2. If you do that again, I will have to tell. (threat of punishment)
3. I'm very disappointed in you. (emotional appeal)
4. Don't take what isn't yours. (action violates norms)
5. It makes me sad when you do that (emotional black mail)
6. That's against the rules. (behavior violates external rules)

Just as the same goal can be expressed by a variety of linguistic forms, the same linguistic form can express diverse intentions, depending on the contextual components of setting, participants, and topics. For instance, the sentence "I love you like my brother" conveys solidarity and emotional closeness when said by a man to his friend, but it conveys limitations on a relationship if spoken by a woman to a man. And it can mean something entirely different if the addressee knows that the speaker actually hates his or her brother (and the speaker knows that the addressee knows this; see Bach and Harnish 1979:5).

In analyzing any given text, we need to analyze the effects of two different kinds of goals. Societal goals that underlie and support a particular sociopolitical system may be differentiated analytically from an individual's goal in performing a particular act. For example, societal goals may impose rules for using titles when referring to or addressing certain people, but each individual makes a choice to use titles in addressing certain people in a given context (Duranti 1985:204). Of course, a person's choice is never completely free of the pressures exerted directly and indirectly through norms that support societal goals. For example, if social rules indicate a preference for the use of titles by subordinates to superiors, a person who chooses not to follow these norms may face negative consequences depending on numerous factors, including context, specific participants, and the perceived seriousness of the failure to follow rules.

Speakers give some indication of goals through what is termed the key of an utterance. Key refers to the manner in which an utterance should be performed and interpreted. For example, speakers may employ a particular constellation of volume, velocity, and intonational contours to indicate that they mean their utterances to be interpreted as serious, joking, affectionate, and so on. Changes in key within discourse dramatize changes in the ways that speech should be interpreted.

SPEECH ACTS

The term *speech act* refers to the fact that, through speaking, a person accomplishes goals. Speakers choose ways of expressing themselves based on their intentions and on what they want hearers to believe, accept, or do. Several linguists and philosophers have proposed typologies that classify differences among speech acts. John Austin's distinction among utterances in terms of their purpose and effect has become a widely used framework (1962:94–101):

Type of Speech Act	Definition	Example
Locutionary Act	Act of verbalization, what the speaker says.	She said to me, "You shouldn't try that."
Illocutionary Act	The purpose of verbalization: informing, warning, assuring, criticizing, identifying, persuading.	She warned against my plan.
Perlocutionary Act	The effect produced on the hearer: feelings, thoughts, actions.	She sat me down, checked me. She stopped me, brought me to my senses. She angered me.

Speech act theorists have given attention to delineating illocutionary acts. Prominent among these theorists is John Searle, whose classification and definitions are as follows (1976:10–13):

1. *Representatives:* Commit the speaker (in varying degrees) to something's being the case, to the truth of the expressed proposition; for example, *state, conclude, represent, deduce.*
2. *Directives:* Attempts (of varying degrees) by the speaker to get the hearer to do something; for example, *command, offer, invite, ask, order, request, beg, permit, dare, challenge.*
3. *Commissives:* Commit the speaker (again in varying degrees) to some future course of action; for example, *promise, pledge, threaten.*
4. *Expressives:* Express the psychological state of the speaker toward a particular state of affairs; for example, *thank, congratulate, apologize, condole, deplore, welcome.*
5. *Declarations:* Bring about the correspondence between the propositional content and reality; for example, *appoint, nominate, sentence, pronounce, fire, resign.*

Speakers can ask questions, make predictions, issue commands, express wishes, and state hypothetical conditional intentions, as illustrated in the following utterances (Searle 1965:225):

1. Will John leave the room?
2. John will leave the room.
3. John, leave the room!
4. Would that John left the room.
5. If John will leave the room, I will leave also.

Underlying the notion of illocutionary acts are certain conditions, most important, that interlocutors share beliefs about speakers' sincerity in expressing their intentions. Participants also accept basic notions that they cooperate with each other and that they expect cooperation from one another. Because it is impossible to know fully what is in someone else's mind, interlocutors have to share assumptions about how linguistic form relates to inner thoughts. They have to base their interpretations of speech on the same or at least very similar presuppositions about the range of intentions and the way the speaker expresses these goals linguistically.

Although Searle and others writing on speech acts imply that their taxonomies and underlying presuppositions reflect universal themes, this claim is open for cross-cultural empirical investigation. Michelle Rosaldo, for instance, contended that Western theorists' emphasis on speakers' internal states as a criterion for speech act distinctions is itself a culture-bound notion, stemming from Western philosophical biases that view "language as a 'resource' that can represent the world (and that the individual can then 'use' as a tool to argue, promise, criticize or lie)" (1982:210). Rosaldo's research among the Ilongot, a tribal people of the Philippines, led her to formulate their appreciation of language in quite different terms. For Ilongots, "words are not made to 'represent' objective truth, because all truth is relative to the relationships and experiences of those who claim to 'know.' We may...think that meaning grows from what the individual 'intends' to say. For Ilongots, it is relations, not intentions, that come first" (ibid.).

Speech act theorists such as Searle stress the importance of sincerity conditions, that is, assumptions about speakers' beliefs in the truth of their assertions, certainty of their promises, necessity of their commands, and the like. However rational these conditions may appear to Westerners, they may not be of equal concern to other peoples. Rosaldo asserted that "Ilongots lack 'our' interest in considerations like sincerity and truth; their lives lead them to concentrate, instead, on social bonds and interactive meanings. For the Ilongots, verbal actions [should] be divided into those which roughly correspond to social situations wherein norms of 'sameness' and autonomy prevail, and those belonging to relationships defined by continuity and hierarchy" (ibid.:222).

Rosaldo classified Ilongot speech acts into two groups: declaratives and directives. *Declaratives* include acts of assertion and comment through which speakers express their beliefs, opinions, and feelings. *Directives* include acts of commanding and requesting that lead to subsequent actions of hearers, most typically in the form of compliance with the directive (i.e., carrying out a command or acceding to a request) (ibid.). Ilongots emphasize directives because these speech acts call forth cooperative bonds between people, and such cooperation is the foundation of their social system. In addition, Ilongots' beliefs about people's rights and obligations, which are based on gender and age inequalities, affect usage of directives; that is, men are more likely to command women; elders are more likely to command juniors.

These facts clearly lead to the conclusion that cultural knowledge and assumptions play a critical role in co-participants' response to each other's messages. The ability to speak and comprehend a particular language is a necessary, but not sufficient, condition for mutual understanding. People also need to share the same set of norms about the kinds of goals expressed in speaking, norms that are learned through socialization in one's culture. The required competence consists of presupposed models of behavior and beliefs and knowledge of the way these are interconnected and manifested verbally.

ROUTINES

Several kinds of speech acts—greetings, partings, apologies, thanks, compliments—are frequently expressed by highly predictable and stereotyped linguistic routines. They combine verbal material and social messages in patterns expressive of cultural values and sensitive to interactional context. Their appropriate use requires that speakers know rules dictating both linguistic form and situational relevance. And their use reflects the language ideologies of speakers in several ways. First, routines display speakers' awareness of conventionalized social/linguistic forms. That is, the social meanings conveyed are not inherent in the linguistic form itself; rather, it is the performance of the routine that is understood to carry social meanings. The word *performance* is important here because routines are essentially accomplishing nonlinguistic tasks. Second, routines demonstrate speakers' understanding that language is not used for only referential functions (i.e., to name or refer) but that social and affective functions are also central to why people talk.

Although each type of routine has unique characteristics, they share several key features. First and foremost is their similarity of function in social interaction. To one degree or another, they all create, reaffirm, and/or negotiate social solidarity. Their primary goal is social rather than referential. Second, routines typically occur as sequences of exchanges between participants, minimally consisting of an utterance by the first speaker followed by a return or acknowledgment by the second speaker.

1a.	Hello.
1b.	Hello.
2a.	Thank you.
2b.	You're welcome.
3a.	I'm sorry.
3b.	Don't worry, it's nothing.
4a.	That's a nice sweater.
4b.	Thanks.

A third common trait of routines is that they are formulaic in structure. Each category (greetings, compliments, etc.) consists of instances of patterned forms used by most speakers on most occasions. The expected and redundant linguistic form of these speech acts is what, in fact, makes them routines.

We will review some research dealing with greetings and apologies, focusing on their structure and the purposes for which they are employed. Analyses of such behavior are principally based on data from two sources: One is elicited, constructing test frames or situations and asking subjects to project their behavior; the other is ethnographic, observing actual speech and collecting large samples of occurrences with attention to situational and interactional parameters. The latter approach is especially useful in revealing recurring forms and functions of routines.

Greetings

Greetings function to begin communicative interactions or to acknowledge the presence of others. In Erving Goffman's words, they "mark the transition to a condition of increased access" (1971:107). Although their basic structure is stereotyped within each culture, optional elaborations or innovations are possible. Speakers can use more or less formal constructions, pronunciations, and/or prosodic features to create diverse introductions to encounters. Different kinds of greetings are offered, depending on situational context, status relationships between interlocutors, and personal goals.

Alessandro Duranti has postulated six recurring features that can be used as criteria for identifying greetings cross-culturally (1997:67):

1. Near-boundary occurrence (greetings occur at the beginning of a social encounter).
2. Establishment of a shared perceptual field (people engaged in greeting recognize each other's presence in the same conceptual field).
3. Adjacency-pair format (greetings are typically part of one or more sets of adjacency pairs, i.e., two-part sequences in which the first pair is uttered by one party and the second is a reply by another).
4. Relative predictability of form and content.
5. Implicit establishment of spatio-temporal unit of interaction (greetings occur only once in an interaction).
6. Identification of the interlocutor as a distinct being worth recognizing.

Greetings in U.S. society are usually variants of "Hello" or "How are you?" Some, such as these, can be employed at any time of day, whereas others are temporally restricted (e.g., "Good morning"). Typical responses to greetings include identical returns or minor modifications, such as "Hello"/"Hi," or formulaic acknowledgments, "Good morning"/"The same to you." In some languages, responses produce an effect of linguistic balance. The following exchange is common in Arabic (Ferguson 1976:143):

1a. *assalāmu ¿alaykum* "Peace be on you."
1b. *wa¿ alaykumu ssalām* "And on you be peace."

Another frequent pattern of response is what Ferguson called "the principle of 'the same or more so,'" exemplified by Arabic rejoinders to *marhaba* ("hello"), which are *marhaba, marhabten, mit marhaba,* or *marahib,* meaning "hello, two hellos, a hundred hellos, hellos" (ibid.).

Anglo-American greetings are used to create impressions, whether real or false, of social equality and camaraderie. Patterns of response also demonstrate this function. Identical or modified returns and acknowledgments are linguistic metaphors for desired social balance.

In contrast, greeting exchanges in some cultures are manipulated in order to affirm status inequalities between participants. This is so among the Wolof, a stratified Muslim society in Senegal. Wolof etiquette dictates that co-presence requires talk, and that talk must be formally initiated (Irvine 1974:168). Social status is immediately relevant because "ideally, one greets 'up': it should be the lower-ranking party who greets the higher" (ibid.:169).

Wolof greeting behaviors reflect an underlying cultural assumption that social relationships are inherently unequal. This cultural model is repeatedly enacted by Wolof speakers as they engage in obligatory linguistic routines. Wolof greetings express status relations by a constellation of verbal and nonverbal behaviors. Prior to speaking, an initiator moves toward the addressee. Movement and activity are conceived in Wolof culture as traits of low-status people, whereas high-status people remain stationary and passive. And, as mentioned, people of lower rank speak first, commencing the exchange. Because moving and speaking are necessary components of greetings, it is impossible to avoid displays of social inequality, succinctly expressed in a Wolof proverb, "When two persons greet each other, one has shame, the other has glory" (ibid.:175).

People can use various strategies to lower or elevate their status vis-à-vis interlocutors. A person may engage in self-lowering in order to deflect social consequences of high status; namely, high-ranked people are obligated to grant financial or material requests of low-ranked individuals. Self-lowering can be accomplished by initiating greetings and/or by showing deference through a proliferation of questions about the addressee and his or her family (ibid.:175–176).

Strategies of self-elevation include attempts to avoid initiating exchanges. Such reluctance can be problematic if both parties have the same intention because eventually someone must begin. Another possibility is to refrain from asking elaborate questions but instead to proceed quickly into topics of conversation (ibid.:178–179).

Apologies

Apologies are verbalized social acts. Their purpose is to maintain or reestablish rapport between participants. They are occasioned by actions that are perceived to have negative effects on addressees and for which speakers take responsibility. In apologizing, a speaker "splits [himself or herself] into two parts, the part that is guilty of an offense and the part that dissociates itself from the delict and affirms a belief in the offended rule" (Goffman 1971:143). Naturally, what counts as a deed or intent necessitating an apology is entirely dependent on cultural models of offensive or regrettable behavior. An act of apologizing is verbal recognition of some social breach either past, present, or future:

1a. I'm sorry I broke your dish.
1b. I'm sorry to be bothering you now.
1c. I'm sorry that I'll have to inconvenience you tomorrow, but I'll be late picking you up.

Apologies are middle segments of three-part sequences. The first part, which may be verbal or behavioral, constitutes the "object of regret" (Coulmas 1981:75). Following an apology, the last segment consists of the addressee's response. In Western societies, such turns typically are acknowledgments, often in a form intended to downgrade the offense, as in the following:

2a. I'm sorry.
2b. Don't worry about it.
  It was nothing.
  Forget it. (and so on)

Responses to apologies may, however, fully acknowledge the weightiness of an offense:

3a. I'm sorry.
3b. Okay, but don't do it again.
  I hope this is the last time it happens.
  You always say that. (and so on)

The two types of replies clearly have different contextual uses and speaker intents. Those in the second group are polite and mitigating, whereas those in the third are potentially aggravating and confrontational.

Apologies are routinized in the sense that they are expressed with stereotyped formats. The following strategies were attested to in research conducted by Janet Holmes in New Zealand, given with examples from her data (1990:167):

  1. *An explicit expression of apology*
    a. Offer apology: "I apologize"
    b. Express regret: "I'm afraid"; "I'm sorry"
    c. Request forgiveness: "excuse me"; "forgive me"

2. *An explanation or account, an excuse or justification*
   "I wasn't expecting it to be you"; "we're both new to this"
3. *An acknowledgment of responsibility*
   a. Accept blame: "it was my fault"
   b. Express self-deficiency: "I was confused"; "I wasn't thinking"; "I didn't see you"
   c. Recognize hearer as entitled to an apology: "you're right"; "you deserve an apology"
   d. Express lack of intent: "I didn't mean to"
   e. Offer repair/redress: "we'll replace it for you"; "I'll bring you another"
4. *A promise of forbearance*
   "I promise it won't happen again"

In Holmes's study of 183 apologies collected ethnographically through observation of spontaneous occurrences, 162 (88.3 percent) employed strategies of "explicit expression of apology" (strategy 1). Apologies were overwhelmingly based on recurring syntactic and semantic components (ibid.:172). The most common, accounting for approximately 80 percent of the data, were variants with "sorry," as in "I'm sorry," "I'm so (very) sorry," and so on. Other patterns included "excuse me," "pardon me," and "I would like to apologize." The most typical offenses found by Holmes's New Zealand research (presumably applicable to other Western societies) were instances of inconvenience; infringements on space, talk, time, or possessions; and social gaffes (ibid.:177). More serious breaches triggered more elaborate apologies.

Social relationships between participants influence the occurrence and form of apologies. In Holmes's data, most occurred between equals (probably because people more often interact with status equals). Of the remaining cases, lower-status individuals were twice as likely to apologize to those of higher rank than the reverse. And low-status participants tended to use more explicit and complex strategies (ibid.:188–189). However, instances of elaborate apology are frequent between intimates (relatives, close friends) as well, possibly because serious offenses, which often trigger elaborate forms, are more likely to occur in these contexts than in formal or public situations.

Comparison with other cultures reveals some similarities and differences in apology routines. For example, Japanese social norms require apologies in more contexts than would be expected in Western societies. According to Florian Coulmas, citing Sugiyama Lebra, Japanese people are highly conscious of their effects on others and concerned with not infringing on others' rights and needs. They strive to avoid embarrassment either to themselves or their interlocutors (1981:82–83). Not only are apologies frequently issued for offenses, they are also "used to line other speech acts such as greetings, offers, thanks with an apologetic undertone" (ibid.). In fact, a common utterance, *sumimasen* (literally: "this is not the end" or "it is not finished"), can be translated as either "I'm sorry" or "thank you" and is used to express apology or gratitude. And in contexts such as upon leaving someone's home where a Westerner might say, "Thank you for a wonderful evening," a Japanese guest often says *o-jama itashimashita* "I have intruded on you" (literally: disturbance have done to you). As in Western societies, Japanese speakers typically respond to apologies with polite downgraders, for example, *iie, iie, do itashimashite* "no, no, don't mention it" (ibid.).

Japanese interactional norms require explicit recognition of people's effects on each other in the form of apology for actual or implicated intrusions, disturbances, and infringements. Apologies are perceived as polite, considerate, and deferential according to Japanese models of social rights. The most common apologies in Japanese are given below:

1. *sumimasen* "This is not the end; it is not finished."
2. *shitsurei shimasu* "I was very rude."

These occur in either intimate or casual contexts when the offense is relatively slight. Serious breaches and/or formal situations invoke more elaborate apologies (ibid.:88–89):

3. *o-yurushi kudasai* "I beg your pardon." (in the literal meaning)

4. *o-wabi itashimasu* "I offer my apologies."

5. *mōshiwake arimasen* "There is no excuse; this is unpardonable."

6. *sore-wa kyoshuku desu* "I feel ashamed."

7. *o-kindodoku-sama degozaimashita* "This must have been poison to your soul."

NARRATIVES

Narratives are stories or framed segments of ongoing discourse that relate or report events in chronological sequence. There are many kinds of narratives: *historical narratives* that recount events in the history of a community or a people, *mythic narratives* that recount happenings in primordial times or in a realm other than our own, and *personal narratives* that relate events in the speaker's life (or in the lives of persons whom the speaker is describing). For our purposes, we will be analyzing the third category, that is, personal narratives.

One of the foremost researchers in the field of narrative analysis, William Labov, noted that "narratives are privileged forms of discourse that play a central role in almost every conversation" (1997:396). That is, in most conversational interactions, people talk about their *experiences,* past events that have meaning in their lives. Although storytelling may not be the focus of all conversations, narratives are frequently included to exemplify or dramatize a person's feelings, thoughts, and opinions. Labov defined a personal narrative as "a report of a sequence of events that have entered into the biography of the speaker by a sequence of clauses that correspond to the order of the original event" (ibid.:398). This definition captures several important features. Narratives are told in chronological order, with beginnings, middles, and ends that follow the sequence of the experienced events. In addition, a personal narrative recounts events that are meaningful to the speaker's life and that are "emotionally and socially evaluated and so transformed from raw experience" (ibid.:199). A narrative is not an exhaustive recounting of every element of the reported experiences but is the outcome of the narrator's editing. Speakers select certain events; highlight some features and episodes; and trim or eliminate others to make a story that is coherent, dramatic, and convincing. Personal narratives must be "reportable." Because narratives tend to occupy more conversational space (i.e., they are longer) than other contributions, the narrative must be of interest to the audience; it must be reportable. Narratives must also have a point. Speakers may assert causality, praise, or blame, or comment on the competence or incompetence of people in the story. Narratives must also be credible; that is, a narrator asserts that the events recounted have actually taken place. Credibility thus distinguishes personal narratives from jokes, tall tales, or fantasies.

Personal narratives are performances that enhance relationships between tellers and audience, revealing events, emotions, attitudes, and themes important to the narrator and presumably of interest to the audience. They are examples of and vehicles for self-disclosure. And in the telling, they also allow for the growth of self-knowledge as the speaker comes to understand his or her own motives and attitudes. As a performance, and as a communicative interaction, personal narratives work to build relationships with others through the telling and through the responses received. In the words of Heidi Rose (1996:429–430), "the relationship between the narrator and the audience invites intimacy, empathy, and understanding as the audience participates in the unfolding of the narrator's life experience, and understands the significance of his/her experience in its larger historical, social, and cultural contexts."

A fundamental issue in narrative analysis is the attempt to understand "how experience is translated from the narrator to the audience" (Labov 1997:411). Personal narratives, unlike literary accounts, relate events seen exclusively through the eyes of the narrator. The chronological sequencing of events contributes to the transfer of experience as the audience becomes aware of the events "as if" they were participants. Finally, successful narratives describe experience in objective terms, avoiding the subjectivity of the narrator's emotions. According to Labov, "those narratives that have the greatest impact on audiences—that seize the attention of listeners and allow them to share the experience of the narrator—are those that use the most objective means of expression" (ibid.:412). Events reported objectively are taken as more credible than events reported subjectively or through the emotional filter of the speaker. In contrast, when narrators add "subjective reports of emotion to the description of an objective event, listeners become aware of that event as if it were the narrator's experience and not their own" (ibid.:413).

The following is a brief, but highly dramatic, personal narrative told by Harold Shambaugh about events that occurred to him while he was in South America (ibid.:398):

   a. Oh I w's settin' at a table drinkin'
   b. And—this Norwegian sailor came over
   c. an' kep' givin' me a bunch o' junk about I was sittin' with his woman
   d. An' everybody sittin' at the table with me were my shipmates.
   e. So I jus' turn aroun'
   f. an' shoved 'im,
   g. an' told 'im, I said, "Go away.
   h. I don't even wanna fool with ya."
   i. An' nex' thing I know I'm layin' on the floor, blood all over me,
   j. An' a guy told me, says, "Don't move your head.
   k. Your throat's cut."

Shambaugh's story satisfies the criteria of personal narrative in every respect. Events are recounted in chronological order with a bare minimum of detail, honing in on the critical features of context, setting, significant characters, and directly relevant actions: the arrival of the Norwegian sailor, Shambaugh's responses (physical and verbal), and the result of the Norwegian's actions. Indeed, these actions are not themselves described but left to the imagination of the listener; only their violent consequences are stated. Notice, too, the use of direct quotation: Shambaugh quotes himself, making what he presumably thought was an appropriate response to the Norwegian's accusations, but that evidently provoked the latter to retaliate, and Shambaugh quotes a companion who reported the dramatic conclusion of events. Although the narrative recounts an occurrence of undoubtedly intense emotion for Shambaugh, it is told in objective, dispassionate language. This is clearly a reportable event, conveyed credibly and succinctly by a skilled narrator.

Since the 1970s, linguistic anthropologists have developed analytic techniques aimed at uncovering the structures of oral narratives. Dell Hymes is one of the important innovators in this field. A number of his foundation essays, drawn together in *In Vain I Tried to Tell You* (1981), examine oral texts from the perspective of ethnopoetics to discover the structural organization underlying their form. According to Hymes, oral narratives are usually structured in terms of lines and groups of lines, together forming units that constitute sets. Hymes proposes that commonly occurring patterns include sets of two and four or three and five. Sets of three reflect a natural sequence of "onset, ongoing, outcome" of action (1985:409). In sets of five, the middle is often a pivot that concludes the first set of three and begins the second set of three. Hymes suggests that the patterning of sets of two and four and of three and five may be universal, although he does not speculate about the origin of this "natural" organization: "This argument obviously only indicates a possibility, it is not a proof. The likely universality of internal organization of spoken narrative in terms of lines (verses) points to a grounding in human nature" (1997:485).

In different texts, different structural features may signal the beginnings of lines and verses. These may include intonation contours (obviously not analyzable in printed texts) or grammatical features, sentence particles, repeated words, or changes in turns at talk. A text's underlying structure can be ascertained on the basis of "the general principle of poetic organization called equivalence":

> Equivalence may involve any feature of language. Features that count to constitute lines are well known: stress, tonal accent, syllable, initial consonant (alliteration), and such forms of equivalence commonly called metrical. Lines of whatever length may also be treated as equivalent in terms of the various forms of rhyme, tone group or intonation contour, initial particles, recurrent syntactic pattern, consistency of contrast of grammatical feature, such as tense or aspect. (1996:166)

Narrative form is built on a series of units, marked and linked by equivalence, that combine and build through sequencing or "succession": "Succession is not a matter simply of linear sequence, of counting. Successive units give shape to action" through development and creation of "an implicit rhythm" that leads to an ending (1994:332).

When the same narrative is recounted or performed on different occasions, the length of the text as well as specific details may vary considerably in response to differences in contexts of performance and differences in the intent of the narrator, but the underlying structure remains constant. For example, Hymes (1985) compared two tellings of a narrative called "Salmon's Myth" in Kachlamet Chinook (recorded from speaker Charles Cultee in 1891 and 1894 by anthropologist Franz Boas) and found that in both versions, lines were organized into sets of three and five. In a close analysis of the two versions, Hymes noted similarities of structure and sequencing of acts, reflecting a "stability of tradition," but differences in detail and variations of order within acts, reflecting selective performances. The second version "shows fuller command of the content of the tradition," stimulated by Boas's visit 3 years earlier that "activated memory of the story" (ibid.:422).

Hymes has also applied the techniques of ethnopoetic analysis to the personal narratives of ordinary people in a study of three short accounts collected from urban African-American children by William Labov (1972:367) and Sarah Michaels (1981:33). Despite the surface simplicity of vocabulary, syntax, and plot development in these stories, Hymes has found that they, too, are built on a framework of lines and groups of lines organized in sets of three and five.

As an outgrowth of his work in ethnopoetic analysis, Hymes has championed the rethinking of procedures for presenting the oral literatures of nonliterate peoples in print form. Rather than previous renditions in which myths and folklore were printed in prose paragraphs, Hymes advocates their presentation by line segmented according to principles of equivalence that reveal their patterning and structure. The same procedures can profitably be applied to every-day narratives of personal experience, as demonstrated by the following printing of an account given by a young African-American boy (Hymes 1996:173–174; Labov 1972:367–368):

A. (a) When I was in fourth grade—
　　　　no, it was in third grade—
　　　　　　this boy he stole my glove.
　　(b) He took my glove
　　　　and said that his father found it downtown on the ground.
[And you fight him?]
B. (a) I told him
　　　　　　that it was impossible for him to find downtown
　　　　　　　cause all those people were walking by
　　　　　　　　and just his father was the only one that found it?
　　(b) So he got all mad.
C. (a) So then I fought him.
　　(b) I knocked him all out in the street.
D. (a) So he say he give.
　　(b) And I kept on hitting him.
E. (a) Then he started crying and he ran home to his father.
　　(b) And the father told him that he ain't find no glove.

Here we see displayed a structure based on sets of three and five. The first three sets (ABC) lead to the outcome of the fight, whereas the second section of three sets (CDE) leads to the outcome of the glove. The third set (C) functions as the pivot, ending the first grouping of three and beginning the second grouping of three.

Another approach to analyzing oral narrative has been pioneered by Dennis Tedlock (1972, 1983) working primarily with the oral literatures of the Zunis, an indigenous nation in New Mexico. Tedlock segments Zuni narrative on the basis of structuring by pause units. Noting that "past translations of Zuni narratives have suffered from neglect of 'oral' or 'paralinguistic' features such as voice quality (tone of voice), loudness, and pausing" (1983:45), Tedlock renders Zuni narratives with transcription conventions that note changes in volume (louder, softer) and notations of raspiness, tightness, and breaks in voice production. The following is an excerpt from "The Boy and the Deer," narrated by Andrew Peynetsa (ibid.:46).

SO' NAHCHI.
The little baby came out.
　　"Where is the little baby crying?" they said.
He was nursed, the little boy was nursed by the deer.
　　"I will go to Kachina Village, for he is without clothing, naked."
When she got back to her children they were all sleeping.
　　"HE SAW A HERD OF DEER.
BUT A LITTLE BOY WAS AMONG THEM."
　　"PERHAPS WE WILL CATCH HIM."
THEN THIS DEER MOTHER TOLD HIM EVERYTHING.
　　"THAT IS WHAT SHE DID TO YOU, SHE JUST DROPPED YOU."

The boy became
Very unhappy.
AND ALL THE PEOPLE WHO HAD COME KILLED THE DEER,
    KILLED THE DEER, KILLED THE DEER
And his uncle dismounting,
Caught him.
    "THAT IS WHAT YOU DID AND YOU ARE MY REAL MOTHER."
He put the quiver on and went out.
There he died.
THIS WAS LIVED LONG AGO. LEE———SEMONIKYA.

Notation of prosodic, tonal, and rhythmic patterns that include shifts in volume, changes in voice quality, and pausing to determine line properly reflects the dramatic and aesthetic elements of performance. These narratives do not describe emotional states but "evoke them" (ibid.:51) by dramatic shifts of pause and voice. Of course, structural linguistic elements of repetition and parallelisms occur in Zuni narratives as found elsewhere. Although Tedlock's presentation provides dramatic markers of performance qualities, it is obviously only possible to render materials in this manner if there are voice recordings or the analyzer is present at the narration.

Both Hymes's and Tedlock's approaches add to our understanding of the underlying structure of narratives and the features that give life to their performance. Because all narratives are text, they have structural and grammatical features, and because they are performed, they also have elements of voice that contribute to their dramatic quality.

Examination of multiple tellings of the same story by the same speaker may reveal intriguing consistencies as well as significant variations. In a comparison of five tellings of a Wasco Coyote story by the same bilingual speaker (the earliest in 1972 and the latest in 1986), Robert Moore provides a "longitudinal, historical perspective on a traditional performance genre [that] enables one to see how alive the tradition really is" (1993:236). Three versions of the story were told in the indigenous language, Wasco Chinookan; one account was given in English; and one in a mixture of English and Chinookan. The versions were told in different social settings, some spontaneously produced and others elicited by researchers Robert Moore in the 1980s (four versions) and Michael Silverstein in 1972 (one account). Remaining constant in all five versions were instances of quoted speech, that is, direct quotations in the voices of Coyote, Raccoon, and other mythic figures. All tellings contained the same five episodes in the same order, but the length of episodes varied and details of events were sometimes elaborated or simplified. Of special significance, even in the accounts that were in English or in a mixture of English and Chinookan, all speech quoted from mythic characters was given in the indigenous language and was identical in all five versions (ibid.:214). In the native culture, "directly quoted character speech is absolutely central to the constitution of myth-recital as a recognizable performance genre, and its enduring centrality suggests analogies to theater and related performing arts" (ibid.:236).

In the study of narrative, attention is often directed toward the analysis of quoted or reported speech. Quoting or reporting the speech of another may serve different functions in different contexts. We saw previously how one narrator, Harold Shambaugh, effectively employed reported speech to highlight dramatic turning points in his story. In other contexts, quoting an absent speaker may absolve the narrator from responsibility for the reported speech. Such a use of language may function strategically in arguments, allowing the narrator to slip into the background of ongoing talk, citing the words of others to substantiate the narrator's own claims or to evade blame and responsibility. But the use of reported speech may not achieve the goal of evading responsibility unless the narrator is seen to be entitled to quote the original source. Indeed, arguments between people may be triggered by the unentitled quotation of previous speech of nonpresent participants. In a study of inner-city junior high school students, Amy Shuman found that disputes sometimes arose over "challenges to entitlement" in the use of reported speech (1992:136). Reported speech might be challenged on the grounds of accuracy or sincerity, but it might also be challenged on the grounds of entitlement, that is, that the narrator is not entitled to repeat privileged speech: "The offense of using reported speech can focus on a lack of correspondence between original and reported remarks (a problem with accuracy), or on an unauthorized use of those remarks (a problem of entitlement)" (ibid.:148). A listener can challenge the reporter's accuracy and can also challenge the competence of the narrator and his or her relationship to the original text. In adolescent dispute narratives studied by Shuman, talking and quoting others were both ways to fight and to avoid fighting: "The girls talked about fights more than they fought. If a girl could shift the focus from an initial offense to some other offense, usually talking behind someone's back, she could successfully divert antagonisms away from herself" (ibid.:149).

Narratives are enmeshed in larger conversational sequences and interchanges, but they also contribute to the construction of the interaction itself. As Shuman observed,

> The relationship between the storytelling situation and the events described is especially complicated in the narratives of everyday life since the storytelling can be part of the ongoing experience. Stories about everyday experiences do not replicate experiences, they construct them. The clarity of an account, the accuracy of the portrayals, and the presentation events in chronological order are conventions for concealing as well as for revealing information. (ibid.)

In a study of speaking styles on the Polynesian atoll of Nukulaelae, Niko Besnier has shown that people frequently used quoted speech in everyday discourse, in part because it is considered inappropriate to speculate about other people's thoughts and emotions. A speaker can quote the words of others even when not a witness to the original speech. Indeed, children are taught the skills of accurate reporting from their early years when they are prompted to repeat messages exactly as originally uttered (1992:165). Believing that speech and action are of equal importance and that speakers and actors are equally responsible for their behavior, people on Nukulaelae believe that a speaker who quotes another must repeat the exact words and the identical prosodic features (voice quality, volume, intensity, pitch) of the source. The reproduction of prosodic features, in fact, is critical because different prosodic cues are associated with different emotional states. However, speakers may misrepresent the quoted source by changing prosodic features if the speaker wishes to present the person negatively (e.g., in gossip). Although this practice violates the norm of accuracy, because prosodic features are less consciously focused on by an audience, the speaker is usually able to evade direct responsibility for the shifts that he or she has made. Nukulaelae speakers thus employ indirect, covert means to characterize the emotions of others while, at the same time, quoting their words accurately. As Besnier concludes, "While adhering to the cultural norm dictating that speech be reported faithfully, Nukulaelae islanders can also superpose affect in a covert off-record manner, in a manner that is also most likely to escape scrutiny" (ibid.:177).

In some cultures, narratives function in complex ways to invoke specific cultural and interactional meanings. Keith Basso's work among Western Apaches reveals the extraordinary depth of meaning conveyed by the telling of "historical tales." Such tales recount events that happened "long ago," typically (but not always) before 1872 when Apaches were forced to settle on reservations (1990:115). On the surface, historical tales inform listeners of significant past events that occurred at specific, named places, but the telling of the stories functions interactionally to warn and criticize individuals who are engaged in behavior deemed undesirable or improper. These stories serve as a means to communicate the social consequences of continued misconduct. (ibid.). Characteristics of Western Apache historical tales conform to a specific set of stylistic devices, especially an opening and closing line containing the place-name where the events occurred. Apache place-names are highly detailed and evocative, describing salient characteristics of the physical environment that allow hearers to visualize the named place and imagine that they are there. Examples include the following: "water flows down on top of a regular succession of flat rocks," "water flows inward underneath a cottonwood tree," and "white rocks lie above in a compact cluster" (ibid.:109). When historical stories are told, they are aimed (to use the Apache hunting metaphor) at a particular hearer who comes to understand that the message in the story is directed at him or her. As a result, the person appreciates the wisdom of one's ancestors in relating the moral of the story to his or her own behavior.

There is a tale about a man who long ago killed a cow off the reservation that had belonged to a Whiteman. He was arrested at "men stand above here and there" by an Apache policeman. Then he was transferred to stand before the head army officer at Fort Apache. When the head army officer inquired of the situation, the policeman could not make the words he wished and instead asked for food and ammunition. The next day, after deciding to report the man's actions again, the policeman was unable to tell the head army officer of the man's offense. Someone was changing the words he spoke. The policeman decided to release the man who had killed the cow, back at "men stand above here and there." (ibid.:119–120)

This story impresses upon Apache listeners the moral obligation to be loyal to their own people, not betray them or act "too much like a Whiteman" (ibid.:120). When the Apache policeman in the story was about to accuse his fellow Apache of theft, someone used witchcraft on him so that he forgot what he wanted to say and instead acted in a way that was "absurd and laughable" (ibid.).

Basso reports the way in which this particular story was used to criticize the behavior of a 17-year-old Apache woman who attended a girls' puberty ritual with her hair rolled up in pink curlers in violation of the norm prescribing that women wear their hair loose when attending such ceremonies. Two weeks after the rite, at a gathering of friends and relatives at the camp of the young woman's maternal grandmother, the grandmother recounted the historical tale of events at "men stand above here and there" and the humiliation of the Apache policeman who acted like a Whiteman. The young woman stood up after the story was told and quietly walked away. About two years later when Basso happened to be driving near "men stand above here and there" in the company of the young woman, she observed "I know that place. It stalks me everyday" (ibid.:123). Her comment exemplifies an analysis offered by one of Basso's Apache consultants, Nick Thompson:

> This is what we know about our stories. They go to work on your mind and make you think about your life. Maybe you've not been acting right. Maybe you've been stingy. Maybe you've been chasing after women. Maybe you've been trying to act like a Whiteman. People don't like it. So someone goes hunting for you...tells a story about what happened long ago. It doesn't matter if other people are around—you're going to know he's aiming that story at you.   (ibid.:124–125)

For example, a study by John Beatty (2006) of four versions of a Mohawk folktale demonstrates the way that each narrator's life experiences intruded on the details of the story. Significantly, other members of the Mohawk community (the reserve called Kahnawake, located just south of Montréal) viewed all the versions as acceptable tellings of the traditional story because their basic moral themes made the same point. Here is one version of the story called "Tehenrasahkwa" (the name of the main protagonist) (Beatty 2006:19):

Tehenrasahkwa was a young man who used to go to the river regularly. One day a creature, half human and half fish appeared. She was very friendly, chatted freely with the young man and suggested that the next day Tehenrasahkwa and she have lunch by the river.

He returned to his home and told his grandmother about his experience. His grandmother warned him not to become involved with the creature, and that he should not go back.

Nonetheless, he went back the next day anyway and after they had a delightful picnic lunch together, the "mermaid" suggested that Tehenrasahkwa and she dive down under the water and visit her home. He agreed and the two dove into the water. It was a splendid place with all kinds of lights shining. Tehenrasahkwa noticed that he was turning into a creature like the mermaid. He was developing a tail and other changes. The people on the land saw the two of them (he now totally changed) swimming down the river to Niagara Falls. Now, every year when the small fish come back up the river, the people know that these are the children of the pair.

Episodes occurring in all four versions studied include the young man going to the river, meeting a half-human creature, and being admonished (either by the creature herself or by the protagonist's grandmother) not to return to the river or to divulge some information pertaining to his visits, and the consequences of violating the interdiction. But the versions vary in intriguing details that, according to Beatty, reflect the personality and/or life history of the individual storyteller. For instance, the version given above was told by an elderly woman who likes romances and thinks of herself as a matchmaker. In her version, the young man and the mermaid become a couple and swim off to Niagara Falls, the iconic North American location for honeymoons. In another version, the mermaid helps the hero catch fish but tells him that if he sells the fish, he should not use the money for anything else. He violates this ban and is subsequently dragged into the river, where he is turned into a half-human, half-fish creature. This story was told by a steelworker who had been injured at work and had collected some insurance payments, which he and his wife then needed to treat some other illnesses, leaving them with few resources. In the third version, the mermaid also helps the young man get fish but warns him not to tell anyone how he gets them. After a while, he does tell a friend and is then dragged into the river when he returns. This version was told by a young woman who had left the Mohawk reserve in order to hide her out-of-wedlock pregnancy. Finally, being lonely, she invited a friend to visit. The friend, of course, found out about her pregnancy and upon returning to the reserve, told everyone, to the embarrassment of the storyteller. A final version centers on a man who goes to a pond, has a headache, feels a bone protruding from his head, takes out the bone, and throws it into the pond. A creature, this time half-man, half-fish, comes out of the water and frightens the man away. His grandmother tells him never to return, but he constantly hears the voice of the merman calling him. He finally goes to the river and is dragged into the water. This version was told by an elderly man who never married and was thought by some members of the community to have been gay.

It is intriguing to notice the differences in the stories, based on common themes, that bear the unique imprint of their narrators. The study also raises questions about the versions of stories that anthropologists or folklorists collect and analyze. Presumably, the patterns of individual variations that Beatty uncovered could be discovered elsewhere as well. Relevant also is Bakhtin's (1981) concept of polyphony or the multiplicity of voices in a community that undermines standard notions of homogeneity and questions the authority of any particular version of a narrative or other type of discourse.

Because personal narratives are speech events told by speakers to co-participants, we should briefly consider how listeners respond. To encourage a narrator, listeners contribute to the interaction by signaling their attentiveness, their interest in the development of the narrative, and their reactions to episodes. They signal active listenership through culturally appropriate strategies. For example, in North American practice, active listenership may be expressed by periodic vocalizations such as "hmm...," "yeah," "really," and by various gestures and facial expressions that communicate their participation and interest. A listener may also ask questions that prompt the narrator to further elaborate on the story.

In Samoan society, listeners employ a range of *affect pronouns,* pronouns that express affect or attitudes of speakers. The Samoan language contrasts neutral forms for first person as subject, object, and possessor with corresponding affect markers. Affect pronouns for first person are employed by speakers in order to elicit sympathy for oneself from addressees. Neutral forms mean "I, me, my," whereas affect pronouns have meanings such as "poor I, poor me, poor my" (Ochs 1987:53). Determiners can also be marked for positive affect, expressing the speaker's sympathy for referents or addressees, for example, *le, se* ("the, a") → *si* ("the dear, a dear"). Additionally, affect can be expressed by various kinds of sentence particles, interjections, and vocabulary choices for verbs and adjectives.

In a study of narrator–listener interactions, Elinor Ochs (1987) recorded Samoan villagers' conversations containing personal narratives that recounted events involving the speaker and others. Participants included men and women of various ages and social statuses. (However, all of the women in the study were at least 50 years of age; the speech of young women was not sampled.) Ochs measured uses of positive, sympathetic affect markers by speakers and also noted listeners' responses, for example, whether they reacted with sympathy toward the speaker and the referent. Ochs found that among narrators, lower-status young men used the most affect forms. And as listeners, both young men and older women employed a high proportion of affect markers, and high-status older men expressed least sympathy.

For men, youthful age and lowly status were consistently reflected in expressions of sympathy toward referents and the elicitation of sympathy for oneself. As listeners, they responded most often with positive affect when sympathy was expressed by other narrators. Older, high-status men demonstrated least affect. Older women's communicative behavior was more complex, tending to express neutrality as speakers but responding with sympathy to the speech of others. Perhaps older men do not need to employ sympathy markers in their narratives because their high status automatically makes addressees respond favorably to them. In contrast, young men used affect forms as speakers to obtain addressees' empathy. And as listeners, they accommodate to elders by their sympathetic replies. Finally, elder women may routinely show sympathy to others as part of politeness strategies.

Summary

We have used the framework of an ethnography of communication to analyze components of communicative events, emphasizing interrelationships among settings, participants, topics, and goals. Language is used by speakers in conformity with culturally shared expectations. Ethnographic-linguistic analysis includes discussion of both behavior and its evaluation. People not only speak in ways considered appropriate in their culture, but they also assess the speech of others by these same norms.

Choices of linguistic form, whether of sounds, grammar, or words, are made, usually nonconsciously, after weighing co-occurrences of significant components. Settings of relative formality or informality provide the background for participants' interactions and help determine topic selection and methods of phrasing personal intentions. Speakers can signal their relations with co-participants by manipulating various aspects of language, revealed especially in their choice of words and in forms of address. Finally, speakers' goals can be expressed through speech acts directly or indirectly after considering cultural rules of propriety and the likelihood of specific outcomes. Some speech acts, such as greetings and apologies, are expressed as stereotyped, formulaic social and linguistic routines. Analyzing discourse functions of speech situates linguistic analyses in ongoing, context-dependent meanings.

References

AUSTIN, JOHN. 1962. *How to Do Things with Words.* Cambridge, MA: Harvard University Press.

BACH, KENT, AND ROBERT HARNISH. 1979. *Linguistic Communication and Speech Acts.* Cambridge, MA: MIT Press.

BAKHTIN, M. M. 1981. *The Dialogic Imagination, Four Essays.* Austin: University of Texas Press.

BASSO, KEITH. 1990. *Western Apache Language and Culture.* Tucson: University of Arizona Press.

BEATTY, JOHN. 2006. Tehenrahsahkwa: Story variations and personalities. In *Information Distribution in English Grammar and Discourse and Other Topics in Linguistics: Festrschrift for Peter Erdmann.* Berlin: Peter Lang, pp. 17–22.

BESNIER, NIKO. 1992. Reported speech and affect on Nukulaelae Atoll. In *Responsibility and Evidence in Oral Discourse,* ed. J. Hill and J. Irvine. New York: Cambridge University Press, pp. 161–181.

BLUM, SUSAN. 1997. Naming practices and the power of words in China. *Language in Society* 26, no. 3:357–380.

BROWN, ROGER, AND MARGUERITE FORD. 1961. Address in American English. *Journal of Abnormal and Social Psychology* 62:375–385.

BROWN, ROGER, AND ALFRED GILMAN. 1960. The pronouns of power and solidarity. In *Style in Language,* ed. T. Sebeok. Cambridge, MA: MIT Press, pp. 253–276.

COULMAS, FLORIAN. 1981. "Poison to your soul": Thanks and apologies contrastively viewed. In *Conversational Routine,* ed. F. Coulmas. The Hague: Mouton, pp. 69–91.

DURANTI, ALESSANDRO. 1985. Sociocultural dimensions of discourse. In *Handbook of Discourse Analysis,* Vol. 1: *Disciplines of Discourse,* ed. T. van Dijk. New York: Academic Press, pp. 193–229.

DURANTI, ALESSANDRO. 1997. Universal and culture-specific properties of greetings. *Journal of Linguistic Anthropology* 7, no. 1:63–97.

FANG, HANQUAN, AND J. H. HENG. 1983. Social changes and changing address norms in China. *Language in Society* 12:495–507.

FERGUSON, CHARLES. 1976. The structure and use of politeness formulas. *Language in Society* 5:137–151.

FISKE, SHIRLEY. 1978. Rules of address: Navajo women in Los Angeles. *Journal of Anthropological Research* 34, no. 1:72–91.

GOFFMAN, ERVING. 1971. *Relations in Public.* New York: Basic Books.

HALLIDAY, M. A. K. 1973. *Explorations in the Functions of Language.* Hawthorne, NY: Elsevier North-Holland.

HILL, JANE, AND KENNETH HILL. 1978. Honorific usage in modern Nahuatl. *Language* 54:123–155.

HOLMES, JANET. 1990. Apologies in New Zealand English. *Language in Society* 19:155–200.

HONG, BEVERLY. 1985. Politeness in Chinese: Impersonal pronouns and personal greeting. *Anthropological Linguistics* 27:204–213.

HYMES, DELL. 1974. *Foundations in Sociolinguistics: An Ethnographic Approach.* Philadelphia: University of Pennsylvania Press.

HYMES, DELL. 1981. *"In Vain I Tried to Tell You": Essays in Native American Ethno-Poetics.* Philadelphia: University of Pennsylvania Press.

HYMES, DELL. 1985. Language, memory, and selective performance: Cultee's "Salmon's Myth" as twice told to Boas. *Journal of American Folklore* 98, no. 390:391–434.

HYMES, DELL. 1994. Ethnopoetics, oral-formulaic theory, and editing texts. *Oral Tradition* 9, no. 2:330–370.

HYMES, DELL. 1996. *Ethnography, Linguistic, Narrative Inequality: Toward an Understanding of Voice.* London: Taylor & Francis.

HYMES, DELL. 1997. When is oral narrative poetry? Generative form and its pragmatic conditions. *Pragmatics* 8, no. 4:475–500.

IRVINE, JUDITH. 1974. Strategies of status manipulation in the Wolof greeting. In *Explorations in the Ethnography of Speaking,* ed. R. Bauman and J. Sherzer. New York: Cambridge University Press, pp. 167–191.

IRVINE, JUDITH. 1979. Formality and informality in communicative events. *American Anthropologist* 81:773–790.

IRVINE, JUDITH. 1998. Ideologies of honorific language. In *Language Ideologies: Practice and Theory,* ed. B. Schieffelin, K. Woolard, and P. Kroskrity, New York: Oxford University Press, pp. 51–67.

KEATING, ELIZABETH. 1994. "Language, gender, rank, and social space: Honorifics in Pohnpei, Micronesia." In *Cultural Performances,* ed. M. Buchholtz et al. Berkeley, CA: Third Berkeley Women and Language Group, pp. 367–377.

KROSKRITY, PAUL. 1985. Growing with stories: Line, verse, and genre in an Arizona Tewa text. *Journal of Anthropological Research* 41:183–199.

LABOV, WILLIAM. 1972. *Language in the Inner City.* Philadelphia: University of Pennsylvania Press.

LABOV, WILLIAM. 1997. Some further steps in narrative analysis. *Journal of Narrative and Life History* 7:395–415.

LEE, MOTOKO. 1976. The married woman's status and role in Japanese: An exploratory sociolinguistic study. *Signs* 1:991–999.

MICHAELS, SARAH. 1981. Sharing time: Children's narrative styles and differential access to literacy. *Language in Society* 10:423–442.

MOORE, ROBERT. 1993. Performance form and the voices of characters in five versions of the Wasco Coyote Cycle. In *Reflexive Language,* ed. J. A. Lucy. New York: Cambridge University Press, pp. 213–240.

MORFORD, JANET. 1997. Social indexicality in French pronominal address. *Journal of Linguistic Anthropology* 7, no. 1:3–37.

OCHS, ELINOR. 1987. The impact of stratification and socialization on men's and women's speech in Western Samoa. In *Language, Gender and Sex in Comparative Perspective,* ed. S. Phillips, S. Steele, and C. Tanz. New York: Cambridge University Press, pp. 50–70.

PAULSTON, CHRISTINA. 1976. Pronouns of address in Swedish: Social class semantics and a changing system. *Language in Society* 5:359–386.

ROSALDO, MICHELLE. 1982. The things we do with words: Ilongot speech acts and speech act theory in philosophy. *Language in Society* 11:203–237.

ROSE, HEIDI. 1996. Inventing one's "voice": The interplay of convention and self-expression in ASL narrative. *Language in Society* 25, no. 3:427–444.

SEARLE, JOHN. 1965. What is a speech act? In *Philosophy in America,* ed. M. Black. Ithaca, NY: Allen & Unwin and Cornell University Press, pp. 221–239.

SEARLE, JOHN. 1976. A classification of illocutionary acts. *Language in Society* 5:1–23.

SHUMAN, AMY. 1992. "Get outa my face": Entitlement and authoritative discourse. In *Responsibility and Evidence in Oral Discourse,* ed. J. Hill and J. Irvine. New York: Cambridge University Press, pp. 135–160.

SILVERSTEIN, MICHAEL. 1985. Language and the culture of gender: At the intersection of structure, usage and ideology. In *Semiotic Meditation,* ed. E. Mertz and R. Parmentier. Orlando, FL: Academic Press, pp. 219–259.

TEDLOCK, DENNIS. 1972. *Finding the Center: Narrative Poetry of the Zuni Indians.* Lincoln: University of Nebraska Press.

TEDLOCK, DENNIS. 1983. *The Spoken Word and the Work of Interpretation.* Philadelphia: University of Pennsylvania Press.

YAMANASHI, MASA-AKI. 1974. On minding your p's and q's in Japanese: A case study from honorifics. *Papers from the Tenth Regional Meeting of the Chicago Linguistic Society.* Chicago, IL: Chicago Linguistic Society, pp. 760–771.

CHAPTER 5

Communicative Interactions

| **A:** | "What is she? Small?" |
| **B:** | "Yes, yes, she's small, smallish, um, not really small but certainly not very big." |

Talk is the primary means by which people interact and satisfy personal and social goals. In the dialogue above, speaker B responds to speaker A's question by performing an intricate series of linguistic moves that accomplish the personal goal of stating an opinion while also accomplishing the social goal of avoiding conflict by being conciliatory and agreeable. If B had not wanted to be polite and avoid conflict, she could have said, "No, she's not small, she's big." But such a statement, by baldly contradicting the implied assumption in A's question (namely, that "she's small"), would have been a challenge to A's competence and therefore to A's social being. In all situations, speakers have options of ways to express themselves. Their choices reveal underlying cultural and linguistic ideologies of behavior, rights, and obligations. In this chapter, we will deal with issues of conversational interaction, beginning with an examination of the structural properties of conversation, proceeding to an analysis of how people accomplish goals through talk, and ending with a discussion of rules of politeness.

STRUCTURAL PROPERTIES OF CONVERSATION

Conversation is based on principles of turn taking that can be structurally defined but that are also influenced by context. The basic structure of turns, their alternation and allocation, are context-free, but the ways that turns are used by speakers, their length and content, are sensitive to situation, allowing greater or lesser opportunities for co-participants.

Harvey Sacks and his co-workers suggested the following mechanisms for turn taking in American practice (1974:700–701):

Speaker change recurs, or, at least, occurs.

Overwhelmingly, one party talks at a time.

Occurrences of more than one speaker at a time are common, but brief.

> Transitions from one turn to a next with no gap and no overlap or with slight gap or slight overlap make up the vast majority of transitions.

> Turn-allocation techniques are used; a current speaker may select next speaker or parties may self-select.

Additional aspects of turn taking, such as order of turns (in multiparty encounters), size of turn, and length of conversation, vary. However, even these features are not totally random but are sensitive to social constraints based on the relative status of participants. Generally, in encounters between unequals, higher-status members assume more rights to turns and to longer turns than do those of lower status. These patterns essentially map social ideologies onto language structure and use.

Conversing includes exchanges of turns, based on certain rules. In two-party interactions, turns alternate automatically between the participants so that each person has the same number of turns. The next speaker normally begins his or her turn at the completion of a *turn-constructional unit* (ibid.:702). Such units are composed of at least a single word but may contain multiple clauses, phrases, and/or sentences.

In multiparty conversations, turns do not rotate in a fixed sequence but are instead variable in their distribution. Turns are allocated in two ways: current speaker selection and self-selection. In the first, the current speaker may select the next speaker directly by asking questions, making requests, or issuing invitations and offers. These are examples of *adjacency pairs,* utterances that are linked automatically to particular kinds of responses (Schegloff and Sacks 1973:295). Adjacency pairs occur as sequences of interaction: question/answer (What time is it?/Four o'clock), request/grant or refusal (May I come in?/Yes), invitation or offer/acceptance or decline (Come for dinner tonight/Sorry, I'm busy).

Linguistic constructions called tag questions are particularly effective mechanisms for ending a turn. *Tag questions* are utterances beginning with a declarative proposition to which a question, or "tag," is added (e.g., "It's hot in here, isn't it?"). They function as "exit techniques" (Sacks et al. 1974:718) because the addressee is obliged to respond by confirming or denying the tag. And this obligation is predicated on the responsibility that conversation participants have to reply to questions.

When the current speaker completes his turn without choosing the next speaker, each participant may self-select, principally by starting first. Sacks and his co-workers noted that self-selectors often "begin with a beginning," typically using such words as *well, but, and,* or *so.* These *turn-entry devices* signal a person's desire to speak next (ibid.:719).

Because conversing is a human activity, it is subject to errors, such as simultaneous talk in the form of overlaps or interruptions. In these cases, *repair mechanisms* are used to correct errors so that one party in simultaneous talk stops and allows the other to complete her turn. Although in theory a participant can either terminate or continue, in practice social norms based on status affect actual outcomes. In accordance with societal rights to speak, higher-status people tend to interrupt or complete their turns when interrupted, whereas lower-status individuals are apt to be successfully interrupted.

Throughout conversation, while speakers talk, listeners have supportive work to do in order to signal their interest, or *active listenership.* Listener responses, or *backchannel cues* (Yngve 1970:574), include words and vocalizations such as *yeah, right, uh-huh,* and *hmm.* These devices are referentially meaningless, but they have great interactional import by indicating one's attention to and ratification of the speaker's talk. They must be well timed to clauses and phrases within the speaker's turn. Too many vocalizations by listeners can be perceived as interruptive, and too few discourage the speaker by implying a lack of interest.

Although conversation is structured in all societies and is everywhere based on principles of turn taking, rules that dictate the timing, length, and allocation of turns differ in accordance with cultural norms. For instance, Native Cree people living in western Canada follow rules for conversational interaction that are quite distinct from those of American-Canadian practice, revealing differing attitudes about language use and social interaction. Whether speaking English or their indigenous language, Cree speakers allow longer pauses within and between turns (Darnell 1985:67). The "no gap" or "slight gap" pattern observed by Sacks and his colleagues for most Americans is not followed. Cree speakers employ pauses in their own turns in order to consider what they will say next. They wait at the end of the previous speaker's turn before beginning their contribution, to show respect for the co-participant. For Cree conversation participants, "Anything serious enough to be worth responding to requires a pause to register and evaluate the words, before speaking in answer" (ibid.).

Cree people actively indicate their attentiveness by using backchannel cues at pauses during interlocutors' turns. The most frequent signal is *ehe* "yes," which is an "acknowledgement of what is said, not an agreement with it" (ibid.). A stronger response, *tapwe* "truly," is reserved for the endings of developed argumentation.

Informal conversation may appear to be loosely structured, but close examination reveals that people follow organizational rules in exchanging turns and in negotiating and achieving the overall format of encounters. Conversations have beginnings and endings that frame the activity of talk. In our society, conversations typically begin with some sort of greeting and end with some sort of closing. Greetings and closings are examples of adjacency pairs and are exchanged sequentially. As we saw in Chapter 4, greetings often consist of routinized formulas having no true semantic content but functioning to mark a person's availability for talk. Both participants signal by their response that they understand and agree to a jointly negotiated behavior, indicating their willingness to engage in talk.

After an initial greeting exchange, participants propose and ratify topics of conversation. Here, too, each party is, in theory, in equal position to introduce topics, but, in practice, people of higher status assume more rights to select topics.

Termination of encounters is usually achieved in our culture through a gradual process at the end of some topic unit. Various techniques for "closing down a topic" are used, including words of agreement, such as *okay, alright,* or *fine,* and other vocalizations, such as *well* or *so* (Schegloff and Sacks 1973:306). Proverbial or conventional expressions of "morals or lessons" commonly occur as initiators of closings, as in the following example (ibid.:307):

DORRINNE:	Uh-you know, it's just like bringin' the—blood up.
THERESA:	Yeah, well, things uh always work out for the best.
DORRINNE:	Oh certainly. Alright Tess.
THERESA:	Uh huh.
THERESA:	Okay.
DORRINNE:	G'bye.
THERESA:	Goodnight.

Another type of closing is the return to a prior topic, highlighting and repeating a main theme. This pattern frequently occurs in telephone conversations where a caller begins with a specific reason for calling and ends by mentioning the same issue. In telephone talk, either party can begin closings by referring to activities immediately prior to the call: "Well, I'll let you get back to your book" or "I gotta go finish making dinner" or simply "I gotta go."

As is the case for all social practices, different cultural norms lead to diverse rules for framing interactions. In contrast to American-Canadian custom, Cree speakers do not employ formal greetings or leave-takings because they interpret such markers as "giving the impression that the relationship is restricted to that occasion" (Darnell 1985:69). Cree speakers choose to emphasize the continuity of social bonds by avoiding indicators of closure.

Conversations are internally cohesive because of their formal structure and because of techniques that speakers use to relate current talk to previous interactions. One of the subtle linguistic devices speakers frequently use to achieve cohesion is repetition. Speakers can repeat entire utterances intact, make partial repeats with variation, and paraphrase previous utterances (Tannen 1987). Repetitions of whatever type involving words, phrases, and sentences bind constructional units to each other, performing an essential cohesive role (Halliday and Hasan 1976:282).

Repetition serves multiple communicative purposes, allowing speakers to stall while formulating their talk, providing redundancy to hearers as an aid in comprehension, and connecting turns of talk. It has varied interactional purposes as well, such as controlling the floor, demonstrating active listenership, ratifying the previous speaker's talk, showing or appreciating humor, and emphasizing one's own or another's contribution (Tannen 1987:583–584). According to Deborah Tannen, repetition in conversation is both a linguistic and an interpersonal device to make experience coherent: "Perceiving meaning through the coherence of discourse, as well as perceiving oneself as coherent in the interaction constituted by the discourse, creates an emotional experience of connectedness; this permits not only participation in the interaction, but also understanding of meaning" (ibid.:584). Use of repetition within discourse also expresses the "eternal tension between fixity and novelty that constitutes creativity. It sends a metamessage of rapport between the communicators, who thereby experience that they share communicative conventions and inhabit the same world of discourse" (ibid.:585).

Tannen identified types of repetition in naturally occurring conversation that can include repetition to indicate participation and familiarity, repetition for humorous effect and repetition for expansion or "scaffolding" of talk (ibid.:589–591).

Here are some examples of each type of conversational repetition:

1. *Repetition to indicate participation and familiarity:*
   [S is serving ice cream, L declines, and her refusal is immediately repeated by N and S, speaking almost in unison.]

   L: I don't eact ice cream.

   N: She doesn't eat ice cream.

   S: Libby (L) doesn't eat ice cream.

2. *Repetition for humorous effect:*
   [D had requested permission to videotape an encounter.]

   P: Just to see if we do anything funny?

   D: No. Just to see how you do nothing funny.

   P: Well I hardly ever do nothing funny.

3. *Repetition for expansion or "scaffolding" of talk:*

   D: Do you run?

   P: Do I run?

   D: Do you run for exercise?

   P: Yes. Right now I run about 3 miles three or four times per week.

Cohesion in discourse can also be accomplished through punning; that is, speakers can tie talk to either their own or previous speaker's talk by conscious or unconscious use of puns. Nondeliberate punning in conversation is often not consciously noticed by either speaker (S) or hearer (H), but its occurrence provides evidence of a linguistic binding mechanism. Puns often occur at the ends of utterances or topic episodes, providing a framing that comments on previous talk. They also function interactively and creatively to pull together participants' talk and their meanings. Some examples from actual conversations follow:

1. Nutritionist talking about intestinal ailments:
   Well, there are nutritional supplements you can take to rectify the problem.
2. Talking about nuclear energy plants:
   The issue of nuclear explosions is a real hot topic now.
3. Sportscaster talking about a baseball pitcher who played in a game even though he had a broken toe:
   He admitted it was bothering him; he made no bones about it.

Additional types of unplanned patterning in everyday speech reflect what Gail Jefferson (1996) refers to as the "poetics of ordinary talk." People often use words that repeat similar sounds, sometimes referred to in artful speech or writing as alliteration. This usage may occur in speech errors, indicating to Jefferson that the errors have an underlying logic. For example, when a woman was asked what time she was planning to leave for a drive, she responded with what Jefferson calls an [s-] row: "Probably, [s]even, [s]even-thirty or [s]omething" (ibid.:5). Here, the repetition of "seven" emphasizes the use of the "s" sound. The mistaken use of consonant clusters also reflects a similar patterning: (from a football announcer): "Staubach goes back in a [dr]eep—[d]eep [dr]opback" (ibid.:6). Sometimes people mix up words, erroneously using one member from a category to which the correct word belongs: "Hi. I'm Carol's sister—uh brother" or "And maybe there's a better way of getting, uh, giving them some power" (ibid.:6–7).

Ordinary poetics can surface across speaker turns as well. For example (ibid.:29),

ALICE:	The speakers cost $20.
BETTY:	Each!
ALICE:	Eatcher heart out!

And

CLAIRE:	(To Barbara) What are you doing?
BARBARA:	I'm looking for.... I'm looking for....
CLAIRE:	(To Jean, with whom she has the lunch date)
	I'm looking forward to Saturday. I hope I'm feeling well enough.

In the following example, two types of poetics occur: The category of body parts is repeated within Jack's turn and Judy responds in her turn with a connecting link (ibid.:35):

JACK:	As long as your parents are [foot]ing the bill, kids, you just go right a[head].
JUDY:	You're not kidding.

In these and other examples, speakers' utterances display a systematic use of sounds and words that reveal "great orderliness" (ibid.:48). While these patterns may not be consciously planned, they are far from random.

CONVERSATIONAL POSTULATES

When people converse, they have certain assumptions about the situation and co-participants based on cultural and linguistic models of interaction, of the fit between behavior and context, and of people's rights and obligations. Cultural norms also dictate what can be said and what should not be said in particular situations, as well as the ways to say what can be said. If interlocutors belong to the same culture, none of these assumptions need be stated or even consciously recognized; they are learned through socialization and presupposed in daily life.

According to H. P. Grice, a "cooperative principle" is presumed to operate in most social encounters (1975:45). Participants have common aims to make "mutually dependent contributions" to conversation. Grice described the *cooperative principle* as "making your conversational contribution such as is required, at the state at which it occurs, by the accepted purpose or direction of the talk exchange in which you are engaged" (ibid.). This statement, although seemingly plausible, glosses over many crucial qualifications. For instance, notions expressed by phrases such as "is required" and "accepted purpose or direction" are influenced both by cultural expectations and by individual motives. What is the "accepted purpose" of a given interaction? Who defines or controls the "direction of the talk exchange"? Do co-participants always share a common aim, or do they merely appear to do so? Or is the "common aim" that of appearing to share a common aim? In analyzing actual speech, attention to intricacies of cooperation reveals a great deal of complexity.

Grice further developed a number of "maxims" that he believed account for and direct communicative interaction (ibid.:45–46):

1. *Quantity: Be informative.*
   a. Make your contribution as informative as required (for the current purposes of the exchange).
   b. Do not make your contribution more informative than required.
2. *Quality: Be truthful.*
   a. Do not say that which you believe to be false.
   b. Do not say that for which you lack adequate evidence.
3. *Relation: Be relevant.*
4. *Manner: Be perspicuous.*
   a. Avoid obscurity of expression.
   b. Avoid ambiguity.
   c. Be brief.
   d. Be orderly.

The first maxim, "be informative," implies a minimum and maximum on quantity, giving as much but no more information than is needed. The second maxim, "be truthful," refers to the speaker's sincerity and obligation not to mislead the hearer. The maxim to "be relevant" means that discourse or conversation should be coherent. Speakers' utterances should be topically, situationally, and interpersonally relevant. Last, the maxims of manner, "be brief" and "be orderly," refer to the use of linguistic form that clearly and succinctly expresses one's ideas, goals, and so on.

All these maxims, of course, are ideals that are relative in their realization. Contextual, social, and cultural constraints limit the degree to which they are appropriately fulfilled. It may be necessary to violate the maxim "be truthful" in order not to insult or betray another individual. Similarly, a speaker may not "be informative" if she wishes to avoid conveying hurtful or upsetting messages. Speakers may choose not to "be brief"; rather, they may use elaborate mitigating linguistic forms in order to blunt the force of their speech.

Grice recognized that conversational maxims are often ignored, evaded, or flouted in actual practice. Indeed, he noted, but did not elaborate on, the possibility of additional maxims of an "aesthetic, social or moral" nature, such as "be polite" (ibid.:47).

Speakers can use certain linguistic devices as prefaces to statements to signal or acknowledge their violations of presupposed maxims. The following examples illustrate such functions of *but* in English (Baker 1975:40–41):

1. *Quantity:* Don't give too much or too little information.
   a. You probably have enough examples by now, but—
   b. This is just a minor point, but—
2. *Quality:* Don't say things you don't believe or don't have adequate evidence for.
   a. This may just be my own intuition, but—
   b. I'm probably totally wrong on this, but—
3. *Relevance:* Stick to the topic.
   a. I don't want to get too far off the topic, but—
   b. I'm not sure if this is relevant, but—
4. *Manner:* Avoid ambiguity and obscurity; be brief and orderly.
   a. I don't know if this makes any sense, but—
   b. It's difficult to state this clearly, but—

Cultural expectations and rules of etiquette affect the way that conversational maxims are fulfilled. For instance, the need to "be truthful" raises the question "How truthful?"; "be brief" leads to the query "How brief?" Even the maxim "be informative" is open for cultural interpretation, as Elinor Ochs Keenan (1976) showed in a study of conversation among the Malagasy of Madagascar. The Malagasy treat information as a valuable commodity and do not share it readily. Keenan attributes this attitude to the fact that, given the public nature of activities in small villages, most of what transpires is seen or quickly known by all. Therefore, "information that is not already available...is highly sought after. If one manages to gain access to 'new' information, one is reluctant to reveal it. As long as it is known that one has that information and others do not, one has some prestige over them" (ibid.:70).

Also, Malagasy speakers hesitate to answer questions fully or make explicit claims because "they do not want to be responsible for the information communicated" (ibid.). The Malagasy blame a person whose statements result in any unpleasantness. Finally, Malagasy villagers are reluctant to make claims about future activities because they would feel shamed if events do not occur as predicted. An example of complicated avoidance of the maxim to "be informative" was a woman's response to Keenan's inquiry about when the woman's brother would return home: "If you don't come after five, you won't find him" (ibid.:71).

Interpersonal relationships existing between Malagasy co-participants also affect whether speakers give information to hearers. The Malagasy classify people into three categories: *havana,* close kin and neighbors; *havan-davitra,* distant kin; and *vahiny,* strangers (ibid.:77). People regularly exchange information with *havana* because they are trusted, but the Malagasy do not give information to distant kin or strangers because they are not trusted. Finally, women are generally more informative than are men because men cultivate an air of caution and polite detachment in their speech, whereas women are more direct and confrontational (ibid.:77–78).

DIRECTIVES

Speakers are expected to respect the rights of others and to be sincere, that is, mean what they say (although they may not always say what they mean). These norms are displayed, for example, in patterns for issuing *directives,* utterances intended to result in an action by the hearer. In order for *directives,* or *requests for action,* to be heard as legitimate, they must satisfy certain sincerity, or felicity, conditions (Gordon and Lakoff 1971:64):

1. Speaker wants hearer to do act.
2. Speaker assumes hearer is able to do act.
3. Speaker assumes hearer is willing to do act.
4. Speaker assumes hearer would not do act in the absence of the request.

Linguistic forms of directives can be tailored to focus on each of these assumptions (ibid.):

1. I want you to take out the garbage.
2. Can you take out the garbage?
3. Would you be willing to take out the garbage?
4. Will you take out the garbage?

Note that none of these requests is expressed as an overt imperative; they are either assertions or questions. However, they are intended as directives and are appropriately understood as such. Hearers are expected to react to speakers' underlying intentions, not necessarily to the surface linguistic form of utterances.

Gordon and Lakoff pointed out that speech acts must be reasonable (ibid.:67). Each kind of speech act—stating, directing, requesting, promising—has its particular basis in reasonableness. Assertions are reasonable inasmuch as the beliefs expressed are reasonable; directives are reasonable if all the sincerity conditions apply.

Speech acts can be challenged if they diverge from the principles of sincerity or reasonableness. Hearers can make challenges by questioning underlying assumptions or by denying assumed conditions. The following utterances are challenges to directives:

1. Why do you want me to close the window? It's hot in here.
2. My arm hurts, so I can't close the window.
3. Why do you think I'd be willing to close the window?
4. You don't have to tell me to do it. I was just going to close the window anyway.

The rights and obligations of participants may be shared equally by all or be monopolized by certain individuals based on status differences. Higher-status speakers are less often challenged when making statements, regardless of the accuracy of their remarks, or when issuing directives, regardless of the inconvenience of complying.

Directives are particularly sensitive to contexts of speaking and to specific social characteristics of the issuer and addressee. They reveal underlying suppositions about certain people's rights to impose and others' rights to be free from imposition. Their complexity stems from the fact that a speaker should phrase requests so that they have the greatest likelihood of positive result, namely, compliance; because a social relationship of some sort exists between interlocutors (even if it is one of "stranger"), however, speakers must be sensitive to addressees' feelings. An issuer of directives needs to navigate between two extremes of clarity: He must make his request clear enough so that the addressee comprehends the directive intent, yet she must also pay attention to the addressee's needs not to be imposed on by a blunt presumption of the speaker's power.

In English, and presumably in all languages, many linguistic alternatives exist for issuing directives. They are generally classified into six types:

1. *Need statement* (speaker asserts her need or want):
   "I need some salt."
2. *Imperative* (speaker commands an action of hearer):
   "Give me the salt!"
3. *Embedded imperative* (command is embedded in another linguistic frame):
   "Could you give me some salt?"
4. *Permission directive* (speaker asks permission, implying action of hearer):
   "May I have the salt?"
5. *Question directive* (speaker asks a question, indirectly implying action of hearer):
   "Do you have any salt?"
6. *Hints* (speaker makes assertion, hinting a request):
   "The salt's not here."

Directives in each of these categories can be expressed with greater or lesser mitigation. For instance, markers of politeness, principally "please" in English, can be added: "May I please have the salt?" Other elaborate linguistic frames are employed in certain contexts: "Would you be so kind as to give me the salt?" In our culture, politeness and mitigation are generally used by speakers who are subordinate to addressees or who, for reasons either of context or personality, wish to soften the force of a directive. In situations socially marked as "formal," blunt demonstrations of authority, even by high-status speakers, are considered inappropriate. In contrast, some speakers select especially bald imperative forms to emphasize their rights to command addressees. Adult speech to children often includes threats or warnings: "Clean up your room, or I'll spank you."

Because many directives are not imperative in form, it is necessary that hearers interpret them appropriately. Hearers need to understand speakers' intent. Comprehension of speakers' intentions is based on knowledge of context, of what kinds of goals people express in language, and of the linguistic alternatives that potentially express those intentions. For example, the interrogative "Do you have any salt?" uttered during a meal is normally interpreted as a directive because a "request for information" about the addressee's possession of salt seems irrelevant. Interpreting this interrogative form as a "request for information" is excluded on the grounds of an absence of legitimacy. A yes or no reply by the addressee, then, would usually be intended as a joke. Otherwise, if an addressee responds to the surface linguistic form rather than the underlying intent of a directive, he or she can be interpreted as making a challenge.

Speakers select among linguistic alternatives for issuing directives based on context and on relationships with addressees. A speaker can mitigate statements of need and many types of imperatives either by deleting the command verb or by supplying additional linguistic frames that soften the speaker's message. The following examples of directives are obtained from actual conversations recorded by Susan Ervin-Tripp (1976:29–45):

1. *Need statements:*
   a. (Physician to technician) "I'll need a routine culture and a specimen."
2. *Imperatives:*
   a. Deleted imperative:
   (Customer to waitress) "Coffee, black."
   b. You + imperative:
   (Passenger to driver) "You should turn right here, then you go straight."

   c. Attention-getters:
   (A child is yelling in the vicinity of a group of adults talking; father to child) "Please!"
   d. Post-posed tags:
   (Professor to colleague) "Carry some of these, will you?"
   e. Rising intonation:
   (Student to another) "Give me a copy?"

The next two categories of directives are indirect in their surface representation, having been converted into the form of questions. Their underlying purpose, however, is still obvious.

   3. *Embedded imperatives:*
   a. (Hospital nurse to aide) "Would you hand me Mr. Adams's chart, please?"
   b. (To stranger in theater) "Can you move your coat over there?"
   4. *Permission directives:*
   a. (Salesperson to clerk) "May I have change for a dollar?"

The final two categories, question directives and hints, provide options for hearers because they can be interpreted as assertions, requests for information, or requests for confirmation rather than as directives. Speakers frequently use negative tag questions if they assume that noncompliance is at least as likely as compliance.

   5. *Question directives:*
   a. (Office worker to another) "Are we out of coffee?" (Give me some coffee.)
   b. (Motorist to gas station attendant) "You don't happen to have any change for the phone, do you?"
   6. *Hints:*
   a. (Child to adult) "I'm hungry."
   b. (Daughter to mother) "Mother, you know I don't have a robe."
   c. "I know."
   d. "Well, we're having a slumber party tomorrow night."

Because utterances often have multiple possible interpretations, reactions to linguistic form can be manipulated for various effects, including humor:

   (Son to mother) "I need a ten-speed bicycle."

   "I'm sure you do."

Linguistic strategies for formulating directives can be classified on the basis of both the orientation of requests and the kinds of linguistic devices employed. Orientation refers to which element of the request matrix is stressed: speaker, addressee, or action to be performed (data from Blum-Kulka and Olshtain 1984:203):

   1. *Hearer-oriented:* Could *you* tidy up the kitchen soon?
   2. *Speaker-oriented:* Do you think *I* could borrow your notes from yesterday's class?
   3. *Speaker- and hearer-oriented:* So, could *we* please clean up?
   4. *Impersonal:* So it might not be a bad idea to *get it cleaned up.*

Directives can be mitigated through various types of linguistic devices (ibid.:203–205):

   1. *Syntactic downgraders or mitigation:*
   a. Interrogative: Could you do the cleaning up?
   b. Negation: Look, excuse me. I wonder if you *wouldn't mind* dropping me home?

     c. Past tense: I *wanted* to ask for a postponement.

     d. Embedded "if" clause: I would appreciate it *if* you left me alone.

2. *Pragmatic mitigation:*

     a. Consultative devices (indirectly asking for addressee's cooperation): *Do you think* I could borrow your lecture notes from yesterday?

     b. Understaters (minimizing request): Could you tidy up *a bit* before I start?

     c. Hedges (avoiding commitment): It would really help if *you did something* about the kitchen.

     d. Downtoner (signaling possibility of noncompliance): Will you *perhaps* be able to drive me?

Languages can provide grammatical means of issuing indirect commands in order to comply with social rules of etiquette and appropriateness. For example, in Malagasy, a Malayo-Polynesian language spoken in Madagascar, cultural norms emphasize values of behaving and speaking in nonconfrontational and nonargumentative manners in most social interactions. Indirect speech is favored in everyday behavior, masking potentially unpleasant interactions. For example, commands are rarely issued with imperative constructions because these directly express speakers' authority. Instead, they are mitigated by several linguistic procedures, including use of the passive rather than active voice. The passive voice focuses attention on patients (direct object) of desired actions rather than on agents (subject) and thereby mutes the force of an order. Compare the following sentences (Keenan 1974:132):

    Active: *Manasa ny lamba amin'ny savony.*
                  Wash the clothes with the soap!

    Passive: *Sasao ny lamba amin'ny savony.*
                  Have the clothes washed with the soap! (literally: have washed the clothes with the soap)

A directive can also be issued in "circumstantial" form in sentences with nouns denoting the instrument used in an activity. This usage highlights the instrument and further detracts from the action being commanded:

    Circumstantial: *Anasao lamba ny savony.*
                     The soap is to be used to wash clothes! (literally: have-washed-with clothes the soap)

Children learn styles of formulating directives as part of socialization and acquisition of communicative norms. Comparison of directives used by Hungarian and Norwegian children demonstrated differences between the two cultures and also between younger (4 to 5 years old) and older (9 to 10 years old) children in each group (Hollos and Beeman 1978). In general, Hungarian children employed direct commands and requests, making a distinction between familiars (friends, family, neighbors) and strangers in selecting linguistic alternatives. For example, a bald imperative *adjal* "give!" is used to familiars, whereas polite, but still direct, forms such as *tessek szives lenni adni* "please to be kind to give" is used to strangers (ibid.:347). When initial requests were denied, Hungarian children resorted to intensified demands, repetition of requests, and forms of begging.

    Norwegian children, in contrast, generally favored indirect means both to initiate and repeat requests. They used need statements, *jeg er sa torst* "I have so thirst"; interrogatives, *kann du hjelpe meg* "can you help me?"; and hints, *kann du finne litt saft* "can you find a little juice?" (ibid.:349). Norwegian children also distinguished between familiars and strangers; in interactions with the latter, they often attempted to enlist an adult's aid in obtaining their goals. When requests were denied, these children either gave up or repeated their requests in even more indirect styles.

As one would expect, older children employed a wider range of syntactic and lexical formulations. Their ability to use more complex grammatical structures is based on their advanced language acquisition. For example, a 5-year-old Norwegian child commanded his father, *Far, kom hit* "Father, come here!" whereas a 9-year-old asked, *Far, kann du komme?* "Father, can you come?" When these children intensified their requests, the younger said, *Nei, kom na* "No, come now"; the older asked, *kann du ikke komm?* "Can you not come?" (ibid.:353).

DIRECTIVES AND RESPONSES IN CONTEXT

Analysis of the form of directives and of addressees' responses often reveals that speakers use indirect means in order to soften the force of their speech and to avoid responsibility for underlying implications. In a discussion of directives, William Labov and David Fanshel formulated the *rule of requests* (1977:78), which is based on assumptions similar to Gordon and Lakoff's *felicity conditions*.

Rule of Requests

If A addresses to B an imperative specifying an action X at a time T, and B believes that A believes that

1. X should be done (for a purpose) (*need for action*).
2. B would not do X in the absence of the request (*need for request*).
3. B has the *ability* to do X (with an instrument Z).
4. B has the *obligation* to do X or is willing to do it.
5. A has the *right* to tell B to do X, then A is heard as making a valid request for action.

This rule is predicated on mutually recognized needs, abilities, obligations, and rights. Such preconditions are usually not stated directly but exist as part of the participants' interactional competence. According to Labov and Fanshel, explicit reference to needs of speakers, abilities of addressees, or existential conditions (e.g., "This place is really dusty") is often perceived as mitigating the force of requests, whereas statement of speaker's rights or hearer's obligations is typically aggravating (ibid.:83). However, Labov and Fanshel's generalization should be tempered with the provision that context, relationship between interlocutors, and prosodic cues affect the mitigating or aggravating force of any utterance. For example, appeals to existential conditions, "Have you dusted yet?" or abilities, "Do you have enough time to dust the room?" that Labov and Fanshel consider mitigating can be intended and interpreted as sarcastic and therefore aggravating.

Just as speakers choose means for making requests, addressees select among alternative means of responding. If an addressee intends to comply with a request, a direct response is usually given. In contrast, noncompliant moves are often accomplished indirectly. Given the social nature of conversation and requirements that participants be cooperative, refusals of directives typically contain an "accounting" (ibid.:88) related to underlying validity conditions. An addressee can question the need for an action, her ability to perform the act, her obligation to comply, and/or the right of speaker to make the request. Most refusals, then, are indirect and call for additional justification by the requester, who can reinstate the directive by responding to the addressee's accounting.

Bald repetitions of directives are perceived in our culture as aggravated assertions of authority. Labov and Fanshel analyzed such responses as challenges to the competence of the addressee. They suggested that most challenges are in practice mitigated to avoid overt confrontation: "Though a challenge to competence is always present when a request is repeated, the more the surface structure is varied, the less strongly is this challenge felt" (ibid.:95). Challenges are often expressed as surface interrogatives. Because, like all questions, challenges are examples of adjacency pairs, they require a response from the addressee in the form of either a defense or an admission. Admissions of the validity of a challenge have interpersonal consequences not only for the moment of a particular episode but also for the future because they form part of the presupposed background of subsequent speech events.

The following examples, from Labov and Fanshel's analysis of a therapy session, demonstrate interactional complexities of conversation and the need to attend to personal histories of co-participants in order to develop a full understanding of what is meant by talk. The patient, Rhoda (age 19), begins an account of a telephone call to her mother, who was visiting Rhoda's married sister, with the following surface question:

> And so–when–I called her t'day, I said, "Well, when do you plan to come home?" (ibid.:155)

Although this utterance takes interrogative form, Rhoda intends it as a directive, a request for action, namely, that her mother return home. Rhoda's question (implied request) satisfies preconditions for validity based on the rule of requests (ibid.:159):

1. Her mother should come home to help do the housework and does not seem to be doing so without being asked.
2. Her mother has the ability to come home.
3. Her mother has an obligation to come home because she is the head of the household.
4. Rhoda has the right to tell her mother to come home.

Because Rhoda's underlying intent differs from the linguistic form she chooses, her question can be expanded to reflect its actual meaning:

> *Rhoda:* When I called my mother today, I actually said "Well, in regard to the subject which we both know is important and is worrying me, when are you leaving my sister's house where any obligations you have already have been fulfilled and returning home where your primary obligations are being neglected as you should do as head of our household?" (ibid.:160)

Finally, Rhoda has accomplished an act of requesting in the context of a specific interaction with her mother. Labov and Fanshel explained the interpersonal communicative work as follows:

> Rhoda requests information on the time that her mother intends to come home and thereby requests indirectly that her mother come home, thereby challenging her mother indirectly for not performing her role as head of the household properly, simultaneously admitting her own limitations.

And how does Rhoda's mother respond to the indirect requests and implications? She also employs covert means to challenge Rhoda's question:

So she said, "Oh, why?" (ibid.:165)

This utterance cannot possibly be intended as a simple question. Labov and Fanshel offered the following expansion:

So my mother said to me: "Oh, I'm surprised; why are you asking me when I plan to come home, and do you have a right to ask that? There's more to this than meets the eye: Isn't it that you can't take care of the household by yourself and I shouldn't have gone away in the first place, as I've told you before." (ibid.:166)

The interactional implications are given:

Mother asks Rhoda for further information, which she already has, thereby putting off R's requests for action and for help and asserts indirectly that she knows that the answer to her own question is that R is asking for help because she cannot perform the obligations of household, thereby challenging R's status as an adult member of the household. (ibid.:166)

POLITENESS

Theories of Politeness

When people converse, they generally adhere to cultural norms, showing that they are "competent" speakers. Robin Lakoff suggested two underlying *rules of pragmatic competence* (1973:296):

1. Be clear.
2. Be polite.

Ideally, speakers try to fulfill both of these requirements. If the rules conflict, however, Lakoff claimed that politeness supersedes because "it is considered more important in a conversation to avoid offense than to achieve clarity...since in most informal conversations, actual communication of important ideas is secondary to reaffirming and strengthening relationships" (ibid.:297–298).

Lakoff's postulates for politeness are as follows (ibid.:298):

1. Don't impose.
2. Give options.
3. Make A feel good—be friendly.

These rules are deceptively concise, but they are actually complex because languages provide multiple forms for expressing them. For example, passive constructions, such as "Dinner is served," are more polite than direct questions, "Would you like to eat?" (ibid.:299). The first sentence, in compliance with Rule 1, avoids intruding into the addressee's wants or needs and is therefore interpersonally distancing.

Speakers comply with Rule 2 (Give options) by using hedges and mitigated expressions that allow hearers to form and hold their own opinions. By not forcefully asserting propositions, hedges and mitigation blunt potential confrontations. Speakers can provide hearers with options to respond either affirmatively or negatively, as in "I guess it's time to leave" or "It's time to leave, isn't it?" (ibid.:300).

Rule 3 (Make A feel good—be friendly) is the most variable in terms of cultural meanings. It implies, as do all of Lakoff's rules, that co-participants share similar ideologies and norms for behavior and that they evaluate speech according to the same presupposed notions.

In a widely acclaimed attempt to discover universal principles of politeness, Penelope Brown and Stephen Levinson (1987) compared linguistic data principally from English, Tzeltal (a native language of Mexico), and Tamil (spoken in India). They suggested that everywhere polite behavior is based on assumptions of cooperation because all social groups need to minimize conflict among co-members. In Brown and Levinson's terms, politeness is concerned with *face,* defined as an "individual's self-esteem" or the "public self-image that every member wants to claim for [him- or herself]" (ibid.:2, 161). The notion of face entails different kinds of desires, or *face-wants,* that all people have and that all people know others to have. These wants are of two basic types (ibid.:13):

1. *Positive face-wants:* desire (in some respects) to be approved of.
2. *Negative face-wants:* desire to be unimpeded in one's actions.

Although these wants are presumably universal, they are "subject to cultural specifications of many sorts—what kinds of acts threaten face, what sorts of persons have special rights to face-protection, and what kinds of personal styles (in terms of things like graciousness, ease of social relations, etc.) are especially appreciated" (ibid.:13).

Brown and Levinson distinguish strategies of polite behavior by differentiating face-wants (ibid.:2, 70):

1. *Positive politeness:* oriented to the positive image which hearer claims; speaker recognizes hearer's desire to have her or his positive face-wants respected. Positive politeness strategies express solidarity, friendliness, and in-group reciprocity.
2. *Negative politeness:* oriented to H's desire not to be imposed upon; S recognizes H's rights to autonomy. Negative politeness strategies express S's restraint and avoidance of imposing on H.
3. *Off-record politeness:* indirect strategies which avoid making any explicit or unequivocal imposition on H.

Speakers choose among these modes and within each they select specific linguistic variants, depending on relationships to addressees within the overriding context of cultural assumptions about rights of co-participants, potential offensiveness of intended messages, and appropriateness of each behavior in any given event. Cultures vary, too, in the emphasis given to interactional qualities—for example, being tactful, modest, agreeable, generous, and sympathetic. People in different social categories may be expected to display any of these qualities to a greater or lesser extent; for example, lower-status people may need to show modesty or tact when speaking to higher-status people.

According to Brown and Levinson, politeness strategies develop to deal with *face-threatening acts* (FTAs) (ibid.:60), acts that intrinsically infringe on H's face-wants. For instance, requests by necessity impose on H's negative face (desire to be unimpeded). Requests and other FTAs can be done "bald on-record," that is, directly. However, most FTAs are accomplished with "redressive action," through some expression of positive or negative politeness. Figure 5.1 represents Brown and Levinson's schema of strategies and risks (ibid.:60).

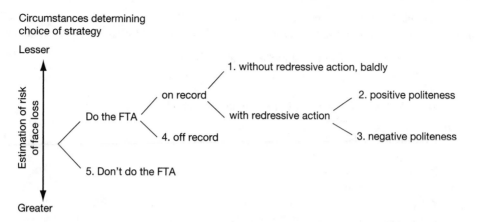

Circumstances determining
choice of strategy

Lesser

Estimation of risk
of face loss

Do the FTA

on record

1. without redressive action, baldly

with redressive action

2. positive politeness

3. negative politeness

4. off record

5. Don't do the FTA

Greater

FIGURE 5.1 **Communication Strategies.** (Brown, Penelope, and Stephen Levinson, 1987:60. *Politeness: Some Universals in Language Usage.* New York: Cambridge University Press.)

The more threatening an act is, the more polite and indirect are the means used to accomplish it. Requests that involve minimal cost to H are made through positive politeness strategies, stressing solidarity between S and H. Requests involving greater imposition on H are made through negative politeness strategies that are more formal and distancing. The most imposing requests are expressed through indirection and hints (ibid.:59).

FTAs vary in terms of the kind of threat involved (ibid.:65–68). Some threaten H's negative face by imposing on H (requests, orders, dares, offers, expressions of anger). Other FTAs threaten H's positive face (desire to be respected) by indicating S's lack of concern for H's self-image (criticism, accusations, insults, contradictions, boasts). Finally, some FTAs are threatening to S rather than to H by either offending S's need not to be imposed upon (thanking, accepting offers, making unwilling promises) or by offending S's need for positive self-image (apologies, confessions, admissions of responsibility).

Speakers select linguistic mechanisms for accomplishing FTAs depending on three types of social factors having varying weight in any given encounter (ibid.:74):

1. *Social distance:* a symmetric relation between S and H.
2. *Power:* an asymmetric relation between S and H.
3. *Ranking:* an assessment of the degree of imposition entailed by the FTA.

Cultural norms obviously affect the interpretation of these factors. Degree of social distance depends on cultural notions of familiarity or formality involved in any given relationship, the relative power of S and H is contingent on social segmentation and the assignment of greater or lesser rights and obligations to members of distinct groups, and relative ranking of FTAs is only appropriate in the context of cultural assumptions about the risks and costs of given behaviors.

Speakers begin by wishing to accommodate H's face-wants to some degree in order to gain cooperation or compliance from H and to demonstrate S's own cooperativeness. Then S decides to what extent she or he should use politeness strategies to minimize the intended FTA, given the encounter's social and personal context and S's need to accomplish the FTA. Speakers consider these factors as they select linguistic means for expressing FTAs. As shown in Brown and Levinson's diagram (Figure 5.1), four types of strategies are possible: bald on-record, positive politeness, negative politeness, and off-record (indirect). Following is a compilation of various linguistic devices employed in English, Tzeltal, and Tamil to realize different strategies (ibid.:94ff):

1. Bald on-record (no effort to minimize threats to H's face):
   a. In emergencies:
   Help!
   eRu! eRu! periya paampu! (Tamil: Get up! Get up! There's a big snake!)
   b. In task-oriented activities:
   Give me the nails.
   c. In unequal power relationships:
   Bring me the wine, Jeeves.
   d. In joking or teasing:
   ʔok'an. ʔilinan. (Tzeltal: Cry. Get angry.)
   e. In alerting H to something in his or her interest:
   Your headlights are on!
   f. In granting H's request:
   yakuk. La? čuka tey ʔa. (Tzeltal: Okay. Come tie it there.)
   g. In greetings, leave-takings; formulaic offers:
   hiȼ 'an tal. la? we?an. [Tzeltal: Pull (your chair) up. Come eat.]
2. Positive politeness (recognize H's desire to be respected):
   a. Claim common ground (indicate that S and H belong to same group, have similar needs, etc.):
   (1) Attend to H:
   You must be hungry; it's a long time since breakfast. How about some lunch?
   (2) Exaggerate approval, sympathy, and so on:
   viiTu payankaramaa kaTTirukkiraar. [Tamil: He built the house terrifyingly (i.e., lavishly).]
   (3) Use in-group identity markers:
   Help me with this bag here, will you pal?
   (4) Avoid disagreement:
   A: What is she? Small?
   B: Yes, yes, she's small, smallish, um, not really small but certainly not very big.
   (5) Assume agreement:
   So when are you coming to see us?
   hk'opon hbakik ȼ'in. (Tzeltal: We'll be talking together then.)
   (6) Hedge opinions:
   You really should sort of try harder.
   memel niwan. (Tzeltal: True maybe.)
   (7) Switch personal focus:
   en paNam elaam poocc alla. (Tamil: All my money's gone, hasn't it?)
   (8) Presuppose H's wants:
   ma ya? we wah me?? (Tzeltal: Won't you eat, Mother?)
   (9) Joke:
   Okay if I tackle those cookies now?
   b. Convey cooperation between S and H:
   (1) Presuppose H's feelings:
   I know you can't bear parties, but this one will really be good—do come!

(2) Be optimistic:
I'll just help myself to a cookie then—thanks!
onka vaNTi kuTukkiriinka, illeyaa? (Tamil: You'll lend me your bike, right?)

(3) Include both S and H:
Let's have a cookie, then.
hk'antik?a?wala?a¢ 'am ?a. [Tzeltal: We (inclusive) want your little salt.]

(4) Give (or ask for) reasons:
bistuk ma ša? wak'betik bel hmahantik?a?son?
(Tzeltal: Why don't you lend us your record player?)

3. Negative politeness (recognize H's desire not to be imposed upon):

a. Be conventionally indirect:
I'm looking for a comb.
inta paattiratt-le neriya koncam teeva paTutu.
(Tamil: This plate needs much more a little.)

b. Don't presume or assume:
muTincaa, koncam paNam kuTunka. (Tamil: If you can, give some money.)

c. Don't coerce H:

(1) Be pessimistic, uncertain:
Could you do it?
onka-kiTTee sikaraTT irukkumaa? (Tamil: Will there be a cigarette on you?)

(2) Minimize the imposition:
I just want to ask you if I can borrow a little bit of paper.
ya kh 'an ala p~esuk. (Tzeltal: I want a little peso's worth, as it were.)

d. Communicate a desire not to impose on H:

(1) Apologize:

(a) Admit imposition:
I'd like to ask you a big favor.

(b) Indicate reluctance:
I don't want to bother you, but....

(c) Give overwhelming reasons:
I can think of nobody else who could....

(d) Beg forgiveness:
mannikkaNum. (Tamil: You should/must forgive me.)

(2) Impersonalize:
(onkalukku) aavasiyum. [Tamil: (To you) it is necessary that....]
ma stak (ya?) pas mene. [Tzeltal: It is not possible (you) do that.]

(3) Use passives:
That letter must be typed immediately.
ceyyaTTum. (Tamil: Let it be done.)

(4) Use indefinites:
One shouldn't do things like that.
?ay bal mac'a ?ay sk'u ya hmahan? (Tzeltal: Is there someone who would have a blouse I could borrow?)

(5) Pluralize pronouns:
We regret to inform you....

(6) Use distance:
I was wondering whether you could do me a little favor.

      (7) State general rules:
           Latecomers cannot be seated until the next interval.

      (8) Nominalize:
           An urgent request is made for your cooperation.

  4. Off-record (indirect strategies):

    a. Give hints:
       It's cold in here.
       etoo paNam vaankinaa, paraville-ille? (Tamil: If some money is received, it wouldn't matter, would it?)

    b. Understate:
       It's not half bad.
       puersa k'ešlal ¢' in mak. (Tzeltal: She's really embarrassed then maybe.)

    c. Overstate:
       I tried to call a hundred times, but there was never any answer.

    d. Be ironic:
       John's a real genius.
       yuʔ ma ʔihk'al čahpuk lah ta yalel ʔa ¢'i. [Tzeltal: Because it's not really bad-as-it-were then (i.e., it's really bad)!]

    e. Use rhetorical questions:
       What can I say? (i.e., Nothing, it's so bad.)
       ancu mailukku varra muTiyaataa? [Tamil: Can't you come five miles (to see us)? (i.e., Why haven't you come to visit?)]

    f. Be vague or ambiguous:
       Perhaps someone did something naughty.

This survey of politeness strategies demonstrates both forms and functions of linguistic alternatives. Certain features of linguistic structure can readily accommodate speakers' needs to mitigate or redress FTAs, the essence of politeness. Grammatical mechanisms such as embedded interrogatives, passives, and impersonal nominalizations have differing forms and frequencies of use in diverse languages. And formulaic expressions and terms of address are part of the repertoire of all languages, although their proliferation and usage vary cross-culturally.

Among the Akan of Ghana, the use of proverbs in conversation functions as a strategy to mitigate FTAs engendered by giving advice and admonitions, thereby protecting the face of both speaker and addressee (Obeng 1996). For example, in the following excerpt, a mother advises her adult son to send money home to contribute to the support of his aged parents by reminding him of his familial responsibility:

Mpaninfo na ekaa se se obi hwe

elders FOC said that if someone looks-after

wo ma wo se fifi a, ese se wo nso

you for your teeth develop if must you also

wo hwe no na ne se tutu.

wo look-after him FOC his teeth uproot

Wonim wo papa yadee yi. Seesi ntumi

you-know your father illness this now he-cannot

nye adwuma; asetena aye den.

NEG-do work life has-become hard

(*Note:* FOC = focus; NEG = negative) (Obeng 1996:532.)

"It is the elders who said, *If someone looks after you when you're teething, you should also look after him when he loses his teeth.* You're aware of your father's illness. Now he's incapable of working. Life is hard these days." Here the mother begins a potential FTA by quoting a proverb handed down by "the elders" in order to soften the implied request for her son's financial assistance. In addition, this usage is based on cultural and linguistic practices that affirm the validity of elders' views and the legitimacy of their role in supporting social norms.

In some societies, polite ritualized speech can be used to mask confrontation and criticism. For instance, among the Malagasy of Madagascar, certain ceremonial occasions involve dialogues between two speakers who competitively use elaborate linguistic and stylistic forms in order to criticize the other speaker. Because overt criticism is socially disvalued, subtle and indirect speech, including mitigated speech, instructive proverbs, and other forms of polite allusion and innuendo, is used in these confrontations. Following is an example of a speaker who is developing a criticism of his rival.

> Thank you very much, sir. The first part of your talk has already been received in peace and happiness. I am in accordance and agreement with you on this, sir. You were given permission to speak and what you said gave me courage and strength. You said things skillfully but not pretentiously. You originate words but also recognize what is traditional. But as for myself I am not an originator of words at all but a borrower. I am more comfortable carrying the spade and basket. You, on the other hand, have smoothed out all faults in the speech; you have woven the holes together. You have shown respect to the elders and respect to the young as well. This is finished. But...[criticism begins]. (Keenan 1974:129)

However, when examining politeness strategies, we should remember that linguistic forms can be manipulated in speech encounters in contradictory ways. Consider the following episode in which a nurse tries to convince an elderly hospitalized patient to take her medicine (data from Coupland et al. 1988:259):

NURSE (N):	Edith. Hallo, my darling. Try and drink that for me. Drink that down for me.
EDITH (E):	I've got to go to school.
N:	Well drink that down first and then you can go to school.
E:	(( ))
N:	Down the hatch with it. And the rest. Straight down. Go on straight down, Edith. It's nice. Drink it straight down then. I've had mine; you drink that up.
E:	Oh, I don't want it.
N:	Yes, drink it down you must. Doctor's orders.
E:	Take it.
N:	Doctor's orders. Come on, drink it down. Drink it down for me. Drink it now.

E:	(( ))
N:	No, drink it now. Come on then, drink it down. Quick, look, Mary is drinking hers. You drink yours straight down. You must quick. If you don't drink it, you'll be very poorly.

(Nurse tries to force medicine)

E:	Ow! Ow! Ow!
N:	Come on. Drink it down.
SECOND NURSE:	I'd leave her then if she don't want it that bad. I don't think she wants it.

In this encounter, the nurse employed many supposedly mitigating politeness strategies: addressing patient with familiar name and term of endearment (Edith, my darling); incurring a debt (drink that for me); using metaphor and humor (down the hatch with it); being optimistic (it's nice); including speaker and hearer in activity (I've had mine); impersonalizing (doctor's orders); exaggerating benefit to hearer (if you don't drink it, you'll be very poorly). Nearly all of the nurse's turns contain at least one of these devices. But they hardly render the interaction any less intrusive or less coercive. Indeed, the proliferation of endearing, optimistic, inclusive formulations has the opposite effect. Rather than belittling the imposition on the hearer, they belittle and demean the hearer herself.

Politeness in Japanese

Situational and cross-cultural studies supplement and illustrate theories about politeness and its linguistic and social meanings. The Japanese language provides a rich body of data for the investigation of politeness. Politeness is demonstrated in Japanese through *honorification*— the use of respect markers with nouns, verbs, and modifiers to show deference toward addressees or referents. Nouns representing worthy people or objects can be marked in several ways. First, Japanese contains some contrasting expressions for persons (Ide 1982:359):

1a. *ano hito* "that person" (plain)
1b. *ano kato* "that person" (honored)

Second, names and kin terms can co-occur with polite respect markers:

2a. Last name/first name/kin term + *san* (honored)
   Hanako-san; otoo-san "father"
2b. LN/FN/kin term + *sama* (exalted respect)
   Hanako-sama; otoo-sama "father"
2c. (LN) + *sensei* (literally: teacher)
   Satoo-sensei

Although *sensei* means "teacher," it can be used politely for any high-status professional, such as a doctor, politician, writer, and so on.

Nouns referring to objects can co-occur with the polite prefixes *o-* and *go-*. They are attached to objects associated with honored people. (*Note:* Examples are from Ide 1982:360–365; HON = honorific; TOP = sentential topic; NOM = nominative; DAT = dative; ACC = accusative.)

3. teacher's book (possession)

sensei	*no*	*go-hon*
teacher		HON-book

Honorification of verbs and modifiers is more complex. Three different politeness devices are used to mark grammatical subjects, objects, or addressees. A fourth type humbles the speaker rather than (or in addition to) honoring the addressee or referent.

To show respect toward grammatical subjects, speakers combine the prefix *o-* or *go-* and the ending *(r) are.*

4. Professor Sato (honored) wrote a book.

Satoo-sensei	*ga*	*hon*	*o*	*kak-are-ta.*
	NOM	book	ACC	write-HON-PAST

The suffix *(r)are* is a homophone of the regular passive suffix in Japanese, confirming one of Brown and Levinson's postulates of universal linguistic practice, that is, use of passives as a politeness strategy.

Adjectives that describe the respected subject are marked with the *o-* or *go-* prefix:

5. Professor Sato (honored) is busy.

Satoo-sensei	*wa*	*o-isogasii*
	TOP	HON-busy

To show respect toward addressees, verbs co-occur with the ending *masu.* In addition, the polite pronoun *anata* is employed:

6. Are you (honored) coming?

Anata	*wa*	*irassyai masu*	*ka*
you	TOP	come (HON) HON	QUESTION

Finally, respect toward referents and addressees can be demonstrated indirectly by humbling the speaker:

7a. I will go (plain).

Watasi ga iku
I   go

7b. I will go (humble).

Watasi ga mairu.
I   go (humble)

Humbling prefixes are sometimes attached to nouns labeling referents associated with the speaker:

8. *tuma*	"wife"	*gu-sai*	"my (stupid) wife"
musuko	"son"	*gu-soku*	"my (stupid) son"
mise	"shop"	*syoo-ten*	"my (small) shop"
bun	"sentence"	*setu-bun*	"my (bad) sentences"

These usages are not intended to insult a wife, son, shop, and so on; rather, they indicate the speaker's modesty, thereby raising the status of the addressee (note, however, that there is no equivalent phrase meaning "my [stupid] husband").

According to Sachiko Ide, Japanese social rules of politeness influence speakers' selection of various linguistic devices. The overriding rule of politeness is to "be polite in a formal setting" (1982:371). Formality is based on relationships among participants (lacking familiarity or solidarity), situational occasion (e.g., ceremonies, public meetings), and topic of talk (seriousness).

In addition to the general rule of formality, three other rules apply in Japanese social etiquette (ibid.:366–368):

1. Be polite to a person of higher social position.
2. Be polite to a person with power.
3. Be polite to an older person.

Social position is an important aspect of one's identity, and it influences the linguistic treatment one receives. However, it is secondary to the operation of Rule 2, which takes precedence. Power is a characteristic of specific encounters and varies with the type of interaction. For example, professionals such as doctors have power over their patients; teachers have power over their students. In these cases, power and social position coincide, but in others, they may not (a police officer issuing a traffic ticket to a doctor has power even though he has lower social status). People who control money have power in interactions (customers to merchants, employers to employees). Finally, a person making a request will be polite to an addressee, reflecting the latter's power to satisfy or deny requests (ibid.:367–368).

Ide reported that some individuals of high social status and power violate expected norms of politeness by using reciprocally polite speech to their subordinates. She suggested that "this may be caused by the egalitarian consciousness of upper-class guilt by which one denies Rule 1.... This trend is strongly observed in the behavior of women in higher positions [resulting from] a clash of the high professional position and the low status of women in general" (ibid.:367). Women typically use more polite speech than do men, characterized by a high frequency of honorifics, formal stylistic markers, and softening devices such as hedges and questions.

Experimental studies with Japanese men and women reveal additional factors contributing to women's more polite speech. When asked to rate numerous sentences containing a range of politeness markers, men and women ranked all sentences in the same relative order, but men rated each sentence as more polite than did women. Therefore, because women perceive each specific structure to be less polite, they must use a more strongly deferential utterance to express the same degree of politeness (Ide et al. 1986:30). When women and men were directed to ask questions of a range of addressees (relatives, friends, superiors, strangers), women generally chose more polite stylistic alternatives than did men. The only exceptions to this pattern were that women spoke less politely to their children and neighbors. Ide and her colleagues contended that notions of sociability and solidarity affect these cases (ibid.:34). Mothers have closer emotional bonds with their children than do fathers, and women establish more solidarity networks in private domains with their children and in their neighborhoods. Therefore, men's use of polite forms in these contexts may indicate social distance rather than deference. In most other situations (e.g., employment and public interactions), women are socially less secure and linguistically more deferential and polite than are men.

To investigate connections between gender and politeness, the National Language Research Institute of Japan conducted an experimental study of the usage of polite speech (reported in Shibamoto 1987:32–33). Subjects were asked how they would make requests, ask questions, and address participants in various situations. Responses were coded as "normally polite" (0), "marked polite" (11), and "rude" (21). Average scores were computed for women and men across situations, and significant gender differences were found: 0.27 for men and 2.90 for women.

Interactions between spouses also indicate women's deferential behavior, as women consistently direct more polite speech to their husbands. And research by Tsunao Ogino found that husbands used their least polite styles when speaking to their wives, although wives employed moderately polite and formal speech to their husbands (1986:43, 47).

While all researchers studying Japanese patterns of politeness and gender agree that cultural and linguistic ideologies encourage both women and men to think of women as using language that is more polite and deferential, in actual practice there is a great deal of variation (Okamoto 2004). For example, age may be a contributing factor because several studies of honorific usage indicate that older women employ a greater number of honorifics than do younger women. The same pattern is exhibited by older and younger men as well. In addition, contextual variation is often significant in affecting the use of honorifics. For instance, a comparison of the speech of salespersons working in two large department stores with the speech of vendors in two open markets revealed some unexpected behavior. According to the rules of politeness, salespeople should use polite speech to their customers, and in fact both men and women working in the department stores did use many honorifics when addressing customers. In contrast, women vendors in the marketplaces often did not use honorifics (ibid.:46). Such behavior, seemingly violating linguistic norms, may express attitudes of equality and friendliness.

In her analysis, Okamoto stressed the importance of varying interpretations of honorific usage. That is, the use of honorifics may reflect the speaker's low social status in relation to the addressee or it may reflect the speaker's desire to express politeness. In addition, the reciprocal use of honorifics by a higher-status person to a lower-status person may reflect the speaker's desire to express solidarity and to minimize power and social distance. Just as the use of honorifics may have several interpretations, the nonuse of honorifics may be ambiguous. Avoiding the use of honorifics in situations where they are expected by social norms may be an expression of rudeness or a reflection of solidarity and familiarity. And it may be a strategy of resistance to dominant cultural and linguistic models. Indeed, according to Okamoto, nonreciprocal use of honorifics seems to be decreasing in contemporary Japan, while reciprocal patterns of either employing or avoiding honorifics are increasing in frequency. (Note similar trends in the use of *tu/vous* pronouns in European countries, as discussed in Chapter 4.) Finally, a speaker's personal attitudes toward the use of honorifics and toward the meanings that they convey are also sources of linguistic variation within the community.

Summary

People interact primarily through talk, most often in informal conversation. Conversation is structured, framed by openings and closings, and internally characterized by rules of turn taking and turn allocation. Although these properties can be defined abstractly, analysis of ongoing talk demonstrates situational and interactional complexities that influence how the structure of conversation is actualized.

Co-participants are expected to adhere to cultural norms or postulates of conversational behavior. Specification and strength of these postulates vary across cultures. They vary across speech events as well, depending on the relationships, rights, and purposes of interlocutors. These bases of variation are especially revealed in issuing directives. Speakers want directives to produce responses or actions by addressees, but the speakers are sensitive to the rights and obligations of co-participants. Directives can be issued in many linguistic forms. Speakers need to take care in their selection of form in order to both make clear their intent and avoid an affront to addressees. Culturally sanctioned rules of politeness affect the form and content of speech and provide participants with shared expectations to guide and evaluate behavior.

References

BAKER, CHARLOTTE. 1975. This is just a first approximation, but.... In *Papers from the Eleventh Regional Meeting of the Chicago Linguistic Society.* Chicago, IL: Chicago Linguistic Society, pp. 37–47.

BLUM-KULKA, SHOSHANA, AND ELITE OLSHTAIN. 1984. Requests and apologies: A cross-cultural study of speech act realization patterns. *Applied Linguistics* 5:196–213.

BROWN, PENELOPE, AND STEPHEN LEVINSON. 1987. *Politeness: Some Universals in Language Usage.* New York: Cambridge University Press.

COUPLAND, NIKOLAS, KAREN GRAINGER, AND JUSTINE COUPLAND. 1988. Politeness in context: Intergenerational issues. *Language in Society* 17:253–262.

DARNELL, REGNA. 1985. The language of power in Cree interethnic communication. In *Language of Inequality,* ed. N. Wolfson and J. Manes. The Hague: Mouton, pp. 61–72.

ERVIN-TRIPP, SUSAN. 1976. "Is Sybill there?" The structure of some American English directives. *Language in Society* 5:25–66.

GORDON, DAVID, AND GEORGE LAKOFF. 1971. Conversational postulates. In *Papers from the Seventh Regional Meeting of the Chicago Linguistic Society.* Chicago, IL: Chicago Linguistic Society, pp. 63–84.

GRICE, HERBERT PAUL. 1975. Logic and conversation. In *Syntax and Semantics, Vol. 3, Speech Acts,* ed. P. Cole and J. Morgan. New York: Academic Press, pp. 41–58.

HALLIDAY, M. A. K., AND RUQAIYA HASAN. 1976. *Cohesion in English.* London: Longman.

HOLLOS, MARIDA, AND WILLIAM BEEMAN. 1978. The development of directives among Norwegian and Hungarian children: An example of communicative style in culture. *Language in Society* 7:345–355.

IDE, SACHIKO. 1982. Japanese sociolinguistics: Politeness and women's language. *Lingua* 57:357–385.

IDE, SACHIKO, MOTOKO HORI, AKIKO KAWASAKI, SHOKO IKUTA, AND HITOMI HAGA. 1986. Sex difference and politeness in Japanese. *International Journal of the Sociology of Language* 58:25–36.

JEFFERSON, GAIL. 1996. On the poetics of ordinary talk. *Text and Performance Quarterly* 16, no. 1:1–61.

KEENAN, ELINOR OCHS. 1974. Normmakers and normbreakers: Uses of speech by men and women in a Malagasy community. In *Explorations in the Ethnography of Speaking,* ed. R. Bauman and J. Sherzer. New York: Cambridge University Press, pp. 125–143.

KEENAN, ELINOR OCHS. 1976. The universality of conversational postulates. *Language in Society* 5:67–80.

LABOV, WILLIAM, AND DAVID FANSHEL. 1977. *Therapeutic Discourse.* New York: Academic Press.

LAKOFF, ROBIN. 1973. The logic of politeness; or, minding your p's and q's. In *Papers from the Ninth Regional Meeting of the Chicago Linguistic Society.* Chicago, IL: Chicago Linguistic Society, pp. 292–305.

OBENG, SAMUEL GYASI. 1996. The proverb as a mitigating and politeness strategy in Akan discourse. *Anthropological Linguistics* 38:521–549.

OGINO, TSUNAO. 1986. Quantification of politeness based on the usage patterns of honorific expressions. *International Journal of the Sociology of Language* 58:37–58.

OKAMOTO, SHIGEKO. 2004. Ideology in linguistic practice and analysis: Gender and politeness in Japanese revisited. *In Japanese Language, Gender, and Ideology: Cultural Models and Real People,* ed. S. Okamoto and J. S. Smith. London: Oxford University Press, pp. 38–55.

SACKS, HARVEY, EMANUEL SCHEGLOFF, AND GAIL JEFFERSON. 1974. A simplest systematics for the organization of turn-taking for conversation. *Language* 50:696–735.

SCHEGLOFF, EMMANUEL, AND HARVEY SACKS. 1973. Opening up closings. *Semiotica* 8:289–327.

SHIBAMOTO, JANET. 1987. The womanly woman: Manipulation of stereotypical and non-stereotypical features of Japanese female speech. In *Language, Gender and Sex in Comparative Perspective,* ed. S. Phillips, S. Steele, and C. Tanz. New York: Cambridge University Press, pp. 26–49.

TANNEN, DEBORAH. 1987. Repetition and variation as spontaneous formulaicity in conversation. *Language* 63:574–605.

YNGVE, V. H. 1970. On getting a word in edgewise. In *Papers from the Sixth Regional Meeting of the Chicago Linguistic Society.* Chicago, IL: Chicago Linguistic Society, pp. 567–578.

CHAPTER 6

Digital Communication and Signed Languages

R:	Hello.
C:	Hello Ida?
R:	Yeah.
C:	Hi, this is Carla.
R:	Hi, Carla.
C:	How are you?
R:	Okay.
C:	Good.
R:	How about you?
C:	Fine. Don wants to know....

This conversation exhibits several features that distinctively mark it as a telephone conversation rather than a face-to-face interaction. In the initial utterance, the caller asks the responder to confirm her identification as "Ida." After receiving confirmation, the caller identifies herself as "Carla." If the two people were face to face, there would be no need to identify themselves because they obviously know each other. In addition, the caller employs a greeting twice, first in the utterance "Hello Ida?" and then in "Hi, this is Carla." Such redundancy is generally unnecessary in ordinary conversations.

In this chapter, we will explore the dynamics of communicative practices in several domains. We will then proceed to investigate the structural and social characteristics of conversations made possible by the modern technologies of telephones and computers. We end the chapter with a discussion of signing employed by Deaf conversation participants.

TELEPHONE CONVERSATIONS

Conversing via telephone has become a daily feature of our public and private lives. Discourse analysts have turned attention to the study of telephone conversation, demonstrating both its similarities and its differences with face-to-face interaction. Like personal conversation, telephone talk is based on the structure of turn taking, each speaker alternating turns and allocating rights to speak. The overall form of an episode of telephone talk begins with a routine greeting, develops into one or more topics, and ends with a formulaic closing. Despite their structural similarity to ordinary conversations, telephone conversations have significant distinct characteristics. Participants do not see each other, so they must rely solely on auditory cues and messages. They recognize each other through sound of voice or through name identification. And each feature of the conversation (greetings, topic introductions and developments, and closings) differs somewhat in structure and in interaction from the comparable features of face-to-face talk. Face-to-face conversation begins with a mutual co-presence, but telephone conversation begins with a caller issuing a unilateral summons. The caller issues a summons by making the call, thereby interrupting the activities of the addressee. By this beginning, the caller is in an advantageous position in the interaction. That is, the two parties are not interactional co-equals, at least not at the beginning of the conversation. The call is planned by the caller but occurs at an unplanned moment for the answerer. Indeed, telephone calls are always interruptive: They always interrupt some activity, even if it is rest or idleness, of the answerer. Although in principle a person chooses whether or not to answer the telephone's ring, most people do answer the phone most of the time. Indeed, "[t]he telephone summons has become a demand to truncate ongoing lines of activity in order to answer the phone" (Hopper 1992:57).

Second, the caller is privileged by the fact that she or he knows the identity of the addressee, or at least of the intended addressee, whereas the answerer hears the telephone ring but does not know the identity of the caller before answering. Finally, because of the structure of the summons and the opening, the caller is in the position of offering the first topic. The first topic is typically the reason for the call. All these features result in what has been termed "caller hegemony" (ibid.:32).

Let us examine some telephone data to demonstrate both their structural and interactional components, keeping in mind that telephone conversations, like all interactions, are dialogic and jointly produced by both participants. That is, we will see the ways in which both parties participate in producing the kinds of exchanges that take place. What happens at the beginnings and at the ends of telephone conversations is consistent with the structure of adjacency pairs that occur in face-to-face conversation as well. Following is an example of a telephone opening (Schegloff 1979:55):

H:	H'llo?
R:	Harriet?
H:	Yeah.
R:	Hi!
H:	Hi!

Here, the answerer (H) responds to the summons of the caller (R) with the formulaic opening, "Hello." Note also that the answerer is providing the caller with a voice sample to be used as an identification. The caller responds by supplying an identification of the addressee, which the answerer then confirms. Note too that by offering an identification of the answerer, the caller is also providing a voice sample that can be used by the answerer to identify the caller. This opening interaction is then followed by an exchange of greetings, again initiated by the caller (R). Degrees of familiarity between caller and answerer affect the content of each of these turns. For instance, a caller making an impersonal call to a business office might first identify him- or herself by name before stating the reason for the call, such as asking for information or making a request. Greeting exchanges are likely to be omitted in such circumstances. And named identifications may be omitted entirely in calls between intimates, moving directly into greeting exchanges.

Following is an extended sample of the beginning of a telephone conversation that exemplifies the opening, identification confirmations, and greetings, and moves into an initial topic (Schegloff 1986:115):

R:	Hello.
C:	Hello Ida?
R:	Yeah.
C:	Hi, this is Carla.
R:	Hi, Carla.
C:	How are you?
R:	Okay.
C:	Good.
R:	How about you?
C:	Fine. Don wants to know...

Analyzing this excerpt, we can infer that the two speakers have some acquaintance with each other but are not intimates. The assumption that they are acquaintances is based on the fact that only first names are used in the identifications. And the assumption that they are not intimates is based on the fact that they do use named identifications rather than rely solely on voice recognition. The initial speech turn is not the initiation of the call but is better viewed as a response turn, a response to the ring of the telephone that was initiated by the caller. This response is followed by a series of identifications (both of self and other) and then by several greeting exchanges. The first set consists of the greeting words *hello* and *hi*. The second set consists of utterances that are grammatically questions but that function as routine openers and markers of social interaction. They are responded to by routine answers (*good, fine*). These questions and answers are entirely formulaic in structure and content, containing no information but simply confirming mutual willingness to engage in talk. The caller's final greeting turn ("Fine") is followed without pause by the topic introduction. This series of turns demonstrates the joint construction of the telephone encounter. Both participants respond in ways that ratify what has just happened and that set up the context for subsequent turns.

Note here that, consistent with the concept of caller hegemony, it is the caller who initiates each type of exchange: The caller makes the identification of the addressee, offers a self-identification, initiates the greeting adjacency pair, and introduces the first topic, thus setting the initial agenda. It is also interesting to note that telephone conversations are typically "about something." Unlike casual encounters that might occur between acquaintances who see each other in the street and might exchange formulaic greetings without engaging in further talk, telephone conversations must move beyond the greeting into specific topics. It would be ludicrous to call someone, exchange greetings, and then terminate the conversation. In calls between intimates, the topic of conversation may be relatively unfocused. That is, the caller's objective may simply be to reaffirm contact with the answerer. Calls between acquaintances tend to have some focus such as a request for information or a confirmation of plans. However, calls between strangers in a business context must have a specific and clear focus. Typically, the answerer identifies the business establishment and may or may not identify oneself by name. The answerer may also ask opening questions, for example (Hopper 1992:78),

> **A:**   Cancer Information Service. May I help you?
>
> **B:**   Yes, I was wondering if there was a possibility of getting a list of the foods that are available to reduce risk of cancer?

Here, after an initial confirmation, the caller immediately proceeds to the specific question that prompted the call. Greetings are omitted entirely. In the following example, however, the caller includes a personal identification and a greeting sequence in order to establish some rapport and thus to succeed in her objective of obtaining special information (ibid.:79):

> **A:**   Metro Allergy Associates. This is Alice.
>
> **B:**   Hi there, Alice, this is Sandy Welch.
>
> **A:**   Hi.
>
> **B:**   Um, I have a problem, my husband is Barry Welch. Do you think maybe Dr Hart might consider calling him in a prescription for amoxicillin instead of having to see him?

Here the caller merges two discourse types, the impersonal request for action and the friendly conversation, interspersing techniques for building rapport into a telephone call between strangers. This strategy leads to a preference for a positive response, making it difficult for the answerer to reject the request. As Richard Hopper comments, "Relationships are, to a degree, what we enact them to be. Greeting a stranger by name and eliciting a return greeting is also relationship development" (ibid.:80).

Studies of telephone conversations in other countries reveal turn taking and adjacency sequences similar to those found in the United States. Answerers respond with an initial segment selected from a fairly narrow range of culturally appropriate choices. Then some sort of greeting exchange takes place, possibly followed by initial routine inquiries before proceeding to topic introduction. However, there are differences in the types of initial responses produced by answerers. For example, in France, the telephone is recognized as an intrusion into one's privacy and activities; therefore, French callers need to demonstrate that they have an acceptable reason to call (Godard 1977). Callers typically may ask for confirmation of the number they have called or they may identify themselves by name, or they may apologize for intruding on the answerer's privacy.

In the Netherlands, both telephone participants self-identify. The answerer's first utterance consists of his or her own name, followed by self-identification by the caller. This sequence may or may not be preceded by a routinized greeting such as "Good morning/evening"

(Houtkoop-Steenstra 2002:276). In a study of telephone calls made randomly to strangers in 1995, Houtkoop-Steenstra found that only 9 percent of the answerers responded with an utterance that was not a self-identification, such as the Dutch version of hello or yes. Women reported that they were sometimes reluctant to give a self-identification before they learned the identity of the caller, but analysis of the data indicated no gender difference in the likelihood of giving a named identification or saying hello (ibid.:282). However, there were gender differences in the type of named identification given by the initial answerer. Both men and women were about as likely to give both their first and last names (33 percent to 32 percent): However, while women were about twice as likely as men to give first name only (25 percent to 15 percent), men were then twice as likely as women to give last name only (52 percent to 21.5 percent) (ibid.:283). Finally, about 21.5 percent of the women gave title plus last name, while none of the men did so. It may be that some of the gender differences can be explained on the basis of choosing informal or formal options. And it may be that women more than men give only a first name in order not to reveal their full identities to an unknown caller.

For the first many decades of telephone usage, the caller was privileged in his or her role as summoner; as initiator of agency pair sequences of identifications, greetings, and initial queries; and as introducer of first topic. In the last decade, however, new technologies have become widely used that return some advantage to the answerer or at least equalize the power dynamic between the participants. The use of answering devices allows the call receiver to choose whether or not to allow their ongoing activity to be interrupted by the call. Technologies that automatically transmit the phone number and therefore the identity of the caller further allow the call receiver to know who is calling them and thereby gives her or him more choice in deciding whether or not to respond to the call. Finally, call-waiting technologies have the potential to disrupt the call itself. Call-waiting gives the subscriber the option of choosing between the current co-participant and a third party. With call-waiting and caller identification systems, the subscriber gains more specific information that can be used to make the choice. And these technologies further the dynamic of interruption because now telephone calls themselves, previously immune to challenge, can be interrupted by other calls.

ONLINE COMMUNICATION

The use of personal computers to facilitate communication has revolutionized linguistic and social interactions, in many ways with comparable significance to the inventions of the printing press and the telephone. Technologies to link computers were first sponsored by the US Defense Department in the 1960s in order to allow computers used by university researchers to communicate with defense contractors. From there, computer technology was developed for business and then for personal use. It became widespread in the 1980s and especially in the 1990s as prices declined and access increased. Computer-mediated communication (CMC) enables people to interact with others far distant in space and time. A growing body of literature in linguistics, communication studies, anthropology, and sociology asks questions about changes in modes of interaction instigated by CMC. We will survey some of the research in linguistics and language studies.

CMC is a worldwide phenomenon, but access to computer technology is clearly not universal. Growth in computer use over the last 15 years is staggering. In 1995, there were 16 million computer users worldwide, accounting for a mere 0.4 percent of the world's population. By 2009, about 1.802 billion people, or 26.6 percent of people in the world, used computers (Internet World Stats 2010). Figures for internet penetration (i.e., the percentage of people living in a particular area who use computers compared to the population of that region) reveal some of the discrepancies in usage. The following list presents the relevant data (ibid.):

Africa: 8.7 percent

Asia: 20.1 percent

Europe: 53.0 percent

Middle East: 28.8 percent

North America: 76.2 percent

Latin America/Caribbean: 31.9 percent

Oceania/Australia: 60.8 percent

World total: 26.6 percent

In addition to regional differences, barriers of class, education, and race/ethnicity within a country are some of the impediments to utilization of computer resources. In the United States, males and females have about equal access to the Internet (78 percent and 75 percent, respectively), but race and ethnicity are significant factors affecting differential access. That is, 78 percent of whites and 75 percent of Latinos are Internet users, while 68 percent of African Americans have Internet access. Income levels are also critical: 61 percent of people with family incomes below $40,000 per year use the Internet, while a much higher 91 percent of those with annual family incomes above $40,000 do so. A person's education level is another predictor of Internet usage: Less than half (41 percent) of those without a high school diploma use the Internet, whereas 69 percent of people with high school diplomas, 86 percent of those with some college experience, and 93 percent of people with advanced college degrees have access to the Internet (Ignite Social Media 2010; Internet Usage Stats 2010).

Internet communication is unequally distributed in the world's languages. Data from December 2009 reported the following languages as the most frequently used on the Internet (numbers represent millions of users):

English: 495.8

Chinese: 407.7

Spanish: 139.8

Japanese: 96.0

Portuguese: 77.6

German: 72.3

Arabic: 60.3

French: 57.8

Russian: 45.3

Korean: 37.5

All other languages: 313.7

(Source: Internet World Stats: www.internetworldstats.com/stats7.htm. Copyright © 2010, Miniwatts Marketing Group. All rights reserved worldwide.)

These data reveal that speakers of the top 10 languages account for 82.8 percent of all Internet users, while the rest of the world's languages are employed by 17.2 percent. And by language,

Internet use is lopsided: Speakers of English and Chinese together account for just over 50 percent (50.5 percent).

An additional significant set of data concerns Internet penetration by language, that is, the percentage of people using the Internet in a particular language compared to the number of people in the world who speak that language as their primary tongue. The following list presents these data:

English: 39.7 percent

Chinese: 29.7 percent

Spanish: 34.0 percent

Japanese: 75.5 percent

Portuguese: 31.4 percent

German: 75.0 percent

Arabic: 17.5 percent

French: 16.9 percent

Russian: 32.3 percent

Korean: 52.7 percent

Total of top ten languages: 33.8 percent

Total of all other languages: 10.2 percent

World total: 26.6 percent

These figures indicate that more than half of speakers of Japanese, Korean, and German use the Internet as one of their means of communication with others. And comparing figures for Internet penetration with those for users of the top 10 languages indicates the uneven distribution of Internet access. That is, while speakers of all of the world's languages except those in the top 10 account for 17.2 percent of Internet users, only 13.2 percent of these speakers actually employ computer-mediated communication.

Among the types of CMC are synchronous and asynchronous interactions. Forms of asynchronous CMC, such as e-mail, chat groups, bulletin boards, and weblogs (or blogs), do not assume that the addressee (for e-mails) or audience (for chat groups, bulletin boards, and blogs) are necessarily aware of the message as it is being written and sent; instead, they may respond at any later time of their own choosing. Therefore, asynchronous CMC does not imply the usual conversational structure of turn allocation. E-mail is closer to ordinary conversation: A particular message may be addressed to one person, but e-mails may also be sent to as many people as the sender wishes or to a composite list containing the e-mail addresses of numerous people. Chat groups or bulletin boards are often formed around a particular subject matter and are joined by people with an interest in that topic. Members of the group can send messages that are stored in the system and are ready to be accessed by other members when they choose to do so. People who read these messages may respond whenever they wish, but there is never any expectation of an immediate reply by anyone in particular. Some chat groups have moderators who can function as gatekeepers, allowing or disallowing contributions depending on whether they are deemed relevant to the topic or are consistent with rules governing the group in terms of language and etiquette.

Despite the possible lack of conversational coherence implied by the structure of asynchronous CMC, participants may employ techniques to establish interactional relevance.

The beginning of a message may explicitly refer back to a previous message, either by using the name of a previous contributor, by asserting a topical connection to the relevant subject, or by quoting or paraphrasing a prior posting. For example, note the following openings (Crystal 2001:141):

> We're all democrats at heart? I don't think so.
> I never thought I'd hear someone talking about people power, not in 2000.
> I was living in a different universe. [pasted from a previous message] Isn't that the truth?

In addition, people use various kinds of sentence openings that link their contributions to prior ones (Crystal 2001:143):

> Another good tool is...
> The last time I tried it...
> Perhaps I should be clearer...
> Or you could just...
> Except you can't...

Synchronous CMC differs significantly from asynchronous forms in terms of structure, linguistic patterns, and social functions. Synchronous CMC, especially chatrooms, facilitates ongoing, simultaneous interaction with at least one other person, although thousands of other individuals may be present. Participants send messages received by a central server that are then posted on a continuously scrolling screen to be read by anyone in the room. These interactions may or may not be moderated, depending on the system, in order to screen out inappropriate language or topics. Like face-to-face interaction, synchronous Internet communication takes place in real time and allows interlocutors to respond quickly to one another's input. Stylistically, CMC is generally characterized as informal, using colloquial vocabulary and grammar. Most often, contributors use first-person pronouns in reference to themselves.

However, synchronous CMC differs in important ways from face-to-face interactions. The transmission of meaning through gesture and facial expression, a feature ubiquitous to ordinary conversation, is obviously not possible in computer-mediated conversations. Computer technology itself does not reflect variations in intonation or emphasis, but these have been added through changes in script, for example, by using fonts in bold, italics, or capital letters. Various emoticons have also been developed to express particular emotional or attitudinal meanings. Emoticons are made by combining certain keystrokes on a keyboard to produce stylized icons that have become conventionalized to indicate attitudes or reactions of the participants, especially those that represent faces to imply joking or humor and express confusion or surprise.

Like other forms of written language, CMC can be preserved as text, reread, and commented upon numerous times. But there are significant differences between CMC and both oral and written language that derive from constraints imposed by the time delay when writing, sending, and receiving computer messages. Because CMC interactions take place rapidly, participants need to write their contributions as quickly as possible. Accordingly, abbreviations are often used to hasten the time when a message can be sent. These can be combined with rebus writing, that is, using a letter or number whose pronunciation stands for an actual word (e.g., 4 to mean, not the numeral, but the word *for*). Common abbreviations for words, or combinations of shortened forms of words and rebus writing, include r (are), u (you), ur (your), c (see), b4 (before), no (know), ryt (right), coz (because), 4 (for), wanna (want to), any1 (anyone), gf (girlfriend), and bf (boyfriend). Shortened forms are also substituted for common phrases: g m (good morning), omg (oh my God), LOL (laughing out loud), brb (be right back), bbfn (bye-bye for now), gmta (great minds think alike), hhok (ha ha only kidding), pmji (pardon my jumping in), t2ul (talk to you later), w4u (waiting for you), and many more (Crystal 2001:85–86). Most punctuation marks (including apostrophes) and capitalization of the first word in an utterance or personal names are omitted.

Some research has explored the particular ways that CMC structural features differ from those of ordinary conversation, especially in terms of patterns of turn allocation, overlap, and selection of the next speaker. People enter the chatroom at different times, coming into the middle of already ongoing conversations. Therefore, they need to read text before they can understand and respond to what is being said. Because CMC is interactive, it follows the expected organization of turn allocation; that is, speaker turns alternate so that when current speaker completes his or her contribution, a next speaker may begin. However, the selection of a next speaker is problematic in several respects. First, some of the cues, such as changes in intonation, facial expression, and body alignment, that current speakers employ in face-to-face interaction in order to indicate that they are about to conclude their turn cannot be used on the Internet. Therefore, a next speaker may erroneously anticipate the end of the previous speaker's utterance and interrupt the current turn. Second, because a CMC message may reach many hundreds of people at the same moment, any of those present may self-select as next speaker, resulting in turn overlaps. Even if the current speaker follows norms of face-to-face interaction and attempts to select a next speaker by using a term of address, someone else may send an intervening message that is posted before the selected next speaker's turn commences. When this happens, adjacent turns may lose their sequential coherence. Third, the lack of sequential cohesion also results from the fact that messages are not sent until the utterance is completed. In this way, CMC differs from face-to-face interaction, in which co-participants listen to and can engage with talk as it is being developed by the speaker. In CMC, an addressee or an audience does not have access to the message until the writer clicks "Send." Some elapse of time is therefore necessary for the receiver to process and respond to the message. Finally, messages are displayed on the computer screen in the order in which they are received by the system without regard to semantic content, leading also to disruptions in cohesion. For example, the following segment recorded from a chat in the research of Susan Herring shows overlap and discontinuous sequences (1999:5):

ASHNA:	hi jatt
***SIGNOFF:	puja
DAVE-G:	kally, I was only joking around
JATT:	hi ashna
KALLY:	Dave-G it was funny
ASHNA:	how are u jatt
LUCKMAN:	ssa all
DAVE-G:	kally you da woman!
JATT:	ashna do we know each other? I'm ok how are you
KALLY:	dave-g good stuff
JATT:	kally so how's life, life in general, love life, family life?
ASHNA:	jatt no we don't know each other, i fine
JATT:	ashna where r ya from?

In this excerpt, multiple conversations are taking place, that is, between Ashna and Jatt, Dave-G and Kally, and then with Jatt and Kally intervening. It requires skill and experience to manage the threads of these interactions and make sense of their development.

Such interactions raise issues of audience. That is, messages can be addressed to one particular participant, usually identified by a webname, or to a generalized addressee that includes all potential co-participants. When a message is directed to a named person, that person is thereby selected as the next speaker, but when a message is sent to a larger audience, the next speaker must self-select. These patterns are similar to those operating in face-to-face interactions except that, in the case of CMC, participants cannot give nonverbal cues about their readiness to speak.

Some chatrooms provide the option of leaving the multiparty discussion and communicating with just one person in a whisper room, to the exclusion of the other members (Islam 2006:76). Retreat into a whisper room makes possible more personal and private communications, including the exchange of biographical information and of actual e-mail addresses or other ways of contacting one another.

An additional feature of CMC linguistic practice is the preference for short utterances so that participants can send replies as quickly as possible to maintain their place in the conversation. Most contributions consist of one sentence or even of fragments of sentences. Indeed, an examination of 100 messages from published data revealed that contributions averaged 4.23 words; 80 percent of the utterances contained five or fewer words (Crystal 2001:156–157). And short words are preferred for similar reasons. Analysis of 300-word samples from chatroom data indicated that 80 percent of the words were monosyllabic, while only 4 percent consisted of more than two syllables. (Comparison of these data with analyses of two British newspapers—*Daily Express* and *The Times*—uncovered significant differences. Samples from the two newspapers contained 63 percent and 62 percent of monosyllabic words, respectively, and 25 percent and 18 percent of disyllabic words) (Crystal 2001:157).

Topics in CMC may change rapidly because of the constant turnover of participants, fueled by newcomers and leave-takers. Although topical shift is a feature of face-to-face interaction as well, the rate of change is more dramatic in CMC. Some analysts emphasize that, just as in face-to-face conversations, CMC has a primarily social focus and function. The exchange of information is usually less important than making contact with other people and engaging in a free flow of short messages that establish and reinforce social connections. Indeed, certain aspects of face-to-face interaction are largely absent from CMC. In particular, extended personal narratives of past events in people's lives rarely appear in chatroom exchanges. Very little of personal biographies is shared and thus commented or reflected on by participants, as so often happens when communicating in person with friends. CMC participants typically remain anonymous despite the surface appearance of engagement.

Another intriguing area of CMC research concerns the issue of identity. When people interact face to face, even if they are strangers, their presence reveals certain features of their identity: their gender, their probable race and/or ethnic membership, and their approximate age. In addition, they reveal something of their regional origins by their speech sounds or stylistic usages, or of their native country if they speak with an accent. But on the Internet, people are potentially anonymous. They may self-identify by name and they may voluntarily disclose information about their gender, race, place of origin, and so on, but they need not do so and indeed the information they give may not be factually true. Therefore, people can create an identity for themselves in CMC interactions that they cannot do in person. Text is the primary means of creating and negotiating identities. For example, participants in chatrooms create webnames for use in this medium. Then, they may create personal profiles containing demographic information about themselves and personal statements about their attitudes, philosophies, and opinions (Islam 2006:75). Of course, the veracity of these personal data and statements is not ensured.

Analyses of chatroom texts reveal that, despite the potential for participants to create identities and in effect free themselves from the constraints of the normative behavior expected of them, people tend to conform to their expected roles and behaviors because of the strength of socialization and the cultural models that have become naturalized. For example, examination of CMC interactions demonstrated strong links between verbal style and gender (Herring 1992, 2003). In Susan Herring's study of Internet communication in English, gender was assigned based on the webname created by each participant. While this method may not be wholly accurate, the data themselves indicate significant correlations. For instance, in asynchronous CMC contributions, males produced longer messages, posted more messages, and received more responses than did females. Females' contributions often contained hedges and qualifiers (e.g., *perhaps, maybe, somewhat*), while males' contributions consisted of absolute statements of certainty. Females were more likely to talk about their feelings, while males' messages were more impersonal. Females often apologized for their actions or statements and asked questions in order to get a response, whereas males asked rhetorical questions that did not lead to further discussion. In general, females were more polite and agreed with the statements of others, whereas males often contradicted or disagreed with other participants. Of course, these traits are not characteristic of the contributions of every male or every female but, according to Herring, "when they are used, they tend overwhelmingly to be produced by one, and not the other, gender" (2003:211).

Gender differences surfaced in synchronous CMC interactions as well, although females and males sent approximately the same number of messages, and the length of their messages was similar (Herring 2003:210). However, females talked more about their feelings and the feelings of others, and they showed appreciation and support to others. Males were more likely to use profanity, sexual references, sarcasm, and insults, while females made more frequent use of emoticons, particularly those representing laughter. Messages posted by females tended to receive more responses than those posted by males, but many of these responses were flirtatious. Many of the findings concerning CMC are consistent with research dealing with gender differences in face-to-face interactions (some of this research will be discussed in Chapter 10).

However, research on chatroom participation in Thailand sheds a contrasting perspective on gender and CMC (Panyametheekul and Herring 2003). Attribution of gender to unknown participants is probably more accurate in Thai than in English because females and males employ different particles at the ends of sentences. In addition, first-person pronouns used by males and females are distinct, although gender-neutral pronouns are an additional option. During the period of study of interactions in the most popular chatroom in Thailand, most of the participants lived in Thailand at the time of their communication and identified themselves as between the ages of 11 and 25. In a two-hour period, 52 participants sent messages to the chatroom. On the basis of usage of sentence final particles, first person pronouns, and webnames, 25 participants were identified as females and 12 as males, while the gender of 15 others could not be reliably ascertained.

Analyzing patterns of turn allocation, Siriporn Panyametheekul and Susan Herring (2003) found that females posted more messages and responded more frequently, especially to other females, often ignoring the contributions of males. Females not only outnumbered males but also produced a comparable majority of messages. That is, 598 messages were sent by females, 269 were sent by males, and 50 were posted by people whose gender could not be identified. In addition, messages sent by females were more than twice as likely as those sent by males to receive a response. The researchers suggest that these patterns may be explained by gender preferences in turn allocation strategies. Females as current speakers preferred to employ the turn allocation technique of selecting the next speaker by use of a term of address or a direct question. Participants selected by a current speaker were likely to reply. In contrast, males more often self-selected as next speaker and were frequently ignored in favor of a female participant already engaged in an ongoing conversation. It may be that the interactional style preferred by members of the gender that is numerically dominant in the chatroom becomes the norm for appropriate behavior, and therefore members who do not conform are less successful.

The Internet and CMC have become worldwide phenomena, affecting linguistic and social practices to some degree in every country. In China, computer communicators have introduced new forms of the Mandarin Chinese language itself. Chinese Internet Language (CIL) is recognized as a distinctive variety with lexical and syntactic innovations (Gao 2006). New words have been coined and/or new meanings have been associated with older forms. These lexical and semantic processes occur in all languages, but the rate of change has accelerated. And a significant source for the introduction of new words and for changes in sentence construction has been contact with English. Indeed, a large proportion of the distinctive CIL vocabulary comes from English. An authoritative dictionary of CIL, compiled in 2001, contained 1,300 lexical items, including 224 words and expressions (about 18 percent) that are derived from English (ibid.:302). Some of these are direct borrowings; others are compounds made from English models and use English word formation processes to construct Chinese words.

English syntax has also affected CIL (ibid.:304). For example, prepositional phrases that usually appear before verbs in Chinese have been shifted to positions after the verb phrase (e.g., I'll have lunch *at home*). Temporal phrases expressing the time when an event takes place have also been moved to positions following verb phrases (e.g., I am going to the United States *next year*).

English influences on Mandarin derive from the prestige of computer usage and of the English language. Communicating via computers and having knowledge of English are skills associated with youth, education, worldliness, and modernity. Young people in China are in the vanguard of linguistic and social innovation because of their creation and use of a prestigious variety of language.

Use of the Roman alphabet for online communication in many languages with writing systems based on other modes has spread throughout the world. This use goes in tandem with the worldwide influence of the English language. For example, analyses of instant messaging in the United Arab Emirates (UAE) and of postings to bulletin boards in Japan uncovered combinations of English words and abbreviations with traditional Arabic script or Japanese characters, respectively (Nishimura 2003; Palfreyman and al Khalil 2003). In the UAE, the use of the Roman alphabet to transliterate Arabic words leads to a further change; that is, the letters are written from left to right in contrast to the normal Arabic system of writing symbols from right to left. Arabic samples were drawn from instant messaging by students at a women's university in Dubai. The students are, by necessity, bilingual in Arabic and English because the majority of the university courses are conducted in English. Not only was the use of the Roman alphabet to represent Arabic words pervasive in their messages, but a substantial number of texts contained instances of code switching between the two languages. Arabic was employed for writing greetings and formulaic expressions, while English was used especially when discussing university courses and other topics related to school life. In interviews, some students mentioned that using English allowed them privacy from parental scrutiny because their parents were not always fluent in English. Finally, one student wrote that mixing Arabic and English was "a funky language for teenzz to use" (Palfreyman and al Khalil 2003:20).

Japanese contributors to bulletin boards also use an array of scripts, some based on traditional Japanese writing systems and some incorporating letters from the Roman alphabet. Indeed, Japanese writers have four scripts at their disposal, each with different characteristics. Two are syllabaries: *hiragana,* the most common script, a simplified form of Chinese characters written cursively, and *katakana,* angular characters used to write foreign names and words borrowed from other languages. A third writing system, *furigana,* consists of symbols of discrete sounds rather than syllables that are smaller in size and written at the side or top of regular characters. The Roman alphabet is used to transliterate names of people or places and occasionally for other Japanese words and to write English words or acronyms.

Samples were taken from postings to a bulletin board dedicated to popular culture (films, music, entertainers). Most of the contributors were young women (teens through thirties) who shared their personal likes and attitudes about the actors, films, and so on. They used techniques similar to those of English speakers and of Internet users worldwide: shortened spelling of words, capitalization for emotion, asterisks for emphasis, abbreviations, rebus writing, and emoticons.

Discursive practices differed somewhat from face-to-face conversation in Japan. In contrast to the trend among young urban Japanese speakers for preferences for verb endings that indicate informality, about two-thirds of the verbs in the samples contained formal endings (Nishimura 2003:22). (See Chapters 4 and 5 for discussion of these variants and their usages.) Many messages contained a mixture of formal and informal styles. Because a writer to a bulletin board cannot know the social identity of all the readers, the use of a formal style could reflect a wish not to offend someone of higher social status (based on criteria of age, class, and/or occupation). Switching to an informal style in the context of discussing pop culture preferences might mark a desire for closeness or familiarity.

In addition to the increase in computer usage for individual communication, computers have changed the way many college and university courses are taught. Online or distance learning is increasingly common. Data collected by the US Department of Education for 2006–2007 reported that 66 percent of the 4,200 accredited 2- and 4-year postsecondary institutions in the country offer distance learning courses. A total of approximately 12,153,000 students were enrolled in these courses. There were 11,240 degree- or certificate-granting programs that were designed to be completed solely through online work (Parsad and Lewis 2008, Tables 1, 4, and 7).

Distance learning may be either synchronous or asynchronous. Research into its effectiveness demonstrates both advantages and disadvantages. Synchronous learning has the advantage of enabling students to take courses not offered in their own institutions. However, the technology presents a number of problems for actual involvement. The technology itself may not always be reliable; therefore, students offsite may not be able to hear everything that is said by the instructor or the onsite students. Their questions and comments directed to the instructor may get only a delayed response, making them feel alienated from the experience. Indeed, observation of students in offsite classrooms revealed that the students asked very few questions even though the course was theoretically interactive; instead, they talked frequently to each other, sometimes asking each other questions about what was being said but more often about extraneous matters (Howard 2002:773–774). They behaved, and felt, like "spectators" rather than like co-participants.

Asynchronous distance learning is not immediately interactive but has several advantages. Although visual and auditory cues are absent in contrast to face-to-face interactions, students are able to review and reflect on the material presented and on discussions with one another. They can access the data whenever it is convenient without the constraint of a scheduled class time. In addition, people living in different cities or even different countries can form the learning community. And because the texts contributed by participants (questions and comments) are preserved by the computer programs, they can be reviewed as often as necessary by each student to understand the material presented.

Contributions to discussions tend to be longer and more complex than in traditional class-rooms. The absence of the physical presence of all participants may allow some students to feel less threatened and insecure than in face-to-face interactions. However, a delay in responses by the instructor or another student to one's contribution can lead to frustration. In face-to-face interactions, if one party to the conversation makes a statement or asks a question, the other party is obligated to respond immediately with an on-topic reply or with a justified deferral (see Chapter 5 for discussions of these conversational patterns). Continual delays in replies to one's question or comment can dissolve a sense of a learning community. A student in one such asynchronous distance course remarked, perhaps with disappointment and frustration, "I don't like discussion boards that aren't used frequently. I keep checking the reflection bulletin for my group and find nothing posted from others on what they are thinking, how they felt about certain readings, etc. I am feeling a lack of involvement here. I'd love to hear from all of you on your perspective, etc." (Hewling 2005:7).

Of course, the effectiveness of asynchronous distance learning depends on the motivation and the engagement of each student, as is true of traditional classrooms. Study of two online courses for teachers of mathematics on the topic of enhancing pedagogical methods demon-strated that, when the instructor intervened more frequently (at least once or twice per week) with open-ended questioning, the participants increased their own involvement with longer and more frequent comments and questions of their own (Hull and Saxon 2009).

Asynchronous distance learning has decided advantages in multicultural and multilinguis-tic environments. Students whose native language is not the language of class interaction are able to spend as much time as needed to read and respond to others' contributions without the pres-sure of immediate understanding and response to oral discourse that disappears as soon as it is spoken. However, the absence of visual cues and the inability to ask for clarification immediately may contribute to misunderstanding based on the kinds of cultural knowledge and interactional presuppositions that people bring to any encounter with members of other cultures.

For students of foreign languages, online chats with native speakers can be beneficial for improving their linguistic skills and cross-cultural knowledge. For example, online chat sessions were part of the curriculum for English-language majors in a Japanese university and students of Japanese-language courses in a university in Australia (Saito and Ishizuka 2005). Each group of students chatted in the language that they were studying rather than in their native tongue, allowing them to practice with native speakers, receive correction, and ask for new vocabulary or idiomatic expressions in their target language. In addition, students gained insights into their own language by seeing the difficulties that it presented to second-language learners. They also gained cultural knowledge through "conversations" with residents of the countries whose language they were learning.

Computer usage influences changes in discursive features and lexical choices worldwide. These processes are affecting the English language itself. Not only are new words being created that relate specifically to computers and computer use, but many of these words and expressions are being employed in ordinary conversation. For instance, David Crystal reports the following examples (2001:19):

It's my turn to download now [i.e., I've heard all your gossip, now hear mine]
She's multitasking [i.e., doing two or more things at once]

Let's go offline for a few minutes [i.e., talk in private]

He started flaming me for no reason at all [i.e., shouting at me]

Are you wired? [i.e., ready to handle this]

E you later [said as a farewell]

Eventually, many of these and similar expressions will become so embedded within the language that speakers will not necessarily know their origin. *Multitasking* and *wired* are already in such common usage that their origin from a particular type of technology even now goes largely unnoticed.

Research into the interrelationships between language and computer use will continue to evolve just as the technology evolves and as access increases. The role of English as a global language is part of this process. But resistance to English as a dominant language in some communities leads to the development of indigenous forms of technological expressions and the use of native languages in computer-mediated communication.

SIGNED LANGUAGES AND COMMUNICATIVE PRACTICES

In Chapter 2, we outlined structural properties of American Sign Language. In this section, we will explore some of the communicative practices employed by Deaf persons. Estimates put the number of prelingual deaf people at 6.8 million people, based on a worldwide ratio of 1 in 1,000 (and a world population of 6.8 billion in 2010). The term *prelingual* refers to people who are born deaf or become deaf before the age of 3, that is, before they acquire language. Approximately twice this number of people become deaf before the age of 19, an onset that is called prevocational deafness. Another significant terminological issue is the distinction between *deaf* and *Deaf*. The term *deaf* refers to an audiological condition, that is, not being able to hear: *Deaf* refers to an identity and membership in a community of Deaf persons.

Deaf people have access to several types of communicative systems (Senghas and Monaghan 2002:74–76). The most widely used is some form of natural signing language. These are full languages, such as American Sign Language (ASL), having systems of sign formation analogous to phonology, morphological systems of word construction, and syntactic rules that determine the order of signs in sentences and discourse. The language database, Ethnologue, listed 130 signed languages worldwide in 2010, although there are undoubtedly many not recorded (Ethnologue 2010). Signed languages are full languages with systems of formation, word structure, and syntax as rule-governed and expressive as spoken language. Signed languages prototypically take advantage of the ability to manipulate hand and finger formations. In addition, they utilize movement of the hands and fingers in space, location of the placement of the sign in relation to the signer's body (face, neck, chest, arms), and direction and orientation of movement and position. These various channels may be used to express grammatical differences in tense and subject/object ordering. Attitudes or emotions of the signer are also expressed through these communicative modes. And specific speech acts, such as questions and directives, can be distinguished with changes in shape, movement, direction, and position.

Another type of signed language, artificial signed languages, is signed versions of spoken languages. These languages are associated with particular spoken languages and follow the grammatical rules of the spoken tongue. For example, Signing Exact English follows the syntactic rules of spoken English and includes articles, auxiliaries, and modals (e.g., *can, should,* etc.) that are absent in ASL. These languages are sometimes called contact languages because they tend to be used by Deaf people when interacting with hearing people whose command of natural signed languages (such as ASL) is not fluent.

In addition, Deaf people sometimes use fingerspelling, which consists of manual signs representing letters in a spoken language's alphabet. Some fingerspelling systems employ signs made with one hand, while others use two hands to form the signs. Fingerspelling may be used to express meanings in a spoken language where there is no corresponding sign in the signed language. Such practice obviously depends on literacy in the spoken language and therefore cannot be employed by deaf people who have not learned to read and write. The ratio of fingerspelled words to signs varies with signers and with natural signed systems. For example, in one study, four narratives told by Deaf people using ASL contained about 7 percent of fingerspelled words (Padden 1996:104). Many signed languages use a smaller percentage of fingerspelling and some do not use this technique at all. Homesign systems are idiosyncratic sets of signs created and used within families to negotiate meaning between deaf and hearing members, for example, between hearing parents and deaf children prior to the child's acquisition of a sign language (such as ASL) in a school setting. Indeed, the great majority of deaf children are born into hearing families and do not acquire a formal system of communication until they go to school; instead, they rely on some sort of homesigning. Estimates suggest that only about 10 percent of deaf children are born to deaf parents (Parasnis 1996:12). Finally, contact signing is a form of communication that combines elements from a natural sign language and another code (e.g., ASL and fingerspelling, or ASL and Signing Exact English); it is often employed by Deaf individuals when hearing people are present.

Recent anthropological and linguistic studies have focused on the creation of Deaf identities and communities of Deaf people. These studies emphasize the social and cultural bases of Deaf identities. In the past, deaf people were isolated in their families and had little contact with other deaf individuals. Of course, this situation prevails for many deaf people in rural and poor communities throughout the world. In these contexts, communication is narrowly focused and limited to homesign methods. But today in urban areas and industrialized nations, Deaf people are increasingly expressing their own model of community that understands deafness as a variation of human existence rather than as a deviation or deficit in a medical model of human life. And one of the most distinguishing features of Deaf communities is the language used by Deaf individuals and by hearing people who communicate with them.

Users of signed languages are confronted by pervasive language ideologies that privilege spoken language and therefore marginalize signed languages. This ideology, favoring so-called oralism, also marginalizes signers who are therefore thought of as functioning with a deficit. Additional attitudes favor standard signed languages in specific countries. For example, ASL is favored over different varieties based on region, class, gender, or race. These bases of linguistic variation exist for signed languages just as they are significant sources of variation for spoken languages (see Chapters 9 and 10 for a discussion of class, race, and gender differences in language usage).

The notion of speech community can be applied to users of signed languages as well as spoken languages. A first unique feature of signed language communities is, until recently, the necessity for face-to-face interaction for communication to proceed. (We will discuss the significance of modern technologies in facilitating communication below.) A second unique feature for signers is that young children rarely learn signed language in their households prior to attending school. Homesigning enables communication within the family, but by its very nature, it is not an elaborate system and cannot convey all of the thoughts and feelings of deaf children in a hearing household. Thus, children do not usually begin to acquire a sophisticated method of communicating until they are schooled. Educational institutions function significantly as the sites of language acquisition, and their social environments lead to the creation of a linguistic community and to the formation of a Deaf identity.

A growing literature on research in signing communities reveals significant variation in signs—in their formation, placement, and movement—among different groups. For example, several studies among African-Americans in the south revealed differences in the signing of Black and white Deaf adults. In Virginia and North Carolina, Blacks and whites differed in a majority of items from a vocabulary list of 134 tokens (Cronenberg 1965:315). A more detailed study of signers in Georgia investigated variation between Blacks and whites (Woodward and Woodward 1976). The researchers analyzed two types of changes: historical and synchronic. In some cases, signs that were used in ASL in the past have changed for white signers but have remained in the repertory of Black signers. For instance, the meaning PREGNANT is made by Black signers with the hand touching the chin twice, while white signers express this meaning with interlocking hands moving out from the trunk of the body (ibid.:212). In addition, many synchronic variations in signs were confirmed; for example, CORNBREAD is made by Black signers by placing the hands together and moving them from side to side, whereas white signers in Georgia did not have a sign for this meaning in their lexicon.

Phonological differences in the formation of signs were also found. For example, the sign for YOUNG was made by Black signers at the waist, whereas white signers have centralized this sign by moving its formation to the chest (ibid.:213). Additional phonological differences include Face-to-Hand variation, 2-Hands-to-1-Hand variation, movement and placement of the Thumb, and Elbow-to-Hand Shift (ibid.:214). Research with 75 signers in Atlanta and New Orleans revealed significant trends in terms of region, race, and age. In Face-to-Hand variation, New Orleans signers used more face variants, whereas Atlanta signers used hand variants. When disaggregated by race, white signers (wherever located) used more face variants, while Black signers used both hand and face variants. Study of the variation of 2-Hands-to-1-Hand revealed that white signers older than 47 years preferred the older two-handed signs, while younger white signers preferred forming signs with one hand. Age was not a significant factor for Black signers because they all tended to use the two-handed signs.

An intriguing discovery made by Woodward and Woodward (two white researchers fluent in ASL) was that it was sometimes difficult in casual conversation with Black signers to elicit distinctive signs because the signers tended to switch to signs used by white people. This tendency is a further demonstration of the incorporation of language ideologies that privilege what is perceived as "standard" language because it is associated with dominant social groups. Members of subordinate groups then learn to accommodate to speech styles of members of dominant groups when interacting with them. From anecdotal evidence, Woodward and Woodward suggest that there are differences in intelligibility between white and Black signers (1976:217). That is, Black signers are likely to understand white signs, whereas the degree to which white signers understand Black signs is unpredictable.

Convergence of Black signing toward signs used by white people is demonstrated in shifts made by Black signers attending integrated schools in Texas after 1965, the year that the state school for the deaf was integrated (Maxwell and Smith-Todd 1986). Because of past discriminatory practices in many southern states, older Black deaf adults often have very limited communication abilities because they did not have the same opportunities to attend special schools as did whites. As Maxwell and Smith-Todd suggest, because of the lack of educational opportunities, "deaf Blacks are excluded from both hearing Black and white deaf society" (1886:82).

To study the effect of exposure to different signing communities before and after school integration in Austin, Texas, researchers compared signs used by Black adults with those of adolescents and children. Participants in the study included nine Black adults (ages 44 to 71) and 10 Black teenagers (ages 15 to 17), all of whom were primary users of signed languages.

The adults attended the same segregated residential school for the deaf in Austin, while the teenagers attend an integrated residential school. Signs used in the study were chosen because they were known to exhibit phonological or lexical variation; that is, seven signs showed Face-to-Hand variation, while eight signs exhibited 2-Hands-to-1-Hand differences. In addition, eight lexically distinct signs were selected because they were part of the lexicon of Black signers in Austin. Participants were given pictures and/or written English words and asked to produce the sign that they would use to express the meaning represented.

Results of this study yielded a number of significant findings. First, signs used by older Black signers in Austin differed for a number of both phonological and lexical features from signs used by Black signers in the study conducted by Woodward and Woodward in Atlanta and New Orleans, thus indicating regional variation among Black signers in the South. Second, lexical differences between teenagers and adults in Austin were the most marked. All of the teenagers gave standard ASL signs for all of the nine prompts, while none of the adults used only ASL signs. Of the adults, four used only Austin Black signs for all of the prompts, while five adults used standard ASL for one of the prompts (although the prompt selected varied) but they used Austin Black signs for all the others (Maxwell and Smith-Todd 1986:86–87). Thus, this study documents decisive generational shifts among Black signers in Austin. The shift toward standard ASL resulted from the common educational experience of young Black signers with their white counterparts in an integrated residential school. Because most deaf children do not acquire signs until their schooling and because children of all races now attend the same residential schools in Texas, it may be that major differences in the signs used by Blacks and whites will decrease. Regional variations, though, are confirmed.

A more recent study suggests some continuing contrasts between the signs of Black and white signers in the Washington, DC, area. When Black participants were conversing with other Black signers, they used a number of signs that they did not use when conversing with whites. According to the Black participants, the distinctive signs were older forms that had been learned when Blacks attended segregated schools. Some of these forms continue to be used but, in the words of a Black signer, not with someone "who is not a part of that culture" (Aramburo 1994:480).

A final finding from studies of Black signing uncovers an additional dominant language ideology. Interviews conducted with participants revealed positive attitudes toward standard ASL as "correct," while the distinctive signs previously common and now restricted to older Black signers were described as "incorrect" or "wrong." For example, one of Woodward and Woodward's participants reported that now that she is receiving vocational training, she is "learning correct signs" rather than those that she learned at a segregated Black residential school (1976:217). Another woman said that she is learning standard ASL signs in order to "better herself." And a white deaf adult teacher interviewed by Maxwell and Smith-Todd suggested that Black students "used many signs that were wrong but in time they learned the right signs" (1986:92). Commenting on differences between adults and teenagers, he stated that the adults "did not go to [the white school] and did not learn the correct signs but the younger Black deaf children do know the correct signs because they went to [the white school]." As we shall see in later discussions of class, race, and language standardization (Chapters 9 and 11), attitudes that privilege standard language and its speakers simultaneously marginalize and denigrate communicative systems that differ. In turn, speakers of these languages are themselves socially marginalized.

Gender differences in signing have been reported among Irish Deaf persons in Dublin (LeMaster 1998). In her research, Barbara LeMaster drew up a list of 153 words distributed across semantic domains in order to study the degree of male and female contrasts. In interviews, she fingerspelled the words to eight men and eight women to elicit the signs they would use. LeMaster found a total of 106 signs that varied, representing 69 percent of the total; 27 signs (17 percent) were the same for women and men; an additional 20 signs (13 percent) differed in the population but in ways that were idiosyncratic, not according to gender (1998:71). Of the 106 signs that exhibited gender differences, 67 signs (63 percent) were ascertained to be "related," while 39 signs (37 percent) were "unrelated." Whether signs were related or not was determined by whether they shared at least one of three possible features of articulation: point of articulation, hand configuration, and movement (ibid.:71–72). Related or unrelated signs were distributed throughout the semantic domains illustrated in the data.

Gender differences in the Dublin Deaf community have their historical origin in the segregation of girls and boys in two separate residential schools for deaf children established in the mid-nineteenth century. These two schools have only recently been replaced by gender-integrated schools in several locations throughout Ireland. Although the original schools began using the same set of signs, almost complete lack of contact between either the teachers or the students in the two schools may have led to localized changes in signs that then became associated with gender differences.

Today, contrasts between the signs used by men and women are disappearing for several reasons. Female and male students or young adults who are recent graduates have been exposed to the same set of signs at the integrated schools. And convergence toward male signs has been the norm. These are the signs that are currently used by most Deaf Irish signers. We see here another example (similar to African-American signers using the standardized white signs of ASL) of accommodation toward the communicative norms of dominant groups, in this case based on gender. The Irish Sign Language is itself not officially taught in most of the schools for the Deaf, which instead emphasize *oralism,* teaching students to either speak or lip-read. However, female forms of signs have not disappeared entirely. They are still used by some older women when conversing with other women who know these signs. And they are sometimes used by women as a secret code when they want to communicate without a wider audience understanding them.

Although signed languages are documented in most countries of the world, research into their structure and internal variations is in the beginning stages. For example, a study of urban and rural signing communication in India uncovers contrasts in their forms and functions (Jepson 1991). Urban Indian Sign Language (UISL) is employed by approximately 1,500,000 Deaf people in India (ibid.:39). These signers are mainly middle-class and professional or semiprofessional people educated in special schools for the Deaf. Despite this large population and their geographic spread throughout India, UISL exhibits little regional variation. Research comparing signs used in the cities of Bombay, Delhi, Calcutta, and Madras recorded a high percentage of cognate signs, between 77 percent and 83 percent (Vasishta et al. 1978, cited in Jepson 1991). Like other signed languages throughout the world, UISL is highly structured, with a complex syntax and large lexicon. The formation of a Deaf community in India is relatively new; schools for the deaf date only to the 1950s and in many urban areas, they are even more recent (Jepson 1991:39). UISL is the primary language of dwellers who self-identify as Deaf and who consciously choose to belong to a community whose members interact frequently in social groups and in organizations dedicated to improving the lives of Deaf Indians.

In contrast, Rural Indian Sign Language (RISL) is not a unified, structured system of communication but rather more like a homesign method. It is developed idiosyncratically as the occasion warrants for use by deaf people in rural villages and by hearing people who need to communicate with them, principally members of their families and small local groupings.

People who are born or become deaf in rural India do not form a cohesive social community with others like themselves and do not have a Deaf identity. Therefore, RISL is somewhat a misnomer because there is not one Rural Indian Sign Language; rather, signed modes of communication developed in each village without contact with other systems.

Given the contrasting contexts in which UISL and RISL develop and function, the systems themselves differ in structure in a number of important features. The syntax of UISL is complex and fully standardized, with rules determining the order of signs and relative placement of nominals, verbals, modifiers, tense markers, and indicators of negation and interrogatives (ibid.:42). RISL lacks standardized syntactic rules. Indeed, Jepson's research only recorded two simple syntactic orderings: Verbs occur in final position in their clause, and question markers are placed at the end of sentences (ibid.:42). The lexicons of the two varieties are also markedly different; that is, UISL has a full lexicon similar to that of other world signed languages, while RISL has a very limited sign inventory. (Jepson was able to observe only about 45 signs in one variety, and even though more signs are probably used, the number is undoubtedly quite small.) In addition, RISL and UISL differ in their use of pantomime, defined as a mode of communication in which "the actor attempts to represent salient features of the referent, using whatever manual maneuvers are necessary" (ibid.:45). RISL communication depends heavily on pantomime, whereas UISL does not. Although both varieties incorporate gestures commonly used in India by hearing individuals, communication in RISL does so more frequently (ibid.:46).

It should be noted that both UISL and RISL accomplish the communicative goals of their users. Their structural properties differ because of contrasts in the social networks in which signers are embedded. UISL is a language used by educated people throughout India who form a community of Deaf individuals. They may reside in different regions, but they are linked together through a standardized system of communication. UISL is a language people learn either as adults or as children in schools for the deaf with the goal of fluency because this is their primary linguistic mode. Indeed, mastery of UISL promotes and reinforces one's Deaf identity. RISL consists of sets of signs that enable interaction between isolated deaf people and their hearing family or village members. It is not a marker of group identity because there are no such groups in rural villages. Instead, deaf individuals identify with their families and their local communities.

A brief survey of some of the world's signed languages reveals a number of recurring themes and issues. In countries with one dominant spoken language, signed languages tend to exhibit somewhat less variation than in countries where members of different ethnic groups promote their own languages. For example, Swedish Deaf signers' use of Swedish Sign Language functions as a marker of their Deaf identity and also as a facilitator of group cohesion (Bagga-Gupta and Domfors 2003). In contrast, Swiss signers do not have one national signed language; instead, they employ one of a number of options. Different signed languages are generally used in French-speaking, Italian-speaking, and German-speaking regions of Switzerland. Indeed, there is also internal variation, especially in the German-speaking regions, where at least five dialects of signed languages have been found (Braem et al. 2003). In Italy, even though there is one national spoken language, there is no standardized signed language. Estimates of as high as 80 percent of the signs employed in one region of Italy differ from the signs used in other areas (Folchi 1994). The language situation in Thailand and Vietnam is even more complex: Seven signed languages have been found in those countries. Several of these languages can be characterized as dialects; others are separate languages. In all, there are three different language families represented (Woodward 2003).

In some countries, particularly postcolonial nations in Africa, signed languages may be imported from English- or French-speaking countries. For example, the dominant signed language in Nigeria is ASL, modeled on practice in the United States. However, problems in fluency and language acquisition arise because many of the teachers in the schools for the Deaf are proficient in neither ASL nor spoken English; their native languages are the indigenous language of their ethnic group (Schmaling 2003).

Educational policies concerning Deaf children vary throughout the world. In only a few countries is a signed language the primary means of communication in schools for the deaf. Instead, most educational systems are oriented toward oralism, the teaching of the national spoken language or a contact version of signing heavily influenced by the grammar of the spoken language. But in Sweden and in South Africa, government policies mandate the use of a signed language (Swedish Sign Language and South African Sign Language, respectively). Both countries have federal legislation regulating the education of deaf children. In South Africa, although government policy is clear on this matter, actual practice often does not meet this requirement because of the scarcity of teachers able to communicate in South African Sign Language (Aarons and Reynolds 2003). In other countries, educational policies are developed on the local level and therefore differ from city to city. And in some, each school may set its own agenda.

Many countries do not have a coherent language policy for the education of deaf students. In Ghana, education for hearing and deaf children proceeds in local indigenous languages and/or in English, but there is no consistent signed language in use (Okyere and Addo 1994). Elsewhere, language policies change depending on the political and social orientation of the federal and local governments at any particular time and depending on the attitudes of the personnel in charge of education on the national and local levels. For example, in Ecuador and Brazil, influences from European countries (Spain and Portugal, respectively) affect the development of national signed languages. The local signed languages often lack a full vocabulary so that signs are imported either from the European signed languages or from those in other South American countries (Garcia 1994).

One of the newest signed languages is Nicaraguan Sign Language (NSL), a code with a very interesting recent history that has implications for our understanding of the development of language. The first school for the deaf did not open in Nicaragua until 1977; a second school opened in 1980, both in the capital city of Managua. Before that time, deaf children and adults used idiosyncratic homesign methods to communicate with family and community members. Although the new schools represented an advance in recognizing the needs of deaf children, they functioned under Spanish-language preferences. The teachers, all of whom were hearing, taught the children to lip-read and to read and write in Spanish. But then the students made a remarkable shift in their communication: They created their own language based on signs without anyone showing them how to do it. At first, their communication consisted of gestures coming out of their homesign environment. However, the students soon developed complex rules of syntactic order and used linguistic resources to form new words. In addition, without any model to copy or learn from, the students began to use spatial location and movement of signs to convey lexical and grammatical meanings (Helmuth 2001:1758).

Research among different cohorts of students, based on when they attended the Nicaraguan school, indicates that changes are continually being made in NSL to expand its lexical inventory and to add grammatical and syntactic complexity. Today, there are more than 800 Deaf users of NSL, ranging in age from 4 to 45 (Senghas et al. 2004:1780). Nicaraguans older than 45 years of age did not have opportunities to attend schools for the deaf, and most continue to use homesign methods. A study conducted by Ann Senghas, Sotaro Kita, and Asli Ozyurek investigated differences in the signing of 30 Deaf users of NSL, divided into three cohorts of 10 each (those who learned NSL before 1983, between 1984 and 1993, and since 1993). The researchers paid special attention to expressions that "describe complex motion events, such as rolling down a hill or climbing up a wall" (ibid.:1780), to determine the ways that the elements involved in these motions are dissected and expressed. In particular, complex motions consist of both manner of movement (such as rolling) and path of movement (such as descending). The signs used were compared to gestures employed by hearing Nicaraguans when speaking Spanish.

The researchers found that all of the hearing Spanish speakers and the members of the first cohort of NSL users employed gestures that expressed path and movement simultaneously, that is, in a way that imitates the motion described. In contrast, members of the second and third cohorts used signs that separated path and movement into distinct units of meaning. Senghas and her associates conclude that the shift to separating path and movement represents a step in the creation of a language rather than a simple gestural system. As we saw in Chapter 2, all known human languages are made up of discrete units of meaning that isolate semantic features so that they can be combined and recombined to produce new words and an infinite number of sentences. Evidently, the student creators of NSL have engaged in similar productive processes.

Just as new technologies have affected communicative practices in hearing speech communities, these technologies, especially computer-mediated communication (CMC), have expanded interactions among Deaf users. With the aid of video cameras (or webcams), Deaf people can employ signed languages to interact with others no matter how far. The webcams are connected to personal computers to transmit images of ongoing communication. A study of four families of Deaf parents and children in Texas demonstrated some of the innovative practices and the adjustments that people made to adapt their signed languages to the opportunities and constraints of computer technology (Keating and Mirus 2003). For example, one participant wanted to convey the meaning of the word *rollercoaster* to a German interlocutor who, although conversant in ASL, did not know the meaning of the ASL sign for the word. The participant found a picture of a rollercoaster and held it up in front of the webcam so that the image was relayed through the computer to his German friend.

Because of the limitations of the visual field on the computer screen, some signs have to be modified. For instance, signs normally produced in the space at the signer's waist have been moved upward: some to the shoulder, some to chin level, and some to the arm and shoulder raised (ibid.:703). In addition, signing on camera usually moves more slowly than in "normal" conversation. Nonsign gestures and movements, such as changes in head position or facial expression, are also slowed or emphasized because, in the two-dimensional space of a computer image, it may be difficult to pick up small movements and the camera or computer may distort images.

One of the major current and continuing issues for Deaf communication concerns the uneven progress in achieving recognition of Deaf people as bilingual and bicultural. In some countries and some school systems, national spoken languages are taught as second or "foreign" languages and as supplemental to the signed languages, which are accepted as the primary modes of communication employed by Deaf people. However, the approach that is still most common is the emphasis on oralism and the acquisition of some form of spoken language, even though organizations that promote the interests of Deaf people advocate for the bilingual approach. Deaf people also want recognition of their bicultural identities as participants in their local and national societies and as members of Deaf communities with a unique status that includes language as a fundamental feature of self-identity.

Summary

Technologies have been developed that permit communication between people who are not speaking face to face. The telephone enables people in different places to communicate almost as though they were in face-to-face interaction. But there are significant differences deriving from the lack of visual signals of gesture and facial expression that transmit essential meaning in ordinary conversation. Styles of greeting, topic introduction, and leave-taking have developed to adapt to the constraints of the medium. Computer technology is a more recent source of innovations in conversational and social interaction. Now, people can communicate with hundreds or thousands of strangers in chatrooms and other venues, creating a new lexicon and new styles of writing as adaptations to the rapid exchange of turns and the comings and goings of participants.

Signed languages enable Deaf people to communicate with others, using all of the linguistic resources of full and complex languages. Signed languages, like spoken languages, differ from country to country and also vary among distinct segments of communities based on region, age, gender, and race or ethnicity. Study of the communicative practices of Deaf conversation participants reveals complex adjustments of form, position, and movement to expand linguistic repertoires and adapt to new situations and technologies.

References

AARONS, DEBRA, AND LOUISE REYNOLDS. 2003. South African sign language: Changing policies and practice. In *Many Ways to Be Deaf: International Variation in Deaf Communities,* ed. L. Monaghan, C. Schmaling, K. Nakamura, and G. Turner. Washington, DC: Gallaudet University Press, pp. 194–210.

ARAMBURO, ANTHONY. 1994. Sociolinguistic aspects of the black deaf community. In *The Deaf Way: Perspectives from the International Conference on Deaf Culture,* ed. C. Erling, B. Snider, D. Smith, and R. Johnson. Washington, DC: Gallaudet University Press, pp. 474–482.

BAGGA-GUPTA, SANGEETA, AND LARS-AKE DOMFORS. 2003. Pedagogical issues in Swedish deaf education. In *Many Ways to Be Deaf: International Variation in Deaf Communities,* ed. Leila Monaghan, C. Schmaling, K. Nakamura, and G. Turner. Washington, DC: Gallaudet University Press, pp. 67–88.

BRAEM, PENNY BOYES, BENNO CARAMORE, ROLAND HERMANN, AND PATRICIA SHORES HERMANN. 2003. Romance and reality: Sociolinguistic similarities and differences between Swiss German Sign Language and Rhaeto-Romansh. In *Many Ways to Be Deaf: International Variation in Deaf Communities,* ed. L. Monaghan, C. Schmaling, K. Nakamura, and G. Turner. Washington, DC: Gallaudet University Press, pp. 89–113.

CRONENBERG, CARL. 1965. Sign language dialects. In *A Dictionary of American Sign Language,* ed. C. Valli. Washington, DC: Gallaudet College Press, pp. 313–319.

CRYSTAL, DAVID. 2001. *Language and the Internet.* New York: Cambridge University Press.

ETHNOLOGUE. 2010. Languages of the World. Deaf Sign Language, http://www.ethnologue.com/show_family.asp?subid=23-16; (accessed June 14, 2010).

FOLCHI, ANNA. 1994. Sign language and deaf culture in Italy. *In The Deaf Way: Perspectives from the International Conference on Deaths Culture,* ed. C. Erling, B. Snider, D. Smith, and R. Johnson. Washington, DC: Gallaudet University Press, pp. 410–415.

GAO, LIWEI. 2006. Language contact and convergence in computer-mediated communication. *World Englishes* 25, no. 2:299–308.

GARCIA, CARMEN VELASQUEZ. 1994. The birth of Ecuadorian sign language. *In The Deaf Way: Perspectives from the International Conference on Deaths Culture,* ed. Carol Erting, et al. Washington, DC: Gallaudet University Press, pp. 123–126.

GODARD, DANIELLE. 1977. Openings and closings in telephone conversations. *Language in Society* 10:1–19.

HELMUTH, LAURA. 2001. From the mouths (and hands) of babes. *Science* 293, no. 5536:1758–1759.

HERRING, SUSAN. 1992. *Gender and Participation in Computer-Mediated Linguistic Discourse.* Washington, DC: ERIC Clearinghouse on Languages and Linguistics, Document ED 345552.

HERRING, SUSAN. 1999. Interactional coherence in CMC. *Journal of Computer-Mediated Communication* 4, no. 4 (http://www.ascusc.org/jcmc/vol4/issue4/herring.html).

HERRING, SUSAN. 2003. Gender and power in online communication. In *The Handbook of Language and Gender,* ed. Janet Holmes and M. Meyerhoff. Oxford: Blackwell, pp. 202–228.

HEWLING, ANNE. 2005. Culture in the online class: Using message analysis to look beyond nationality-based frames of reference. *Journal of Computer-Mediated Communication,* vol. 11, no.1, article 16:1–19. http://jcmc.indiana.edu/vol11/issue1/hewling.html; (accessed February 28, 2012).

HOPPER, RICHARD. 1992. *Telephone Conversation.* Bloomington: Indiana University Press.

HOUTKOOP-STEENSTRA, HANNEKE. 2002. Gender differences in telephone conversations. In *Studies in Language and Social Interaction,* ed. P. Glenn, C. LeBaron, and J.Mandelbaum. pp. 275–287.

HOWARD, JAY. 2002. Do college students participate more in discussion in traditional delivery courses or in interactive telecourses? A preliminary comparison. *The Journal of Higher Education* vol. 73, no. 6:764–780.

HULL, DARRELL, AND TERRILL SAXON. 2009. Negotiation of meaning and co-construction of knowledge: An experimental analysis of asynchronous online instruction. *Computers & Education* vol. 52:624–639.

IGNITE SOCIAL MEDIA. 2010. Internet usage by age, gender, race and more, http://www.ignitesocialmedia.com/internet-usage-by-age-gender-race; (accessed June 26, 2010).

INTERNET USAGE STATS. 2010. Internet growth and stats. http://www.allaboutmarketresearch.com/internet.htm; (accessed June 26, 2010).

INTERNET WORLD STATS. 2010. Internet usage and population statistics. http://www.internetworldstats.com/stats.htm (accessed June 26, 2010).

ISLAM, GAZI. 2006. Virtual speakers, virtual audiences: Agency, audience and constraint in an online chat community. *Dialectal Anthropology* 30:71–89.

JEPSON, JILL. 1991. Urban and rural sign language in India. *Language in Society,* 20:37–57.

KEATING, ELIZABETH, AND GENE MIRUS. 2003. American sign language in virtual space: Interactions between deaf users of computer-mediated video communication and the impact of technology on language practices. *Language in Society* 32:693–714.

LEMASTER, BARBARA. 1998. Sex differences in Irish sign language. *In The Life of Language: Papers in Linguistics in Honor of William Bright,* ed. J. Hill, P. J. Mistry, and L. Campbell. Berlin and New York: Mouton de Gruyter, pp. 67–86.

MAXWELL, MADELINE, AND SYBIL SMITH-TODD. 1986. Black sign language and school integration in Texas. *Language in Society,* 15, no. 1:81–93.

NISHIMURA, YUKIKO. 2003. Linguistic Innovations and Interactional Features of Casual Online Communication in Japanese. *Journal of Computer-Mediated Communication* 9, no.1: 1–33 (http://www.ascusc.org/jcmc/vol9/issue2/nishimura.html).

OKYERE, ALEXANDER, AND MARY ADDO. 1994. Deaf culture in Ghana. In *The Deaf Way: Perspectives from the International Conference on Deaf Culture,* ed. C. Erting, B. Snider, D. Smith, and R. Johnson. Washington, DC: Gallaudet University Press, pp. 97–101.

PADDEN, CAROL. 1996. Early bilingual lives of deaf children. *In Cultural and language Diversity and the Deaf Experience,* ed. I. Parasnis. New York: Cambridge University Press, pp. 99–116.

PALFREYMAN, DAVID, AND MUHAMED AL KHALIL. 2003. "A funky language for teenzz to use": Representing Gulf Arabic in instant messaging. *Journal of Computer-Mediated Communication* 9, no. 1:1–25 (http://www.ascusc.org/jcmc/vol9/issue2/palfreyman.html).

PANYAMETHEEKUL, SIRIPORN, AND SUSAN HERRING. 2003. Gender and turn allocation in a Thai chat room. *Journal of Computer Mediated Communication* 9, no. 1:1–20.

PARASNIS, ILA. 1996. On interpreting the deaf experience within the context of cultural and language diversity. In *Cultural and language Diversity and the Deaf Experience,* ed. I. Parasnis. New York: Cambridge University Press, pp. 3–19.

PARSAD, BASMAT, AND LAURIE LEWIS. 2008. *Distance Education at Degree-Granting Postsecondary Institutions: 2006–2007.* Washington, DC: National Center for Education Statistics, Institute of Education Sciences, US Department of Education.

SAITO, RITSUKO, AND NORIKO ISHIZUKA. 2005. Practice of online chat communication between two countries and across different curricula. *Journal of Multimedia Aided Education Research* 2, no.1:151–158.

SCHEGLOFF, EMMANUEL. 1979. Identification and recognition in telephone conversation openings. In *Everyday Language: Studies in Ethnomethodology,* ed. G. Psathas. New York: Irvington Press, pp. 23–78.

SCHEGLOFF, EMMANUEL. 1986. The routine as achievement. *Human Studies* 9:111–151.

SCHMALING, CONSTANZE. 2003. A for apple: The impact of Western education and ASL on the Deaf community in Kano State, Northern Nigeria. In *Many Ways to Be Deaf: International Variation in Deaf Communities,* ed. L. Monaghan, C. Schmaling, K. Nakamura, and G. Turner. Washington, DC: Gallaudet University Press, pp. 302–310.

SENGHAS, ANN, SOTARO KITA, AND ASLI OZYUREK. 2004. Children creating core properties of language: Evidence from an emerging sign language in Nicaragua. *Science* 305, no. 5691:1779–1782.

SENGHAS, RICHARD, AND LEILA MONAGHAN. 2002. Signs of their times: Deaf communities and the culture of language. *Annual Review of Anthropology* vol. 31:69–97.

VASISHTA, MADAN JAMES WOODWARD, AND KIRK. WILSON. 1978. Sign language in India: Regional variation within the deaf population. *Paper presented at the 5th International Congress of Applied Linguistics,* Montréal, Canada.

WOODWARD, JAMES. 2003. Sign languages and deaf identities in Thailand and Vietnam. *In Many Ways to Be Deaf: International Variation in Deaf Communities,* ed. L. Monaghan, C. Schmaling, K. Nakamura, and G. Turner. Washington, DC: Gallaudet University Press, pp. 283–301.

WOODWARD, JAMES C., AND JAMES WOODWARD. 1976. Black southern signing. *Language in Society* 5, no. 2:211–218.

CHAPTER 7

Learning Language

ADULT:	Adam, say what I say: Where can I put them?
ADAM (3 YEARS OLD):	Where I can put them?

Adam, a young child learning English, demonstrates a remarkable capacity to acquire language. He accomplishes this, as do all children, not without problems and not in one moment, but over a period of years, advancing through stages of linguistic, cognitive, and social development.

Let us first try to understand the complex task facing every human being in the early months and years of their lives. An infant is surrounded by people who make gestures, movements, and noise. The child becomes aware of distinctions between herself and others and develops desires to interact with those others. In some nonconscious manner, she gradually grasps the notion that the behaviors and noises that people make have meaning, that they are purposeful and useful in social interactions. This, in itself, is a profound discovery, made once by each of the billions of people who have ever lived. But this discovery leads to an enormous problem of deciphering the code, of figuring out meanings expressed through sounds and gestures. Young children cannot consult dictionaries or grammar books; they have to construct their own set of rules. In a sense, children are the best linguists, analyzing an unknown language and discovering its grammar based solely on evidence presented by experience.

The process of learning is multifaceted. Children develop knowledge of their language through unfolding and maturing cognitive and linguistic abilities internal to themselves while they are helped by their parents or caregivers, who, in various ways, provide social contexts where these abilities become focused and meaningful. In this chapter, we identify linguistic processes of learning in English and then consider comparative data from other types of linguistic systems. Finally, we review some studies of instructional techniques that adults employ to guide children in learning language.

ACQUISITION OF LANGUAGE

Development of linguistic ability is linked to maturation of cognitive processes. It is based on growth of the capacity for symbolic representation, resulting in awareness that sounds that are abstract and arbitrary can be used to stand for both present and absent objects and activities. Increased ability to remember experiences and to associate them with present and future events is also critical to a child's language acquisition. Language also implies an understanding of causality, realizing that people and objects can affect others through their actions or states. Children express relations between objects, people, and/or activities; they do not merely compile a catalog of labels. Finally, interactions with other people lead to a child's understanding that language can be used to express personal attitudes and goals.

Linguistic discovery and creativity are universal processes, inherent in human experience. Children learn language primarily through their own cognitive efforts utilizing the genetic potential that is part of their human endowment. Noam Chomsky has stated that a fundamental question in the study of language is to account for a "speaker's ability to produce and understand instantly new sentences that are not similar to those previously heard.... It seems plain that language acquisition is based on the child's discovery of what from a formal point of view is a deep and abstract theory—a generative grammar of his/her language" (1965:57–58). And Chomsky asserted that because all children, regardless of intelligence, motivation, or emotions, learn language, "it seems reasonable to suppose that a child cannot help constructing a particular sort of grammar to account for the data presented.... Thus, it may be that the general features of language structure reflect the general character of one's capacity to acquire knowledge—one's innate ideas and innate principles" (ibid.:59).

Although researchers generally agree that children have an innate capacity to learn language and that the processes of language learning consist at least in part of an unfolding of principles of universal grammar, there are differences of opinion about the relative significance of cognitive maturation and social interaction in language acquisition. These two themes owe their origin, respectively, to language theorists Jean Piaget and Lev Vygotsky. Piaget (1955) stressed the role of individual cognition in language learning. He explained developmental changes in speech as the result of cognitive maturation, itself based on changes in sensorimotor processes. Just as children use "tools" to manipulate objects and perform actions, they use words and other elements of language to achieve desired results. If they cannot obtain what they want through their own actions, they use language to enlist caregivers in helping them in their pursuits. In this view, then, speech has a fundamentally goal-directed, instrumental function. Gradually, as the child matures, she or he is able to broaden her or his understanding of motivation and begins to appreciate the perspective of others. In recognition of others' feelings and attitudes, children begin to use more complex grammatical forms that encode politeness and other forms of indirection that recognize the rights of others. Explanations for the acquisition of additional aspects of language are similarly based on adaptive processes that mediate between a child's egocentric impulses and his or her ability to accommodate to others.

The work of Lev Vygotsky (1962, 1978) takes a different view of childhood speech and development. For Vygotsky, the driving force motivating language acquisition is the social needs of children as they expand their interactions with others. Although Vygotsky recognizes that children's earliest linguistic and cognitive development is oriented toward obtaining objects and attaining other goals, he stresses social needs that emerge with and are related to the use of signs, that is, language. Social development begins to overshadow sensorimotor development in a child's maturation. Signs (or language) are employed not only to express thoughts and goals but also to transform other kinds of activities. A child's thoughts about his or her experiences become expressible primarily through these signs, and therefore the signs themselves affect the way in which a child thinks about him- or herself and the world. That is, as signs are internalized in the process of language acquisition, they come to mediate thought itself. Language is then used both as a means of interaction with others and as a way of representing the world to oneself. Language and thought are thereafter inextricably interdependent.

Speech Sounds

The first step in acquiring language is learning to differentiate and produce sounds occurring in one's language. Children must realize that the stream of noise they hear is made up of discrete, individual sounds combined in a significant linear order. Then they must learn to control muscular movements in their throat and mouth to produce those sounds with consistency so that they are understood by addressees. Before children actually begin to speak, to say words, they go through a period of practicing, or babbling, consonant-like and vowel-like articulations. During the first 4 months of life, infants demonstrate a rapid increase in the number of sounds that they produce. After the fourth month, there is an abrupt drop in rates of change; relatively few new sounds are introduced into their repertory. Once a child begins the actual speaking process, normally by the age of 1 year, expansion of sounds stops altogether (McNeill 1987:132). From this point onward, children focus attention on the sounds that are significant in their language. They learn to control their production, make appropriate phonemic contrasts, and follow allophonic patterning.

In addition to forming consonants and vowels, speakers must learn intonational contours specific to their language and follow normative patterns of pitch and rhythm. These are evidently learned quite early. Infants as young as 5 months are sensitive to intonational changes and are able to produce language-appropriate contours in their own babbling (Weir 1966:155–157).

Cross-linguistic studies provide evidence for some universal sequences in acquiring sound systems. Front consonants /p/ and /m/ and the back vowel /a/ are the first to appear in spoken words, although other sounds (back consonants and front vowels) continue to be present in contemporaneous nonspeech babbling. Roman Jakobson (1941) postulated a universal order of differentiation of sounds beginning with a distinction between consonant /p/ and vowel /a/. These two represent extremes of articulation: /p/ is a voiceless stop consonant, formed in the front of the mouth, with complete closure of the vocal channel; /a/ is a voiced vowel, formed in the back of the mouth, characterized by complete opening of the vocal tract. After this fundamental contrast, a child gradually differentiates sounds to fill in articulatory space and/or add complexities in manners of articulation. According to Jakobson and Halle (1956), the first consonantal distinction results from contrast between oral and nasal sounds, that is, oral /p/ and nasal /m/. The next change involves labial/dental differentiation, leading to addition of /t/ to a child's inventory. The first vocalic distinction results from contrasting an open back sound /a/ with a closed, high front vowel /i/. Then distinctions are made in dimensions of frontness/backness (e.g., /i/ and /u/) or in height (e.g., /i/, /e/, and /a/; ibid.:38–41).

This universal pattern of differentiation explains why children's first words are often made up of sequences like "mama, papa, tata." And it may provide insight into the common, worldwide occurrence of consonants /p, m, t/ in words for "mother" and "father," particularly in address forms. Because parents are the earliest significant people in a baby's universe, it is linguistically and cognitively appropriate to name them with sounds that a baby can most easily produce.

Although children eventually learn all the sounds employed in their language, some sounds present relatively greater difficulty. Consonants requiring more control of muscular movements and timing, such as /θ/, /ð/, /s/, and /r/, are acquired later than simpler sounds such as /p/, /t/, or /m/ (Fry 1966:194).

One-Word Utterances

Children are clearly able to understand language before they themselves start to speak. *Passive language* is demonstrated by the fact that children respond appropriately to commands and suggestions made by others. They comply with directives given to them in more complex structures than they themselves are able to produce (Sachs and Truswell 1976). (Although adults do not remember their earliest childhood learning experiences, comprehension of language in advance of performance abilities is familiar to anyone acquiring a second, or "foreign," language. We can all understand native speakers or read textbooks long before we are able to remember words or construct grammatical forms.)

Usually by the end of their first year, children begin to speak single words. These utterances are *holophrastic*; that is, each word expresses broad semantic and contextual meanings. Because earliest utterances are functionally complex, they can be understood only in the context of a child's experience. Goals expressed through children's speech emanate from the interaction of a child with objects and persons in his or her environment. Children have desires for others to attend to their needs and wants (imperative function), they want to relate emotional states (expressive function), and they want to name objects or people with whom they interact (referential function). Of course, each spoken word may serve several purposes simultaneously.

Studies of holophrastic utterances demonstrate that each word has a complex semantic scope. Many of a child's earliest words are associated with ritualized interactions, such as saying "hi" or "bye-bye," or they express desires that caregivers can fulfill, such as "up," "down," and other demands and refusals (Greenfield and Smith 1976:70). Even young children know that speaking is a human strategy for achieving personal and social goals.

The following table presents data from Patricia Greenfield and J. H. Smith (1976), noting onsets of each semantic function, marking the age at which it first occurred in the speech of one child (age given in months and days), and providing linguistic forms and behavioral contexts.

Onset of Semantic Functions in a Child's One-Word Utterances

Semantic Function	Age	Instance
Performative	7 (22)	*hi,* accompaniment to waving
Performative object	8 (12)	*dada,* looking at father
Volition	11 (24)	*nana,* turning away from stairs in response to mother's "no"
Dative	11 (28)	*dada,* offering bottle to father
Object	13 (0)	*ba(ll),* having just thrown ball
Agent	13 (3)	*daddy,* hearing father come in door and start up steps
Action or state of agent	13 (16)	*up,* reaching up, in answer to question, Do you want to get up?
Action or state of object	14 (6)	*down,* having just thrown something down
Object associated with another object or location	14 (29)	*caca* (cracker, cookie), pointing to door to the next room where cookies are kept
Location	15 (20)	*bo(x),* putting crayon in box

(continued)

Semantic Function	Age	Instance
Animate being associated	15 (29)	*fishy,* pointing to empty fish tank with object/location
Modification of event	ca.18 (1)	*again,* when he wants someone to do something for him again

Two-Word Grammars

Appearance of two-word combinations marks the beginning of true grammatical constructions. This critical advance is normally made in a child's second year, usually by 18 months. It depends on cognitive growth, learning to differentiate words within classes, and recognizing that sequential ordering of words has meaning. Children realize that grammatical relations must be overtly expressed. This is another remarkable insight made independently by every individual.

Emergence of two-word grammars and their continual expansion and refinement indicate a change in the character of a child's thinking. In David McNeill's terms, young children's thought is first *global* and *imagistic* and then becomes *syntactic.* Language acquisition basically involves *unpacking* images through syntactic order. "Unpacking these images into word and morpheme segments and simple linearizations of words are [sic] the first steps of language learning at ages one to two years. Children at this age are learning how to think syntactically" (1987:254). The next stage is equally significant: developing abilities to synthesize two kinds of thought—imagistic and syntactic. This kind of thinking "consists of a synthesis in which images are subdivided and linearized without losing sight of the global whole. Thinking in language is not simply subdividing into segments.... The synthesis of global and syntactic thinking that we observe in each act of speaking draws on this new form of thinking; and this synthesis appears in the earliest stages of linguistic development" (ibid.:255).

McNeill suggested an adaptive advantage in human evolution offered by a synthesis of imagistic and syntactic thinking that may have accounted for the development of human language. "[T]hinking in terms of images that are synthesized with linearly arranged segments of the image—a syntax—could confer adaptive advantages [because] it creates, not a narrow linguistic capacity, but a form of thinking that is necessary for culture and a mechanism for the brain's storage of cultural information" (ibid.:257).

Expressing, or unpacking, experience into linguistic form is a creative process both syntactically and semantically. Children grasp the critical meaning of word order and also understand meanings contained in words themselves. They use this awareness in forming new words and constructions and in comprehending the speech of others.

Research concerned with language in the two-word stage reveals a consistent distinction between two classes of words: a "pivot" class and an "open" class, terms introduced by Martin Braine (1963). The *pivot* category contains a few words used with high frequency in combination with items from the open category. Types of words often occurring as pivots are ritualized greetings or comments (*bye-bye, all-gone*), demonstratives (*this, that*), locatives (*here, there*), possessives (*my*), and adjectives. The *open* class generally consists of nouns and verbs with which a child communicates his or her referential, imperative, or expressive intentions. Possible two-word constructions consist of combining either two items from the open class or a pivot plus an open word. Two pivot words do not co-occur as a complete utterance. This fact gives evidence of a child's developing grammar, involving notions of syntactic restrictions.

Pivot and open categories are found in many languages with different surface and syntactic characteristics. Thus, they appear to reflect a stage in universal cognitive development. Samples are given in Figure 7.1 of two-word sentences from several languages: three Indo-European languages (English, German, and Russian) and three unrelated languages—Finnish, Luo (spoken in Kenya), and Samoan.

Even within restrictions of two-word sequences, children can express varied relations between and among people, objects, and actions. Although children's speech contains only a limited number of words, young speakers can express complex propositions and intentions. For example, the recorded utterances below are the speech of a young girl (18 months old) in contexts of giving and/or receiving objects (Antinucci and Parisi 1973). The experience of giving/receiving involves several underlying semantic components and their interrelations: an action, an agent performing the act, an object being transferred, and a recipient. The girl's utterances express various combinations of these critical components:

Action: *Give* (giving something to her mother)

Object: *Water* (asking her mother for some water)

Recipient: *To me* (asking for something)

Recipient + object: *To me candies* (asking for candies)

Action + object: *Give ball* (asking for a ball)

Action + actor: *Give mommy* (asking for something from mother)

Recipient + action: *Mommy give* (giving something to mother)

COMPLEX GRAMMARS

However ingenious and creative a young child can be operating within restrictions of a limited verbal range, two-word utterances soon become too confining. Cognitive development and experiential maturation stimulate children to expand their linguistic abilities. A number of interconnected discoveries and advances are made. A child begins to express additional grammatical relations through expansion in the number of words in a sentence and through employment of morphological processes affecting the structure of individual words. According to McNeill, "Two-word sentences grow to three-word sentences and beyond because a child observes the *relative* position of words. By learning that a word is first in a phrase and that a phrase is first in a sentence, a child learns that the sentence is hierarchically organized. Thus, positional learning, extended through contextual generalization, leads to [complex] sentence structure" (1970:68).

McNeill's statement captures two important themes. First, a child develops awareness that organization within sentences is significant. She recognizes that words are not simply strung along in adjacent slots, but that they combine in functional units (noun phrases, verb phrases) that are affected by rules of placement and movement. Second, a child transfers her learning from one context to others by processes of analogy and rule generalization. These two capacities are demonstrations of human cognitive endowments and are universal in children's learning.

Morphological Development

Morphological processes are employed to express grammatical concepts. Some of the most common concepts are person, number, case, and verb categories such as tense, aspect, and mode. In early stages of speech (one- or two-word constructions), affixes denoting these concepts are

Function of Utterance	English	German	Russian	Finnish	Luo	Samoan
LOCATE, NAME	there book that car see doggie	buch da [book there] gukuk wauwau [see doggie]	Tosya tam [Tosya there]	tuossa Rina [there Rina] vettä siinä [water there]	en saa [it clock] ma wendo [this visitor]	Keith lea [Keith there]
DEMAND, DESIRE	more milk give candy want gum	mehr milch [more milk] bitte apfel [please apple]	yeshchë moloko [more milk] day chasy [give watch]	anna Rina [give Rina]	miya tamtam [give-me candy] adway cham [I-want food]	mai pepe [give doll] fia moe [want sleep]
NEGATE[1]	no wet no wash not hungry allgone milk	nicht blasen [not blow] kaffee nein [coffee no]	vody net [water no] gus' tyu-tyu [goose gone]	ei susi [not wolf] enää pipi [anymore sore]	beda onge [my-slasher absent]	le 'ai [not eat] uma mea [allgone thing]
DESCRIBE EVENT OR SITUATION[2]	Bambi go mail come hit ball block fall baby highchair	puppe kommt [doll comes] tiktak hängt [clock hangs] sofa sitzen [sofa sit] messer schneiden [cut knife]	mama prua [mama walk] papa bay-bay [papa sleep] korka upala [crust fell] nashia yaichko [found egg] baba kreslo [grandma armchair]	Seppo putoo [Seppo fall] talli 'bm-bm' [garage 'car']	chungu biro [European comes] odhi skul [he-went school] omoyo oduma [she-dries maize]	pa'u pepe [fall doll] tapale 'oe [hit you] tu'u lalo [put down]

INDICATE POSSESSION	*my shoe* *mama dress*	*mein ball* [my ball] *mamas hut* [mama's hat]	*mami chashka* [mama's cup] *pup moya* [navel my]	*täti auto* [aunt car]	*kom baba* [chair father]	*lole a'u* [candy my] *polo 'oe* [ball your] *paluni mama* [balloon mama]
MODIFY, QUALIFY	*pretty dress* *big boat*	*milch heiss* [milk hot] *armer wauwau* [poor dog]	*mama khoroshaya* [mama good] *papa bol'shoy* [papa big]	*rikki auto* [broken car] *torni iso* [tower big]	*pipiy kech* [pepper hot] *gwen madichol* [chicken black]	*fa'ali'i pepe* [headstrong baby]
QUESTION[3]	*where ball*	*wo ball* [where ball]	*gde papa* [where papa]	*missä pallo* [where ball]		*fea Punafu* [where Punafu]

The examples come from a variety of studies, published and unpublished. Data from the three non-Indo-European languages are drawn from the doctoral dissertations of Melissa Bowerman (Harvard, in progress: Finnish), Ben Blount (Berkeley, 1969: Luo), and Keith Kernan (Berkeley, 1969: Samoan). The examples given here are representative of many more utterances of the same type in each language. The order of the two words in the utterance is generally fixed in all of the languages except Finnish, where both orders can be used freely for some utterance types by some children.

[1]Bloom (1968) has noted three different sorts of negation: (1) nonexistence (e.g., "no wet," meaning "dry"); (2) rejection (e.g., "no wash," meaning "don't wash me"); and (3) denial ("no girl," denying a preceding assertion that a boy was a girl).

[2]Descriptions are of several types: (1) agent + action (e.g., "Bambi go"); (2) action + object (e.g., "hit ball"); (3) agent + object (e.g., "mama bread," meaning "mama is cutting bread"); (4) locative (e.g., "baby highchair," meaning "baby is in the highchair"); (5) instrumental (e.g., "cut knife"); (6) dative (e.g., "throw daddy," meaning "throw it to daddy"). (The use of terminology of grammatical case is suggestive here; cf. Filmore's [1968] discussion of deep cases as underlying linguistic universals.)

[3]In addition to wh-questions, yes–no questions can be made by pronouncing any two-word sentence with rising intonation, with the exception of Finnish. (Melissa Bowerman reports that the emergence of yes–no questions is, accordingly, exceptionally late in Finnish child language.)

FIGURE 7.1 Functions of Two-Word Sentences in Child Speech. (SLOBIN, DAN, I. Psycholinguistics, 1st. Edition. ©1979. Reprinted by permission of Pearson Education, Inc., Upper Saddle River, NJ.)

generally omitted. With no overt expression of relations, speech is heavily context-bound. As more grammatical information is made explicit in words themselves, speech moves toward freeing itself from immediate contexts. This process is gradual, but its direction is toward increasing the communicative potential available for speakers. Linguistic form that overtly expresses grammatical meanings is informative and can therefore be used in interactions with people who do not share all of one's experiences, thus expanding social possibilities for a maturing child. And as a child's cognitive capacities develop, she or he has understandings of the world and of her or his own thoughts that the child wants to express to others. As the child's linguistic abilities progress, she or he is better able to establish satisfying social involvements.

English nouns and verbs contain suffixes to mark certain grammatical categories. Inflections are characteristics of the surface form of words, carrying important information about agents, objects, or recipients associated with activities or states. The following table displays the timing and ordering of the emergence of nominal and verbal suffixes for two children studied by Ursula Bellugi (1964). Of importance is the fact that both children introduced inflections in the same order, even though ages at their appearance differed considerably.

The Emergence of English Inflections

Inflection	Adam	Eve
Present progressive, -ing	28 (months)	19.5 (months)
Plural on nouns, -s	33	24
Past on regular verbs, -ed	39	24.5
Possessive on nouns, -s	39.5	25.5
Third person on verbs, -s	41	26

A potentially confusing feature of English inflections is that the same sound, -s, appears as a suffix marking number on nouns, possession of nouns, and third-person singular subject of verbs. Ordering of inflections in Adam's and Eve's speech demonstrates that learners differentiate among grammatical functions of -s, keeping their applications distinct.

An important process in children's acquisition of morphological features is their extension of rules learned in one context to others through analogy and generalization. They add affixes to newly encountered words by recognizing sounds and applying appropriate morphological rules. In a clever and now classic experiment, Jean Berko (1958) developed a test situation to study how children apply plural and possessive suffixes to nouns that they have never heard before and how they apply past-tense and third-person singular suffixes to new verbs. She presented children (ages 4 through 7) with drawings of cartoonlike animals and objects and of men performing various actions. Creatures and activities were named with nonsense words; for example, cartoon characters were labeled "wug" /wÇg/, "kazh" /kæz/, "gutch" /gÇc/; activities were also named with non-English words.

Berko elicited children's selection of affixes to previously unencountered forms through the following kinds of test frames (ibid.:155–157):

Plural: One birdlike animal, then two. "This is a wug (/wÇg/). Now there is another one. There are two of them. There are two _____."

Past tense: Man doing calisthenics. "This is a man who knows how to mot (/mat/). He is motting. He did the same thing yesterday. What did he do yesterday? Yesterday he____."

Children were able to apply known affixes to new linguistic material, although a noun's or a verb's sound affected the ease or difficulty of application. Age differences also affected abilities to generalize rules: Speakers in the younger group (4–5 years) behaved less consistently than those in the older cohort (5½–7 years). However, relative ease or difficulty of suffix formation was the same at all ages for the different types of inflections. Among nouns, correct plurals were added to words ending in stops, liquids, and vowels. Nouns ending in sibilants (/s, z, š, ž, č, ǰ/) caused more problems. Among verbs, affixation of past-tense markers proved most difficult with verbs ending in -*t* or -*d* (ibid.:159–160). Nouns and verbs that were problematic share the requirement of inserting an "epenthetic" or "filler" vowel between stems and underlying forms of an affix, that is, plural {-s}→/-ʌz/ (e.g., /kɔz/ → /kɔzʌz/) and past tense {-d} /-ʌd/ (/mat/ ʌ /mat-ʌ d/). On the whole, though, "the picture that emerged was one of consistency, regularity and simplicity. The children did not treat new words according to idiosyncratic patterns. They did not model new words on patterns that appear infrequently…. Their best performance was with those forms that are the most regular and have the fewest variants" (ibid.:176–177).

Another significant reflection of children's drive to generalize rules is their tendency to overregularize affixes, very frequently applying allomorphs to nouns and verbs that actually select unusual allomorphs: "mouses" for plural and "comed" or "goed" for past tense. Perhaps the most revealing indicator of children's cognitive process is the fact that they apply analogous rules in a secondary wave after they have already learned irregular forms. This procedure, first described by Susan Ervin (1964), applies to many English verbs common in children's speech environments (as speakers and listeners) that have aberrant past-tense markings, such as "came," "went," "did." Children learn these forms first as invariant and unanalyzed wholes. Later they acquire the regular past-tense suffix and extend it to all verbs, resulting in displacement of irregulars: "came" "comed," "did" "doed." Although this process produces forms that are "incorrect" from the viewpoint of adult speech, it demonstrates a child's cognitive and creative capacities. Children generate innovative combinations in order to express newly understood grammatical relations.

Growth in Vocabulary

An obvious aspect of language acquisition is the expansion of vocabulary to include names for people and objects, descriptors of qualities, and indicators of actions and states. Learning new words is based on an interplay of growing cognitive abilities for comprehension, memory, and discrimination and of a widening social environment that presents children with new objects and activities.

Children employ several procedures in developing their vocabularies. From the earliest stages of language acquisition, children restructure the meanings of words either by broadening or narrowing the senses of individual words. For example, a word can first be used to refer to a large category of similar objects, for example, "apple" applied to a pear (Huttenlocher and Smiley 1987:75). Use of object names by young children involves associations between objects and locations or activities, for example, "door" applied to the request to have a door opened (ibid.:78). Later, words are restricted in their usage when children develop awareness of more specific meanings. Changes in semantic ranges of words result when children perceive similarities and contrasts and realize that words are organized into hierarchical categories. This process begins in the one-word stage but continues for many years.

Children also enrich their vocabularies creatively by generating their own words from preexisting words and grammatical material. Anyone who has listened even casually to children speaking can no doubt provide numerous anecdotal examples of such innovations. They arise in order to fill lexical gaps in a child's vocabulary, stimulated by the appearance of new objects or involvement in new activities for which the child has no descriptor. To study children's spontaneous creation of words, Eve Clark (1982) collected recordings of natural speech and analyzed occurrences of *denominal* verbs, that is, verbs that are derived from nouns. Denominal verbs occur frequently in English to fulfill various grammatical roles. The following list gives examples of legitimate English denominals (ibid.:392):

Placement of object: He *plastered* the ceiling.

Location of object: He *stabled* the horses.

Agent of action: She *authored* the books.

Goals of activity: They *knotted* the rope.

Instrument used: She *wedged* the door open.

Experiencer: They *witnessed* the crime.

Duration of event: He *summered* in Canada.

In Clark's samples of children's speech, young speakers independently created their own denominal verbs based on structural and semantic possibilities provided by words that they heard in adult speech. Some examples follow (ibid.:402–410). Ages are given in years and months (e.g., 3;11):

Placement:	(3;11, putting crackers in her soup) *I'm crackering my soup.* (5;0, to his mother) *Will you chocolate my milk?*
Location:	(5;0) *I'm going to basket those apples.*
Agent:	(5;1, talking about someone dancing in a ballet) *She's ballerining.*
Goal:	(3;1, watching a cement truck with its back revolving) *That truck is cementing.*
Instrument:	(2;11, not wanting his mother to sweep his room) *Don't broom my mess.*
Action:	(2;4, eating soup) *I'm souping.* (2;6, seated in a rocker) *Rocker me, Mommy.*

These data indicate children's eagerness to express concepts that they newly recognize. If words do not already exist in their limited vocabulary, they spontaneously create their own. In so doing, children utilize their language's operative procedures, learned from other sources. They model innovations on legitimate linguistic forms. Children use their own inherent cognitive processes in a generative sense, demonstrating their creative human intelligence. As the Soviet linguist A. N. Gvozdev aptly remarked:

> The keenness of the child's observations and the artistic clarity of many childish words are common knowledge. They are truly very close to the linguistic creativity of literary artists. We are therefore dealing here with authentic creativity, attesting to the linguistic endowment of children. (cited in Slobin 1966:132)

Syntactic Development

Children's grammars expand by introducing new propositions. Sentence length increases with additional words specifying aspects of an event—for example, adding modifiers or predicates and expressing more complex relations such as negation or dependent clauses. Grammatical development involves the ability to understand and express concepts about people and objects, and relations to states and activities. Among the best documented areas of propositional growth are the formation of negatives and interrogatives.

When acquiring negation in English, propositions are first negated simply by adding words such as *no* or *not,* usually at the beginning of sentences (Klima and Bellugi 1966:192):

No wipe finger.

No the sun shining.

Not a teddy bear.

Wear mitten no.

The form of these utterances is syntactically simple. Negative markers are added to otherwise affirmative statements: Neg + S (or less commonly, S + Neg). In the second stage, children soon progress, usually from two to four months later, to greater complexity by incorporating negation within the internal structure of sentences, for instance (ibid.:194):

He not little, he big.

I no want envelope.

There no squirrels.

None of these sentences is well formed (from an adult standard), but they show an advance over the earlier stage because negative markers are placed within sentences rather than simply added to them.

The third stage of development, occurring two to six months later, involves more complex incorporation of negation into sentences (ibid.:196):

I not see you anymore.

You didn't caught me.

This not ice cream.

Don't touch the fish.

Ask me if I not make mistake.

At this stage, negative marking is productively applied to auxiliaries (*can, do*). Another feature of this period is that an earlier sentence structure, /Neg + S/, has been omitted from children's grammars. In addition, *no* as an internally positioned marker disappears, replaced either by *not* or by more complex negative forms.

During this stage, several childlike constructions remain, including lack of copulas in some sentences. Also, past-tense forms of main verbs occur in surface structure (e.g., "You didn't *caught* me"), although adult grammar expresses these verbs in present tense ("You didn't *catch* me"). However, children rapidly develop appropriate negative syntax after this phase.

Another area of propositional and linguistic growth is comprehension and expression of *wh-questions*—questions introduced by /what/, /who/, /where/, /why/, /when/. Children readily make distinctions on both structural and semantic grounds between yes–no and wh-questions. The former are indicated simply by rising intonation. The latter are more complex and involve gradual development of syntactic constructions (Bellugi 1968; Brown et al. 1968; Klima and Bellugi 1966).

In the first stage, a simple wh-word is prefaced to declarative sentences (examples from Klima and Bellugi 1966:200):

Who that?

What cowboy doing?

Where Mama boot?

The second stage of development incorporates auxiliaries acquired in declarative contexts and applies them to interrogatives (ibid.:204–205):

> Where small trailer he should pull?
>
> What he can ride in?
>
> What did you doed?
>
> Why the kitty can't stand up?
>
> How he can be a doctor?

A striking feature of this second stage of wh-formation is that, although auxiliaries are properly introduced into sentences, children do not perform subject–auxiliary inversion, that is, in adult English grammar, /NP + aux aux + NP/. If this transformation had affected children's sentences, the question "What he can ride in?" would have been realized as "What can he ride in?" Bellugi suggested that children's difficulties lie in what she termed *performance constraints* on simultaneous operation of multiple transformations. Children obviously comprehend meanings of sentences with inverted subjects and can produce sentences of the same length, composed in fact of identical words. A child begins by adding wh-words to declarative sentences as a first step in transformational cycles and initially can perform only this single operation. Bellugi tested her subjects by asking them to imitate her speech, as in the brief exchange that opened this chapter (ibid.:38):

> **ADULT:**   Adam, say what I say: Where can I put them?
>
> **ADAM:**   Where I can put them?

In the next stage, Adam learned to invert subject + auxiliary but was able to do so only with affirmative questions. Negative questions were not inverted. During this period, Adam could perform two operations (wh-word introduction and subject inversion), but when a third proposition was added, his handling of syntax could not incorporate all three simultaneously. Because negation must be included in order to capture the meaning of the sentence, he opted for omitting the subject-inversion transformation. Note the following dialogue from a game in which Adam was directed to ask questions of an "Old Lady" puppet (ibid.:40):

> **ADULT:**   Adam, ask the Old Lady where she can find some toys.
>
> **ADAM:**   Old Lady, where can you find some toys?
>
> **ADULT:**   Adam, ask the Old Lady why she can't run.
>
> **ADAM:**   Old Lady, why you can't run?

These exchanges provide further evidence of performance constraints. Significantly, they also support notions in generative grammar of the independent status of transformations. It is obvious that children do not acquire language only from surface phenomena presented in adult speech but also operate on the basis of innate principles that require cognitive maturation. Children develop their capacity to use these principles in distinct stages. Multiple transformations involving multiple propositions present conceptual difficulties, resulting in constraints on performance.

Children gradually develop abilities to comprehend and produce complex sentences, including processes of conjoining and embedding. Following are examples of a child's (age 2;4) attempts to imitate some model sentences (Slobin and Welsh 1973):

ADULT:	Here is a brown brush and here is a comb.
CHILD:	Here's a brown brush an' a comb.
ADULT:	The man who I saw yesterday got wet.
CHILD:	I saw the man and he got wet.
ADULT:	The boy the book hit was crying.
CHILD:	Boy the book was crying.

In the first sentence, with the simple conjunction *and,* the girl produced an imitation incorporating a regular English transformation (deletion of redundancies) that the model sentence did not apply. She responded in a normal, colloquial style. The second sentence presented difficulties for her in carrying out sentence embedding. She obviously understood the model but could only repeat the semantic content encoded in each underlying sentence separately. Thus, the girl actually disembedded the sentences and produced them in conjoined form, a structure well handled at this stage.

The child's attempt to imitate the third model failed because she did not understand the relations of complex clauses. She merely extracted content words (boy, book, crying) and repeated them without changing their order but did not express underlying semantic roles. One difference between the second and third sentences is that the relative pronoun *who* occurs in the former, providing a clue about underlying structure. It alerts hearers to the existence of an embedded relative clause. In contrast, the third sentence lacks this signal and instead presents a young speaker/hearer with only a string of words.

A significant phenomenon occurring in all imitation-response elicitations is that children do not imitate on demand any linguistic structures that they do not produce spontaneously in their own speech. Thus, there is a lag in expression despite ability to comprehend meaning. Even directed attempts by caregivers in natural settings to "correct" a child's speech fail if they conflict with the child's own grammar. Note the following mother–child exchange as evidence (McNeill 1966:69):

CHILD:	Nobody don't like me.
MOTHER:	No, say "nobody likes me."
CHILD:	Nobody don't like me.
	(Eight repetitions of this dialogue)
MOTHER:	No, now listen carefully; say "nobody likes me."
CHILD:	Oh! Nobody don't likes me.

Examples such as this, as well as those elicited in testing, demonstrate that children do not mimic adults in acquiring language but develop their own grammars. Children refine their grammars by discarding some rules and altering applications of others until they finally arrive at appropriate constructions. But throughout, it is a creative process of observation and production, consistent with maturing cognitive capacities.

In addition to acquiring the sounds, words, and grammatical rules of their language, children need to learn appropriate discourse patterns. Discourse rules are both linguistic and extra-linguistic. That is, discourse consists of ties created among utterances, referring back to previous speech (anaphoric reference) and forward to anticipated speech (cataphoric reference). In addition, discourse consists of linkages between speech and nonlinguistic context, including relations among participants, goals of speakers, and cultural models or schema of communicative interactions. Studies investigating children's acquisition of these complex discourse rules will be explored further in the following chapter.

COMPARATIVE EVIDENCE

Although researchers concerned with language acquisition accept the notion that children learn through growth of universal cognitive processes, each language presents its own specific structure to be deciphered and reproduced. Studies of many distinct languages confirm hypotheses about universal tendencies but also reveal significant differences in rates of acquisition of various surface phenomena. In this section we review some relevant research in order to understand both universal and unique processes better.

Complex Inflectional Systems

As we have already seen, noun and verb inflections are not included in a child's earliest words. Children first recognize and reproduce the unvarying parts of words (stems or roots), omitting variable segments (affixes). Inflectional affixes are confusing to a child because their occurrence on a word depends on semantic roles intended by a speaker; they are not obvious attributes of objects or events. Affixes are omitted because children do not attend to grammatical content and also because a child's simple words are usually understood by her or his caregivers in contexts of ongoing experience. Later, as children become aware of underlying semantic relations, they begin to learn that inflectional affixes express critical concepts.

Many languages have complex inflectional systems that present problems for learners in sorting their forms and meanings. Russian and other languages within the Slavic family are examples of this type of language. As shown in Chapter 2, Russian nouns are marked for each of six cases: nominative (subject), genitive (possession), dative (indirect object), accusative (direct object), locative, and instrumental. Case suffixes are also differentiated for two numbers (singular and plural) and three genders (masculine, feminine, and neuter). To complicate matters even further, some suffixes have several allomorphs, conditioned by the shapes of noun stems. Finally, some sounds or combinations of sounds signal multiple case and/or gender and/or number combinations—for example, /-a/ marks feminine singular nominative, masculine singular genitive, neuter singular genitive, neuter plural nominative, and neuter plural accusative.

At first, children omit all case distinctions, using nominative forms in every context (Slobin 1966:136). According to Gvozdev's longitudinal study of his son (cited in Slobin 1966), case suffixes did not appear until age 1 year, 10 months. But then rapid acquisition occurred. In only one month, the boy employed nominative/accusative and gender markers in addition to number and some special diminutive suffixes. Verb inflections for tense also appeared in this same period of morphological blossoming. As Slobin remarked, "Once the principles of inflection and derivation are acquired, the principle is immediately applied over a wide range of types" (ibid.).

Just as an English-speaking child overgeneralizes number and tense inflections, a Russian child similarly applies some case suffixes beyond their appropriate scope. Russian children select the case marker having the most consistent form and the least number of functions. For instance, examine the following suffixes for singular nominative and accusative cases, distinguished for three genders and for animate/inanimate masculines (Slobin 1979:95).

Notice that three of the accusative suffixes have shapes similar to other endings (e.g., {-a}: masculine animate accusative/feminine nominative; {-o}: neuter nominative or accusative; masculine nominative/masculine inanimate accusative). Only one suffix, {-u}, has a uniquely accusative function. Therefore, this is the suffix that children seize upon and generalize for all nouns in the accusative case. It is the one with the clearest stable semantic content.

	Masculine—			
	Animate	**Inanimate**	**Neuter**	**Feminine**
Nominative	ø	ø	-o	-a
Accusative	-a	ø	-o	-u

In a similar process, once instrumental suffixes are learned, children overgeneralize again, this time choosing the masculine/neuter singular suffix {-*om*} to apply to all nouns because this phonological shape has only one other function, whereas the feminine singular instrumental, {-*oy*}, marks five additional semantic roles (Slobin 1966:138).

Russian children first acquire those inflectional suffixes expressing the most concrete semantic content. Number is learned before any of the case markers. Nominative/accusative patterns are acquired next, probably because this distinction reflects a basic dichotomization of action, from agent to acted-upon. Other cases are then added. The last category to be learned is gender, probably because it is the most abstract of the grammatical concepts involved in Russian inflection. It is an arbitrary classification of nouns, having nothing to do with actual perception or experience.

Agglutinating Languages

In agglutinating languages, many morphemes are combined in one word, which can potentially result in long sequences. But rather than presenting unusual difficulties (as an English speaker might assume from the length of words), such languages actually seem to promote easier learning. Turkish is a good example of a highly regular agglutinating language. For instance, note the following list of case inflections applying to nouns in Turkish (Slobin 1982:150):

Nominative	ø
Genitive	-in / -ʌn / -ün / -un
Accusative	-i / -ʌ / -ü / -u
Instrumental/comitative	-le / -la
Dative	-e / -a
Locative	-de / -da
Ablative	-den / -dan

Allomorphic rules selecting variants of suffixes are based on only two principles of vowel conditioning (vowel harmony) and are applied consistently. The vowel in stems determines vowels in suffixes. Genitive and accusative suffixes have four allomorphs, varying with four vowels, conditioned by principles of front/back location and of rounding/unrounding. These allomorphs are affected by the following rules:

Vowel in Stem	**Vowel in Suffix**
Front unrounded	i
Front rounded	ü
Back unrounded	ʌ
Back rounded	u

The four remaining cases contain e/a vowels, based solely on a front/back dichotomy. Stems with front vowels select suffixes with /e/; stems with back vowels select suffixes with /a/, as in these examples:

ev-	ev-im	ev-ler-im	ev-ler-im-ı
house	house-my	house-plural-my	house-pl.-my-accusative
house	my house	my houses	my houses (direct object)

According to Slobin, the entire system of noun inflections, including case, number, and possession, as well as much of verb morphology marking subject and tense, is acquired "well before the age of two" (ibid.). Recall that this is the age at which a Russian-learning child is just beginning to use case suffixes. Slobin suggested that several factors contribute to easy acquisition of Turkish: Each suffix has one distinct grammatical role (there are no homonyms); noun and verb paradigms are regular, without exceptions; allomorphs are also conditioned by regular rules; the same set of case suffixes is applied consistently to several word classes; and each suffix has a unique semantic content so that two or more meanings are never collapsed into one form.

Turkish word order is usually SOV (subject + object + verb), but order is not fixed because the inflectional system indicates a noun's grammatical role. Words are shifted within sentences to focus on a particular element. Difficulties in acquiring syntax seem to emerge with more complex sentence types, particularly those requiring embedding of relative clauses (ibid.:166).

Research in learning other agglutinating languages indicates similar developmental processes. In a study of children acquiring Tamil, a Dravidian language spoken in southern India, Parimala Raghavendra and Laurence Leonard (1989) focused on the use of verb inflections by young speakers, ages from 2;2 (2 years, 2 months) to 2;7. In Tamil, verbs are inflected for tense (past, present, future); several aspects and moods; and also for person (first, second, third), number (singular, plural), and gender for third person (masculine, feminine). Inflectional suffixes are highly regular; for example, present tense is always {-r}, past {-nd}, future {-v}. Person markers are likewise regular. Only neuter singular has some variation.

Raghavendra and Leonard found that children, even the youngest at just over 2 years, applied rules correctly in nearly all instances. The only suffix whose correct appearance did not reach at least 90 percent of possible occurrences was the third-person singular feminine. This suffix has the shape {-a:}, which is identical in sound to two other Tamil suffixes and therefore is the only one not having a unique meaning (ibid.:320). But even the feminine marker was used correctly in 73 to 87 percent of its potential occurrences, indicating that it too was acquired with little difficulty.

Raghavendra and Leonard concluded that, in addition to structural regularity of Tamil's inflectional system, ordering of suffixes attached to stems promotes easy acquisition. That is, they "follow the stem in order of decreasing relevance to the inherent meaning of the stem: verb + tense/aspect + person + number + gender. There is semantic clarity in semantic mapping in Tamil" (ibid.:321). Structural and semantic properties present a conceptually orderly system.

Polysynthetic Languages

Polysynthetic languages differ significantly from other types. They share with agglutinating languages the characteristic of including many kinds of meanings and grammatical forms within a single word, but, in contrast, their affixes are not easily segmented. Several markers collapse into one form that may or may not retain any overt trace of its origin. In addition, each affix can have numerous allomorphs, some of which may be phonologically conditioned, whereas others must be learned separately for specific stems. Thus, these languages present problems for children that are not encountered by learners of morphologically simpler systems.

PRT	TRANS	PAST	DU	FUT	REP	PRO	RFL	NOUN	VERB
COIN				OPT	CIS		SRF	ROOT	ROOT
CONTR									
NEG									

→

←

REV	CAUS	INST	DAT	DIST	DISL	HAB	FORMER PAST
INCH							CONT
						STAT	REMOTE PAST
							PROG
						PUNC	

Abbreviations:

PRT	partitive	REP	repetitive	DAT	dative
COIN	coincident	CIS	cislocative	DIST	distributive
CONTR	contrastive	PRO	pronoun	DISL	dislocative
NEG	negative	RFL	reflexive	HAB	habitual aspect
TRANS	translocative	SRF	semi-reflexive	STAT	stative aspect
PAST	past tense	REV	reversive	PUNC	punctual aspect
DU	dualic	INCH	inchoative	CONT	continuative
FUT	future tense	CAUS	causative	PROG	progressive
OPT	optative	INST	instrumental		

FIGURE 7.2   Morphological Structure of Mohawk Verbs. (Mithun, Marianne. 1989. The acquisition of polysynthesis. *Journal of Child Language* 16:285–312)

Mohawk is a polysynthetic, fusional language with complex verb morphology. Verbs contain a large number of prefixes and suffixes having many different kinds of meanings and grammatical functions. The chart in Figure 7.2 indicates structural possibilities. As can be seen, this verbal system creates complexity in terms of both length of words and proliferation of semantic categories.

Data on the acquisition of Mohawk have been obtained by a longitudinal study of one boy, beginning at age 2;10 and ending at age 4;1 (Feurer 1980a, 1980b) and by brief observations of five children ranging in age from 1;9 to 4;9 (Mithun 1989). First, because of the length of Mohawk words and children's early inability to produce long sequences, a strategy for word reduction was employed. It was based on reproducing only the stressed syllable of adult words. In Mohawk, most words are stressed on the penultimate (next to last) syllable, and this is the one that appeared in the speech of the youngest child, age 1;9. By age 2;10, two-syllable words occurred, containing the stressed and following syllables (Feurer 1980a:120):

kí:ra	reduced from	*~Çkhnekí:ra*[?]	(I will drink liquid)
sé:ra	reduced from	*~Çyethiyatk~Ç[?]sé:ra*	(I will see her)

In the first verb, the child by chance reproduced part of the stem, but in the second example, stress falls on a suffix. Thus, children's speech is not based on the most informative part of words but rather on their acoustic and phonological properties.

After the two-syllable stage, children expand their verbs by moving toward beginnings of words. They first discover the category of pronoun prefixes, the only category that must occur in all verbs. These prefixes often immediately precede verb stems, although other morphemes may intervene. In any case, once children begin to distinguish the pronoun system, they acquire it fairly rapidly. Subject and object pronouns are learned first, followed by transitive markers indicating co-occurences of subject and object, for example, "I to him," "she to us" (ibid.:125). Within the category of grammatical person, first and second are distinguished earliest, followed by third person (Feurer 1980b:35). Mohawk third person is the most complex morphologically and semantically because it also expresses gender (masculine, feminine/indefinite, and feminine/neuter).

Children gradually acquire numerous optional affixes expressing complex grammatical meanings. The boy in Feurer's study did not attempt to combine as many as three prefixes in one verb until age 3;8 (1980a:125). Children observed by Mithun also advanced from ends to beginnings of words and from the most frequent and semantically obvious affixes to those more complex in form and function.

When compared with children learning Turkish or Tamil, these Mohawk speakers seem to take a longer time to acquire fully the verbal affixes of their language. Once they begin to use the markers, however, they make very few errors of overgeneralization or confusion of forms (Feurer 1980b:33; Mithun 1989:311). These comments confirm the obvious point that no language can be too complex for its speakers to learn, or, from the other view, every child is innately equipped to decipher whatever complexity a natural language presents.

SOME UNIVERSAL SEQUENCES

Negation

The research by Klima and Bellugi (1966) showed that children's negative constructions begin with Neg + S and end with appropriate application of English transformations. Similar patterns have been documented in other languages. In Russian, adult grammar usually expresses negative propositions with double negation, employing the independent word *nyet* "no" + negative particle *ni* prefaced to a following pronoun or verb, as in *nyet nikavo* "not no-one" (there is no one) or *nyet ni dam* "no, not I-will-give" (I won't give). In the earliest learning phase, children omit the negative particle *ni,* using only the word *nyet* at beginnings of sentences, as in *nyet kavo* and *nyet dam* (Slobin 1966:133).

Children learning Japanese use similar procedures, beginning by using the independent word *nai* as a constant marker of negation. Later, they incorporate negation within sentences themselves, eventually developing the adult system that includes the words *iya* and *iiya* in addition to *nai* (McNeill and McNeill 1968:53–54). Children acquire negative markers in a sequence related to their cognitive function. They learn the proper forms as they are able to understand and express underlying concepts and relations. Examples follow (ibid.:60–61):

1. *nai* (adjective); existence/nonexistence:
   There's not an apple here.
2. *nai* (auxiliary); truth/falsity:
   That's not an apple.

3. *iya;* disapproval or rejection:
No, I don't want an apple.
4. *iiya;* entailment/nonentailment:
No, I didn't have an apple; I had a pear.

Children learning the polysynthetic language Mohawk follow processes found in other types of systems. Feurer noted that her subject first employed separate words *yah* "no" (reduced from *iyah*) and *tosa* "don't" (reduced from *tohsa*) prefaced to otherwise affirmative statements. Adult speech marks negation with these words plus a negative prefix attached to verbs. Although Feurer's subject began expressing negation at age 2;10, he did not incorporate negative markers into verbs until age 3;5 (1980a:127). Similarly, among Mithun's subjects, only the oldest child (4;9) used appropriate negation (1989:306).

Wh-Questions

Studies of acquisition of wh-questions in several languages support claims about universal sequences in their development. Children start by employing independent question words at the beginning of declarative sentences (wh + S) and later progress to more complex interrogative structures.

The most striking regularity, though, is the semantic sequencing of wh-propositions. Data from the acquisition of wh-questions in English, German, Serbo-Croatian, Japanese, and Korean show that propositions learned first are "what" and "where," followed closely by "who." The last concepts to emerge are "why" and "when" (Clancy 1989:327, 329).

Age at emergence of various concepts also seems to be roughly comparable for all languages studied. Children learn "what" and "where" questions before the age of 2; "who" questions usually appear by age 2;6, with some variations both earlier and later. Finally, "when" and "why" seem to be most problematic, often not emerging until well beyond the third year (ibid.). Feurer's study of a Mohawk child confirms this pattern. In fact, although the boy expressed "what" and "who" questions by age 2;8, he had not acquired "how" or "why" propositions by the end of the field study, age 4;1 (1980a:128).

Patricia Clancy suggested that cross-linguistic similarities are due to universal cognitive processes in comprehending concepts underlying wh-propositions (1989:337). "What" and "where" questions relate to objects and people in a child's physical sensory experience, referring to his immediate world. They require only that children be able to form and remember mental representations of objects. "What is" simply elicits a label for an object or activity, whereas "where is" depends on an additional ability to understand placement of objects and people in space. Concepts underlying "how," "why," and "when" are more abstract. They involve "notions of means/manner, causality and temporality" (ibid.).

Locative Concepts

Locative expressions refer to placement of objects, persons, and/or events in space or time. According to Dan Slobin, emergence of various locative concepts is based on their cognitive complexity. The concepts are listed below in order of their postulated development (cited in Slobin 1982:160):

IN/ON/UNDER: containment/support/occlusion
BESIDE: spatial proximity
BACK(i)/FRONT(i): proximity to objects with inherent backs and fronts (e.g., cars, houses, people)

BETWEEN: coordinates two proximity relations
BACK/FRONT: proximity to objects without inherent backs and fronts (e.g., trees, blocks, drinking glasses)

Data from acquisition studies of 48 children (aged 2;0–4;4) who spoke either English, Italian, Serbo-Croatian, or Turkish supported the developmental sequence outlined above (Slobin 1982:161). Concepts of IN/ON/UNDER were acquired by approximately 80 to 90 percent of the subjects; BESIDE emerged nearly as often (72 to 79 percent). BETWEEN/BACK(i)/FRONT(i) form the next cluster, handled by roughly 20 to 50 percent of the children. The final concepts to be acquired were the more abstract relational notions of BACK/FRONT (for objects lacking inherent backs and fronts). These were found in the speech of relatively few children by age 4.

In sum, the fact that universal processes affect acquisition of negation, wh-questions, and locatives confirms contentions that language learning is interdependent with cognitive maturation. Because growth in ability to comprehend concepts is a natural development of human minds, it is reasonable to expect that expressing these concepts in language will proceed along a common path for all speakers.

INSTRUCTIONAL STRATEGIES

In all societies, caregivers are involved in the linguistic development of their children. Adults often use strategies to help children acquire language. These strategies accomplish several tasks. First, they function as culturally prescribed frames for language-learning situations, directing a child's attention to language as a focus of interaction. Second, they teach children appropriate norms of communicative behavior. Most of this process is covert, but it may be overtly expressed, as in teaching politeness routines such as "Say 'thank you' to the nice lady." Linguistic instruction, then, contributes to overall socialization. Third, instructional strategies implicitly impart beliefs about the functions of language in social interaction and the goals that can be accomplished through speech. Finally, exchanges between adult and child display affect and involve the two in social interaction that can be entertaining and playful as well as instructive.

Strategies in the United States

In the United States, children are often spoken to in a specialized register, referred to as "baby talk" or "motherese," that consists of simplified sound patterning (especially the elimination of consonant clusters), simplified words (especially the reduplication of syllables), and simplified grammatical structure. Adults often repeat single words or entire phrases when addressing children. In addition, adults, particularly caregivers, speak more slowly, more loudly, with higher pitch and with exaggerated intonation patterns when talking to children (Thomas et al. 2004:126). Children are frequently addressed with terms of endearment (*honey, baby*), diminutive forms of their given names, or pet names. While these practices may appear to indicate a positive cultural assessment of children, they can also be interpreted as demeaning. Children are seen as not fully competent speakers and perhaps as not fully competent persons. Finally, children are typically overlapped, interrupted, or ignored in conversations with adults. And it is striking that there are similar ways of talking and ways of conceptualizing elderly persons as not fully competent (ibid.:125–127).

Caregivers use several instructional techniques in response to children's speech in natural contexts. Adults often repeat children's utterances with an *expansion* of the basic sentence, filling in missing words, as the following examples show (Brown and Bellugi 1968:417):

Child	Mother
Baby highchair	Baby is in the highchair.
Eve lunch	Eve is having lunch.
Throw Daddy	Throw it to Daddy.
Pick glove	Pick the glove up.

In this example, when the mother repeats utterances, she maintains the child's word order. The child uses simple nouns and verbs; the mother then provides grammatical elements, including copulas, pronouns, determiners, and locative prepositions. Expansions direct learners to parts of sentences that they have omitted. Although at this stage of development, children are not able to produce extended sequences, these interactions can form a basis for future acquisition. In addition, these techniques of interacting with children dramatize and demarcate a dichotomy between the statuses of adult and child.

Caregivers also use a technique called *modeling,* commenting on the semantic content of children's words. Here are some examples (Slobin 1968:442):

CHILD:	His name Tony.
ADULT:	That's right.
CHILD:	We got some more.
ADULT:	There's a lot in there.

Expansion and modeling contribute to linguistic development in part by supplying additional words and sentences that children can later use as sources of data. Also, instructional techniques ratify a learner's speech. By accepting what a child has said, adults encourage the child to make further contributions to talk.

These styles of adult–child speech have been observed in interactions in middle-class American families. They are based on cultural assumptions that children need to be carefully instructed and socialized and that caregivers have a duty to teach language and conversational skills. These attitudes are not held by all Americans, however. For instance, in a study of adults' interaction with children in a lower-class African-American community in rural Louisiana, Martha Ward (1971) found that adults expect children to naturally learn to speak. In their view, overt adult intervention is not required. Rather than expanding or modeling on children's utterances, adults frequently expanded their own speech, providing both repetitions and alternations in syntax. Repeating and changing syntax indirectly teach children grammatical possibilities. They also demonstrate to a child that dissimilar forms can have similar meanings. Note the following examples of mothers' speech to their children (ibid.:48–49):

MOTHER:	Tell the lady your name.
	What your name?
	Tell Joan what your name.
	Tell her your name.
MOTHER:	What Scott ate today for dinner?
	What you ate for dinner?
	What did you eat for dinner?

Although linguists may debate the relative advantages of each strategy of adult–child verbal interaction, in actual learning processes, none is solely necessary. Children acquire language as long as they are exposed to it in communicative experiences with others. However, specific strategies may be embedded within cultural models of childhood and adulthood. For example, Elinor Ochs suggests that some American strategies, which she characterizes as typical among mainstream, white, middle-class families, are built on principles of "high accommodation" to young children (1992:347). Through these interactional techniques, caregivers (especially mothers) transmit messages that communicate a low opinion of themselves while simultaneously centering on the child. According to Ochs, verbal registers, commonly referred to as "baby talk" or "motherese," simplify speech in order to accommodate the child's level of understanding. Baby talk therefore accommodates children's needs. Adult accommodation is also demonstrated in pseudo-conversations that caregivers have with infants and young children. In these types of conversations, the adult interprets and responds to the gurgling and babbling of the child as though they were actual turn-taking contributions. In addition, when young children attempt to communicate but their words are unintelligible, the adult caregiver will guess at the child's possible meanings. Finally, Ochs describes certain "praising strategies" (ibid.:352) as another indication of child-centered principles. When the child is engaged in an activity that requires assistance, the caregiver responds with aid but typically praises the child for his or her behavior, ignoring the fact that success was a joint accomplishment. The child then constructs an image of him- or herself as more competent than he or she may be while at the same time underrating the competence of the caregiver. Cultural models of gender are also implicated in these behaviors because mothers or other women typically serve as primary caregivers for children.

STRATEGIES IN OTHER SOCIETIES

In this section we briefly review some studies of instructional interactions in other cultures, demonstrating the effectiveness of many different techniques.

Samoans

Samoans, inhabitants of the South Pacific island of Samoa, practice language strategies that contrast with those of mainstream, white, middle-class Americans because they do not accommodate children but rather expect children to learn accommodate to others. Such accommodation is consistent with Samoan etiquette appropriate to hierarchical relationships (Ochs 1992). In Samoan society, lower-status people accommodate to those of higher status. Social rank and seniority are the two principal criteria determining status, and children are inherently of lower status than their caregivers. These principles affect the interactional strategies that adults employ with children. In contrast to mainstream American norms, preverbal Samoan children are not treated as co-participants in conversations. Adults do not engage in pseudo-conversations with young children but wait for the child to develop linguistic skills that enable them to engage in meaningful conversations. In addition, a child's unintelligible utterances are either ignored or noted as unintelligible (ibid.:351–352). And finally, when adults engage in activities with children where success is jointly accomplished, Samoan praising strategies are typically "bidirectional" (ibid.:354). That is, one of the participants generally uses the expression "Maaloo!" (Well done!); the second participant then repeats this phrase, directed at the original speaker, overtly recognizing and signaling their joint endeavor.

Samoan strategies, like those of Americans, are embedded in cultural models of interaction. Whereas American strategies focus on the individual, Samoan etiquette stresses cooperation and people's familial and societal interdependence.

Kaluli

The Kaluli, a small horticultural community of 1,200 people living in New Guinea, believe that it is necessary to begin teaching language to young children as soon as they say their first words. In the Kaluli view, infants are "soft" and need "hardening" or "firming up" of both their physical and mental attributes (Schieffelin 1987:256). Although adults believe that children learn most behavior by observing others, they feel that language must be directly taught or "shown" to a child. Adults teach children with routines that encourage them to repeat adult utterances. An adult makes a statement, followed by the imperative *elema* "say like that." Children are expected to respond with the adult's model sentence. This type of exchange is often used when another person is present. Caregivers tell children what to say to others, thereby teaching norms of communicative interaction.

Elema routines are used by caregivers (usually mothers) with both boys and girls until children are about 3 years old. Differences exist between girls' and boys' participation in *elema* routines. Because girls are socialized very early to take on caregiving responsibilities, they initiate *elema* routines with their mothers. Girls as young as 28 months prompt with *elema* "say like that" and their mothers repeat (ibid.:258). Young girls also use these routines while teaching even younger siblings. Because boys are not expected to be caregivers to children, they do not engage in *elema* routines as initiators but only as recipients. Finally, these routines teach children to respond appropriately with compliance to their caregivers' requests, therefore teaching social as well as linguistic messages.

Kwara'ae

Among the Kwara'ae, people living in the Solomon Islands in Melanesia, a different set of routines is used in intensive teaching of language. Kwara'ae adults begin talking to infants and including them in conversations. Because babies cannot talk, adults speak for them by "translating" their babbling into Kwara'ae words (Watson-Gegeo and Gegeo 1986:18). By the age of 9 or 10 months, various routines are directed to children until they reach their third or fourth year. A common routine involves *calling out* (ibid.:19). This strategy teaches linguistic form and communicative style. Adults instruct children to *ako uana* "call out" to someone, providing the child with sentences to repeat. Children as young as 18 months are able to produce the expected responses.

Adults frequently employ calling-out routines with children to give messages, directives, and instructions to other people. For example, note the following exchange (translated into English) between an adult and a 3-year-old child (ibid.:21–22):

ADULT:	Call out to grandpa.
CHILD:	Grandpa!
ADULT:	"The rice is done now."
CHILD:	The rice is done now.
ADULT:	"Come and eat rice."
CHILD:	Come and eat rice.

Another instructional technique used by Kwara'ae caregivers is that of *repeating routines,* initiated by the word *uri,* "like this," followed by propositions to be repeated. This routine is first used to teach politeness formulas, such as greetings and farewells (ibid.:25). Adults praise children when they repeat correctly in order to encourage them to learn. Linguistic skills and social etiquette are taught through repeating adult models. In the following routine, an older sister instructs her 27-month-old brother (ibid.:29–30):

SISTER:	Then when you're full, you just speak like this, "I don't want any more now." "I don't want to eat any more now."
CHILD:	I don't want?
SISTER:	Then you just speak as I said, like this, "I don't want any more now."
CHILD:	I don't want.
SISTER:	"I'm full now."
CHILD:	Full now.
SISTER:	"I'm full, I don't want to eat any more now."
CHILD:	Don't want to eat any more now.
SISTER:	Then you speak like this, "Put it away now." Then speak like this, "Put the stew away now."

Repeating routines are often used when a third person is present in order to teach children how to make requests, give directives, or convey information. Children are told to repeat a message intended for another person present. As among the Kaluli, Kwara'ae children's compliance with these routines is often used by adults to accomplish their own communicative goals, particularly those of asking favors or expressing opinions because explicit statement of these speech acts by adults is considered inappropriate. In these interactions, children are employed as surrogates by adults in accomplishing sensitive goals.

Basotho

The Basotho, the people of Lesotho, an independent country surrounded by South Africa, believe that children must be taught directly so that they will learn to speak properly. Importance of speech is reflected in a Basotho proverb: "A quiet person will perish" (Demuth 1986:54).

Various kinds of *prompting routines* are used in different contexts. Three common prompts are *ere* "say," *echo* "say so," and *juetse* "tell." They can be used separately or together in a single utterance, for instance (ibid.:58):

ere	m-phe	ntho	ena,	*echo,*	mo	*juetse*
say	me-give	thing	this,	say so,	her	tell
Say	"Give me	this thing,"		say so,	tell her.	—

In this example, an adult interprets a child's desires, and, through the prompting routine, ratifies the child's rights. Prompts also teach verbal skills for asking questions and making requests. They are especially helpful in instructing children to express polite forms of address and formulas for greetings. And, as in other cultures, Basotho adults use prompting routines with children as intermediaries to transmit messages to other people. In doing so, adults accomplish their own purposes, but they also teach children norms of proper communicative behavior. As Katherine Demuth remarked, through prompting "social competence is realized as verbal competence" (ibid.:78).

Summary

Acquisition of language involves a number of complex processes. It is inherently interrelated with cognitive development. Language learning proceeds through stages of growth beginning with a child's first awareness that sounds made by others have meaning and that speech can be used to facilitate social interaction. As children develop, they realize that various personal goals are accomplished through language: They can enlist others in satisfying their needs and wants (imperative function), they can convey information (referential function), they can express thoughts and feelings (expressive function), and they can entertain and amuse themselves and others (creative function).

Children begin learning to form sounds and control pitch, rhythm, and volume. They then produce comprehensible words that at first are highly context-bound, referring to multiple aspects of ongoing experience. Later, as children are able to express increasingly complex concepts, their speech becomes free from immediate contexts and can be used for a wider range of functions in varied social situations.

Children in all cultures, learning the language of their society, proceed through similar stages of linguistic and cognitive development. Although languages with different types of morphological and syntactic structures present different kinds of problems for novices, no language presents insurmountable difficulties. All languages are acquired in more or less similar sequences during approximately the same time periods.

Although children acquire language through growth of their own innate cognitive and linguistic skills, adults are involved in the process overtly and covertly as instructors and guides. Caregivers in different cultures employ a variety of strategies to help young learners. These strategies often include explicit routines that teach linguistic structures, cultural norms of communicative behavior, and ideologies about language and its interactional functions.

References

ANTINUCCI, F., AND D. PARISI. 1973. Early language acquisition: A model and some data. In *Studies in Child Language Development,* ed. C. Ferguson and D. Slobin. New York: Holt, Rinehart & Winston, pp. 607–619.

BELLUGI, URSULA. 1964. The emergence of inflections and negation systems in the speech of two children. *Paper presented at New England Psychological Association.* City, ST: New England Psychological Association.

BELLUGI, URSULA. 1968. Linguistic mechanisms underlying child speech. In *Proceedings of the Conference on Language and Language Behavior,* ed. E. M. Zale. New York: Appleton Century Crofts, pp. 36–50.

BERKO, JEAN. 1958. The child's learning of English morphology. *Word* 14:150–177.

BRAINE, MARTIN. 1963. The ontogeny of English phrase structure. *Language* 39:1–13.

BROWN, ROGER, AND URSULA BELLUGI. 1968. Three processes in the child's acquisition of syntax. In *Contemporary Issues in Developmental Psychology,* ed. N. S. Endler et al. New York: Holt, Rinehart & Winston, pp. 411–424.

BROWN, ROGER, COURTNEY CAZDEN, AND URSULA BELLUGI. 1968. The child's grammar from I to III. In *The 1967 Minnesota Symposium on Child Psychology,* ed. J. P. Hill. Minneapolis, MN: University of Minnesota Press, pp. 28–73.

CHOMSKY, NOAM. 1965. *Aspects of the Theory of Syntax.* Cambridge, MA: MIT Press.

CLANCY, PATRICIA. 1989. Form and function in the acquisition of Korean wh-questions. *Journal of Child Language* 16:323–347.

CLARK, EVE. 1982. The young word maker: A case study of innovation in the child's lexicon. In *Language Acquisition: The State of the Art,* ed. E. Wanner and L. R. Gleitman. New York: Cambridge University Press, pp. 390–425.

DEMUTH, KATHERINE. 1986. Prompting routines in the language socialization of Basotho children. In *Language Socialization Across Cultures,* ed. B. Schieffelin and E. Ochs. New York: Cambridge University Press, pp. 51–79.

ERVIN, SUSAN. 1964. Imitation and structural change in children's language. In *New Directions in the Study of Language,* ed. E. Lenneberg. Cambridge, MA: MIT Press, pp. 163–189.

FEURER, HANNY. 1980a. The acquisition of Mohawk: Preliminary observations of first language development. *Studies on Iroquoian Culture* 6:119–130.

FEURER, HANNY. 1980b. Morphological development in Mohawk. In *Papers and Reports on Child Language Development,* No. 18. Stanford, CA: Stanford University Press, pp. 25–42.

FRY, D. B. 1966. The development of the phonological system in the normal and the deaf child. In *The Genesis of Language,* ed. F. Smith and G. Miller. Cambridge, MA: MIT Press, pp. 187–206.

GREENFIELD, PATRICIA, AND J. H. SMITH. 1976. *The Structure of Communication in Early Language Development.* New York: Academic Press.

HUTTENLOCHER, JANELLEN, AND PATRICIA SMILEY. 1987. Early word meanings: The case of object names. *Cognitive Psychology* 19:63–89.

JAKOBSON, ROMAN. 1941 (1968). *Child Language, Aphasia and General Sound Laws.* The Hague: Mouton.

JAKOBSON, ROMAN, AND MORRIS HALLE. 1956. *Fundamentals of Language.* The Hague: Mouton.

KLIMA, EDWARD, AND URSULA BELLUGI. 1966. Syntactic regularities in the speech of children. In *Psycholinguistic Papers,* ed. J. Lyons and R. Wales. Edinburgh: Edinburgh University Press, pp. 183–208.

MCNEILL, DAVID. 1966. Developmental psycholinguistics. In *The Genesis of Language,* ed. F. Smith and G. Miller. Cambridge, MA: MIT Press, pp. 15–84.

MCNEILL, DAVID. 1970. *The Acquisition of Language.* New York: Harper & Row.

MCNEILL, DAVID. 1987. *Psycholinguistics: A New Approach.* New York: Harper & Row.

MCNEILL, DAVID, AND N. MCNEILL. 1968. What does a child mean when he says "no"? In *Language and Language Behavior,* ed. E. M. Zale. New York: Appleton Century Crofts, pp. 51–62.

MITHUN, MARIANNE. 1989. The acquisition of polysynthesis. *Journal of Child Language* 16:285–312.

OCHS, ELINOR. 1992. Indexing gender. In *Rethinking Context,* ed. A. Duranti and C. Goodwin. New York: Cambridge University Press, pp. 335–358.

PIAGET, JEAN. 1955. *The Language and Thought of the Child.* Cleveland, OH: Meridian Books, World Publishing Company.

RAGHAVENDRA, PARIMALA, AND L. LEONARD. 1989. The acquisition of agglutinating languages: Converging evidence from Tamil. *Journal of Child Language* 16:313–322.

SACHS, J. S., AND L. TRUSWELL. 1976. Comprehension of two-word instructions by children in the one-word stage. In *Papers and Reports on Child Language Development,* No. 12. Stanford, CA: Stanford University Press, pp. 212–220.

SCHIEFFELIN, BAMBI. 1987. Do different worlds mean different words? An example from Papua New Guinea. In *Language, Gender and Sex in Comparative Perspective,* ed. S. Philips, S. Steele, and C. Tanz. New York: Cambridge University Press, pp. 249–260.

SLOBIN, DAN. 1966. The acquisition of Russian as a native language. In *The Genesis of Language,* ed. F. Smith and G. Miller. Cambridge, MA: MIT Press, pp. 129–148.

SLOBIN, DAN. 1968. Imitation and grammatical development in children. In *Contemporary Issues in Developmental Psycholinguistics,* ed. N. S. Endler and H. Osser. New York: Holt, Rinehart & Winston, pp. 437–443.

SLOBIN, DAN. 1979. *Psycholinguistics,* 2nd ed. Glenview, IL: Scott, Foresman.

SLOBIN, DAN. 1982. Universal and particular in the acquisition of language. In *Language Acquisition: The State of the Art,* ed. E. Wanner and L. R. Gleitman. New York: Cambridge University Press, pp. 128–170.

SLOBIN, DAN, AND C. WELSH. 1973. Elicited imitation as a research tool in developmental psycholinguistics. In *Studies in Child Language Development,* ed. C. Ferguson and D. Slobin. New York: Holt, Rinehart & Winston, pp. 485–497.

THOMAS, LINDA, ISHTLA SINGH, AND JEAN PECCEI. 2004. *Language, Society, and Power,* 2nd ed. New York: Routledge.

VYGOTSKY, LEV. 1962. *Thought and Language.* Cambridge, MA: MIT Press.

VYGOTSKY, LEV. 1978. *Mind and Society: The Development of Higher Mental Processes.* Cambridge, MA: Harvard University Press.

WARD, MARTHA. 1971. *Them Children: A Study in Language Learning.* New York: Holt, Rinehart & Winston.

WATSON-GEGEO, KAREN, AND DAVID GEGEO. 1986. Calling-out and repeating routines in Kwara'ae children's language socialization. In *Language Socialization Across Cultures,* ed. B. Schieffelin and E. Ochs. New York: Cambridge University Press, pp. 17–50.

WEIR, RUTH. 1966. Some questions on the child's learning of phonology. In *The Genesis of Language,* ed. F. Smith and G. Miller. Cambridge, MA: MIT Press, pp. 153–168.

CHAPTER 8

The Acquisition of Communicative Competence

Compare the following two dialogues. The first is an interaction between a Japanese mother and her child (translated into English):

ADULT:	What color is this?
CHILD:	No!
MOTHER:	What are you saying! You should say, "Green."
CHILD:	Green.
MOTHER:	There is no one who says things like "No!"

The second dialogue occurred between two 13-year-old boys in Philadelphia, talking about slings they were making for a slingshot fight:

TOKAY:	All right we got enough already.
MICHAEL:	No—man! *You* must be *crazy. Must* be. Talking about I got *enough.* Boy. You must—I *know* you have never played *now.* Thinkin I got *enough.* Man you need three *thousand* to have *enough.*

Both these dialogues serve to teach children how to behave with others. In the first, the Japanese mother teaches her child to comply with other people and to avoid direct refusals or rejections. These behaviors are consistent with Japanese norms that stress harmony and agreement in social relations. In the second dialogue, Michael uses insults to emphasize disagreement and to question the competence of his companion.

Through interactions with parents and peers, children acquire *communicative competence,* that is, the ability to function according to cultural models for communicative behavior. In this chapter, we focus on children's acquisition of competence as speakers and listeners. We examine research concerned with learning different stylistic strategies. These strategies reflect cultural beliefs about the ways people can use language to achieve communicative goals, for example, issuing directives, reaching agreement, and expressing opinions. Cross-cultural studies enhance our understanding of the diversity of methods employed to obtain desired results.

ACQUIRING COMMUNICATIVE STYLES

Language fulfills diverse functions either separately or simultaneously. M. A. K. Halliday observed that "language is, for the child, a rich and adaptable instrument for the realization of [his or her] intentions" (1973:2). As children mature and have varied social experiences, they develop models of language based on its social functions. In Halliday's terms, these models are the following (ibid.:3–8):

Instrumental: Getting things done, satisfying needs.

Regulatory: Controlling others, giving instructions.

Interactional: Establishing and maintaining social interactions, defining and consolidating groups.

Personal: Expressing one's individuality, emotions, and thoughts.

Heuristic: Exploring one's environment, learning about the world, questioning others, and gaining information.

Imaginative: Creating and expressing one's fantasies about oneself, others, and the world.

Representational: Communicating about ideas, conveying messages.

Although these functions of language are universal, methods of achieving them differ in both linguistic form and cultural style. Children acquire communicative behavior through the course of daily experience. Direct instruction or correction is sometimes formalized, as in prompting or repeating routines. Children also extrapolate cultural norms from caregivers' responses to them. And they test their understanding when interacting with others, eventually developing competence in communicative behavior. This competence includes knowledge of how to express intentions in various linguistic forms provided by one's language. For example, one needs to learn appropriate means for issuing commands in different social contexts, whether with bald imperatives, mitigated or embedded directives, or hints. In addition, competence includes knowledge of how to assert one's rights and to respond to the rights of others. Finally, people become sensitive to social distinctions in their community and apply this awareness by choosing among styles of communication.

Learning Politeness

Each culture socializes its members to display behaviors that reflect values it upholds. Although some basic themes are universal, they receive different emphases among various peoples. For instance, research concerned with ideals of communicative style in Japan reveals the importance of *omoiyari,* or empathy with others (Clancy 1986:214). Speakers and listeners join in negotiating responses to each other's feelings, attitudes, and needs. Indirect expression is favored over explicit statements of opinions and wants. Both speakers and hearers help achieve harmonious relations. Speakers must learn to be sensitive to feelings (or "face") of addressees and to be aware of how their statements might affect others. People learn to express their own attitudes ambiguously to avoid potential conflict. Listeners also have a responsibility in negotiating harmony.

They must learn to interpret speakers' underlying intentions and opinions from inexplicit surface statements. That is, they come to understand that the surface expression of language may hide the speaker's feelings and intentions and that it is the listener's obligation to decipher these messages.

Japanese caregivers teach communicative skills to children by example and direct admonition. Children's behavior is commented upon and corrected in order to instill virtues of politeness and attentiveness toward others. Adults often appeal to an explicit value system that classifies certain behaviors as acceptable and just and others as deviant. Corrections are also made by reference to people of higher social status. Caregivers teach children that they must be sensitive to interlocutors' wishes and needs as expressed in questions and directives. Lack of response signals self-absorption that, according to Japanese etiquette, is rude. Note the following exchanges documented in Patricia Clancy's study of Japanese families. In the examples, mothers chastised their children for not responding to an adult's questions (ibid.:220–221, 235, 233, 237).

1. (Child, age 2;1, is pretending to eat food from a toy dish)

ADULT:	*Mahochan wa nanika tabeten no? Koko nani ga haitten no?* Are you eating something? What is in there?
CHILD:	[No response]
MOTHER:	*Nani ga haitteru no ka naa. Oneesan nani ga haitten no tte kiiteru yo.* I wonder what could be in there. Older sister is asking "What is in there?"
CHILD:	*Purin.* Pudding.

Consistent with Japanese emphases on learning to interpret others, mothers issued directives with rationales based on their own needs and feelings or attributed wishes to others. A total of 45 percent of mothers' stated rationales were of this type, thus teaching young children to be considerate and responsive.

1. (to child 2;1) *Mama mo nomitai naa.*
Gee, I want to drink too [so give me something to drink].

2. (to child 2;1) *Ano oneechan mo hoshii tte itteru yo.*
That girl is also saying: "I want some."

Because Japanese culture highly values the expression of accommodation and agreement and the avoidance of overt conflict, children are taught to respond positively regardless of their personal inclinations. One of the mother's directives, issued to a child (age 2;0) who had refused to lend his toy to a younger child, not only teaches her child to accede to another's wishes but tells him to make an outright offer of the desired object. And through means of the final tag question, she asks the boy to join with her in an overt positive assessment of the younger baby regardless of his inner feelings:

Dame tte yuu no? Hirochan ni mo doozo tte kashite agenakya. Takusan aru kara, hitotsu doozo tte kashite agenakya. Akachan kawaii deshoo?

Do you say "no"? You must lend one to Hirochan, saying, "Help yourself." The baby is cute/lovable, isn't he?

As in all cultures, certain behaviors are considered appropriate, and deviations from them trigger negative reactions. Japanese mothers often evinced somewhat exaggerated responses to a child's nonconformity: (Child, 2;1, was playing hostess and suddenly began pretending to eat one of the toy dishes).

MOTHER:	*Sonna koto shite osara taberu to okashii deshoo? Osara tabeteru hito inai deshoo? Ne? Osara dare ga tabeteru no?*
	Isn't it strange to do that kind of thing, if you eat a plate? No one eats plates, do they? Who eats plates?
CHILD:	*Kore Mahochan.*
	Maho [child's name] (eats) this.
MOTHER:	*Mahochan ga tabeteru no? Kaijuu mitai. Kowai. Iya. Kowai, obake mitai. Mama obake kirai yo.*
	You're eating it? Like a beast. It's scary. I don't like it. It's scary, like a monster. I hate monsters.

Learning to Express One's Feelings

In contrast to Japanese values, which teach children to guard their feelings and defer to others, Samoan culture encourages discussion and display of emotions, both positive and negative. People openly talk about their own and another's attitudes, reactions, and sentiments. Language and talk are therefore thought of as vehicles for the expression of feelings and attitudes. The Samoan language has numerous methods of indicating speakers' emotions and attitudes, including affect particles or interjections signaling anger, *tae* ("shit"), annoyance, *'isa,* or disapproval, *a'a,* or signaling sympathy, *talofae, ota* (Ochs 1986:260). In addition, Samoan has two sets of personal pronouns, one that is semantically neutral for affect and the other that expresses sympathy for the speaker, hearer, or referent, for example, *a'u* "I," *ta' ita* "poor I" (ibid.:268). Neutral and sympathy articles can also be used to express speakers' attitudes toward referents, for example, *le* neutral article, *si* sympathy ("the dear"; ibid.:263).

Children acquire affect markers early in their linguistic development. They learn particles and pronouns that express sympathy for themselves before those that indicate empathy for others. Children begin to use affect markers, typically by 20 months of age, prior to their use of neutral pronouns or articles, which often emerges three or four months later (ibid.:266–267).

Affect pronouns are frequently used in formulating directives. By stating sympathy for oneself, a speaker elicits empathy from addressees and obtains compliance with her or his request. The following example is illustrative (ibid.:267):

(child, age 2;5, asking mother for water)

mai	ua	vai	deika
bring	question	water	poor me
"bring	water	for	dear me"

Children acquire most of the positive and negative affect markers before the age of 4 (ibid.). Early learning of this system reflects the emphasis in Samoan culture on expressing and discussing emotions. By encouraging addressees to empathize with speakers, people achieve personal goals, especially in reaching consensus of opinion and obtaining compliance with directives.

Learning to Dispute

In some speech communities, conflict is openly displayed. In a study of preadolescents in a working-class African-American neighborhood of Philadelphia, Marjorie Goodwin and Charles Goodwin (1987) found that these children did not avoid conflict by deferring to others or mitigating criticisms but instead frequently engaged in open verbal confrontation.

Like all other interactions, disagreements are rule-governed events. Children tended to use several stylistic patterns in their disputes. Speakers clearly signaled opposition, often at the beginning of their turn, resulting in explicit, unambiguous rejections or refusals. Note the following examples (ibid.:207, 209–210, 212, 218, 233):

EARL (AGE 11):	[asking for rubber bands]: Just two.
DARLENE (10):	No! Y'all losin all my rubber bands up.
EDDIE (12):	You didn't have to go to school today, did you.
TERRI (12):	Yes we *did* have to go to school today!

Children repeated part of a previous speaker's talk as a preface to their opposition, highlighting linguistic elements where disagreements are located:

(on reaching a city creek)

PAM (12):	Y'all gonna walk in it?
NETTIE (11):	*Walk* in it? You know where that water come from? The toilet.

Children also focused on disagreement by repeating linguistic sequences and replacing the locus of a verbal challenge with a correction:

DENIECEY (10):	And that happened last year.
TERRI (12):	That happened *this* year.

In these examples, speakers not only do not mitigate their disagreements with the previous speaker's talk, they also emphasize opposition both by repeating or substituting for the opposed word and by employing strong stress and changes in pitch. These techniques focus on the source of conflict and additionally "call into question the competence" of the previous speaker. "In essence what is opposed is not simply a position but also an actor responsible for stating such a position" (ibid.:208–209).

Speakers question the interlocutor's competence even more overtly by negative characterizations and insults, for example:

MICHAEL (13):	Me and Huey saw—we saw, um, the Witch and the Hangman.
HUEY (14):	The *Hangman* and the *Witch*, knucklehead.

Another linguistic technique that maintains and in fact prolongs contradiction is recycling or repeating challenges:

RAYMOND (10):	Boy, you broke my skate board.
EARL (11):	No I *didn't*.

RAYMOND:	Did *too.*
EARL:	Did *not.*
RAYMOND:	Did *too.*

All these strategies were observed in the speech of both girls and boys. However, some gender differences occurred in topics for dispute and by some styles of confrontation. Boys' arguments typically involved assertions of power and challenges to others (initial talk refers to an incident in which Cameron was reported to have cried because he lost a key):

JOEY (7):	He—he was gettin ready to cry.
CAMERON (6):	But that wasn't mine.
CAMERON:	Mole!
JOEY:	Mole.
CAMERON:	Ah shud up.
JOEY:	Ah shud up.
CAMERON:	*Make* me.
JOEY:	*Make* me!
CAMERON:	Why donchu make me?

In contrast, girls tended not to confront each other directly but to make negative assertions about someone's behavior to a third party. Disputes often took the form of reporting other people's statements, engaging in he-said-she-said arguments (ibid.:230). In the process of reporting previous episodes, speakers attempted to justify their actions or statements and to seek support from co-participants in their dispute with others. The following is an illustrative interaction:

PAM (12):	Terri said you said that I wasn't gonna go around *Poplar* no more.
DARLENE (10):	You *said* you weren't.
NETTIE (11):	She—Terri say—
PAM:	And Terri said that, um, that you said that *Pam* wasn't gonna go around *Poplar* no more.
DARLENE:	That's what Terri said.
PAM:	Well, I *know* what Terri said that you said. She said—She sat there and looked at you. And Terri—And *she* said—And if you have anything to *say* about *me* you come and say it in front of my *face.* And *here* and *right here* you say whatever you got to say cuz *everytime* you go around Poplar you always got something to say.
NETTIE:	Terri *said* it too.
PAM:	And I'm telling Terri *too* that she said it.
DARLENE:	I gotta go somewhere.

These examples illustrate the children's understanding that language can be used simultaneously to question the competence of others explicitly and to assert one's own competence and knowledge implicitly.

LEARNING STATUS AND ROLE

Children learn through socialization that people's rights and obligations differ, depending on their status and the kinds of roles they perform. Status is a concept applying to relations in society, but it is manifested within families as well. In familial interactions, children first become aware of different categories of people based on characteristics such as age and gender. In a society stratified by age, gender, and status, a child eventually learns that social rights are unequally distributed, that certain types of people have more rights or powers than others. Thus, unequal status within families is a reflection of inequality in the larger society. And it is a necessary component in the continual reproduction of social segmentation. People must learn as children how to order themselves hierarchically as adults. Language usage is one means of transmitting this knowledge. Children observe, as onlookers and participants, the varied interactions among family members. They formulate conceptions of themselves and of their place in the world in accordance with cultural models that are enacted on a daily basis in their households.

Status and Role in American English

Communicative competence related to social stratification is acutely displayed in people's rights to speak and obligations to defer to or comply with others. On the basis of age, children have restricted rights and limited ability to control others. Children's lack of power is shown in several ways. First, they are often unsuccessful in getting the attention of adult addressees. This is obviously a critical problem because desired social interaction is blocked without some attentive response by potential co-participants. In a study of language use in family settings, Susan Ervin-Tripp and her co-workers found that when children of age 2 to 4 tried to get the attention of someone already engaged in conversation, they were unsuccessful 94 percent of the time. Older children, age 4 to 7 years, fared somewhat better but still met with overwhelming failure at a rate of 79 percent (1984:124).

Second, children's lack of power is shown by the fact that adults often interrupt their speaking turns. Although our cultural stereotypes portray children as talkative and likely to interrupt others, laboratory and natural observations of familial interactions demonstrate just the opposite. Children are more often interrupted by their parents (Gleason 1987:197). Age, then, confers abilities to demand and maintain the floor. Gender of adult and child also emerges as significant. A number of experimental and home studies indicated that fathers interrupted children more than did mothers, and both parents interrupted daughters more often than sons (ibid.). Children themselves replicate this gender-differentiated pattern quite early. In a study by Anita Esposito, children age 3;6 to 4;8 were observed in male/female encounters; boys interrupted girls twice as frequently as the reverse. In fact, in each of the 10 pairs in Esposito's study, boys were the most frequent interrupters (1979:218).

Esposito's findings on interruption among children differ in an important respect from studies of adults (West and Zimmerman 1983; Zimmerman and West 1975). (See Chapter 10.) Among adults, women tend to become silent when interrupted by men (Zimmerman and West 1975:123), but in Esposito's observations of children, girls did not react to interruptions in this way (1979:219). Young girls appear not to defer to boys to the same extent that women do to men. However, studies of children indicate that even at very early ages, they are already socialized to produce and/or experience unequal encounters.

Power is also displayed in the context of giving and receiving directives. Frequency of issuing directives is correlated with social rights to control others. Linguistic styles chosen to issue commands are sensitive indications of the speaker's rights. Bald imperatives assert power overtly, whereas mitigated expressions, questions, and statements of rationales soften the speaker's control and acknowledge the addressee's feelings, or "face." Studies of parent–child interactions indicate that adults consistently issue more directives to children than they receive. Gender differences are relevant too, especially in the type of directive issued. In studies of behavior in natural home settings, Gleason (1987) found that fathers produced bald imperatives twice as often as did mothers. A total of 38 percent of all fathers' utterances were overt commands. Mothers, in contrast, tended to issue requests with mitigating polite constructions and questions. In laboratory observations, parental gender differences were minimal; fathers evidently were sensitive to the public nature of the context and therefore demonstrated less explicit power (ibid.:195). But in daily encounters, children experienced adults' lack of concern for their autonomy.

Fathers socialize sons into competitive behavior not only by issuing direct imperatives but also by adding threats or insults. Commands such as "Don't go in there again or I'll break your head" and references such as "wise guy" and "nutcake" were addressed to sons (ibid.). These encounters no doubt serve as "training grounds" for boys when they interact with other boys in competitive displays and challenges. Later, when they become parents, they reproduce the same hierarchical system with their children.

Children themselves acquire gender-sensitive patterns for expressing directives. Gleason found that by the age of 4, girls and boys issued directives in a similar style to those given by the same-sex parent (ibid.:198). Susan Ervin-Tripp and her co-workers reported that children recognize addressee's gender because they issued less polite directives to their mothers but made mitigating rationales when making requests of fathers (1984:131).

Results of laboratory studies conducted by Elaine Andersen (1986) revealed children's keen awareness of prerogatives of age and gender. Andersen observed 24 children in play sessions in which 5-year-old subjects were given family-role puppets (Mother, Father, and Baby) and were asked to make up stories, speaking the roles of the characters. In the dialogues, Father-puppets issued direct commands, rarely providing rationales or explanations, whereas Mother-puppets mitigated or explained most of their requests; for example (ibid.:155):

> **MOTHER-PUPPET:**   Gotta get the baby tucked into beddy bye. She's not a sleepy. [To baby] Go to sleep, sleep, sleep, darling. Go to sleep. [Turns to father] Don't you think it's time to go to bed? It's midnight—we should go to bed.

Mothers' and Babies' style of commanding differed from that of Fathers, paralleling Gleason's findings of actual speech behavior. But Mothers and Babies also exhibited contrasts. Mothers commonly phrased indirect commands as hints such as "Dinner's ready" (come and eat) or "Now it's time for your naptime" (go to sleep). Babies employed statements of need to soften their commands: "I need breakfast" or "I want to go to the park and play" (ibid.:159, 156).

Various styles of issuing directives imply differences in the rights of the speaker and the addressee. Bald imperatives assert the speaker's power to control the actions of others. Hints are expressed as declarative propositions that leave open the possibility of compliance or noncompliance with underlying requests. Hints, therefore, are sensitive to the addressee's autonomy. Finally, rationales of needs and wants imply that addressees have some obligations to satisfy speakers, as parents have to care for children.

In another study of experimental play, 5-year-olds were asked to enact roles of doctor and patient (Sachs 1987). Observations of pairs of same-sex children focused on the incidence of "obliges" in children's speech. An *oblige* is a linguistic construction that obligates the addressee to respond. It includes imperatives, prohibitions, directives, and questions. The following are some examples from Sachs (ibid.:182):

Oblige	Example
Imperative	Bring her to the hospital.
Prohibitive	Don't touch it.
Declarative directive	You have to push it.
Pretend directive	Pretend you had a bad cut.
Question directive	Will you be the patient?
Tag question	That's your bed, right?
Joint directive	Now we'll cover him up.
State question	Are you sick?
Information question	What does she need now?
Attentional device	Look it.

Girls and boys expressed obliges with different linguistic structures. The following table presents percentages of each type in children's speech (ibid.).

Percentage of Obliges for Boys and Girls

Category	Boys (%)	Girls (%)
Imperative	25	10
Prohibition	11	2
Declarative directive	6	5
Pretend directive	4	11
Question directive	0	2
Tag question	16	35
Joint directive	3	15
State question	11	2
Information question	22	16
Attentional device	2	2

Girls and boys used approximately the same absolute numbers of obliges (174 and 186, respectively), but differences in stylistic choice are clear. Boys produced more than twice the percentage of unmitigated (direct and overt) obliges that girls did (42 versus 17 percent), whereas girls used mitigated forms (polite, indirect, implied, and explained) nearly twice as often as did boys (65 versus 34 percent; ibid.:183).

    Responses made by recipients of directives have also been studied. Research with four middle-class white families revealed that girls and boys exhibited different kinds of reactions to directives (Ervin-Tripp et al. 1984). Although boys and girls (age 3 and 4 years) complied with directives at approximately the same rate, they used contrasting modes of noncompliance. Boys were more likely than girls to refuse directives overtly (54 percent versus girls' rate of 35 percent). Girls, however, more often than boys used the strategy of ignoring directives (33 percent for girls and 16 percent for boys; ibid.:126). This gender difference indicates boys' greater power because an outright refusal is an assertion of autonomy, implying rights to control oneself and challenging the authority of an issuer of commands. Ignoring directives is also an act of self-assertion but in a covert manner. It may not be any more compliant than a refusal, but it is deferential to the issuer's authority.

Communicative competence includes knowledge of interpretive norms that listeners can use to evaluate speech. Speech informs listeners in two respects. First, it transmits speakers' knowledge, intentions, and attitudes. Second, it provides listeners with data from which to make judgments about speakers. When people listen, they learn more than simply the content of messages addressed to them; they also learn something about a speaker's social identity. Cultural stereotypes abound concerning the way different categories of people are thought to communicate. Children acquire these stereotypes as part of their cultural knowledge. And, like any other learning process, children's interpretive rules develop gradually over time with increased experience and exposure to community norms.

For example, cultural ideologies of gender are replete with models of how women and men are thought to act and speak. As we have seen, children begin to acquire these models early in their socialization. (Topics of gendered styles of speaking will be explored in Chapter 10.) To study degrees of gender stereotyping among different age groups, Carole Edelsky (1977) conducted experiments with four cohorts: first-graders, third-graders, sixth-graders, and adults. Subjects were presented with 24 sentences containing variants of modifiers, intensifiers, and directives and were asked to decide whether each sentence would likely be spoken by men only, women only, or by men and women with equal likelihood. The following sentences were used, although their order was mixed in presentation so that similar sentences were not sequential (ibid.:228):

1. That's an *adorable* story.
2. *Oh dear,* the TV set broke!
3. *My goodness,* there's a friend of mine!
4. *Won't you please* close the door?
5. I was *just* exhausted.
6. I was *so* tired.
7. I was *very* tired.
8. That was a great show, *wasn't it?*
9. *Get* me that pencil.
10. *Damn it,* I lost my keys!
11. *I'll be damned,* there's a friend of mine!
12. You're *damn* right.

The youngest children (first-graders) were not sensitive to vocabulary markers of gender, showing only a low consensus to associating *adorable* with women and *damn it* with men. By third grade, children agreed on assignment of gender for two-thirds of the variables. Responses of sixth-graders were the most interesting when compared to adult interpretations: Sixth-graders assigned gender consistent with adult judgments but actually reflected even stronger consensus about some of the variables than did adults. The following table presents relevant data (ibid.:233).

The three items for which sixth-graders' judgments differed from adults were higher consensus on *damn* and *damn it* associated with men, higher consensus on *won't you please* attributed to women, and exclusive assignment of commands to men. When Edelsky asked children to explain their judgments, a frequent comment was "Men swear but ladies don't" (ibid.:235). Although this cultural stereotype is prevalent in our society, adults certainly know that women do swear, and therefore they are less likely to assign profanity exclusively to men. Two children's remarks about directives and politeness are relevant to the other variables for which children had stronger reactions than adults did. In discussing home situations, they observed that "She *has* to be polite because we won't do it if she doesn't say 'please,' but if a man doesn't say it, we sure will anyway" and "The man is thought of as the king of his house or something and he can tell you what to do, and the lady just *wants* you to close the door while the man tells you to and expects you to do it" (ibid.:238; emphasis in original).

Variable	Age Groups			
	First-Graders	**Third-Graders**	**Sixth-Graders**	**Adults**
Adorable	W	W*	W*	W*
Damn it	M*	M*	M*	M
Damn + adjective	—	M*	M*	M
I'll be damned	—	M*	M*	M*
Oh dear	—	W*	W*	W*
My goodness	—	W	W*	W*
Won't you please	—	W	W*	W
Tag question	—	M/W	W	W
So	—	—	W	W
Very	—	—	W	W
Just	—	—	W	W
Command	—	—	M	M/W

W* = female, high consensus; W = female, low consensus;
M* = male, high consensus; M = male, low consensus; M/W = neutral;
— = not meeting criteria.

The results of Edelsky's study and the comments of the children themselves provide rich evidence of the strength of gender categorization and of the acquisition of knowledge about social meanings of language. Children learn these meanings as part of their enculturation. Once learned, their judgments appear to be more constrained by stereotypes than are adults'. Perhaps because children have less real-life experience with actual variation among speakers, they are more influenced by idealized models.

One of the ways that children acquire models of gender and social relations is through their exposure to and incorporation into family interactions. In their study of dinnertime narratives, Elinor Ochs and Carolyn Taylor observe that "certainly from the point of view of a child, routine moments of family communication are the earliest and perhaps the most profound medium for constructing gender understandings" (1995:98). Rights of family members were constructed and enacted through their participation in various roles in accounts of past and present activities. Based on recordings of 100 spontaneous narratives, Ochs and Taylor describe a "Father knows best" family dynamic in which "father is set up to be primary audience, judge and critic of family members' actions, thoughts and feelings" (ibid.:99). Children figured as "protagonists" (person who the story was about) in 60 percent of narratives; mothers were protagonists in 23 percent and fathers in 19 percent. Therefore, children's actions and thoughts were most open to the scrutiny of others, whereas fathers were the "least vulnerable family members" (ibid.:102). The preponderance of children as protagonists was reversed by their rarity as narrative "introducers" (the person selecting the topic). Only about one-third of the stories about the children were introduced by the child him- or herself. Instead, parents (especially mothers) focused the narrative on the child's actions, thus reflecting and reinforcing the child's lack of privacy and powerlessness by exposing the child to the scrutiny of others. Finally, stories were most often oriented to fathers as "primary recipients," thus setting up father as the "family judge" with rights to evaluate others. Although fathers sometimes held this role by virtue of self-selection, most often mothers introduced narratives with fathers as recipients. And while protagonists were most often children, mothers were more likely to orient stories about themselves to fathers than fathers were to orient stories about themselves to mothers. By doing so, women not only set up fathers as judges but also set themselves up as targets of fathers' evaluation and criticism.

A complex play of family and interactional power is enacted through the narrative dynamics. In the most frequent pattern, women hold the powerful role of selecting narrative topics and protagonists, but they then transfer family power to fathers, who act as judges of members' actions and thoughts. Ochs and Taylor conclude, therefore, that mothers' "exercise of power is ephemeral and may even be self-destructive by giving fathers a platform for monitoring and judging wives and children…. Women may wittingly or unwittingly contribute to—and even set up—the daily reconstruction of a 'Father knows best' ideological dynamic" (ibid.:116–117). Children are socialized into the ideology of asymmetric gender relations both because they are witnesses to it as audience and because they are engulfed in it when they are chosen (usually by others) as protagonists in the drama.

Status in Samoan

Children in all societies are sensitive to the status of individuals in their households and their communities, and need to learn to recognize people's rights. Every society expresses meanings related to social status in specific linguistic form. In the speech of Samoan children, use of two imperatives, *aumai* "bring/give" and *sau* "come," is correlated with status and expresses a child's understanding of the status differences between speaker and addressee (Platt 1986). These verbs are significantly distinguished in Samoan speech in terms of hierarchical orderings between speaker and addressee. The verb *aumai* "bring/give" implies the speaker's right to expect and demand a portion of available objects, goods, and resources. All members of a household, including children, reciprocally share these rights. In contrast, *sau* "come" expresses social power to direct and control another's actions. This power is not evenly distributed among people but is given to those of high status. Within households, people's status is based on age: Children, therefore, are of lower rank than adults; older children have higher status than younger ones. *Sau* "come" is appropriately used by higher-ranked people to those of lower status because the former have authority to control the latter. It is therefore seldom used by children. The verb *aumai* "bring/give" is not restricted in this way and is commonly employed by lower- to higher-status people (ibid.:141–142).

Samoan children learn the culturally prescribed social meanings of *sau* and *aumai* at a very early age. As might be expected, they acquire *aumai* much earlier than *sau* because they most often interact with older, that is, higher-status, people. The authority expressed in *sau* is not available to children in most daily encounters. Children use *sau* mainly to infants or to domesticated animals (ibid.:142).

Relationships in Hungarian

Terms of address are sensitive indicators of social status and interpersonal relationships. In languages with complex pronoun systems based on participants' identity, children need to learn social meanings expressed by these linguistic forms. In Hungarian, adult speakers select among four possibilities: familiar (T), formal (V), polite (P), and formal-polite (VP). Children typically use either familiar T or polite P (Hollos 1977:213). Hungarian address is marked in pronouns and verbs according to the following conventions (ibid.:222):

Familiar T: *te* + second-person singular verb

Formal V: *maga* + third-person singular verb

Polite P: title/honorific + last name or title/honorific + first name + third-person singular of verb "to wish, like, please" + infinitive of main verb

Formal-Polite V/P: *on* + third-person singular verb

Adults use these forms depending on similarities or differences in age, gender, status, and familiarity in relation to addressees. Pronoun use is an elaborate system, requiring awareness of both social relations and complex linguistic rules. Familiar T is exchanged between kin of similar ages and between same-sex nonkin with whom one has a close friendship. Formal V is exchanged between status equals who are socially distant. Nonreciprocal P/T is used by participants who are of markedly different ages or statuses; the younger/lower-status individual employs Polite P and receives Familiar T. Children use reciprocal T with other children or young people and nonreciprocal P/T with their elders (ibid.:223).

In a study of children's knowledge of social meanings in address forms, Marida Hollos (1977) presented subjects (age 7 through 9) with two sets of tasks. In one task, Hollos showed children pictures of scenes with figures engaged in daily activities, such as shopping and visiting. Subjects were asked to play the roles of various figures. They were directed with questions such as: "How does your mother greet the shopkeeper when she goes shopping? Ask for some eggs, as your mother would." In a second task, Hollos again presented children with pictures of scenes, but dialogue was supplied; the children were asked to decide which of three addressees would be the appropriate recipient of each question or command. The utterances contained three kinds of pronominal usage: familiar T, formal V, and polite P; for instance, Mother, using P, asks: "Did you leave the door open?" The choices were [a] grandfather (appropriate form P); [b] child (T); and [c] veterinarian (V). In another example, Doctor, using V, states: "You have to take this medicine three times a day." The choices were [a] a stranger from the city (appropriate form V); [b] grandmother (P); and [c] teacher (V) (ibid.:217).

Children at all ages in Hollos's study recognized and used appropriate pronouns in depicted interactions between children (mutual T) and between children and adults (nonreciprocal P/T). They also correctly employed mutual T between familiar adults (ibid.:218). Children's ability in these tasks is based on the scenes' compatibility with daily life. Because they interact with other children and with adults and because they observe conversations between familiar adults in their households, they easily comprehend and apply the underlying social meanings of T and P pronouns.

Children had the most difficulty in assigning or producing appropriate forms of address for encounters between unfamiliar adults. They erroneously assumed that unfamiliar adults consistently exchange P because this is the address form that a child would use to an adult. In other words, children's judgments are influenced by their own experience. Nine-year-olds made fewer errors than younger subjects, demonstrating that they were acquiring keener sensitivity to the social semantics involved. As Hollos observed, they were also developing the cognitive ability to "switch perspectives with others" (ibid.:222).

LEARNING DISCOURSE

Speaking is a social activity, involving intentions related to co-participants. Discourse entails knowledge of how utterances are connected to prior talk and to prior experience. Children gradually acquire techniques for tying speech to previous talk, following both grammatical and social interactional rules. They also need to learn the distinct structural and interactional norms that define different types of discourse. For instance, discourse genres, such as conversations, arguments, narratives, and interviews, each have their own distinctive components and each occurs in specific interactional settings with particular participants. Because children's earliest speech is conversational, their growing competence includes knowledge of rules for beginning, maintaining, and ending conversations. Because talk occurs in specific speech events, it must therefore be relevant to the context that includes topics, participants' interests, and ongoing activities. Children need to learn how to converse in a relevant, coherent manner. They need to learn the complex rules that organize talk. A child's ability to perform successfully depends on cognitive, linguistic, and social maturation. These three aspects of development are interrelated, each one aiding the others in progressing toward full social engagement.

Knowledge of Conversation Structure

As we saw in Chapter 5, conversation is based on alternation of turns. In two-party encounters, roles of speaker and listener are continually exchanged. Turns to speak are automatically assigned so that, when one speaker ends, the next turn belongs to the listener. Even infants are exposed to this rule when adults carry on "dialogues" with them. Adults talking to babies typically pause at the end of each discourse unit, leaving an empty turn for the infant. An adult may continue with another statement or may fill in a baby's turn by "translating" the latter's intentional or unintentional vocalizations.

It is not until children are nearly 3 years old that they learn to take speaker turns. By then they know that they need to make some response, even if just with audible sound fillers such as "mm," when the previous speaker has ended. They also know to wait to speak until the interlocutor has completed her or his turn. In studies of young children's conversations, Catherine Garvey (1984) observed very few overlaps in children's conversation (only about 4 to 5 percent of utterances), indicating that these young speakers had acquired the "one-turn-at-a-time" rule (ibid.:55).

Children also learn quite early that when questions are asked, addressees are obliged to respond. Through prompting and other routines, they realize that when questioned, they must answer or at least make a minimal response. As speakers, children strategically employ questions to engage others in talk. Children often issue a rapid sequence of questions in order to secure responses from otherwise uncooperative addressees. Another ploy children use to gain the floor is the "Y'know what?" or "Guess what?" gambit. The addressee's automatic response ("What?") gives the turn back to the child. The fact that children resort to these tactics indicates their relative difficulties in social encounters and their creativity in persevering to establish their right to talk.

Young speakers do encounter obstacles, however. First, as already discussed, their turns are often interrupted by adults (Gleason 1987:197). Second, although they manage well in two-party encounters, they have problems with multiparty interactions, particularly those involving older children or adults. Their problems are both linguistic and social. Because of the fast pace of conversation, young children are not always able to ask for explanations or clarifications of words that they do not understand. Even when a child is given an opportunity to ask for clarification, she needs to learn how to focus on the troublesome element. This is not as simple as it might appear. We can recall David McNeill's characterization of children's early thinking as "imagistic" (1987:254). But language is linear and requires segmenting (or "unpacking") thought into units that are arranged syntagmatically. Just as a young child's thought is holistic, so is his comprehension. Therefore, when children do not understand an utterance, it is difficult for them to locate the specific segment causing problems.

Children encounter additional difficulties in conversing. Because young children have not developed the skill needed to time their turn to the end of the previous speaker's, their intention to speak next may not be recognized by co-participants. Additionally, children have trouble retaining the floor even after it has been allocated to them. A helpful strategy is usage of fillers such as "y'know" or "um," "uh," and the like. These allow the current speaker to maintain his or her turn while pausing to check thoughts or wordings. Children need to acquire this tactic because "empty" pauses are quickly colonized by interlocutors. Very young children do not employ sophisticated means but resort to simple repetition of sounds or words while trying to organize their speech. Note the following utterance of a boy (age 2;8) trying to explain why his stomach hurt: "Cause i-/i-/i-/i-/i-/it was hurting cause i-/it was hurting because it was hurting/... and/... and it feels all better now" (Garvey 1984:38). By the age of 4 or 5, however, children begin to use more conventional fillers.

A child also learns to give appropriate signals to speakers indicating active listenership. These signs, or **backchannel cues**, include behaviors such as nods and smiles and vocalizations like "um," "yeah," or "uh huh." In adult interactions, backchannel cues need to be well timed to the speaker's utterances. Because they involve attention to linguistic units as well as to content, their appropriate use depends on more complex processing than young children can manage. Not surprisingly, they do not appear until late in childhood and are not well utilized until adolescence (ibid.:37).

Cohesion in Conversation

Another important feature of conversation is its cohesion across speaker turns. Talk is linked to prior talk not only within turns but also to one's previous statements and to those of other speakers. Directive-response pairs (e.g., question–answer, command–action) obviously depend on this association. A response must be related to the directive, either by supplying/performing appropriate information/actions or by explaining one's noncompliance. Children recognize this cohesive bond in their use of serial questioning as a conversational strategy.

Declarative propositions exhibit cohesion within and across turns as well. Cohesion is achieved through content and linguistic form. First, conversations are about something, about topics. Topics normally shift during encounters, but the content of talk should be focused or relevant to current issues. More complex, however, are the linguistic devices used to organize discourse. Lack of skill in employing such markers is, in fact, a distinctive trait of young children's speech.

In English, cohesion is achieved through various means, including use of pronouns and demonstratives (*this, that*) and processes of substitution, comparison, conjunction, and clausal dependency. Pronouns and demonstratives relate or refer to previously mentioned entities. Comparatives (*same, other, more*) have similar functions. These devices also serve to eliminate redundancies that could potentially overwhelm verbal output. They are an aspect of language's economy, allowing speakers to delete long sequences and replace them with single words. Conjunctions serve a similar function, permitting omission of portions of underlying sentences.

Children acquire these basic cohesive devices quite early. In fact, experiments asking for imitation reveal children's drive to produce naturally efficient speech in their occasional nonimitation of models. Recall Dan Slobin's dialogue (see Chapter 7) in which an adult prompted with "Here is a brown brush and here is a comb" and the child (age 2;4) responded, "Here's a brown brush an' a comb."

Garvey's research indicated that children acquire some cohesive devices by the age of 2;6 to 3 years. The most commonly used forms were pronouns (56 percent), followed in frequency by demonstratives (21 percent); comparatives were rare (1984:86). The conjunction *and* is learned even earlier, usually by age 2, although its first uses are somewhat indiscriminate. For example, a child (age 2;3), wanting her mother to read a book, said, "Would you read it to me? And I'll listen." Another use occurred in "Hold the ladder and it won't fall down."

Cohesion is also achieved through substitutions of words. One type is the use of synonyms or paraphrases that minimize the appearance of repetitiveness but link current to prior talk. Young children's substitutions are at first global—"thing," "stuff," "do"—but gradually they become more selective and informative.

Another cohesive process that reduces output is ellipsis. **Ellipsis** involves omission of textual material that is assumed to be shared by co-participants; for example, "What's in there?"/"Cookies" (are in there). Sharing of knowledge, or **presupposition**, is based on expectations that participants recall and can refer to prior talk. Young children begin to use ellipsis systematically by the age of 3. The following table presents Garvey's data for incidence of elided segments in the speech of 3- to 5-year-olds (ibid.:83–84). Note that percentages indicate proportion of all elided utterances in the corpus (accounting for 22 percent of all of the children's speech).

Type of Signal Retained	Example	Percentage
1. Polarity marker	Are you ready? Yes (I am ready).	40
2. Modal element	Can you see it? I can (see it).	13
3. Wh-component	There's only one thing to do. What (is the one thing to do)?	11
4. Logical connective	Why don't you want to do anything? (I don't want to do anything) 'Cause I'd rather be back in school.	9
5. Complement	What do we have to use? (We have to use) A raincoat.	7
6. Subject	What's in there? Cookies (are in there).	6
7. Matrix clause	Where did the table go? I'll show you (where the table went).	6
8. Adjunct of clause	Where's the man? (Is the man) At the factory?	2
9. Lexical verb	I go get some ice cream after my mommy comes. You won't go (get some ice cream after your mommy comes).	2
10. Simple verb	There's no playhouses. Yes, there is (playhouses).	2

Connected discourse makes use of several kinds of reference, both nonlinguistic and intra-linguistic. That is, speakers make reference to activities or entities in nonlinguistic contexts and they also make reference to previous utterances in discourse. For example, in the following dia-logue, both Speaker A and Speaker B use deictic markers (*that, it*) that refer to some entity in their view:

SPEAKER A: "Look at that!"

SPEAKER B: "Yes, it's flying really fast." (Hickmann 1987:168)

In contrast, note the referential meaning of "it" in the following sentences:

"All of a sudden a bird appeared in the sky. It was flying really fast."

Here, "it" refers to the previously mentioned "bird," an element in a prior linguistic string. Young children, age 4 through 7, have difficulties making reference to linguistic contexts, although they employ deictic markers to refer to nonlinguistic contexts (ibid.:170). Their utterances make reference to entities and events in their environment, but these utterances "…are not fully bound to each other through intralinguistic relations" (ibid.). For example, the following narrative by a 7-year-old describes sequences of events in pictures: "The horse is running. The horse was staring at him. The horse is getting ready to jump over the fence and the horse died. And then the bird came, that bird doctor." Here, the narrator continually repeats nominal labels instead of replacing second and subsequent mentions with anaphoric pronouns.

In addition, young children only gradually acquire the ability to understand and mark the difference between reported and reporting speech as illustrated in the following con-trast: A friend of mine said (yesterday), "I will come tomorrow." And "A friend of mine said (yesterday) that he would come today." It is not until children reach the age of about 10 that they begin to make explicit differentiation between these two types of narrative reference (ibid.:172).

Interactional Cooperation

To converse appropriately, children need to learn that communicative interaction is coopera-tive. Participants normally signal their attentiveness not only to each other's talk but also to each other as people through markers of politeness, including phrases such as *please* and *thank you,* forms of address, ritualized greetings and partings, and apologies. Many of these are overtly taught to children as part of their socialization. Polite signals indicate one's concern for participants and help minimize potential conflict because they recognize addressees' rights to fair treatment.

Interactions often involve requests between co-participants. In children's encounters, a frequent type of request is a request-for-permission, including entreaties for use of toys and play areas or admission to playgroups. To obtain one's goals, speakers need to phrase their desire in an appropriate form. A request that is too abrupt and demanding may be rejected, although one that is too unobtrusive risks being ignored. Children learn a multitude of strate-gies, adjusting their choice to perceived situations and interlocutors. In the following dia-logue, two children, Judy (age 2;8) and Tom (2;9), mutually construct their play (Garvey 1984:112).

Tom	Judy
Can I play here?	
	Yeah, you can.
(Sits down by Judy and points to a plate.) Can I have some muffins?	
	Don't touch them, 'cause they're very hot.
I'm gonna put a little sugar in your muffins, all right?	
	(Judy watches as Tom pretends to sprinkle sugar on the imaginary muffins.)

In this delicate situation, Tom requests permission while recognizing Judy's prior claim to space and objects. Although Judy denies Tom access to the muffins, she acknowledges the legitimacy of his wishes by justifying the denial. Tom obeys Judy's prohibition against touch but interacts with the imaginary muffins nonetheless, after again asking permission, that is, "all right?"

When their desires are blocked by others, children try to achieve their goals by resorting to repetitions, rephrasings, explanations, and additional claims. The following encounter between Judy and Tom is an example of request and response moves (ibid.:124).

Judy	Tom
(Stands beside wooden car) Can I have a turn now?	(Driving wooden car)
	(No response)
I have a turn now?	
	I'm doing it right now.
When you finished?	
	I'm not finished yet.
Awright. (Continues to stand by car and look at Tom)	
	(Drives for seconds) Now I'm finished. (Climbs off car)
(Gets on car)	

Children frequently seek permission to join playgroups. When groups are already established, children need to use various strategies in order to gain admittance. For example, examine the following scene of nursery school children (Corsaro 1979:320–321):

Two girls, Jenny (4;0) and Betty (3;9) are playing around a sandbox, putting sand in pots, pans, and bottles. Another girl, Debbie (4;1), approaches. Neither J nor B acknowledges her presence. D doesn't speak to them and no one speaks to her. After watching for five minutes, she circles the sandbox three times and stops. After a few more minutes of watching, D moves to the sandbox and reaches for a teapot in the sand. J takes the pot away from D and mumbles "No." D backs away and again observes J and B. She then walks over next to B, who is filling the cupcake pan with sand. D watches B for just a few seconds, then says:

D-B:	We're friends, right? We're friends, right, B?
	(B, not looking up at D, continues to place sand in pan and says)
B-D:	Right.
	(D now moves alongside B, takes a pot and begins putting sand in it.)
D-B:	I'm making coffee.
B-D:	I'm making cupcakes.
B-J:	We're mothers, right, J?
J-B:	Right.

D employs several strategies in this encounter. Although her first overt attempt at admission is rebuffed, she had carefully prepared the way through nonverbal cues. After an interval of time, she changes moves and begins with a personal appeal to prior status as a friend of B. When this is acknowledged, she engages in independent, but parallel, activity (making coffee). B responds with a correlated action and explanation (making cupcakes). Finally, the triad is completed by placating and reaffirming bonds with J.

In his study of nursery school encounters, William Corsaro isolated a large number of "access strategies," some of which proved more successful than others (ibid.:324). Among the more helpful were these:

1. Producing a variant of ongoing behavior
2. Questioning participants
3. Offering of object
4. Greeting
5. Reference to affiliation

In contrast, the least likely to achieve positive results were the following:

1. Disruptive entry
2. Reference to adult authority
3. Claim on area or object

Children typically do not abandon their attempts to gain entry when they receive a negative response. Instead, they often try again (as in the scene above), selecting an alternative tactic. On the whole, indirect strategies tend to be more successful than direct or intrusive moves. Indirection in verbal and nonverbal behavior is considered a feature of politeness and thereby acknowledges people's rights and claims. Politeness on the part of one actor tends to be answered by polite responses by others.

Narratives

As discussed in Chapter 4, conversations frequently include reportings of previous experiences. These personal narratives recount events having immediate relevance to the speaker as part of her life. Narrators are obligated to make their stories relevant to addressees as well. Events reported should be shown to exemplify a more general point or to have some extrasituational value, to be entertaining or enlightening. In other words, they should be "newsworthy."

Reporting one's experiences is a skill that develops gradually in children. Young children encounter a range of difficulties. First, they often choose to relate events that are not particularly interesting to listeners, especially to adult listeners. And children have trouble making their stories engaging on the basis of other criteria, for example, by being dramatic or enlightening. A child's limited experiences naturally restrict the kinds of events he or she can report. But more important is his or her inability to employ narrative devices that contribute linguistically to a story's appeal.

Personal narratives are constructed with six different components (Labov and Waletzky 1967):

1. *Abstract:* Summarizes the main point or result of the story.
2. *Orientation:* Identifies time, place, characters.
3. *Complicating action:* Recounts events, in chronological sequence.
4. *Evaluation:* Transmits attitudes or emotions of speaker and/or other characters.
5. *Result or resolution:* Provides point of story.
6. *Coda:* Terminates story, so that listeners do not ask: "And then what happened?"

Narratives must contain complicating action and resolution, but the other components are optional. Even if all segments are included, speakers may elaborate certain sections while providing scant treatment of others. Very young children tend to relate actions but omit orientations and codas. A serious flaw in their narratives is the lack of evaluative material. Young children evidently assume that actions are important or newsworthy enough to maintain audience interest. They are less likely than adults to include material on the feelings and motivations of story participants. Absence of these elements is due to children's inexperience and failure to take the perspective of others. However, they gradually develop storytelling skills in keeping with the models or schema of narrative content and form. Western narrative models emphasize plots that focus on a central character who encounters a difficulty, danger, or conflict that he or she must overcome or learn from. These plot devices provide the themes of risk, struggle, and accomplishment that are basic to narrative grammars. Young storytellers gradually learn to develop their narratives consistent with these themes.

The impetus to tell stories stems from social relations and social interactions. That is, people construct narratives in order to fulfill social needs and to relate to others. And children learn techniques of narrative development, structure, and content by hearing stories told to them and by responding to questions asked of them in the course of their narrative performance. Indeed, the earliest stories that children tell are those that they have heard many times or those that are prompted by pictures in books (Lund and Duchan 1994:269). These early stories do not originate independently but rather derive from social interactions with others.

In studies examining the "social origins" of storytelling, Gillian McNamee (1987) conducted two types of experiments focusing on the role of adult interactions with children in helping the child develop his or her narrative techniques. In the first study, children age 5 and 6 were read a story and were then asked to retell it three times, once each week for three weeks. Each retelling was preceded by hearing the story again. Then the children were read a second story and asked to retell it. In every retelling, the adults offered help by asking questions and encouraging the child to frame statements in narrative form. McNamee found that the amount of help that children needed diminished considerably between the first and second retelling (ibid.:293). In addition, children needed to be prompted by very specific questions at first, but in subsequent retellings, they responded appropriately to more open-ended questions. And, significantly, when asked to retell the second story, children needed much less help than they did for the first story. These data indicate that children incorporate aid received from adults into their schema or grammars of narrative structure and content. They use assistance creatively to expand their stories and render them increasingly complex.

The second experiment involved children age 3, 4, and 5 attending preschool or day-care programs. The children were divided into experimental and control groups. The children in all groups were read stories twice a week for 12 weeks by adults and could also compose their own stories, dictating them to an adult who wrote them down. In the experimental (but not control) groups, the adult and children stories were subsequently dramatized in the classroom. Results of the experiments revealed several interesting comparisons between the experimental and control groups in the children's narrative abilities. Children in the experimental groups developed greater narrative skills over the 12-week course of the study than those in the control groups (ibid.:297). Their stories were more complex and coherent. In addition, when prompted by the adult, children in the experimental groups responded with more editing and reviewing of story episodes and dialogue. According to McNamee, these children were "becoming reflective and more aware of and concerned about the stories they were writing" (ibid.:298). Finally, children in the experimental groups shared and borrowed more elements from each other's stories, incorporating specific incidents and characters. For example, events or characters that evoked group laughter in one story were used by other children in their own stories. McNamee concludes that dramatizing the stories was a social activity through which children shared and learned. Children were both the creators of the stories and their audience, sharing and commenting on narrative elements. Such involvement was one of the means through which narrative skills were acquired and improved because of the children's "desire to be more effective in their communications with one another" (ibid.:299).

Research by Keith Kernan (1977) on narratives produced by African-American girls in an urban California community revealed differences in structural and linguistic devices used by younger and older speakers. Stories told by young girls (age 7 to 8) were predominantly composed of complicating action. Only one story in this group contained an abstract. Orientations did introduce the texts but were quite short and typically were confined to a brief note of characters or places. Young children often mentioned the names of characters, giving no other identifying features, even though their audience was unfamiliar with the people named (ibid.:94–95).

Older girls (age 10 to 14) usually began their stories with abstracts or introductions, such as:

1. We almost drowned in L.A.
2. First time I ever got scared is when, when you know, that them two mens got killed down there.

Orientation sections by older children were elaborate, making up roughly 20 percent of an entire story. Girls included statements of mood and motivation as well as characters and places in making their narratives relevant and appealing to audiences. Within stories, older speakers effectively evaluated or attributed evaluations of ongoing events to others. They also used stylistic devices such as repetition, paraphrasing, or exaggeration in order to capture and maintain audience interest, for instance (ibid.:98):

An girl, you know, half of the cake was gone. I was so mad I almost cried, girl. I say "Mama, I told you Tommy was gonna eat all that cake," I mean, Tommy had him a big, giant piece, girl. That cake was gone. (ibid.: 98)

Older girls were more skilled at terminating their stories. Some simply brought the narrative to a concise close, and others ended with condensed statements of the moral point of the text (ibid.:96):

1. And they still letting her play no matter what they say.
2. I felt sorry. I shouldn't did that in the first place.
3. That's how they get killed. By going in other people's business.

Linguistic framing is an important element in any kind of communicative activity. Co-participants have to signal their awareness of an event's beginning and ending. Young narrators are not aware of this necessity. Their interactional strategies tend to be oriented toward their own interests and needs, whereas older speakers understand that they have to make personal experiences relevant to listeners.

In a collection of narratives produced by boys and young men living in Harlem, younger speakers described events in simple chronological order with little or no introduction, identification of characters, or evaluation. For example, the following story was told by a young child about an episode in a television program.

> This kid got shot and he had to go on a mission. And so this kid, he went with Solo. So they went and this guy—they went through this window, and they caught him. And then he beat up them other people. And they went and then he said that this old lady was his mother and then he—and at the end he say that he was the guy's friend. (Labov 1972:367)

Older children were able to dramatize and evaluate events, as in the next story, told by a boy of 11.

> When I was in fourth grade—no, it was in third grade—This boy he stole my glove. He took my glove and said that his father found it downtown on the ground. I told him that it was impossible for him to find downtown 'cause all those other people were walking by and just his father was the only one that found it? So he got all mad. Then I fought him. I knocked him all out in the street. So he say he give. And I kept on hitting him. Then he started crying and ran home to his father. And the father told him that he ain't find no glove. (ibid.:368)

The first story is hard, if not impossible, for a listener to follow. Pronouns are used without previous mention of referents. It is a skeletal recounting of facts. In striking contrast, the second narrator provides enough contextual information so that listeners can easily understand events. In addition, the speaker uses stylistic devices to continually highlight the story's major point. Each statement develops the theme by adding new and pertinent information. Finally, the story ends with reference to the antagonist's father, succinctly justifying the narrator's actions.

Use of evaluative comments increased with the age of storytellers, and older speakers employed more elaborate embedding of evaluation into their stories. They effectively used quantifiers ("he had cuts all over") and repetition ("You bleedin', you bleedin', Speedy you bleedin'!") to intensify the impact of actions (ibid.:379).

Research by McNamee, Kernan, and Labov demonstrates that older children acquire sophisticated linguistic techniques in narration. But employment of these skills rests on social maturity. Older speakers realize that they must attract and maintain listener interest on the basis of shared assumptions about relevance existing outside the narrative itself.

Expository Discourse

Although conversation and personal narrative are the major discourse genres in children's talk, young speakers are also exposed to additional types of discourse that they need to acquire in their early years of growing competence as members of their speech communities. In school settings, children learn both to produce and to interpret expositions and quizzes (Lund and Duchan 1994). Speakers employ expository discourse to transfer information to other people. It is used in explaining or reporting information. It is "factual, impersonal, timeless, and nonfictional" (ibid.:271). The speaker who uses expository discourse, the imparter of information, takes on the role of "teacher," while the recipient of the information takes on the role of "student." Lund and Duchan describe several kinds of logical relations that occur in expository discourse (ibid.):

> Comparison/contrast (describing how things are the same or different)
>> The moon is much smaller than the earth.
>
> Problem solving (stating a problem and offering a solution)
>> The problem with global warming can be addressed only through international cooperation.
>
> Cause–effect (giving reasons why something happens)
>> Water runs downhill because of gravity.
>
> Temporal relations (used in instructions necessitating sequences of actions)
>> First shake the container well. Remove the red tab. Holding the container upright, press the black top firmly.
>
> Description (used in giving definitions)
>> A noun is the name of a person, place, or thing.
>
> Enumeration (used in listing related events or entities)
>> When you go camping you need a tent, a sleeping bag, warm clothes, and insect repellent.

To use and interpret these types of discourse patterns, children need to understand the underlying logical relations that the discourse patterns incorporate. Cognitive maturation is obviously a necessary precondition for acquiring these notions, but the educational setting helps to formulate the concepts and the grammatical structures through which they are expressed. Teachers facilitate this process by providing models of expository discourse and by involving children in their enactment. Many of the formulations for expository discourse use statements of factual knowledge that are abstracted from context and experience. Interpreting and employing such discourse differs fundamentally from early childhood speech, which is tied directly to the child's activities and inner thoughts.

Quizzes are another discourse type that occurs frequently in educational settings but may occur earlier in adult–child interactions. A quiz is similar to expository discourse in its focus on information, but it differs because both participants are assumed to share the knowledge. Quizzes have a structure that consists of a three-part exchange: initiation, reply, and evaluation (ibid.:272). The exchange is initiated by the "teacher" (this is a structural role that may be carried out by an adult or child) who asks a question or makes a request. The second part of the exchange consists of the "student's" response providing an answer or performing an action. Finally, the third part consists of the teacher's evaluation of the student's response. The evaluation may be an acceptance or ratification of the response, or it may be a correction or request for a modified or substitute response.

Although quizzes dominate school discourse, they occur in the earliest adult–child communication interactions. Caregivers "test" young children by requesting the names of objects and the participants in activities and by asking for descriptions of events and experiences. Through these quizzes, children acquire vocabulary and they learn how to respond appropriately to questions.

Summary

Communicative competence is the knowledge of cultural rules for appropriate use of language in social interaction. It includes the ability to utilize these rules in situated speech events and to recognize the intentions of speakers and the needs and rights of listeners. As part of socialization processes, children learn that language can fulfill a variety of functions. Through example, prompting, and correction, they are encouraged to adopt communicative behaviors consistent with prevailing values about the propriety of expressing one's opinions, directing another's actions, or deferring to co-participants.

Children become aware of the social order of their community through daily interactions within their households. They learn that classifications of people based on factors such as age, gender, and status are reflected in styles of conversational interaction. These styles manifest and maintain cultural models of people's differentiated claims to rights and authority in relation to others. Children acquire communicative competence through development of linguistic and sociolinguistic skills. They improve their ability to employ formal rules of their language, and they learn that stylistic variants have social and situational meaning. This learning takes place in the context of increasing interpersonal maturity, recognizing that speaking is a social activity and must be attuned to the expectations, assumptions, and needs of others as well as of oneself.

References

ANDERSEN, ELAINE. 1986. The acquisition of register variation by Anglo-American children. In *Language Socialization Across Cultures,* ed. B. Schieffelin and E. Ochs. New York: Cambridge University Press, pp. 153–161.

CLANCY, PATRICIA. 1986. The acquisition of communicative style in Japanese. In *Language Socialization Across Cultures,* ed. B. Schieffelin and E. Ochs. New York: Cambridge University Press, pp. 213–250.

CORSARO, WILLIAM. 1979. "We're friends, right?" Children's use of access rituals in a nursery school. *Language in Society* 8:315–336.

EDELSKY, CAROLE. 1977. Acquisition of an aspect of communicative competence: Learning what it means to talk like a lady. In *Child Discourse,* ed. S. Ervin-Tripp and C. Mitchell-Kernan. New York: Academic Press, pp. 225–243.

ERVIN-TRIPP, SUSAN, MARY CATHERINE O'CONNOR, AND JARRETT ROSENBERG. 1984. Language and power in the family. In *Language and Power,* ed. C. Kramarae, M. Schulz, and W. O'Barr. Newbury Park, CA: Sage, pp. 116–135.

ESPOSITO, ANITA. 1979. Sex differences in children's conversation. *Language and Speech* 22:213–220.

GARVEY, CATHERINE. 1984. *Children's Talk.* Cambridge, MA: Harvard University Press.

GLEASON, JEAN B. 1987. Sex differences in parent-child interaction. In *Language, Gender and Sex in Comparative Perspective,* ed. S. Philips, S. Steele, and C. Tanz. New York: Cambridge University Press, pp. 189–199.

GOODWIN, MARJORIE, AND CHARLES GOODWIN. 1987. Children's arguing. In *Language, Gender and Sex in Comparative Perspective,* ed. S. Philips, S. Steele, and C. Tanz. New York: Cambridge University Press, pp. 200–248.

HALLIDAY, M. A. K. 1973. *Explorations in the Functions of Language.* Hawthorne, NY: Elsevier North-Holland.

HICKMANN, MAYA, ed. 1987. The pragmatics of reference in child language: Some issues in developmental theory. In *Social and Functional Approaches.* New York: Academic Press, pp. 165–184.

HOLLOS, MARIDA. 1977. Comprehension and use of social rules in pronoun selection by Hungarian children. In *Child Discourse,* ed. S. Ervin-Tripp and C. Mitchell-Kernan. New York: Academic Press, pp. 211–223.

KERNAN, KEITH. 1977. Semantic and expressive elaboration in children's narratives. In *Child Discourse,* ed. S. Ervin-Tripp and C. Mitchell-Kernan. New York: Academic Press, pp. 91–102.

LABOV, WILLIAM. 1972. The transformation of experience in narrative syntax. In *Language in the Inner City,* ed. W. Labov. Philadelphia, PA: University of Pennsylvania Press, pp. 354–396.

LABOV, WILLIAM, AND JOSHUA WALETZKY. 1967. Narrative analysis. In *Essays on the Verbal and Visual Arts,* ed. J. Helm. Seattle, WA: University of Washington Press, pp. 12–44.

LUND, NANCY, AND JUDITH DUCHAN. 1994. *Assessing Children's Language in Naturalistic Contexts,* 3rd ed. Englewood Cliffs, NJ: Prentice Hall.

MCNAMEE, GILLIAN. 1987. The social origins of narrative skills. In *Social and Functional Approaches to Language and Thought,* ed. M. Hickmann. New York: Academic Press, pp. 287–304.

MCNEILL, DAVID. 1987. *Psycholinguistics: A New Approach.* New York: Harper & Row.

OCHS, ELINOR. 1986. From feelings to grammar: A Samoan case study. In *Language Socialization Across Cultures,* ed. B. Schieffelin and E. Ochs. New York: Cambridge University Press, pp. 251–272.

OCHS, ELINOR, AND CAROLYN TAYLOR. 1995. The "Father knows best" dynamic in dinnertime narratives. In *Gender Articulated: Language and the Socially Constructed Self,* ed. K. Hall and M. Bucholtz. New York: Routledge, pp. 97–120.

PLATT, MARTHA. 1986. Social norms and lexical acquisition: A study of deictic verbs in Samoan child language. In *Language Socialization Across Cultures,* ed. B. Schieffelin and E. Ochs. New York: Cambridge University Press, pp. 127–152.

SACHS, JACQUELINE. 1987. Preschool boys' and girls' language use in pretend play. In *Language, Gender and Sex in Comparative Perspective,* ed. S. Philips, S. Steele, and C. Tanz. New York: Cambridge University Press, pp. 178–188.

WEST, CANDACE, AND DON ZIMMERMAN. 1983. Small insults: A study of interruptions in cross-sex conversations between unacquainted persons. In *Language, Gender and Society,* ed. B. Thorne, C. Kramarae, and N. Henley. Rowley, MA: Newbury, pp. 103–118.

ZIMMERMAN, DON, AND CANDACE WEST. 1975. Sex roles, interruptions and silences in conversation. In *Language and Sex,* ed. B. Thorne and N. Henley. Rowley, MA: Newbury, pp. 105–129.

CHAPTER 9

Societal Segmentation and Linguistic Variation: Class and Race

What do the following three speakers reveal about themselves?

"Where's toity-toid street?"

"We has a little fire, keeps us warm."

"It's just not convenient cause the office be closed on weekends."

In these sentences, the speakers use language that differs from the "standard" forms of English spoken in the United States and Great Britain. But their pronunciations, words, and grammatical constructions are not random or idiosyncratic. They conform to definite sets of rules that obtain within their speech communities or speech networks. Many, if not most, of the people these speakers converse with also use the sounds and words that they employ. Such use of speech signals people's membership in particular communities or networks. The first example, "Where's toity-toid street?" is typical, stereotypical in fact, of a lower-class regional dialect spoken in New York City. The speaker replaces the fricative sound (written as "th") with the stop /t/ and replaces the vocalic segment (written "ir" in thi<u>r</u>ty-thi<u>r</u>d) with the diphthong /oy/. The second example comes from a lower-class British speaker. Here the speaker replaces the standard plural form of "have" with the singular "has." The third speaker uses an invariant, unconjugated form of the verb "be," common in the dialect of US English known as African-American Vernacular English (AAVE). Speakers of AAVE use the invariant "be" to mark verbs that report activities or states that are habitual.

   As these three examples show, members of different speech communities use styles of speaking that are distinctive, consistent, and rule-governed. These styles may differ from forms of speech generally held to be "standard" in their choices of pronunciation, words, or grammar, but they are nonetheless "correct" and follow the rules accepted and used by speakers in their neighborhoods and networks.

Within speech communities, people are differentiated on the basis of many social factors, including gender, age, class, race, ethnicity, and occupation. In this chapter, we focus on the interconnections between speech and the factors of social stratification and race because these bases of segmentation are significant in many societies throughout the world. Social distinctions influence both the production of speech and its evaluation by community members.

SOCIAL STRATIFICATION

Social stratification is the hierarchical structuring of groups within a society, reflecting inequalities among sectors of a population. Inequality may be based on many factors, including income, occupation, education, and access to social, economic, and/or political power. These factors are in practice not distinct; rather, they interact in complex ways to produce and reproduce societal segmentation. Theories about origins and processes of stratification are controversial in sociology and anthropology and will not be explored here, but the concept itself has generally been adopted into sociolinguistic research as useful for understanding one of the parameters of linguistic variation. Speakers of socially ordered groups exhibit differences in frequency of use of certain sounds, words, and grammatical features. Of equal importance is the fact that members of all groups within a society are aware, either consciously or unconsciously, of speech styles characteristic of various social strata, and they use this knowledge in assessing their own and other people's speech. These reactions are indications of beliefs that language can be employed as a marker of social identity both in speakers' use and in listeners' patterns of evaluation.

CASTE

Social stratification can be stable and absolute, as in systems of caste, or potentially fluid and fluctuating, as in class systems. **Caste** is a term associated with a social hierarchy in which people are separated according to criteria of birth and are usually unable to change their group membership. It is a system that prevails in India, for example, determining many aspects of a person's behavior. Residence, occupation, and marriage choices are all linked to caste groupings; members of particular castes live in certain areas of Indian villages, have specified occupations, and generally marry within their own group. In many cases, ritual activities and even styles of clothing further demarcate the castes. Language, too, is a marker of the pervasive social hierarchy.

Speech samples from Khalapur, a north Indian village of some 5,000 inhabitants that is divided into 31 castes, indicate that the population varies in the pronunciation of several sounds (Gumperz 1971). Higher castes—the Brahmins (ritually the purest) and Rajputs (or warrior-rulers)—use the sound system of the standard local dialect of Khari Boli, a subdialect of Hindi, India's official language. Lower castes, or "untouchables," in the village—chamars (landless laborers), leatherworkers, and sweepers—employ variants of some of the standard forms. The following list summarizes contrasting patterns of pronunciation observed in Khalapur (adapted from Gumperz 1971:32–33):

A. Diphthongs /aɪ/, /uɪ/, /oɪ/ before consonants contrast with single vowels /a/, /u/, /o/:

Standard	Sweepers	
1. baiL	Bal	ear of corn
2. JhuiL	Jhul	cattle blanket
3. khoir	Khor	cattle trough

B. /u/ before a stressed vowel in next syllable contrasts with /ʌ/:

Standard	Sweepers	
1. nulána	nʌlána	(to) weed
2. Dut√l	dʌt√'i	Blanket

C. Oral vowels contrast with nasal vowels:

Standard	All Untouchables	
1. ik	ĩk	sugar cane
2. Jua	Jũa	Joke

Interviews with residents of Khalapur revealed that they were well aware of caste styles of speech. Members of higher castes often characterized nonstandard forms as "ignorant" or "backward." Lower castes were sensitive to the same norms. In one instance, when questioned about a chamar variant, two chamar men "evidenced a great deal of emotion on hearing the form. They did not answer the question, but entered into long explanations to the effect that chamars have hitherto been denied educational opportunities by the higher castes" (ibid.:32). These reactions indicate people's knowledge that speech differs and that certain pronunciations and their speakers are stigmatized.

Fundamentally it is not language in the abstract that is evaluated negatively or positively, but language as it is used by specific segments of a population. Criticizing linguistic variants is actually a mask for the social denigration of speakers. We shall see this dynamic demonstrated again and again in the ways that members of a community judge their own and others' speech.

CLASS

In societies like the United States, social stratification takes the form of *classes* that are structured in terms of economic, political, and social relations. Most sociolinguistic studies assign consultants to classes based on arbitrary indices compiled from various attributes, including occupation, income, and education. This procedure is problematic because it accepts and applies automatically a superficial definition of class. Unlike castes, which are named and overtly recognized groupings, the concept of class seems fuzzy, at least as it is applied by sociolinguists. In sociolinguistic research, class and class membership are generally assumed rather than investigated. Despite these real difficulties, social and economic differences among members of a community are reflected in many aspects of lifestyle, educational and occupational opportunities, and political power. These differences, perhaps summarized under the notion of class, have interdependent effects on linguistic performance as well. Language use both reflects and reinforces class differences. Analysis of class styles is further complicated by the inherent variability of patterning. Most speakers use upper-class and lower-class features, but it is the frequency of usage that identifies speakers. That is, class styles are not exclusive to any particular class but are instead inherently variable. It is not, therefore, the feature itself that distinguishes classes but rather the frequency of its use in particular contexts.

In the following review of research, we examine studies of class and language that draw on data from several countries and highlight different aspects of social and linguistic interconnections. An important caution should be noted regarding the methodologies used in some of the studies. Sociolinguistic research is usually based on one of two approaches. In the first approach, researchers gather samples of speech from as many speakers as possible, numbering in the hundreds or even thousands. William Labov's study of New York City speech demonstrates the validity of research based on speech samples from large numbers of people. The second approach uses a small number of consultants who are assumed to be typical speakers of their class. Their speech is then taken to be representative of the features prevalent in their class style. The research by Jacqueline Lindenfeld on French and Jan van de Broeck on Netherlandic are examples of this type of study. Their results are intriguing and certainly consistent with findings in general on class-based speech styles, but the methodology does raise questions about whether the consultants used are in fact representative inasmuch as their representativeness is assumed rather than proved.

Class and Network

Before discussing research on class and language, we should examine an additional theoretical issue, the distinction and interplay between class and network analysis. The distinction between class and network is useful in sharpening the focus on two different kinds of societal organizations. As stated by Lesley Milroy and James Milroy, "Social class is a concept designed to elucidate large-scale social, political, and economic structures and processes, whereas social network relates to the community and interpersonal level of social organization" (1992:2). According to Milroy and Milroy, two very different types of relationships exist on the levels of class and of network. Systems of class are based on "conflict, division, and inequality," whereas networks are held together through "consensus" (ibid.:3). Linguistic variation, of pronunciations and grammatical forms, occurs between classes, whereas linguistic conformity tends to occur within social networks. Close-knit networks where members share geographic location, family ties, and workplaces exert the strongest pressures for maintaining group norms.

In the opinion of Milroy and Milroy, close-knit networks are more typical of lower-class communities, whereas weak social networks, characterized by greater geographic mobility, looser kinship ties, and relationships with a wider range of people, predominate among the middle classes. Because of the strength of interpersonal bonds and community pressure in close-knit networks, members may maintain distinctive forms of speech that may actually be severely stigmatized by the society as a whole. Indeed, within such groups, "the persistence over centuries of stigmatized linguistic forms and low-status vernaculars in the face of powerful national policies of diffusing and imposing standard languages is remarkable" (ibid.:6).

Much of the research discussed in the following sections is based on analysis of class, although the data can be interpreted through appeal to the concept of social network as well.

These two approaches are, in fact, complementary because they refer to the two levels of organization and integration: the societal level of class and the interpersonal level of network.

Although analyses of class often differentiate speakers into isolable groups, class membership and, more important, the meaning of class are not categorical but rather are enacted through discourse and practice. That is, class is partly a presentation of socially recognized symbolic behavior associated with each group based on cultural norms. This symbolic behavior may be constituted through public demeanor and through linguistic and communicative behavior. Individuals adopt the discourse strategies associated with their class as a feature of their personal identity. Through discourse, speakers assume their place in a hierarchical system of status. Some individuals exert their rights to speak, to introduce and direct topics of conversation, and to ratify or dismiss the contributions of others. Other individuals limit their rights to speak and in other ways allow themselves to be treated as subordinate participants. These choices are rarely made consciously, but instead, through socialization, become normative and naturalized. Patterns of use reflect linguistic ideologies of class and identity and can be reflections of conformity or resistance to dominant norms.

New York City

Studies of linguistic diversity by William Labov, beginning with *The Social Stratification of English in New York City* (1966), have become classics in the field. In his analysis of the speech of employees in three New York City department stores, Labov focused on the phonological variable known as *postvocalic /-r/,* the pronunciation of /-r/ following a vowel—for example, *car* and *card*. The presence of /-r/ in this context is a marker of standard American English; its absence is generally stigmatized. Labov obtained data through rapid, anonymous observations by asking store employees the question "Excuse me, where are the women's shoes?" knowing the answer to be "Fourth floor." Emphatic speech (in which speakers pay more attention to pronunciation) was then elicited by repeating the question. These elicitation frames tested occurrences of /-r/ in both words (*fourth floor*) and provided comparable data from all consultants.

Labov found that workers differed in their use of /-r/ and that this differentiation was linked to their employment in stores of ranked relative prestige, that is, Saks Fifth Avenue, Macy's, and S. Klein. He found that rates of /-r/ pronunciation among employees paralleled the stratification of the stores: highest in Saks, somewhat less in Macy's, and much lower in S. Klein. Ranking of the stores resulted from differences in the quality and cost of merchandise, attracting a clientele from specific social classes. Labov concluded that workers identified with the prestige of their employer and customers, and that this identification was reflected in language use. The following tables present Labov's findings.

When employees were separated according to gender and race, some changes in frequencies of /-r/ were noted, but the overall patterning was confirmed.

Overall Distribution of /-r/

	Saks Fifth Avenue	Macy's	S. Klein
All /-r/	30%	20%	4%
Some /-r/	32	31	17
No /-r/	38	49	79
Number of subjects	68	125	71

Source: Labov 1966:73.

Distribution of /-r/ for African-American Employees

	Saks Fifth Avenue	Macy's	S. Klein
All /-r/	50%	12%	0%
Some /-r/	0	35	6
No /-r/	50	53	94
Number	2	17	18

Source: Labov 1966:77.

Distribution of /-r/ by Gender

	Women	Men
All /-r/	30%	22%
Some /-r/	17	22
No /-r/	54	57
Number	194	70

Source: Labov 1966:89, n. 10.

Distribution of /-r/ for Native-Born White Women

	Saks Fifth Avenue	Macy's	S. Klein
All /-r/	34%	31%	26%
Some /-r/	33	28	4
No /-r/	33	41	70
Number	49	65	27

Source: Labov 1966:79.

In a more complex survey among residents of New York City's Lower East Side, Labov studied the speech behavior of a large sample of speakers from different classes. Class membership was established on the basis of three equally weighted factors: occupation of main earner, education of respondents, and family income. Ten socioeconomic levels were delineated, grouped into four strata: lower class (LC), working class (WC), lower middle class (LMC), and upper middle class (UMC) (Labov 1972b:112–113). Labov incorporated the variable of contextual style by recording pronunciations of certain sounds in five contrasting situations in interviews with speakers (adapted from Labov 1966:92–98):

A. Casual speech (observed with members of the family)
B. Careful speech (recorded during interview questioning)
C. Reading style (subjects were asked to read stories)
D. Word lists (subjects read lists of isolated, random words)
E. Minimal pairs (subjects read pairs of minimally differentiated words, for example, dock/dark, sauce/source)

Through this procedure, linguists can observe whether respondents change their pronunciation in different contexts. The advantage of focusing on sounds is that speakers are generally not consciously aware of their pronunciation and therefore are unlikely to be able to control it. Linguists assume that as speakers become more attentive, they unconsciously select variants that they perceive to be closer to standard or prestige norms. The graph in Figure 9.1 for postvocalic /-r/ indicates that this assumption is valid for speakers of all social classes.

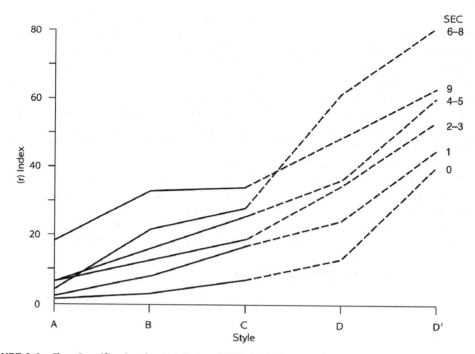

FIGURE 9.1   Class Stratification for /-r/. (Labov 1972b:114) Class stratification of a linguistic variable in process of change: (r) in *guard, car, beer, beard, board,* and so on. Socioeconomic class (SEC) scale: 0–1, lower class; 2–4, working class; 5–6, 7–8, lower middle class; 9, upper middle class. A, casual speech; B, careful speech; C, reading style; D, word lists; D′, minimal pairs.

A number of important conclusions can be drawn from the data. First, members of disparate social classes use different amounts of /-r/ in their speech, demonstrating that the variable is a significant marker of social stratification. Second, members of all classes increase their use of /-r/ as context focused more attention on pronunciation, indicating that they are aware of the same general norm giving value to /-r/ pronouncing. And third, in speech in the most careful contexts, members of the second highest class (LMC) use more /-r/ than do members of the highest group (UMC). According to Labov, such *"crossover" patterning* demonstrates that LMC speakers are most sensitive about negative evaluations of their own speech and most desirous of achieving prestige norms (1972b:117). Such patterning also reveals the speakers' conformity to beliefs that link language use and social identity.

Social class differences are exhibited not only in people's speech but also in their judgment of the speech of others. "The correlate of regular stratification of a sociolinguistic variable in behavior is uniform agreement in subjective reactions towards that variable" (ibid.:249). Speakers' assessment of /-r/ was measured by asking them to rate tape-recorded speech on a scale of occupational suitability, judging whether the speech would be acceptable for a television personality, executive secretary, receptionist, switchboard operator, salesperson, or factory worker (Labov 1966:411). Following are scores for sensitivity to postvocalic /-r/ (Labov 1972b:131):

LC	50%
WC	53
LMC	86
UMC	75

These subjective reactions show that just as members of the LMC are most attentive in their own use of /-r/, they are also most sensitive to its occurrence in the speech of others, once again outdoing members of the highest group. Labov referred to LMC patterns as evidence of "linguistic insecurity" (ibid.:133). However, it is the societal circumstances of these people that motivate their reactions. In other words, linguistic insecurity is a reflection of social insecurity stemming from disadvantages due to education, income, occupation, and the like, that members of this class experience. Perhaps, they exhibit crossover behavior more than people of even lower groups because they are closest to the highest stratum and attempt to model their speech more directly on prestige norms.

When additional sounds were studied, Labov found similar patterns of class stratification in use and evaluation. Vowels /oh/ (as in _off, caught, chocolate_) and /eh/ (as in _pass, dance_) fluctuate from standard American English pronunciation to stereotyped and stigmatized New York City dialect. Figures 9.2 and 9.3 present data for three class groupings across contextual styles.

Responses for subjective reactions to these features in tape-recorded speech reveal the following percentages of negative judgments of nonstandard forms (Labov 1972b:130):

Negative Response to Nonstandard /oh/

LC	24%
WC	61
LMC	79
UMC	59

Negative Response to Nonstandard/eh/

LC	63%
WC	81
LMC	86
UMC	67

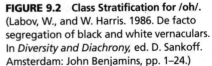

FIGURE 9.2   Class Stratification for /oh/. (Labov, W., and W. Harris. 1986. De facto segregation of black and white vernaculars. In _Diversity and Diachrony,_ ed. D. Sankoff. Amsterdam: John Benjamins, pp. 1–24.)

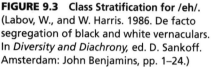

FIGURE 9.3   Class Stratification for /eh/.
(Labov, W., and W. Harris. 1986. De facto
segregation of black and white vernaculars.
In *Diversity and Diachrony,* ed. D. Sankoff.
Amsterdam: John Benjamins, pp. 1–24.)

Crossover behavior exhibited by the LMC for the variables /-r/, /oh/, and /eh/ shows a consistent pattern in their own speech and their reactions to others. These three variables are undergoing change in New York City dialects. The prestige value of pronouncing post-vocalic /-r/ spread to this area after World War II, undoubtedly accelerated by use of the American standard /-r/ in the mass media. Vowel variants of /oh/ and /eh/ are also unstable and changing.

When speech behavior and judgments of these three variables are compared with two stable pronunciations, significant contrasting patterns emerge. The relevant stable features are the pronunciation of /th/ and /dh/ in words such as th*ing* and th*is,* respectively. In standard English, these sounds occur as fricatives /θ/ and /D/, with corresponding stigmatized use of stops /t/ and /d/, for example, *t*irty ("thirty"), *d*ese ("these"). Labov found a complete, sharp stratification for all classes. All speakers decrease their use of stigmatized /t/ as context invokes more attentive speech. And for each style, each class is ranked consistently in relation to the other classes; the higher the class, the greater is the use of the standard fricative. The same pattern occurs for voiced /dh/. Figure 9.4 shows stylistic and class differentiation for /th/.

Subjective reaction tests for stable markers /th/ and /dh/ reveal a contrast to those for the three changing features /-r/, /oh/, and /eh/. Negative judgments to nonstandard /t/ were (Labov 1972b:131):

LC	58%
WC	76
LMC	81
UMC	92

In subjective judgments, class stratification is sharp; negative reactions increase as class ranking increases. Crossover behavior of LMC speakers occurs only for phonological markers in the process of change. Thus, crossover behavior can be used as a reliable and consistent indicator of linguistic change, responding to overall social and linguistic stratification.

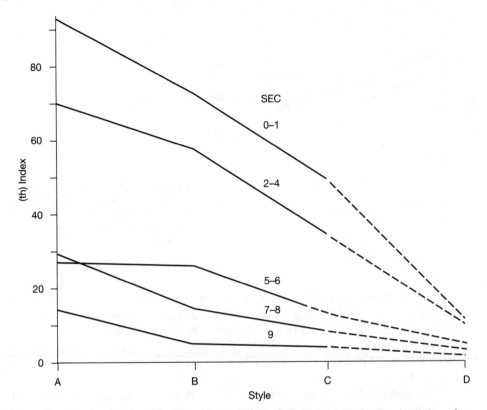

FIGURE 9.4   Class Stratification for /th/. (Labov, W., and W. Harris. 1986. De facto segregation of black and white vernaculars. In *Diversity and Diachrony,* ed. D. Sankoff. Amsterdam: John Benjamins, pp. 1–24.)

Norwich, England

Interconnections between social stratification and language have also been researched in Great Britain. In Peter Trudgill's study of class styles among speakers in Norwich, England, the following phonological features were measured (Trudgill 1974a):

1. /ng/: frequency of replacement of /-ng/ by /-n/ in words such as *walking, running, walkin, runnin*
2. /t/: frequency of replacement of /t/ by glottal stop /ʔ/ in words such as *butter, bet, buʔer, beʔ*
3. /h/: frequency of dropping /h/ in words such as *hammer, hat, 'ammer, 'at*

Consultants were assigned class membership on the basis of six factors: occupation, income, education, housing, locality, and father's occupation.

Trudgill found that members of social classes are stratified by their use of the three variables in parallel patterning. For all features, higher-class speakers use less nonstandard forms, meaning, of course, that they use more standard pronunciations. The reverse pattern is demonstrated by members of lower classes, whose speech is characterized by stigmatized pronunciations. Although all five class groupings are differentiated, Trudgill's research reveals a marked distinction between middle-class and working-class usage. Speech patterns among all middle-class speakers are more similar to each other, as are speech patterns among members of working-class categories.

The following table summarizes data for all classes, distinguished as middle middle class (MMC), lower middle class (LMC), upper working class (UWC), middle working class (MWC), and lower working class (LWC). Percentages reflect use of stigmatized variants: /n/ rather than /ng/, /$^?$/ rather than /t/, and loss of /h/ (Trudgill 1974b:47).

	ng	t	h
MMC	31%	41%	6%
LMC	42	62	14
UWC	87	89	40
MWC	95	92	59
LWC	100	94	61

As the data show, distinctions among the three phonological variables occurred. Frequencies for nonstandard loss of /h/ at beginnings of words are much less for all classes than are rates for the other nonstandard forms, /n/ and /$^?$/, indicating that loss of /h/ carries greater stigma.

In addition, class differences were correlated with use or nonuse of the morphological marker on present-tense verbs for third-person singular, written as "-s," for example, she/he/it moves. The following table displays rates of omission of the suffix (Trudgill 1974b:44).

Percentage of Verbs Without /-s/	
MMC	0%
LMC	2
UWC	70
MWC	87
LWC	97

Although class stratification for the suffix follows the same trend as that for sounds, several significant differences occur. First, distinction between middle-class and working-class aggregates is especially sharp, from 0 to 2 percent for the former and from 70 to 97 percent for the latter. Second, behavior of the highest and lowest groups is almost reversed: MMC speakers always use standard /-s/, but LWC speakers use it only 3 percent of the time. These values can be compared to findings on pronunciations where differences between MMC and LWC speakers are not as extreme. Although LWC speech contains more nonstandard pronunciations, MMC speakers also use nonstandard variants; for example, they use nonstandard /-n/ at a rate of 31 percent.

Paris and Rouen, France

Class differences are reflected in the use of syntactic alternatives as well as in phonological or morphological features. Jacqueline Lindenfeld's (1969) research in Paris and Rouen demonstrated correlations among syntactic complexity, degree of formality of speech events, and speakers' class membership. Twelve subjects were selected and grouped into high (Class I) and low (Class II) strata based on education, occupation, and income, although the latter factor was given less weight. Class I occupations included lawyer, teacher, psychologist, and bank manager. Some Class II occupations were factory worker, practical nurse, and nursery school assistant. All members of Class I had at least three years of college education, whereas no Class II members had gone beyond junior high school.

Speech samples were obtained from subjects in an experimental situation designed to elicit formal and informal speech. Lindenfeld asked each respondent to role-play, speaking first to a large audience about his or her occupation and second to a family member or friend about his or her summer vacation. This methodology is problematic in its reliance on the speaker's out-of-context performance, although Lindenfeld claims that the linguistic differences among speakers are reliable.

The analysis focused on syntactic structure and the degree of complexity used by speakers where syntactic options are available. Three syntactic features were investigated: subordination, relativization, and nominalization. Contrasting examples, demonstrating alternatives of use or nonuse of these features, are given (ibid.:894):

1. **Subordination**
   a. No subordination:
      On a fini de déjeuner. On peut sortir. "We are finished with lunch. We can go out."
   b. Subordination:
      Puisqu'on a fini de diner, on peut sortir. "Since we are finished eating supper, we can go out."

2. **Relativization**
   a. No relativization:
      On est allées à Delos. On a vu toutes sortes de choses. "We went to Delos. We saw all kinds of things."
   b. Relativization:
      Nous sommes passés par Amsterdam, où nous avons fait un tour du musée. "We went through Amsterdam, where we visited the museum."

3. **Nominalization**
   a. No nominalization:
      Elle était toute triste. Jean était parti. "She was very sad. John had gone."
   b. Nominalization:
      J'étais content qu'il soit parti. "I was glad that he was away."

In addition to recording occurrences of these grammatical features, Lindenfeld noted sentence length, measured in number of words. She hypothesized that syntactic complexity and sentence length would increase along with factors of higher class and greater situational and topical formality. Indeed, results of the study confirmed all but one of the hypotheses. Nominalization, relativization, and sentence length were significant indicators of class and context. Although Class I and II speakers produced sentences of roughly equal complexity in their informal style, marked differences occurred in formal speech. Class I speakers employed higher rates of nominalization and relativization in formal contexts than in their informal speech, whereas members of Class II showed no difference between their formal and informal styles. Numerical results are presented in the following table (ibid.:894):

Thus, it is the differences in formal speech that distinguish members of Classes I and II. The former use greater syntactic complexity in formal contexts, whereas the latter employ the same kinds of sentence constructions in all contexts. Although sentence length is greater on average in formal situations for all speakers, the increase is sharper for members of Class I than of Class II (from 14 to 23 words for Class I and 13 to 17 words for Class II).

The Correlation of Linguistic Variation, Sociological Variation, and Contextual Variation*

	Formal Context		Informal Context	
	Class I	Class II	Class I	Class II
Subordination	7	7	7	7
Relativization	11	7	8	8
Nominalization	13	8	9	7
Sentence length (number of words)	23	17	14	13

*Figures represent averages for six subjects on the basis of 400-word samples.

Members of distinct classes thus exhibit differences in sensitivity to social context, at least as measured by their use of optional syntactic formations. This contrast is probably due, in part, to educational levels attained, inasmuch as people who have advanced educations are more familiar with and more comfortable using complex grammatical constructions. Exposure to linguistic markers of social class, then, contributes to the reproduction of social and class identity.

Maaseik, Belgium

Relationships between social stratification and degrees of syntactic complexity in speech have also been found among speakers in Maaseik, a small town in Belgium (van de Broeck 1977). Jef van de Broeck selected eight male subjects and assigned them to middle-class or working-class groups on the basis of occupation, income, and education. Speech was recorded in a formal interview between the subject and a stranger and in an informal discussion with a friend in order to study the influence of both social stratification and context on linguistic performance (ibid.:152–153). Relevant features of syntactic complexity in Netherlandic (Dutch) were identified. Note that sentence equivalents are given here in English (ibid.:155–157):

1. Average length of main clause plus any attached or embedded clauses.
2. Subordination—for example: "I was glad that John had seen Mary."
3. Multiple embedding—for example: "After he had spoken to his father, whom he had not seen for a long time, John went to his mother's place, where he ate the best meal he had had in years."
4. Passives.
5. Passives without agents—for example: "My car was stolen" [compared to "they (someone) stole my car"].

Indices for each type of complexity were developed and measured. The same correlations among class, context, and syntax emerged for all features. Although middle-class (MC) and working-class (WC) speakers showed no significant differences in sentence complexity in informal situations, there was a marked distinction between the classes in formal contexts. In these situations, MC speakers used a high degree of complex constructions, consistent with Lindenfeld's findings for French. When speech was analyzed within each class, a striking contrast emerged in class behavior in the two contexts. MC formal syntax was always much more complex than MC informal speech, but WC formal syntax was actually somewhat less complex than WC informal style. Van de Broeck represented this finding by a diagram (Figure 9.5) indicating directions of shifts from informal to formal speech for the two classes.

MC and WC speech move in different directions in formal situations—the former toward greater complexity and the latter toward greater syntactic simplicity. Such behavior requires an

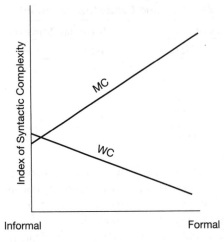

FIGURE 9.5 Class, Context, and Syntactic Complexity. (van de Broeck, Jef. 1977. Class differences in syntactic complexity in the Flemish town of Maaseik. *Language in Society* 6:149–181.)

explanation that focuses on interconnections between class and context. Van de Broeck suggested that two attitudinal factors are operative. First is the desire of MC speakers to distinguish their style from that of the WC in formal situations, that is, in situations where all people feel "on display." They use linguistic mechanisms as an "act of conspicuous ostentation, a marker of social distance" (ibid.:169). The second factor concerns WC speakers, who also feel "on display" in formal circumstances but who recognize their relative powerlessness in those situations. They respond to their social subordination by moving away from prestigeful speech, possibly because they want to actively reject MC norms or because they are unsure of their linguistic abilities and prefer to use simpler speech rather than make mistakes (ibid.:170–171). Van de Broeck concluded: "The MC behaves linguistically 'with an eye on' the WC, not independent of them. And partly because the MC displays their handling of complex syntax, the WC refrains from trying to achieve the same norms. They react in the opposite way by underperforming, by appearing to a certain extent less verbally skilled than they actually are" (ibid.:171). The behavior of WC speakers may also be a strategy of resistance to dominant notions of language and prestige.

Class-Based Codes

Use of different linguistic styles, or codes, may affect the ways that speakers participate in society. Basil Bernstein made the point that class-based styles of speaking lead to differences in styles of thinking and how one experiences the world. He described two kinds of linguistic codes that he associated with different social classes. According to Bernstein, middle-class speech is characterized by use of an "elaborated" code that expresses "universalistic" meanings by use of nouns, adjectives, and verbs having explicit referents. In contrast, working-class style tends to employ a "restricted" code, expressing "particularistic" meanings by use of words that are more context-bound (1971b:175). (Bernstein's choice of terms is unfortunate because the words *elaborated* and *restricted* have value-laden connotations.)

Bernstein supported his thesis with examples of speech of middle- and working-class children. The following excerpts are illustrative. They are composites of speech of 5-year-old children who were asked to describe the actions in a series of four photographs. Although the excerpts illustrate Bernstein's hypothesis, it is important to remember that they are not the children's verbatim speech (ibid.:178).

1. *Middle-class sample:* Three boys are playing football and one boy kicks the ball and it goes through the window the ball breaks the window and the boys are looking at it and a man comes out and shouts at them because they've broken the window so they run away and then that lady looks out of her window and she tells the boys off.
2. *Working-class sample:* They're playing football and he kicks it and it goes through there it breaks the window and they're looking at it and he comes out and shouts at them because they've broken it so they run away and then she looks out and she tells them off.

A major difference between the two styles is that working-class children employ words with inexplicit references and pronouns lacking stated antecedents (e.g., "he kicks it and it goes through there"). Their language use, therefore, presupposes shared knowledge and experience with their interlocutors. In contrast, middle-class speakers make their meanings explicit, not relying as much on presuppositions (e.g., "one boy kicks the ball and it goes through the window").

Bernstein contended that use of explicit references in elaborated codes can allow speakers to think about meanings and relationships separate from their immediate context, potentially permitting them to "enter into a reflexive relationship to the social order." In contrast, restricted codes are limited in their ability to express abstract meanings, leading speakers to understand their experience primarily in relation to a specific context. Significantly, "one of the effects of the class system is to limit access to elaborated codes" (ibid.:176).

According to Bernstein, because members of different social classes use different modes of expression, they develop different patterns of thought and thus understand their world in different ways. In terms echoing Sapir and Whorf (who Bernstein credits with influencing the development of his ideas), Bernstein stated:

> Language is one of the most important means of initiating, synthesizing, and *reinforcing* ways of thinking, feeling and behaviour which are functionally related to the social group. It does not, of itself, prevent the expression of specific ideas or confine the individual to a given level of conceptualization, but certain ideas and generalizations are facilitated rather than others (emphasis in original). (1971a: 43)

Through their use of elaborated or restricted codes, members of stratified social classes orient and express their experiences and thoughts in different forms, thus affecting the ways that they participate in society. In addition, lack of familiarity and competence in middle-class ("elaborated") styles renders working-class speakers uncomfortable with members of higher classes (see also van de Broeck 1977). Working-class speakers' discomfort with elaborated codes makes it difficult for them to read and write using formal styles of language.

All the studies of language and class demonstrate that classification of people into different social strata is powerfully reflected in linguistic variation. Speakers' sensitivity to context, their awareness of their own behavior and that of others, and their reactions both in subjective judgments and in modifications of speech all converge to mark one's place in a hierarchical system.

Speech styles associated with members of upper classes obtain and retain prestige because of the status of their speakers. People with lower status often exhibit speech patterns (e.g., crossover behavior) reflective of their linguistic (and social) insecurity. Their awareness of negative judgments toward their speech, judgments that they also hold, makes them attempt to use prestige norms of upper-class speakers. Class membership not only affects life circumstances but also influences the construction of personal identities. In the process, personal identities become socialized. Language use is a recognized and recognizable reflection of one's social identity.

In the context of family life, people are socialized into their roles, not only as actors but also as speakers. Children learn their rights and obligations from the kinds of communicative interactions in which they are enmeshed. In a study taking its basic premises from Basil Bernstein's work on language and class, Erica Huls (1989) investigated normative interactions in two Dutch families, one headed by a factory director (called the "High" family) and the other by a janitor (called the "Low" family). (Note that Huls uses the father's occupation to describe the families, although both mothers are employed: The factory director's wife is a kindergarten teacher and the janitor's wife is a home help worker.) Both families have young children ranging in age from 2 to 11 and both have daughters age 5. These latter children are the principal focus of this study.

Huls's research centered on three types of structural and interactional forms: turn-taking processes, issuing and receiving directives, and participating in "school speech acts." The analysis of turn-taking considered the ways that interactants competed with each other for the floor through interruptions of others' turns and simultaneous starts in order to gain the opportunity to speak and to limit the talk of others. Turn-taking dependency was also studied, reflected in the use of *prestarts,* strategies in which a prospective speaker requests attention and/or permission to speak (e.g., "Mom, you know what?"). These strategies reflect the dependence of a prospective speaker on another participant. The two families differed significantly in their use of competitive techniques both in absolute and relative terms. That is, examples of competitive turns constituted 7.8 percent of the total number of turns in the High family, but only 4.6 percent of the total of turns in the Low family (ibid.:127). And each member of the High family used competitive strategies more than his or her comparable member in the Low family, indicating a consistent prevalence of competition in the former.

Within families, social position and age contributed to the likelihood of a person's winning in competitive interactions. In both families, mothers were the most likely winners, having a success rate of 70 percent. Fathers were successful 50 percent of the time. The success rate of the oldest children was about 40 percent, while younger children had declining chances of success (ibid.:129). Analysis of dyadic interactions reveals that mothers are more likely winners in each pair, regardless of with whom they are interacting. Children are especially unlikely to win when competing with their mothers. Fathers have an intermediate role, more frequently losing to their wives but winning against their children. The children in the High family are socialized to compete with each other, to attempt to hold their own in conversation, and even to compete with people of higher social power such as their parents and older siblings. Although they may lose in competition with social superiors, the interactions teach them winning techniques that they can use later in life and in other contexts.

Analysis of prestarts or dependency signals reveals that, although this is a common strategy for all children, the children in the High family scored higher for this feature. Prestarts were used more with mothers than with any other conversation participant, but they were used as well by younger children when interacting with older children, reconfirming the social- and age-based hierarchies in both families.

Analysis of directives indicates similarities in the frequencies with which they are issued in both families. In addition, mothers in both families issued more directives than anyone else, accounting for about half of all the directives given. Differences emerge, however, in the styles chosen. That is, in the High family, directives are more often embedded in complex linguistic structures, while in the Low family, commands are more often stated indirectly. Directives also vary in force and appeal. In the High family, appeal is often made to the personal wishes or needs of the speaker or other concerned parties, while in the Low family, directives are formulated in the context of rights of speaker, duties of addressee, and sanctions that might result from non-compliance (ibid.:132).

The category of "school speech acts" includes positive reinforcements (e.g., praise, ratification, and agreement), corrections, and continuations. Because these are features of speech that occur in school, their use at home familiarizes the child with behaviors that will be expected of them in the school context. Huls found that each type of "school speech act" occurred more frequently in High family interactions than in Low family interactions. Although parents often instigate these behaviors, children also use them when interacting with other children (ibid.:134).

In sum, the two families differed in significant ways, socializing their children into different expectations about their rights and obligations, their orientation to others in interaction, and their familiarity with the kinds of behaviors expected of them in school. Overall, High family children learn to compete with others, to develop strategies enabling them to hold their own in conversation, to appreciate personal relationships and orientations, and to value explicit rules of grammar and behavior. In contrast, Low family children are less used to and less skilled at competitive verbal interactions, learn to comply with directives based on appeals to external rules and sanctions, and are less practiced in the kinds of interactions that take place in school settings. These differences do not in themselves carry positive or negative meanings, but in the context of a hierarchical class society in which certain forms of speech and communicative interactions are privileged, speakers who manipulate the prestige forms are able to present themselves as people worthy of respect. And in a class-based society, they are granted such respect by others. Therefore, we can see the ways that socialization into norms of language use contributes to the production and reproduction of social inequality.

RACE

African-American English in the United States

In the United States and elsewhere, race has an impact on language use. Many (but, of course, not all) African Americans in the United States speak a variety of English known as African-American Vernacular English (AAVE). Some speakers use this dialect in all their communication; others use it only in certain contexts, such as among family and friends, and speak standard English (SE) in other situations, such as in school or at work. They may also switch from one style to the other during any speech event, depending on the topic, attitude, and co-participants. In these cases, stylistic choices are reflections of the links between language use and personal identity.

Studies of AAVE have documented both its linguistic and social features. We will begin with an examination of structural differences between AAVE and standard English. We then discuss the complex ways that use and evaluation of AAVE reflect and interconnect with societal attitudes and speakers' identities.

AAVE is a dialect that, like all other dialects, has phonological and grammatical rules. Most of these rules are identical to those of the standard language, but there are some regularly occurring patterns in AAVE that, taken as a whole, distinguish it from other varieties. There has been much debate in linguistics about the origins of AAVE, principally whether it is derived from regional southern speech or from Creole languages of African slaves, incorporating syntactic and semantic traits of African languages. The current consensus among linguists is that both historical sources have contributed to the development of AAVE. Some features are derived from the speech of rural white southerners, whose language reflects the dialect of their Scots-Irish ancestors. Other features, particularly several grammatical aspects in the verb system, have their origins in earlier Creoles. Labov summarized the basic position as follows (1982:192). Note that Labov's *Black English Vernacular* is the older term for *African-American Vernacular English*:

1. Black English Vernacular is a subsystem of English with a distinct set of phonological and syntactic rules that are now aligned in many ways with the rules of other dialects.
2. It incorporates many features of southern phonology, morphology, and syntax; Blacks in turn have exerted influence on the dialects of the South where they have lived.
3. It shows evidence of derivation from an earlier Creole that was closer to the present-day Creoles of the Caribbean.
4. It has a highly developed aspect system, quite different from other dialects of English, which shows a continuing development of its semantic structure.

In discussing linguistic features of AAVE, it should be remembered that speakers employ different styles, depending on relative formality or informality of situations, and on other social factors, including relationships with co-participants and topics of conversation.

The Structure of African-American Vernacular English

Major phonological and morphological characteristics of AAVE are listed and exemplified first, followed by a discussion of AAVE's unique aspectual system. The unique grammatical features of AAVE are characteristic of the dialect spoken by many African Americans throughout the United States. Although it may have originated geographically among speakers in the South, AAVE is now a national, not a regional, dialect.

REDUCTION OF WORD-FINAL CONSONANT CLUSTERS. In all dialects of English, when two (or more) consonants occur at the end of a word and the next word in an utterance begins with a consonant, speakers in normal, colloquial style reduce the cluster in the first word by eliminating the final consonant; for example, *last night* becomes *las' night.* Speakers of AAVE exhibit the same pattern but also modify word-final clusters at the ends of utterances or when the next word begins with a vowel, for example, *She came in las'.*

Reduction of clusters, though, is not always a simple phonological process. In English, some final consonants have an important role in marking morphological changes. In addition to their status as phonemes, the sounds /t/ and /d/ can occur at the ends of verbs to denote past tense, as in "I liked (/laykt/) the movie" or "they solved (/salvd/) the problem." When the final consonant has a grammatical function, it is less likely to be deleted. John Baugh (1983) collected large samples of adult speech in Los Angeles and computed probability values for the likelihood of occurrences of phonological and morphological features in what he calls "Black street speech." Based on a scale from 0.000 (for full manifestation in all contexts) to 1.000 (for deletions of variables), the probability value for omission of /t/ and /d/ is .683 when the sounds have no grammatical function, but it is only .353 when they mark past tense (ibid.:98). This clearly proves that speakers are well aware of the importance of the grammatical roles of sounds and are responsive to the meanings of words.

Similar patterning occurs for omission or retention of word-final /-s/. This phoneme can represent three different grammatical morphemes: plural (two cats), possessive (the cat's dish broke), and third-person singular (she likes it). Speakers of AAVE are most likely to retain /s/ at the end of words when it marks plurality of nouns. In fact, for this meaning, /s/ is rarely deleted. It is often omitted, however, when it represents the possessive and especially when it denotes third-person singular. Baugh's probability values for loss of /s/ with these three meanings are plural, .173; possessive, .611; and third-person singular, .753 (ibid.:95).

Studies among African Americans in Detroit revealed gender differences in reducing final consonant clusters (Wolfram 1969). Men tended to delete final consonants in clusters more often than did women, with percentages of 57.8 and 43.7, respectively.

VARIATION OF /r/.   Another phonological feature of AAVE is the variation of postvocalic /-r/. Its occurrence in this dialect is similar to patterning in other variable dialects, as noted, for instance, in Labov's New York City research. African Americans tend to delete postvocalic /-r/ at higher rates than white speakers do in all contextual styles. In addition, /r/ is sometimes omitted between vowels, especially when a preceding vowel is stressed—for example, Carol → Ca'ol, interested → inte'ested (Labov 1972a:14).

CONTRACTION AND DELETION OF THE COPULA.   The English copula (the verb *to be*) can be contracted in present tense in colloquial speech, as in "she is smart" → "she's smart." This rule describes the normal process in most dialects. A further development takes place in AAVE: deletion of present-tense forms entirely, as in "she smart." But AAVE does not omit the copula in all linguistic contexts. Deletion of the copula in AAVE is related to its contraction in standard English; that is, "wherever SE can contract, AAVE can delete *is* and *are,* and vice versa" (ibid.:73). In SE, the copula cannot be contracted in "exposed position," particularly at the ends of sentences. For example, it must occur in "Here I *am*" or "that's the kind of person he *is.*" Forms like "Here I'm" or "that's the kind of person he's" are not possible. Similarly, AAVE retains the full copula in these environments.

Deletion of the copula in AAVE also depends on the kind of grammatical form that follows. Some possibilities (examples from Labov 1972a:67–68) are the following:

1. *Noun phrase:* She the first one started us off.
2. *Predicate adjective:* He fast in everything he do.
3. *Locative:* We on tape.
4. *Negation:* They not caught.
5. *Progressive* (verb): He always coming over to my house to eat.
6. *Future* ("gonna" or "gon"): He gon' try to get up.

According to Baugh's probability values, speakers are most likely to omit the copula preceding *gonna* or a progressive verb (values of .691 and .662, respectively) and most likely to be retained preceding locatives and noun phrases—.294 and .315, respectively (1983:101).

Studies in Detroit demonstrated gender and class differences in the pattern of this grammatical feature. Women tended to retain the copula with greater frequency than did men. And men and women who were members of higher classes tended to retain the copula. Walt Wolfram's data (1969), separated for gender and class, are presented in the following table:

Percentage of Copula Deletion

Class	Men	Women
Upper middle	6.4%	3.1%
Lower middle	16.4	5.3
Upper working	45.3	28.7
Lower working	66.3	47.5

For all phonological and morphological features—consonant reduction, variation of /r/, and deletion of the copula—AAVE seems to be advancing rules of the standard language: Standard English allows reduction of final consonant clusters before a next consonant, but AAVE allows reduction of all final clusters; several regional dialects omit /r/ following vowels, but AAVE omits /r/ between vowels as well; SE contracts the copula in certain environments, but AAVE deletes the copula in these same contexts. Rules in AAVE, therefore, are sensitive to phonological and morphological traits of SE but manifest innovative expansions.

Some speakers of AAVE exhibit behavior referred to as hypercorrection. **Hypercorrection** is a process of extending linguistic rules in an overly generalized and regularized fashion. For example, Baugh quoted a teenager who said, "They act like they think I really likes going to school" (1983:65). This speaker attaches the suffix /-s/ to a first-person verb even though it normally occurs only on third-person forms. Another hypercorrection in some AAVE speech is overgeneralization by analogy of the past-tense suffix /-d/, written "-ed," resulting in: look → lookted (/lʊktɪd/), love → loveded (/lʌvdɪd/).

Baugh suggested that hypercorrection occurs more frequently in formal contexts when speakers are particularly aware that their speech is stigmatized (ibid.). Hypercorrection is a response to social pressures and to people's sensitivity to the fact that their colloquial style is criticized by the "general" population. Speakers of AAVE know that they sometimes delete /-s/ and /-d/ on verbs and so they include them in linguistic environments where they do not belong. In attempting to correct their speech, speakers actually outdo standard norms by overextending grammatical rules. This kind of reaction is similar to pronunciations by lower-middle-class speakers in Labov's New York City research who exhibited crossover rates of standard speech in formal contexts. In both cases, people respond through their use of language to social perceptions of them, knowing that they are judged negatively and hoping to make a better impression by changing the way they speak. But, as we have already seen, negative evaluations of a linguistic style are actually metaphors for the powerlessness of its speakers.

The unique character of AAVE is demonstrated especially by its development of complex aspectual systems in verbs. *Grammatical aspects* indicate the manner or duration of an event's occurrence. For example, the progressive denotes action throughout a time period: "I was reading all morning." AAVE contains many more kinds of aspect marking than are available in standard English. These properties of AAVE may have originated in Creoles derived from African languages, although Anglo-Irish influences are also possible (Baugh 1983:73; Labov 1982:140). Whatever the historical antecedents, AAVE continually expands on aspectual meanings using contemporary forms. (Examples in the following discussion are taken from Baugh 1983:70–87, with the exception of number 6, which is taken from Labov 1972a:188.)

1. Invariant *be*: Use of *be* generally marks habitual and/or durative aspect. The habitual refers to events that occur and are expected to recur, and the durative denotes an action over time.
   a. It's just not convenient…y'know…cause the office *be* closed on weekends.
   b. She say, "Why you *be* runnin in the street so much?"
   c. But the teachers don't *be* knowing the problems like the parents do.
      Invariant *be* sometimes has only a durative meaning.
   d. …and we *be* tired from the heat, but he just made everybody keep on working.
      Finally, invariant *be* can occur in diverse syntactic environments.
   e. Preceding progressive verbs: He *be* hiding when he knows she's mad.
   f. Preceding locatives: They don't *be* on the streets no more.
   g. Preceding noun phrases: Leo *be* the one to tell it like it is.
   h. Preceding adjectives: It's not right to act like you *be* stupid in school.

2. Perfective *done*: Perfective aspect denotes an action that is completed.

   a. The teacher *done* lost her keys.

   b. We *done* told him 'bout these pipes already.

     Done also has meanings comparable to standard *already* and the emphatic *really.*

   c. It don't make no difference 'cause they *done* used all the good ones by now.

   d. Well, we useta get into trouble and if Pop'd catch us, he say, "Boy—you *done* done it now."

3. Future perfective *be done*: This form is used for an event that will occur and be completed in the future. Its form is *be done* + past-tense verbs.

   a. We *be done* washed all the cars by the time Jojo gets back with the cigarettes.

   b. I'll *be done* bought my own radio waitin on him to buy me one.

4. Stressed *been:* Stress (or accent) on the word *been* marks an event that began in the past. In some cases, it marks completion of an event in the past, whereas in others, the action or state continues into the present.

   a. We *been* lived here.

   b. I *been* had that job.

5. Aspectual *steady*: *Steady* functions as an intensified continuative, emphasizing consistent and persistent continuation of an event. It usually occurs with progressive verbs and always takes an animate subject.

   a. He all the time be *steady* complainin bout somethin.

   b. Them fools be *steady* hustlin everybody they see.

6. Multiple negation: Speakers of many English dialects use multiple negation in colloquial speech. AAVE is characterized by a proliferation of negation to mark emphasis and stylistic effect.

   a. They didn't never do nothing to nobody.

   b. He ain't not never gon say it to his face.

   c. They can't do nothing if they don't never try.

     AAVE allows for the inversion of standard word order of noun + auxiliary + verb auxiliary + noun + verb with negation.

   d. Didn't nobody see it, didn't nobody hear it!

Settings and Contexts

As with speakers of all other languages, speakers of AAVE are sensitive to situational requirements and adapt their linguistic performance to context. As Baugh points out in his analysis of street speech, people employ stylistic alternatives, depending on the degree of familiarity and solidarity with co-participants in speech events. "All people are more comfortable when they are interacting with others who share common norms, and linguistic performance is one of the most important criteria for establishing rapport" (Baugh 1983:33). Features of AAVE occur with greatest frequency in informal contexts when speakers share life experiences, expectations, and values. In contrast, speakers use standard English in situations of formality and social distance. In a mathematical measure of sensitivity to context, Baugh's probability values for phonological variables in different speech events reveal that speakers' deletion of the suffix /-s/ (described above) has the probability value of .615 (out of 1.000) in the most informal situations, whereas its value is .378 in the most formal contexts (ibid.:95). Other linguistic features showed similar situational variation.

    Speakers are often acutely aware of their status in relation to co-participants and adjust their behavior accordingly. Research among adolescent boys in Harlem (Labov 1972a) revealed that when boys were interviewed in a somewhat formal manner, they typically gave minimal responses, answering in few words and in a hesitant and pause-filled fashion. But when the children felt relaxed, they were very talkative and exhibited a great deal of verbal creativity. In the first instance, "[t]he child is in an asymmetrical situation where anything he says can literally be held against him. He has learned a number of devices to avoid saying anything in this situation and he works very hard to achieve this end" (ibid.:206). In the second instance, when people are socially at ease and do not feel that they are being evaluated and judged, they willingly express their individuality, knowledge, and opinions in a free and easy style. Evidence from other research on speech contexts and language use supports these same conclusions. Recall, for example, van de Broeck's work in Belgium showing that lower-class speakers used simpler syntactic constructions in formal situations than in informal ones where they felt more comfortable.

A number of studies have demonstrated the significant use of African-American Vernacular English as a device to display solidarity between speaker and addressee. In particular, code switching from standard speech to the vernacular was seen to emphasize community membership and create affective and supportive bonds. When Linda Nelson (1990) analyzed life-history narratives from African-American women in New York City, southern New Jersey, and Philadelphia, she noticed that the women began speaking in standard English but often switched to the vernacular at key points in the interviews. In some cases, switches were made to highlight incidents or feelings expressed, and others were triggered by Nelson's responses and/or her own use of vernacular features. Nelson later "translated" the women's utterances from AAVE into standard speech and asked the women whether they perceived a difference in meaning. Responses usually focused on the affective meanings transmitted by the vernacular, but not by the standard forms. For example, when talking about the poverty experienced by her family in her childhood, one woman said, "Girl, you better get that 5-cent pack of Kool-Aid!" And when Nelson asked about the difference between her statement and a standard equivalent statement the woman explained that it was more than a focus on the words. Meaning was found in how those words and concepts could represent something larger, it was a label that could be used on a wider range of things. The woman noted, "We had to improvise on a lot of things that weren't always available to us" (ibid.:150). Speaking about the influence of her elders, the woman said, "I always had an ear to what older folks talkin bout." When Nelson asked her to compare her statement with a standard equivalent statement, the woman responded:

> I tried to convey a sense which meant I would sit and listen but also more, I would try to be in their presence, more than just eavesdropping. I'm trying to communicate a shoebox full when you only give them [the words] a matchbox. I'm trying to relate the spiritual meaning. (ibid.:151)

The speaker also conveyed her camaraderie with Nelson and her desire to display that relationship, but using her "home tongue" she expressed her message more clearly and showed that she was comfortable. (ibid.).

The use of AAVE as a means of establishing rapport and solidarity was also demonstrated in a study of teacher–student interactions in a community college (Foster 1995). During classroom interactions, the teacher framed some of class time as "performance" by switching into vernacular language and style. "In performances, there is a shift away from mainstream language to language and behavior that is more Black. The resulting talk is more participatory, with students contributing spontaneously" (ibid.:337). Shifts included changes in rhythm, grammar, intonational patterns, and use of "images, symbolism and gestures" characteristic of African-American styles. The teacher's talk incorporated features of a "Black sermonic tradition" (ibid.:140). In interviews with the teachers, Michele Foster found that the women switched within discourse from standard to vernacular speech, sometimes to highlight emotional aspects of their narratives, sometimes to set off episodes or reported speech within the narrative, and sometimes to display solidarity with the researcher. The significance of the latter function was revealed especially by contrasts when Foster interviewed male teachers. The men exhibited many fewer instances of code switching, suggesting that "gender plays some part in facilitating or inhibiting codeswitching behavior" (ibid.:346).

Studies such as those of Nelson and Foster have helped extend knowledge of the use of AAVE by including research among women. Nearly all studies conducted during the 1960s and 1970s focused on language used by boys and men. As John Rickford observed, "Research on discourse and verbal genres has highlighted male-centered activities and male sexual exploits. As a consequence, African American women are either erased from the urban landscape because of their purported linguistic conservatism or portrayed as willing interlocutors and audiences for the plethora of street hustler raps and misogynistic boasting reported by researchers" (1997:171). Thus, Nelson and Foster have contributed insights into the creative rather than passive use of the vernacular by women in both private and public interactions.

Social issues related to the use of AAVE have arisen, particularly in contexts of school and educational practices. In these situations, institutional attitudes evaluate speech against a perceived "standard" and view deviations as "incorrect." Children who speak AAVE are faced with multiple conflicts stemming from numerous factors, including teachers' negative judgments of a child's speech, children's desire to succeed in school, and their sometimes incompatible desire to be accepted by their own peers. Children have to resolve these conflicts in environments that they perceive to be hostile, not only to their behavior but also to themselves as persons. Because of the distinct grammatical rules of AAVE that differ from standard English, teachers are often not able to comprehend fully what the children say, or they may misinterpret a child's speech. Negative attitudes of teachers toward nonstandard language lead them to reject children who use this style.

Some of these issues were raised in a case brought to federal court in Michigan in 1977. The case arose because of parents' concerns about their children's poor school performance and their feeling that such performance did not reflect the children's ability but rather a lack of cultural and linguistic understanding between teachers and students. The plaintiffs argued that the local school in Ann Arbor had not taken any remedial action to address children's educational problems. After hearing testimony from many linguists about the origins and structure of AAVE, Judge Joiner handed down a historic decision in 1979, finding for the plaintiffs and ordering the Ann Arbor school board to institute procedures to correct teachers' misconceptions about AAVE and to help students better learn the standard language. Judge Joiner found that "the language barrier that did exist was in the form of unconscious negative attitudes formed by teachers towards children who spoke AAVE, and the reactions of children to those attitudes" (cited in Labov 1982:193). The school board began instructing teachers about the characteristics of AAVE and developing ways to help children learn the standard dialect.

In school settings, children who have difficulty with or refuse to use standard English are sometimes perceived as hostile and can even be labeled as learning disabled or mentally handicapped. Children's linguistic problems should be seen, however, as resulting from their awareness of teachers' negative judgments and their ensuing rejection of teachers' demands.

Use of AAVE in these contexts may therefore be understood as a form of resistance to dominant norms.

Additionally, the effects of peer pressure can be considerable. Other children often ridicule and reject students who speak standard English and perform well in school. Because most children want to be accepted by their peers, and because they believe that they will never get teachers' approval, they frequently rebel against standard norms. Labov's research found a close correlation between peer-group acceptance and reading failures among Harlem boys. An inverse relation was found between a boy's status in street groups and his reading abilities; the more prestige he had among his peers, the lower were his reading scores (1972a:247). Difficulties in reading clearly affect attainment of other educational skills and can result in lifelong underachievement with concomitant economic impact.

Attitudes of parents toward their children's speech are also factors affecting children's performance. Parental attitudes are often complex; parents want their children to be able to speak standard English, and they recognize the social and cultural validity of the vernacular. In a study of language preferences of parents in Oakland and East Palo Alto, California, Mary Hoover documented parental attitudes toward their children's speech styles in different social contexts. Hoover distinguished between "Black Standard English" and the "Black vernacular." The former is characterized by standard syntax but contains some phonological features common among African-American speakers, including simplification of consonant clusters, high rates of *r*-lessness, and weakening of final consonants, although if word-final consonants function as morphological markers (possessive or third person /-s/, past tense /-ed/, future /-l/), they are retained. Additionally, standard AAVE has distinctive intonational patterns and some specialized vocabulary (1978:69). Speakers of the vernacular employ linguistic features outlined in earlier sections of this chapter.

Parents of diverse income levels and social groupings were questioned about the acceptability of their children's use of either of the two styles in both formal and informal speech in home, community, and school. Hoover also noted parents' preferences in various channels of listening, speaking, reading, and writing. Hoover's study indicated that parents' attitudes were not rigid but were sensitive to setting, context, and channel. Parents recognized the value of both vernacular and standard speech, approving of the former's use in home and community for speaking and listening, but not for reading or writing. Most parents rejected the use of vernacular speech in school, preferring that their children be educated in the standard. The following table summarizes Hoover's findings (ibid.:78).

Positive evaluation of AAVE was correlated with other positive attitudes toward distinctive African-American culture, political involvement, and self-pride. People in higher-income

Sociolinguistic Rules for Vernacular Black English

Channel	Home		Community		School	
	Informal	**Formal**	**Informal**	**Formal**	**Informal**	**Formal**
Listening	+	+	+	+	−	−
Speaking	+	+	+	=	−	−
Reading	NA	−	NA	−	=	−
Writing	−	−	−	−	=	−

+ Accepted.
− Rejected.
= Close to acceptance.
NA = Not applicable.

brackets more readily accepted AAVE in informal home and community contexts in combination with their overall greater positive evaluations of African-American culture (ibid.:83). Hoover explained this finding in terms of parents' control of the standard in their own speech: People who themselves easily use standard speech do not object to the vernacular in certain contexts, whereas parents who have difficulty with standard English tend to want their children to learn this style (ibid.:81). These parents "reveal an acute awareness of an economic system in which one of the indices to discrimination can be speech" (ibid.:82).

Once again, when people know that they are judged by linguistic performance, they try to modify their behavior and that of their children. But it is the larger social context that constructs both positive and negative attitudes and that stigmatizes certain sectors of a population indirectly by criticizing their speech. In situations of inequality, unequal burdens are placed on members of groups lacking power, who then are expected to adjust to norms imposed by the dominant society. Many African-American speakers are caught in this dilemma, compounded by conflicting attitudes toward AAVE and standard English. Geneva Smitherman writes about social values of speech styles, and has identified the dilemma of language use within the Black community. Distinctly black language is valued and reserved for use within the community. Proper language or "talkin white" has a negative association, but is seen as imperative for admission to U.S. mainstream culture. (1984:108).

Although teaching literacy is a primary goal of the educational system, teacher–student interactions can significantly mold the way in which literacy learning takes place and the covert lessons children learn about what literacy involves. In a study of third-grade classrooms in a working-class African-American neighborhood in Chicago, James Collins (1996) found that teachers approached the task of literacy in different ways for children judged to be at different levels of skill. Collins observed classrooms in which children were separated into workgroups based on high or low reading levels, each group working separately with the teacher at different times. The teacher exerted greater control over the behavior and interactions of children in the low-skill group than in the high-skill group. For example, although disruptive behavior occurred about equally in both groups, the teacher tended to ignore disruptions in the high-skill group, continuing to proceed with the lesson, whereas disruptions in the low-skill group led to interruptions in the flow of lessons. Children who called out of turn in the low-skill group were more likely to be reprimanded, whereas such behavior by children in the high-skill group was either ignored or treated as an appropriate comment or response. Children's responses were also dealt with differently. When high-skill children offered answers, the teacher responded positively, either embedding the child's answer in the teacher's comment or in the teacher's next question, but the answers of low-skill children were not taken up and incorporated into the teacher's next utterance.

Of special importance was Collins's surprising observation that, although both groups of children were strong users of AAVE, the speech of children in the low-skill group was corrected twice as often as that of the high-skill group. Although the suppression of "nonstandard" dialects and of AAVE in particular is a pervasive feature of American prescriptive conventions, Collins's study demonstrates that dialect suppression is not uniform but arises in specific contexts: "Despite its historical durability, we must avoid viewing prescriptivism simply as some abstract cultural-linguistic authoritarianism, immanent in American culture. It is authoritarianism, but viewing it abstractly obscures its nature and dynamic" (1996:211).

Although the children in both groups learned to read, their strategies and orientations were directed toward different goals. As Collins notes, " 'Poor readers' acquire early and maintain consistently a view of reading as fluent pronunciation of text. Conversely, 'good readers' acquire early and maintain consistently a view of reading as an interpretive process, a learning from text" (ibid.:223). These different strategies and goals cohere with a system of hierarchical distinctions based on class and race that characterizes societies like our own.

Research among African Americans in an inner-city neighborhood in Detroit showed that, even within a small community, differences exist in the rates of speakers' use of vernacular pronunciations and grammatical forms. Walter Edwards (1992) found that such differences were correlated with the strength of speakers' involvement with their neighborhood and their emotional attachment to their community. Edwards first constructed an index to measure people's cultural identification. The Vernacular Culture Index was compiled from responses to 10 questions, including whether most of a respondent's relatives and friends live in the neighborhood, whether most of their daily interactions are with neighborhood residents, whether they hope to remain in the neighborhood, and whether they think their neighborhood is a good place to raise children.

Edwards collected samples of speech from 33 male and 33 female consultants and noted the occurrence of four features of AAVE pronunciation (three vowel pronunciations and the presence or absence of /r/) and one grammatical trait (absence of copula in the present tense). As might be expected, he found that a person's use of AAVE speech was strongly correlated with his or her score on the Vernacular Culture Index. That is, the stronger a person's identification with the neighborhood and the person's involvement in a network of residents, the more likely he or she was to use more AAVE features (ibid.:107). This finding applied equally to men and women: Edwards found no significant difference in the rates of AAVE usage by gender.

However, age was an important factor. Groups of older speakers (age 40–59 and 60 plus) used more AAVE features than groups of younger speakers (18–25, 26–39; ibid.:102). According to Edwards, the vernacular dialect and standard English are converging for younger speakers, leading to a merging of speech styles and a lack of distinctive AAVE traits. If this conclusion is correct, the Detroit community is markedly different from a community in Philadelphia studied by Labov and Harris (1986) that indicated increased separation of AAVE and SE. In addition, Edwards found that, of the two younger groups, the age group of 26- to 39-year-olds used the most SE pronunciations and the least AAVE forms. Edwards applied network theory to explain this pattern, concluding that these speakers "are most geographically mobile and come into contact more often with speakers of SE," whereas members of the youngest group "interact more with their parents and elders" (ibid.:104).

The requirements of available jobs may be an additional factor motivating people to conform linguistically. In a study of African-American communities in Georgetown County, along the South Carolina coast, Patricia Nichols (1983) found relationships among employment, gender, age, and linguistic style. At one end of the speech continuum is a variety influenced by Gullah, a Creole derived from English and African languages, still spoken by residents of islands off the Carolina and Georgia coasts. The two other linguistic codes are an African-American vernacular and regional standard English.

Older women used the most creolized, nonstandard forms, whereas younger women showed greatest use of standard English. Although differences in style exist among men, they do not seem to be significantly affected by age. Gender distinctions are especially sharp between younger women and men, women using standard speech and men speaking the vernacular. Nichols interpreted these findings as related to differential employment opportunities for gender and age groups. Male jobs, concentrated in farm and construction work, have remained relatively constant over time. Neither of these occupations requires standard language skills, particularly because men usually work in local communities with friends and family. Jobs available to women, in contrast, have changed considerably. Older women most often worked as domestics in households and hotels and as farm laborers, jobs similarly involving few interactions with standard English. Women have recently obtained an increasing number of white-collar jobs in sales, nursing, and teaching. Because these jobs clearly require knowledge and use of standard English, young women continue their education in order to acquire linguistic and other job-related skills (ibid.:61–63).

In sum, then, attitudes of African Americans toward AAVE are ambivalent and not fixed within the community itself. Indeed, to speak of the "African-American community" is misleading, implying that it is homogeneous. In fact, like all other communities, it is stratified by class and differentiated by experience and attitude. Still, most African Americans recognize, whether explicitly or implicitly, the advantages and values of bidialectalism. That is, AAVE is a speech style that emphasizes a unique identity. Its use both builds and symbolizes group solidarity. While there is pressure from both within and without the community to conform to standard American norms of speech, there is also pressure to be proficient in AAVE. Educational, media, and other public discourses exert pressure on African Americans to conform to standard norms in order to obtain employment and to be taken seriously in public spheres. These are attitudes that derive from the context of prejudice and discrimination faced by African Americans. However, African Americans themselves also absorb some of these attitudes, reflecting the intensity of socialization and exposure to prejudice. But African Americans who speak only standard English may face negative reactions from their families and peers because AAVE is a marker of group solidarity. Therefore, an African American who completely rejects AAVE may be perceived as rejecting his or her own identity and community.

The relative merits and values associated with AAVE and standard English are not easily reconciled. The same person is likely to hold conflicting opinions and have ambivalent reactions. These issues undoubtedly will remain subjects of lively debate within the African-American community itself, as witnessed by the frequency with which political officials, community leaders, writers, and media and entertainment celebrities raise the topics for public discussion (Lippi-Green 1997:185–197). The complexity of these debates and attitudes notwithstanding, AAVE remains a vibrant means of communication despite all of the pressures against it and despite stigmatization of the dialect and its speakers.

The research conducted by Hoover, Edwards, Nichols, and Lippi-Green demonstrates that speech communities are not homogeneous, that use of linguistic styles is affected by conditions of life, and that people's choices depend on their economic and social participation in the community.

Most African Americans, both children and adults, like nearly all speakers of any language, are bidialectal. That is, they are fluent speakers of more than one dialect of their native language. Most African Americans switch back and forth between some variety (or varieties) of standard English and some variety (or varieties) of AAVE. This is a phenomenon, known worldwide, as **code switching**. Code switching is practiced within connected discourse, often within the same sentence. It is reflection and signal of a bicultural identity, of engagement with varying familial, social, and occupational networks (McWhorter 1998:145), and demonstrates the speakers' facility in both dialects. Standard English and AAVE are not monolithic entities; rather, they have various levels differentiated by vocabulary and grammar. Some speakers are more likely to employ distinct levels of their repertory of dialects, varying with education and with the interactional networks in which they participate.

The Ebonics Controversy

In December 1996, the Oakland, California, school board passed a resolution to implement new methods and goals of teaching reading and language skills in its district. The directive unleashed a firestorm of controversy that actually distorted the thrust of the resolution, in part because of ambiguous wording in the resolution itself and in part because of underlying assumptions and prejudices in the nation as a whole. The Oakland school board's action was prompted by the poor performance of African-American children on reading and language arts tests. Because the children's poor performance was judged to derive from differences between the vernacular language that they used at home and in the community and the standard speech demanded in the school setting, the board resolved to implement a program of instruction that would inform and train teachers in the legitimacy of AAVE and that would enable speakers of the vernacular to acquire standard English. It is worth quoting the resolution because much of the ensuing controversy was sparked by a misreading of its stated goals:

> The Superintendent shall devise and implement the best possible academic program for imparting instruction to African-American students in their primary language for the combined purposes of maintaining the legitimacy and richness of such language…and to facilitate their acquisition and mastery of English language skills. (quoted in *The Black Scholar* 1997:4)

While there is considerable variability in research findings concerning standard and alternative approaches to reading instruction (McWhorter 1997b:2–3; Rickford 1997:180–181), the approach to teaching language skills advocated by the Oakland school board is consistent with some research demonstrating children's reading improvement when instruction and testing are carried out in their "primary language." For example, when test items in the Boehm Test of Basic Concepts were "translated" from standard into vernacular language, children in kindergarten and first and second grades scored significantly higher (Williams 1997:212).

In addition, in the 1970s, researchers developed a reading program called Bridge. The program began with reading material written only in the vernacular, then presented texts that were written 50 percent in AAVE and 50 percent in standard English, and finally switched completely to the standard. Reading selections were followed by comprehension exercises and language arts drills. To motivate the students, stories were introduced by a recording made by a young man:

> What's happenin', brothers and sisters? I want to tell you about this here program called "Bridge," a cross-cultural reading program. Now I *know* what you thinkin'. This is just another one of them jive reading programs, and that I won't be needin' no readin' program. But dig it. This here reading program is really kinda different. It was done by a brother and two sisters, soul folk, you know…. (quoted in Rickford 1997:179)

To evaluate the effectiveness of the Bridge approach, children in grades 7 through 12 were tested after four months and compared to a group who had not been exposed to the program. Reading scores of the Bridge children increased an average of 6.2 months, whereas those in the standard school programs increased only by 1.6 months. The Bridge children not only surpassed children in standard programs but also did better than the norm (four months' gain for four months of instruction; ibid.:179). Unfortunately, the Bridge readers were discontinued by their publisher because of criticism by educators and the media and not because they had been ineffective.

Despite evidence of the potential usefulness of a variety of alternative teaching methods, the intent of the Oakland school board was distorted by focus on the resolution's initial claim that what the board called "Ebonics" is derived from "Niger-Congo African languages" and is "genetically based and not a dialect of English." The claim that Ebonics is a separate language rather than the more accepted linguistic view that it is a dialect of English cannot be substantiated by linguistic data. And although AAVE certainly shares syntactic, semantic, and stylistic features with some African languages, its historical origins are much more complex than suggested by its roots in "Niger-Congo African languages." Finally, the statement that Ebonics is "genetically based" is at the least odd.

Although the board later modified or retracted these claims, its initial wording was unfortunate because it merely gave fuel to people opposed to the more important intent, that is, the desire to develop special educational programs to serve the needs of African-American children. The board's statement that teachers should recognize the legitimacy of AAVE as a rule-governed and valid form of language was distorted by opponents to mean that children would be taught to read, write, and speak AAVE and not be taught to communicate in standard English. Even some influential African Americans such as Jesse Jackson and Maya Angelou voiced opposition to the Oakland resolution, probably because they had not read the full text but had only heard media reports that took some of the board's statements out of context. Their quick reactions were unfortunate because they only helped to engender even less reasoned responses by people who never in the past showed any sympathy for African-American children. In response to the barrage of criticism in the media, the Linguistics Society of America voted unanimously to support the Oakland school board's resolution, but the society's voice was not widely reported nationally.

The important issue is not whether one agrees or disagrees with the Oakland text but rather what is to be done to teach reading and language skills to children whose "home" language differs from the standard. Some argue that the Oakland board's dual-language approach is the best answer; others believe that immersion in standard English is preferable. These divergent opinions were expressed by researchers and public figures in special journal issues of both *The Black Scholar* (1997) and *The Journal of Black Psychology* (1997).

In the midst of the controversy, however, it is well to remember the significance of social context and the multiple kinds of meanings conveyed not just by a language but by *choice* of language (or dialect). The lack of interest or even resistance of some African-American children to acquiring standard English must be seen in the historical and social contexts in which African Americans find themselves. Their educational difficulties are not due to the standard's incomprehensibility because of its divergence from their home dialect. As John McWhorter points out, children in countries such as Switzerland, Germany, and Scotland easily learn a standard dialect of their language when they enter school (1997a:12–13). But African-American children are confronted not merely with some relatively limited linguistic differences. They are also confronted with social attitudes that typically stigmatize their own style of speech, denigrating not only their language but their selves as well. Therefore, educational programs that respect their home speech and encourage their community-based verbal skills may facilitate their acquisition of the standard. As Geneva Smitherman and Sylvia Cunningham conclude:

> Many of our students resort to not-learning as a means of resistance.... We need to help them move beyond the resistance that keeps them stifled and saddled in the same place. We are advocating that educators provide Black youths with the history of Black and Standard English and encourage them to critically examine these two linguistic forms and the social and political situations that created them. Merging this knowledge with the pride and confidence that comes from a healthy sense of self and peoplehood, Black youths can move forward knowing the differences between

languages and the value of language and culture, never having to surrender one language (Black English) for another (Standard English). (1997:230–231)

We also need to understand the performance of African-American children in the context of failing public school systems in many parts of the country (McWhorter 1998:223). Although this failure affects people of all races, it affects poor people disproportionately and it therefore affects African Americans and other people of color disproportionately.

Afro-Caribbean Speakers in Great Britain

Migration of Caribbean peoples to Great Britain increased during the 1940s and 1950s as a result of postwar economic growth in Britain and a decline in economic and social conditions in the Caribbean. Also, in 1952, the US Congress passed the Walters-McCarran Act, which established a quota system for immigration, thus forcing a majority of people wanting to leave the West Indies to settle in Great Britain rather than in the United States. At the same time, several British employer organizations, including London Transport, National Health Service, and British Hotels and Restaurants Association, actively recruited West Indian workers (Wong 1986:111–112). In 1961 and 1962, however, the British government enacted two Commonwealth Immigration Acts that severely restricted immigration from the Caribbean. Therefore, most young Afro-Caribbean Britons today are native-born (Sebba 1986:150).

The speech repertory of young Afro-Caribbean Britons is complex. People of Caribbean ancestry living in London use at least two, often three, varieties of English. Most speakers employ a dialect of London English that Mark Sebba identifies as Afro-Caribbean London English. It is similar to the Cockney dialect. In addition, many Afro-Caribbean Londoners, especially young men, speak London Jamaican, a form of English heavily influenced by the Jamaican Creole of their parents. Finally, older residents who were born in Jamaica usually speak the Jamaican English or Creole of their native country (ibid.:151).

Afro-Caribbean London English diverges from white London English in a number of sounds, grammatical features, and vocabulary (ibid.:151–154):

1. *Pronunciation:* Afro-Caribbean London English replaces the interdental voiceless fricative /θ/ with labiodental /f/, as in thing →/fɪŋ/ or through →/fru/. Although this replacement occurs in Cockney English as spoken by whites as well, its use is increasing in the Afro-Caribbean community and decreasing among whites.
2. *Prosodic features:* Afro-Caribbean English contains several prosodic features that differ slightly from white speech. These include qualities of "pitch, rhythm, volume, vowel length, nasality, aspiration, breathiness [which] add up to a 'Black accent' " (ibid.:152).
3. *Vocabulary:* A few words are used distinctively in Afro-Caribbean English. For example, *hug up* "hug, cuddle," *picky-picky* "peppercorn hair," *duppy* "ghost," *facety* "impertinent."
4. *Grammar:* Afro-Caribbean English contains a syntactic particle *se* or seɪ (pronounced "say") that occurs following a verb of knowing, believing, or perceiving. It is related to a similar form in Jamaican Creole and has obviously been borrowed from this source into Afro-Caribbean London speech. *Se* functions as an equivalent to the standard English *that* but is restricted in its use, occurring only after a limited category of "psychic state" verbs, as in the following examples (ibid.:154):
   a. If we lose, we lose, we know *se* we tried. (female, age 16)
   b. A all white jury found out *se* 'e was guilty. (male, age 15)

c. Sometimes fings 'appen, right [pause] and you know *se* really an' truly it ain't gonna work out. (female, age 20)

d. I feel *se* they're 'olding it over there you know. (female, age 15)

Another Afro-Caribbean London dialect, London Jamaican, contains several sounds that differ from both white London English and Afro-Caribbean London English. These distinctive traits are derived from Jamaican Creole (Sebba 1986: 162):

a.	ay [ɛI]	→	ie [ʌ]	*niem*	"name"
b.	ow [aw]	→	ou [ow]	*soun*	"sound"
c.	th [θ]	→	t [t]	*tiif*	"thief"
d.	th [D]	→	d [d]	*di*	"the"
e.	u [ʌ]	→	o [ɔ]	*mekop*	"makeup"
f.	[ɔ:]	→	[a:]	*kaal*	"call"
g.	[æ]	→	[å]	*man*	"man"

In a study of an Afro-Caribbean British community in West Midlands, Viv Edwards described numerous grammatical characteristics in the dialect she identified as "patois." Patois is spoken by teenagers and young adults of Jamaican ancestry living in Dudley, West Midlands (1986:97). The relevant traits are as follows:

a. Third-person singular present-tense verbs:
John *swim* fast. Kevin *eat* a lot.

b. Plurals:
Six *car*

c. Simple past tense:
Winston *see* di boy. Beverly *walk* away.

d. First-person singular pronoun:
Mi feel happy.

e. Third-person singular pronouns:
Im put *im* coat away.

f. Third-person plural pronouns:
Dem see di baby. Look at *dem* hat.

g. Negatives:
Di boy *no* see it. (The boy doesn't see it.)

h. Adjectival verbs:
Di man *happy*. (The man is happy.)

i. Continuatives:
John *a* come. (John is coming.)

j. Focus:
A John do it. (*John* did it/it was John who did it.)

k. Questions:
>Mary *a go* home? (Is Mary going home?) Harvey *see* di man? (Did Harvey see the man?)

l. Infinitives:
John aks *fi* see it. (John asked to see it.)

   m. Other pronouns:
       Unu want it. (You [plural] want it.)

   n. Psychic state transitive verbs:
       Tony tell me *seh* im no know. (Tony told me he didn't know.)

   o. '-dem' plurals:
       Give me *di* book-*dem*

   p. Locating verb:
       Mary *deh* a yaad. (Mary is at home.)

   q. Equating verb:
       Patrick *a* di winner. (Patrick is the winner.)

   r. Past markers:
       Roy *did* ready in di morning. (Roy was getting ready in the morning.)

Speakers of Afro-Caribbean dialects in Great Britain vary their linguistic usage, as do speakers of all languages and dialects, on the basis of attitudes and contexts. Edwards found that a speaker's use of patois was correlated positively with her or his integration into the Afro-Caribbean community and her or his "critical attitudes towards mainstream white society" (1988:38). Its use therefore is simultaneously a marker of social identity and solidarity and a subversion of linguistic norms. Allegiance to the Afro-Caribbean community was assessed by residence, participation in local churches, and socializing primarily with other Afro-Caribbean Britons. Attitudes toward white society were determined by responses to questions about school and the speaker's perceptions of white racism, particularly on the part of teachers and the police.

Speakers of Jamaican descent in Dudley used several dialects ranging from patois to the regional West Midlands standard. People chose their speech style based, in part, on whom they were talking to. They used fewer patois features in talk to whites and other blacks who were not members of their own community. Use of patois is therefore a marker of racial and ethnic identity. It functions both to solidify in-group membership and to exclude outsiders.

Switching between styles is a common practice of Afro-Caribbean British speakers. Note the following excerpts of switching within and between turns (Sebba 1986:164–165):

   B: [A]nd then I just laughed and then 'e—'e just pulled me for a dance I didn't mind
        dancing wiv 'im' cause *mi nuo se, mi n' av notin in a* my mind but to dance, and then
        we star'ed to talk and all the rest of it and that's it. *ful stap*

   I: *dem tomp im an kil im*

   F: (fhm)

   I: an' as I said righ', *im iz a*—he he's a baxer innit

   F: yeah

   I: *an i kan tek lik, i kan tek gud lik*

   J: you 'ave a nice day then

   C: 'course. 'e bough? me—*im bai mi dis kiipa* [keeper?] *ring guol chien*

Speakers are well aware of the varieties of language used in their community and of the frequency of switching styles. The following comments were made by a young woman in Dudley describing her friend's speech patterns. (Note dialectal variants: *ay,* corresponding to "isn't," *day* to "didn't," and *bay* to "be.")

With Melanie right, you have to say she speaks *tri different sort of language when she want to. Cos she speak half Patois, half English and when im ready im will come out wid,* "I day and I bay and I ay this and I ay that. I day have it and I day know where it is."… And then she goes, "*Lord God, I so hot.*" Now she'll be sitting there right and she'll go, "It's hot, isn't it?" (Edwards 1988: 48–49)

There is much debate in Great Britain, as in the United States, concerning the use of Afro-Caribbean vernacular speech in educational contexts. Within the range of positions are those advocating exclusive use of standard English in schools (in order to provide speakers with linguistic means for upward mobility) to those supporting use of Black English in school (recognizing the importance of language to speakers' identity) (Richmond 1986:124).

Underlying this controversy are assumptions about the intelligence and worthiness of children based on (mis)perceptions about their speech. John Richmond pointed out that many teachers, although wanting to help children overcome what they see as barriers to advancement, unwittingly transmit negative messages about the children's own code. He also noted that the lower-class status of most Afro-Caribbean Britons contributes to teachers' biased perceptions of these children (ibid.:129).

Richmond proposed a combination of approaches, stressing the value of acquiring competence in standard English, balanced with recognition of personal and creative roles of the vernacular. He contends that students should be taught to write and speak in standard style, appreciating its usefulness in formal, public contexts, and also be permitted and encouraged to use the vernacular in activities such as narrative writing, poetry, and drama (ibid.:130–131). This approach is a reasonable compromise because it respects children's identity and their use of a linguistic code that marks that identity and yet recognizes social realities of the need for standard English in some contexts.

Summary

Linguistic variation is systematically interconnected with societal segmentation. Language is an important marker of a person's identity, and language use is one way for speakers to display their personal and social identities. Differentiation of sectors within a population can be based on various factors, including class and race. Group membership is often signaled by sharing linguistic styles and attitudes toward language use. Separation of social groups, in contrast, can be marked by differences in forms and functions of language. Similarities in linguistic performance not only reflect social solidarity but also contribute to maintaining solidarity, just as linguistic divergence transmits and reinforces segmentation.

Social stratification is basic to the structuring of many modern societies. Speakers employ varieties of language as markers of their place within a hierarchical order. Status relations, stemming from nonlinguistic factors, are expressed through linguistic use and are further reflected in evaluations of the speech behavior of different sectors of society. For people belonging to subordinate groups, sensitivity to negative judgments about their speaking styles is often manifested in both negative self-appraisals and reluctance to display verbal abilities in situations where they are most aware of their relatively low status. The continued use of "nonstandard" forms can be a reflection of group membership and/or a strategy of resistance. Attitudes, either favorable or unfavorable, toward linguistic styles associated with particular groups are actually messages about existing social relations.

Racial differences in the United States and Great Britain are also reflected in linguistic and stylistic devices employed by some (but not all) people of African ancestry that diverge from standard English. African-American Vernacular English (AAVE) in the United States and Afro-Caribbean English in Great Britain have some unique features, although they share most linguistic rules with the standard English spoken in their respective country. Attitudes toward vernacular speech are complex, both on the part of the speakers themselves and in the rest of society. Controversies in both countries focus primarily on proposals to incorporate vernacular speech in schools.

References

BAUGH, JOHN. 1983. *Black Street Speech*. Austin: University of Texas Press.

BERNSTEIN, BASIL. 1971a. A public language: Some sociolinguistic implications of a linguistic form. In *Class, Codes and Control*, Vol. I, ed. B. Bernstein. London: Routledge and Kegan Paul, pp. 42–59.

BERNSTEIN, BASIL. 1971b. Social class, language and socialization. In *Class, Codes and Control*, Vol. I, ed. B. Bernstein. London: Routledge and Kegan Paul, pp. 170–189.

The Black Scholar. 1997a. *The Black Scholar Reader's Forum: Ebonics.* 27, no. 1:2–37.

The Black Scholar. 1997b. *The Black Scholar Reader's Forum: Ebonics.* 27, no. 2:2–14.

COLLINS, JAMES. 1996. Socialization to text: Structure and contradiction in schooled literacy. In *Natural Histories of Discourse*, ed. M. Silverstein and G. Urban. Chicago, IL: University of Chicago Press, pp. 203–227.

EDWARDS, VIV. 1986. *Language in a Black Community*. Avon, UK: Clevedon.

EDWARDS, VIV. 1988. The speech of British black women in Dudley, West Midlands. In *Women in Their Speech Communities*, ed. J. Coates and D. Cameron. London: Longman, pp. 33–50.

EDWARDS, WALTER. 1992. Sociolinguistic behavior in a Detroit inner-city black neighborhood. *Language in Society* 21:93–115.

FOSTER, MICHELE. 1995. "Are you with me?" Power and solidarity in the discourse of African American women. In *Gender Articulated: Language and the Socially Constructed Self*, ed. K. Hall and M. Bucholtz. New York: Routledge, pp. 329–350.

GUMPERZ, JOHN. 1971 (1958). Dialect differences and social stratification in a North Indian village. *American Anthropologist* 60:668–681.

Reprinted in *Language in Social Groups: Essays by John J. Gumperz*. Stanford, CA: Stanford University Press, pp. 25–47.

HOOVER, MARY. 1978. Community attitudes toward Black English. *Language in Society* 7:65–87.

HULS, ERICA. 1989. Family interactions from an interactional sociolinguistic perspective. In *Conversation: An Interdisciplinary Perspective*, ed. D. Roger and P. Bull. Clevedon, UK: Multilingual Matters Ltd., pp. 116–139.

The Journal of Black Psychology. 1997. 23, no. 3.

LABOV, WILLIAM. 1966. *The Social Stratification of English in New York City*. Washington, DC: Center for Applied Linguistics.

LABOV, WILLIAM. 1972a. *Language in the Inner City: Studies in the Black English Vernacular*. Philadelphia: University of Pennsylvania Press.

LABOV, WILLIAM. 1972b. *Sociolinguistic Patterns*. Philadelphia: University of Pennsylvania Press.

LABOV, WILLIAM. 1982. Objectivity and commitment in linguistic science: The case of the Black English trial in Ann Arbor. *Language in Society* 11:165–201.

LABOV, WILLIAM, AND WENDELL HARRIS. 1986. De facto segregation of black and white vernaculars. In *Diversity and Diachrony*, ed. D. Sankoff. Amsterdam: John Benjamins, pp. 1–24.

LINDENFELD, JACQUELINE. 1969. The social conditioning of syntactic variation in French. *American Anthropologist* 71:890–898. Reproduced by permission of the American Anthropological Association.

LIPPI-GREEN, ROSINA. 1997. *English with an Accent: Language, Ideology, and Discrimination in the United States*. New York: Routledge.

MCWHORTER, JOHN. 1997a. Wasting energy on an illusion. *The Black Scholar* 27, no. 1:9–14.

McWhorter, John. 1997b. Wasting energy on an illusion: Six months later. *The Black Scholar* 27, no. 2:2–5.

McWhorter, John. 1998. *The Word on the Street: Fact and Fable About American English.* New York: Plenum Trade.

Milroy, Lesley, and James Milroy. 1992. Social network and social class: Toward an integrated sociolinguistic model. *Language in Society* 21:1–26.

Nelson, Linda. 1990. Code-switching in the oral life narratives of African-American women: Challenges to linguistic hegemony. *Journal of Education* 172:142–155.

Nichols, Patricia. 1983. Linguistic options and choices for black women in the rural South. In *Language, Gender and Society,* ed. B. Thorne, C. Kramarae, and N. Henley. Rowley, MA: Newbury House, pp. 54–68.

Richmond, John. 1986. The language of black children and the language debate in the schools. In *Language and the Black Experience,* ed. D. Sutcliffe and A. Wong. Oxford: Blackwell, pp. 123–135.

Rickford, John. 1997. Unequal partnership: Sociolinguistics and the African American speech community. *Language in Society* 26:161–198.

Sebba, Mark. 1986. London Jamaican and Black London English. In *Language and the Black Experience,* ed. D. Sutcliffe and A. Wong. Oxford: Blackwell, pp. 149–167.

Smitherman, Geneva. 1984. Black language as power. In *Language and Power,* ed. C. Kramarae, M. Schultz, and W. O'Barr. Beverly Hills, CA: Sage, pp. 101–115.

Smitherman, Geneva, and Sylvia Cunningham. 1997. Moving beyond resistance: Ebonics and African American youth. *Journal of Black Psychology* 23:227–232.

Trudgill, Peter. 1974a. *The Social Differentiation of English in Norwich.* New York: Cambridge University Press.

Trudgill, Peter. 1974b. *Sociolinguistics.* New York: Penguin.

van de Broeck, Jef. 1977. Class differences in syntactic complexity in the Flemish town of Maaseik. *Language in Society* 6:149–181.

Williams, Robert. 1997. The Ebonics controversy. *Journal of Black Psychology* 23:208–213.

Wolfram, Walt. 1969. *A Sociolinguistic Description of Detroit Negro Speech.* Washington, DC: Center for Applied Linguistics.

Wong, Ansel. 1986. Creole as a language of power and solidarity. In *Language and the Black Experience,* ed. D. Sutcliffe and A. Wong. Oxford: Blackwell, pp. 109–122.

CHAPTER 10

Language and Gender

What clues do the following sentences contain that tell us whether the speakers are men or women?

"You're driving rather fast, aren't you?"

"Well, I guess it's approximately four feet high."

Both sentences are more typical of the speech of women than of men. The most significant stylistic feature is their use of mitigation to blunt a direct statement. In the first sentence, the speaker employs two devices to minimize the force of her criticism of the addressee's behavior. She uses a **hedge** word, *rather,* to qualify the following word *fast.* And she uses a linguistic device called a **tag question** ("aren't you?") that has the effect of questioning the declaration "you're driving rather fast." By asking a question rather than making an assertion, the speaker asks the addressee to confirm or deny the proposition contained in the statement. That is, the speaker lets the addressee decide whether she or he is driving fast.

In the second sentence, the speaker employs a series of hedges: "*Well,* I *guess* it's *approximately* four feet high." These words have the effect of creating uncertainty about the speaker's claims, uncertainty that she herself expresses about her own knowledge. Use of such devices blunts the intended statement, undermines the speaker's competence, and anticipates the possibility that she may be contradicted by the addressee.

The styles of speech illustrated here are more typical of women than of men because women and men are socialized to express themselves in different ways in accordance with cultural norms that teach and reinforce differentiated gender roles. Gender itself is a social construct. It is through concepts of gender that society transforms female and male human beings into social women and men, assigning them roles and giving them cultural value. Social norms construct and reinforce attitudes about women's and men's proper work roles, their participation in family and community life, modes of dress and demeanor, and their appropriate styles of communicative behavior. In this chapter, we review research concerning the ways that men and women speak and interact. We examine data from English-speaking societies and from studies that document gender differences in other societies.

The interrelationship of language and gender can be approached from several perspectives. Sociolinguistic analyses inform us about women's and men's styles of speaking, including differences in pronunciation, use of prosodic cues (intonation, velocity, volume), grammatical forms, and choices of vocabulary. Speech performance can also be examined in order to discover gender differences in conversational interaction such as modes of topic introduction, topic control, and supportive or nonsupportive mechanisms used by speakers and listeners. Linguistic and semantic analyses inform us about categories in a language itself and the ways that cultural attitudes toward people are both expressed and reinforced in grammar and vocabulary.

It is probably a universal fact that all cultures show differences in how men and women communicate because in all cultures the genders are socially distinguished. As we have seen from studies of class and race, wherever societal distinctions are made among community members, linguistic and stylistic variations arise to reflect and reinforce existing segmentation. It is important to stress that, although the obvious sexual female–male dichotomy is used in social differentiation of gender, it does not absolutely determine the roles and values given to women and men. If it did, behavior and evaluations of the two genders would be identical in all societies. This clearly is not the case. Cross-cultural differences in roles performed and rewards given to the genders are well documented. And societal roles and attitudes are subject to change as part of social processes resulting from economic and ideological transformations.

In English, and in many other languages, speech styles of women and men vary in the frequencies with which they employ particular sounds, grammatical features, or words. No patterns are exclusive to either gender; rather, different styles are culturally associated with each. These associations have become stereotypes in many cases so that members of the culture believe that certain communicative behavior is typical of women and other communicative behavior is typical of men. Stereotypes are sometimes based on people's actual behavior, but stereotypes also serve to reinforce conformity with prescribed norms. And reactions to people's behavior based on stereotyped assumptions can be complex because overt approval or criticism may actually carry conflicting messages. We will see that this is often the case in evaluations of gender-linked speech.

Before examining data revealing gender-related tendencies in language use, it is critical to caution against overstating differences between women and men. Numerous reviews of studies of linguistic behavior conclude that men's and women's speech are far more similar and overlapping than they are different. Stereotypes about people's behavior are often believed to be true without systematic evidence to support them. As Nancy Henley and Cheris Kramarae (1991) point out, Western societies tend to exaggerate linguistic, social, and psychological differences between women and men. It could be argued that such exaggerations construct and reconstruct divisions between the genders. And Penelope Eckert and Sally McConnell-Ginet caution that we need to untangle the web of gendered practices: "[I]t is precisely because gender seems natural, and beliefs about gender seem to be obvious truth…that we need to uncover the process of construction that creates what we have so long thought of as natural and inexorable—to study gender not as given, but as an accomplishment, not simply as cause, but as effect (2004:9). Linguistic behavior exhibited by women and men should be seen within the social context that gives it meaning and interpretation. Gender itself is not immutable or static but is a "holistic and dynamic concept" that affects language use (Uchida 1992:564). By examining linguistic behavior, we can "see how we, in the social context, are *doing* gender through the use of language" (ibid.). We need to understand gender in terms of "performativity" (Butler 1990); that is, we need to examine how people perform or enact a gendered identity. We also need to keep in mind that the expression of our gendered identity (or identities) is not static but adapts to many features of context, including the setting, the other participants, the topics discussed, and our interactional goals.

It is also necessary to caution that, while research findings may point to differences between women's and men's speech, the data are suggestive of tendencies and frequencies of use, not of prediction about any particular individual's speech in all or any context.

All women do not employ typical female styles, nor do all men employ male styles. In addition to individual variation, the context of communicative interactions is also significant. Contextual factors of formality/informality, speaker goals, and relationship between interlocutors influence the alternatives that people employ. Features of identity such as age, class, status, and race also help determine a speaker's choices. We need to be careful not to overgeneralize and therefore stereotype speakers when discussing gender differences. Although gender is central to a person's social identity, how one chooses to signal one's gender varies for individuals and for contexts. Gender is an aspect of identity that is enacted through discourse practices. It is a dynamic, not static, feature of interactions. When people communicate with others, they make choices from a complex array of behaviors having symbolic as well as referential meanings.

With these cautions in mind, we will review and evaluate some of the research concerning women's and men's speech. We need to investigate the ways that gender is enacted through structural linguistic features of pronunciation, lexicon, and grammar, and we need to investigate the range of discourse strategies that men and women use in interactions with others. Through learning how to express or enact gender, people come to understand two sets of norms: what to do and what not to do. These norms are equally significant. And violating expected gendered behaviors may be more or less risky, again depending on context and participants. People may employ the stance or "voice" (Ochs 1992:342) deemed socially appropriate for their gender, thus signaling or indexing this aspect of their identity, but they may also choose to avoid that stance or voice and therefore signal resistance to dominant cultural stereotypes.

PRONUNCIATION

Phonological Variants

Except for some regional variations, speakers of English use the same inventory of sounds. There are differences, however, in the frequencies with which men and women use particular sounds. In a pioneering study of children's speech in a small New England town, John Fischer (1958) found gender-related patterns in the pronunciation of -ing, the progressive suffix on verbs. Relevant variants are -Iŋ ("-ing") and -In ("-in"), as in rʌnIŋ (running) or rʌnIn (runnin). In Fischer's study, speech samples were obtained from children age 3 to 10 in both formal and informal contexts. The boys showed a slight preference for -In, but for the girls, the discrepancy was much more marked, nearly all of them preferring -Iŋ. Fischer concluded that "in this community, -ing is regarded as symbolizing female speakers and -in as symbolizing males" (ibid.:49).

No significant differences were reported for any ages, indicating that children learn this gender-appropriate behavior very early. But given that there is a gender-related preference, what motivates the specific choice of -Iŋ for girls and -In for boys? Fischer found a strong correlation between -Iŋ and formal situations and -In and informal situations. The variant -Iŋ, then, carries social meaning of contextual formality as well as "symbolizing female speakers." His data also suggest that -Iŋ may be associated with compliance and politeness.

A similar association of -Iŋ/-In and gender was found among adult speakers in Norwich, England (Trudgill 1972). In discussing the data, we should keep in mind two other factors that produce linguistic variation: class and contextual style. Recall that class segmentation in Trudgill's Norwich study (see Chapter 9) was reflected in differences in occurrences of -Iŋ/-In. Higher-class speakers tended to use standard -Iŋ, whereas lower-class speakers used -In. In addition, for all phonological variables, speech context was an important influence on stylistic choices. In formal contexts, speakers regularly shifted to standard pronunciations. The Norwich data reveal that, within class and context, women employed standard features at greater frequencies than did men. Women exhibited marked style shifting, significantly increasing their use of -Iŋ as contexts became more formal.

Gender differences in Norwich were particularly significant for highest and lowest social groups. In the middle middle class (MMC), women used standard pronunciation all the time, whereas men used -I*n* in casual speech about one-third of time. In the next group, the lower middle class (LMC), women continued to use -Iŋ in all contexts except casual speech. At the lower end of the class hierarchy, men used nonstandard -I*n* in all contexts except the most careful style ("word lists"), whereas women in the lowest group began to shift to standard -Iŋ in "formal style."

These data agree with the results of other studies that show women's greater use of standard pronunciations, and quicker and more marked style shifting to the standard in increasingly formal speech contexts. The phonological variable of postvocalic /-r/ (we saw in Chapter 9 that it is sensitive to class distinctions and stylistic variation) has been analyzed in several US dialects in relation to gender differences. For example, William Labov's study (1966) of New York City speech demonstrated women's greater use of prestige /-r/.

Gender is also related to the use of postvocalic /-r/ among white speakers in North Carolina (Levine and Crockett 1967). In their study, Levine and Crockett asked speakers to read aloud a list of sentences containing words with the targeted /-r/ feature and a list of words to be spoken in isolation. The following table compares "R scores" (use of /-r/) for different contexts and also shows net increases for the more careful context of word-list readings (ibid.:95).

	Sentences	Words	Net Increase
Men	52.3	57.4	5.1
Women	52.9	61.1	8.2

Men's and women's sentence readings do not differ, but it is the "net increase" to isolated words that is most significant, showing that women have greater sensitivity to prestige norms, as evidenced by their increased use of the prestige variable in a context where more attention is given to speech.

Another study demonstrated that African-American speakers follow the same patterns as do whites. Investigations of African-American Vernacular English (AAVE) in Detroit indicated that gender had an impact on pronunciations, again given class and contextual parameters (Wolfram 1969). In this speech community, women used more of the prestige postvocalic /-r/ than did men.

Percentage of Postvocalic/-r/

	Upper Middle Class (UMC)	Lower Middle Class (LMC)	Upper Working Class (UWC)	Lower Working Class (LWC)
Men	66.7	52.5	20.0	25.0
Women	90.0	70.0	44.2	31.7

Male and female speakers in Detroit varied their use of other sounds as well, including omission of standard labiodental /θ/ at ends of words (e.g., *tooth*) or between vowels (e.g., *nothing*) or its replacement with either a bilabial fricative /f/ or an alveolar stop /t/. Frequencies of such patterns are exhibited in the following table (ibid.). Note that for both this and the /-r/ variable, gender differences among lower-working-class (LWC) speakers are less than among the other socioeconomic classes.

Percentage of /θ/ Deletion or Replacement

	Upper Middle Class (UMC)	Lower Middle Class (LMC)	Upper Working Class (UWC)	Lower Working Class (LWC)
Men	14.6	21.9	70.1	72.3
Women	9.6	12.3	47.5	70.2

All these studies support the contention that pronunciations act, in part, as sociolinguistic markers of gender. Whether the research has been conducted among children, among speakers of American or British regional dialects, or among African Americans or whites, the conclusions are identical: Females use standard and prestige pronunciations at higher rates than do males of similar age and social or racial groups. And in studies that take account of context, females demonstrate quicker and sharper stylistic shifting toward prestige norms in increasingly formal styles.

Again, we need to think about why this is so. One explanation is that women are more conscious of prestige norms and strive to use them because they are judged by their social self-presentation and are socialized to behave in ways that are considered polite and refined. Aware of strong social sanction if they do not conform, women use linguistic style as one manifestation of their "proper" behavior. Labov's notion of "linguistic insecurity," characteristic of members of the lower middle class (LMC), can be applied to women as well. Just as LMC speakers' linguistic patterns reflect their position in a system of class hierarchy in which they are stigmatized, women's "linguistic insecurity," manifested by careful speech, reflects their "social insecurity" in a hierarchical system of gender in which they are culturally relegated to second place.

Trudgill developed another explanation of gender differences that is compatible with the one just offered. He introduced the concept of covert prestige to account for the fact that men use less standard pronunciations and less style shifting toward the standard than do women. Although standard language is given overt social prestige, shown by comments about one's own or another's speech, a competing norm gives covert prestige to male behavior that rejects the standard. In other words, men and women are acting in accordance with different norms. An important indication of this is found in self-reports about one's own speech. Trudgill's subjects were given self-evaluation tests, asking them to specify which of two variants they used. Each set was paired for standard and nonstandard features (*yu,* as in the word "tune" (tyun/tun); *-er,* as in "ear" or "here"; and the vowel *-o-,* as in "road" or "nose"). Women tended to claim greater use of standard pronunciations, whereas men tended to claim greater use of the nonstandard than actually occurred in their speech. These patterns recurred for a number of consonants and vowels. Both women and men overreport but they are overreporting use of different forms. In the case of women, it is the standard; for men, it is the nonstandard. Whereas women claim to produce pronunciations having overt prestige, men model their behavior purposely, although nonconsciously, toward nonstandard forms having covert prestige.

Trudgill also noted an interesting link between masculinity and working-class behavior. In male self-reports, the nonstandard pronunciations that men often claim to use are stereotypical traits of working-class speech. In a significant finding, no differences were shown in men's self-reports when separated for class, so that middle-class men were just as likely to claim nonstandard speech as were working-class men (ibid.).

This observation raises additional questions about sociocultural models of gender. Perhaps an explanation lies in the complexities of gender dichotomization. Given that women are socialized to behave with propriety and politeness (reflected by middle-class speech), and given a system of gender stratification in which men are privileged and in which men who act like women are strongly criticized, men consciously or unconsciously strive toward speech norms that reject styles associated with women. Because women model their behavior on middle-class styles, men covertly prefer working-class speech.

Elizabeth Gordon approaches the question of women's use of standard speech from the opposite direction. Rather than explaining women's speech as reflecting a desire to model their behavior on middle-class norms for positive reasons, Gordon suggests that they may do so in order to avoid inferences associated with lower-class speakers. Whereas men may value stereotypical images of masculinity that are linked to the lower class, women avoid the stereo-typical images of "immorality" or "sexual promiscuity" associated with members of the lower class (1997:48). Women are particularly vulnerable to condemnation for even the hint of sexual promiscuity because of the existing double standard that either overlooks or rewards men's sex-ual behavior but criticizes that of women. In this social context, "style-shifting to a more pres-tigious speech variety conveys the information that the female speaker is not lower class, and is consequently a 'respectable' person" (ibid.:50).

Penelope Eckert (1998) notes that many of the jobs available to women require the use of standard language. Because white-collar workers, such as secretaries, receptionists, flight attendants, and other "front-end" workers, represent their organizations to the public, they must employ standard or prestige speech in order to make a good impression. And women's work as elementary and high school teachers especially encourages knowledge and use of standard language. The relationship between language style and employment in white-collar and service occupations has also been demonstrated in Patricia Nichols's (1983) study of dialect and style shifting among African-American women in coastal Georgia (see Chapter 9).

Studies from a small number of languages detail pronunciation differences that apply to particular sounds in the speech of men and women exclusively. That is, women always use a certain sound, while men always use another sound. In Chukchee, an indigenous language of Siberia, consonants č and r in male speech are consistently replaced by s in female speech. Similarly, consonant clusters čh and rk spoken by men are spoken as šš by women. Compare the following words (Bogoras 1922:665):

Men	Women	
čūmñáta	šūmñáta	"by a buck"
rámkıčhın	sámkıššın	"people"

From these examples, it appears that male speech is the basic linguistic form and that female speech is derived from it. That is, š in female speech is predictable from either č or r in male speech, but the choice of č or r by males cannot be predicted from female š. However, another sound pattern in Chukchee indicates the opposite development. Consonants n and t appearing in basic women's speech are omitted between vowels in derived men's speech, as in the following words (that Bogoras does not translate):

Women	Men
nıtváqěnat	nıtváqaat
tírkıtir	tírkiir

According to Bogoras, when women and men quote a statement made by a male or female character in storytelling or personal narrative, they use pronunciations appropriate for the charac-ter. However, "in ordinary conversation, the pronunciation of men is considered as unbecoming a woman" (ibid.). This comment indicates that Chukchees gave social evaluations to gender-appropriate behavior; however, we should be wary of taking the statement at face value inasmuch as Bogoras did not specify his sources or context for the remark.

Studies of several Native American languages have documented gender distinctions. For example, in Koasati and other languages in the Muskogean family spoken by Native Americans in the southeastern United States, male and female pronunciations contrasted in certain classes of words in various ways. Mary Haas (1944) established Koasati female forms as basic and derived male forms from them because changes were better described in this direction. Following are lists of rules and examples from Koasati (ibid.:142–144).

1. If the female form ends in a nasal vowel, male forms denasalize the vowel and add -*s*:

Women	Men	
lakawwā·	lakawwa·s	he will lift it
lakawtakkō	lakawtakkos	I am not lifting it

2. If the female form ends with falling pitch on a final short vowel followed by -*l,* male forms have rising pitch and replace -*l* with -*s*:

molhîl	molhís	we are peeling it
lakawhôl	lakawhós	lift it! (you pl.)

3. If the female form ends with falling pitch on a final short vowel followed by -*n,* male forms retain falling pitch, replace -*n* with -*s,* and lengthen the final vowel:

tačilwân	tačilwâ·s	don't sing!
iltočihnôn	iltočihnô·s	don't work!

4. If the female form ends in a vowel followed by one or two consonants, male forms add -*s* (unless affected by any previously stated rule):

mól	móls	he is peeling it
tačílw	tačílws	you are singing

Koasati men and women used each other's speech when quoting a speaker or formerly when correcting a child's speech in order to reinforce gender-appropriate styles. Women's speech was evidently on the decline by the mid-twentieth century, however, because Haas noted that "only middle-aged and elderly women use the women's form, while younger women are now using the form characteristic of men's speech" (ibid.:146). Even so, one of Haas's male informants said that he thought women's speech to be "better" than men's. Because Haas did not pursue this issue in her writing, it is impossible to know precisely what the speaker meant by his remark.

Disappearance of female forms of speech in favor of male forms has been documented in other Native American languages, including Hitchiti (Muskogean), Biloxi (Siouan), and Gros Ventre (Algonkian) (see Flannery 1946, Gatschet 1884, and Haas 1944, respectively). This process of replacement, more than the linguistic differences themselves, indicates gender inequalities. Although gender-specific styles demonstrate social differentiation, they do not necessarily imply a hierarchical relationship between women and men. But when one style is consistently replaced by the other, status and value distinctions between men and women must be assumed. Such distinctions have increased in many native cultures along with other aspects of assimilation to Euro-American society. Gender differentiation certainly existed in earlier aboriginal cultures, but it seems to have stressed complementary roles more often than unequal status relations.

Although differences in sounds have been studied in relatively few languages, it is reasonable to assume that such patterns exist or existed elsewhere. Gender-exclusive usages may have gone unnoticed by linguists, particularly if they dealt only with either male or female speakers. Processes of change, similar to those documented in Native American languages, may well have obscured or eliminated gender differentiation previously expressed in other languages.

Intonation

Intonation is a crucial feature influencing how people sound. **Intonation** is a complex combination of rhythm, volume, and pitch overlaying entire utterances. It is heard by listeners as relative changes in these prosodic features rather than as absolute qualities. Some intriguing research has investigated differences in female/male intonational patterns and has discovered cues people use in evaluating the speech of others. In general, women use more dynamic intonational contours than do men. They employ a wider range of pitches within their repertory and a more rapid and marked shift in volume and velocity. In studies of judgments by subjects asked to listen to tape-recorded speech and evaluate the "femininity" or "masculinity" of speakers, speech that varied more in overall rhythmic and pitch patterns was identified as "feminine," whereas speech within narrower limits was identified as "masculine" (Bennet and Weinberg 1979; Terango 1966).

In a review of research on gender differences in English intonation, Sally McConnell-Ginet noted that dynamic patterns are interpreted as indicating emotionality and natural impulses, whereas use of narrow intonational ranges is taken as evidence of control and restraint (1983: 76–77). It is important to remember that this is primarily a cultural interpretation (although intonational changes may result from internal emotional states that have respiratory and muscular effects). By employing more monotonic styles, men are perceived as being in control of their emotions, as opposed to women, who are seen as more expressive. "Masculine speech melodies can be heard as metaphors for control and feminine speech melodies as uncontrolled" (ibid.:82). But "[t]he problem is that the culture does not simply categorize [women] as emotionally expressive but also views [women] as unstable and unpredictable" (ibid.:77).

Intonational patterns may also serve social functions. McConnell-Ginet suggested that women's frequent changes in pitch and volume "may serve the important function of attracting and holding the listener's attention. Women may need this device more than men because of their relative powerlessness and their frequent contact with young children who are not yet socialized to attend reliably to verbal signals" (ibid.:83).

Studies of intonational patterns suggest that women and men employ sentence contours in distinctive ways in some linguistic or interactional contexts. For instance, women may raise pitch levels at the end of declarative sentences, whereas men use a steady or lowering pitch. Because rising pitch is a regular indicator of a question, some linguists, such as Robin Lakoff (1975:17), believe that when women use rising pitches, they are interpreted as hesitant, uncertain, and lacking assertiveness. Other linguists, including McConnell-Ginet (1983) and Pamela Fishman (1983), agree that rising pitch is heard as a question and suggest that women use this style in order to secure a response from hearers.

GRAMMATICAL VARIANTS

Studies of gender-related grammatical alternatives are suggestive of differences but they are often problematic. One reason is that many discussions of the subject are anecdotal or introspective. Also, results of experimental or observational studies sometimes present contradictory findings. Both of these issues deserve further clarification. Regarding the first problem, claims are made about characteristics of women's and men's speech without any testing or controlled observations. Examples to support hypotheses are constructed and presented not as data, but as illustrations. A major difficulty encountered in this technique is the perplexing question of whether the claimed gender-based styles are actual or stereotypical. That is, do they reflect how women and men actually speak, or do they reflect cultural stereotypes of how people are thought to speak? Because people's perceptions of men's and women's speech are influenced by underlying cultural models, we need to be wary of statements about differences without careful analyses of the data presented.

This leads to the second problem of inconsistent results. Some research demonstrates clear distinctions, whereas other work does not. Part of the problem may be the small samples selected in research projects. Another problem is more difficult to address: The speaker's gender is only one of many factors that influence choice of grammatical forms. Additional factors include addressee, context, and speaker's intentions and goals. It is difficult to tease out all the contributing influences on a speaker's use of language. With these cautions in mind, we now turn to an examination of some of the relevant research and debates dealing with gender and grammar.

Gender differences have been found in usage of nonstandard grammatical constructions by adolescent girls and boys in a working-class district of Reading, England (Cheshire 1982:153–154). The following linguistic features were targeted:

1. Present-tense *-s* with nonsingular subjects:
   "We go*es* shopping on Saturdays."
2. *Has* with first- and second-person subjects:
   "We *has* a little fire keeps us warm."
3. *Was* with plural subjects and singular "you":
   "You *was* outside."
4. Multiple negation:
   "I'm *not* going *nowhere*."
5. Past-tense *never,* replacing standard "didn't":
   "I *never* done it, it was him."
6. *What,* replacing "who, whom, which, that":
   "Are you the boy *what's* just come?"
7. Auxiliary *do* with third-person singular subjects:
   "How much *do* he want for it?"
8. Past-tense *come:*
   "I *come* down here yesterday."
9. *Ain't* used for negative auxiliary "have":
   "I *ain't* got any."
10. *Ain't* used for negative auxiliary "be":
    "I *ain't* going to help."
11. *Ain't* used for negative copula:
    "It's her proper name, *ain't* it?"

In the Reading community, boys consistently employed nonstandard grammatical constructions more often than did girls (only the feature *do* was an exception). This finding is not surprising; rather, it is consistent with other research showing that females use more standard and prestige features than do males, who prefer nonstandard forms. However, rates of usage varied for different features. The most marked contrast between boys and girls occurred for *what, come,* and *ain't,* while smaller contrasts were shown for *-s, has, never,* and the use of multiple negation (ibid.:163).

In an influential book on gender differences, Robin Lakoff (1975) pointed out, from anecdotal evidence, that a number of grammatical patterns appear in women's speech more frequently than in men's. Of the syntactic constructions she discussed, the one receiving the most subsequent attention is the tag question. *Tag questions* are sentences in which a speaker makes a declarative statement and adds on a "tag" in the form of a question about the assertion, as in

> Jane came home, didn't she?
>
> It's cold in here, isn't it?

Lakoff stated that women use tag questions because they are reluctant to make direct assertions. They "can avoid committing [themselves] and thereby avoid coming into conflict with the addressee" (ibid.:16–17). Although such deferential style can be favorably evaluated, it can also be perceived as indicating uncertainty and a lack of definite opinions.

Some studies of actual behavior, however, demonstrate no clear gender preferences for use of tag questions (e.g., Dubois and Crouch 1975). Others indicate the critical effect of context and goals on linguistic usage. Tag questions may serve a variety of social functions. For instance, *modal tags* (Holmes 1984:53) are used to request information from the addressee or request that the addressee confirm a statement about which the speaker is unsure. Janet Holmes calls these tags speaker-oriented because they function to supplement the speaker's knowledge, as in

> She's coming around noon, isn't she?

Another type, called *affective tags,* is addressee-oriented, indicating the speaker's interest in or concern for the addressee. One class of affective tags functions as softeners to mitigate the force of a command or criticism:

> Open the oven door for me, could you?
>
> You're driving rather fast, aren't you?

Another class of affective tags are facilitative and indicate the speaker's desire to engage the addressee in continuing conversation (ibid.:55):

> Still working hard at your office, are you?
>
> The hen's brown, isn't it?

These tags are essentially mechanisms to establish speaker turns. They facilitate conversation by inviting the addressee to build on a topic offered by the current speaker.

Holmes discovered a significant difference in the functional role of tags in women's and men's speech. Men more often use tags for speaker-oriented goals, to obtain or confirm information for themselves, whereas women more often use tags for addressee-oriented goals, particularly as strategies to engage addressees in talk. (Recall a similar possible function of women's use of rising or questioning intonational contours.) By taking account of interactional meaning, Holmes's research demonstrates the inadequacy of simply tabulating occurrences of form without attending to function in discourse.

Another study of tags pointed out their use in asymmetric status interactions (Cameron et al. 1988). Deborah Cameron and co-workers recorded television and radio talk show and classroom programs and noted differences between powerful (e.g., medical expert, teacher, program host) and powerless (e.g., client, student, program guest) roles. Sampling included a balance between women and men in each asymmetric role. Although they found that women used more tags than men did, the numbers were not significant (61 and 55, respectively). However, role power seemed to influence the kind of tag employed. Using Holmes's terminology for classifying tags, Cameron and her co-workers found that powerful participants employed affective tags, whereas powerless speakers preferred modal tags. The following table presents their results (ibid.:89):

Tag Questions in Unequal Encounters

Type of Tag	Women		Men	
	Powerful	Powerless	Powerful	Powerless
Modal	3 (5%)	9 (15%)	10 (18%)	16 (29%)
Affective				
Facilitative	43 (70%)	0	25 (45%)	0
Softeners	6 (10%)	0	4 (7%)	0
Total	Women: 61		Men: 55	

Although status asymmetry is an operative factor in the use of tags, gender is also significant. Cameron and her co-workers do not discuss gender differences in the asymmetric roles, but an examination of their data shows support for Holmes's findings that powerful men were more likely than powerful women to employ modal tags (18 percent versus 5 percent) and, contrastingly, powerful women were more likely than powerful men to use affective tags (80 percent versus 52 percent).

In a few languages, morphological constructions vary depending on the gender of the speaker and/or hearer. For example, in Kũṟux, a Dravidian language spoken in North India, verb suffixes marking tense (past, present, future) and imperatives are distinguished in a complex pattern based on same-sex or cross-sex interactions (Ekka 1972). One set is used by men speaking to men and another set by women speaking to women. When men and women interact, they use the male forms.

> The acceptance of [male] grammatical features by women and the rejection of [female] grammatical features by men in Kũṟux speech system are both linguistically and sociologically interesting phenomena…. It may be mentioned that Kũṟux community is patriarchal where men enjoy higher social status than women. Perhaps it might be that the dominance of [male] grammatical features reflects men's superiority over women in Kũṟux speech behavior. (ibid.:31)

Hints about the possibilities of ideological struggle in gendered styles are provided by Chiquita, spoken by native people in Bolivia. In women's speech, all nouns are treated in identical fashion, but in men's speech, nouns are divided into two classes that are marked morphologically. One class consists of nouns referring to men and supernatural beings; the other consists of all other nouns (reported in Bodine 1975b). Men's speech, therefore, links the category of "male" to that of supernatural beings. This style is employed by men only when speaking to other men; women never use it, and the style is never used when speaking to them. Ann Bodine speculated that "Chiquita men have tried to use language to symbolically elevate themselves, but…Chiquita women have refused to go along with it" (ibid.:144). Use of a particular form can demonstrate a social attitude, just as refusal to use that form can signify a rejection of implied cultural meaning.

Examples documenting pronunciation and grammatical and vocabulary differences are actually rather restricted when viewed in terms of each linguistic system as a whole. They involve either a small number of sounds, a few morphological markers, or a handful of words. They do not alter the fundamental character of a language. However, despite the evidence of such patterns, it is well to be cautious about their interpretation. It may well have been true that the speech usually associated with the gender other than the speaker was used in some contexts or for pragmatic and stylistic functions. Unfortunately, because of the loss of women's speech in some communities (or of the extinction of the language altogether), contextual data cannot be retrieved.

Some insights into pragmatic possibilities may be gleaned from a study of Lakhota particles that are inserted after verbs to denote the gender of the speaker (Trechter and James 1994). The particles also carry affective meaning, conveying attitudes of the speaker toward self, addressee, and topic. For example, the "opinion/emphasis" particle associated with women (/yele/) connotes nurturance and concern for the addressee, whereas the particle associated with men (/yelo/) connotes authority, seniority, and rights to discipline or assert (ibid.:749–750). As in other Native American languages, when quoting other people, speakers use the particles of the person they are quoting. But people may also use particles stereotypically associated with the other gender to convey particular affective and contextual meanings. Sara Trechter and Eli James cite several instances of men's use of women's speech: a man talking to his young nephew to indicate affection, an elderly man speaking about a dead relative to indicate his respect for the deceased, and a middle-aged man expressing an opinion that might upset or anger the addressee. The researchers also note an example of a woman using a particle associated with men when giving permission to a younger female relative to engage in an activity (singing in public) that contravenes Lakhota mourning observances (ibid.:752–754). These data uncover a critical distinction between stereotypical ideals and actual usage, a distinction that can presumably be found in most, if not all, societies.

CHOICES OF VOCABULARY

Numerous researchers have discussed differences in choice of vocabulary used by women and men, observing that certain words or categories of words appear with greater frequency in the speech of one or the other. Some domains of vocabulary are more elaborated by each gender. Men and women are expected to know the meanings of words within domains reflecting culturally stereotyped areas of their assumed expertise, as, for example, cooking and other domestic skills for women, sports and machinery for men.

One well-studied category of words with relevance to gender differences in English is that of profanity. It has often been claimed that, given class and context, men use curse words with greater frequency and greater profane force than do women, while women tend to employ milder expletives. Although both genders use less profanity in cross-sex interactions, many women refrain from its use even in casual conversations with other women who are not their familiars (Bailey and Timm 1976; Jay 1980). It is unclear, however, whether these claims are actually substantiated or whether they reflect cultural stereotypes and assumptions. In a study of South African teenagers, Vivian DeKlerk (1992) found no significant differences in the number of or semantic force of the words used by boys and girls to describe males and females. Age was a more important indicator of knowledge and behavior than was gender. Susan Hughes (1997) also criticized the accepted notion of men's greater use of profanity. She contends that vernacular speech of lower-class women, including the use of profanity, functions as a linguistic mechanism that reflects and reinforces solidarity and bonding between women.

Another area of vocabulary differences is that of modifiers (adjectives and adverbs). Ever since the Danish linguist Otto Jespersen's chapter "The Woman" appeared in his *Language* (1922), observers have pointed to women's tendency to use intensifiers such as *very, so,* or *extremely* and what some have called "empty" adjectives, such as *wonderful* or *lovely*. Jespersen interpreted these usages as an example of women's tendency to exaggerate and as a sign of linguistic and cognitive superficiality (ibid.:347). But adjectives such as *lovely* are not empty or devoid of meaning. They express personal affective judgments.

One last area of vocabulary differences in English is the noted tendency for women to use more *hedge words* in discourse—that is, words or expressions that covertly comment on assertions in one's statements, for example:

> *Perhaps* we *could try* fixing it.
> I've been *sort of wondering whether* I should go.
> *Well,* I guess it's *approximately* four feet high.

These constructions function to signal a speaker's uncertainty about the validity of her statement. In doing so, they create an impression of indecisiveness and lack of clarity. Because females are socialized to defer to others and avoid conflict, they choose to state opinions interspersed with hedges to minimize confrontation with an addressee who may hold a different view. And making assertions in a tentative style allows speakers to modify or retract statements if they are challenged.

Hedges can also function to "express the speaker's attitude to the addressee, that is, to signal affective meaning" (Holmes 1984:48); for example,

> *Well,* I *think* George is a *bit, er, perhaps* foolish.

This statement was made by a woman commenting on the behavior of her friend's husband. By hedging the assertion that "George is foolish," the speaker demonstrated concern for the addressee by not making a blunt criticism.

Using hedges as part of a politeness strategy is invoked not only by gender, but also by status and context. Note the following excerpt from an interviewer's questioning of the prime minister of New Zealand (quoted in Holmes 1984:49):

> I *had the feeling* that with all the talk about the future that *perhaps* some of the Ministers were not talking *quite so strongly* in an election year context and I *wondered whether perhaps* you were surprised that....

To test the relative weight of gender, status, and context on stylistic choice, Faye Crosby and Linda Nyquist (1977) examined speech produced in three different situations: laboratory experiments involving college students discussing a given topic, information-booth question-and-answer exchanges, and police-station interactions between personnel and clients. They measured usage of what they called the female register (ibid.:314), based on Lakoff's characterization of women's speech. As they point out, the female register can be used by either women or men. "The distinguishing feature of the female register is not that it is used exclusively by women but rather that it embodies the female role in our society. The female register is both expressive (e.g., polite rather than direct and informative) and nonassertive. Both of these attributes are central aspects of the stereotyped feminine role in our culture" (ibid.).

Traits measured by Crosby and Nyquist included hedges ("kind of," "stuff like that," "I don't know"), expressive adjectives ("charming," "cute," "weird"), tag questions, intensifiers ("so"), and politeness formulas ("please," "thank you"). They discovered that in college experiments and police-station interactions, women more often produced speech conforming to the female register. In police-station observations, status also proved important because clients of either gender used the female register more than police personnel did. Consistent results in information-booth exchanges were not found except that male-to-male speech tended to show least use of the targeted traits (ibid.:316–319). This context is highly artificial. Interpersonal contact is extremely brief, routinized, and impersonal. It is therefore not unexpected that speakers do not use affective styles in such situations.

In sum, although both men and women sometimes employ linguistic styles characterized by indecisive, imprecise, or mitigated speech, these traits are perceived to be more typical of women. They are, in actuality, more likely to be used by women (given contextual similarities) and also by people of either gender in subordinate roles. Subordinates (and women in general) are expected to behave politely and show deference to higher-status people. Through these processes linking style, gender, and status, cultural models of personal and gender images are reinforced and justified.

In the Japanese language, some words are contrasted on a scale of politeness and formality, and those deemed more polite tend to be used by women, whereas less polite forms tend to be used by men. Some examples follow (ibid.:28):

	Less Polite Forms	More Polite Forms
Water	mizu	ohiya
Delicious	umai	oisii
Eat	kuu	taberu

Nouns that contain the prefix {o-} (as in the preceding list) carry connotations of politeness. This prefix is a polite or honorific marker that can be used by either gender but occurs in women's speech with greater frequency. It can be attached to any noun to render the speaking style more polite or refined. Other politeness prefixes are {go-} and {omi-}, also appearing in women's speech at high rates. However, the relative status of speakers in any dyadic interaction is also significant. Both men and women use polite forms to superiors. But because women are socially defined as inferior in status in many intergender interactions, they tend to use polite forms with greater frequency than do men, for instance:

	Less Polite Forms	More Polite Forms
Chopsticks	hasi	ohasi
Book	hon	gohon

In Japan, as in the United States, people stereotypically identify certain linguistic constructions with female speakers and others with male speakers. And in Japan, as in the United States, the validity of some of these stereotypes is questionable.

GENDER-RELATED CONVERSATIONAL STYLES

Differences between the genders are demonstrated in conversational style as well as in linguistic structures. Much of the research investigating women's and men's conversation concerns alternatives in speaker turns, topic introduction and control, and mechanisms of signaling active listenership.

In the study of gender-related styles, two different explanatory perspectives have emerged. One contends that men's and women's behavior stems from their socialization into contrasting "cultures," beginning in childhood and continuing into adulthood. It is claimed that girls and boys tend to play and interact in same-sex groups and develop different communicative skills based on different individual and social goals. The other approach analyzes linguistic behavior within a social context of male power and dominance. Men use communicative strategies that assert their control and prerogatives, whereas women employ strategies that are deferential, conciliatory, and sensitive to the other's "face"—to use Penelope Brown and Stephen Levinson's (1987) term.

Among the prominent proponents of the "cultural differences" theories are Daniel Maltz and Ruth Borker (1982) and Deborah Tannen (1986, 1990). Maltz and Borker place gender differences within the framework of research concerning "cross-ethnic miscommunication" (ibid.:196). To them, cross-sex conversation is sometimes problematic because of "cultural differences between men and women in their conceptions of friendly conversation, their rules for engaging in it, and their rules for interpreting it" (ibid.:200). Maltz and Borker note the major reported conversational tendencies of women and men: women's tendencies to ask questions, encourage responses from interlocutors, make "positive minimal responses," and allow interruptions into their speaking turns; and men's tendencies to interrupt, challenge, and/or ignore the speech of interlocutors, introduce and control topics, and make direct assertions of fact and opinion. These modes of adult speech are the outcomes of childhood training in same-sex groups where girls learn "to create and maintain relationships of closeness and equality, to criticize others in acceptable ways, and interpret accurately the speech of others," and boys learn "to assert positions of dominance, to attract and maintain an audience, and to assert [themselves] when other speakers have the floor" (ibid.:205, 207). As a result, when women and men converse "as friends and equals" (ibid.:212), they misinterpret each other's cues.

Maltz and Borker criticize explanations based on gender-linked social power, stating that such explanations "do not provide a means of explaining why these specific features appear as opposed to any number of others.... They do not really tell us why and how these specific interactional phenomena are linked to the general fact that men dominate within our social system" (ibid.:199). In fact, though, theories based on situating speech in the social context of gender hierarchy do indeed explain why "these specific features" appear and how they are linked to male dominance. Stylistic strategies associated with men are (as Maltz and Borker themselves note) those of asserting control and dominance (interrupting another's turn, insisting on introducing and developing topics while ignoring those introduced by others, failing to encourage another's talk), whereas women's strategies are indicative of relative powerlessness (encouraging another's talk through questions and positive responses, mitigating criticism, deferring to others' interruptions and attempts at control).

The "cultural differences" approach has also been championed in the academic and popular writings of Tannen (1986, 1990). Tannen states the claim even more strongly than do Maltz and Borker: "Boys and girls grow up in different worlds.... And as adults they travel in different worlds, reinforcing patterns established in childhood" (1986). Boys and girls "talk differently" because "[f]rom the time they're born, they're treated differently."

Although Tannen acknowledges that girls and boys are "treated differently," she never attempts to understand why. Instead, she focuses on the "misunderstandings" between men and women because of their "incongruent expectations" and differences in how they "view the role of talk in relationships." Going one step further than Maltz and Borker, Tannen states that male–female conversations are not similar *to* but actually *are* instances of "cross-cultural communication" (1990:47). Just as people from different cultural backgrounds misinterpret the stylistic intents and meanings of each other's speech, Tannen cautions her readers that "not seeing style differences for what they are, people draw conclusions about personality or intentions.... Understanding the other's ways of talking is a giant leap across the communication gap" (ibid.:298).

However, Tannen herself has been accused of "not seeing style differences for what they are." For example, by "regard[ing] socialization as the main influence shaping identified patterns of adult linguistic behaviour," Tannen fails to address "both what the triggers for such behaviour patterns in the first place are and what ensures [their] continuation from child to adulthood" (Davis 1996:75). And as Uchida (1992) points out, "the sexual division of labor in conversation is not a mere result of cultural differences." Instead, it reflects "a hierarchy, a power structure in the society [that] affects our everyday interaction" (ibid.:559–560). In addition to the differences in communicative strategies that result in women working harder to maintain conversation than do men, the negative consequences of "miscommunication" are borne more by women. Men's behavior (being in control, assertive, rational) is given public approval, whereas women's behavior (being deferential, unassertive, emotional) is devalued or trivialized. Again quoting Uchida:

> An analysis of miscommunication must take into consideration who gets what they want, who is punished, who is forgiven, and in what ways—both on the individual level and on the societal level—after the miscommunication.... The approach that dismisses this aspect has the danger of being used to legitimize blatantly misogynist behavior on the ground that it is a case of innocent miscommunication caused by cultural differences. (ibid.:562)

Senta Troemel-Ploetz discounts Tannen's premise that women and men do not understand each other:

> On the contrary, they understand each other quite well. They know who is allowed to use dominant speech acts, like commands, orders, explanations, contradiction, criticism, evaluations, definitions, attacks, challenges, accusations, reproaches; and who has to apologize, defend, ask for favors, beg, request permission, justify herself, agree, support, adjust, accommodate, and accept someone else's definition of the situation. (1998:447)

In conversation, men and women reproduce their social rights by the way that they present themselves and interact. Men are typically able to get their interactional needs fulfilled more often than women do. Communication differences between men and women are, therefore, not simply differences of style that can be resolved by attempting to understand each other. By taking linguistic interaction out of the social context that produces it, the meaning of the interaction is lost. And any fundamental remedy is made impossible. As Troemel-Ploetz notes, by avoiding the social and political implications of conversation and by "selling the status-quo, [Tannen's] by-intention apolitical book becomes a highly political act" (ibid.:450).

Rather than explaining men's and women's behavior as derived from separate cultures, other researchers emphasize the context of power and dominance that permits men to assert control while it teaches women to support and defer to the goals of others. Henley and Kramarae draw similarities between the social relations of the genders and those of unequal ethnic, racial, and class groups and note similarities in conversation interaction and interpretation:

> Hierarchies determine whose version will prevail; whose speech style will be seen as normal; who will be required to learn the communication style, and interpret the meaning, of the other; and who will be required to imitate the other's style in order to fit into the society. (1991:19–20)

It is typically men's speech style that is considered "normal" and that of women as deviant or in need of explanation. Women bear more of the burden of interpreting men's interactive style.

And in order to be considered serious and competent, women must use speaking styles generally associated with men. As Henley and Kramarae point out, "Females, not males, [must] learn to read the silence, lack of emotional expression, or brutality of the other sex as not only other than, but more benign than, it appears" (ibid.:23).

The facts of male control of conversation (through mechanisms that will be detailed in following sections) are best understood within the social context that produces them. But not only are the communicative strategies of men and women created by a system of hierarchy and inequality, the strategies themselves serve to maintain that very system: "One may in fact ask how well male dominance could be maintained if we had open and equally-valued communication between women and men. The construction of miscommunication between the sexes emerges as a powerful tool, maybe even a necessity, to maintain the structure of male supremacy" (ibid.:42).

Power is not abstract, however. It is embodied in people's identities. And those identities are based, in part, on the roles that people expect to have in the society. As Scott Kiesling observed, "When a man constructs a powerful identity, it is usually connected in some way to 'real' power. Thus, the expectation of a 'powerful' identity for men is not symmetrical to the expectation of a 'powerless' identity for women, since a man's powerful identity is *rewarded* (with power), whereas a woman's non-powerless identity may be *punished*" (italics in original; 1997:65–66).

The role women play in this system is, of course, complex. They may at times contribute to maintaining their own subordination by acquiescing to men's control, they may collude with male power by interpreting men's speech as more worthy than their own, and they may counter male prerogatives either through overt objections or through covert resistance. Resistance may be demonstrated informally through comment and gossip, or it may be formalized through special speech genres such as women's poetry and songs (see, for example, Lila Abu-Lughod's studies of Bedouin women's genres).

A number of studies have investigated whether cultural stereotypes concerning men's and women's speaking styles have any basis in practice. One such stereotype is that women are more talkative than men. However, an experiment aimed at measuring verbosity (amount of talk) demonstrated the opposite pattern. Male and female college students were presented with three pictures drawn by Albrecht Dürer, a fifteenth-century Flemish artist, and were asked to describe the drawings as thoroughly as possible, taking as much time as they liked (Swacker 1975). Results showed striking gender differences. The mean time for all three pictures was 13.0 minutes for males and only 3.17 for females (ibid.:80). Choosing only the second description, men's speaking length averaged 333.41 seconds, and women's 96.0 seconds. Verbosity differed significantly, but rather than confirming the stereotype of talkative women, the study showed that male speakers talked more. Persistence of the erroneous stereotype has been explained by Cheris Kramer, who suggested that because females are socialized to defer to their co-conversationalists, "perhaps a 'talkative' woman is one who does talk as much as a man" (1975:47). Because men have more rights to talk, they are not considered talkative when they exercise those rights. In contrast, women who speak in moderation are judged to be talkative.

In actual (rather than experimental) settings, men also tend to be more talkative than women. Observation of conversation in university faculty meetings revealed that speaking turns of male teachers were from one and one-quarter to nearly four times longer than those of females (Edelsky 1981:415). When topics and context of meetings were more formal, men's contributions to discussions lengthened and those of women were shortened. In more relaxed, give-and-take exchanges, women's and men's turns were equal.

Extending the meaning of these findings, Jack Sattel (1983) found that, although men may be more talkative than women in some settings, they are more silent in regard to discussion of emotions. Sattel contended that men's tendency for emotional inexpressiveness or unwillingness to talk about affect either with women or with other men stems from their desire to maintain and assert power. "What better way is there to exercise power than *to make it appear* that *all* one's behavior seems to be the result of unemotional rationality.... Keeping cool, keeping distant as others challenge you or make demands upon you, is a strategy for keeping the upper hand" (italics in original; 1983:120). Silence functions as part of competitive displays of dominance because "to not say anything is to say something very important indeed: that the battle is to be fought by [his] rules and when [he] chooses to fight" (ibid.:122). This tactic is particularly effective when used in interactions with women because of women's tendencies for emotional self-disclosure. Sattel notes that it is women rather than men who have to interpret the other's speech and adjust to it (ibid.:123). Sattel urges that these interactions be understood in the context of male dominance and female subordination:

> Male dominance takes shape in the positions of formal and informal *power* men hold in the social division of labor; greater male prestige includes, and is evidenced by, the greater *reward* which attaches to male than to female activities. What our culture embodies is not simply two stereotypes—one masculine, one feminine—but a set of power and prestige arrangements attached to gender. (ibid.:119–120)

This system, which rests on social power, cannot be changed by "simply changing men's capacity to feel or express themselves" because "men are not oppressed *as men,* and hence are not in a position to be liberated *as men*" (ibid.:123).

In a study of interactions between spouses that substantiated Sattel's insights, Victoria DeFrancisco reported that men's silence had the effect of silencing women. Although men directed topics and their development through interruption and minimal responses, they most often exerted their control by silence, especially in the form of "no response" to their wives' prior statement (1998:179). While women sometimes employed this strategy as well, they did so much less often (68 percent of "no response" were done by men, 32 percent by women). Men's "no response" turns were followed either by their wives' silence (giving up) or attempts to introduce an alternative topic.

Two influential studies by Candace West and Don Zimmerman (1975, 1983) investigated dyadic (two-person) interactions, focusing on instances of one speaker's turn limited or interrupted by a co-participant. West and Zimmerman recorded casual conversations in public places (coffee shops, stores, university buildings) between people who knew each other and later conducted experiments involving college students who were unacquainted. In both studies, they noted violations of speakers' turns in the form of interruptions, defined technically as an intrusion into current speaker's talk "prior to the last lexical constituent [word] that could define a possible terminal boundary" (Zimmerman and West 1975:114). An "interruption" contrasts significantly with an "overlap," which is "simultaneous speech where a speaker other than the current speaker begins to speak at or very close to a possible transition place in a current speaker's utterance (i.e., within the boundaries of the last word)" (ibid.). Overlaps are errors of judgment in transitions and timing to the next turn, whereas interruptions are violations of a current speaker's rights.

Although Zimmerman and West's samples were small, their findings are quite striking and consistent with other research concerning men's and women's status in our society. First, they found a marked difference in patterns of overlap and interruption in same-sex and cross-sex conversations. In the former, overlaps and interruptions were evenly distributed, each speaker contributing approximately the same number. But in cross-sex conversations, almost all errors and intrusions were initiated by men. The following tables present data obtained in the 1975 study (ibid.:115, 116):

Interruptions/Overlaps in 20 Same-Sex Conversations

	First Speaker	Second Speaker	Total
Interruptions	43% (3)	57% (4)	100% (7)
Overlaps	55 (12)	45 (10)	100 (22)

Interruptions/Overlaps in 11 Cross-Sex Conversations

	Males	Females	Total
Interruptions	96% (46)	4% (2)	100% (48)
Overlaps	100 (9)	—	100 (9)

In addition to marked gender differences in cross-sex conversations, another significant fact displayed in these tables is that, in same-sex interactions, most conversational errors are overlaps (minor mistakes of timing), whereas in interactions between men and women, most intrusions are interruptions (violations of current speaker's turns).

The following table presents findings from West and Zimmerman's (1983) experimental study of unacquainted students (1983:107):

Interruptions in Five Cross-Sex Conversations

	Number of Interruptions		
Conversation	Male-initiated	Female-initiated	Total
Dyad 1	75%	25%	100% (4)
Dyad 2	100	0	100 (4)
Dyad 3	67	33	100 (6)
Dyad 4	83	17	100 (6)
Dyad 5	63	37	100 (8)

Zimmerman and West's research demonstrates a clear inequality in the rights of women and men engaged in conversation. Men use mechanisms of power and control in interactions with women, whether previously acquainted or not. Interruptions are strategies that disregard the current speaker's talk and attempt to disallow that person an opportunity to express herself fully as she had intended. In so doing, interruptions also function as tactics to exert control over topics of conversation because they frequently lead to changes in topics, establishing the interests of the interrupter. West and Zimmerman concluded:

> When viewed from a perspective encompassing the fate of women in the various institutional domains of society, the many small insults women suffer in face-to-face interaction do perhaps seem trivial. Yet…the gestures of power are an integral part of

women's placement in the social scheme of things. These daily gestures are constant "reminders" which help constitute women's subordinate status. (1983:110)

In research designed to test hypotheses concerning relative influences of gender and occupational status on frequency of interruption, Nicola Woods (1988) tape-recorded triadic (three-party) interactions in work settings. Subjects included both male and female supervisors and subordinates. Woods discovered that the two factors of status and gender significantly affected several conversational strategies, but that gender was the most important influence on behavior. "Essentially, while the power base of occupational status did influence the way that both men and women organised conversation, nevertheless even when women held high-status occupational positions male subordinates still organised the interaction in a way that allowed them to dominate the floor" (ibid.:149).

Woods found that powerful people (high status and male) were more likely to interrupt co-participants successfully and were least likely to be interrupted in their turns. And when men intruded on other speakers, they were usually successful in gaining the floor (data indicate 17 out of 20 attempts), whereas women interrupters were not as likely to succeed (only 11 of 21 attempts; ibid.:151).

Woods's data show that men are usually successful in interrupting current speakers. They violate other speakers' turns, even when the men are subordinates and particularly when subordinate to a higher-status woman. And women are the most likely targets of successful interruptions even when they are in higher-status positions. When the double factors of low status and female gender co-occur, women are especially vulnerable. The lowest-status woman was interrupted successfully 11 times and the second-ranked woman seven times.

In a study of dyadic conversations between physicians and their patients, West found that both status and gender were significant factors in the frequency of interruption but, like Woods's findings, gender outweighed status. In interactions between male physicians and their patients, the doctors initiated 67 percent (126) of the interruptions, whereas patients were responsible for only 33 percent (62); but in encounters between female physicians and their patients, the doctors initiated 32 percent (19) of the interruptions, and patients were responsible for 68 percent (40) (1998:399–400). An additional significant finding is that, in all dyads involving a male physician, the doctor always interrupted the patient more often than the patient interrupted the doctor, whereas there was variation in dyads involving female physicians. When both doctor and patient were women, both interrupted the other with about equal frequency, whereas male patients interrupted the doctor much more often than the doctor interrupted the patient (ibid.:404–405).

Women and men employ different strategies for conversational interaction in casual and familiar settings as well as in structured contexts. In studies of talk between couples, Pamela Fishman (1983) collected 52 hours of tape-recordings made in the homes of three white, middle-class couples (with their approval and ability to censure material if they wished). In her research and analysis, Fishman developed the notion of the "work of conversation":

Interaction requires at least two people. Conversation is produced not simply by their presence, but also by the display of their continuing agreement to pay attention to one another. That is, all interactions are potentially problematic and occur only through the continual, turn-by-turn, efforts of the participants.... For an attempt to succeed, the other party must be willing to do further interactional work. That other person has the power to turn an attempt into a conversation or to stop it dead. (ibid.:90–91)

Fishman's data revealed a "variety of strategies to insure, encourage and subvert conversation" (ibid.:93). On the whole, women do more of the interactional work, attempting to gain their partner's attention and responding to their partner's talk. The following devices were used to initiate conversation or to introduce topics (ibid.:94–95):

1. *Attention beginnings* (e.g., "this is interesting"): These expressions function to establish the interest or legitimacy of statements or topics to follow. "Attention beginnings" were used twice as often by women as by men.

2. *Asking questions:* Questions help guarantee subsequent talk because they are bound in a paired sequence with answers. Addressees are usually obliged to give at least some response. In Fishman's transcripts, women asked questions two and a half times more often than did men.

3. *Asking "D'ya know what?"* These ritualized questions trigger a three-part exchange of the form: question–question–answer. The initiator asks, "D'ya know what?" the addressee asks "What?" and the initiator returns with the intended topic. This tactic was used by women twice as much as by men.

A significant ingredient in the work of conversation is the response one gives to co-participant(s). Responses can encourage speakers to continue or discourage and block interaction. One type of reaction is the "minimal response," often in the form of "umm," "oh," or "yeah," uttered by the listener during or following the current speaker's turn. According to Fishman, men and women used these mechanisms for different purposes. Men's responses tended to occur at the ends of women's turns, taking the place of their own turn. This actually discourages the current speaker because it displays no interest in the speaker's topic, requests no elaboration, and contributes no informational comment that the previous speaker can build on. In contrast, women as listeners tended to place responses within the current speaker's turns, signaling ongoing listener interest and encouraging the speaker to continue (ibid.:95–96).

Fishman discovered that, whereas women suggested nearly twice as many topics as men, they were successful in establishing only about one-third of the accepted topics. Men's topics were almost always accepted, whereas women had a failure rate of nearly 2–1 (ibid.:97). After analyzing the evidence contained in the recordings, Fishman concluded:

> As with work in its usual sense, there appears to be a division of labor in conversation. The people who do the routine maintenance work, the women, are not the same people who either control or benefit from the process. Women are the "shitworkers" of routine interaction, and the "goods" being made are not only interactions, but, through them, realities.… Because this work is obscured, because it is seen as an aspect of gender identity rather than of gender activity, the maintenance and expression of male-female power relations in our everyday conversations are hidden as well. (ibid.: 99–100)

One of the complexities in research on gendered conversational styles is the issue of interpretation. Many studies characterize women's conversational contributions as supportive and cooperative because women build on each other's utterances, strive for agreement, and give listener responses indicating encouragement for the speaker. In contrast, men's styles are often described as competitive because they make direct assertions, challenge each other's statements, and often use insults to characterize co-participants. However, Jane Pilkington (1998) suggests that these descriptions of gendered styles may not be how the participants perceive their behavior.

In particular, in analyzing all-male and all-female gossip groups in Australia, Pilkington noted the types of behavior familiar in the research literature on gendered styles, but men did not experience their interactions in negative ways. Instead, they enjoyed their "verbal sparing" (ibid.:268) and understood their linguistic interactions as means of establishing and reinforcing a kind of camaraderie or "mateship culture."

In Scott Kiesling's (2005) analysis of conversations among fraternity men, "discourses of masculinity" include an emphasis on gender differences (i.e., that men are not women), heterosexism, dominance, and male solidarity (ibid.:701). Interactions among the fraternity men often stressed feelings of loyalty and unity, demonstrating "homosocial" desires (i.e., the social, not sexual, desire to be with other men). But the very expression of these desires, while augmenting the discourse of male solidarity, puts the men at risk of damaging their masculinity because it subverts the discourses of dominance and might potentially question their heterosexuality. For example, at a group meeting, a recently graduated fraternity member reminisces about his experiences:

> I can tell you one thing made all the problems go away. It's unity.… I can tell you the best times I ever had were when all the brothers were together. When we're together, it didn't matter, it was cool. I felt safe. I felt comfortable. I'm surrounded by all these people. I feel OK. Those were the best feelings ever. (ibid.:708–709)

In another study, an analysis of an interaction involving four male college roommates uncovers some of the strategies these young men use to affirm their masculinity while at the same time employing characteristics often thought to be typical of the behavior of women (Cameron 1999). In the conversation analyzed, two topics dominated: basketball (the men were engaged in watching a basketball game on television) and the negative attributes of supposedly gay classmates. The latter topic clearly was an example of "gossip," a stereotypically female pastime. In Cameron's analysis, the men identified several of their classmates as "gay" because of these classmates' choice of attire and personal grooming habits, not because of specific knowledge about their sexual activities. But in so doing, the four friends revealed that they paid close attention to the bodies and clothing of other men, a supposedly taboo behavior. For example, note the following exchange:

BRYAN:	You know that really gay guy in our Age of Revolution class who sits in front of us? He wore shorts again, by the way, it's like 42° out, he wore shorts again. It's like a speedo, he wears a speedo to class. He's got incredibly skinny legs.
ED:	It's worse, you know, like those shorts women volleyball players wear? It's like those. French cut spandex.
BRYAN:	He's either got some condition that he's got to like have his legs exposed at all times or else he's got really good legs.
ED:	He's probably, he's like at home combing his leg hairs.
BRYAN:	He doesn't have any leg hair though.
AL:	Very long very white and very skinny.
BRYAN:	Those ridiculous Reeboks that are always…and goofy white socks always striped, tube socks.
ED:	He's the antithesis of man.

In analyzing this conversation segment as part of the young men's overall display of their heterosexual gender identity, Cameron points out the contradiction in which they find themselves: "They are impelled, paradoxically, to talk about men's bodies as a way of demonstrating their own total lack of sexual interest in those bodies" (ibid.:449). In gossiping about the "gay" classmates, the men were revealing their keen observation and attention to their target's body and style of dress. But in this conversation, as always, context and participants are critical components in the negotiation and display of meaning. As Cameron notes, "performing masculinity or femininity 'appropriately' cannot mean giving exactly the same performance regardless of the circumstances" (ibid.: 454). As she observes, it is safer for heterosexual men to comment on the appearance and clothing of "gay men" than it would be for them to talk so intimately about other heterosexual men.

Japanese

Research into topics of language and gender in other societies uncovers relationships between cultural models of gender and stylistic choices. The Japanese language provides speakers with sentence-final particles, that is, morphemes occurring at ends of sentences that mark speakers' attitudes. Common particles in women's speech indicate "femininity" {*wa*}, "childishness" {*no*}, and "uncertainty" {*-te*}. In contrast, particles most often used by men are "emphatics": {*ze*}, {*zo*} (ibid.:33–34). Gender styles in particle usage can thus be compared to patterns of vocabulary or syntactic choices in English. As we have seen, American-Anglo women tend to mark their speech with indicators of mitigation and uncertainty (hedges, tags), whereas men tend to use more direct (emphatic) constructions.

To study the actual usage of Japanese gender markers in speech, Janet Shibamoto (1987) conducted a study of casual conversations among friends, recorded in groups of three. On the basis of these recordings, Shibamoto identified three syntactic features occurring at different frequencies in women's and men's speech: omission of subjects, objects, and other noun phrases in sentences; transposition of subjects from their usual place of preceding verbs (as in English) to positions following verbs, often to the end of sentences; and omission of case markers on subjects and direct objects (ibid.:36, 38). Women consistently employed the relevant features at much higher rates than did men, demonstrating differences in gendered styles.

However, evidence indicates changes in usage of gender markers in speech of younger Japanese women. Although the normative reactions of many Japanese people continue to recognize gender-linked styles, actual behavior is not consistent with these images. To document young women's speech in informal contexts, Shigeko Okamoto (1995) analyzed tape-recordings of dyadic conversations between female college students (age 18 to 20) residing in Tokyo. The analysis centered on sentence-final particles, auxiliaries, and verb forms that are traditionally classified as "feminine" (used primarily by women), "masculine" (used by men), and "neutral" (used by women and men). The linguistic forms were further identified as "moderately" or "strongly" feminine or masculine. Okamoto found that all ten subjects employed neutral forms most. And eight of the ten used masculine forms more often than feminine forms (ibid.:303). Of the feminine forms used, the majority were "moderately feminine." And, significantly, most of the "strongly feminine" forms used were quotations of the speech of older women. Most of the masculine forms employed were "moderately masculine," although a few speakers used words or expressions perceived as "strongly masculine" or "vulgar" (ibid.:305). In another study, Okamoto and Shie Sato found that middle-age women tended to use more "feminine" forms than did younger women (1992). Okamoto (1995) cites additional research by Midori Takasaki indicating that women in different occupations employed different levels of "feminine" (or polite) markers: Homemakers used more "feminine" speech than did students, and office workers used more markers of politeness than did professional or self-employed women (ibid.:307).

As roles of Japanese women have become more varied and flexible, the emphasis on "feminine" speech has diminished. Young women's use of perceived "masculine" markers may serve to distinguish them from older women and foster solidarity as a group. And the fact that professional women use less "feminine" (polite or deferential) speech may serve both to "express power and to empower themselves" (Okamoto 1995:314). Some Japanese women are exploiting a recent resource, the use of loanwords from English, to escape the parameters of politeness and status inherent in the Japanese language. Contemporary songwriters and poets especially use English loanwords to express modernity and equality, allowing them to convey images and sentiments that are deeply personal without the restrictions of linguistic and interpersonal expression deemed appropriate for women in Japanese (Stanlaw 2004:133–139).

Change may also be taking place in men's use of gender markers. Styles of speaking and use of particles stereotypically identified as "feminine" occur in men's speech with greater frequency than in the past, possibly leading to "neutralization" of these markers. These facts make it clear that gender itself is not the sole contributor to speech styles. Rather, factors such as age, occupation, and class influence linguistic strategies that people employ.

In a study of men's conversational styles, Cindi Sreetharan (2004) analyzed interactions of male friends living in two regions of Japan, Kansai and Kanto (in western and eastern Japan, respectively) to investigate whether the men actually used the so-called masculine sentence-final particles and, if so, in what contexts. In their conversations, all of the men preferred to use "neutral" particles most frequently, with secondary emphasis on "masculine" particles and last on "feminine" particles (ibid.:281–282). The specific rates of use of neutral particles varied somewhat in the different regions (from 40 percent to 49 percent). Rates for masculine particles also varied (from 13 percent to 22 percent), but among the masculine particles, those identified as moderately masculine occurred with higher frequency than those identified as strongly masculine. The men in all conversations occasionally employed "feminine" particles (from 4.4 percent to 9.1 percent of all usages), preferring those identified as moderately feminine over strongly feminine particles.

Looking at the contextual occurrence of the strongly masculine particles, Sreetharan found that they were used more often to emphasize stereotypical masculine qualities of authority and confidence. For example, they were used to assert expert knowledge, register disagreement with a previous speaker, and express confidence in one's opinions (ibid.:283). In addition, in one of the conversations, the two men used strongly masculine particles and word choices in a comical role-playing interaction in which they acted out a hypothetical collision between two tough bike riders. These data attest to the contextual significance of sentence-final particles and their ability to display masculine or feminine stereotypes chosen for specific pragmatic purposes.

Javanese

The language spoken in Java, an island in the Indonesian chain, contains complex indicators of politeness and deference. These markers occur in both women's and men's speech, but their use by each gender differs significantly. Of equal importance, gender-related usage is evaluated in distinct ways by men and women, raising a critical issue concerning the ability of groups of people to define their own or another's behavior.

Javanese culture contains conflicting notions of gender status. An egalitarian ideology stresses women's and men's autonomy. Women participate in work inside and outside the home, with primary responsibilities for managing household income and for hosting social gatherings. An important nationwide reflection of one attitude toward gender is the fact that girls and boys are equally educated. However, other societal norms restrict women's actual participation in public life: Women do not usually become political or religious leaders, although they can occasionally function in place of their husbands (Smith-Hefner 1988:538–539). Javanese culture, then, gives some support for gender equality, but in practice inequality exists in certain areas of life.

The Javanese language has two speech levels, chosen by speakers to reflect their relationship with addressees. One is a familiar style called *ngoko,* used with intimates and people of lower status, and the other is a formal style called *kromo,* for speech to people who are unfamiliar, older, or of higher social status. In addition to this basic distinction, Javanese has some 250–300 markers indicating various degrees of honorific attitudes. One class of honorifics (*Kromo inggil*) is used to "elevate the addressee" in relation to the speaker, and the other class (*Kromo* and *hap*) "humbles" the speaker in relation to the addressee (ibid.:540). The two types combine with the familiar and formal speech styles in complex ways in order to express and transmit images of personal status.

In Javanese, gender inequality is reflected in word choices, in differential use of speech levels and honorifics, and in the interactional significance attached to such usage. One manifestation of unequal relationships between women and men is the pattern of address terms used by wives and husbands that indicates the lower status of wives. In Javanese households, a husband generally calls his wife either by her first name, a nickname, or the kinship term *dhik* meaning "younger sibling." In contrast, wives address their husbands with the kin term *mas,* "older brother" (ibid.:541). Although Javanese husbands usually are older than their wives, this asymmetric expression of seniority is employed even by couples of similar ages who had addressed each other as equals before marriage, demonstrating that the marital relationship is symbolized as hierarchical. Wives are also expected to speak to their husbands with styles replete with polite and deferential honorifics, whereas husbands use plainer, familiar forms of speech with their wives.

Nancy Smith-Hefner (1988) described a significant contrast in evaluations of women's speech styles given by the two genders. Javanese men interpret women's style as indicating their lower status within the family, while women assert that their speech reflects politeness and refinement. As Smith-Hefner remarked, "It is very possible for speakers to interpret their own speech behavior in a given speech interaction as statusful, while the other interlocutor regards it as deferential" (ibid.:540–541). Accepting that women's evaluation of their own behavior is legitimate from their perspective, the question still arises as to why women speak in a polite and refined manner. One possible explanation derives from women's role in socializing children to speak in culturally appropriate styles, reflecting a child's junior and subordinate status. Children must learn to use respectful speech to their elders and superiors, including fathers and older siblings. Mothers are the primary teachers of this style. They instruct children by using the desired speech, and the children model their own language after that of their mother (ibid.:542–543). This responsibility compels mothers to employ polite speaking styles. And because women's activities take place predominantly within their households, they are not likely to develop a wide range of speech styles.

Politeness can express several underlying cultural premises and therefore can have ambiguous meanings. Both Javanese men and women use polite speech, but they do so in different contexts. Although women employ polite *kromo* styles at home, men use elaborate *kromo* speech in other situations, particularly in public roles as officials or ceremonial leaders. Men, in fact, often develop skilled use of complex honorific markers in order to manipulate and reaffirm their status in personal interactions. Such skill is positively perceived by the community, further enhancing speakers' prestige. According to Smith-Hefner, intricate social messages are transmitted by men's polite speech:

> Humility is given a positive value in Javanese society, but there is a very different feel to an interaction in which the speaker is constrained to speak humbly or politely and one in which the speaker uses artful control of the language to signal linguistic skill and responsiveness to complex linguistic norms. Such speech may sound polite inasmuch as it respects language norms, even while subtly communicating the speaker's skill and status superiority. It is this ambiguity in the social message of the polite forms which renders them powerful. In any single speech interaction they may express deference on the one hand and refinement and power on the other. Deference here can hint—or even openly wink—at social superiority. (ibid.:548)

Javanese language and culture, then, contain complex connections between politeness and gender. In many cultures, where polite speech is most typical of women (e.g., American-Anglo societies, Japan), it is interpreted as a signal of deference and lower status. However, in other societies (e.g., Java), polite speech is manipulated by men to convey messages of power and superiority.

Kuna

A complex pattern of gender-differentiated communicative behavior exists among the Kuna, a native people of San Blas, Panama. Kuna society is basically egalitarian both in its social and political structures and in relationships between women and men. In theory, men and women can hold leadership roles in political and ritual activities, although in practice female leaders are rare. Kuna people conceptualize economic and social responsibilities of women and men as distinct yet complementary and harmonious. Men are expected to supply their families with food obtained from farming and hunting; women perform domestic labor, including food preparation, childcare, and other household duties. In addition, women's artistry in making *molas* (appliquéd cloth blouses) for market sale is highly prized and praised. These products are not only important in economic terms but also as valued symbols of Kuna ethnicity (Sherzer 1987:95, 101).

Distinctions between women's and men's communicative behavior occur in speech genres associated with each. Some of these genres occur in public or ceremonial contexts, and others take place in private, familial settings. Each is typified by linguistic and topical characteristics that distinguish it from everyday speech. Men's genres include political oratory and ritual incantations. Two types of speaking occur at political gatherings: extemporaneous speeches and debates of community leaders, and the formalized chanting of chiefs. These roles are nearly always held by men. Curing chants are performed by (usually) male specialists who gather medicines and administer them in rituals (ibid.:102–103).

There is some overlap between women's and men's speaking roles. Women hold public political gatherings too, mostly concerned with issues related to *mola* cooperatives. At these meetings, women make speeches, engage in debates, and express their opinions. Ritual speech is also performed by some women who recite curing chants taught to them by spirits in their dreams. But women's distinctive genres are lullabies and "tuneful weeping" chanted to dying and deceased relatives. These genres are similar in their focus on individual, family happenings (ibid.:102–105).

According to Joel Sherzer, the egalitarian and complementary division of labor in Kuna society is reflected in the division of speech genres generally performed by women or men. Although the genres are different, no single linguistic style is considered appropriate only to men or women. Each gender has occasion to employ elaborate, rhetorical styles replete with metaphor and symbolic allusions. Each also uses chanting and rhythmic patterns or tunes in certain contexts. Finally, both men and women speak directly and confidently when voicing their opinions (ibid.:110–111). Gifted speakers, whether they are women or men, are equally praised.

LANGUAGE AND SEXUALITY

Until fairly recently, most studies of language and gender assumed an unstated binary dichotomy between men and women. Again not often stated, these studies assumed the heterosexuality of their subjects.

Since the 1980s, some linguistic research has focused on issues of sexuality in particular, attempting to delineate whether there are features that distinguish the speech of gay men and lesbians. Although this is a field of increasing interest, it is often difficult to determine what these features are. One difficulty stems from deeper questions about language and identity. Just as not all women or men employ features of "women's" or "men's" speech, not all gay men or lesbians speak in ways that might enact or "perform" their sexual orientation. Another question concerns the types of features that might be diagnostic, i.e., phonological, lexical, grammatical. The earliest treatments focused on determining whether there were specific words or terms used by gay men (note the bias in this research toward gay men rather than lesbians). Lists were compiled of expressions thought to be employed by gay men whose meaning would not be understood by heterosexual men (for example, see Legman 1941). These were not novel words but rather expressions that were invested with new meaning. For example, "playing checkers" meant "moving from one seat to another in a motion-picture theater to find a willing youth" and "sister in distress" referred to a "homosexual male in trouble, usually with the police." It turns out, not surprisingly, that these terms were not necessarily understood by gay men either. Another reputed attribute of gay men's speech was a tendency to use feminine pronouns or terms of address (*she, her, Miss, sister,* etc.) to refer to males. Although some gay men may use such terms in some contexts, the practice could hardly be said to be characteristic of all.

Turning attention from compiling lists to understanding their interactional meaning, Joseph Hayes (1981) analyzed the functions of *gayspeak* (Hayes's term). Prominent among these was its use as a secret code that would both identify speakers to each other and shield them from "exposure" to others through the use of indirection and innuendo. Hayes stressed the multiplicity of roles that people could adopt within the gay community and the various uses of language to express these roles. Finally, *gayspeak* could be employed to reverse socially stigmatizing labels (e.g., *fag, dyke, queer*) to make political statements that enable gay men and lesbians to assert agency and take control of linguistic and social meanings rather than being objects of the meanings of others. Still, the features that characterize *gayspeak* continue to be difficult to delineate. And there remains the issue of speech and identity. Clearly, just as women can use stereotypical features of "women's speech" to index their gender in some contexts for some interactional goals, gay men and lesbians can use language to index their sexual orientation in contexts and for goals of their choosing, while in other contexts and for other goals, specific features can be avoided.

A number of studies have been carried out in experimental contexts to investigate whether gay men and lesbians are identifiable to others based on their voices. One study used tape-recordings of eight men (four self-identified as gay, four as nongay) reading two passages (Gaudio 1994). These recordings consisted of excerpts lasting 15 seconds each from two sources: a text about accounting and a play called *Torch Song Trilogy* by the playwright Harvey Feirstein. The tapes were played to 13 undergraduate students (10 women and three men) who rated the speakers on scales of gay/straight, reserved/emotional, masculine/effeminate, and ordinary/affected. Results demonstrated that the listeners correctly identified the sexual orientation of seven of the eight speakers. Examining the tapes for vocal differences, Gaudio found that the gay men used a wider pitch range and varied their pitch changes more frequently than did the straight men, but these differences were only significant when speakers read the accounting text. There were no significant contrasts among the men in pitch ranges or variability when reading the play.

A study of vocal segments produced by women was even less conclusive. In this experiment, 30-second tapes of natural speech recorded by six lesbians and six straight women were played to 21 undergraduate students (whose gender was not noted in the report) (Moonwomon-Baird 1997). Listeners were asked to judge speakers' identities, including their age, class, educational level, region of origin, sexual preference, and Jewish/non-Jewish ethnicity (why this last identity was chosen was also not noted in the report). Results indicated that listeners were correct in identifying the sexual preference of the speakers in only "about half" of the cases. While there were no correlations found between vocal qualities of lesbian and straight women, when compared to the results from studies of male speech, this research does give further evidence of the stereotypical attitude that gay men are more identifiable by their speech patterns than are lesbians.

This interpretation is consistent with some features of gender crossing in other realms of behavior. For example, men who wear the clothing or cosmetics typically associated with women are more "noticeable" than women who wear men's clothing. In fact, most women occasionally (or often) wear clothing (i.e., pants) that in previous decades was associated primarily with men. And, in the words of Deborah Cameron and Don Kulick (2003:97), writing on issues of language and sexuality, because " 'men's language' as a cultural category or stereotype is less focused and elaborate than 'women's language,'…perhaps this is one reason why linguistic gender crossing has not provided the same kind of resource for lesbians as it has for (some) gay men."

A further experiment investigating voice patterns collected samples of speech from 25 men, 17 of whom self-identified as gay and eight as straight (Smyth et al. 2003). The samples included reading of a scientific text about rainbows, a dramatic paragraph about a fire, and a segment of spontaneous speech about a true incident that happened to the speaker. Excerpts of about 30 seconds were taken of each sample type and played to 46 listeners (14 who self-identified as gay men) and 32 (13 men and 19 women) whose sexual orientation was not requested. The listeners were asked to decide whether the voices "sounded" gay or straight. Results showed that five voices were rated as straight-sounding and six as gay-sounding by at least 80 percent of the listeners. The type of discourse was a significant factor as well. Judgments about speakers who "sounded gay" were more confident when the speaker read the scientific text compared to readings of the dramatic passage or of the spontaneous speech sample. The researchers interpret this finding as demonstrating that "formal speech is considered more gay-sounding" and that "gay men tended to use this style in all three discourse types, while the straight men used it only for the scientific passage" (ibid.:337). In addition, straight speakers were misidentified as gay-sounding more often when reading the scientific passage, while discourse type did not affect the rates with which gay speakers were misidentified as straight-sounding.

Although the results of these studies are intriguing and indicate that listeners are picking up on some cues in order to correctly identify the sexual orientation of speakers, it is still not clear what these cues actually are. And because these studies rely on self-identifications of sexual orientation, they may be reflecting issues of gender performativity and enactment rather than actual sexuality. Whatever cues listeners interpret as conveying any particular gender or sexual identity, these cues can be manipulated by speakers, just as cues about one's region of origin, class, and race or ethnicity can be manipulated in order to convey (or not to convey) one's identity.

Indeed, a study of the discourse practices of telephone sex workers in San Francisco, California, demonstrated the ways that the fantasy makers (as they like to be called) manipulate their style to approximate what they think the clients (in these cases, heterosexual men) want to hear in order to be aroused (Hall 1995). The workers create a world of fantasy through linguistic features such as voice quality, pitch, intonational rhythms, and word choices. Successful fantasy makers had to "sound" like young, attractive, sexually available women regardless of their actual age, physical appearance, or even gender, In interviews with the researcher, Kira Hall, the workers talked about their use of "feminine" speech features (lilting voice, changes in volume, word choice (i.e., adjectives, elaborate noun phrases instead of simple nouns)) in order to create characters whose persona they transmit. One successful worker, a Mexican-American man, uses a variety of regional, racial, ethnic, and foreign styles (i.e., stereotypes) in order to appeal to particular clients.

Research involving gay and lesbian language use in other countries has focused on discursive practices. The studies often demonstrate that the influence of English reaches many disparate communities worldwide. English loanwords and mixes of English and other languages, for example, have been adopted by members of gay and lesbian communities in a number of countries when speaking of sexual identities. For instance, a French magazine marketed to the gay community has as its subtitle the phrase, *le magazine des gays et lesbiennes* ("the magazine of gays and lesbians"). Referring to *coming out*, the magazine uses a combination of French and English: *faire son come-out* (to make one's coming out) (Provencher 2004:29). Similarly, German magazines employ mixed German and English terms such as *das Outing* and the reflexive verb *sich outen* ("to out oneself") (Minning 2004:48).

In Thailand, sexual categories are complex due to a long history of publicly acknowledged gendered identities. Traditionally, four categories of sexuality (or *phet*) were identified and named (Jackson 2004:210): normatively masculine men (*phu-chai*), normatively feminine women (*phu-ying*), an intermediate category (*kathoey*), and Buddhist monks (considered to be an asexual *phet*). Recently, new categories of sexuality have emerged and have been labeled. Some use English terminology, such as "gay king," "gay queen," "tom," and "dee." The latter two terms differentiate masculine and feminine lesbians: "tom" from the first syllable of *tomboy* and "dee" from the second syllable of *lady*, respectively.

And in Israel, where the official national languages are Hebrew and Arabic, there is a gradual shift to English preference in gay and lesbian communities (Moriel 2004). English usage can be seen as a unifying linguistic practice because it is not identified with any particular Jewish, Muslim, or Christian constituency. In addition, because both Hebrew and Arabic are languages that mark gender on all nouns and have obligatory gender marking for the subjects of verbs, English can function as a comparatively genderless code, especially attractive to people who do not conform to stereotypically gendered identities.

IMAGES OF GENDER IN LINGUISTIC FORM

Language is a vehicle for expressing cultural models, in part through the way people, activities, and ideas are named. In societies with gender hierarchies, where women and their behavior are disvalued, inequalities in linguistic images are one sign of the denigration of women. By continual usage of words and expressions that demean females, speakers unconsciously (or consciously) reproduce and reinforce negative stereotypes. These stereotypes become internalized symbols for both genders, resulting in male attitudes toward females as deviant and female acceptance of negative self-assessments. In this section, we review some of the literature and findings related to gender bias in linguistic form.

English

CLASSES OF VOCABULARY.   The English language expresses gender distinctions in many classes of vocabulary, including the labeling of people (nouns), their qualities (adjectives), and their actions (verbs). But English does not simply record differences; it covertly (and overtly) demeans or trivializes females, presenting males as normative and females as deviant or secondary.

First of all, English creates a context for the interaction of genders with the term *opposite sex*. Certainly the sexes are different, but in what sense are they "opposite"? The word itself connotes a polarity, denying possibilities of overlap or congruence. It also implies conflict and antagonism, as in "they have opposing views" or "the Mayor opposes the new legislation."

Second, words referring to human beings are often paired for female and male exemplars, but in ordinary usage, males precede and females appear in linguistic "second place." Some instances of this common ordering are *male and female, man and woman, he or she,* and *husband and wife.* Such pairing denotes primary status of males in two ways. First, order of linguistic components is generally of cognitive importance; that is, more important elements usually occur earlier in sentences. For example, many languages make use of a procedure known as "focus-fronting," through which words and clauses are manipulated to place important or emphasized segments earlier than they would appear in unmarked sentences. English employs passive constructions to accomplish this goal (compare *the child caught the ball* with *the ball was caught by the child*). Therefore, arguing that the first member of a pair carries greater importance is consistent with widespread linguistic processes. The second kind of evidence supporting the contention of covert inequality in male–female pairs is provided by comparing similar constructions denoting age and status hierarchies. Older or higher-status individuals precede younger or lower-status people: *older and younger, parent and child, dominant and subordinate.* Other sets of paired words reflect positive connotations given to the first member and negative connotations to the second: *good and bad, happy and sad, rich and poor.* Gender, then, merges with these constellations of social and semantic categories.

Two counterexamples to the "male + female" ordering are *ladies and gentlemen* and *bride and groom.* The first is typically used in public formal situations where polite speech is preferred. Perhaps its use is akin to chivalrous behavior that often masks underlying power. The second, *bride and groom,* is also a conventionalized expression relevant in a formal ceremonial context. Note, however, that after the wedding, the couple is transformed from *bride and groom* to *husband and wife.* Variation in the usual ordering occurs in kin-term pairs; for example, *mother and father* is as likely as *father and mother.* Perhaps this flexibility reflects individual choice based on attitudes toward relatives and may also indicate our society's stereotypes of closer emotional bonds between children and their mothers.

Third, the English language provides evidence of gender hierarchy in marital relationships, first in the traditional, although disappearing, formula "I now pronounce you man and wife," in which the male is labeled by his humanness, but the female is defined in relation to her husband. Second, our culture decrees that women give up their maiden names at marriage and assume their husband's last name. A wife can be referred to by her husband's full name (first + last) with the preposed address term *Mrs.,* as in Mrs. John Smith. The couple can then be called "the Smiths" or even "the John Smiths," depriving the wife of her own identity. Finally, couples are frequently described by the use of the husband's name + "his wife," as in "John Smith and his wife." In such usages, the wife appears almost as a possession or appendage without an autonomous existence. A contrasting construction, "Jane Jones and her husband," has marked meaning and would typically occur only if special attention is given to "Jane Jones" for particular contextual or emotional purposes.

Another symbolic reflection of females' subsidiary status is the possibility of deriving girls' names from male sources. Feminine endings *-a, -ette, -ine, -y* (or *-ie*) are thus added to male names: Roberta, Bernadette, Geraldine, Stephanie. Any male name can idiosyncratically be converted into a girl's name by this procedure. The only boy's name obtained from a female source is Marion, which occurs rarely in contemporary US society but in any case has a special derivation, originating from the religious symbol of Mary.

In a further reflection of the semantics of gender, feminine suffixes *-ette* (or *-et*) and *-y* (or *-ie*) can function as diminutives, that is, as markers of smallness, for example, *booklet, itsy-bitsy.* Diminutives also carry meanings of endearment, reflected in nicknames and affectionate or youthful versions of personal names: Cathy, Tommy. Although both girls and boys are addressed with these forms as children, males tend to outgrow their diminutive names (except among kin), whereas females often retain them throughout life.

Fourth, the interaction of age and gender is also differentially marked for males and females in the terms *boy, girl, man, woman.* Boys typically become men at roughly the age of adulthood, although exact demarcation of the change is often vague. But girls can remain girls long after they become adults. It is true that this usage is unacceptable today among many people, but it is still frequently employed. Comparable use of the word *boy* to refer to an adult man is restricted to certain regional varieties, as in the American South. These examples demonstrate that although the words *girl* and *boy* have definitions that might appear to be distinguished solely on the basis of gender, they actually have uses and implications that are quite different in recognizing or denying adult status.

Fifth, some sets of words for males and females illustrate another process of inequality in images of gender. Consider the following pairs: *lord/lady, sir/dame, master/mistress, king/queen, bachelor/spinster, governor/governess.* In each pair, there is one level of meaning equating the paired individuals. But a critical process has affected females in a consistent manner. That process is often referred to as *semantic derogation,* changes in meaning by which negative attributes become attached to senses of words. Semantic derogation of words for women has historically resulted in secondary meanings that demean or trivialize women and their activities or that emphasize their sexuality. The words *mistress* and *dame* are examples of words taking on sexual connotations, whereas *governess* is a trivialization. *Queen* also has a sexual meaning, although it is applied to men, rather than women, in a derogatory fashion. *Spinster* implies negation of sexuality, so that a spinster is not an "unmarried woman" in the same way that a bachelor is an "unmarried man." A bachelor is a man who is desirable as a potential husband, whereas a spinster is an undesirable mate. Because of this negative implication, the expression *bachelor girl* (or even *bachelorette*) has evolved.

The word *lady* has special complexities. In one of its uses, it retains the polite, respectful implications of its origin. However, it also occurs in casual contexts as a label for a woman whose name is unknown to a speaker: "Hey, lady, move your car!" Perhaps its most interesting function is as a euphemism for "woman." The word *woman* needs a euphemistic replacement because it too has acquired sexual connotations. Compare the following (adapted from Lakoff 1975:26):

> She's only 12, but she already acts like a woman.
>
> She's only 12, but she already acts like a lady.

These sentences highlight two cultural images of females that our society promulgates. The first suggests her sexuality; the second notes the polite and "proper" behavior expected of her.

Sixth, the pair *woman/man* also deserves attention. *Woman* refers specifically and only to females, whereas *man* is used not only for males but for "people" in general, as in *mankind*. In addition, *man* appears as a verb meaning "operate" or "control": "We need someone to man the elevator." In addition, many English words and terms are based on roots or compounds with *man, master,* or other male-oriented sources: *bachelor's degree, bedfellow, brotherhood, fore-father, fraternize, freshman, manpower, masterful, mastermind, patronize, statesmanship* (Nilsen 1977:36).

As Muriel Schulz pointed out, many words associated with females that began with innoc-uous or even positive connotations have undergone processes of derogation, most often with sexual implications. For example, *hussy* is derived from Old English *huswife* ("housewife"), originally meaning "female head of household." It gradually came to mean "a rustic or rude woman" and finally "a lewd, brazen woman or a prostitute." The words *nymph* and *nymphet* were first endearments referring to "beautiful young girls or women" and then became euphemisms for prostitutes, finally meaning "a sexually precocious girl; a loose young woman." Semantic narrowing and derogation also affected the word *whore,* which originally was a polite term for "a lover of either sex." It then narrowed its meaning only to women and degenerated as a label for prostitutes (1975:66–69).

Seventh, *sex object* is a more recent expression and another instance of defining females by their sexuality. The term removes not only females' full personalities and activities, but also their very personhood, and metaphorically transforms them into inanimates. Similar semantic processes have not affected words for males. In fact, although words referring to male sexuality, such as *stud,* are not used in polite speech, they have positive rather than negative connotations.

Terms in AAVE similarly express derogatory or trivialized meanings for females. In AAVE slang, most words for women emphasize physical characteristics, including variations in skin color—*redbone, spotlight, high yaller, pinky*—or apply animal terms to females—*fox, filly, but-terfly* (Scott 1974:220).

Female/male differences are also found in adjectives describing people's attributes and in verbs denoting their activities. Most verbs can be used for male or female activities, but others are restricted to describing the actions of females. For example, men/women "yell," but only women "screech" or "shriek"; men/women "talk" and women "chat" or "gossip"; men/women may "laugh," but women "giggle." Notice that all of the specialized "female" verbs have deroga-tory or trivialized nuances. Adjectives or adverbs derived from these verbs are employed for women with negative meaning: *chatty, screechy, talkative, giggly.*

Adjectives referring to physical characteristics of females are often used in contexts where comparable modifiers for males would not likely occur. Even public figures and political leaders who are women typically have their appearance or clothing commented on by the media. This practice reminds women that they are never free from scrutiny and that their physical image is a crucial part of their being.

GENERIC *He* AND *Man*.   One of the most frequently debated examples of linguistic favoritism toward males is the use of the so-called generic *he* and *man* to refer to people without regard to gender. In some contexts, the prescribed pronoun *he* has a singular referent—"A child learns his reading skills in the first grade"—but in others, it has underlying nonsingular semantic referents, as in "Everyone should take his coat." Here, "everyone" may be morphologically singular (lacking the plural suffix *-s*), but it obviously refers to more than one individual. Insistence by grammarians that *he* is the "proper" pronoun for an indefinite person or for people in general dates to the eighteenth century (Bodine 1975a). Prior to that time, the pronoun *they* was used for singular or plural indefinites and generics, as shown in writing and presumably in speaking. In a discussion of English pronouns, George McKnight (1928) collected quotations from no less than William Shakespeare's *Much Ado About Nothing:* "God send every one their heart's desire" and "Each leaning on their elbows and their hips." Later authors continued to use *they,* as did Jane Austen, for example, in *Mansfield Park:* "Nobody put themselves out of the way" and "Each had their favorite." Although people are taught in school to use *he* in formal speech and especially in writing, even casual observation shows that speakers employ *they* in ordinary conversation. And while prescriptivists argue about the confusion of number and person in the use of *they* to refer to one individual, they ignore the fact that the second-person pronoun *you* is employed for both singular and plural (McWhorter 1998:122). In addition to overlooking semantics and failing to hear actual speech, the grammarian approach ignores the existence of a linguistic context in which only the pronoun *they* can occur. In tag questions, when the subject of a statement is a generic or indefinite person, the underlying pronoun replacement surfacing in the tag is clearly *they:*

> Everyone left the room, didn't they?

Even when an indefinite noun refers to a single individual, its pronoun is *they:*

> Somebody left the room, didn't they?

Experimental tests of people's reactions to sentences with "generic he or his" consistently support the contention that "he or his" is never gender-neutral. Rather, it always contains some of its basic masculine sense. This is not surprising; it is even expected in terms of semantic theory in linguistics. That is, every word has a central or focal meaning that is carried with it in all contexts of its extended use. Underlying notions of gender associated with generic pronouns were studied in several experiments conducted by Donald MacKay (1983). One study presented male and female students at the University of California at Los Angeles (UCLA) with sentences containing pronouns, such as "When a botanist is in the field, he is usually working." Test sentences were mixed, so that some referred to stereotypically "male-related" antecedents (*engineer, doctor*), others to "female-related" antecedents (*model, secretary*), and still others to "neutral" referents (*student, musician*). Subjects were asked to decide quickly whether or not sentences could refer to females. Results revealed that 95 percent of respondents (10 women and 10 men) judged that the sentences could not refer to females. Male and female subjects had similar reactions. And subjects excluded females at constant rates regardless of whether sentences had gender-stereotyped or neutral antecedents (ibid.:41).

In a related experiment in the same study, MacKay presented subjects with sentences identical to those in the first test except that pronouns were omitted, for example, "A botanist who is in the field is usually working." Results were strikingly different: 43 percent of the subjects (as compared to 95 percent in the prior study) responded that the sentences could not refer to females. The identity of antecedents became significant. Subjects thought that 68 percent of sentences with male antecedents could not refer to females, 42 percent with neutral antecedents could not refer to females, and 19 percent with female antecedents could not refer to females. The sex of the subject also affected judgments. Men were more likely than women to restrict sentences to male referents. MacKay concluded, "These findings suggest that adding prescriptive he dramatically increases the exclusion of females and washes out effects of subject sex and nature of the antecedent" (ibid.:42).

Supposedly neutral interpretations of *man* face similar problems. This word has an interesting history, beginning in Old English to mean "a human being" with no gender association. Separate unambiguous words existed to denote females, *wif,* and males, *wer* or *carl. Man* could combine with these to refer specifically to adults of their respective genders: *wifman* and *werman* or *carlman. Wifman* eventually became "woman," and male designators were replaced by semantic narrowing of *man* to refer to males (Miller and Smith 1977:25). Experimental studies have revealed that even when *man* is used in generic contexts, male images surface.

In one experiment, college students were asked to select and submit illustrations for an introductory sociology textbook (Schneider and Hacker 1973). Each of two groups was presented with alternative titles for chapters, one phrased as "Urban Man," "Political Man," or "Social Man" and the second as "Urban Life," "Political Behavior," or "Society." In the first group, 64 percent of respondents chose photographs of males only, whereas half of those in the second group chose male-only illustrations (ibid.:14). The likelihood of including women in photographs varied for different titles. The only one in which women appeared in a majority of illustrations was "Social Man" in which case a male was typically shown surrounded by females in contexts of social or leisure activities. The title "Urban Man" elicited nearly equal representation, "males only" in 55 percent of illustrations. For the "Political Man," "Industrial Man," and "Economic Man" chapters, women appeared in a small minority of photographs (ibid.:16). On the basis of their study, Schneider and Hacker asserted that uses of *man* as a label "may serve to 'filter-out' women, largely by suggesting imagery appropriate only or primarily to men" (ibid.:12).

In response to concerns over the symbolic preference for males expressed covertly and overtly by words such as *man, he,* and *his,* advocates of gender equality in language have suggested replacing these words with genuinely neutral forms such as *person, people,* and *she or he,* and *his or her.* However, a curious development has occurred in the case of *-person* when used in compounds such as *spokesperson* or *chairperson.* In common usage, there is currently a tendency to restrict *-person* nouns to females, retaining *-man* for males. *Spokesperson,* therefore, has replaced *spokeswoman* but not *spokesman.*

A similar failure to get the point of an advocated change concerns address designations of Ms./Miss/Mrs. The title Ms. was introduced in order to eliminate labeling women according to their marital status. Although intended as a replacement for both Miss and Mrs., it has come to be employed (if at all) to refer solely to unmarried women. The only context in which it is generally used for all women is in business and official letters to address unfamiliar women, thus providing senders with the ability to avoid offending receivers by mistaking their marital status.

All the data uncovered in analyses of English linguistic forms indicate a pervasive, covert ascription of positive and normative qualities to males and negative or secondary ones to females. Continual repetition of English words and expressions, both as speakers and hearers, reinforces cultural evaluations that enhance males' status and disvalue females'. These judgments do not originate in the language but arise linguistically to express, supplement, and justify entrenched cultural models.

French

French contains a singular pronoun, *on,* that is not marked for gender. It occurs in sentences with indefinite or generic subjects, such as:

> Ici *on* parle français.
>
> They (people, one) speak(s) French here.

Because French possessive pronouns (comparable to *his* and *her*) agree in grammatical gender with possessed nouns rather than sex of possessors, the English problem of using the masculine form *his* or the neutral *his or her* or *their* does not arise. However, even though French expresses neutrality in singular pronouns, bias in favor of males surfaces in plurals. Whereas English has one plural third-person pronoun (*they*) that is not marked for gender, French has two, distinguishing female and male aggregates, *elles* and *ils,* respectively. *Elles* is used only if all members are female; *ils* occurs for all-male or male-and-female groups. Therefore, the presence of even one male is enough to tip the semantic balance toward that masculine pronoun.

Since the 1980s, changes in the social roles and public participation of women in France have prompted discussion of the expression of grammatical gender in French. Pronouns in French generally agree with the grammatical gender of the noun that the pronouns replace, regardless of the actual gender of the person referred to. For example, the noun meaning "captain," *le capitaine,* is grammatically masculine, indicated by the masculine definite article *le*. However, with changes in the military and police forces, some French captains are female. In discourse concerning female captains, the woman's name would be preceded by the proper masculine noun *le capitaine,* but in the next mention where the full noun is replaced by a pronoun, rules of standard grammar select the masculine pronoun *il* or "he."

Inconsistencies between grammatical and biological facts stirred debate that led to formation of a government commission in 1983 charged with creating feminine equivalents of professional and occupational titles then existing only in masculine grammatical form (Fleischman 1994:189). The commission issued proposals that addressed the dilemma faced by speakers of French when they need to choose between pronominal agreement on the basis of grammar or biological gender. However, French academics, journalists, and the public at large gave a cool reception to the proposals, demonstrating little interest in changing their linguistic habits. During the same period, other Francophone communities such as Canada, Switzerland, and Belgium, as well as the European Union, were making more successful efforts at eliminating sexist reference in language (ibid.:190). Their progress indicates that it is not the French language that creates barriers to linguistic equality, but rather the social norms and language ideologies of France itself. Through educational institutions, governmental discourses, and the media, French citizens have been persuaded to espouse strong allegiance to and respect for standard grammar and vocabulary (Bourdieu 1991). Similar processes have prevailed in most modern state societies and have resulted in similar beliefs in the superiority of standard speech, but according to Suzanne Fleischman, "France has had a particularly heavy tradition of academism, purism, and linguistic control, dating back to the 17th-century" (1994:193). Furthermore, speakers believe that any deviation from the authoritative style is not simply an alternative but rather an error. Language ideologies in France have become entwined with attitudes toward the history, culture, and international prestige of the nation. Women as well as men adhere to these beliefs and uphold the virtues of the language despite the fact that it disadvantages them in its grammar and imagery.

German

The German language classifies nouns as masculine, feminine, or neuter and marks articles, adjectives, and verbs to agree with the gender of nouns. Whereas grammatically feminine nouns for persons refer only to females, some masculine nouns can be used for either males or females. The following masculine nouns may have male or female referents (Hellinger 1989:275):

der Bürger	citizen (Bürger)
der Wähler	voter
der Kunde	customer

Feminine subjects can co-occur with masculine nouns, but masculine subjects never co-occur with feminine nouns. For example, one can say

"He/She is a second Einstein."

Er/Sie ist ein zweiter Einstein.

But one cannot say

"He is a second Marie Curie."

Er ist eine zweite Marie Curie.

Some masculine nouns can be transformed by feminizing suffixes to refer to females—for example, *der Lehrer* "the teacher" → *die Lehrerin* "the woman teacher" (ibid.:276), and *die Kundin* "the female customer." The unmarked words symbolize men as neutral or expected exemplars, whereas the marked feminine words symbolize women as derivative or unusual.

In the few cases where feminine nouns are used for men, they take on derogatory meanings. The words *die Memme, die Tucke,* and *die Tunte,* all meaning "coward," are used as insults in referring to homosexuals (ibid.:275).

Recent changes in usage reflect sensitivity to gender issues. Although not officially codified in dictionaries, feminine forms of some masculine nouns are frequently used, especially in colloquial speech.

Spanish

In some pairs of words having male–female counterparts, the Spanish language expresses sexual meanings for females. Compare the following words and their meanings (Hellinger 1989:277, 284–285):

Masculine	**Feminine**
un reo: "a criminal"	*una rea:* "an impoverished prostitute"
el inocente: "an innocent person"	*la inocente:* "a virgin"
un doncel: "a young nobleman"	*una doncella:* "a virgin"

In addition, when feminine suffixes are added to some masculine occupational terms, the derived word does not refer to a woman of that profession but rather to a wife (ibid.:285):

el médico "doctor"

la médica "doctor's wife"

Russian

Analysis of the meanings of male–female kinship terms in Russian also shows a restricted representation of females. Roots that occur in kin terms can be extended to name other people or entities, but female and male forms show different patterns. Derivations from female bases generally refer to domesticity and/or sexuality, whereas those derived from male bases have wider "semantic space," referring to activities or qualities of a more social character (Wobst 1981:42–43). And female words tend to acquire negative connotations, most strongly so when applied to men, whereas male terms are positive even when applied to women. For example, roots for "grandmother," *bab-,* and "grandfather," *dyed-,* can both be extended to nonkin. (Note that in reference to one's grandmother, the root word *baba* is never used; rather, it always appears with a diminutive suffix in *babushka.*) Words derived from *bab-* have meanings including "old woman," "wife" (in slang), and (scornfully) "stout or loutish woman." Words with *dyed-,* on the other hand, are "ancestors" or "village elders" (ibid.:36–38).

The mother–father pair, *mat-/otyets-,* also is extended. Words with *mat-* include "maternity" and "motherhood" in positive tone, but others can be applied to males as terms of abuse. Words derived from *otyets* mean "protector, benefactor, leader, founder, and ancestors" (ibid.:38–39).

The roots for "sister," *syestr-,* and "brother," *brat-,* demonstrate now-familiar patterns. *Syestr-* has limited use, appearing only as a kin term and in restricted contexts as a female friend. In contrast, *brat-* has rich connotations, including "companionship, friendship, someone who loves people as brothers" (comparable forms in English are "brotherhood, brotherly love"). In addition, the root *brat-* can combine with a feminine suffix and be used to refer to females in a positive light, as in expressions for "a sister who is a friend" or a greeting to any woman (ibid.).

Mohawk

In contrast to European languages that restrict feminine meanings, the Mohawk language elaborates feminine semantics. In Mohawk, there are three third-person singular pronoun markers for subjects, occurring as prefixes in verbs. One prefix, {*la-*}, is used exclusively for males (human and animal); another, {*ka-*}, denotes female animals, some female humans, and all inanimate objects; and a third, {*ye-*}, refers to some female humans and all indefinite or generalized persons (Bonvillain 1973:85–87). The following is a set of Mohawk verbs with human subjects:

layʌ́thos	he's planting it
kayʌ́thos	she's planting it
yeyʌ́thos	she's planting it; someone's planting it

Pronoun prefixes for human females are semantically complex. Speakers can use either {*ka-*} or {*ye-*}, the choice depending on context, attitude, and relationship to addressee. Most people employ {*ye-*} to refer to older women, relatives, and/or any woman toward whom the speaker has a feeling of respect or admiration. {*Ka-*} is used more often as either a form neutral for attitude or actually negative in affect.

Mohawk speakers use these prefixes somewhat idiosyncratically because there are no absolute grammatical rules governing their occurrence. Alternatives are selected for personal and contextual reasons. This seems not to have always been the case. Samples of Mohawk spoken in the early twentieth century indicate a different, presumably traditional, pattern in which the semantics of feminine prefixes included a focus on female reproductive capacities. The prefix {*ye-*} was evidently used to refer to both young girls and older women, whereas {*ka-*} was selected for women in their childbearing years. The Mohawk language, then, directly symbolized the distinctiveness of women's ability to reproduce.

Remembering that the significance of linguistic form can be understood in specific contexts of culture, Mohawk emphasis on reproduction as expressed by the prefixes was a positive reflection of women's status. The Mohawk kinship system is based on matrilineal clans (i.e., descent traced through women). In addition to their prominence in kinship groups, women had important economic roles in traditional Mohawk culture. They were food producers, providing their families with basic crops of corn, beans, and squash. These crops are symbolized as female, referred to as "The Three Sisters" or "Our Life Supporters." In Mohawk sacred narratives, they are derived from the body of a female mythic personage. Given religious and economic concerns with fertility of the land, kinship groups, and the Mohawk nation itself, special note of women's childbearing role reflected the acknowledged contributions of women to society.

Meanings of {*ye-*} and {*ka-*} have changed, the former now employed to mark respect or positive feeling toward a female, probably as a result of its traditional use for elder women. Although some of the meanings of feminine pronouns have shifted, linguistic attention to females and the use of {*ye-*} to mark indefinite or generic person can be interpreted as continuing a valued symbolization of women in Mohawk culture.

Summary

Because men and women are socially distinguished in all cultures, contrasts in some of their communicative behavior presumably occur everywhere. But degrees of difference and specific linguistic patterns that display gender distinctions vary cross-culturally. Women and men may use alternatives in pronunciation, word selection, and grammatical construction. Gender-appropriate styles of communicative interaction may further mark the identities of women and men. Words and expressions in a language itself may reflect gender differences in how they symbolize males and females.

In societies such as the United States or Japan, where men have more prestige and rights than women do, language and style are used to underscore male privilege. Women tend to use sounds that are marked as standard, correct, and/ or prestigeful. Their choice of words and grammatical constructions can be characterized as polite or deferential. And women's interactional moves tend to defer to rights of interlocutors. In contrast, men are more likely, given similarities of class, race, and context, to use less formal, less prestigeful, and less polite forms of speech. And through their conversational styles, men more often exert control and dominance.

Explanations for these behaviors should be sought in social systems that not only distinguish between the genders but structure men's and women's relationships in a hierarchical order, endowing men with more valued status and rights and restricting or subordinating women.

In societies where gender equality exists, communicative behavior and meanings accord value and worth to both genders. Through communicative processes, cultural models of gender are both portrayed and reinforced, contributing to the socialization of females and males into their expected roles and also creating their ideas about themselves and each other. Language usage and language form are thus revealed as partners in generating cultural models and symbols of gender.

References

BAILEY, LEE ANN, AND LENORA TIMM. 1976. More on women's—and men's—expletives. *Anthropological Linguistics* 18:438–439.

BENNET, SUZANNE, AND BERNS WEINBERG. 1979. Sexual characteristics of pre-adolescent children's voices. *Journal of the Acoustical Society of America* 65:179–189.

BODINE, ANN. 1975a. Androcentrism in prescriptive grammar. *Language in Society* 4:129–146.

BODINE, ANN. 1975b. Sex differentiation in language. In *Language and Sex,* ed. B. Thorne and N. Henley. Rowley, MA: Newbury, pp. 130–151.

BOGORAS, WALDEMAR. 1922. Chukchee. In *Handbook of American Indian Languages.* Bulletin No. 40, Part 2. Washington, DC: Bureau of American Ethnology, pp. 631–903.

BONVILLAIN, NANCY. 1973. *A Grammar of Akwesasne Mohawk.* Mercury Series No. 8. Ottawa: National Museum of Canada.

BOURDIEU, PIERRE. 1991. *Language and Symbolic Power.* Cambridge, MA: Harvard University Press.

BROWN, PENELOPE, AND STEPHEN LEVINSON. 1987. *Politeness: Some Universals in Language Usage.* New York: Cambridge University Press.

BUTLER, JUDITH. 1990. *Gender Trouble: Feminism and the Subversion of Identity.* New York and London: Routledge.

CAMERON, DEBORAH. 1999. Performing gender identity: Young men's talk and the construction of heterosexual masculinity. In *The Discourse Reader,* ed. A. Jaworski and N. Coupland. London: Routledge, pp. 442–458.

CAMERON, DEBORAH, and DON KULICK. 2003. *Language and Sexuality.* Cambridge UK and New York: Cambridge University Press.

CAMERON, DEBORAH, FIONA MCALINDEN, AND KATHY O'LEARY. 1988. Lakoff in context: The social and linguistic functions of tag questions. In *Women in Their Speech Communities,* ed. J. Coates and D. Cameron. London: Longman, pp. 74–93.

CHESHIRE, JENNY. 1982. Linguistic variation and social function. In *Sociolinguistic Variation in Speech Communities,* ed. S. Romaine. London: Edward Arnold, pp. 153–166.

CROSBY, FAYE, AND LINDA NYQUIST. 1977. The female register: An empirical study of Lakoff's hypotheses. *Language in Society* 6:313–322.

DAVIS, HAYLEY. 1996. Theorizing women's and men's language. *Language & Communication* 16:71–80.

DEFRANCISCO, VICTORIA. 1998. The sounds of silence: How men silence women in marital relations. In *Language and Gender,* ed. J. Coates. Malden, MA: Blackwell, pp. 176–184.

DEKLERK, VIVIAN. 1992. How taboo are taboo words for girls? *Language in Society* 21:277–290.

DUBOIS, BETTY LOU, AND ISABEL CROUCH. 1975. The question of tag-questions in women's speech: They don't really use more of them, do they? *Language in Society* 4:289–294.

ECKERT, PENELOPE. 1998. Gender and socio-linguistic variation. In *Language and Gender,* ed. J. Coates. Malden, MA: Blackwell, pp. 64–76.

ECKERT, PENELOPE, AND SALLY MC-CONNELL GINET. 2004. *Language and Gender.* Cambridge: Cambridge University Press.

EDELSKY, CAROL. 1981. Who's got the floor? *Language in Society* 10:383–421.

EKKA, FRANCIS. 1972. Men's and women's speech in Kũṟux. *Linguistics* 81:25–31.

FISCHER, JOHN. 1958. Social influences on the choice of a linguistic variant. *Word* 14:47–56.

FISHMAN, PAMELA. 1983. Interaction: The work women do. In *Language, Gender and Society,* ed. B. Thorne, N. Henley, and C. Kramarae. Rowley, MA: Newbury, pp. 89–101.

FLANNERY, REGINA. 1946. Men's and women's speech in Gros Ventre. *International Journal of American Linguistics* 12:133–135.

FLEISCHMAN, SUZANNE. 1994. Eliminating gender bias in French: A case of language ideologies in conflict. In *Cultural Performances, Proceedings of the Third Berkeley Women and Language Conference,* ed. M. Bucholtz, A. Liang, L. Sutton, and C. Hines. Berkeley, CA: Third Berkeley Women and Language Group, pp. 187–196.

GATSCHET, ALBERT. 1884. *A Migration Legend of the Creek Indians.* Philadelphia, PA: Brinton.

GAUDIO, RUDOLF. P. 1994. Sounding gay: Pitch properties in the speech of gay and straight men. *American Speech* 69: 30–57.

GORDON, ELIZABETH. 1997. Sex, speech, and stereotypes: Why women use prestige speech forms more than men. *Language in Society* 26:47–64.

HAAS, MARY. 1944. Men's and women's speech in Koasati. *Language* 20:142–149.

HALL, KIRA. 1995. Lip service on the fantasy lines. In *Gender Articulated: Language and the Socially Constructed Self,* ed. Kira Hall and Mary Bucholtz. London: Routledge, pp. 183–216.

HAYES, JOSEPH. 1981. "Gayspeak." in *Gayspeak: gay male and lesbian communication.* (ed. James Chesebro). New York: Pilgrim Press, pp. 45–57.

HELLINGER, MARLIS. 1989. Revising the patriarchal paradigm: Language change and feminist language policies. In *Language, Power and Ideology,* ed. R. Wodak. Philadelphia. PA: John Benjamins, pp. 273–288.

HENLEY, NANCY, AND CHERIS KRAMARAE. 1991. Gender, power and miscommunication. In *"Miscommunication" and Problematic Talk,* ed. N. Coupland, J .M. Wiemann, and H. Giles. Newbury Park, CA: Sage, pp. 18–43.

HOLMES, JANET. 1984. Hedging your bets and sitting on the fence: Some evidence for hedges as support structures. *Te Reo* 27:47–62.

HUGHES, SUSAN. 1997. Expletives of lower working-class women. *Language in Society* 21:291–304.

JACKSON, PETER. 2004. Gay adaptation, tom-dee resistance, and Kathoey indifference: Thailand's gender/sex minorities and the episodic allure of queer English. In *Speaking in Queer Tongues: Globalization and Gay Language,* ed. William Leap and Tom Boellstorff. Urbana: University of Illinois Press, pp. 202–230.

JAY, TIMOTHY. 1980. Sex roles and dirty-word usage. *Psychological Bulletin* 88: 614–621.

JESPERSEN, OTTO. 1922. *Language: Its Nature, Development and Origins.* London: Allen and Unwin.

KIESLING, SCOTT. 1997. Power and the language of men. In *Language and Masculinity,* ed. S. Johnson and U. Meinhof. London: Blackwell, pp. 65–85.

KIESLING, SCOTT. 2005. Homosocial desire in men's talk: Balancing and re-creating cultural discourses of masculinity. *Language in Society* 34, no. 5:695–726.

KRAMER, CHERIS. 1975. Women's speech: Separate but unequal. In *Language and Sex,* ed. B. Thorne and N. Henley. Rowley, MA: Newbury, pp. 43–56.

LABOV, WILLIAM. 1966. *The Social Stratification of English in New York City.* Washington, DC: Center for Applied Linguistics.

LAKOFF, ROBIN. 1975. *Language and Woman's Place.* New York: Harper & Row.

LEGMAN, GERSHON. 1941. "The language of homosexuality: an American glossary." *Sex Variants: a study of homosexual patterns,* volume II. (ed. George W. Henry). New York: Paul B. Hoeber, Inc., pp. 1149–1179.

LEVINE, LEWIS, AND HARRY CROCKETT. 1967. Speech variation in a Piedmont community: Postvocalic r-. In *Explorations in Sociolinguistics,* ed. S. Lieberson. Bloomington: Indiana University Press, pp. 76–98.

MACKAY, DONALD. 1983. Prescriptive grammar and the pronoun problem. In *Language, Gender and Society,* ed. B. Thorne, C. Kramarae, and N. Henley. Rowley, MA: Newbury, pp. 38–53.

MALTZ, DANIEL, AND RUTH BORKER. 1982. A cultural approach to male-female miscommunication. In *Language and Social Identity,* ed. J. Gumperz. New York: Cambridge University Press, pp. 195–216.

MCCONNELL-GINET, SALLY. 1983. Intonation in a man's world. In *Language, Gender and Society,* ed. B. Thorne, C. Kramarae, and N. Henley. Rowley, MA: Newbury, pp. 69–88.

MCKNIGHT, GEORGE. 1928. *Modern English in the Making.* New York: Appleton.

MCWHORTER, JOHN. 1998. *The Word on the Street: Fact and Fable About American English.* New York: Plenum Trade.

MILLER, CASEY, AND KATE SMITH. 1977. *Words and Women.* New York: Anchor.

MINNING, HEIDI. 2004. Qwir-English code-mixing in Germany: Constructing a rainbow of identities. In *Speaking in Queer Tongues: Globalization and Gay Language,* ed. William Leap and Tom Boellstorff. Urbana: University of Illinois Press, pp. 46–71.

MOONWOMON-BAIRD, B. 1997. Toward a study of lesbian speech. In *Queerly Phrased: Language, Gender and Sexuality,* ed. A. Livia and K. Hall). Oxford: Oxford University Press, pp. 202–213.

MORIEL, LIORA. 2004. Dancing on the needle's edge: Gay lingo in an Israeli disco. In *Speaking in Queer Tongues: Globalization and Gay Language,* ed. William Leap and Tom Boellstorff. Urbana: University of Illinois Press, pp. 105–133.

NICHOLS, PATRICIA. 1983. Linguistic options and choices for black women in the rural South. *Language, Gender and Society,* ed. B. Thorne, C. Kramarae, and N. Henley. Rowley, MA: Newbury, pp. 54–68.

NILSEN, ALLEEN, ed. 1977. Sexism as shown in the English language. In *Sexism and Language.*

Champaign, IL: National Council of Teachers of English, pp. 27–42.

OCHS, ELINOR. 1992. Indexing gender. In *Rethinking Context,* ed. A. Duranti and C. Goodwin. New York: Cambridge University Press, pp. 335–358.

OKAMOTO, SHIGEKO. 1995. "Tasteless" Japanese: Less "feminine" speech among young Japanese women. In *Gender Articulated: Language and the Socially Constructed Self,* ed. K. Hall and M. Bucholtz. New York: Routledge, pp. 297–325.

OKAMOTO, SHIGEKO, AND SHIE SATO. 1992. Less feminine speech among young Japanese females. In *Cultural Performances: Proceedings of the Third Berkeley Women and Language Conference,* ed. M. Bucholtz, A. Liang, L. Sutton, and C. Hines. Berkeley: University of California, Berkeley Women and Language Group, pp. 478–488.

PILKINGTON, JANE. 1998. "Don't try and make out that I'm nice!" The different strategies women and men use when gossiping. *Language and Gender: A Reader,* ed. J. Coates. Oxford: Blackwell Publishers, pp. 254–269.

PROVENCHER, DENIS. 2004. Vague English Creole: (Gay English) cooperative discourse in the French gay press. In *Speaking in Queer Tongues: Globalization and Gay Language,* ed. William Leap and Tom Boellstorff. Urbana: University of Illinois Press, pp. 23–45.

SATTEL, JACK. 1983. Men, inexpressiveness and power. In *Language, Gender and Society,* ed. B. Thorne, C. Kramarae, and N. Henley. Rowley, MA: Newbury, pp. 118–124.

SCHNEIDER, JOSEPH, AND SALLY HACKER. 1973. Sex role imagery and use of the generic "man" in introductory texts: A case in the sociology of sociology. *American Sociologist* 8:12–18.

SCHULZ, MURIEL. 1975. The semantic derogation of women. In *Language and Sex,* ed. B. Thorne and N. Henley. Rowley, MA: Newbury, pp. 64–75.

SCOTT, PATRICIA B. 1974. The English language and black womanhood: A low blow at self-esteem. *Journal of Afro-American Issues* 2:218–224.

SHERZER, JOEL. 1987. A diversity of voices: Men's and women's speech in ethnographic perspective. In *Language, Gender and Sex in Comparative Perspective,* ed. S. Philips, S. Steele, and C. Tanz. New York: Cambridge University Press, pp. 95–120.

SHIBAMOTO, JANET. 1987. The womanly woman: Manipulation of stereotypical and non-stereotypical features of Japanese women's speech. In *Language, Gender and Sex in Comparative Perspective,* ed. S. Philips, S. Steele, and C. Tanz. New York: Cambridge University Press, pp. 26–49.

SMITH-HEFNER, NANCY. 1988. Women and politeness: The Javanese example. *Language in Society* 17:535–554.

SMYTH, RON, GREG JACOBS, and HENRY ROGERS. 2003. Male voices and perceived sexual orientation: An experimental and theoretical approach. *Language in Society* 32, no. 3:329–350.

SREETHARAN, CINDI. 2004. Japanese men's linguistic stereotypes and realities. *Japanese Language, Gender, and Ideology: Cultural Models and Real People,* ed. S. Okamoto and J. Shibamoto Smith. New York: Oxford University Press, pp. 275–287.

STANLAW, JAMES. 2004. *Japanese English: Language and Culture Contact.* Hong Kong: Hong Kong University Press.

SWACKER, MARJORIE. 1975. The sex of the speaker as a sociolinguistic variable. In *Language and Sex,* ed. B. Thorne and N. Henley. Rowley, MA: Newbury, pp. 76–83.

TANNEN, DEBORAH. 1986. *That's Not What I Meant.* New York: Ballantine.

TANNEN, DEBORAH. 1990. *You Just Don't Understand.* New York: Ballantine.

TERANGO, LARRY. 1966. Pitch and duration characteristics of the oral reading of males on a masculinity-femininity dimension. *Journal of Speech and Hearing Research* 9:590–595.

TRECHTER, SARA, AND ELI JAMES. 1994. "Appropriate" gendered speech in Lakhota society. In *Cultural Performances: Proceedings of the Third Berkeley Women and Language Conference,* ed. M. Bucholtz, A. Liang, L. Sutton, and C. Hines. Berkeley: University of California, Berkeley Women and Language Group, pp. 746–756.

TROEMEL-PLOETZ, SENTA. 1998. Selling the apolitical. In *Language and Gender,* ed. J. Coates. Malden, MA: Blackwell, pp. 446–458.

TRUDGILL, PETER. 1972. Sex, covert prestige and linguistic change in the urban British English of Norwich. *Language in Society* 1:179–195.

UCHIDA, AKI. 1992. When "difference" is "dominance": A critique of the "anti-power-based" cultural approach to sex differences. *Language in Society* 21:547–568.

West, Candace. 1998. When the doctor is a "lady": Power, status and gender in physician-patient encounters. In *Language and Gender,* ed. J. Coates. Malden, MA: Blackwell, pp. 396–412.

West, Candace, and Don Zimmerman. 1983. Small insults: A study of interruptions in cross-sex conversations between unacquainted persons. In *Language, Gender and Society,* ed. B. Thorne, C. Kramarae, and N. Henley. Rowley, MA: Newbury, pp. 103–118.

Wobst, Susan. 1981. Male and female reference in semantic space in Russian. *Russian Language Journal* 35:35–44.

Wolfram, Walt. 1969. *A Sociolinguistic Description of Detroit Negro Speech.* Washington, DC: Center for Applied Linguistics.

Woods, Nicola. 1988. Talking shop: Sex and status as determinants of floor apportionment in a work setting. In *Women in Their Speech Communities,* ed. J. Coates and D. Cameron. London: Longman, pp. 141–157.

Zimmerman, Don, and Candace West. 1975. Sex roles, interruptions and silences in conversation. In *Language and Sex,* ed. B. Thorne and N. Henley. Rowley, MA: Newbury, pp. 105–129.

CHAPTER **11**

Multilingual Nations

Note the contentious language in the following dialogue between two bilingual Canadians, one (the man) a native speaker of English and the other (the receptionist) a native French speaker:

MAN:	Could you tell me where the French test is?
RECEPTIONIST (IN FRENCH):	Pardon? ("Pardon?")
MAN:	Could you tell me where the French test is?
RECEPTIONIST:	En français? ("In French?")
MAN:	I have the right to be addressed in English by the government of Québec according to Bill 101.
RECEPTIONIST (TO A THIRD PERSON):	Qu'est-ce qu'il dit? ("What's he saying?")

Both speakers are bilingual in English and French, so they can well understand each other. Either speaker could have chosen to use the language preferred by the interlocutor. Because the man spoke first, in English, the receptionist could have responded in English. Failing that, the man could have next repeated his question in French after the receptionist's French response. But neither speaker was willing to accommodate the other. Instead, they both insisted on continuing to use their own native language. Such an interaction is symbolic of linguistic and, as we shall see later in the chapter, social, economic, and political conflicts in Canada. It is commonly played out elsewhere in the world as well where different ethnic groups compete for economic and political control in their communities and nations.

All modern nations are multilingual in the sense that some sectors of their population speak more than one language. Presumably even in earlier, smaller societies, at least some members were bilingual or multilingual. Because trade, travel, and intermarriage between neighboring or distant peoples have always occurred, the convenience and/or need to speak the language of another group has been an obvious social fact. Of all the countries in the world, Papua New Guinea has the highest number of languages used as a first language, an impressive total of 830 in a population of about 3,833,000. This number accounts for an equally impressive 12.01 percent of all of the languages spoken in the world. Papua New Guinea is followed by Indonesia, with 722 languages (10.45 percent) and a population of 222,700,000.

After that, the numbers decline considerably, but major multilingual countries include Nigeria (521 languages, or 7.54 percent), the United States (364 languages, or 5.27 percent), Mexico (297 languages, or 4.30 percent), the Democratic Republic of the Congo (217 languages, or 3.14 percent), and Australia (207 languages, or 3.00 percent) (Ethnologue 2010). The United States differs from the other countries listed because of its high number of immigrant languages (about two-thirds of the total), whereas elsewhere most of the languages spoken are indigenous to that nation.

The following table presents similar data by world area (note that languages are counted once, specified in the world area of their origin) (Ethnologue 2010):

Distribution of Languages by Area of Origin

Area	Number of Languages	Percent of World's Languages
Africa	2,110	30.5
Americas	993	14.4
Asia	2,322	33.6
Europe	234	3.4
Pacific	1,250	18.1
Total	6,909	100.0

In this chapter, we begin by examining relations of languages in two multilingual countries, India and Canada. We then describe and analyze linguistic diversity, public policies, and attitudes concerning languages in the United States.

In multilingual communities, each language has a particular status, one (or some) having greater prestige than others. Many factors contribute to linguistic ranking, including the social status of native speakers and economic, political, and social contexts of contact. In some cases, relatively benign attitudes are maintained, but elsewhere, conflict among members of different linguistic groups disrupts societal cohesion. We now turn to a discussion of these issues in the context of India and Canada.

INDIA

Linguistic Diversity

Linguistic diversity in India is enormous. An estimated 415 different languages are spoken, 30 of which have more than 1 million speakers each. India's languages are distributed among four distinct language families: Indo-Aryan (74 percent); Dravidian (24 percent); Austro-Asiatic (1.2 percent); and Tibeto-Burman (0.6 percent) (Census of India 2001). The map in Figure 11.1 illustrates areas of concentration of the language families.

Prior to India's independence in 1947, English was the country's governmental language. Its prominence originated from Great Britain's economic and political control from the eighteenth century until India's independence. English was the language of the colonizers and became a second language of indigenous elite classes. After independence, as part of a rejection of India's colonial era, the governing Congress Party gave "official" status to Hindi, an Indo-Aryan language presently spoken by more than 422 million people, or 41.03 percent of the Indian population. The government also hoped that establishing one official language would help to integrate the hundreds of ethnic groups living in India.

FIGURE 11.1   Linguistic Divisions in India. (APTE, MAHADEV. 1976. Multilingualism
in India and its socio-political implications: An overview. In Language and Politics,
ed. W. O'Barr and J. O'Barr. The Hague: Mouton, pp. 141–164.)

India's constitution of 1948 recognized linguistic diversity by granting "national" status
to the following 15 languages, listed here with the number of speakers according to the Indian
Census taken in 2001:

In the early 1950s, the Indian government began to reorganize its internal polities and
confronted the serious problem of linguistic and ethnic diversity within its borders. A principle
of linguistic homogeneity was used to establish states. In all but two of India's 18 states, a
majority of residents speak a common language. However, *homogeneity* is a misleading term,

implying complete or near-complete similarity. Such a situation does not exist in any Indian state. Although states may have a majority of speakers of a single language, percentages vary from just over 50 percent (Assamese in Assam) to 95 percent (Malayalam in Kerala). And despite goals of linguistic uniformity, some states have no numerically dominant language (e.g., Himachal Pradesh) (Apte 1976:155).

		Number of Speakers	
		In Millions	**In Percent**
1.	Assamese	13.1	1.28
2.	Bengali	83.4	8.11
3.	Gujarati	46	4.48
4.	Hindi	422	41.03
5.	Kannada	37.9	3.69
6.	Kashmiri	Number unknown, no census data from Kashmir	
7.	Malayalam	33	3.21
8.	Marathi	71.9	6.99
9.	Oriya	33	3.21
10.	Punjabi	29.1	2.83
11.	Sanskrit	Not spoken as a first language	
12.	Sindhi	2.5	0.25
13.	Tamil	60.8	5.91
14.	Telugu	74	7.37
15.	Urdu	51.5	5.01

Conflicts over boundaries between states have continued. As late as 1966, the former state of Punjab was subdivided into Hindi-speaking Haryana and Punjabi-speaking Punjab. Some regional border disputes are still ongoing, for example, between Kannada-speaking Mysore and Marathi-speaking Maharashtra. A number of areas in dispute between two states have become "union territories" and are administered by the central government. For example, Goa declined to become merged with the neighboring state of Maharashtra. Both the states of Punjab and Haryana have claimed the city of Chandigarh, but the city has so far remained independent (ibid.:147). These conflicts indicate the complexity of ethnic and linguistic divisions in India and the difficulties in reaching compromise.

In addition to Hindi (the country's "official" language) and 14 other "national" languages, each state can choose its own "regional" language. A state can adopt Hindi as its regional language, or it may select another code from among those spoken in its territory for use in local government affairs and in education. India's constitution further guarantees the rights of all citizens to communicate in their own language and allows them to interact with any government agency in a code of their choice (ibid.:144).

Of the 18 states, six (Bihar, Haryana, Himachal Pradesh, Madhya Pradesh, Rajasthan, Uttar Pradesh) have selected Hindi as their sole regional language, one state (Gujarat) has chosen Hindi and an indigenous code (Gujarati), English is the regional language of two states (Kerala, Nagaland), and English and Oriya are the languages of the state of Orissa. In the remaining states, indigenous regional languages have been designated (Andhra Pradesh: Telugu; Assam: Assamese; Jammu/Kashmir: Urdu; Karnataka: Kannada; Kerala: Malayalam; Maharashtra: Marathi; Punjab: Punjabi; Tamil Nadu: Tamil; West Bengal: Bengali). Of ten union territories, five have English as their regional language, two have English and Hindi, one has English and French, and only one has a local language (Bengali) as its regional code (ibid.:161–163).

Not only are there problems in state boundaries and selection of regional languages, there are also controversies in choosing writing systems for local and national languages. Eleven different scripts are used in India. Minority languages that have historically not been associated with a written form have particular problems adopting scripts. To illustrate possible complexities, consider the situation of Santhali, a language spoken in four states (Assam, Bihar, Orissa, West Bengal). Each of the four states uses a different script for its own regional code. Therefore, if Santhali is written in the script of its state, four versions would coexist. The central Commission of Linguistic Minorities has tried to solve the problem by suggesting adoption of either Devangari, the script in which Hindi is written, or the Roman alphabet, but the states involved have been unable to reach an agreement (Dua 1985:362).

English remains an optional language in several societal domains throughout most of India. It is the mother tongue of only about 260,000 people in India, but it is the second or third language of an additional 90 million, according to the census of 2001. This represents a large increase from the 1981 census reporting 25 million people able to speak some English. Despite the Congress Party's desire to establish Hindi as the sole official language, either Hindi or English is used in the Indian Parliament and in communication between states and with the central government. In addition, English is sometimes used as a medium of instruction in schools, particularly in universities. In fact, knowledge of English has become a marker of advanced education and elite social status. The courts function primarily in English, especially at higher levels of adjudication. In town courts, proceedings are often conducted in local languages, although official records are maintained in English. In High Courts and the Supreme Court, lawyers and judges employ English, even though it may not be understood by other participants (Kidder 1976:238–239). Use of English creates a language barrier, or "blackout" (ibid.:247), that helps maintain the privileged position of lawyers and other professionals. By translating proceedings for their poorly educated clients, lawyers may filter information in a way that secures their advantages and the disadvantages of their clients.

Speakers of Hindi constitute the largest single linguistic group—that is, approximately 41 percent of the people are native speakers and another 27 to 43 percent are able to speak or understand the language. Although Hindi is strongly endorsed by the central government, several sectors of the Indian population oppose its use as the official language and instead advocate English. Members of elite classes, most of whom are proficient in English, prefer English because its use enhances their prestige and control over governmental, technological, and educational institutions. Opposition to Hindi is also voiced by people in South India, where Hindi is sparsely represented or absent altogether. These people resent economic and political control by Hindi-speaking regions and therefore resist Hindi linguistic dominance (Apte 1976:148).

Rivalry among the numerous and diverse ethnic and linguistic groups in India has blocked the smooth adoption of Hindi. Governmental and educational institutions have had little effect on encouraging employment of Hindi. In fact, according to S. N. Sridhar (1988b:312–313), the spread of Hindi throughout India is attributable more to its use in the popular cinema and television than to official policies.

Standardization

The ascendancy of Hindi is complicated by linguistic standardization. Standard Hindi differs from colloquial speech in pronunciation and vocabulary, borrowing many words from Sanskrit, India's ancient literary and ceremonial language. Hindi's social prestige is strengthened by its incorporation of Sanskrit vocabulary, "showing that an Indian language can be independent of English and other international languages" (Southworth 1985:232). But this process of Sanskritization also separates standard Hindi from the speech of ordinary people. Most Indians in all regions speak colloquial or vernacular styles of their languages, so even native speakers of Hindi have problems understanding standardized, literary Hindi.

Similar processes of standardization have affected regional languages in each state, resulting in problems for native speakers and other state residents. For instance, a survey of speakers of Malayalam, the majority language of Kerala, a state having the highest literacy rate in India, revealed only slight ability of respondents to understand standardized Malayalam (ibid.). Franklin Southworth prepared two levels of written text, administering one to adults with an average of eight years' education and a simpler version to adults with 4.4 years of schooling. On a comprehensibility scale from 0.0 to 5.0, the first group averaged 1.5 and the second, 2.0. Although the sample was small, results clearly showed that speakers had difficulty understanding standardized forms of their native tongue (ibid.:234). Only well-educated elites are functionally fluent in standardized literary forms of language; thus, they are able to maintain their status over an uneducated or poorly educated populace through the medium of linguistic code.

Many Indian languages are in the process of modernization, that is, adapting or expanding their vocabularies to include new items or activities. This linguistic process is accelerated by socioeconomic trends toward increased urbanization, industrialization, and access to education. It is furthered as well by the use of borrowed and coined words in the mass media (Daswani 1989:85). Modernization includes borrowing words from other languages, especially from Hindi, Sanskrit, English, or another of the major Indian languages (Sridhar 1988a:356). Borrowed words are often integrated into compounds with native words to label modern entities. For example, the following expressions are used in Kannada, a Dravidian language of South India (ibid.:357):

aspirin matre: "aspirin tablet"

cancer roga: "cancer" (literally: cancer disease)

Another common process involves compounding two (or more) native words to form a new construction:

vicara sankirana: "symposium" (literally: thought confrontation)

Meanings of existing words are sometimes reinterpreted to apply to innovations:

akasavana: "radio" (literally: voice from the sky)

Linguistic procedures such as these expand a language's contextual usefulness. However, they can also result in development of "style strata" (ibid.:359), which segments a linguistic community into unequal groups based on degrees of familiarity with a more technical or educated language variety.

In some cases, modernization of local languages has led to rapid linguistic changes affecting not only incorporation or creation of new words for technological innovations, but also replacement of indigenous words by others derived from a language with higher societal status.

For instance, Tripuri, a local language spoken in West Bengal, has adopted many Bengali words, including labels for colors and numbers as well as grammatical indicators such as "who, which, until" (Dua 1985:363). If this process gains momentum, it could potentially erode the distinctiveness of some local languages under pressure from competing regional or national codes.

Linguistic Minorities

All Indian states contain linguistic minorities, people who speak neither Hindi nor the official state language. Some of these minorities constitute large sectors, numbering in the millions, whereas others are members of small, isolated, mostly rural tribal enclaves. Languages having large numbers of speakers are more likely to receive public recognition and be used as mediums of instruction and mass communication than are those spoken by only a few.

Each state government determines which of its languages can be used in education. A state's regional language and/or Hindi are always options. Many people throughout India oppose instruction in Hindi because native speakers of Hindi have an advantage in schooling (they already command the official code), whereas speakers of other languages (who constitute the majority of Indians) must learn a second language. Because the Indian constitution assigns control over education to states rather than to the central government, most states have developed their own instructional policies.

Minority languages receive support for schooling in some states, but in others they do not. In states where minority languages are used in school, they are typically employed only in the early grades. Students are later required to learn the regional language or Hindi (ibid.:364).

Practical problems undoubtedly exist in supporting minority languages because educational uses necessitate economic investments in teacher training and preparation of texts and other instructional materials. However, pedagogical decisions are often based on societal attitudes toward speakers of each language. Refusal to acknowledge minority or tribal languages is tantamount to asserting economic and/or political control over their speakers. But minority linguistic communities are not united on issues of language choice because class or caste differences affect people's goals. Elites may choose not to advocate their own native language for state recognition and instead favor Hindi or English because these have national and international stature. Inasmuch as elites are likely to be well educated, their fluency in Hindi and/or English enables them to participate in national culture; at the same time, this fluency separates them from others in their linguistic community who are subordinate.

Mass communication also promotes marginalization of minority linguistic communities. Print and broadcast media are rarely available in local languages. Even when they are available, most sectors of minority groups do not support these media because topical coverage is generally limited to local events. In most cases, newspapers printed in minority languages have circulations of under 3,000 (ibid.:368). Thus, because minority media have only narrow appeal, they cannot adequately legitimate or strengthen local identities.

Despite obstacles, however, hundreds of minority languages continue to be spoken in India. Even languages spoken by very few people can maintain their vigor. In a review of minority languages in the state of Kerala, V. I. Subramoniam identified the following circumstances favoring continued use of local codes in a small community: (1) little or no job contacts with speakers of dominant languages, (2) low levels of formal education, (3) tendency for marriages to take place between people of the same community, and (4) lack of migration to other areas either for work or schooling (1977:23–26).

Although such communities exist by the thousands throughout India, the people pay a price for their isolation because they have few educational and economic opportunities that could potentially lead to improved standards of living.

Nationalist philosophies often relegate minority languages and their speakers to peripheral status. Expansion of standardized codes through mass communication, education, and government encourages uniformity not only of language, but also of "ideology and culture" (Dua 1985:370). The government advocates linguistic uniformity as a necessary adjunct to centralization and coordination of economic development and modernization. Minority languages and their speakers thus become stigmatized as obstacles to societal integration and advance.

CANADA

Language in Canada

The linguistic situation in Canada, although apparently simpler than in India, is replete with long-standing ethnic tensions that finally erupted into political conflicts. Canada was colonized by French and British traders and settlers beginning in the sixteenth and seventeenth centuries. French settlement was concentrated around ports along the St. Lawrence River from Montreal eastward to the Atlantic Ocean. British control expanded westward, eventually reaching the Pacific coast. In 1762, France's colony of Québec was ceded to the British after France's defeat in the Seven Years' War. Rural French farmers were geographically, economically, and linguistically separated from urban English workers, business owners, and politicians in Québec. Members of French upper classes entered professions such as medicine, law, and the clergy. After Canadian independence from Great Britain in 1867, these francophone elites controlled provincial government as anglophone Québecers turned their interests to federal politics (Heller 1985:76). (Note that **anglophone** refers to a monolingual English speaker or a bilingual with English dominance; **francophone** refers to a speaker who is monolingual in French or a French-dominant bilingual.)

The fairly stable separation of French and English speakers in Québec began to change after World War II. A growing French middle class was absorbed first by the expanding provincial bureaucracy. In the 1960s, this group entered private business sectors previously monopolized by anglophones. According to Monica Heller, as French prominence increased, francophone politicians championed the cause of Québec nationalism in part to strengthen their control over the political apparatus. They wanted to keep Québec's anglophones out of provincial politics and to block inroads by the immigrant populace, most of whom ally themselves with anglophones and adopt English rather than French as their second language (ibid.:77).

Many of Québec's francophone residents continued to resent the fact that the province's economy was controlled by anglophones, often by corporations located in English-speaking provinces. As a result, calls for Québec's independence from Canada increased throughout the 1960s and led to urgent responses by federal authorities, including passage of the Official Languages Act in 1969. As stated in the act's Declaration of Status of Languages, "the English and French languages are the official languages of Canada for all purposes of the Parliament and Government of Canada, and possess and enjoy equality of status and equal rights and privileges as to their use in all the institutions of the Parliament and Government of Canada" (quoted in Grosjean 1982:16–17).

This policy means that Canada is a bilingual country in the sense that services must be provided in two languages so that any (monolingual) resident can benefit. It does not specifically advocate individual bilingualism, that is, that people should speak two languages. In accordance with the law, all government documents are published in both languages and speakers of either have rights to interact with agencies in a language of their choice. In the opinion of Frank Vallee and John de Vries (1978), this approach accomplishes two goals. First, by granting symbolic recognition to French and its speakers, it blunts the appeal of francophone nationalism. Second, by attracting francophones into federal employment, it offers an economic lure to weaken Québec separatism (ibid.:765).

In the domain of education, the federal government provides funds to help provinces set up bilingual education programs in districts where at least 10 percent of the population speaks the minority language (English in Québec; French elsewhere). This goal has not been uniformly or adequately met, however (Grosjean 1982:17).

Federal attempts at reconciliation did not succeed. Most of Canada remained indifferent or hostile to Québec's grievances. In Québec, francophones rejected official bilingualism and instead established French monolingualism in the province. In 1977, Québec's government enacted the Chartre de la Langue Française (Charter of the French Language), known as Bill 101, which recognizes French as the only official language of Québec. Official documents are published in French only. French is the language of education for the francophone majority and for immigrants speaking other languages. Anglophones may send their children to English-speaking schools if the parents had been educated in English in Québec (ibid.:18). In addition, French has become the routine language of public and private employment. All job seekers must speak French, as must current employees who apply for promotions (Heller 1985:77). These provisions for language use in education and in workplaces at first applied to Native Canadian communities as well, but Native Canadians succeeded in establishing their rights to use either their native language or English or French as they see fit.

This historical review provides a background for examining language abilities, situational usage, and attitudes toward speakers of French and English. Canadians' linguistic proficiencies remained stable throughout most of this century. Since the 1970s, some significant changes have occurred in proportions of those speaking only French and in rates of bilingualism. The following table compares figures from the 1971 census as reported by Vallee and de Vries (1978:776) and the census of 2001 (*Statistics Canada* 2005):

Proportions of Speakers of Official Languages

	1971	2001
English only	67.1%	67.5%
French only	18.0	13.3
Both English and French	13.4	17.7
Neither	1.5	1.5

Although the proportion of Canadians who speak only English has remained relatively constant, fewer Canadians speak only French. Therefore, French speakers have primarily contributed to the increase in bilingualism. Another reflection of English prominence in Canada is the fact that most people who speak a nonofficial language and only one of the official languages choose English rather than French. Figures from the 2006 census are fairly stable except that the percentage of speakers of neither English nor French rose slightly, to 2.0 percent.

The census of 2006 also reports the "home language" of Canadian residents, that is, the language most often spoken at home. In these data, English is the home language of 67.1 percent of Canadians; French is the home language of 21.5 percent; and 11.4 percent of Canadians speak a language at home that is neither English nor French (*Statistics Canada* 2010).

Rates of French–English bilingualism are highest in Québec and neighboring New Brunswick (40.8 and 34.2 percent, respectively). In other provinces, bilinguals account for much smaller proportions of the population: Ontario is highest with 11.7 percent; the Prairie provinces average about 6.0 percent (*Statistics Canada* 2005). These figures indicate some increases in bilingualism throughout Canada since 1971.

Across Canada, percentages of francophone bilinguals significantly outnumber anglophone bilinguals. Based on 2006 figures, 46 percent of native speakers of French also speak English, whereas only 11 percent of anglophones speak French. Overall, 85 percent of all Canadians can speak English. Rates of francophone bilinguals are highest in the two provinces neighboring Québec, New Brunswick and Ontario. And the only province where anglophone bilinguals outnumber francophone bilinguals is in Québec. Throughout the country, bilingualism is highest among residents who are native speakers of neither French nor English. In most of Canada, these allophones learn English, but in Québec, French is the language more often chosen. The following table summarizes some of the data on French–English bilingualism, comparing Québec with the rest of Canada (Statistics Canada 2010):

French–English Bilingualism

Anglophones	Francophones	Allophones	Percent
Québec	66.1	36.6	50.4
Rest of Canada	7.1	85.1	5.7

Finally, there is a significant age difference in English–French bilingualism. Most anglophones outside Québec who learn French do so in the context of schooling and tend to lose their ability to speak French beginning in their twenties. In contrast, many francophones who learn English do so after they have completed school, reaching a peak in their late twenties.

In Canada, there is concern over the strong separation of French and English communities. Surveys of personal values, political opinions, and voting patterns indicate a consistent difference between these populations (Meisel 1978). And when respondents were asked to assess diverse ethnic groups, English Canadians gave lowest ratings to French Canadians, preferring members of other non-English ethnicities. French Canadians, though, rated English Canadians higher than other non-French groups (ibid.:687). Although language is not the only cause of these attitudes, it can be used as a signal of and catalyst for arousing prejudicial stereotypes.

The attitudes of the Québécois about language and linguistic groups were heightened following passage of Bill 101 (Charter of the French Language) in 1977. Surveys conducted in Québec revealed that both anglophones and francophones recognized the existence of two ethnic/linguistic blocks whose opinions and interests diverged sharply. Members of both groups thought that francophones favored Bill 101 and that anglophones opposed it, and both thought that anglophones felt threatened by the legislation (Taylor and Dube-Simard 1985). Although Québec's anglophones claimed that the bill's provisions were unjust, they reported that they had not received unfair treatment. Donald Taylor and Lise Dube-Simard suggested that media accounts of fears and problems of a few individuals may have contributed to the widely held perception of injustice even though that perception is not validated by personal experience (ibid.:165).

Situational Use

In the current context of political strife concerning the rights of linguistic minorities in Canada and the rights of the linguistic majority in Québec, situational language choice assumes symbolic and personal meanings. In Montreal, a predominantly French-speaking city but with the largest percentage of anglophones in Québec, selection of code between bilingual speakers may reflect underlying attitudes about each language. By choosing one language over another, speakers assert their identity and show their sensitivity to the linguistic rights of others. For instance, in the dialogue quoted at the beginning of this chapter, a receptionist in a government agency and an anglophone who wanted to take an official French test made symbolic statements with their choice of code in a clearly confrontational encounter. Recalling the interaction, one can assume that the anglophone applicant had some ability to speak French because he planned to take (presumably with hopes to pass) a test in French, yet he demanded his right to use his native language. The francophone bilingual receptionist countered his challenge by pretending not to understand English.

A decidedly nonconfrontational interaction is illustrated in the following telephone conversation between a hospital clerk and patient. Both speakers attempted to accommodate each other. The clerk answered the telephone in English, noticed the patient's French response, and proceeded to match her language to the code of the patient's prior turn. However, this strategy did not lead to an entirely trouble-free interaction because the patient was uncomfortable not knowing the clerk's ethnic identity (Heller 1985:80–81):

CLERK:	Central Booking, may I help you?	
PATIENT:	Oui, allô?	("Yes, hello?")
CLERK:	Bureau de rendez-vous, est-ce que je peux vous aider?	("Appointments Desk, may I help you?")
PATIENT:	(French)	(The patient begins to try to make an appointment)
CLERK:	(French)	
PATIENT:	(English)	
CLERK:	(English)	
PATIENT:	(French)	
CLERK:	(French)	
PATIENT:	Êtes-vous française ou anglaise?	("Are you French or English?")
CLERK:	N'importe j'suis ni l'une ni l'autre.	("It doesn't matter; I'm neither one nor the other.")
PATIENT:	Mais…	("But…")
CLERK:	Ça ne fait rien.	("It doesn't matter.")
PATIENT:	(French)	

(The conversation continues in French.)

In conversations between friends and colleagues who are aware of each other's linguistic abilities, various adjustments can be made. Some speakers repetitively translate previous statements in order to include all interlocutors in multiparty discussions. In the following excerpt, three co-workers are conversing, two francophone bilinguals (Albert and Claude) and an anglophone (Bob) with slight French proficiency (ibid.:85):

| ALBERT: | Il nous reste plus de temps après ça pour discuter les problèmes majeurs t'sais les choses qui vraiment you understand that Bob? I say if we lose less time in going over the routine we have more time to discuss the important uh… | ("We'll have more time after that for discussing major problems you know the things that really…") |

A final example illustrates another option: that each speaker uses the native language of her or his preference in an exchange for autonomous turns (ibid.:88):

HÉLÈNE:	Va-t-on manger de la soupe aujourd'hui?	("Are we going to have soup today?")
IAN:	I'm going to, I don't know if anyone wants to join me.	
HÉLÈNE:	Je veux bien, qu'est-ce qu'on mange?	("Sure, I do, what will we have?")
IAN:	Oh, I'll take care of it.	

Attitudes Toward Languages and Speakers

Although overt behavior reflects speakers' adjustments to interlocutors, covert attitudes also significantly affect both personal interactions and communitywide relations. Canadians' reaction to French and English speakers and their behavior in interlinguistic encounters have been studied using several techniques. Results of research in the 1950s and 1960s will be discussed first, followed by comparison with later studies. The first experiments employed the **matched-guise technique** (Lambert et al. 1960), in which subjects listen to tape-recorded speech in two versions of the same content, both spoken by the same fluent bilingual person. In one version, the bilingual speaks French and in the other, English. Subjects are asked to rate speakers (thinking they are different people) according to various dimensions of personality, intelligence, competence, and sociability.

Studies by Wallace Lambert and his co-workers in the 1950s and 1960s revealed consistent patterns. In their experiments, using male guises and male and female judges, anglophone subjects, as expected, rated guises more favorably when they spoke English rather than French. But, surprisingly, francophone subjects expressed similar preferences for English speakers except on ratings for kindness and religiousness. On other measures (intelligence, leadership, self-confidence, dependability, attractiveness, ambition, sense of humor), francophone subjects preferred English speakers. Francophones gave significantly higher ratings to English speakers than did anglophones for qualities of leadership, intelligence, and self-confidence (ibid.:47).

The various dialects of French spoken by the four bilingual guises in Lambert and his co-workers' experiments had an effect on subjects' assessment. Two spoke standard Canadian French, one a rural, heavily accented Canadian French, and the fourth Parisian French. All subjects rated the Parisian French guise most favorably and the rural Canadian guise most negatively (ibid.:50). These results indicated that both anglophones and francophones hold strong negative stereotypes of French Canadians.

A subsequent study used male and female guises in order to assess the variable of speaker's gender on hearer's attitudes. Among anglophone subjects, both men and women attributed more negative characteristics to French-speaking male guises, but more positive traits to French-speaking females. Among francophone judges, men consistently rated English speakers (male and female) more positively than French speakers. Francophone women, though, preferred French-speaking men on certain measures, rating them as more competent and sociable (Lambert 1967:95–97).

Matched-guise experiments with children as speakers and judges revealed the age at which socially derived stereotyping begins. One study involved 10-year-old subjects, half of whom were monolingual French speakers and half were bilingual francophones. They were told that the purpose of the experiment was to see how well people can evaluate personalities of speakers solely on the basis of their voice. Speaker guises were all 10-year-old bilingual girls. The results of this study indicated a split between reactions of monolingual and bilingual subjects. Monolinguals rated French-speaking guises much more favorably on all personality traits, demonstrating strongly negative attitudes toward English speakers. In contrast, bilinguals did not show any significant preference for either speaker (Anisfeld and Lambert 1964:91–92). They exhibited no prejudice toward other groups and no strong preference for their own group. By around age 12, however, negative attitudes on the part of francophone bilinguals toward French speakers were found in further research. The social class of respondents influenced these ratings: Middle- and upper-class children had stronger biased reactions than did children from working-class families (Lambert 1967:98–99).

Employing a different research strategy, a series of experiments applied speech accommodation theory to Canadian linguistic performance and its evaluation. **Speech accommodation theory** basically suggests that when speakers have positive attitudes toward interlocutors, they accommodate or converge to the latter's speech styles. In contrast, they maintain their own style, and possibly even exaggerate it, if they have negative opinions about co-participants (Giles et al. 1973:179).

In tests of speech accommodation theory with Canadian bilingual subjects, anglophone bilinguals listened to the recorded speech of a francophone bilingual man giving directions from a map of Montreal. Subjects were informed that the speaker knew his hearers would be English-dominant and that he was free to speak whatever language he wished. Each subject heard one recording, although four different versions were distributed among them. The versions were spoken in French; mixed French and English; fluent English; and nonfluent, hesitant, heavily accented English. After listening to a tape, anglophone subjects were asked to make recordings of their own descriptions of a city route, intended to be played later to the francophone speaker they had heard.

The study revealed that subjects who had heard the French version responded in English, whereas those hearing nonfluent English replied in French or apologized for their lack of French proficiency (ibid.:187). According to Howard Giles and his co-workers, when the speaker on tape used French, he was seen as nonaccommodating to his anglophone hearers; subjects responded by refusing to accommodate to him. When he spoke English with difficulty, subjects thought he was making a great effort to accommodate to them and they reciprocated his effort by trying to reply in French (ibid.). Another possible factor explaining this behavior, though, is that subjects hearing nonfluent English might have assumed the speaker had difficulty comprehending English and so they tried to reply in French simply to be understood.

A subsequent study of francophone bilingual subjects hearing a taped message from an anglophone speaking in French added a further manipulation to the same basic procedure. This time, one group of subjects was informed that the anglophone bilingual speaking French had been permitted to speak whatever language he wished, whereas another group knew that he had been told to speak in French. Subjects evaluated speakers more positively when they assumed they were hearing a voluntary French taping (voluntarily accommodating to them) than when they heard a speaker who had been instructed to speak French (Simard et al. 1976:382–383).

All the various reactions to speech exhibited in these experiments can be understood in the sociopolitical context of language in Canada in the 1960s and early 1970s. Attitudes toward language are not linguistic in their origin; rather, they are social. People attribute qualities to speakers of particular languages as a reflex of their opinions about members of given linguistic or ethnic communities. In some cases, prejudice against outgroups is uniform, for example, anglophone negative stereotyping of francophones. But members of stigmatized groups may themselves adopt self-denigrating bias; although in these cases, attitudes frequently are mixed, approving of ingroup people on certain measures.

Studies by Lambert and Giles and their co-workers were conducted prior to the 1977 passage of Bill 101, which established French as the only official language of Québec and that promotes French usage in education and business as well as in government. Surveys and experiments conducted since 1977 are important indicators of both change and stability in Canadian attitudes toward language and language users. Richard Bourhis (1985) reported three types of studies designed to investigate different aspects of linguistic and social interconnections. First, Bourhis administered a questionnaire to francophone undergraduates at the University of Montreal and to anglophones at McGill University (also in Montreal). Respondents were asked a number of questions concerning their linguistic behavior in situations of interlinguistic contact. They were specifically queried about which language they used in conversing as customers to outgroup clerks in stores and restaurants (an outgroup clerk is an English speaker to a francophone, a French speaker to an anglophone).

Although both groups reported initiating conversations in their native language in such settings, adhering to the traditional norm that "the client is always right," anglophones claimed that they were more likely to change to French with francophone clerks "today" than they had been "in the past" (i.e., prior to Bill 101). These respondents also noted that francophone clerks were less likely to switch to English than had been characteristic of past encounters. In contrast to anglophone respondents, francophones did not report a changed pattern in their choice of language in these interlinguistic contacts; they still maintained French or changed to English at the same rates as in the past.

In a finding with similar implications, anglophone respondents said that francophone clerks were less likely today to accommodate to an English-speaking client than in the past, whereas francophones reported that anglophone clerks were currently more likely to accommodate French-speakers than in previous years (ibid.:182).

This survey documents a change in expectations, attitudes, and experiences of young people in Montreal since discussion of language issues has become public and governmental intervention has created a legal and social climate encouraging the use of French.

However, overtly expressed sentiments are not always consistently reflected in actual behavior. Bourhis reported two related experiments asking subjects (age 16 and 17 years) to evaluate speakers on tape-recordings of three-part dialogues in which two male actors portrayed clerks and customers. In both tests, dialogues had the same format of turns: salesperson/customer/salesperson. In the first study, the following language choices were employed: (1) F-E-F,

(2) F-E-E, (3) F-F-F, and (4) F-F-E. Both anglophone and francophone respondents rated ingroup speakers more positively than outgroup speakers (ibid.:186). This is an important finding because it demonstrates a significant change from earlier studies (e.g., Lambert 1967) in which francophones had negative biases against speakers of French. In addition, francophone subjects were positively impressed by anglophone customers who accommodated the French-speaking clerk. All subjects reacted negatively to the francophone clerk when he failed to switch to English in response to an anglophone customer and thus violated norms of politeness to customers.

In the second study, the same procedure was followed in dialogues beginning with an English-speaking clerk: (1) E-F-E, (2) E-F-F, (3) E-E-E, and (4) E-E-F. Here, all subjects reacted favorably to the anglophone clerk when he switched to French in his response (Bourhis 1985: 188–189). Positive responses were greater toward the anglophone clerk changing to French (study 2) than for a francophone changing to English (study 1). Perhaps such reactions imply that some degree of hierarchical relations continues between English and French. That is, a speaker of a higher-status language (English) is especially rewarded for switching to a lower-status language (French).

A third series of studies by Bourhis was aimed at eliciting actual language use by interlocutors in natural settings. In this research, a perfect bilingual asked directions of pedestrians in Montreal. In encounters conducted in 1977 (shortly after passage of Bill 101), 95 percent of francophone pedestrians converged to English when the experimenter spoke English, whereas only 60 percent of anglophones converged to French when the experimenter spoke French. Note that a response was counted as convergence if it contained even as little as one word of the "foreign" language (ibid.:193).

This study was followed in 1979 by an identical procedure to test whether changes in behavior had occurred. Experiments were conducted with middle-age subjects chosen at random in downtown Montreal and with young university students at McGill University and the University of Montreal. Among older subjects, 100 percent of francophones switched to English when queried in English, and 70 percent of anglophones switched to French in response to a question in French. In contrast, young francophone university students converged to English at a rate of 83 percent, matched by 84 percent of anglophone students who converged to French (ibid.:196–197).

A number of important conclusions can be drawn from studies by Bourhis and his colleagues. Overt attitudinal responses by francophones have changed markedly from earlier studies by Lambert and others. By the late 1970s, francophones were at least consciously demonstrating positive reactions to their own group, as shown by students' claims to maintain their own language in interlinguistic contacts. In addition, anglophone students claimed a current greater tendency than in the past to converge to French.

Covert attitudes, as revealed by the "dialogue" experiments, show some shift from earlier reactions but also demonstrate that English continues to have some prestige. In addition, the fact that older anglophones resist converging to French and that older francophones are willing to converge to English, as elicited in the "asking directions" studies, similarly indicates inequalities between the two linguistic communities. However, future trends may be indicated by the fact that younger respondents, both francophone and anglophone, were equally willing to converge to the outgroup language (at rates of 83 and 84 percent, respectively). Although this last point may auger well for possibilities of linguistic tolerance on a nonconscious level, recent political developments in Québec indicate sharpening differentiation among various linguistic/ethnic groups.

A historic referendum on the question of sovereignty for the province of Québec was held on October 30, 1995. Since the 1960s, a separatist movement had grown in Québec, organized since the 1970s as a political party (Parti Québécois) whose goal was independence for Québec. Along with demands for political and economic ascendency of francophones in Québec, the Parti Québécois spearheaded the campaign for passage of Bill 101, making French the only official language of the province. In recent years, as francophone political and economic control was consolidated, cultural and linguistic issues that were always present took center stage, at least in rhetorical efforts to gain public favor for independence. Several referenda on the question were easily defeated in earlier years, but in 1995, proponents of sovereignty came within one percentage point of achieving their goal, in part by rallying people around the issue of their cultural and linguistic distinctiveness—a distinctiveness that is readily apparent and elicits emotional as well as intellectual reactions.

The final vote (50.5 percent against separation, 49.5 percent in favor) indicates a divided province, but the specific figures for diverse linguistic groups are even more revealing: 60 percent of francophones voted for independence, while only 10 percent of anglophones and a mere 5 percent of allophones (native speakers of neither French nor English) did so. Indigenous peoples, called the First Nations in Canada, were especially opposed to Québec independence. In fact, a week before the provincial vote, the Crees and Inuit held a referendum in their communities in which the Native groups voted nearly unanimously that if Québec has the right to separate from Canada, they have the right to remain. Regional diversity among francophones also surfaced. Pro-sovereignty voting was lower in the city of Montreal and in areas of Québec that border other provinces (Ontario to the west, New Brunswick to the east) or the United States than elsewhere.

Leaders of the separatist movement vowed to renew their efforts and seek another referendum in a few years. The issue of linguistic and political distinctions in Canada, begun more than 400 years ago, will obviously not be resolved immediately.

THE UNITED STATES

Language in the United States

The United States is a multilingual nation inhabited by millions of people who speak more than one language. Although English is the country's dominant language, it is not the first language of many native-born citizens. And, of course, numerous immigrants continue to use their original language in most social interactions. No federal legislation specifically grants official status to English, but a "complex web of customs, institutions and programs has long fostered well-nigh exclusive reliance upon English in public life" (Fishman 1981:517). This was not always the case. From the late-eighteenth through the mid-nineteenth centuries, political leaders and prominent citizens contended that all Americans should be encouraged to learn English but not be hindered from maintaining whatever other languages they spoke. These leaders understood that different languages express different thoughts and cultural orientations, and thus they believed that linguistic diversity strengthened the development and exchange of ideas (Health 1977:272). In this period, some states promoted languages other than English by publishing laws in additional codes, for example, German in Pennsylvania and French in Louisiana. Some laws affecting Native Americans were printed in indigenous languages in the nineteenth century (ibid.:273).

Change in attitudes toward multilingualism came in the latter half of the nineteenth century. Policies promoting or protecting other languages were repealed. Educators and public figures stressed the necessity for all to learn "correct" standard English. Many states enacted laws requiring sole use of English in schools and mandated fines for teachers who spoke other languages in the classroom. Children were often punished for speaking non-English mother tongues. The US Supreme Court ruled in 1923, however, that minority communities have a constitutional right to speak their own languages in private, but not public, schools if they so wish (Grosjean 1982:69–70). Because most people attend public schools, they are subject to public restrictions on the use of their native language. Standardization of code was increasingly stressed. "Textbooks emphasized the co-occurrence of 'good talk' with good behavior, a moral character, and an industrious nature.… The way of dealing with 'strangers' and their differences was to educate them to use 'good American speech' and motivate them to conform in the Americanizing process" (Health 1977:274). This trend was strengthened in the twentieth century, especially during World War I and World War II, when speakers of some foreign languages were suspected of being traitors.

Despite social pressures and the prominent image of English as the code of US residents, the reality of linguistic diversity continues. According to statistics collected by the US Bureau of the Census in the census of 2000, 47.0 million people (18 percent of the total population age 5 and over) reported non-English mother tongues. This figure represents a steady increase since 1980 and 1990, when 23.1 million and 31.8 million residents (11 percent and 14 percent of the population) were native speakers of a language other than English. The census reported that some 380 languages were spoken in homes in the United States, including 120 Native American languages.

Of all non-English languages, Spanish was spoken at home by the largest number of people, having 28.1 million speakers, or more than half of all people claiming a non-English mother tongue. This figure, too, represents an increase from 1980 and 1990, when there were 11.1 and 17.3 million Spanish-speaking residents. In addition to Spanish, the most frequently spoken non-English languages were Chinese (2.0 million speakers), French (1.6 million speakers), German (1.4 million), Tagalog (1.2 million), Vietnamese (1.0 million), and Italian (1.0 million). Taken as a group, Asian and Pacific Island languages had 7.0 million speakers, and Native American languages were spoken by some 332,000 people.

The ability of speakers of non-English mother tongues to speak English varied considerably. Approximately 55 percent reported that they spoke English "very well," while 8.1 percent said they did not speak English "very well."

Although Spanish dominates as a non-English home language in the nation, some regional variation exists. Among speakers of non-English languages, French is the most frequently spoken language in Louisiana, Maine, New Hampshire, and Vermont. German is most used in Montana, Minnesota, and North and South Dakota. Portuguese is first in Rhode Island. The Native American language called Yupik dominates in Alaska, and Japanese is most commonly spoken in Hawaii.

States varied in their numbers and proportions of speakers of non-English languages. The four states having at least 2 million such residents were California (12.4 million), Texas (6.0 million), New York (5.0 million), and Florida (3.5 million). California also had the highest proportion of speakers of non-English languages (39 percent), followed by New Mexico (37 percent). Areas with the smallest ratios of people with non-English mother tongues are in the South (except Louisiana and Florida), the Central and Mountain states, and the Northwest (Figure 11.2).

According to the 2000 Census, a final category of households consists of those identified as "linguistically isolated," that is, any household in which no person age 14 or over speaks English at least "very well." Any person living in such a household is counted as a "linguistically isolated person." Using these definitions, census data for 2000 indicate that there were some 11.9 million people living in 4.4 million linguistically isolated households.

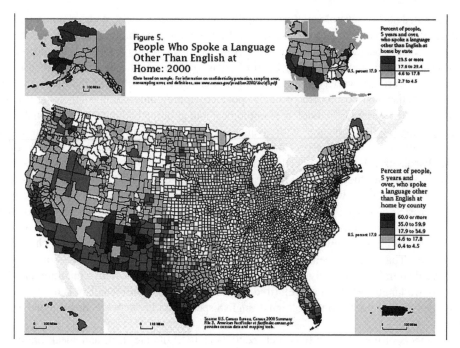

FIGURE 11.2 **Distribution of Minority Languages in the United States.** (Grosjean 1982:47, based on 1976 Survey of Income and Education, National Center for Education Statistics Bulletin. 78, B-5.)

Puerto Rican Speakers in New York City

The number of immigrants from Puerto Rico living in New York City has risen over the past 50 years. Immigration continues to bring in a steady flow of people from Puerto Rico, but many residents of Puerto Rican communities in New York City were born in the city, not on the island. Although people from Puerto Rico and their descendents live in every borough and every neighborhood, they are concentrated in certain neighborhoods. One of these, called El Barrio, is located on the east side of upper Manhattan. The linguistic repertory of its residents is complex, choosing options among three varieties of Spanish [Popular Puerto Rican (PR) Spanish, Standard PR Spanish, English-dominant Spanish] and four varieties of English (PR English, African-American Vernacular English [AAVE], Hispanized English, Standard NYC English) (Zentella 1997:41–48). Few speakers are skilled in all these varieties, but most are conversant in several, selecting a current variety depending on contexts, co-participants, and proficiency. Standard PR Spanish is a dialect of Spanish that shares most of its lexicon, grammar, and phonology with other dialects but has some distinctive intonational and pronunciation features and some special vocabulary. Popular PR Spanish is a nonstandard variety distinguishable by some pronunciation, grammatical, and lexical elements. It is a stigmatized dialect, associated with people who are poor and uneducated. The term *English-dominant Spanish* refers to a variety of Spanish spoken by English-dominant bilinguals, mostly children and young adults, that shows some tendencies toward convergence to English syntax, particularly a preference for subject-verb-object (SVO) word order and some regularization of Spanish irregular verbs.

As noted above, several varieties of English were spoken widely in the community. Puerto Rican English is a nonstandard dialect spoken by Puerto Rican immigrants, their descendents, and other second-generation Latinos living in New York City. It is generally used by members of the lower and working classes. Many Puerto Ricans, particularly young males, may also speak AAVE. They learn this variety and use it as members of social networks that include African Americans. "Hispanized English" is likely spoken by immigrants who lived their early years in Puerto Rico. This variety is marked by phonological and grammatical interference from Spanish, replacing some English phonemes with Spanish sounds, simplifying English consonant clusters, and using Spanish tense and aspect translations in English. In the context of New York City speech, Hispanized English is heavily stigmatized.

In an extensive study of one El Barrio block, Ana Zentella (1997) found that nearly all residents were bilingual and were able to switch between Spanish and English and among several varieties of each language. Their linguistic repertory, tied to context and participants, revealed a flexible rather than compartmentalized bilingualism. Research also demonstrated a current and projected future shift toward English, a projection supported by trends among children and young adults. That is, 62 percent of residents between the age of 3 and 20 were more proficient in English than in Spanish. Only 15 percent were Spanish-dominant. The remaining 23 percent spoke the two languages about as well (ibid.:49). The strength of bilingualism is reflected in the fact that only one child was a monolingual English speaker and none were monolingual Spanish speakers.

Members of the community (which Zentella calls El bloque) hear and speak English and Spanish in an almost seamless overlapping of contexts and topics. When speaking English or Spanish, the other language might be heard in the background on the radio, in stores, on the street. And speakers switched easily from one language to the other even within a single encounter. There are some gender differences that help predict the amount of Spanish or English a person is likely to hear and speak (ibid.:51–52). Girls' experiences tend to locate them in contexts where Spanish dominates, especially in the home. Women are more likely than men to retain Spanish because of their relatively narrower social networks. They tend to socialize with family members and with other Spanish-dominant speakers. Because girls' lives also revolve more around family, performing household chores and childcare tasks, they frequently hear and participate in extensive Spanish conversations. Boys' networks often draw them out of the household into neighborhood groups that consist not only of other bilinguals, but also of monolingual English speakers, especially speakers of AAVE. Still, gender alone does not determine one's language proficiency. Children of either gender who were born and spent formative years in Puerto Rico are more likely to be Spanish-dominant, whereas children born in the United States or who arrived at an early age are more likely to be proficient in English. Siblings born to immigrant parents might also vary in their language proficiency, depending on their seniority. That is, elder siblings might be more likely to be Spanish-dominant than younger siblings because the home environment would have been more oriented toward Spanish during their early years.

Pressures toward English are ubiquitous within the bilingual community. The use of English is predominant in school, entertainment and other media, and much of public discourse. Puerto Rican parents understand the value of their children learning English in order to advance in school and in the local and national economies. However, Spanish is maintained in the community as well. A continual influx of immigrants from Puerto Rico and other Spanish-speaking countries in Central and South America constantly reaffirms the vitality of the language. In addition, Spanish is seen as a marker of ethnic identity and continuity. And children need to be at least passively bilingual because they frequently interact with elders who are either monolingual

Spanish speakers or who are clearly Spanish-dominant. Even when faced with increasing use of English in many if not most activities, children still hear Spanish spoken at home at least some of the time and by at least some of their kinfolk, and "…overlapping networks guaranteed constant visiting, sharing, and exposure to both languages" (ibid.:78). Knowledge of both languages and the ability to navigate in and out of each one mark membership in both Spanish-oriented and English-oriented communities.

Bilingual Education

Recognizing the reality of multilingualism in the United States, public policies shifted in the direction of protecting the rights of linguistic minorities. First steps were taken in the domain of education. In 1963, the Coral Way School in Dade County, Florida, established a federally funded bilingual education program for Spanish-speaking immigrants from Cuba. The next year, Texas's Webb County schools began operating bilingual classes for Spanish speakers. Congress encouraged such programs by passing the Bilingual Education Act of 1968, or Title VII of the 1965 Elementary and Secondary Education Act. This act provides federal funding for bilingual education in public schools. Congress periodically updates the act, most recently in 1979–1980, to give additional funding for increased services. Under the law, federal monies are given to state education departments and local school districts to provide bilingual education programs for students of limited English-speaking ability. The current statement of eligibility specifically includes Native Americans and others who may be native speakers of English but "who come from environments where a language other than English has had a significant impact on their level of English language proficiency" (quoted in Leap 1986:601).

Federal legislation did not spell out characteristics of programs or length of time students should remain in bilingual classes. It encouraged states and local districts to develop curricula and train teachers. Seventy-six programs were funded during the first year of applicability, nearly all for Spanish-speaking students. Massachusetts was the first state to implement mandatory bilingual education with passage of its Transitional Bilingual Education Act in 1971, providing that school districts with at least 20 children of one language group who have limited English proficiency must institute bilingual programs (Grosjean 1982:72).

Bilingual education in the United States is usually based on a **transitional model**, oriented toward assimilation of foreign-speaking communities. Its goal is to encourage speakers to shift to English, eliminating reliance on their native languages. For example, the Massachusetts law specifies that a child remain in a bilingual program for a maximum of three years. During the first year, the native language is used in 95 percent of class time, and it is reduced to 50 percent in the second year and 5 to 10 percent in the third (ibid.:73). In contrast to transitional programs, some countries such as India adopt **maintenance models** that encourage acquisition of fluency and literacy skills in both native and second languages. Although the Bilingual Education Act is a progressive step in recognizing difficulties for children in classrooms dominated by what for them is a foreign language, it does not actually promote multilingualism. According to Joshua Fishman, "the Act was primarily an act for the Anglification of non-English speakers and not an act for bilingualism…. Thus, it is basically an act against bilingualism" (1981:517–518).

In 1974, the US Supreme Court handed down a landmark decision in the *Lau v. Nichols* case that resulted from an action brought by members of the Chinese community in San Francisco who alleged that school systems without bilingual programs effectively deny non-English-speaking students an equal education. The Court agreed that such systems violate the 1964 Civil Rights Act. Although remedies were not specified by the Court, the Department of Health, Education, and Welfare subsequently issued guidelines for corrective actions, including bilingual instruction and teaching English as a second language. Generally, school districts with at least 20 children of the same language group must institute bilingual programs (Grosjean 1982:73–74).

Bilingual projects are concentrated in California, New York, and Texas, but most states and US trust territories participate in some ways to satisfy legal requirements for educating children whose native language is not English. California has the major share (41 percent) of the nation's schoolchildren whose primary home language is not English, followed by Texas (15 percent), New York (7 percent), Arizona (7 percent), and Florida (5 percent). Although most bilingual programs are geared for speakers of Spanish (80 percent), other languages include French; Greek; Yiddish; Haitian Creole; Armenian; Japanese; Vietnamese; Chinese; Ilocano (of the Philippines); and several Native American languages such as Navajo, Apache, Algonkian, Ojibwa, and Oneida (US Department of Education 1990).

These programs enable many children with limited English proficiency to benefit from schooling. However, they do not reach the majority of children who need them. Grosjean reports that 3.6 million children are eligible but that less than 40 percent receive bilingual education (Grosjean 1982:78). Reasons for the discrepancy between needs and services include lack of adequate funding, low priority given to these programs by some states and local districts, and the possibility that the number of eligible children in any one school does not reach the required threshold of 20. In the last decade, some states have passed legislation or ballot initiatives that limit or terminate funding for bilingual education. Some of these regulations mandate a different type of approach. For example, in Massachusetts, bilingual education has been replaced by English immersion strategies.

Debates continue among professionals and the public about the effectiveness of bilingual education. Detractors claim that it is unnecessary, that children will learn by being "immersed" in a second language (English), and/or that it is harmful to their educational advancement. In contrast, supporters cite advantages to a minority child's self-esteem by recognizing the worthiness of her or his language and culture. They also point to numerous studies that demonstrate enhanced learning not only of English, but also of other academic subjects by students in bilingual programs.

Research by Beverly McConnell (1985) among children of migrant Mexican workers in two parallel bilingual programs showed that bilingual schooling aids learning abilities. One school was located in southern Texas and the other in Washington State. Both programs, beginning in preschool and extending through third grade, include teaching math and oral and written Spanish and English. Although these programs are identical, the communities served are vastly different. In Texas, most extrafamilial contacts (e.g., in stores, churches, and through the media) are conducted in Spanish, whereas in Washington State, English dominates. McConnell compared achievement scores over a seven-year period of some 700 children in the two bilingual programs with similar groups of Spanish-speaking children in Washington who were in monolingual English classes and found significant differences in performance in all subjects. At the earliest ages, the Washington bilingual group acquired English vocabulary more rapidly than did the Texas group, but this distinction disappeared by age 7. A major finding was that children in either of the bilingual programs learned English vocabulary at a much faster rate than did the children educated monolingually in English. McConnell explained:

> When Spanish-speaking children enter a traditional classroom where the teacher does not understand Spanish, the children often become silent, and are not expected to respond by a teacher unable to communicate with them. Without practice they do

not learn either Spanish or English very fast. With a bilingual teacher, communication is never lost—what is said in Spanish is understood and responded to, and the teacher is able to help the child rephrase the question or comment into English so that there is more language practice in both languages and more active learning. The result is significantly greater learning of English by children in the bilingual program than for children from traditional, English immersion classrooms. (1985:205)

Children in Texas made greater improvements in their Spanish linguistic skills than did those in Washington, undoubtedly because their use of Spanish was reinforced in their homes and communities. These children demonstrated greater competence in math as well. McConnell suggested that, for the Washington children, "the process of language shift [away from their Spanish mother tongue to English] is somewhat detrimental to the learning of math" (ibid.:210).

Another study compared cognitive functioning of sixth-grade monolingual children in Pennsylvania with Spanish–English bilingual students in Texas (Kessler and Quinn 1985). The latter had been in bilingual programs through third grade and were fluent and literate in both Spanish and English. Carolyn Kessler and Mary Quinn devised an experiment to test children's ability to formulate their own scientific hypotheses after viewing films dealing with science problems. Both the monolingual and bilingual children were divided into two groups, an experimental and a control. Those in experimental groups were taught to distinguish between types of scientific hypotheses, for example, differences between explanations such as "Magic did it" and "I could test my idea by putting several little bottles with different amounts of water in them in a tub and then see which ones would sink." Children in control groups were not given overt instruction of this sort. All students were told to devise hypotheses to explain the science problems they had seen on film. Although both experimental groups formed much more complex hypotheses than did the control groups, bilingual children far surpassed monolinguals. Based on a standardized rating system, the mean for the monolingual experimental group was 53.3, but for bilinguals, it was 176.0 (ibid.:289–290).

Kessler and Quinn relate bilingual children's achievement to superior cognitive functioning. They contend, along with other researchers, that "bilingual children have a cognitive flexibility and a more diversified set of mental abilities than monolinguals" (ibid.:283). Consistent with the notion that intellectual development is triggered by exposure to "discrepant events," "bilingualism presents an additional element of conflict within the linguistic environment since the child must adapt to two languages. In learning to manipulate language structures, the child may develop a general cognitive skill useful in other domains." Finally, "it may be that certain relevant aspects of the problem situations may be brought to the bilingual child's attention by the availability of two different linguistic perspectives" (ibid.:285–286). This conclusion is compatible with Sapirian–Whorfian insights about relationships between language systems and thought processes. Monolinguals speak and therefore think primarily within frameworks provided by a single language, whereas bilinguals inherently have at their ready disposal a wider range of alternative linguistic and cognitive options.

A small number of schools in the United States are dedicated to achieving two-way bilingualism: teaching English to children from non-English-dominant homes and teaching Spanish to English-speaking children. The Oyster Bilingual School in Washington, DC, has the oldest such program. The school's population represents more than 25 countries and is racially and ethnically diverse: 58 percent Hispanic, 26 percent white, 12 percent African American, and 4 percent Asian (Freeman 1996:558). Although the two-way language program is successful in teaching children both English and Spanish, the ways in which children employ the languages differ. They are more likely to switch from Spanish to English than from English to Spanish. The fluency of Spanish-dominant students in English is better than that of English-dominant students in Spanish. These facts indicate an English orientation that underlies the school culture, obviously reflecting societal values and norms.

Recent Trends in the Law

Laws protecting the rights of linguistic minorities affect several societal areas in addition to education. In 1975, Congress passed voting rights amendments containing provisions that mandate distribution of information for registering and voting in languages of minority ethnicities if these people make up at least 5 percent of the voting age population in a district (Rubin 1985:144). In 1978, Congress passed the Court Interpreter's Act to provide court interpreters in cases where defendants, plaintiffs, and/or witnesses "speak only or primarily a language other than English" (quoted in Rubin 1985:136). Deaf people who use American Sign Language are also protected by this act, guaranteeing them the services of an interpreter in court proceedings in which they are a witness, defendant, or party to a dispute (*Gallaudet University Encyclopedia of Deaf People and Deafness* 1987:212). The act sets guidelines for determining and certifying the qualifications of bilingual interpreters.

Numerous federal and state agencies have also instituted policies to help non-English speakers and people with limited English proficiency avail themselves of public services. For example, the New York City Department of Social Services hires bilingual workers to aid clients who apply for welfare benefits. In the health field, the California Department of Health Services recommends dissemination of bilingual material concerning hospital procedures. And the US Department of Labor regulates provision of bilingual services to people seeking unemployment compensation (ibid.:146, 138).

Although these laws and administrative regulations safeguard the rights of citizens and residents who lack full English proficiency, efforts began in the 1980s to reverse these protections. In 1981, a constitutional amendment was introduced to make English the nation's official language, but it has not been enacted despite repeated reintroductions in both the House and Senate (Baron 1990). Working in the legislative forum, in 1996 the House of Representatives passed the Language in Government Act (HR-123) that would mandate the use of English by "all employees and officials of the Government of the United States while performing official business" (quoted in Hornberger 1998:446–447). The legislation has not become law, however, because of its repeated failure to be enacted by the Senate. In the words of one former senator, Paul Simon of Illinois, it is a "not very subtle symbolic attack" on Hispanic and Asian Americans (ibid.:447). Using local strategies, numerous states, either through legislatures or voter referenda, have passed laws that establish English as the official language of the state and do not allow use of public monies to prepare; print; or distribute information, forms, or brochures in languages other than English. Regulations favoring English in some manner are in force in 27 states, dispersed throughout the country. Many of these are states with relatively small immigrant populations (Kentucky, Mississippi, Nebraska), but others have high proportions of foreign-born residents (California, Hawaii, Illinois, Florida).

In California, voters approved a ballot initiative in 1998, called Proposition 227, that aims to reverse bilingual education policies. Under the plan, "nearly all" bilingual classes must be conducted in English rather than in the children's native language, usually Spanish. However, the law does not define what "nearly all" means, so school districts have interpreted the plan in diverse ways. Some districts use a formula of 20 percent Spanish/80 percent English, others use a 30–70 percent formula, and some have classes taught 40 percent in Spanish and 60 percent in

English (*The New York Times* 1998). In any case, only about 30 percent of foreign-language-speaking children are actually enrolled in bilingual programs because of the scarcity of qualified teachers.

The diversity of policies and attitudes concerning language and multilingualism indicates the complexity of these issues. Unfortunately, the facts of language use in the United States are often obscured or even ignored in the debate. While 18 percent of Americans either speak a language other than English or live in a household where one is spoken, more than 92 percent of all US residents speak English with no difficulty. And about 90 percent of Americans are monolingual speakers of English (Baron 1990:177). Despite the rhetoric that arouses totally unfounded fears of the future shrinkage of English use, fewer US residents do not speak English today than at the beginning of the nineteenth century. The shift to greater English dominance currently than in the past can be accounted for by gains in educational achievement and by the decline in the proportion of immigrants to the total population. That is, while the proportion of foreign-born residents was 14 percent in 1920, it was 12.6 percent in 2007 (US Census Bureau, American Community Survey Reports 2010).

Residents of the United States who speak English with a foreign accent sometimes face difficulties in the workplace that might include outright discrimination. People who believe they have been discriminated against because of their accent have recourse to sue in court under Title VII of the Civil Rights Act of 1964, which outlawed discrimination on the basis of race, color, religion, sex, or national origin. And in 1988, national origin discrimination was extended to include denial of equal employment opportunity because "an individual has the physical, cultural or linguistic characteristics of a national origin group" (US Equal Employment Opportunity Commission 1988:1606.1). Despite this broad protection, however, employers have some discretion about the extent to which a person's accent interferes with job performance. The settlement of cases involves three phases. First, the plaintiff who seeks redress must prove that she or he was qualified for the job for which she or he applied, that she or he was rejected in spite of her or his qualifications, and that the employer continued to seek applicants. Second, the employer needs to offer a rebuttal giving a legitimate, nondiscriminatory reason for rejecting the applicant. And third, the plaintiff needs to show that the employer's stated reasons are merely pretexts for discrimination (Lippi-Green 1997:154).

In a review of 25 cases that centered on language-based discrimination from federal and state courts, Lippi-Green found that the issues at stake are often confused by conflicting claims of personal judgments about intelligibility and appropriateness. The scope of the problem is indicated by a report of the federal General Accountability Office (GAO) finding that about 10 percent of their sample (or 461,000) companies "openly, if naïvely, admit that they discriminated on the basis of a person's foreign appearance or accent" (quoted in Lippi-Green 1997:157). The burden of proof generally rests more heavily with the plaintiff in part because judges and juries accept standard language ideologies that privilege English spoken with a standard or prestige accent. These ideologies are so thoroughly naturalized that people are unaware of the biases that discriminate against foreign or other stigmatized speakers. For instance, in a case brought by an employee of a radio station, a native speaker of English who speaks with a Hawaiian Creole accent, "the judge discounted the testimony of the linguist who stated that Hawaiian Creole pronunciation is not incorrect, rather it is one of the many varieties of pronunciation of standard English. The linguist, the judge stated, was not an expert in speech" (Lippi-Green 1997:160). Of the 25 cases brought to trial since 1972, the plaintiff suing on the basis of language-related discrimination won in only seven instances. Of these, two were speakers of AAVE. The others were immigrants, one each from Poland, India, the Philippines, Cambodia, and Korea. Plaintiffs who lost their cases came from Asia (six), the Caribbean (three), South America (two), Eastern

Europe (two), and Africa (three). A final losing plaintiff was a Native Hawaiian (ibid.:156). It is interesting to note that winning plaintiffs came from countries in Asia and Eastern Europe, while no immigrant from Africa or the African diaspora won their case except the two African Americans. These data confirm by both supporting and deepening language attitudes derived from social stereotypes and stigmatization.

Native American Languages

Many speakers of non-English languages come from communities that have resided in this nation for decades or centuries. In the case of Native Americans, their ancestors have lived here for millennia. Analysis of 2000 census data indicates that some 361,000 Native Americans speak an indigenous language as their mother tongue. Native American speakers of indigenous languages represent numerous linguistic families. Some languages are currently spoken by only a small number of people, whereas others are well represented. Navajo, the largest, has about 150,000 speakers. According to federal statistics, the following linguistic families have at least 10,000 speakers: Algonkian, 48,000; Athabaskan (non-Navajo), 17,000; Iroquoian, 17,500; Muskogean, 16,500; Uto-Aztecan, 30,000; and Siouan, 28,000.

Figures available from the 2000 US Census also report the number of people speaking a Native language at home (note that others may be speakers of indigenous languages but do not use the language "at home"). By far the most frequently spoken language is Navajo (148,530 people reporting it as their home language). Other languages with more than 10,000 speakers include Dakota/Lakhota, Yupik, Apache, Cherokee, and Pima and Papago. Those with between 5,000 and 10,000 speakers are Choctaw and Chickasaw, Keres, Zuni, Muskogee/Creek, Hopi, and Ojibwa. In addition, some 17,000 respondents reported their home language as "Indian" or "American Indian." And approximately 10,000 people stated that they were monolingual speakers of an indigenous language.

The linguistic needs of Native American children are addressed by several federal laws, including the Bilingual Education Act of 1968, amended specifically for Native Americans in 1972 as the Indian Education Act. This law provides funds for programs serving Native American communities (Spolsky 1977:59). Extension of the Bilingual Education Act in 1979–1980 also benefits Native Americans even if they do not speak their tribal language.

Various reservations have developed educational programs designed to meet their specific needs. Some groups accept a transitional model advocated by the federal government. Among the Northern Cheyenne, Choctaw, Ute, and Zuni, bilingual programs seek to teach students English in early grades and switch exclusively to English in third grade. Other Native American peoples employ a maintenance model of bilingual education, stressing acquisition of skills in English while simultaneously developing literacy and fluency in their indigenous language. For example, the Navajo, Yupik, and Cree continue instruction in their native language in elementary school (ibid.:65). In addition, Navajo is spoken in community colleges on the reservation. For groups whose native language is no longer spoken as a first language, linguistic programs aim at revival, usually in conjunction with instruction in other aspects of traditional culture.

In an important statement of policy, the US Congress in 1990 recognized the importance of languages to the continuation of distinctive Native American cultural identity. The Native American Languages Act (PL 101–477) states:

> The status of the cultures and languages of Native Americans is unique and the
> United States has the responsibility to act together with Native Americans to ensure

the survival of these unique cultures and languages. The traditional languages of Native Americans are an integral part of their cultures and identities and form the basic medium for the transmission, and thus survival, of Native American cultures, literatures, histories, religions, political institutions, and values.

In addition to generally encouraging use of Native American languages, the act specifically endorses use of these codes as "mediums of instruction in order to encourage and support Native American language survival and educational opportunities, increase student success and performance, increase student awareness and knowledge of their culture and history and increase student and community pride."

Efforts to protect and promote the use of Native American languages are especially critical, given the fact that many of these languages have few speakers at this time. The paucity of speakers has resulted from many factors, not the least of which was the federal government's policies, lasting from the nineteenth until the middle of the twentieth century, that banned the use of Native American languages in schools and dormitories for Native American children. Officials targeted the maintenance of indigenous languages as impediments to the "assimilation" of Indians into American society. The government, in collusion with missionaries and secular teachers, established boarding schools for Native American children in order to separate children from their families and break their emotional and cultural ties with their communities. In the words of John Atkins, Indian commissioner in 1887, "The instruction of Indians in the vernacular is not only of no use to them, but is detrimental to the cause of their education and civilization, and no school will be permitted on the reservations in which the English language is not exclusively taught" (Commissioner of Indian Affairs 1887:xxii).

Strong social and political pressures have been exerted for centuries to compel Native Americans to abandon their traditional cultures. In addition to forcing children to speak English, American authorities had two important goals: (1) They wanted Indians to abandon traditional religious beliefs and practices and convert to Christianity, and (2) governments wanted to indoctrinate Native American children into sharing American values and finally acquiesce to American authority and control. As a result of decades of such pressures, many Native American languages were forgotten. And many of those still spoken today have uncertain futures even though the direct assault on them has ended. Of course, some remain strong, especially Navajo (in the Southwest), Inuit-Inupiat (in Arctic Canada and Alaska), Cree (in subarctic Canada), and Lakhota (in the Great Plains), among others. In the context of the history of US (and Canadian) policy toward Native American languages, the recent statement by Congress is most welcome, although its practical effect is yet to be seen.

Creole Languages in the United States

Three unique languages developed in the United States in the past several hundred years. These are Gullah (spoken mostly on the Sea Islands off the coast of South Carolina), Louisiana Creole, and Hawaiian Creole. As are all **creoles**, these languages are amalgams of sounds, grammatical forms, and vocabularies from several linguistic sources. Creoles arise in contact situations where speakers of different languages interact and need to develop a mutually intelligible code. Gullah and Louisiana Creole are derived from various African languages and English or French, respectively. Hawaiian Creole is a complex mixture of English, Native Hawaiian, and several Asian and Pacific languages.

FIGURE 11.3   Coastal South Carolina and Georgia. (Nichols, Patricia 1981:72. Creoles of the USA. In *Language in the USA,* ed. C. Ferguson and S. Heath. New York: Cambridge University Press, pp. 71–91.)

GULLAH.   Gullah is spoken by possibly as many as 300,000 people on the Sea Islands and along the mainland Atlantic coast from southern North Carolina to northern Florida. Most speakers of Gullah are descendants of Africans whose languages contributed to this creole. Figure 11.3 depicts the relevant area.

Gullah changed significantly in the twentieth century because of increasing contact with speakers of standard English and southern regional dialects. As English elements have been incorporated into Gullah, many creole features have become attenuated. Although no "pure" Gullah speakers remain, the language retains many distinct forms and rules, differing considerably from standard English. The following sample of Gullah is taken from the speech of a 9-year-old girl (Nichols 1981:74). The text is written in standard English orthography, with added underlining of distinctive Gullah traits:

When Christmas come I had gone to my Aunt house. Then my aunt say have to beat my little sister 'cause she had, she had broke a glass, with the cocoa in um. And then we had gone up to we other cousin house name. And then we had see-then we-then that night we had gone up to Jerome. Then when we <u>come</u> from there, the dog had come and <u>bite</u> my little sister and my little sister <u>say</u>, "Owww, Ooooo." And then <u>ee</u> say, "Unnn." And then she-and then after that-Monday, we-I had gone to my <u>aunt</u> house <u>fuh</u> see my baby sister. And then we had gone and <u>play</u>. And then I <u>had ride</u> her bicycle. And she bicycle had broke. And say, "Oh, see what you <u>done do</u>; broke that <u>girl</u> bicycle."

I <u>say</u>, "I ain't do <u>um</u>; you do <u>um</u> 'cause you want me <u>fuh tote</u> you."

Characteristic grammatical features of Gullah include the following (unless otherwise specified, examples are from ibid.:74–75):

1. Third-person subject pronouns are not distinguished for gender. The original Gullah form for all third-person singular subjects was *ee, /i/.* Among some speakers there is a tendency now to include aspiration /hi/, but its occurrence is unstable. Some speakers employ the standard feminine pronoun /ši/ ("she"), using it contrastively with /i/ or /hi/ for masculine and neuter subjects. This pattern, too, is currently unstable (Jones-Jackson 1984:355). In the sample above, for example, the girl uses both *she* and *ee* as pronouns for female subjects.
2. The third-person possessive pronoun *ee /i/* is used for all three genders (masculine, feminine, neuter). Again, variation is found, with use of /i/ or /ši/ for feminine possessors, and occasional adoption of standard "her." Examples are "he took *ee* mother long with um" (his); "but I ain't see *she*" (her). Also note in the quoted story: "And then I had ride *her* bicycle. And *she* bicycle had broke."
3. The third-person objective case pronoun is *um /ʌm/* for all three genders: "but I ain't see she fuh tell *um* nothing" (her); "I ain't know fuh get *um* off" (it). Current variation includes /ši/ for feminines: "but I ain't see *she*" (her); "she took *she* time for get here" (ibid.:358).
4. Nouns are not inflected for possession; for example, in the girl's story: "I had gone to my *aunt* house." Similarly, plural objects are not marked for number, for example: "There was this big snake with two horn."
5. Simple past tense is usually not marked: "Then my aunt *say* have to beat my little sister."
6. Several verbal aspects are overtly marked:
   a. Habitual: "This summer, when my daddy *be working,* they always have lot of peaches."
   b. Progressive, marked by *duh:* "Gregg *duh* hide."
   c. Perfective, marked by *done:* "I *done* know."
7. Clauses with infinitive verbs are introduced by *fuh,* as in "I come *fuh* get my coat" or in the narrator's "you do um 'cause you want me *fuh* tote you."
8. Embedded sentences are introduced by sε, as in the following excerpt quoted by Dreyfuss (1978:66) from Lorenzo Turner's transcription of Gullah (1949:211): /dεn di čI/εn dε In nyu yak s ε n wʌd sε de ẽ gain gIt nʌtn/ "Then the children in New York sent word <u>that</u> they weren't going to get anything."

Gullah's distinctive grammatical features are similar to those of several West African languages. For instance, just as Gullah does not mark gender differences, neither do Yoruba, Igbo, and Efik (Jones-Jackson 1978:426). Unlike English, West African languages contain highly developed aspectual systems, a characteristic also found in Gullah. Finally, the particle sε occurs with identical functions in Gullah and some West African languages such as Twi (Dreyfuss 1978:66). (On a comparative note, recall that sε appears in Jamaican English or patois spoken by people of Jamaican descent in Great Britain; see Chapter 13.)

Gullah's inventory of sounds is similar to that of English, but it contains some distinctive elements:

1. Gullah replaces English interdental fricatives /Ø/ and /ð/ with corresponding alveolar stops /t/ and /d/, respectively (Jones-Jackson 1978:427–428).
2. Gullah contains bilabial fricatives /Ø/ and /B/. Voiceless /Φ/ appears in place of English labiodental /f/, whereas voiced /B/ replaces English labiodental /v/ and bilabials /b/ and /w/. Bilabial fricatives do not occur in standard English, although they are common sounds in West African languages (ibid.:427).
3. Vowels /i/, /e/, /o/, and /u/ are monothongs in Gullah, whereas they are diphthongs in English, that is, /iy/, /ey/, /ow/, and /uw/ (Dreyfuss 1978:66).

Although Gullah vocabulary is primarily derived from English, Turner reported some 250 words in Gullah that originated from 20 West African languages (Dreyfuss 1978:65; Turner 1949). The following examples were recorded in Jones-Jackson's study of Gullah in the 1970s (1978:425–426).

Gullah	English	Source Language
gulu	pig	gula "pig, hog" (Kongo)
guba	peanut	ŋguba "peanut" (Kimbunda)
gɔmbo	okra	tšiⁱŋgɔmbɔ "okra" (Tshiluba)
jiga	small flea	ɟiga "insect" (Wolof)
nansi	spider	anansi "spider" (Twi)
tot	to carry	tota "to pick up" (Kikongo)
cikabod	a see-saw	cika "to lift" (Mandingo)
hudu	bad luck	húždužba "to arouse resentment" (Hausa)

LOUISIANA CREOLE.   Louisiana Creole is derived from French and from African languages spoken by slaves brought to the area principally from West Africa. Creole coexists today with two varieties of French; a rarely spoken dialect descended from the speech of colonial settlers; and a widely used Acadian, or "Cajun," dialect originating with eighteenth-century émigrés from Nova Scotia. Regional and standard English are now spoken in Louisiana as well. The number of creole speakers is unknown, but estimates of 80,000 have been suggested (Dreyfuss 1978:67). Most speakers of creole are African American, although many whites also speak the language. Speakers of creole are often bilingual in Cajun French or multilingual speakers of Cajun, standard French, and/or English. As expected in a situation of such constant contact, changes in all these varieties have taken place.

Distinctive traits of Louisiana Creole include the following (examples compiled from Dreyfuss 1978:68–70 and Nichols 1981:79–80):

1. Replacement of standard French rounded front vowels by unrounded vowels:

French				Creole	
ü	fumer	/fümé/	→	i /fimé/	"to smoke"
ɔ̈	seul	/sɔ̈l/	→	ɛ/sɛl/	"alone; only"
ö	peu	/pö/	→	e/pe/	"a little"

2. Use of feminine definite article *la* for all nouns, including nouns that are masculine in standard French. Definite articles either follow or precede their nouns in creole, whereas they always precede in standard French:

Creole	French	
Fɔm-la	la femme	"the woman"
la-kɔrd	la corde	"the string"
ti-košõ-la	le petit cochon	"the little pig"

3. Gender is not distinguished for third-person subjects, both marked by the pronoun *li*:
Li vini pu-mõte ãho-là.
She/he managed to climb up there.

4. Standard third-person plural pronouns *ils/elles* ("they" masculine/feminine) are replaced by *ye. Ye* also occurs following nouns to mark plurality:
Creole: /sa fɛ trwa lapɛ̃-*ye* ki muri. m-alɛ šarše *ye*/
French orthography: ça fait troit lapin-*ye* qui mouri. Moi aller chercher *ye*
"That makes three rabbits who are dead. I'll go look for *them*."

5. Tense is not marked on verbs. Particles indicating aspects precede verbs:

mo fini	"I finish, I finished, I will finish"
mo te-fini	"I have finished" (completive)
m-ape-fini	"I am finishing" (progressive)
m-ape-kupe	"I am running" (progressive)
mo te-pe kupe	"I was running" (progressive)
m-ale-kupe	"I will run"

6. Embedded sentences are introduced by sɛ (note the similarity to Gullah):
Creole: /buki tɛ krwa sɛ ɛ̃ nɔt lapɛ̃/
French orthography: Bouki te croire <u>se</u> un autre lapin.
"Bouki believed that it was another rabbit."

Due to multilingualism and dialect mixing in Louisiana, creole has had an impact on local varieties of English. The following constructions in English are derived from Louisiana Creole (Marshall 1982:314–315):

1. Omission of tense markers:
He come and see you. (past)
  She expect in September. (present)
2. Omission of noun plurals:
sixty-two stitch
  in other word
3. In interrogative sentences, the auxiliary "do" (or "did") is not included:
How she write dat?
  What he used to do?
4. Shifts in meaning (translations of creole constructions):
I made $200 worth of damage. (from creole/French *faire* "to make, do")
What he used to do for a life?
  She remarried back.

HAWAIIAN CREOLE Hawaiian Creole is one of many languages spoken in Hawaii. The complex linguistic situation in that state is a result of contact among indigenous Hawaiians; American colonizers; and Asian, Pacific, and European immigrant workers. American colonization of the Hawaiian Islands began in the late eighteenth century and intensified in the nineteenth. The Hawaiian monarchy was overthrown in 1893, and the territory was annexed by the United States in 1898. During this era, American plantation owners and traders brought in workers from many countries, principally China, Japan, the Philippines, and Portugal. In this multilingual context, a Hawaiian pidgin language developed for use among workers, merchants, and residents of diverse linguistic backgrounds (Sato 1985:255–258).

Pidgins are similar to creoles in their origin, arising in contact situations among speakers of varied languages. The difference is that pidgins have simplified grammatical structures and a limited vocabulary, containing primarily those words necessary to carry on restricted conversations between people who interact in specific contexts, as in work or trade. Pidgins are not first languages of any speaker but are acquired for use with limited functions. Pidgins sometimes eventually develop into creoles, that is, full languages, through expansion of grammatical elements and vocabulary. The creoles can be learned as first languages by children, possibly beginning with offspring of interethnic marriages. Such a potential situation arose in Hawaii and probably accounts for the origin of Hawaiian Creole (ibid.:261).

Creole is currently spoken by about 600,000 of the 1,285,000 residents of the state, or nearly half of Hawaiians. Most speakers are bi- or multilingual, speaking variants along a creole-standard continuum.

Distinctive traits of Hawaiian Creole include the following (examples compiled from ibid.:85–86; Dreyfuss 1978:72):

1. Absence of definite articles. Indefinite article is expressed as *wan*:
   I go see *wan* movies. (I went to see a movie.)
2. Past tense is either not marked or signaled by *wen* preceding a verb:
   My cousin go. (past)
      I *wɛn* go climb up when I was *wan* baby. (I climbed up when I was a baby.)
3. "Neutralization" or elimination of past-tense markers occurs in two syntactic contexts (Day 1973:307–308):
   a. In sentences containing multiple past-tense verbs, only the first verb is marked; subsequent verbs are not marked:
      So he went down there and open the door and trying to drag the guy out.
   b. In sentences containing adverbs referring to past times, verbs are not marked for tense:
      In those days, when I get only one two baby I go with Papa all over. (In those days, when I had only one or two babies, I went with Papa all over.)
4. Future tense is signaled by *gon* preceding a verb:
   I *gon* see wan movie.
5. Progressive or habitual aspect is marked by *stay* preceding a verb:
   Us *stay* playing basketball over there.
6. Negation is marked by:
   a. *no* or *not* in nonpast tenses:
      I *not* joking.
   b. *never* in past tense:
      He *never* go. (He didn't go.)
7. Clauses with infinitive verbs are introduced by *for*:
   Ask him *for* iron my shirt.

The following passage illustrates many features of Hawaiian Creole. It was spoken by a 45-year-old man who resided on one of the most remote islands in the chain.

/luk nau, a bin go si Toni abaut go spansa da kidz, ae, da b skitbawl tim, da wan ai ste koch fo—ai tel, e. Toni, hauz abaut, a, spansa da kidz, boi, yu no æfta awl iz awl Puhi kidz, yu no—æn awl as gaiz awl y unyen membaz, ae? a tel am yu—yu gaiz kæn spansa ada gaiz—ai no si wai yu gaiz no kæn spansa da kidz/

look-now, I-been-go-see-Tony-about-go-sponsor-the-kids, eh, the—basketball-team, the-one-I-stay-coach-for—I-tell, hey, Tony, how's-about, uh, sponsor-the-kids, boi. you-know-after-all-it's-all-Puhi-kids-you-know—and-all-us-guys-all-union-members, eh? I-tell-him-you—you-guys-can-sponsor-other-guys—I-no-see-why-you-guys-no-can-sponsor-the-kids

"Look now, I went to see Tony about [their] sponsoring the kids, eh, the basketball team that I'm coaching. I said, 'Hey, Tony, how about sponsoring the kids, boy? You know after all they're all Puhi [name of a town] kids, you know—and all of us [parents] are union members, eh?' I told him, 'You—you guys can sponsor other guys—I don't see why you can't sponsor the kids.'"(Sato 1985:262)

All three American creoles (Gullah, Louisiana, and Hawaiian) share certain structural similarities. Morphological complexities are minimal because of an absence of markers for plurality on nouns, gender on pronouns, and tense on verbs. Aspectual distinctions, however, are well developed.

In all three speech communities, speakers of creoles are rarely, if ever, monolingual. They employ various dialects and/or languages on a continuum, from heavily creolized to regional standards. Speakers of creoles tend to be among the poorest, least educated sectors of their communities, usually living in rural or isolated regions. Because of a combination of their class, limited education, and often race, and influenced by dominant societal attitudes favoring standard English, these speakers are generally stigmatized. Their language is denigrated as ungrammatical or incorrect. Needs of creole-speaking children in schools are ignored; they are expected to learn standard English with no special instruction in bilingual programs. Negative stereotypes no doubt contribute to the erosion of some distinctive characteristics of the creoles, yet they remain fully functional languages spoken by substantial numbers of people.

Summary

In all societies, some people speak more than one language. Multilingualism results from universal experiences of meeting and living with people of diverse linguistic and ethnic backgrounds. In modern nations, conflicts based on economic and/or political conditions often surface as conflicts over languages spoken by different groups. The language one speaks is an important aspect of individual identity and can be used to galvanize and focus group consciousness. We have examined aspects of these issues in India, Canada, and the United States, each having its own specific problems and outcomes.

In India, linguistic diversity reflects a complex history of uniting many distinct cultural groups into a modern political entity. In Canada, two large ethnic divisions compete for economic and political status. Multilingualism in the United States stems from past and present immigration. Immigrants have continually interacted with previously established communities, whether native or themselves descendants of prior immigrants.

Government policies in the United States have undergone historical changes regarding support or nonsupport of minority language rights. These policies, and public opinion, are still in flux and will undoubtedly continue to arouse controversy. But the fact remains that millions of people in the United States are speakers of languages other than English. Native-born and immigrant, monolingual and multilingual, all add to society's complexity and diversity.

References

ANISFELD, ELIZABETH, AND WALLACE LAMBERT. 1964. Evaluational reactions of bilingual and monolingual children to spoken languages. *Journal of Abnormal and Social Psychology* 69:89–97.

APTE, MAHADEV. 1976. Multilingualism in India and its socio-political implications: An overview. In *Language and Politics,* ed. W. O'Barr and J. O'Barr. The Hague: Mouton, pp. 141–164.

BARON, DENNIS. 1990. *The English-Only Question: An Official Language for Americans?* New Haven, CT: Yale University Press.

BOURHIS, RICHARD. 1985. The Charter of the French Language and crosscultural communication in Montreal. In *Conflict and Language Planning in Québec,* ed. R. Bourhis. Avon, England: Clevedon, pp. 174–204.

CENSUS OF INDIA. 2001.

COMMISSIONER OF INDIAN AFFAIRS. 1887. *Annual Report.* Washington, DC.

DASWANI, C. J. 1989. Aspects of modernization in Indian languages. In *Language Adaptation,* ed. F. Coulmas. New York: Cambridge University Press, pp. 79–89.

DAY, RICHARD. 1973. Tense neutralization in the Hawaiian post-creole gradatum. In *New Ways of Analyzing Variation in English,* ed. C. Bailey and R. Shuy. Washington, DC: Georgetown University Press, pp. 306–312.

DREYFUSS, GAIL. 1978. Pidgin and creole languages in the United States. In *A Pluralistic Nation,* ed. M. Lourie and N. Conklin. Rowley, MA: Newbury, pp. 61–77.

DUA, HANS. 1985. Sociolinguistic inequality and language problems of linguistic minorities in India. In *Language of Inequality,* ed. N. Wolfson and J. Manes. The Hague: Mouton, pp. 355–372.

ETHNOLOGUE. 2010. Languages of the World. Statistical Summaries by Area, by Country, http://www.ethnologue.com/ethno_docs/ distribution (accessed 6 May, 2010).

FISHMAN, JOSHUA. 1981. Language policy: Past, present and future. In *Language in the USA,* ed. C. Ferguson and S. Heath. New York: Cambridge University Press, pp. 516–526.

FREEMAN, REBECCA. 1996. Dual-language planning at Oyster Bilingual School: "It's much more than language." *TESOL Quarterly* 30:557–582.

Gallaudet University Encyclopedia of Deaf People and Deafness 1987. New York: McGraw-Hill, vol. I.

GILES, HOWARD, DONALD TAYLOR, AND RICHARD BOURHIS. 1973. Towards a theory of interpersonal accommodation through language: Some Canadian data. *Language in Society* 2:177–192.

GROSJEAN, FRANÇOIS. 1982. *Life with Two Languages.* Cambridge, MA: Harvard University Press.

HEALTH, SHIRLEY. 1977. Language and politics in the United States. In *Linguistics and Anthropology,* ed. M. Saville-Troike. Georgetown University Round Table on Languages and Linguistics. Washington, DC: Georgetown University Press, pp. 267–296.

HELLER, MONICA. 1985. Ethnic relations and language use in Montreal. In *Language of Inequality,* ed. N. Wolfson and J. Manes. The Hague: Mouton, pp. 75–90.

HORNBERGER, NANCY. 1998. Language policy, language education, language rights: Indigenous, immigrant, and international perspectives. *Language in Society* 27:439–458.

JONES-JACKSON, PATRICIA. 1978. Gullah: On the question of Afro-American language. *Anthropological Linguistics* 20:422–429.

JONES-JACKSON, PATRICIA. 1984. On decreolization and language death in Gullah. *Language in Society* 13:351–362.

KESSLER, CAROLYN, AND MARY QUINN. 1985. Positive effects of bilingualism on science problem-solving activities. In *Perspectives on Bilingualism and Bilingual Education,* ed. J. Alatis and J. Staczek.

Washington, DC: Georgetown University Press, pp. 283–296.

KIDDER, ROBERT. 1976. Language and litigation in South India. In *Language and Politics,* ed. W. O'Barr and J. O'Barr. The Hague: Mouton, pp. 235–251.

LAMBERT, WALLACE. 1967. A social psychology of bilingualism. *Journal of Social Issues* 23:91–109.

LAMBERT, WALLACE, R. C. HODGSON, R. C. GARDNER, AND S. FILLENBAUM. 1960. Evaluational reactions to spoken languages. *Journal of Abnormal and Social Psychology* 60:44–51.

LEAP, WILLIAM. 1986. American Indian English and its implications for bilingual education. In *Dialect and Language Variation,* ed. H. Allen and M. Linn. New York: Academic Press, pp. 591–603.

LIPPI-GREEN, ROSINA. 1997. *English with an Accent: Language, Ideology, and Discrimination in the United States.* London: Routledge.

MARSHALL, MARGARET. 1982. Bilingualism in southern Louisiana: A sociolinguistic analysis. *Anthropological Linguistics* 24:308–324.

McCONNELL, BEVERLY. 1985. Bilingual education and language shift. In *Spanish Language Use and Public Life in the US,* ed. L. Elias-Olivares et al. The Hague: Mouton, pp. 201–215.

MEISEL, JOHN. 1978. Values, language and politics in Canada. In *Advances in the Study of Societal Multilingualism,* ed. J. Fishman. The Hague: Mouton, pp. 665–717.

The New York Times, 1998. California bilingual teaching lives on after vote to kill it (Don Terry). October 3:A1, 7.

NICHOLS, PATRICIA. 1981. Creoles of the USA. In *Language in the USA,* ed. C. Ferguson and S. Heath. New York: Cambridge University Press, pp. 71–91.

RUBIN, JOAN. 1985. Spanish language planning in the US. In *Spanish Language Use and Public Life in the US,* ed. L. Elias-Olivares, E. A. Leone, R. Cisneros, and R. Gutierrez. The Hague: Mouton, pp. 133–152.

SATO, CHARLENE. 1985. Linguistic inequality in Hawaii: The post-creole dilemma. In *Language of Inequality,* ed. N. Wolfson and J. Manes. The Hague: Mouton, pp. 255–272.

SIMARD, LISE, DONALD TAYLOR, AND HOWARD GILES. 1976. Attribution processes and interpersonal accommodation in a bilingual setting. *Language and Speech* 19:374–387.

SOUTHWORTH, FRANKLIN. 1985. The social context of language standardization in India. In *Language of Inequality,* ed. N. Wolfson and J. Manes. The Hague: Mouton, pp. 225–239.

SPOLSKY, BERNARD. 1977. American Indian bilingual education. *International Journal of the Sociology of Language* 16:57–72.

SRIDHAR, S. N. 1988a. Language modernization: Structural and sociolinguistic aspects. In *Conference on the Basque Language.* Lisbon, Portugal, pp. 351–368.

SRIDHAR, S. N. 1988b. Language variation, attitudes and rivalry: Spread of Hindi in India. In *Language Spread,* ed. P. Lowenberg. Georgetown University Round Table in Languages and Linguistics 1987. Washington, DC: Georgetown University Press, pp. 300–319.

Statistics Canada. 2005. Ottawa.

Statistics Canada. 2010. Ottawa.

SUBRAMONIAM, V. I. 1977. A note on the preservation of the mother tongue in Kerala. In *Indian Bilingualism,* ed. P. G. Sharma and S. Kumar. Agra, India: Kendriya Hindi Sansthan, pp. 21–33.

TAYLOR, DONALD, AND LISE DUBE-SIMARD. 1985. Language planning and intergroup relations: Anglophone and francophone attitudes toward the Charter of the French Language. In *Conflict and Language Planning in Québec,* ed. R. Bourhis. Avon, England: Clevedon, pp. 148–173.

TURNER, LORENZO. 1949. *Africanisms in the Gullah Dialect.* Chicago, IL: University of Chicago Press.

US CENSUS BUREAU, AMERICAN COMMUNITY SURVEY REPORTS. 2010. Washington, DC: US Government Printing Office.

US DEPARTMENT OF EDUCATION. 1990. Office of Bilingual Education. Printout. Washington, DC: US Government Printing Office.

US EQUAL EMPLOYMENT OPPORTUNITY COMMISSION. 1988. Report. Washington, DC: US Government Printing Office.

VALLEE, FRANK, AND JOHN DE VRIES. 1978. Trends in bilingualism in Canada. In *Advances in the Study of Societal Multilingualism,* ed. J. Fishman. The Hague: Mouton, pp. 761–792.

ZENTELLA, ANA. 1997. *Growing up Bilingual.* London: Blackwell.

CHAPTER 12

Bilingual Communities

In the following two examples from the speech of bilinguals, the speakers combine elements from each of their two languages for stylistic and emphatic effect:

(Mother to child, using English and Spanish):
"Go sit down, go. SIEN-TA-TE (SIT DOWN)!"

(Father to child, using English and French):
"Now it's really time to get up. Lève-toi! (Get up.)"

These are two simple examples of the ways that bilinguals exploit the resources of their languages to convey thoughts and emotions. The speakers here are members of bilingual communities, one in the United States and the other in Canada. Bilingual communities exist throughout the world, wherever members of different ethnic groups meet, interact, and exchange ideas.

Contact between speakers of different languages has diverse linguistic and societal consequences. For people in contact situations to communicate, at least some of them must be bilingual. These bilinguals are often catalysts for language change. Exposure to different languages may lead bilingual speakers gradually to incorporate new linguistic material into their primary languages. Innovations eventually spread beyond bilingual communities so that new sounds, morphemes, and/or syntactic constructions can be incorporated into an indigenous system. In addition, words are often borrowed or old meanings adjusted because of influences from foreign sources. Over a period of time, languages can be altered as a result of linguistic and social contact.

In bilingual (or multilingual) communities, speakers develop strategies for use of their languages. They may restrict each language to particular contexts, participants, or topics. Each language then performs distinct situational or social functions. This division of roles can remain stable for centuries, or it can lead to shifts in statuses of languages spoken.

In this chapter, we begin by briefly reviewing recent research in understanding the cognitive processes involved in bilingualism. We then discuss a number of changes in languages derived from foreign cultural and linguistic influences. Next, we turn our attention to examining functional uses of and attitudes toward languages in bilingual communities. Finally, we discuss several conversational strategies used by bilinguals and some consequences of interlinguistic or interethnic communication.

COGNITIVE BENEFITS OF BILINGUALISM

As reviewed in Chapter 11, studies of bilingual schoolchildren indicate that bilingualism confers some advantages to learning beyond the knowledge of language itself. Although the bilingual brain has to do extra work in order to process linguistic data, both in encoding (to speak) and decoding (to understand), that extra work pays off in improved cognitive functioning. Bilinguals need to control their two languages in order to access data from their target language and at the same time avoid interference from their second language. Their ability to do so relies on what are called **cognitive control functions** or **executive functions**. These functions are defined as "mechanisms involved in conflict monitoring, planning, attentional control, and the suppression (inhibition) of habitual responses" (Kovacs and Mehler 2009: 6556). Recent studies have investigated cognitive processes in bilingual infants and in aging adults to see whether the onset of these cognitive advantages can be determined and to see whether they continue through adulthood.

Agnes Kovacs and Jacques Mehler (2009) developed an experimental design to study responses to auditory and visual cues by monolingual and bilingual infants at 7 months of age. A total of 40 infants were studied; 20 were monolingual and 20 were crib bilinguals, that is, infants who were exposed to two languages from their birth. The bilingual babies had two parents, each of whom spoke to them in their own (different) native language on a daily basis. All of the infants resided with their parents in Trieste, Italy, and were exposed to Italian. Their second languages varied considerably and included Spanish, English, Slovenian, French, Russian, Arabic, and Danish. The particular sets of languages had no bearing on the results.

The experiment consisted of two phases. In the first, called a preswitch, the infants were given an auditory cue of a three-syllable nonsense word followed by a visual reward, namely, a puppet appearing in a white square on one side of a computer screen. This phase consisted of nine trials in which the puppet always appeared on the same side of the screen. Monolingual and bilingual infants had no trouble learning to look at the correct side of the screen following the auditory cue in order to see the puppet. In the second postswitch phase, also consisting of nine trials, the puppet appeared in a white square on the opposite side of the screen. To see the puppet, the infants had to redirect their gaze. Correct learning was measured by anticipatory eye movements in the direction of the puppet. Results demonstrated that monolingual infants did not learn to look in the direction of the puppet but instead continued to look toward the side of the screen where the puppet had first appeared. In contrast, the bilingual infants changed their anticipation to the correct location of the new puppet. They were flexible in their cognitive processes and adjusted quickly to the new situation. These findings suggest that "a multilingual environment improves aspects of Executive Functions even in preverbal infants" (Kovacs and Mehler 2009: 6557).

Two additional variations on the experiment were conducted to test the effects of auditory and nonauditory cues, and both experiments led to the same conclusions; that is, bilingual infants were more adaptable in their cognitive processing and were able to adjust spontaneously to new cues and learn new responses, whereas the monolingual infants were unable to learn to redirect their gaze.

Because a bilingual's two languages are both active when speaking or listening to either one, they need to rely on cognitive executive functions to keep their two languages separate and to prevent interference. This reliance entails inhibitory controls that suppress data from the unwanted language. Evidence for this kind of processing comes from both behavioral studies and from brain imaging (Bialystok et al. 2009:93). Studies with adult bilinguals demonstrate that the cognitive advantages for executive functions continue throughout the lifespan. Findings from experiments comparing monolingual and lifelong bilingual adults in several tasks confirmed that, in fact, the advantages accruing to bilinguals increased with age (Bialystok et al. 2004). That is, although some cognitive functions performed by both monolinguals and bilinguals decrease with age, the decline is steeper for monolinguals, whereas bilinguals exhibit a slower rate of loss. It is important to note that the bilingual participants are lifelong speakers of two languages; that is, they learned their second language early in life and continued to use both languages throughout their lives.

For example, in one experiment, participants were asked to rapidly name colors when shown colored squares on a screen (the congruent condition), but then were asked to name the color of a word written on the screen in a different colored font than the color name (the incongruent condition). That is, the words *red, green, blue* were presented in different colors; for example, *red* was written in green ink. (Bialystok et al. 2009:99). Results showed that there was no difference in the timed responses of monolingual and bilingual participants when naming the colored squares in the congruent condition. However, there was a consistent significant advantage for bilinguals in the incongruent condition, that is, when naming the color word rather than the color in which the word was written. And indeed, this disparity increased with age.

This kind of evidence raises questions about the possible advantages that bilinguals have in forestalling age-related cognitive decline. Several studies of elderly monolinguals and bilinguals did indicate that bilinguals tend to have later onsets, by perhaps four or five years, of dementia and Alzheimer's than do monolinguals. And when they do suffer from Alzheimer's, bilinguals' cognitive decline is slower than that of monolinguals.

LINGUISTIC CHANGE

Languages change over time. Change sometimes results from processes internal to a language itself. For instance, a language may gradually eliminate case markers on nouns or reorder words within phrases. Evidence of such patterns can be found in the history of English. Old English had noun suffixes that indicated three genders (masculine, feminine, neuter) and four cases (nominative, genitive, dative, accusative), but Modern English nouns lack these markers.

Languages also change as a result of influences from other linguistic systems. All languages contain elements derived from other codes—a normal universal process because no language is a completely closed system. A few examples from English sounds, grammar, and vocabulary will suffice to illustrate this process.

The Modern English consonant /ž/ was not present in the sound system of Old English (or Anglo-Saxon). It is a sound derived from French, heard by eleventh-century inhabitants of the British Isles in the speech of Norman invaders after AD 1066. At first, when Anglo-Saxons borrowed French words, they replaced the foreign, and to them unpronounceable, /ž/ with their native sound /ǰ/. Compare the following French and English words written phonemically:

	English	French
just	ǰʌst	žüst
judge	ǰʌǰ	žüz
Jack	ǰæk	žak

The English consonant /ǰ/ replaced French /ž/ because it is the native sound closest to the French one. Both /ǰ/ and /ž/ are voiced, palatal consonants, although they differ in their manner of articulation: /ǰ/ is an affricate, whereas /ž/ is a fricative. As a result of centuries of contact between English and French speakers, the French /ž/ was eventually incorporated into the sound system of Modern English. It currently occurs in some words of recent French origin—for example, *lingerie* (/lãžeri/), *rouge* (/ruž/)—as well as in a few other words such as *pleasure* (/plɛžɣ/) and *casual* (/kæžual/).

French influence on English grammar occurs in some comparative and superlative adjectival constructions. Old English employed the suffixes -*er* and -*est* as in fair/fairer/fairest. Modeling on French *plus* ("more") and *le plus* ("most") is reflected in sets like beautiful/more beautiful/most beautiful.

Syntactic change is another possible result of linguistic contact. English syntax has been modified by Latin and French sources. G. L. Brook suggested that influence from Latin, and to a lesser extent from French, became particularly strong because these languages were important in British schooling. Because educators believed that Latin was a superior language, they used it as a model (1958:147–148). Examples of Latinate origin include use of infinitive verbs following accusative constructions, for example, "I know him to be a good person" or "I told her to arrive by noon." Grammarians also copied Latin structure in their opposition to ending sentences with prepositions. Brook noted the fact that John Dryden, a seventeenth-century writer, revised some of his own works to fit the preferred style, altering his original "the age I live in" to "the age in which I live" (ibid.:148).

Borrowing foreign words is the most widespread result of linguistic and cultural contact. Although rates of borrowing vary, all languages incorporate words of foreign origin. When new items or activities are introduced from other cultures, donors' labels for these entities or events are often added to native lexicons. Hundreds of words in Modern English are derived from Latin and French, the two most frequent sources. English has also borrowed words from dozens of other languages. The following list contains only a handful of **loanwords**, representing a variety of origins (collected from Pyles and Algeo 1982:297–316):

Source	Loanwords
Greek	agnostic, chlorine, idiosyncrasy, telephone
Irish Gaelic	brogue, leprechaun, shamrock
Scots Gaelic	clan, plaid, slogan, whiskey
Scandinavian	muggy, rug, ski
Spanish	bonanza, canyon, patio, ranch
Portuguese	albino, flamingo, molasses
Italian	balcony, bandit, studio, umbrella
Dutch	boss, cookie, pit (of fruit), sleigh
German	hamster, pretzel, semester
Yiddish	kibitzer, nebbish, phooey, schlep
Russian	czar, mammoth, tundra, vodka
Turkish	fez, tulip, turban
Arabic	candy, mattress, orange, sugar
Hebrew	cherub, hallelujah, jubilee, kosher

(continued)

Source	Loanwords
Persian	caravan, bazaar, shawl
Sanskrit	karma, yoga
Hindi	bungalow, dungaree, jungle, pajamas
Chinese	tea, kowtow, tycoon
Japanese	hara-kiri, samurai, soya
Pacific languages	bamboo, kangaroo, launch, tattoo
African languages	gorilla, jazz, tote, yam
Native North American languages	bayou, moccasin, moose, pecan
Native Central American languages	chocolate, maize, tomato, potato

In some cases, foreign words whose meanings are similar to native words are borrowed, but each takes on specialized usage. For example, indigenous Anglo-Saxon animal terms are now complemented by French words to refer to foods:

Animal	Food	French Source
steer	beef	boeuf
pig	pork	porc
calf	veal	veau
sheep	mutton	mouton
chicken	poultry	poulet

Foreign influences sometimes result in contrasting stylistic uses for native or borrowed words. In English, some words of French origin are considered more formal or polite than their Anglo-Saxon equivalents:

Anglo-Saxon Source	French Source
smell	odor
sweat	perspiration
eat	dine
dead	deceased
want	desire
look at	regard
go away	depart
come back	return

Processes of linguistic change can be easily and abundantly demonstrated in all languages of the world, although the locus and extent of modification vary depending on duration, context, and intensity of contact between speakers of different languages. Just as hundreds of English words are borrowed from foreign sources, other languages have loanwords from English. And just as English has modified foreign words to fit native phonological patterns, so other host languages have altered sounds of English words to fit their systems. A few examples are offered on page 321 to illustrate this process, with explanations of changes.

LANGUAGE USE IN BILINGUAL COMMUNITIES

In bilingual or multilingual communities, language ideologies may develop that privilege particular languages, granting them social value and legitimacy while at the same time marginalizing other languages. The privileged language or languages are perceived as complex, with regular rules of structure and elaborated meanings. In contrast, marginalized languages are perceived as simple, irregular, lacking in formal structure, and restricted in meanings. The use of both privileged and marginalized languages becomes associated with particular contexts and invokes distinct social and personal meanings. All of these beliefs arise out of specific social and historical contexts. The functional specialization of languages and related social attitudes may remain stable or they may result in shifts in linguistic preference, possibly even in the loss of one language entirely. In this section, we describe several examples of language use in bilingual communities. The cases discussed illustrate different sets of features and patterns of linguistic choice.

English Donor		**Host Language**		
Spelling	**Pronunciation**	**Language**	**Loanword**	**Change**
Roof	ruf	Spanish (Puerto Rico)	rufo	Add final vowel
Ginger beer	jɪnjɚ bir	Spanish (Costa Rica)	člnčlbi	Replace voiced /ǰ/ with voiceless /č/; delete syllable- final /r/
Police	pʌlíys	Swahili	polisi	Add final vowel
Car	kar	Swahili	kaa	Delete final /r/
Ruler	rulɚ	Ganda	luula	Replace initial /r/ with /l/
Railway	reylwey	Ganda	leerwe	Replace initial /r/ with /l/; replace medial /l/ following a front vowel with /r/
Thumbtacks	θʌmtæks	Mohawk	tamtaks	Replace fricative /θ/ with stop /t/
Matches	mæčlz	Mohawk	majis	Replace voiceless /č/ with voiced /ǰ/; replace voiced /z/ with voiceless /s/
Number	nʌmbɚ	Navajo	nóomba	Delete final /r/
Christmas	krɪsmls	Navajo	késmiš	Simplify initial consonant cluster; replace alveolar /s/ with palatal /š/
Elevator	ɛllveytor	Japanese	erebeta	Replace /l/ with /r/; replace /v/ with /b/; delete final /r/
Baseball	beysbɔl	Japanese	beisuboru	Add epenthetic vowel; replace /l/ with /r/; add final vowel
Casual	kæžual	Tagalog	kazwal	Replace /ž/ with /z/; simplify vowel cluster
Budget	bʌɛt	Tagalog	badyɛt	Replace affricate /ǰ/ with stop /d/ + glide /y/

Sources: Puerto Rican Spanish: Zentella (1985:45); Costa Rican Spanish: Appel and Muysken (1987:169); Ganda: Halle and Clements (1983:51); Mohawk: Bonvillain (1978:37); Navajo: Young and Morgan (1987:7); Swahili, Japanese: Berlitz (1982:299–300); and Tagalog: Molony (1977:141–142).

An **ethnography of communication** among bilinguals includes analysis of their choice of language in various speech events. Factors such as context, participant, topic, and goal influence bilinguals' decisions. For instance, two speakers of Spanish and English in the United States may converse at work in English but speak Spanish to each other on their way home. They may talk about a current international crisis in English but gossip about their neighbors in Spanish. And they may use Spanish to signal their mutual solidarity as members of an Hispanic ethnic group.

The term **diglossia** refers to situations where each language is systematically employed in certain domains or events. The term was introduced by Charles Ferguson to apply to circumstances where two varieties of the same language coexist in a community, for example, a national standard and a regional form; however, diglossia currently includes both bilingual and bidialectal conditions. Ferguson referred to the sets of contexts and values assigned to each language as high or low (1959:327). A **high language** is used in public arenas, such as school, church, and government. It has a long literary tradition and may be linked to prestigeful social groups. In contrast, a **low language** is used in private or informal domains with family and friends. It may have less social prestige than the high variety, but it is often associated with strong emotional loyalty and can be used to signal ingroup membership.

Bilingualism in Paraguay illustrates such divergent associations demarcating Spanish and Guarani, an indigenous language spoken by more than 90 percent of the population. Paraguay's 1967 constitution recognized Guarani and Spanish as "national" languages, although Spanish is given status as the "official" language. Nearly everyone living in rural areas speaks Guarani, but even in Paraguay's capital, Asuncion, 76 percent of the populace are bilingual. Monolingual Guarani speakers usually reside in rural villages, whereas monolingual Spanish speakers typically live in large cities (Rubin 1985:112).

Among bilinguals, who constitute the overwhelming majority of Paraguayans, a diglossic pattern is evident. According to Joan Rubin, four contextual factors influence a bilingual's choice of code: location of interaction, degree of formality, degree of intimacy, and seriousness of discourse (ibid.:116). In general, Spanish is the language of urban life and is used in formal situations such as speaking to officials, doctors, teachers, and others with whom a speaker is socially distant. Guarani predominates in rural areas but is spoken throughout Paraguay in interactions with family and friends, especially when conversing about informal or personal topics (ibid.:116–117).

Attitudes toward the two languages are somewhat contradictory, particularly regarding Guarani. Spanish has prestige because of its association with an international culture and an important literary tradition. Guarani is favorably perceived as a symbol of Paraguayan nationalism. But it is also sometimes disparaged as unsophisticated. For this reason, young men in the countryside reported that they try to use Spanish when initiating courtship, although couples tend to switch to Guarani when they become better acquainted (ibid.:117). Despite some negative attitudes toward Guarani, it is thought to be emotionally expressive. Rubin also noted that Paraguayans traveling abroad typically speak Guarani to each other "in order to establish their solidarity by the use of the more unusual and intimate language" (ibid.).

Patterns of language use in many African countries illustrate the coexistence of local tribal codes and international lingua francas, each assigned various communicative functions. A **lingua franca** is a language that is used by non-native speakers when interacting with speakers of different codes. It enables members of diverse ethnic and linguistic groups to communicate with one another. In many parts of Africa, an indigenous language, Swahili, has functioned for centuries as a lingua franca. During the era of European colonization in Africa, European languages, principally English and French, assumed roles as international and interethnic languages. Even though African nations are now independent, English and French often continue to function as codes for administration, business, advanced education, and elite discourse. Therefore, despite the small ethnic base of European languages in Africa, they are frequently employed in public domains.

In addition to the lingua francas, linguistic usage in Africa is complicated by the multitude of codes spoken within each nation. These languages are native to different indigenous ethnic or tribal groups, each of which uses its own code among co-members. The languages all maintain their vitality in a social context of ethnic diversity.

Linguistic choices are made on both the societal and interpersonal levels. Since independence from colonial rule, African governments have developed their own policies regarding language use in educational and administrative contexts. Kenya and Tanzania provide instructive contrasts in linguistic policies. The Tanzanian government recognizes Swahili as its official code, and it is used in all public domains, including schools and government institutions. Although it is not the first language of most Tanzanians, Swahili is a member of the Bantu linguistic family, as are the native codes of 90 percent of the population (Appel and Muysken 1987:56). Therefore, because of the linguistic similarities between Swahili and the vast majority of languages spoken in Tanzania, Swahili is acceptable as a lingua franca for use in public encounters and in interactions between people from different ethnic groups.

The government in Kenya also acknowledges Swahili as an official language, but in practice English is employed in many societal domains. English is the language of business, legal proceedings, and most government administration. The first three years of schooling are conducted in local native languages, but beginning in the fourth year, instruction is given in English (Zuengler 1985:244).

A critical difference between language policies in Tanzania and Kenya is the use of Swahili in Tanzanian schools and of English in Kenyan education. According to Jane Zuengler (1985), the Kenyan government chooses English because it wants to encourage a select minority to pursue advanced education and participate in economic development projects in conjunction with international business groups. In contrast, Tanzania selects Swahili because it wants the entire population to achieve an adequate level of literacy and education as preparation for either rural or urban employment (ibid.:246–248).

Language choices may play a critical role in national development strategies. As Wiseman Magwa and Davie Mutasa (2007: 59) suggest, an official language that is spoken only by a minority "will produce a wealthy few whilst a language shared by many should ensure greater productivity and fairer distribution" of a country's economic, political, and intellectual resources. If development is understood as processes of growth not only in economic terms but also in increases in literacy, education, and health-care services, then linguistic participation becomes crucial. A nation's people need to be able to participate in the dissemination of information about economic opportunities, political and judicial matters, and the provision of health-care and other social services. But linguistic barriers may cause an uneven and unequal distribution of such information.

Magwa and Mutasa argue that "a language can contribute to nation building" (2007:65) in several ways. National identity is fostered by the symbolic and emotional meanings transmitted through one's language, helping to create a linguistic shared community. In addition, the ability for people to communicate to all others in their country, voicing their opinions, attitudes, and needs, also contributes to the formation of a national consciousness.

When members of different ethnic groups interact, they must select an appropriate code. Choice of the tribal language of one participant obviously carries social messages concerning relative status, prestige, or authority. Because such messages can potentially lead to antagonism, interethnic interactions often take place through the medium of a neutral language. Carol Scotton's study of language usage in workplaces in the capitals of Kenya, Uganda, and Nigeria showed that, although co-workers may be multilingual and share one or more tribal languages, they often choose to speak a nontribal lingua franca as a "strategy of neutrality" (1976:919). In West Africa, English and/or pidgin English predominate as such languages, whereas in East Africa, Swahili is often selected. A neutral code is "nobody's language," so its use does not transmit messages of inequality between interlocutors. Speakers thus engage in "reciprocal accommodation" (ibid.:920) by implicitly recognizing the affront people may feel when their own code is disparaged.

Despite the use of English as a neutral language in public domains, attitudes toward it may be mixed. For instance, people who speak English with a British or American accent rather than with the local African accent may be resented because they are negatively viewed as "putting on airs" and flaunting their wealth and access to education abroad (Saah 1986:372).

New varieties of languages arise in multilingual contexts in some African cities, merging lexical, grammatical, and syntactic resources from local languages. These varieties may serve to unify people whose native tongues differ, enabling communication among people of many cultural and linguistic backgrounds. They may also serve to distinguish an ingroup familiar with the new and popular codes. Such a variety is Sheng, an innovative speech style used by mostly urban and mostly young speakers in Nairobi, the capital of Kenya. Sheng's major grammatical structure is based on Swahili, with some notable divergences (Githiora 2002). It also includes grammatical and lexical material from other Kenyan languages as well as from English. Sheng is reported to have arisen in a particular neighborhood (called Kaloleni) in the 1960s and spread from there to other areas of the city, even reaching rural communities outside the city. It started with young people, mostly identified as poor and unemployed or underemployed. Sheng then became perceived as a street language, spreading through contact among peers of similar age and social status. By the turn of the twenty-first century, Sheng had become an increasingly popular linguistic variety, spoken by many residents in their teens and twenties. Surveys of Nairobi revealed that more than 50 percent of male university students employ Sheng when speaking with their peers, and about 25 percent of the people interviewed, who were between the ages of 11 and 25, said that they use Sheng as their "principal language of solidarity" (Githiora 2002:160).

Although Sheng derives much of its phonological, morphological, and syntactic patterning from Swahili, there are some contrasts. Sheng rearranges the order of sounds in Swahili words: for example, Sheng *analaku* comes from Swahili *anakula* "s/he is eating," Sheng *fundi* comes from Swahili *ndifu* "handyman," and Sheng *mmoja* comes from Swahili *mjamo* "one person." And final syllables may be deleted, with a lengthening of the previous vowel: for example, Sheng *saa* comes from Swahili *sasa* "now," and Sheng *mii* comes from Swahili *mimi* "I."

Lexical borrowing, particularly from English, is a major feature of Sheng. Nouns, verbs, and modifiers may be borrowed and incorporated into Sheng's morphological structure. For example, *ku-dishu* "to eat" (from *dish*). *ku-kreki* "to go mad, crack up," *nibring-ie* "bring it to me," *ku-chill* "to chill out," *ku-kidi* "to kid, to joke," and *ku-piga stori* "to have a chat with friends" (from *story*).

Attitudes of Nairobi residents toward the use of Sheng vary, as one might expect, depending on age and class. Younger speakers, from their teens through their twenties, stress the positive aspects of this code, citing its novelty and association with popular culture. Because it is a language that incorporates elements from several African languages, Sheng is seen as a language of unity that does not favor or discriminate against any particular group. This is a significant feature for language in a multicultural country. In contrast, older speakers, and especially members of middle- and upper-class segments of society, report negative views about the use of Sheng. They consider Sheng to be ungrammatical, difficult if not impossible to understand, and reflective of lower-class street culture.

It will be interesting to see if Sheng remains predominantly a language of young people, spoken by youth and then abandoned as people mature, only to be taken up by the next cohort of young speakers. It may become even more widely spoken, however, if it is retained as people age, thereby increasing its usage in a growing linguistic community.

Language ideologies in Africa and in other postcolonial regions of the world can be viewed as outcomes of historical processes originating in the colonial era, when missionaries and government agents doubled as linguists studying indigenous languages in their work to convert native peoples to colonial religious and social policies. For instance, the language now known as Thonga or Tsonga, spoken in parts of eastern South Africa and Mozambique, was a creation of Swiss missionary-linguists in the late nineteenth century (Harries 1988). In particular, two linguists working for the Paris Missionary Society were perplexed by the variety of languages and dialects spoken by people then living in small communities in the eastern Transvaal. This was a region of great cultural and linguistic diversity due in part to stable communities of people who had lived in the region for generations and in part to an influx of refugees from other areas. Although the immigrants were not unified and had no particular linguistic or cultural ties, they were viewed by the indigenous people as similar and were identified as the outgroup. One of the names used to identify the immigrants was *Tonga,* a term with derogatory meanings (ibid.:30).

In the missionaries' attempt to expand their area of operation and to deepen their entrée into the African communities, they developed a writing system and standardized a language to be used in translating the Bible and other texts. The Swiss missionaries at that time referred to the language as Gwamba, a language that one of the priests described as "a fruit salad of Hlengwe, of Djonga, of Boer, of English, of Newaloungou, of Hlavi, of Venda, of Sotho" (quoted in Harries 1988:33). The language was disseminated among a disparate population from several regions in southeastern Mozambique, functioning as a lingua franca to facilitate intercommunication. At the same time that the missionaries were promulgating use of Gwamba as a common language, the indigenous communities themselves tended to emphasize their linguistic differences as a means of upholding cultural and territorial boundaries. By the late 1880s, the term *Gwamba* was replaced by the more commonly used *Thonga* (ibid.:35).

The next step in the process of creating a language was the Swiss linguists' delineation of dialect areas or zones. These zones were entirely constructed by the linguists themselves and did not reflect any linguistic facts. Instead, the zones functioned to categorize peoples whose actual ties and distinctions were fluid and changing. It was a process that had political meanings.

After and along with establishing Thonga as the dominant language, the missionaries developed a writing system and worked to standardize forms. The creation of a standardized and written form of Thonga was consistent with the goal of "modernization" that helped justify and legitimize the missionaries' presence. It also privileged this code and established it as distinct from languages spoken by illiterate pagans. By controlling written forms of Thonga, the missionaries were able to control the content of texts available to African readers. Literacy in Thonga became associated with people in power, privileging them and the language they spoke. African members of elite classes employed Thonga to facilitate their interactions with colonial agents, in the process adopting dominant and dominating linguistic and social ideologies. As one local chief remarked when shown a copy of a book, "Ah! This is the book they spoke about! Look after it. Thus we are conquered by this book alone!" (quoted in Harries 1988:45). Once Thonga was legitimated as the standard language, speakers of other languages also adopted it to participate in the new communicative networks being formed in the region. And as the language gained status, people began to self-identify as its speakers, stimulating the development of a new, historically based ethnic group.

In some countries, linguistic choices in bilingual communities indicate a clear, permanent shift away from a local language. For example, Susan Gal's (1978) research in an eastern Austrian province near Hungary uncovered a changing preference for German and away from Hungarian. Gal's study concentrated on the town of Oberwart (Felsoor in Hungarian), located in an area that was originally part of Hungary but has been in Austria since 1921, when boundaries were realigned after World War I. Following World War II, Oberwart became a county administrative and commercial center, populated by immigrant monolingual German speakers from Austria and an indigenous community of Hungarian/German bilinguals and Hungarian monolinguals. The latter two groups constitute approximately one-quarter of the town's more than 5,000 residents.

Austrians and Hungarians are differentiated economically and socially. Austrians tend to hold professional, administrative, and commercial positions. Hungarians were previously peasant farmers, but currently most are industrial workers (ibid.:3). Because of economic changes, Hungarian has become disparaged as the language of peasants, associated with a way of life that is now negatively perceived.

Gal found that several factors were reliable predictors of language choice among bilinguals in Oberwart, including speech situation, age and gender of the speaker, and the speaker's usual social networks. When conversing with doctors, government officials, and young people, most bilinguals chose German. When talking to parents and elders, most spoke Hungarian. Interactions with siblings and age mates varied, depending on the age of the speaker. Older people tended to speak Hungarian with familiars, whereas younger residents spoke German. Bilinguals who regularly associated with monolingual German speakers were more likely to use German in their encounters with other bilinguals than were those whose social networks consisted mainly of monolingual Hungarian peasants and farm workers (ibid.:6–7).

Gender was an important factor in shifts of language preference in Oberwart. Women and men made different linguistic choices based on differing economic alternatives. Although some young men continue to value peasant life, most young women reject it entirely. Farming retains some traditional prestige for a man and gives him economic independence, but for a woman it is burdensome and allows her little autonomy, given male-dominated gender relations in traditional farm households (ibid.:10). Young women therefore opt for industrial employment and/or marriage to industrial workers. Whereas farming families tend to be Hungarian monolinguals or Hungarian-dominant bilinguals, industrial workers and their families tend to be German speakers. Women therefore use the German language as a symbol of their social values. Shifts to German will no doubt become even stronger in the future because children in households with at least one German-speaking parent are always monolingual German speakers.

An additional possible social and linguistic configuration is exemplified by many Hispanic communities in the United States. Research among Puerto Ricans, for example, reveals several trends regarding use of and attitude toward Spanish and English. Studies in New York City indicate shifts toward English usage and simultaneous approval of Spanish maintenance (Pedraza 1985). In the community known as El Barrio (an area of 125 square blocks with a population of 175,000, approximately 60 percent of whom are Hispanic), age and length of residence are factors in language choice. Older people and recent immigrants continue to use Spanish in all or nearly all contexts. In contrast, second- and third-generation Puerto Ricans lose their ability to speak Spanish, although they may retain passive comprehension. But the community is united in strongly favoring acquisition of skills in both Spanish and English (ibid.:61, 63).

Although a shift toward English is discernible, the community as a whole remains solidly bilingual. This pattern results from a high level of individual bilingualism and from a continual influx of Hispanic immigrants. In communities in other parts of the United States where Hispanic people are not as heavily concentrated as in large urban centers, shifts toward English are more pronounced. For instance, among members of Hispanic groups living in Indiana, 46.2 percent report English as their best language, 35.4 percent claim to be equally fluent in both languages, and only 18.4 percent report Spanish as their best language. These figures contrast with statistics from New York City Hispanics, where 29.7 percent of a sample reported English as their best language, 39.6 percent were fluently bilingual, and 29.7 percent considered Spanish their dominant code (Attinasi 1985:45).

Even though the two communities differed in language usage, positive attitudes toward Spanish maintenance were just as strong in Indiana as in New York. In both areas, people recognize the value of Spanish as an indicator and symbol of ethnicity. Among Hispanics in Indiana, 98.5 percent believed that being bilingual is advantageous, 92.3 percent wanted Spanish to be maintained in their community, and 89.2 percent advocated bilingual education for their children (ibid.:49). These attitudes indicate robust continuation of Spanish in Hispanic communities even in the context of individual shifts to English dominance.

More recent research carried out among Puerto Ricans speakers in New York City indicated continuity of the two sets of attitudes and practices: approval of English as the language of advancement, and simultaneous adherence to Spanish as the language of personal and community identity (Zentella 1997). In this vibrant bilingual community, speakers' choice of language is constrained by setting and participants. That is, in certain settings, either Spanish or English may be required, and the presence of a monolingual Spanish or English speaker will trigger use of that language. Among bilinguals, speakers generally accommodate the dominant language of their co-participant. Children and young adults are especially likely to accommodate the communication needs of their elders, responding in the language spoken to them, be it Spanish or English (ibid.:83–84). These norms result in continual language shifts within familial and other community settings. For example, children defer to the dominance of Spanish spoken by their parents and grandparents but switch to English when interacting with their siblings. Similar shifts occur rapidly outside the household as well. Children expect to speak Spanish to older community members but use English with their peers, many of whom are monolingual speakers of English and particularly of African-American Vernacular English (AAVE). Children whose Spanish is weak may attempt to use English even with elder Spanish-dominant bilinguals. Conversations between these participants may involve two languages in which the child speaks English and the elder speaks Spanish (ibid.:89).

The situation of native peoples in Guatemala and Mexico illustrates tendencies to limit use of indigenous languages in favor of the language of a dominant national culture. In both Mexico and Guatemala, speakers of Mayan languages whose ancestors developed the powerful Mayan states of pre-Columbian times have come under increasing social and economic pressure to shift to use of Spanish. Degrees of shift vary, however, depending on a community's isolation from or integration into the nation in which they reside. Several Mayan communities exemplify distinctive choices of language use.

A first Mayan group, the Chol Maya, who live in the southern Mexican state of Chiapas, are one of the most traditional groups in the region. They have been able to maintain their indigenous culture and language because of their location in rural towns isolated from main transportation routes. In addition, their participation in Mexico's economy is marginal, limited to growing a small amount of coffee as a cash crop. The Native language, Chol, is employed by nearly all community members, two-thirds of whom are monolingual speakers. Use of Spanish is common only among some young men who have the desire to leave their towns and migrate to Mexico City or other cities in the country (Fought 1985:28–29).

The second group, Chorti Maya, who live nearby in eastern Guatemala, are more heavily influenced by Spanish language and culture. They reside in small, dispersed hamlets outside towns inhabited by Guatemalan Ladinos, who are Spanish speakers. Most Chorti are bilingual; monolingual Chorti speakers are found only among very young children. Whereas Chorti is the primary language used in native homes, Spanish is necessary for public interactions in towns. Interethnic contacts are generally conducted in Spanish despite the fact that the Chorti outnumber Ladinos by nearly 10 to 1 (ibid.:24). Therefore, the relative social and economic power of participants determines choice of language. It is the Chorti rather than the Ladinos who become bilingual. Knowledge of Spanish is essential for upward social mobility, as well as for daily contacts with Ladino storekeepers and with authorities in government agencies and schools.

Although the Chorti language has little social prestige, it is used in the domain of religion. Resident missionaries of both the Roman Catholic and Quaker faiths have learned Chorti and employ it in religious services and instruction. They recognize that people have strong emotional ties to their native language (ibid.:27).

Among a third Mayan group, the Chontal of Chiapas, linguistic shift is most marked. The Chontal live in an area of recent industrial development. Oil refineries employ some Chontal as well as Spanish-speaking Mexicans. Networks of highways have been built to link the area to other centers. Although most Chontal speak their native language, nearly all are bilingual in Spanish as well. The only societal domain in which Chontal predominates is in the home, but even there many bilingual speakers employ Spanish rather than their native code (ibid.:23).

In addition to different patterns of linguistic use in these three Mayan communities, the languages themselves reflect varying degrees of influence from Spanish. All three languages contain many loanwords from Spanish, a result of incorporating numerous features of Mexican and Guatemalan culture. In Chol Mayan, spoken by the least assimilated group, loanwords are limited to these cultural borrowings. In contrast, Chontal Mayan, spoken by the most assimilated group, contains Spanish words that have replaced native labels for many indigenous objects as well as for borrowed items. Spanish grammar has also influenced Chontal Mayan, resulting in displacement of conjunctions and prepositions and in reformulation of sentence structure (ibid.:23, 28). The extent of linguistic change in Chontal Mayan is a clear and direct effect of extensive contact between natives and speakers of Spanish. It is also a clear and direct reflection of social and economic pressure experienced by the Chontal in their subordinate position relative to the dominant culture.

Patterns of language use and shift exemplified by Mayan peoples are by no means unique. Similar restrictions on functions of indigenous languages in situations of expanding national cultures and their codes occur throughout Latin America and indeed throughout the world. In some countries where large populations of indigenous peoples are concentrated, however, governments have occasionally attempted to address problems of speakers of native languages. For example, such attempts have been made in Peru. Although Peru is officially a Spanish-speaking country, it has an estimated 3.5 million speakers of indigenous languages, accounting for one-third of the country's total population (Briggs 1985:297). In the 1960s and 1970s, the Peruvian government established bilingual education programs for speakers of Quechua, who constitute the largest native group, numbering more than 3 million. Although these programs have not received consistent governmental support (ibid.:302), they do acknowledge the strength of native languages. The large numbers of speakers of Quechua in Peru and of other indigenous languages elsewhere help ensure their survival despite overall trends toward assimilation of native peoples and the spread of national languages.

Languages that have experienced constriction in usage and loss of speakers can be revitalized when particular attention is focused on the association between linguistic and ethnic identity. The resurgence of Basque in Spain since the 1960s is a telling example of the strength of a once-forbidden language when its speakers reassert their rights to cultural autonomy. Basque (or Euskera, also spelled Euskara) is spoken in seven provinces of northern Spain (and one in southern France) that are referred to as Euskal Herria ("Basque Country"). The link between land and language is explicit in the designation of the region since Euskal Herria literally means "land of the Basque language." Ethnicity and language are also made explicit by the term for a Basque person, *euskaldun,* meaning "someone who possesses the Basque language" ("euskera"; Hoffmann 1996:78). Basque was the majority language of the region until the eighteenth century, but it has since been marginalized by the spread of Castilian (and French in France). According to Spanish government estimates for 1991, of some 2,900,000 residents of Euskal Herria, there were approximately 660,000 fluent speakers of Basque and an additional 455,000 people with some knowledge of the language (Zuazo 1995:5).

The shift away from Basque was intensified during the rule of General Francisco Franco, beginning at the end of the Spanish Civil War in 1939 and ending with his death in 1975. The use of Basque was forbidden because of its association with political radicalism and agitation against the central government. A gradual lessening of official restrictions began in the 1960s, leading to the development of Basque-language schools for children as well as programs aimed at teaching Basque to adults (ibid.:21).

Promoters of Euskera had to grapple with the complexity of dialectal differences because the language had evolved in different communities. Some dialects are mutually intelligible, but others are not. Therefore, efforts were undertaken to develop a standardized form that could be used throughout the region. In 1968, a basic text of *euskera batua* ("unified Basque") was published by the Academy of the Basque Language. Euskera batua is based primarily on an educated variety of one of the regional dialects, but it is not understood by all speakers of other regional forms. For some speakers, "it is almost a new language" (ibid.:77). Still, it is the variety now taught in schools and used in public domains, and regional dialects continue to be spoken in home and community settings.

Use of Basque has grown considerably, especially since the establishment of Basque autonomy in 1979. Euskera is taught at all levels of education, beginning in the primary grades and continuing through the university level. The number of speakers has risen steadily. According to surveys conducted in 1986, 26.7 percent of Basques understood Euskera, while 24.6 percent were able to speak it. Smaller percentages of people were able to read (18.7 percent) or write (16.2 percent) the language (Artigal 1993:32). The Autonomous Community of the Basque Country, or Euskadi (established in 1979), is officially bilingual. Newspapers, other public media, government documents, and street and business signs are bilingual. Public sector employees must be bilingual.

Religious services are held in Spanish and Euskera. And a growing literature of prose and poetry is published in Basque. Throughout the region, governmental, educational, and cultural agencies actively promote the use of Basque in ever-widening social contexts. Members of the Basque community recognize the direct link between the political autonomy of Euskadi and the maintenance of their linguistic and cultural heritage.

Endangered Languages

In many parts of the world, speakers in bilingual communities have abandoned their native language in favor of their second language. When an entire community does so, the native language dies as an effective means of communication. This process of **language death** or **language obsolescence** is a worldwide phenomenon affecting different types of communities. In some cases, indigenous peoples abandon their native language after being subjected to invasion, conquest, and subsequent control by an overwhelming power. For example, many Native American societies throughout North and South America have stopped speaking their own languages and have replaced them with the dominant national code in their countries. Many indigenous peoples of Australia and of the small islands in the Pacific have also ceased using their native languages. Similar processes have taken place in Africa, Asia, and Europe. Replacement of native codes by dominant languages is usually a gradual process, first restricting native languages to limited interactional spheres and eventually leading to their complete abandonment. Once replacement is complete, the indigenous language disappears, the classic case of language death.

Processes leading to language loss are the consequence of dominant and dominating social and political ideologies, of which ideologies about language are an integral feature. In some cases, indigenous peoples are forced to abandon their own language through educational policies that separate children from their communities and instruct them in the dominant language. In other cases, language shift may appear to be "voluntary," but even then the choice is made in the context of negative attitudes toward indigenous codes that become accepted by the people themselves.

The future of the majority of the world's languages is very much in doubt. According to Michael Krauss's estimates, about half of the world's current 6,000 or 7,000 languages will no longer be spoken by the end of the twenty-first century (1992:6). In an even more dire prediction, Krauss suggests that as many as 90 percent of the world's languages will be either extinct or on their way to extinction by that time (ibid.:7). Many languages spoken today are what Krauss calls "moribund" (ibid.:4). These languages are spoken by adults but are no longer being learned as the mother tongue by children and are therefore "no longer viable." Their lack of generational continuity dooms these languages unless steps are taken to promote their use through education and encouragement in familial and informal settings. In the United States and Canada, of some 187 languages still spoken by Native Americans, 149 are no longer being learned by children. Conditions are somewhat better in Central America, where 50 of 300 (17 percent) indigenous languages are likely to die out, and in South America, where 110 of 400 (27 percent) are likely to disappear. Native languages probably face extinction. According to Krauss, the worst conditions are found in Australia, where 90 percent of the 250 aboriginal languages are moribund (ibid.:5).

In an attempt to focus on issues of indigenous rights in the international arena, including language rights, the General Assembly of the United Nations approved a Declaration on the Rights of Indigenous Peoples in 2007 that protects "the right to maintain and use their own languages, including for administrative, judicial, and other relevant purposes; the right of children to have access to education in their own languages; and to establish, structure, conduct, and control their own educational systems and institutions." Only four countries voted against the Declaration: Australia, Canada, New Zealand, and the United States, although these governments (beginning with Australia and ending with the United States) have since reversed their vote and approved the declaration. Education in one's native language and the promotion of its use in society are clearly key to maintaining a language's vitality and averting the worldwide trend that Krauss warns against. As Nancy Hornberger notes, where languages are in danger, bilingual communities should undertake "bottom-up revitalization efforts" that encourage the transmission of a language from one generation to the next because of its usefulness in the widest possible range of communicative contexts. "Such revitalization efforts are not about bringing the language back, but rather about bringing it forward" (1998:453).

Processes of language shift and loss are exemplified in many Native American communities in the United States. Some research raises questions concerning the role of native ideologies about language itself in the abandonment of indigenous languages and in the subsequent attempts to maintain or restore native codes. One key issue is the association between language and identity. Language tends to become a marker of identity when the survival of one's language is threatened either from external dominating forces or from the internalization of negative attitudes that results from this domination. In a discussion of Native American language ideologies, Margaret Field and Paul Kroskrity suggest that language becomes a "badge of identity" when the number of remaining speakers dwindles and when community members become alarmed at its approaching loss (2009:20).

Differences in the speech of younger and older community members may also affect the goals and successes of language maintenance programs. For example, older speakers may promote a kind of "linguistic purism" that denigrates speech that contains borrowings from English or patterns of **code mixing**, the amalgamation of native and foreign structures and lexicon (see discussion of these processes later in the chapter).

Concepts related to the issue of "language and thought" underlie the desire to maintain native languages in some communities. One's indigenous language is felt to express cultural models of the world that differ fundamentally from those expressed by English; therefore, the loss of language is seen as a loss of cultural distinctiveness. For instance, analysis of a Hopi tribal court hearing revealed that a Hopi tribal advocate representing a defendant repeatedly insisted on the use of the Hopi language. She stated: "You can't separate Hopi and religion and land, language, court, Constitution. It's all tied up into one. That's why we need special courts, hear us in our language" (Richland 2009:93). And the Yukon Native Languages Project, sponsored by the Yukon First Nations in Canada, adopted the motto: "We Are Our Language" to stress the interconnections among language, identity, and worldview (Meek 2009:158). Religious rituals and prayers are often thought to lose their power if not spoken in the indigenous language.

Jeffrey Anderson's (1998) study of the Northern Arapaho at the Wind River Reservation in Wyoming demonstrates complexities in attitudes and behaviors associated with the indigenous code and with English. In the mid-nineteenth century, knowledge of English began to be valued as a means of communicating with federal officials, who came to have increasing influence and control over reservation communities. Those few Arapahos who spoke English became interpreters and brokers in relations between the native people and outsiders. By late in the century, federal education policies restricted or even eliminated the use of native languages in schools, thus limiting young people's fluency in their own code. People who were the most proficient English speakers eventually rose to positions of tribal leadership in part because of their linguistic skills.

Bilingualism was considered an asset. For much of the twentieth century, both Arapaho and English were valued for their usefulness in different contexts. Arapaho was spoken in homes, at community meetings and celebrations, and in religious contexts, whereas English was used in school, business, and government domains. Gradually, however, the pattern of stable bilingualism "gave way to language loss when the speech community could no longer maintain the boundaries between the two languages" (ibid.:57).

Beginning in the 1950s, most children learned English as their first language. The change was so abrupt that many families were divided between older siblings who were fluent speakers of Arapaho and younger siblings who spoke only English (ibid.:55). As a result, by the 1990s, only about 500 or 600 people out of a reservation population of approximately 5,000 are fluent speakers of Arapaho. Most are more than 60 years old. As a further indication of the future, few parents speak Arapaho to their children (ibid.:54). Arapaho is typically employed only in "speech situations involving elders (e.g., meetings of elders as consultants, ceremonial speech acts, and informal gatherings)" or in educational settings specifically aimed at teaching the language (ibid.).

Members of the Arapaho community have diverse attitudes toward the changes that have taken place. Elders view the loss of Arapaho as "one stream in a larger shift in everyday social relations—that is, in ways people talk to each other, …in the loss of respect, hospitality, and modes of visiting" (ibid.:101). Perhaps in an attempt to regain a traditional sense of community, many young people are trying to learn the indigenous language in concert with renewed interest in Arapaho ceremonial and social practices.

The role of parental (or other caregivers') use of indigenous languages in the maintenance of the native code is demonstrated in a study conducted at the Alabama-Coushatta Reservation in eastern Texas (Halmari 1998). While people age 45 years or older were likely to be fluent in Alabama or Coushatta (or both) and to consider one of the native languages to be their "dominant" language, people younger than 45 varied in their fluency. Among the younger tribal members, 55 percent stated that English was their dominant language, 21 percent noted equal dominance of English and one of the indigenous languages, and the remaining 24 percent reported that they were dominant in either Alabama or Coushatta (ibid.:415). Age differences were also significant in language usage patterns. Older speakers typically employed an indigenous language when conversing with peers, whereas younger speakers were more likely to speak English to siblings and age mates (ibid.:419). Parental language use was the prime predictor of linguistic abilities of younger speakers. Young tribal members who were bilingual (or trilingual) typically grew up in households where one or both parents regularly spoke a native language to their children (ibid.:423). On the basis of findings such as these, Halmari notes the importance of "community language planning," which encourages parents to speak indigenous languages to their children and that creates other "opportunities for younger and older members of the community to interact with each other in native languages in natural and mutually rewarding speech situations" (ibid.:423–424).

Efforts at revitalizing and maintaining Native American languages have accelerated considerably in the last decade. Innovative learning projects have been initiated in many communities in the United States and Canada. Each project develops in the context of specific language needs based on the number of speakers present in the community and the current vitality of the language as a means of communication. Where languages are still spoken by a sizable percentage of the community, such as among the Inuit in Arctic Canada, Navajo in the southwestern United States, and Cree in central and northern Canada, programs are aimed at language maintenance. The native language is used in schools as either a primary or secondary code of instruction, books and other teaching materials are printed in the native languages, and children are encouraged to speak their native tongue in all appropriate settings. Parents and other relatives also need to be involved because the best hope for survival occurs when languages are used in ongoing, spontaneous, and meaningful social interaction. In communities where there are only a small number of native speakers, other techniques of reintroduction need to be developed. Language immersion programs and the presence of elders as role models help develop the necessary motivation for young children to learn the native tongue. And, of course, there are intermediary cases where people utilize a variety of strategies. For example, in the Mohawk settlement of Kahnawa:ke, located just south of the Canadian city of Montreal, the community operates two elementary schools, one in which English is the language of instruction and the other in which Mohawk immersion predominates. While the majority of Mohawk residents are monolingual English speakers, a sizable (and now growing) minority are fluent in the native language. In the 1970s, people began to fear steep declines in speaker abilities and began to take steps to develop language programs for children. The Mohawk immersion program began in 1984 and was originally used in nursery, kindergarten, and first grade. Since then, the program has gradually extended through older grades, finally reaching the sixth grade by 1989. A further modification took place in 1994. At that time, full-day language immersion programs were instituted in kindergarten through fourth grade, while in the fifth and sixth grades, language maintenance rather than immersion became the goal (Jacobs 1998:120). Parents can choose to send their children to either school. Presently, about half of the community's children attends the Mohawk immersion school, while the other half attends the English language school.

In California, in contrast, most of the remaining native languages have only a handful of elderly speakers. In the 1990s, the Master-Apprentice Language-Learning Program was initiated (Hinton 1998). In this program, each "master speaker" was teamed with an apprentice from the same community. Master speakers were first trained in informal interactional teaching techniques (such as managing repetition and rephrasing). Apprentices were also trained in learning strategies, emphasizing the importance of active learning. That is, they were encouraged to take an active role in shaping the learning context, asking questions, and speaking as much as possible. Following their initial work together, the master and apprentice speakers returned to their communities and attempted to involve a wider network of participants. These programs have generated a great deal of interest in Californian Native communities, but they are unlikely to lead to widespread language use; however, they are important strategies in language survival.

One of the most remarkable instances of language revitalization, or, more accurately, language reclamation, is the achievement of members of Wampanoag communities in Cape Cod and Martha's Vineyard. Jessie Little Doe Baird started these programs in 1993 after recurring dreams in which voices spoke in an unknown language. Since then, the Wampanoag language has come from a state of near-extinction to become a language with a growing number of speakers and at least one child who is a native speaker.

Little Doe Baird began working with Ken Hale of the Department of Linguistics at the Massachusetts Institute of Technology (MIT) in Cambridge, Massachusetts. Together they used two major types of sources to reconstruct Wampanoag. First, they used the extensive body of colonial documents written in Wampanoag and English dating from the seventeenth and eighteenth centuries. Indeed, there are more documents written in Wampanoag than in any other indigenous language of North America. These manuscripts included deeds, property transfers, letters to colonial authorities, and agreements between Wampanoag representatives and British and American officials. The documents provide the basis for understanding Wampanoag sentence structure and word formation processes as well as a large vocabulary. The second source of information comes from comparative material gleaned from the several dozen languages belonging to the Algonkian linguistic family, of which Wampanoag is a member. Study of these languages, some of which are spoken today and some of which are welldocumented by linguists and earlier observers, provides data for the reconstruction of Wampanoag grammar and lexicon as well as clues to pronunciation.

The Wampanoag Language Reclamation Project has involved many community members in organizing immersion camps, master-apprentice teams, and language classes. They have also developed materials for use in these programs, such as grammar workbooks, computer files, and board games. The success of this project demonstrates that a community of dedicated people can achieve what might seem impossible if materials are available. Their work is captured in a documentary entitled *We Still Live Here, As Nutayunean* (Makepeace Productions 2010).

Language revival has been the goal (and an impressive success) of the indigenous communities in Hawaii. Once the language of a strong and thriving island society, Hawaiian was spoken by less than 1,000 native residents of the state by the 1970s. Fearing further loss and eventual language death, some Native Hawaiians embarked on an ambitious project to develop language immersion programs for the Hawaiian language. The first program, established in 1984, created language immersion classes paid for privately by tuition fees. An additional feature of the project, and one necessary for successful language revival, stipulated that parents whose children participated must also take language classes. Three years later, the state-run Department of Education initiated its first publicly funded immersion programs in elementary schools. And in 1989, the Hawaiian state legislature established an agency, housed at the University of Hawaii, that supports and trains teachers of the Hawaiian language as well as develops and disseminates curriculum materials. Another significant milestone was reached in 1996 when the state opened its first total-immersion school from kindergarten through high school. By the end of the twentieth century, approximately 1,600 students were participating in public-school immersion classes, and some 2,500 students were taking second-language classes in Hawaiian (Nettle and Romaine 2000:183).

Efforts at maintaining or restoring indigenous languages in other regions of the world have also intensified in the last several decades. The increasing spread of dominant languages, especially English, has alerted members of indigenous communities to the imminent danger of language loss and death. A special issue of *Cultural Survival Quarterly* (2001), a publication of an organization dedicated to promoting indigenous rights, documents the worldwide growth of programs teaching Native languages. These programs differ in their strategies depending on the linguistic situation in each community. Some communities emphasize immersion programs that provide continual and contextual language use; others are attempting to restore languages that have only a few living speakers remaining. As many members of remote indigenous communities move to towns and cities where their languages are marginalized, further pressure is exerted on their languages, leading to increased rates of loss. Indigenous peoples as diverse as the Saami in northern Sweden, the Quechua in Chile, the Yahgan in Tierro del Fuego, and the Kamchatka in Siberia are investigating ways to avert further language loss. In some cases, national governments provide funds for developing teaching materials and employing instructors, but in other cases, local communities receive little governmental support.

Speakers of minority languages in Zimbabwe have embarked on ambitious initiatives in order to protect their languages in a multilingual and multiethnic environment. Representatives of six minority languages established an organization called the Zimbabwe Indigenous Languages Promotion Association (ZILPA) with the goal of obtaining government recognition and support for their native tongues. Zimbabwe has one official language, English, and two national languages, Shona and Ndebele. These African languages are spoken by about 75 percent and 16 percent of the population, respectively (Nyika 2008:459). There are at least a dozen additional indigenous languages spoken by minority communities and, together, they are the native tongues of about 7 percent of the people. Approximately 1 percent of the Zimbabwe people are native speakers of English, while another 1 percent speak a different non-African language (Hindi, Chinese, and other European languages). ZILPA specifically represents the interests of speakers of Tonga, Kalanga, Venda, Shangani, Nambya, and Sotho (ibid.:461), but its efforts may help to promote other indigenous languages as well.

English, Shona, and Ndebele are privileged in several respects. These languages are employed in the Zimbabwe educational system, as set forth by the Education Act of 1987. Shona and Ndebele are employed as the language of instruction in primary school through the third grade and then are taught as subjects in secondary schools and in colleges and universities. English is the major language of instruction in the upper grades and in postsecondary educational settings. The Education Act allows for the teaching of minority languages at the discretion of the Minister of Education, whose policies can be implemented locally. Given the lack of governmental commitment to minority communities, actual implementation of language protection policies was not forthcoming. In this context, ZILPA was formed in 2001 and immediately pressed for amendments to the Education Act to allow minority languages to be employed throughout the educational system. They achieved some success the following year when the government amended the legislation, thus permitting instruction in minority languages throughout the primary school years.

In addition to official policies, however, resources need to be committed in order for real implementation to occur. At a minimum, these resources must include training of teachers and development of curricula and teaching materials in minority languages. In some regions of Zimbabwe, such resources are provided, but advocacy on the part of ZILPA and other organizations continues to ensure their availability nationwide. ZILPA also strives to have minority languages taught as subjects in secondary and postsecondary education, but this has not yet happened. They see the educational system as a primary site of contestation because the fact that a language is promoted in schooling gives it official acknowledgment. Such status can contribute to positive attitudes by the speakers themselves, helping to avert further language shift. ZILPA has had some success in establishing collaborative relationships with the African Languages Research Institute at the University of Zimbabwe to train speakers of minority languages as researchers and teachers.

The status of minority languages varies from region to region. Some of the languages are used as the daily code of interaction by people of all ages, especially in rural communities. Still, bilingualism in the minority and at least one of the national languages is common, leading to some degree of shift away from minority speech. These shifts have already occurred in many urban areas, even for interactions within the family. Efforts to maintain minority languages are therefore focused on promoting the value of these speech forms as markers and transmitters of cultural identities in a multicultural country. For example, ZILPA organizes neighborhood cultural festivals "as a strategy for language and cultural affirmation as well as an avenue for grassroots mobilization" (Nyika 2008:463). These festivals include crafts, foods, songs, and dances that enhance pride in one's heritage. Local, regional, and even national political figures attend the events as an acknowledgment of the rights of ethnic communities in Zimbabwe.

The media (i.e., radio, television, and newspapers) in Zimbabwe generally employ English, Shona, and/or Ndebele both in national and regional outlets. After ZILPA and other organizations pressed the Zimbabwe Broadcasting Corporation, the national broadcasting service, to allocate airtime to programming in minority languages, a separate radio station was established dedicated to programming in these languages.

The lessons learned from the Zimbabwe experience include the important role that dynamic and committed minority communities can play in advocating for their rights to promote their languages in public domains. By forming organizations that unite several groups, their voices become stronger. Of course, receptive and responsive government agencies are also part of a successful equation.

Unlike indigenous communities, immigrant populations often give up their native language in favor of the language of the society into which they have moved. Immigrant groups in the United States are good examples of this process. In general, many immigrant families in the United States retain some knowledge of the parental language in the second generation, but by the third generation, much, if not all, of that knowledge is lost. Social pressure toward English monolingualism is an important factor in this trend. And the trend is supported and encouraged by an educational philosophy that often disparages bilingualism and claims, contrary to the findings of most academic research, that children who speak two languages have difficulty learning either one well (see the discussion in Chapter 11). The loss of native languages in immigrant communities does not mean that the language itself is undergoing language death, however, because it continues to be spoken by people remaining in the country of origin.

Gaelic, the indigenous Celtic code of Scotland and Ireland, exemplifies the process of loss and restriction. Gaelic is an endangered language whose eventual fate is uncertain. Once spoken by the entire population of these countries, Gaelic is now in active use only in isolated areas in the northern and western edges of the territories. This restriction has been a long-term process, beginning centuries ago when the English invaded and conquered the native Celts. The English language then gradually replaced the local code. Although Gaelic is still spoken in some rural areas, even there its use is limited, becoming more so with each generation. In fact, since the 1970s, few parents speak Gaelic to their children (Watson 1989:42).

Attitudes toward Gaelic are somewhat mixed. In Ireland, Gaelic is officially recognized by the constitution as the "national language" and the "first official language" (Constitution of Ireland, Article 8). The Irish government promotes a standardized form of Gaelic that is taught in schools and used in published official documents. Gaelic is also promoted through radio programs and other cultural outlets (ibid.:47). Still, its actual use is decreasing despite government support for its revival (ibid.:44). Many factors contribute to its decline, notably the influx of English-speaking people, incorporation of isolated areas into regional and national economies, and the desire of young rural residents to leave the area for economic opportunities elsewhere. These trends result in the association of Gaelic with an uneducated, poor, rural population that translates into a negative attitude toward maintaining the language.

In Scotland, Gaelic is not given official recognition and support, as it is in Ireland. And it is generally disparaged by nonspeakers as representing a backward, traditional past. However, those few people who still speak the language are fiercely loyal to it and have high regard for other speakers. As one elderly Gaelic speaker commented to Seosamh Watson, "Because we have a side [a liking] to anyone that'll speak the Gaelic. It draws us like a magnet. Anybody that'll speak the Gaelic I've a side to them and I'll trust my life to them" (ibid.:45). Despite such positive associations, older speakers rarely employ Gaelic with their children, and its use is declining rapidly in Scotland.

English is replacing Gaelic in Scotland and Ireland because of social and economic pressures that have accelerated during the twentieth century. As traditional economic pursuits such as fishing and sheepherding have declined, many rural people have had to seek employment away from their isolated communities. Knowledge of English has become a requirement for successful outmigration and integration into national labor markets. In addition, the prestige of English filters throughout the educational establishment in Ireland and Scotland, regardless of official policies that promote Gaelic in Ireland. Speaking English carries social prestige, especially for the young who associate it with pop music, sophisticated fashions, and sports. The spread of English is also enhanced by its exclusive use in the mass media (ibid.:49).

In contrast to English, Gaelic has no prestigious written tradition but is associated with folk culture, which is often disparaged in modern society, especially by the young. A further sign of Gaelic's vulnerability is the fact that it has borrowed many English words not only for innovations in technology and science, but also as replacements for indigenous Gaelic nouns, adjectives, and verbs (ibid.:50). As a result of a lack of native words for modern objects and activities, speakers of Gaelic often switch to English in order to talk about "subjects more complicated than the weather, community news, or basic farming or fishing" (ibid.:55).

Given Gaelic's limited usefulness and the high rates of English monolingualism among the young, it is unlikely that Gaelic will survive as a vibrant, living language for much longer unless official policies have more than a superficial effect. It may well suffer the language death all too typical of codes of indigenous peoples throughout the world whose lands and cultures have been overwhelmed by conquering nations.

The fate of Gaelic as an indigenous language in Ireland and Scotland is matched by its fate as the language of Celtic immigrants to other countries. Gaelic is still spoken by small groups of people whose ancestors migrated from Scotland to Nova Scotia, Canada, in the eighteenth and nineteenth centuries, but its use is highly restricted and the number of Gaelic speakers has fallen sharply since the 1930s and 1940s. According to researcher Elizabeth Mertz, the case of Gaelic in Cape Breton is an example of what Nancy Dorian has termed a *linguistic tip,* a situation in which "a language which has been demographically highly stable for several centuries may experience a sudden 'tip,' after which the demographic tide flows strongly in favor of some other language" (Dorian 1981:51). In two communities studied by Mertz, residents were bilingual in English and Gaelic until the 1930s and 1940s, but thereafter Gaelic was no longer transmitted to the younger generations. Currently there are no fluent Gaelic speakers under the age of 40. And many people in their forties who speak Gaelic are not fluent speakers but rather use the language rarely and with difficulty (Mertz 1989:105–106).

Although Gaelic was spoken by most residents in the 1930s, it had already become a language of private, familial contexts and was rarely used in public. But at that time, a dramatic change occurred when parents no longer spoke Gaelic to their children. Mertz explains this sudden shift, or "tip," in economic, social, and ideological terms. The economy of Cape Breton had been marginal for centuries, dependent on small-scale fishing and farming. During the economic depression of the 1930s, residents' livelihood deteriorated even further. People realized that the economic potential of isolated areas was severely limited and responded by trying to seek occupations elsewhere in Nova Scotia and Canada. Their desire to disassociate themselves from their isolated background was reflected in their pejorative attitudes toward speaking Gaelic, a language that had long suffered from a lack of prestige compared to the high status of English.

The educational system contributed to the decline of Gaelic by promoting the notion that bilingual speakers are at a disadvantage because each of their languages interferes with their ability to learn either one well. One of Mertz's consultants recalled: "Parents thought teaching Gaelic would sort of confuse the two languages in their minds" (ibid.:111). This ideology, erroneous though it was, convinced parents to stop speaking Gaelic to their children in order to better the youngsters' chances of speaking "good" English, assimilating into mainstream Canadian society, and advancing socially and economically.

Older Cape Breton speakers continue to employ Gaelic with friends and families in informal settings. Greetings, affectionate names, and exclamations are often expressed in Gaelic. And its use can succinctly mark the distinction between insiders and outsiders. But with the passing of older generations, Gaelic will soon die out as an immigrant language of Nova Scotia.

The International Dominance of English

One consequence of the historic colonial experience has been the spread of the languages of colonizers far beyond their own national boundaries. The expansion of European languages to other parts of the globe is but the latest example of this process. The worldwide prominence of specific European languages has risen and fallen with their colonial fortunes. Presently, although direct imperial control has disappeared or at least weakened, linguistic dominance of former colonial languages has survived. French is still spoken in many countries of Africa, the Caribbean, and the Pacific. Spanish is the major language of most of South and Central America. And English is spoken by residents of former British and American colonies or possessions in the Americas, the Pacific, and Africa. Use of English has spread to many additional countries because of the economic, political, and cultural influence of the United States. In fact, such influence has accelerated since World War II, and the English language has gained increasing worldwide dominance. Estimates suggest that some 341 million people are native speakers of English and between one-quarter and one-third of the world's people understand and speak English to some degree (Ethnologue 2000). English is the most frequently taught foreign language in the world's schools. It is the sole official language of 25 countries and functions, along with others, as official languages in some 36 more. Its closest rival is French, which is the sole official language in 14 independent countries and in 16 island countries in the Caribbean or the Pacific still linked to France, and it is one of two or more official languages in 18 additional nations (Ethnologue 2010). English dominates as the primary language of international business. An estimated 75 percent of all mail and 80 percent of computer data are written in English (Baron 1990).

Reflecting the deepening influence of the language, varieties sometimes called New Englishes have developed. According to Platt, Weber, and Lian, New Englishes are "localized" or "nativized" dialects that have adopted "language features of [their] own, such as sounds, intonation patterns, sentence structures, words, expressions, ...[and] different rules for using language in communication" (1984:3). These are not creoles because they have not developed from pidgins; rather, they have developed from a form of English disseminated through formal education. New Englishes are in use in numerous countries throughout the world. They have developed in Africa (Ghana, Liberia, Nigeria, Sierra Leone, Cameroon, Kenya, Tanzania, Uganda, Zimbabwe), the Caribbean (Barbados, Guyana, Jamaica, Puerto Rico, Trinidad and Tobago), Asia (Bangladesh, Hong Kong, India, Malaysia, Philippines, Singapore, Sri Lanka), and the Pacific (Fiji, Guam, Hawaii, Samoa, Papua New Guinea) (ibid.:15). John Platt and his co-workers apply the term to varieties of English that are spoken in areas where English is typically used as a medium of instruction, especially in higher education, and has important societal functions in government, business, high-status professions such as law and medicine, and mass communication. Some speakers of New English also employ it in familial and casual settings. The language is typically perceived by the speech community as a neutral language and/or a language of high status. Its neutrality derives from the fact that it is not associated with any particular native ethnic or regional group, and its high status comes from its association with advanced education and public uses. These latter features obviously imply privileges of class and social power as well. Remarking on the social clout of English, a Zambian reported that "in Tanzania and Zambia people carry English newspapers just to be seen…even if they cannot read it and hold it upside down" (ibid.:29). And in Japan, inclusion of English loanwords in Japanese speech has complex meanings. On the one hand, it can sound "modern and cosmopolitan, technical and scientific," but on the other hand, the speaker can come across as "affected and pretentious" (Stanlaw 2004:268). The dominance of English as a second language in Japan is part of an international trend, and although most Japanese have positive reactions to English, some react against the seepage of English into Japanese. These attitudes are embedded in cultural beliefs about cultural, linguistic, and racial purity (ibid.:276–277).

New Englishes are characterized by unique local features of sound, syntax, lexicon, and style; however, a number of general patterns distinguish these varieties. Among the distinctive phonological traits, the most common is the replacement of the interdental fricatives /θ/ and /ð/ with the corresponding stops /t/ and /d/ because of the lack of the fricatives in most languages. Consonant clusters are often simplified, again in accordance with phonotactic rules of the dominant language spoken in the area. Nouns in many New Englishes are typically not marked for number. In addition, markers or separate words denoting definite or indefinite are also generally omitted. And third-person subjects or objects are often not distinguished for gender. New Englishes often rework or omit markings on verbs, particularly for events in the past (all examples are from Platt, Weber, and Lian 1984):

I *graduate* there in 1975. (Papua New Guinea)
I was new here and I *don't know* where to go. (Philippines)
My wife, she *pass* her Cambridge. (Singapore)

Instead, some New Englishes indicate tense with adverbs or special words:

Before I always go to that market. (Malaysia)
My father *already* pass away. (Singapore)
You *eat finish,* go out and play. (When you've finished eating, go and play.) (Singapore)

In addition, New Englishes may use the "be + verb + ing" construction for stative verbs, as well as for action or process verbs:

Mohan *is having* two houses. (India)
I *was doubting* it. (India)
She *is knowing* her science very well. (East Africa)

The lexicons of New Englishes often borrow from the "background" languages of the area:

When we get home, we ask daddy to *changkol* the garden. (Singapore: *changkol* "hoe")
If you don't like, *yaya* will give you water. (Philippines: *yaya* "nursemaid")
Don't *kacho* (or *kacau*) me when I want to work! (Malaysia: *kacau* "disturb")

New Englishes also contain locally coined words:

dry coffee (coffee without milk and sugar: East Africa)
change-room (dressing room: India)
bed-spacer (someone who rents a bed in a room or dormitory: Philippines)

Some words exemplify processes of shifts in word classes:

> to friend (to be friends with: Malaysia, Jamaica)
> to be aftering something (to look for something: Papua New Guinea)
> My gentleman naked himself. (got undressed, undressed himself) (Singapore)

And words may change their meanings:

> You did not give me any *balance*. (change: West Africa)
> Take some water to the *stranger*. (guest: Nigeria)
> You can *drop* here. (get out: Singapore)

BILINGUAL CONVERSATIONAL STRATEGIES

Bilingual speakers have more linguistic resources at their disposal than do monolingual speakers. Words in each language express somewhat different meanings, either because they refer to different entities or activities or because they express divergent perspectives. Therefore, bilinguals often employ strategies for maximizing the potential expressiveness of their linguistic repertory.

Code Switching

When bilingual speakers converse, they frequently integrate linguistic material from both of their languages within the same discourse segment. This process, called **code switching**, differs significantly from borrowing. When words are borrowed, host languages adapt sounds and intonation patterns to suit their native rules. In code switching, alterations do not occur. Instead, switched elements retain the sound patterns of their origin.

Code switching has a variety of linguistic and interactional functions. It can have simple uses in expanding vocabulary. Bilingual speakers may employ a word from one language in sequences spoken in another because the latter lacks a comparable word expressing the desired meaning. In some cases, both languages may actually have words with similar meanings, but the structure of one may be more cumbersome than the other. Speakers often opt for the simpler expression.

Some examples from Mohawk can illustrate switching for ease of vocabulary. The indigenous Mohawk language did not contain specific words for each day of the week and month of the year. After contact with Europeans, Mohawks constructed their own native labels for seven days and 12 months. In current usage, however, most speakers switch to English even though a word exists in their vocabulary. In the following sentences, the speaker incorporated English "Sunday morning" in place of Mohawk *awʌ̃tatokʌ̃ htí:ke*[?] "holy day" and "July" in place of *ohyali*[?] *kó:wa* "the fruit ripens a lot" (Bonvillain 1988:15, 13):

1. *ó:nʌ̃) ki*[?] *ki*[?] Sunday morning *wà:kye*
   (then this this) (I woke up)
   "Then I woke up Sunday morning."

2. *yà:yak niwáhsa wisk yakoyelí:tu* July
   (sixty-five she turned)
   "She turned sixty-five in July."

In subsequent examples throughout this section, abbreviations are used to indicate languages: E = English, F = French, H = Hindi, M = Mohawk, S = Spanish. English translations are given in parentheses of segments spoken in other languages. Sources of examples are not indicated in the text but have been obtained from Bonvillain 1988 (Mohawk); Grosjean 1982 (French); Gumperz 1982 (Hindi, Spanish); Kachru 1978 (Hindi); McClure 1977 (Spanish); Pandit 1986 (Hindi); Pfaff 1979 (Spanish); Sridhar 1978 (Kannada); and Zentella 1985, 1997 (Spanish).

Instances of using the more accessible word may depend on speakers' linguistic abilities in their two languages or momentary lapses of memory:

3. [S/E]:   *Necesito un* string   *para la* kite
(need a)   (for the)
"I need a string for the kite."

Words may be transferred from one language to another because of social values associated with knowledge of a prestige code. Switches from Hindi to English exemplify this tendency:

4. society *hii aisii hai*
"The society is like that."

5. *itanaa* money *aayaa kahaan se?*
"Where did so much money come from?"

Code switching has numerous discourse and interactional functions, such as emphasizing, marking discourse boundaries, expressing emotions or opinions, and signaling ingroup/outgroup membership. Some of these functions are exemplified in the remainder of this section.

Code switches sometimes involve use of routine phrases or markers of politeness and solidarity:

6. [S/E]: *Dale un beso a Pucho* (Give Pucho a kiss). Julie, please.
Tag questions also make use of switched elements:

7. [E/S]: She is, *verdad?* (right?)

Because code switching involves two languages, it inherently results in contrast and therefore can be used as an attention-getting device. In the following two examples, from the speech of a 9-year-old Mexican-American girl, equivalent words "look/*mira*" are switched, depending on the base language; that is, "look" is switched into Spanish, whereas "*mira*" is transferred into English. Thus, it is the fact of switching itself that carries contrastive meaning:

8. Now let me do it. Put your feets down. *Mira!* (Look!) It's Leti's turn again. Hi Leti.

Code switching within sentences or discourse highlights transferred elements and can be used as a dramatic device in narrative. In the next extract from a personal story, the narrator switches from Mohawk to English to focus on her father's formal attire and demeanor:

9. *tehoji²jahlʌ́hhoh   ki²ná:²* a blue suit   *lótstū   tanú²* white shirt
(he was all dressed *up   this*) (*he wore   and*)
kwah ki² na² it was starched, the collar was starched, necktie *lótstú*
(*very   this*) (*he wore*)

"He was all dressed up, he wore a blue suit and a white shirt, it was very starched, the collar was starched, he wore a necktie."

Speakers may express the same meaning in both languages sequentially, using repetition as an emphatic device. Such switches are particularly effective in issuing directives:

10. (Mother to child [S/E]): *Callate* (shut up). Shut up!
Repetitions sometimes include expansions or clarifications:

11. (Child to younger child [E/S]): Roli, you stay here. *Tu quedate 'jito con Suzy.* (Stay with Suzy, Honey!)

12. (Father to son learning to swim in a pool [H/E]): *Baju-me jao beta, andar mat* (Go to the side son, not inside.) Keep to the side.

Switches are sometimes used to signal changes in types of syntactic constructions occurring within a speaker's turn:

From statement to command [E/F]:

13. Now it's really time to get up. *Lève-toi!* (get up!)

From statement to question [E/S]:

14. I wiggle my fingers. *Qué más?* (what else?)

Speakers frequently switch at boundaries of internal quotes within narratives:

15. [S/E]: *El me dijo* (he told me), "Call the police."

16. [E/H/E]: I went to Agra, *to maine ʌpne bhaiko bola ki* (then I said to my brother that), if you come to Delhi you must buy some lunch.

Switching can occur within a sentence to segment phrases or clauses that mark qualification, explanation, or elaboration:

17. [H/E]: *mujhe duusaron se acchii hindii bhii aatii hai lekin phir bhii main samajhatii huun* (I know Hindi better than others, even then I feel) that it is not up to the mark.

18. [E/S]: That has nothing to do *con que hagan ese* (with the fact that they're doing this).

19. [E/S]: Those are friends from Mexico *que tienen chamaquitos* (who have little children).

20. [F/E/F/E]: *Va chercher Marc* (go fetch Marc) and bribe him *avec un chocolat chaud* (with a hot chocolate) with cream on the top.

Code switching may perform several kinds of shifts within discourse.

Shift of focus: from action to a comment or evaluation:

21. [S/E]: *Lo pegó aqui* (he hit him here). I saw it.

22. [H/E/H] [Narrator telling a traditional story]: *sharmishthaa ye sun letii hai to sharmishthaa kahatii hai* (Sharmishtha overhears this and says) I like this sentence very much, *pitaajii jab raajpuut laraaii men jaate hain to pitaa aashiir-vaad dete hain kii tum laraaii men* successful *ho.* (When the Rajputs go to the battlefront their fathers bless them by wishing them success in the battle.)

Shift of addressees:

23. [E/S]:   **A (SPEAKING TO B):** Why you cry baby?
         A (SPEAKING TO C): *Esta llorando* (he is crying).

Shift of topic within conversations (next speaker switches code to mark discontinuity with previous speaker's topic):

24. [S/E]:   **A:** *Dile que es una casa sin techo* (tell her that it's a house without a roof).
         B: We have a pretty, uh, Christmas tree.

The following example, from Hindi to English, demonstrates the speaker's internal comment and topical shift:

25. *yah ek nazuk mamla hai* (it is a delicate matter); let's not talk about it.

Code switching may separate a speaker's turn into segments that fulfill contrasting functions. In the following telephone conversation, both speakers switch for a variety of interactional and emotional purposes [S/E]:

26. A: *Qué pasa?* (what's happening?) Can't you come over today?

   B: I would love to, but I don't know if we can for sure. *Dejame hablarte des-pues que llegue Joe* (let me talk to you later after Joe arrives). I don't know what to tell you right now.

   A: Okay *y* don't forget, *llamame despues* (call me later).

In A's first turn, she switched to English after the routine opening *Qué pasa?* Her friend responded in English, switching internally to Spanish to set apart her explanation for not making definite plans.

The following example reflects emotional attitudes expressed in a bilingual's two languages. The speaker, whose native language is Spanish, is discussing her attempts to stop smoking:

27. ...they tell me "How did you quit Mary?" I don't quit...I just stopped. I mean it wasn't an effort that I made *que voy a dejar de fumar por que me hace dano o* (that I'm going to stop smoking because it's harmful to me or) this or that uh-uh. It's just that I used to pull butts out of the waste paper basket, yeah. I used to go look in the...*se me acababan los cigarros en la noche* (my cigarettes would run out on me at night). I'd get *desperate y ahi voy al basarero a buscar, a sacar* (and there I go to the wastebasket to look for some, to get some), you know.

According to John Gumperz's analysis of this text, code switches symbolize the speaker's "involvement in the message. Spanish statements are personalized, while English reflects more distance. The speaker seems to be talking about her problem in English and acting out her problem through words in Spanish" (1982:81).

Such emotional associations with one's native language are common. Bilingual speakers often feel more emotionally attuned to their first language and more apt to express feelings through it. In some cases, however, speakers may switch from their native language in order to avoid sensitive issues and to adopt emotional distance or neutrality. In the next extract, from an Indian woman's discussion of her opposition to traditional arranged marriages, the speaker switches from Hindi to English:

28. *mere saath to kabhii aisaa nahiin ho sakataa* (it can never happen to me). I feel very odd *kii* how can you share the bed, share the feelings with the boy whom you don't know.

Because words and expressions often presuppose underlying cultural values, speakers sometimes switch from their primary language in order to avoid expectations associated with native norms. In an example from another Indian language, Kannada, the request "*nanagondu* favor *ma:dti:ra?*" (will you do me a favor?) involves a switch to English "favor" from Kannada *upaka:ra*. Use of English here distances speakers from the strength of obligations to return favors that are basic to Kannada customs (Sridhar 1978:116).

Code switching sometimes appears to be motivated or triggered by words within sentences. If a foreign word is transferred into the base language, it often triggers subsequent switches of words or clauses. In the next examples, words, titles, or names spoken in English lead to a complete change to English:

29. [S/E]: *Porque allí hay* (because here are some) cashews. You don't like them?

30. [M/E]: *tkathé:thahkwe* (there used to be a gristmill at) Millrush; he was talking way back fifty years ago.

In some cases, use of a particular language by one bilingual speaker can trigger another bilingual speaker to match the language choice of the first. Research by Guadalupe Valdes-Fallis

(1978) indicated that this kind of switching may be influenced by the interlocutor's gender. In a sample of Mexican-American women recorded in same-sex and cross-sex conversations, the women matched the language of their male interlocutors more frequently than they matched the language of female co-participants. Valdes-Fallis concluded that these women switched to the language of males as a sign of their deference or accommodation to addressees. The fact that women accommodated more to men than to other women can be interpreted as their recognition of gender inequality. And as was discussed above in the analysis of the use of Spanish and English in a Puerto Rican bilingual community in New York City, age may be a factor in language switching. Children and young adults are likely to switch into the language of elder interlocutors, accommodating to their language dominance (Zentella 1997).

In sum, code switching is a complex process having many grammatical and interactional functions. It requires a firm knowledge of the formal grammars of both languages because of the structural constraints in each language that determine what kind of elements can and cannot be switched and where (and where not) they can be placed. Switching also requires communicative competence, learning how to use linguistic devices as emphatic, contrastive, and/or emotional signals. Studies of Mexican-American children (from 3 to 13 years old) found that linguistic proficiency must be fairly advanced before code switching can occur (McClure 1977). Fluent bilinguals (usually older) switched more often, in more complicated structural environments, and with greater interactional sophistication than did less linguistically competent (usually younger) children (ibid.:99, 111). Erica McClure concluded by commenting that "the adept use of code-switching by the bilingual can be viewed as analogous to the creative use of language by a skilled monolingual author or orator" (ibid.:112).

Code Mixing

Code mixing is a linguistic process that incorporates material from a second language into a base language, adding morphological markers of the base to introduced elements. It differs from code switching by integrating mixed material more deeply into the host's linguistic system. For instance, consider the following extract from Kannada, a Dravidian language of South India. In the text, the speaker employs many English words despite the fact that Kannada contains equivalents. English elements obey English grammatical rules within mixed units (e.g., commercial-minded, holy alliance of marriage), but English units obey Kannada rules in their placement within larger clauses. For example, the construction translated as "the sacred occasion of arranging the holy alliance of marriage" is governed by Kannada order placing relative clauses before head nouns (i.e., holy alliance of marriage + sacred occasion) (Sridhar 1978:111). The sample is from a contemporary play, spoken by a father angered by his prospective son-in-law's demand for dowry.

> ...kshamisu, *dear boy,* na:nu use ma:dida *strong language*-u eshto: *control*-ma:do:k no:dde. a:dre na:nu *educated*-u, man of *culture*-u, *broad-minded*-u, ambo:dnella martubittu nannello: halli:kade:l huttid *commercial-minded* gama:ra anta tilkondu *holy alliance of marriage arrange*-ma:do: *sacred occasion*-nalli *dowry* eshtu anta ke:lti:yalla, nan *blood*-u *boiling point*-ge barde iddi:te?
>
> (...Forgive me, dear boy, I tried so much to control the strong language that I used. But, on this sacred occasion of arranging the holy alliance of marriage, forgetting that I am educated, a man of culture, broad-minded, and taking me for a village-born, commercial-minded rustic, you ask me how much "dowry" I would give! Wouldn't my blood come to a boiling point?) (ibid.:110)

Another instance of code mixing in the text is the application of Kannada morphological markers on transferred material. Suffixes *-u, -ma, -ge,* and *-nalli* are added to appropriate English words: educated-*u,* control-*ma,* boiling point-*ge,* sacred occasion-*nalli.*

Like code switching, code mixing has social functions. In India, speakers who use English are perceived as well educated, sophisticated, and refined. In the quoted text, the speaker employs English to contrast his own enlightened opinions with those of traditional, backward people (ibid.:114).

The Navajo language provides some further examples of code mixing. Two processes operate to integrate English material into Navajo structure. First, English verbs occur in conjunction with Navajo helping verbs: "make" with transitives and "do/be" with intransitives. Navajo verbs then carry obligatory markers for person, number, mode, and aspect (Canfield 1980:219). For instance:

1. Nancy *bich'ı˜?*   show *ánílééh*
Third person:to   second person:make
"Show it to Nancy."

2. Swimming *asht'ı˜*
first person:do/be
"I'm swimming."

A second type of mixing is characterized by substituting an English word in place of a Navajo verb stem. In this case, Navajo affixes are added to transferred forms:

3. *shil   naweasy* (from "queasy")
first person:with   third person:sick
"I feel sick."

4. *shiléechãã?i   anáyíílturn* (from "turn")
my dog   third person:died
"My dog died."

Navajo/English code mixing occurs in the speech of bilinguals, often young speakers, reflecting their exposure to the English language and to Anglo culture.

In the following examples from Canadian francophone speech, speakers embed English words into French morphological and syntactic structure. In the first utterance, French suffixes are added to an English adjective; in the second, an English unit, "high-rise building," is adjusted to French word order that places a modifier after, rather than before, its head noun (Poplack 1988:97):

1. Sont *spoilés* rotten.
"They're spoiled rotten."

2. A côté il y en a un autre gros *building high rise.*
"Next door there's another big high-rise building."

INTERETHNIC MISCOMMUNICATION

Because cultural expectations are part of communicative competence, interlocutors who come from the same culture are likely to operate with the same rules for speaking and interpreting speech. In contrast, interlocutors of different cultural backgrounds may misinterpret each other's messages despite the fact that they comprehend the language spoken. Quoting Susan Gass and Evangeline Varonis, "No natural speech utterance is ever made in a linguistic vacuum. Each is enriched and empowered by a social history that considers the relationships of class, status, power, and solidarity, and a linguistic history that includes culturally specific rules of discourse, politeness, conversational maxims, conversational inference, and patterns of interpretation" (1991:121). When people converse, they use their own culture's norms to interpret messages and to evaluate interlocutors. Positive or negative judgments are often based not necessarily on speakers' actual intentions, but on hearers' own culturally derived norms about how social and personal meanings are expressed in language. Listeners attribute to speakers the kinds of motives they would have if they had expressed themselves with the linguistic forms they are hearing. Because most cultural and linguistic presuppositions are nonconscious, interlocutors most often interpret each other's speech subjectively. Exposure to another culture or frequent interethnic contacts may modify subjective reactions. However, misinterpretations may become entrenched and contribute to creating and maintaining stereotypes about other people.

Miscommunication can occur in any encounter, even between people of the same culture, or, for that matter, the same family. But cultural differences increase the chances of divergent understandings. Problems can arise when participants attribute direct or indirect meanings to each other's speech. Consider the following exchanges between wives and husbands. In both cases, the wives are American and the husbands are Greek (Tannen 1982:220, 222):

1. **WIFE:**   John's having a party. Wanna go?
   HUSBAND: Okay.
   (Later)
   WIFE: Are you sure you want to go to the party?
   HUSBAND: Okay, let's not go. I'm tired anyway.
2. **HUSBAND:** Let's go visit my boss tonight.
   WIFE: Why?
   HUSBAND: All right, we don't have to go.

In both episodes, spouses misinterpreted questions and statements. American wives intended their questions as straightforward requests for confirmation or clarification. But Greek husbands interpreted them as indirect expressions of hesitation or disinterest. Even though participants obviously knew each other well, they were incorrect about interactional meanings implied by assertions and questions. Such lack of synchrony can become a way of life and can lead to deeper conflicts. Quoting Deborah Tannen on this issue, "Misjudgment is calcified by the conviction of repeated experience" (ibid.:220).

When family members who come from different cultural backgrounds interact, their statements and assessments of ongoing communication are based on unstated presuppositions of which they are unaware. These "taken-for-granteds" (Fitch 2003) become part of conversational cues that form the basis of participants' judgments. The problem faced by people in such situations is that they do not state assumptions that they believe everyone shares. Indeed, to state the obvious in conversations is generally considered rude. As Fitch explains, "To make explicit something that a competent hearer could be assumed to know calls into question how competent this particular hearer actually is" (ibid.:100). Because cultural presuppositions or "taken-for-granteds" are naturalized through socialization and through hearing talk in "well-worn grooves of inference," they become part of a background ideology that goes unquestioned. If people were more aware of these assumptions, they might challenge or resist them in ways that would be socially destabilizing. Although people often disagree with each other overtly, the disagreements are usually about options of how to act within boundaries that are not themselves challenged. For example, in her study of a dinnertime conversation involving an American wife, her Colombian husband, and their two children, Fitch points out that the parents' disagreement over how to handle their 9-year-old son's request for an allowance only touches the surface of the actual difference in their social perspectives. The parents argue about whether the son should divide his money into two jars, one with funds to spend and one to save, or whether he should let his father hold on to the money that he wants to save. The mother argues for the child to be self-reliant, while the father wants to help his son by keeping the money for him. Fitch interprets their words as an argument over much more fundamental issues that neither one consciously espouses, that is, whether people should value independence and individuality or should emphasize interdependent, mutually reliant relationships with others.

When people of different ethnic backgrounds interact frequently, they can become aware of their divergent interpretations, possibly as a result of arguing about each other's meanings. But when interethnic encounters are brief, routinized, or limited to specific contexts, miscommunication can easily lead to negative stereotypes. For example, in a study of the speech of Chinese businesspeople, Linda Young identified linguistic features that render their style problematic for American interlocutors. The structure of Chinese sentences and discourse differs fundamentally from that of English. English sentences are based on a subject–predicate order, whereas Chinese follows a topic–comment format. Compare the sentences below (1982:74):

English:	A giant squid	ate the blue surfboard.
	Subject	Predicate
Chinese:	Blue surfboard	giant squid ate.
	Topic	Comment

Chinese structure also contains subordinate clauses that evaluate assertions made in main clauses. Subordinate clauses precede main clauses, each introduced by specific markers, described by Young as causal (because…, therefore; since…so); conditional (if…, then); and concessive (although…, yet or but) (ibid.:75).

These linguistic patterns apply not only to sentences but to the organization of discourse as well. Chinese speakers use a topic–comment format in ordering the presentation of their opinions, judgments, and requests. Chinese speakers respond to questions by first stating their reasons or explanations and ending with their judgments. Consider the following two exchanges (ibid.:76):

AMERICAN: How does the Nutritional Institute decide what topics to study? How do you decide what topic to do research on?

CHINESE: *BECAUSE,* now, period get change. It's different from past time. In past time, we emphasize how to solve practical problems. Nutrition must know how to solve some deficiency diseases. In our country, we have some nutritional diseases. But now it is important that we must do some basic research. *SO,* we must take into account fundamental problems. We must concentrate our research to study some fundamental research.

(In response to question about qualifications for salespeople): My business is textile. The salesman is…. The quality of the salesman, need something different. *BECAUSE* the volume of making a sales in textiles is at least over ten thousand US dollars, sometimes. Whenever anybody who makes a decision to buy such…willing to pay such amount, we'll make sure their financial aid is strong. And, then…sometimes the market may suddenly drop in textile. Maybe we're willing to buy one month ago, but may not be buying…want to buy now. Things like that. *SO,* for a salesman, also have to understand about the financial situation and things like that.

When Americans listened to tapes of these conversations, they had difficulty following the arguments or understanding the points being made. They described the Chinese speakers as hesitant, unclear, and evasive. Americans prefer a concise presentation of views, stating conclusions first and then, if necessary, proceeding to explanations. In contrast, Chinese people prefer to provide their reasoning initially, gradually developing shared knowledge so that when a conclusion is finally stated, its legitimacy will be mutually recognized. Chinese speakers intend this style as a display of cooperation and a desire to avoid confrontation (ibid.:80). Americans typically failed to appreciate underlying Chinese social values and instead became impatient with surface forms. In comparing these ethnic differences, a bilingual Chinese student living in the United States commented that Chinese speakers.

at the same time as [they] are speaking, are reasoning with the listener to allow the listener to see whether what they say makes sense or not. This Chinese speech style is more open-minded, less biased, not as constrictive as the American style, where it immediately sets you up to a particular frame of mind. You see, with the American style, you can react immediately to what the speaker says without listening to the rest of [her or his] explanation. (ibid.:82–83)

When participants have divergent interpretations of underlying intentions, serious consequences can ensue, especially in situations where one participant has authority over another. In these cases, dominant people can discriminate against subordinates with justifications based, in part, on stereotypes triggered by communicative styles.

In complex, multiethnic societies, ethnic stratification is interwoven with other kinds of unequal relationships. Ideally, all participants help construct social meanings of encounters, but in situations of inequality, meanings and interpretations given by high-status people override those of low-status participants. For instance, analyses of interactions and outcomes in job interviews reveal that divergent assumptions about meanings of questions and answers can work against the ability of minority people to be understood and taken seriously. Consider the following extract from an interview for a job as a librarian in a college in Great Britain. The interviewers are British and the applicant is a South Asian man with a British professional degree (Jupp et al. 1982:252–253):

INTERVIEWER: One last question, Mr. Sandhu, why are you applying for this particular type of job in a college—a librarian's job in a college?

APPLICANT: Well, in fact, I have, up till now—um—previous to my—this job which I'm at present doing, I did send about 150 applications and my present job that was the only interview I got and I was accepted there and I was given that job doing and that is a temporary job as you know. Job is going to finish next December—so I desperately need another job—I've already sent about 50 applications but this is my second interview.

INTERVIEWER:	I see, thanks very much.
SECOND INTERVIEWER:	What attracts you to this particular librarian job and, in particular, why do you want to come to Middleton College?
APPLICANT:	Well, as I have said, I have already applied for 50 other jobs, you know, sent 50 applications and—er—this is my second interview. I'm not particularly interested in this particular job. I'm interested in a job maybe in an academic library maybe in a public library—any job in this field, you know—I'm qualified for this and I desperately need one.
SECOND INTERVIEWER:	Um—well, we, I think, perhaps might be looking for someone who's really committed to working for the college for the next at least three or four years.

The critical problem faced by the applicant has nothing to do with his linguistic skills; he is a fluent speaker of English. His handicap is his lack of knowledge about underlying sociolinguistic rules for conducting interviews. According to British (and American) norms, interviewers often ask indirect questions and expect applicants to respond by focusing on their special qualifications and interests. The candidate here did not recognize the implied meanings of interviewers' questions. In discussing the episode afterward with researchers, Mr. Sandhu "confirmed that he was puzzled and somewhat insulted by being asked a question that he interpreted as meaning, 'Why do you want a job?' " (ibid.:252).

This exchange was obviously problematic for all parties. The interviewers were confused by Mr. Sandhu's response, as shown by the fact that the second interviewer pursued the question of the candidate's specific qualifications and interests. Because this inquiry was also stated indirectly, Mr. Sandhu again failed to respond according to British norms. The applicant made two errors of interpretation and reply. First, he responded to surface forms of questions rather than to their indirect, implied meanings; second, he answered directly and perhaps too honestly. His basic message was that he is qualified for this (and any comparable) job and therefore ought to be hired. Because the interviewers did not directly state their confusion or dissatisfaction with Mr. Sandhu's replies, they did not give him any clues that he could use to satisfy their concerns. Each subsequent turn only served to deepen and solidify or (to use Tannen's term) "calcify" misinterpretations by all participants. These are serious problems because interviewers are in a position to make decisions that critically affect applicants' lives. Thus, members of ethnic minorities may be discriminated against, albeit unconsciously, because they and dominant decision makers, or gatekeepers, rely on divergent behavioral and interpretive frameworks. Examination of interviews such as this and others (Gumperz 1993) indicates that the problems that arise in communication materially affect the outcome, often to the disadvantage of non-native speakers.

The likelihood of cultural misinterpretation actually increases with the greater linguistic fluency of non-native speakers. When conversing with someone whose knowledge of the language of discourse is clearly limited, people are more likely to make allowances for their performance, but when the interlocutor demonstrates linguistic competence, people tend to ignore possible cultural causes of divergent meanings.

Interpretations of communicative behavior are embedded in cultural matrices consisting of attitudes and expectations about the ways that actions and words convey values. Much has been written about differences between American and Japanese norms and their influence on linguistic and cultural interpretation. For example, the linguistic style of Americans stresses directness, avoidance of ambiguity, and expression of personal tastes and opinions. This style contrasts with Japanese norms that stress indirectness, ambiguity in expression of personal judgments, and qualifying or mitigating opinions. These two styles are embedded in cultural differences emphasizing distinct attitudes about people and their relationships. In the United States, cultural norms focus on the value of personal independence and individual achievement, while in Japan, cultural norms emphasize people's interdependent relationships and the familial or community contexts that support them (Gudykunst and Nishida 1994). While Americans value direct expression of opinions and tend to favor truthfulness that is abstract and not tied to context, Japanese frame their statements in keeping with the expectations of others and the possible effect that their own opinions and ideas might have on their interlocutors. For Japanese speakers, truthfulness depends on understanding the context in which it is expressed. Japanese distinguish between what may be said in public and what may in fact be one's personal opinions. If personal opinions conflict with what is acceptable to their conversation participant, Japanese speakers refrain from stating their own ideas.

Americans and Japanese may use greetings differently as well. In the United States, greetings are used to initiate interactions with strangers and to establish new relationships, but in Japan, greetings are generally not exchanged with strangers, but only with people with whom one already has a relationship (ibid.:45). In addition, Americans ask more questions of strangers than do Japanese, and they are more willing to disclose information about themselves (ibid.:65).

Turn-taking patterns also differ in American and Japanese conversations. American speakers may compete with each other for the floor and take long turns in order to hold the floor, especially when they have introduced a topic. In contrast, Japanese speakers tend to take short turns and to distribute turns equally among co-participants regardless of who has initiated the topic (ibid.:48–49).

While members of all societies are attuned to the possibility of face-threatening acts, people differ in respect to the kinds of acts that they consider to be a threat to their face. Japanese define face as "honor, pride, trustworthiness, politeness, respect extended to others, considerateness, and dignity," while Americans tend to understand face as "credibility, reputation, self-respect, appearance of strength, pride, status, and self-defense" (ibid.:79). Given these values, Japanese feel that they lose face when they are insulted, criticized, or are treated inconsiderately by others, whereas Americans lose face when they personally fail or are treated as not credible. And these differences in turn affect the ways in which people attempt to persuade others. For example, when business managers were asked how they would persuade employees who were consistently late to change their behavior, Japanese managers reported that they "appeal to the employees' sense of 'duty'" ("It is your duty as a responsible employee of this company to begin work on time"). In contrast, American managers said that they "threaten" their workers ("If you don't start reporting to work on time, I will have no choice but to dock your pay.") or issue ultimatums ("If you can't come to work on time, go find yourself another job"; ibid.:47).

Summary

Language contact frequently results in changes in linguistic systems. New sounds may be introduced and/or grammatical constructions may be altered. In addition, all languages borrow words from foreign sources to name introduced items, activities, or ideas.

Within multilingual communities, speakers adjust to their languages and to each other in several ways. They often employ each language in certain situations, and they are also sensitive to topics or participants. Stable patterns of language use can become established, but shifts in values and preferences may occur as a result of changing economic, social, and/or political conditions. In such situations, some languages may gain ascendancy because members of the community employ them in more contexts, while others may become limited in their communicative functions. In the most extreme cases, some languages may die out.

Common strategies of bilingual interlocutors include code switching and code mixing, techniques of blending material from each language. Use of these techniques enables bilingual speakers to maximize both their available linguistic inventories and their methods of signaling personal, interactional, and social meanings.

Although contact with members of diverse ethnic and linguistic groups is a culturally and individually enriching experience, it can result in miscommunication. Interlocutors interpret messages on the basis of their own socialization about linguistic and sociolinguistic cues. People enculturated into different systems have learned divergent normative cultural models and therefore may misinterpret the behavior and speech of others.

References

ANDERSON, JEFFREY. 1998. Ethnolinguistic dimensions of Northern Arapaho language shift. *Anthropological Linguistics* 40:43–108.

APPEL, RENE, AND PIETER MUYSKEN. 1987. *Language Contact and Bilingualism.* London: Edward Arnold.

ARTIGAL, JOSEP MARIA. 1993. Catalan and Basque immersion programmes. In *European Models of Bilingual Education,* ed. H. Beardsmore. Philadelphia, PA: Multilingual Matters, pp. 30–53.

ATTINASI, JOHN. 1985. Hispanic attitudes in northwest Indiana and New York. In *Spanish Language Use and Public Life in the US,* ed. L. Elias-Olivares. The Hague: Mouton, pp. 27–58.

BARON, DENNIS. 1990. *The English-Only Question.* New Haven, CT: Yale University Press.

BERLITZ, CHARLES. 1982. *Native Tongues.* New York: Grosset and Dunlap.

BIALYSTOK, ELLEN, FERGUS CRAIK, DAVID GREEN AND TAMAR GOLLAN. 2009. Bilingual Minds. *Association for Psychological Science , Psychological Science in the Public Interest* 10, no. 3:89–129.

BIALYSTOK, ELLEN, FERGUS CRAIK, RAYMOND KLEIN, AND MYTHILI VISWANATHAN. 2004. Bilingualism, aging, and cognitive control: Evidence from the Simon Task. *Psychology and Aging* 19, no. 2:290–303.

BONVILLAIN, NANCY. 1978. Linguistic change in Akwesasne Mohawk: French and English influences. *International Journal of American Linguistics* 44:31–39.

BONVILLAIN, NANCY. 1988. Dynamics of personal narrative: A Mohawk example. *Anthropological Linguistics* 30:1–19.

BRIGGS, LUCY. 1985. Bilingual education in Peru and Bolivia. In *Language of Inequality,* ed. N. Wolfson and J. Manes. The Hague: Mouton, pp. 297–310.

BROOK, G. L. 1958. *A History of the English Language.* New York: W. W. Norton.

CANFIELD, KIP. 1980. A note on Navajo-English code-mixing. *Anthropological Linguistics* 22:218–220.

Cultural Survival Quarterly. 2001. Endangered languages, endangered lives: The struggle to save indigenous languages. *Cultural Survival Quarterly* 25 no. 2.

DORIAN, NANCY. 1981. *Language Death: The Life Cycle of a Scottish Gaelic Dialect.* Philadelphia: University of Pennsylvania Press.

FERGUSON, CHARLES. 1959. Diglossia. *Word* 15:325–340.

FIELD, MARGARET, AND PAUL KROSKRITY. 2009. Introduction: Revealing Native American language ideologies. *Native American Language Ideologies: Beliefs, Practices, and Struggles in Indian Country,* ed. M. Field and P. Kroskrity. Tucson: University of Arizona Press, pp. 3–28.

FITCH, KRISTINE. 2003. Taken-for-granteds in (an) intercultural communication. In *Studies in Language and Social Interaction,* ed. P. Glenn, J. Mandelbaum, and C. LeBaron. Mahwah, NJ: Lawrence Erlbaum, pp. 91–102.

FOUGHT, JOHN. 1985. Patterns of sociolinguistic inequality in Mesoamerica. In *Language of Inequality,* ed. N. Wolfson and J. Manes. The Hague: Mouton, pp. 21–39.

GAL, SUSAN. 1978. Peasant men can't get wives: Language change and sex roles in a bilingual community. *Language in Society* 7:1–16.

GASS, SUSAN, AND EVANGELINE VARONIS. 1991. Miscommunication in nonnative speaker discourse. *"Miscommunication" and Problematic Talk,* ed. N. Coupland, H. Giles, and J. Wiemann. Newbury Park, CA: Sage, pp. 121–145.

GITHIORA, CHEGE. 2002. Sheng: Peer language, Swahili dialect or emerging Creole? *Journal of African Cultural Studies* 15, no. 2:159–181.

GROSJEAN, FRANÇOIS. 1982. *Life with Two Languages.* Cambridge, MA: Harvard University Press.

GUDYKUNST, WILLIAM, AND TSUKASA NISHIDA. 1994. *Bridging Japanese/North American Differences.* Thousand Oaks, CA.: Sage.

GUMPERZ, JOHN. 1982. *Discourse Strategies.* New York: Cambridge University Press.

GUMPERZ, JOHN. 1993. Interviewing in intercultural situations. In *Talk at Work: Interaction in Institutional Settings,* ed. Paul Drew and John Heritage. New York: Cambridge University Press, pp. 302–327.

HALLE, MORRIS, AND GEORGE. N. CLEMENTS. 1983. *Problem Book in Phonology.* Cambridge, MA: MIT Press.

HALMARI, HELENA. 1998. Language maintenance on the Alabama-Coushatta Reservation. *Anthropological Linguistics* 40:409–428.

HARRIES, PATRICK. 1988. The roots of ethnicity: Discourse and the politics of language construction in South-East Africa. *African Affairs* 87:25–52.

HINTON, LEANNE. 1998. The role of women in Native American language revival.

HOFFMANN, CHARLOTTE. 1996. Monolingualism, bilingualism, cultural pluralism and national identity: Twenty years of language planning in contemporary Spain. In *Monolingualism and Bilingualism: Lessons from Canada and Spain,* ed. S. Wright. Philadelphia, PA: Multilingual Matters, pp. 59–90.

HORNBERGER, NANCY. 1998. Language policy, language education, language rights: Indigenous, immigrant, and international perspectives. *Language in Society* 27:439–458.

JACOBS, KAIA'TITAHKHE ANNETTE. 1998. A chronology of Mohawk language instruction at Kahnawa:ke. In *Endangered Languages: Current Issues and Future Prospects,* ed. L. Grenoble and L. Whaley. New York: Cambridge University Press, pp. 117–123.

JUPP, T. C., CELIA ROBERTS, AND JENNY COOK-GUMPERZ. 1982. Language and disadvantage: The hidden process. In *Language and Social Identity,* ed. J. Gumperz. New York: Cambridge University Press, pp. 232–256.

KACHRU, BRAJ. 1978. Toward structuring code-mixing: An Indian perspective. *International Journal of the Sociology of Language* 16:27–46.

KOVACS, AGNES, AND JACQUES MEHLER. 2009. Cognitive gains in 7-month-old bilingual infants. *Proceedings of the National Academy of Sciences* 106, no. 16:6556–6560.

KRAUSS, MICHAEL. 1992. The world's languages in crisis. *Language* 68:4–10.

MAGWA, WISEMAN, AND DAVIE MUTASA. 2007. Language and development: Perspectives from Sub-Saharan Africa. *NAWA Journal of Language and Communication.* June:57–68.

MCCLURE, ERICA. 1977. Aspects of code-switching in the discourse of Mexican-American children. In *Linguistics and Anthropology,* ed. M. Saville-Troike. Georgetown University Round Table on Languages and Linguistics. Washington, DC: Georgetown University Press, pp. 93–116.

MEEK, BARBARA. 2009. Language ideology and aboriginal language revitalization in the Yukon, Canada. *Native American Language Ideologies: Beliefs, Practices, and Struggles in Indian Country,* ed. M. Field and P. Kroskrity. Tucson: University of Arizona Press, pp. 151–171.

MERTZ, ELIZABETH. 1989. Sociolinguistic creativity: Cape Breton Gaelic's linguistic "tip." In *Investigating Obsolescence: Studies in Language Contraction and Death,* ed. N. Dorian. New York: Cambridge University Press, pp. 103–116.

MOLONY, CAROL. 1977. Recent relexification processes in Philippine Creole Spanish. In *Sociocultural Dimensions of Language Change,* ed. B. Blount and M. Sanches. New York: Academic Press, pp. 131–159.

NETTLE, DANIEL, AND SUZANNE ROMAINE. 2000. *Vanishing Voices: The Extinction of the World's Languages.* New York: Oxford University Press.

NYIKA, NICHOLUS. 2008. "Our languages are equally important": Struggles for the revitalization of the minority languages in Zimbabwe. *Southern African Linguistics and Applied Language Studies* 26, no. 4:457–470.

PANDIT, IRA. 1986. *Hindi English Code-Switching: Mixed Hindi English.* Delhi: Datta Book Centre.

PEDRAZA, PEDRO. 1985. Language maintenance among New York Puerto Ricans. In *Spanish Language Use and Public Life in the US,* ed. L. EliasOlivares, E. A. Leone, R. Cisneros, and R. Gutierrez. The Hague: Mouton, pp. 59–71.

PFAFF, CAROL. 1979. Constraints on language mixing: Intrasentential code-switching and borrowing in Spanish/English. *Language* 55:291–318.

PLATT, JOHN, HEIDI WEBER, AND HO MIAN LIAN. 1984. *The New Englishes.* London: Routledge and Kegan Paul.

POPLACK, SHANA. 1988. Language status and language accommodation along a linguistic border. In *Language Spread,* ed. P. Lowenberg. Georgetown University Round Table in Languages and Linguistics, 1987. Washington, DC: Georgetown University Press, pp. 90–118.

PYLES, THOMAS, AND JOHN ALGEO. 1982. *The Origins and Development of the English Language,* 3rd ed. New York: Harcourt Brace Jovanovich.

RICHLAND, JUSTIN. 2009. "Language, court, constitution. It's all tied up into one": The (Meta)pragmatics of tradition in a Hopi tribal court hearing. In *Native American Language Ideologies: Beliefs, Practices, and Struggles in Indian Country,* ed. M. Field and P. Kroskrity. Tucson: University of Arizona Press, pp.77–98.

RUBIN, JOHN. 1985. The special relation of Guarani and Spanish in Paraguay. In *Language of Inequality,* ed. N. Wolfson and J. Manes. The Hague: Mouton, pp. 111–120.

SAAH, KOFI. 1986. Language use and attitudes in Ghana. *Anthropological Linguistics* 28:367–377.

SCOTTON, CAROL. 1976. Strategies of neutrality: Language choice in uncertain situations. *Language* 52:919–941.

SRIDHAR, S. N. 1978. On the functions of code-mixing in Kannada. *International Journal of the Sociology of Language* 17:109–117.

STANLAW, JAMES. 2004. *Japanese English: Language and Culture Contact.* Hong Kong: Hong Kong University Press.

TANNEN, DEBORAH. 1982. Ethnic style in male-female conversation. In *Language and Social Identity,* ed. J. Gumperz. New York: Cambridge University Press, pp. 217–231.

VALDES-FALLIS, GUADALUPE. 1978. Code-switching among bilingual Mexican-American women: Towards an understanding of sex-related language alternation. *International Journal of the Sociology of Language* 17:65–72.

WATSON, SEOSAMH. 1989. Scottish and Irish Gaelic: The giant's bed-fellows. In *Investigating Obsolescence: Studies in Language Contraction and Death,* ed. N. Dorian. New York: Cambridge University Press, pp. 41–60.

YOUNG, LINDA. 1982. Inscrutability revisited. In *Language and Social Identity,* ed. J. Gumperz. New York: Cambridge University Press, pp. 72–84.

YOUNG, ROBERT, AND WILLIAM MORGAN. 1987. *The Navajo Language,* rev. ed. Albuquerque: University of New Mexico Press.

ZENTELLA, ANA. 1985. The fate of Spanish in the US: The Puerto Rican experience. In *Language of Inequality,* ed. N. Wolfson and J. Manes. The Hague: Mouton, pp. 41–59.

ZENTELLA, ANA. 1997. *Growing Up Bilingual.* London: Blackwell.

ZUAZO, KOLDO. 1995. The Basque country and the Basque language: An overview of the external history of the Basque language. In *Towards a History of the Basque Language,* ed. J. Hualde, J. A. Lakarra, and R. L. Trask. Philadelphia, PA: John Benjamins, pp. 5–30.

ZUENGLER, JANE. 1985. English, Swahili, or other languages? The relationship of educational development goals to language of instruction in Kenya and Tanzania. In *Language of Inequality,* ed. N. Wolfson and J. Manes. The Hague: Mouton, pp. 241–254.

CHAPTER 13

Language and Institutional Encounters

Note the italicized words in the following excerpt from a doctor's advice to a patient seeking to choose a method of birth control:

> *"If you take them* right, *you are going to be in* pretty good shape…*and of course,* everybody uses birth control pills."

Were the doctor's words neutral? Or did they reveal the doctor's attitudes? When patients seek advice from doctors, they usually assume that the doctor has impartial information and expertise that they themselves lack. But a patient's ability to make an informed, independent decision is often undermined by the words doctors use to convey covert messages and assert their authority.

Talk is situated in interactions that are themselves situated in social contexts within an overall framework of cultural meanings. In addition to the words spoken in encounters, messages about people's worthiness and rights are communicated. These messages are the subtexts of human interaction. We have already seen that societal divisions based on categories of gender, class, race, age, and ethnicity affect speaking styles and conversational strategies. In this chapter, we focus on interconnections between language and hierarchical roles. We begin with a general discussion of this issue and then proceed to analyses of institutional settings, where power and control versus powerlessness and constraint are systematically actualized. We will discuss institutional interactions in the United States and Great Britain. Examination of behavior in other societies might demonstrate the extent to which comparable institutional controls are exerted.

LANGUAGE IDEOLOGIES

In most modern nations, language ideologies entail practices that select and promulgate a standard or "legitimate" language for use in public contexts, for example, in schools; the media; and political, economic, and religious life. Other varieties or dialects are then evaluated negatively in relation to the standard and their speakers are stigmatized. The selection of a particular dialect as a standard is the result of complex linguistic, social, economic, and political processes. The variety chosen as standard is usually one associated with an elite segment of society. In Great Britain, the standard (now usually referred to as Received Pronunciation [RP]) was a dialect originally associated with upper-class speakers regionally centered around London. By the late nineteenth century, that regional elite dialect spread through the English public school system (in US terms, private schools). Any young man desiring to advance his education at a prestigious university was well advised to adopt the accent as well (Milroy 2000:72). At first, RP was a regional dialect, but it became the standard once it was redefined on the basis of class. RP speakers were perceived as upper class, whereas speakers of other dialects were stigmatized because of their language and its class associations.

In the United States, in contrast, issues of class were publicly less salient than in Great Britain; instead, racial and ethnic distinctions were more prominent. Until the late nineteenth century, bilingualism and multilingualism were accepted as normal features of language life; indeed, several states officially recognized bilingualism by publishing statutes in languages other than English (French in Louisiana; German in Pennsylvania). By the early twentieth century, however, the tide had turned against an official view of the United States as a multilingual nation. Increasing immigration from Europe and elsewhere aroused antagonism on the part of the US citizenry, resulting in a general pattern of loss of foreign mother tongues by the second or third generation. Influences from other languages on American English pronunciation were disparaged. Racial distinctions became especially marked, leading to the strong stigmatization of African-American English that continues into the present. The dialect recognized as standard in the United States is perceived to have the least distinguishing features and is therefore thought to be the most easily understood no matter what the regional background of the hearer. In contrast to the situation in Great Britain, where most people are able to identify the standard Received Pronunciation whether they speak it or not, in the United States there is a much lower degree of consensus about exactly what standard pronunciation is. In fact, it is more readily identified by what it is not—that is, it is not the speech of regional stigmatized groups, especially Southerners, New Yorkers, and Appalachian dwellers, and not the language of racially or ethnically marginalized groups, especially African Americans and Hispanics. There is no general agreement, even among professional linguists, about the regional origin of the US standard (ibid.:59).

But in both the United States and Great Britain, there is strong adherence to a standard language ideology, a belief that there is only one correct form of spoken and written language. Deviations from the given standard are wrong and in need of correction. Positive and negative attitudes toward standard or nonstandard speech are extended to the speakers themselves. Speakers of nonstandard forms are thought to be stupid, lazy, or even morally deficient.

The emergence of a dominant and dominating standard language in the United States and Great Britain is indicative of a widespread process. Bourdieu has written extensively about a similar generation of standard or "legitimate" language in France (1991:46–48). There the dialect of French spoken by the social and political elite was elevated to official status beginning in the sixteenth century, relegating other regional varieties to the status of "patois." Before their subordination to the standard, regional dialects had both oral and written uses. Local ordinances, contracts, and literary forms (especially poetry) were written in the regional dialects, but these gradually gave way to the dominance of the standard and lost their deep traditions, becoming marginalized forms of speech.

Struggles over standard language choice are evident in many former colonial nations of Africa, where the focus is not so much on dialects within a language, but on choices among separate languages. Decisions about which language to use as the official or national language, whether to choose a colonial language (English or French) or whether to select an indigenous language, are often fraught with conflict based on class and ethnicity as well as on the prevailing social, economic, and political goals of the central government.

The development of a standard language often coincides with processes of state formation and centralization through which the state exerts both linguistic and cultural control. Such is the case of the development and spread of the language known as Indonesian in the modern state of Indonesia. Indonesian has roots in several Malay dialects indigenous to some areas of the collection of islands known as Indonesia as well as several varieties of lingua francas that were spoken throughout the islands before European colonial encounters in the sixteenth century (Errington 2000:207). The origin of Indonesian dates to the period of Dutch colonial occupation. Because the Dutch avoided using their own language with their native clients, they sought to select an indigenous dialect for use in trade, missionary, and other colonial enterprises. Dutch efforts to deepen their control in the islands led to further attempts to standardize a native language. By the beginning of the twentieth century, a standard Malay orthography was introduced, leading to codification of a "general, cultured Malay" (ibid.:207). The language was formally given the name of Indonesian in 1928 at a meeting of Dutch-educated native and political elites in a declaration of purpose, stating the goal of creating a "unified people" speaking "one language" in a "single homeland" (ibid.:208).

Through its promulgation in schools and its use in public governmental and economic contexts, Indonesian has become the dominant language of Indonesia. As is common in many colonial and postcolonial nation-states, the national language is the mother tongue of relatively few people, but its dominance and authority are acknowledged by all. Indeed, the state can hardly conceive of itself without a dominant language ideology. In the words of a government publication, "the concept of national society cannot be fully understood if one national language does not exist. A country that has one general/common language known throughout society will be more advanced in development and its political ideology will be safer and stable" (Burhan 1989; quoted in Errington 2000:211). Indonesian has thus become associated inextricably with the identity of Indonesia as a nation, and the language has become part of the identity of the nation's citizens.

As currently spoken, Indonesian has incorporated numerous borrowings from English. This tendency is applauded by some of the country's language commentators and authorities who, at the same time, are critical of the use of words derived from archaic Old Javanese and Sanskrit. Attitudes favoring English words reflect the desire to appear "modern," while the use of Old Javanese and Sanskrit words is criticized as "nativistic" and "traditional" (ibid.:216). The extent of English influence on Indonesian is evident not merely in the number of borrowed words, but also in their meanings. English borrowings have been adopted into Indonesian for new items of modern technology, a process that is nearly worldwide in its scope. In addition, however, English borrowings have replaced some perfectly adequate Indonesian words. English has therefore exerted its dominance as the major international language, infiltrating the local dominant language of Indonesia.

In all modern countries, the educational system is one of the prime arenas for the promulgation of standard languages and standard language ideologies. Dell Hymes's observations about language dynamics in the United States apply equally well elsewhere:

> Language has been a central medium of cultural hegemony in the United States. Class stratification and cultural assumptions about language converge in schooling

to reproduce the social order. A latent function of the educational system is to instill linguistic insecurity, to discriminate linguistically, to channel children in ways that have an integral linguistic component, while appearing open and fair to all. All have equal opportunity to acquire membership in the privileged linguistic network. If they fail, it is their fault, not that of the society or school. (1996:84)

The insistence on linguistic uniformity, coupled with criticisms of any deviation, is among the building blocks of educational systems in most modern state societies. Linguistic hegemony is manifested both in the use of the standard and the recognition of its prestige and authority, even by people who do not themselves employ it. And failure to conform, whether due to choice or to lack of access, justifies the exclusion of marginalized groups. As Bourdieu observed:

Produced by authors who have the authority to write, fixed and codified by grammarians and teachers who are also charged with the task of inculcating its mastery, the language is a *code,* in the sense of a cipher enabling equivalences to be established between sounds and meanings, but also in the sense of a system of norms regulating linguistic practices. (1991:45)

However, the fact that nonstandard, nonprestige varieties continue with great vigor should be understood, not in negative terms but as a positive reflection of individual and group values. Nonstandard varieties must have "covert prestige" (Trudgill 1972) or they will eventually disappear. Discovering what these competing values are is a complex matter. As Kathryn Woolard observes, "Competing sets of values exist, creating strong pressures in favor of the 'illegitimate' languages in the vernacular markets, and not just an absence of pressure against them" (1985:744). Nonstandard varieties may be supported by ingroup membership identification, especially in close and dense networks in which members exert strong pressures toward conformity as an emblem of their group. Group solidarity may have meanings of opposition to domination by elite segments of society. Quoting Woolard again, "It is critical to understand that vernacular practices are productive, not merely reproductive, that they arise not from a mere bending to the weight of authority, but are paradoxically a creative response to that authority, mediated by the opposition value of solidarity" (ibid.:745). The continuation of "devalued linguistic strategies and genres" (Gal 1989:349) can be seen as forms of resistance by their very survival and also by their transmitting "alternate models of the social world" (ibid.).

Studies of language ideologies and resistance to dominant varieties can attempt to connect the processes of face-to-face interaction with social, economic, and political orders. Members of some stigmatized communities may sharpen or exaggerate their differences from the dominant forms. For example, a dialect of Caribbean immigrants and their descendents in Great Britain, called Afro-Lingua, turns the tables on standard English, opposing some widespread metaphoric constructions that transmit negative images of "black" and positive images of "white" (see Chapter 6 for a discussion of Afro-Lingua and other Black dialects in Great Britain and the United States). Afro-Lingua originated and spread with the popularity of the Rastafarian movement and especially with the reggae music closely identified with it. Rastas, as they are often known, challenge some basic cultural models transmitted through standard English metaphors:

For example, black is depicted as bad or dangerous. "A black day" means that on a particular day things have gone badly for the whites. "A black sheep" in the family means the worst or most detested member of the family. One sees, quite clearly, that black is associated with the devil and hell and with death. At the same time the assumption is that white is good, right, pure. There is no doubt that the black/white opposition is racial and racist. (Bones 1986:46)

Some English words are altered in Afro-Lingua by changing syllables to highlight cultural and political meanings. For example, the word *politics* is transformed into *politricks,* the word *system* becomes *shitstem,* and *oppression* becomes *downpression* (Wong 1986:119). By transforming these words, speakers of Afro-Lingua deliberately attack underlying meanings that exemplify the control of the dominant language ideology on subordinate and stigmatized peoples.

In societies with standard language ideologies, the standard becomes naturalized; that is, community members regard the standard as natural, commonsensical, and unquestioned. They accept the fact that any variation from the standard is either ignored or discredited. Language ideologies develop and are maintained in specific cultural contexts. It is appropriate to ask whose interests are served by the dominant ideologies, who benefits from the beliefs that are promulgated, and who is disadvantaged. Languages and beliefs about language have social and political implications. Beliefs about the correctness of the dominant language become so much a part of people's everyday thinking that they fail to see that these beliefs are socially constructed. Rather, the dominance of the standard becomes part of their everyday consciousness, unexamined and naturalized. As Michael Silverstein remarked,

> Many speakers of languages in such cultural orders [where dominant languages are standardized] cannot even conceive of any other kind of linguistic phenomena, for instance, unwritten languages, languages without standards, and so on.... The very concept of language rests upon finding the various institutional paraphernalia of standardization, for example, literacy in relation to standard register, grammars and dictionaries, authoritative judgment of correctness enforceable in certain institutional rights of power over discourse, and so forth. Within cultures of standard, forms of language that lack these to some significant degree are relegated to some classificatory category other than language. (2000:122–123)

In addition to its role in the development of a standard language, state control exerts its influence in language practices that impose social and cultural values and promulgate particular dominant language ideologies. For example, although literacy is usually seen as a positive process, or at worst a benign one, literacy may in fact be embedded in social and political processes that are detrimental to the survival of an indigenous culture.

Bambi Schieffelin's study of the introduction of literacy among the Kaluli of Papua New Guinea demonstrates the ways that literacy practices contributed to transforming Kaluli identity. Although Kalulis first met white people in 1935, it was not until the early 1970s that Australian missionaries entered their territory, bringing Christianity, education, and literacy in an attempt to alter Kaluli society. The missionaries, soon joined by others, produced grammatical sketches and readers that introduced Christian and European concepts and values. New ideas were transmitted with sample verbs and nouns such as *write, book, wireless radio, letter,* and *do school*. In some cases, Kaluli words were expanded in their meanings to fit borrowed concepts, whereas in others the missionary linguists created new words out of native morphemes (Schieffelin 2000:302–303). Christian concepts and characters were introduced in sentences given to illustrate Kaluli vocabulary: "Do you pray to God every day?" and its accompanying response "Yes, I pray every day" (ibid.:304). Other sentences included vocabulary and concepts depicting European activities that were presented to Kalulis in a positive light. Especially common were sentences about buying goods such as cloth, beads, and tinned fish that could be purchased at mission stores. Stories in primers and readers depicted Kaluli families in traditional subsistence activities but also included foreign activities such as going to the mission store, church, or school. One of the most startling introductions is the word employed for the Kaluli themselves. Instead of using an indigenous name for the people, the readers employ the term *ka:na:ka,* derived from the New Guinean trade pidgin Tok Pisin. Although the formal definition of *ka:na:ka* is "native, nonindentured person," it has long been used with derogatory connotations to mean "uncivilized, backward" (ibid.:308). Through the introduction of this word for the Kaluli, the books "(re)formulate, (re)present, (re)construct" Kaluli social identity and present the Kaluli themselves in negative terms (ibid.:309).

Literacy practices have also transformed Kaluli modes of acquiring knowledge and forming opinions. Traditionally, knowledge was imparted through oral learning, dialogue, and conversational feedback, whereas consensus was built through open discussion with the participation of all interested parties. In contrast, the literacy practices imparted to the Kaluli are authoritative, regimented, and controlled through the printed text and through a new group of local experts such as teachers and missionaries. Replacing patterns of egalitarian discussion and community involvement, a hierarchical system wielded by foreign experts and their students has taken shape in indigenous communities.

Language ideologies entail beliefs and practices about the use of authoritative speech, that is, the speech of culturally validated voices of authority. Quoting an authority [or what Mikhail M. Bakhtin (1981:342) referred to as "authoritative discourse"] creates distance among the narrator, the text quoted, and the listener. According to Bakhtin,

> ...the authoritative word demands that we acknowledge it, that we make it our own; finds us, quite independent power it might have to persuade us internally; we encounter it with its authority already infused to it. The authoritative word is located in a distant zone, organically connected with a past, that is felt to be hierarchically higher. Its authority was already acknowledged in the past. It is a prior discourse. It is therefore not a question of choosing it from among other possible discourses that are its equal. (ibid.)

Reported speech, especially the reported speech of authority, can be used to manipulate an audience for a desired end. Quoting authoritative sources can be a move to legitimate one's own position and persuade an audience to accept one's word without question. Depending on the cultural and situational context, however, use of authoritative speech can be controversial and may not necessarily achieve the desired ends. In societies like our own, authorities quoted may be from a variety of sources: so-called experts (scientists, doctors); public, political, or media figures; historical personages who have come to be considered near-legendary (e.g., most prominently, our founding fathers).

In many other societies, traditional lore, proverbs, and mythological characters may be cited as authorities for everyday experience. In a study of the use of authoritative speech in a political controversy on the Micronesian island of Belau, Richard Parmentier demonstrated the ways in which language use signaled changing norms associated chiefly with language. During a village meeting prompted by political disputes over a new constitution, a middle-age woman suddenly began to scream, stomp her feet, repeat the names of the two chiefs present, adding, "I hate it, I hate it, I hate it!" (1993:266). The woman later claimed to have been speaking the words of one of the community's traditional gods. This claim proved to be controversial; some villagers accepted it as valid, while others (including the chiefs) questioned the woman's right to speak for the gods, noting that she did not have the proper cultural credentials to use the divine authoritative voice. During the uproar that followed this outburst, a villager asked one of the chiefs whether he would in fact support the new constitution. The question itself violated traditional norms because high-ranking chiefs are never asked to publicly state their opinions. Overhearing the question, another chief interjected, "Who was it that asked this? I cannot approve of this *boy* asking Ngirtur for his thoughts" (ibid.:267). Another meeting was soon held to discuss the political turmoil and events of the previous meeting. After several attempts to be recognized as a speaker, the high-ranking chief referred to the past incidents and spoke at length about his reactions to the political controversy, quoting traditional proverbs to substantiate his interpretation of events and the need for traditional norms of interaction and procedure. As Parmentier observed,

> [the chief] is using his authority as a high-ranking title holder and as an accepted expert on Belauan tradition and village history to typify rather than to merely report discourse. The function of citing traditional proverbs can be understood in terms of the speaker's need to legitimize his own position as an authoritative voice. In attempting to remind the village of certain traditional norms of language use and to perform a resolution of political tension exacerbated by recent violation of these rules, the chief obviously places great store not only in his own political weight but also in the power of speech to affect the goals sought. For some people in the village, however, the speech accomplished an unintended purpose—that of standing as a historical marker of the demise of chiefly authority and respect. (ibid.:284)

In the traditional view, "high-ranking chiefs have little need to persuade others of their views through public oratory, since their final decisions were not subject to questioning or even debate. In fact, passive silence was one of the hallmarks of presupposed chiefly authority. So the chief's highly persuasive speech about the relevance of traditional rules of speaking belies its own message" (ibid.:284).

LANGUAGE AND STATUS

Differences in rights and values given to various categories of people are manifested in several features of language. First is the ability to name and classify:

> The ability to bestow meanings—to "name" things, acts and ideas—is a source of power. Control of communication allows the managers of ideology to lay down the categories through which reality is to be perceived. Conversely, this entails the ability to deny the existence of alternative categories, to assign them to the realm of disorder and chaos, to render them socially and symbolically invisible. (Wolf 1982:388)

Examples of how society labels people demonstrate this process. For instance, many English words for females tend to take on derogatory, limiting, and often sexual meanings. Similarly, members of nonwhite racial groups are negatively labeled. The right to name and thereby either legitimate or trivialize others is not only expressed in vocabulary but also enacted in daily encounters whereby it reflects and reproduces the prevailing social order. The following episode is recalled by Alvin Poussaint, an African-American doctor (1967:53):

> "What's your name, boy?" the policeman asked.
> "Dr. Poussaint, I'm a physician."
> "What's your first name, boy?"
> "Alvin."

These four utterances poignantly give witness to conflicts inherent in many unequal social interactions. They are overt here, although they are generally enacted covertly. In struggles for the right to name, powerless individuals lose the ability even to name themselves.

In stratified societies, elites or majorities often employ derogatory words for subordinate groups. Use of these words "may promote prejudice by enhancing the perception of out-group members as like each other and unlike in-group members" (Greenberg et al. 1988:76). Derogatory labels express negative attitudes by speakers toward members of targeted groups and produce negative stereotypes about people defined as "other." In statements reminiscent of ethnolinguistic discussions of relationships between language and thought, Jeff Greenberg and his colleagues contend:

> Because DELs [derogatory ethnic labels] have the power to communicate all the negative beliefs about a given group in a single word, they are likely to be especially potent communicative devices. Words have the power to make a concept seem like something that actually exists in the world. [They] crystallize [negative] beliefs into concept or prototype that has a sense of concrete reality to those who use the term. Essentially, the DEL is a cultural legitimization of a negative conception of members of a particular out-group; the mere existence of the term implies at least some cultural sanctioning of the concept it represents. (ibid.:77)

Use of derogatory labels for people based on their gender, ethnicity, or race is an example of expressing and imposing social beliefs through rights to name and refer. Subordinate groups are thus demeaned and depersonalized.

Interrelationships between language and hierarchical social models can also be demonstrated by contrasts in evaluations of speaking styles associated with different groups. For example, women's speech is negatively judged because of its reputed use of numerous devices to hedge or disclaim speakers' opinions and generally to show deference to interlocutors. Although it is positively perceived as "polite," women who employ this style are dismissed as inconsequential. But women who use direct ("masculine") speech are criticized for being abrasive and aggressive. A cross-cultural view, though, quickly demonstrates that it is the speakers, female or male, who are socially evaluated and not their linguistic output in the abstract. For instance, recall that among the Malagasy (Keenan 1974), women's direct and sometimes confrontational style is denigrated, whereas men's inexplicit, vague, and deferential speech is praised and in fact likened to that of the ancestors. (See Chapter 8 in this text.)

Differences in status are not only expressed in words and speech patterns but also demonstrated in assignment of rights to speak and determine topics of talk. Rights or constraints are displayed in interpersonal encounters on a daily basis where high-status people can exert their influence. We have seen examples of this process in relation to male–female and adult–child interactions, where higher-status individuals often interrupt or disregard contributions of lower-status interlocutors. The latter learn strategies of indirection, mitigation, or manipulation in order to eke out some communicative space. According to Bonnie Erickson and her co-workers, low-status speakers react to their situation by developing a style that the researchers identify as "powerless." It is characterized by the use of intensifiers, hedges, hesitations, rising intonations, and polite forms (1978:267–268). These examples are appropriate illustrations of Bourdieu's observation that "the competence adequate to produce sentences that are likely to be understood may be quite inadequate to produce sentences that are likely to be *listened to,* likely to be recognized as *acceptable* in all the situations in which there is occasion to speak" (1991:55).

Immediate contexts of encounters shape the behavior taking place within. Volosinov believed in the significance of the "hierarchical factor" in influencing the form of utterances and the manner in which they are communicated. He applied this insight to understanding the forms and functions of all utterances. Utterances are interpreted by participants within the context of specific situations and thus are socially driven. This social element dictates tone and content of communication, depending on the function of the expression. This will dictate if an utterance is issued as plea instead of a warning, or as a demand instead of a request. The manner of communication is also dependent on the situation and audience, it determines if the expression should be a formal or casual utterance, one that is expressed boldly or with reserve. (1973: 21, 86–87)

A Non-Western Comment

As with all aspects of language use, cultural models of behavior may give alternative interpretations of similar stylistic variants. Although differentiation of status exists to some extent in most, if not all, societies, whether within households, communities, or wider social systems, linguistic and sociolinguistic forms that reflect inequality may vary. Behavior exemplifying high or low status in one culture may have quite different social meanings in another. For instance, in Japan, the so-called "powerless" style, identified by Erickson and her co-workers (1978), is valued for all Japanese speakers (Wetzel 1988). Within Japanese culture, these behaviors are not markers of powerlessness; rather, they are are indicators of the speaker's basic humanness, expressed by *ningen-rashii* and *yutaka,* concepts stressing interpersonal harmony and empathy (ibid.:560). Favored models of interaction and communication emphasize "sensitivity to the other, demonstrations or signals of empathy, solicitation of agreement, concern about what others are thinking, silent protest as a strategy for signalling disagreement or displeasure" (ibid.:561). In contrast, Japanese speakers view communicative behaviors that are considered signals of power in our society (control through interrupting, challenging, or ignoring another's comments; direct assertions of opinions) as "immature or childish" (ibid.).

This comment does not negate the relevance of analyzing interactions between social structures and language. Indeed, it cautions us to attend to the continually interconnected nature of linguistic form and cultural context that gives talk its meaning and potency.

INSTITUTIONAL CONTEXTS

In our society, institutional settings, wherein roles are distributed and interactions are managed in terms of preassigned rights and constraints, are important in orienting, explaining, and influencing our lives. Jürgen Habermas referred to development of a "technocratic consciousness" that affects our ways of thinking (our worldview) in institutional spheres and is extended to other interactional contexts. It has become a "background ideology," replacing interpersonal and symbolic understandings of experience with its own emphasis on "purposive-rational action." We accept this mode of thought and behavior as normal, natural, and legitimate. In fact, "the concealment of the difference [between alternate modes of thinking] proves the ideological power of the technocratic consciousness" (1970:105–107).

Numerous institutions affect our lives and through their hierarchical structure elicit characteristic kinds of behaviors within them. Two prominent examples are institutions that provide education and health care. Everyone has direct experience with schools and medical providers, coming under their authority for extended periods of time and/or in critical periods of life. A third major institution in US society is that of the legal establishment. Although many people do not have direct contact with courts, courtroom behavior is so explicitly linguistic and controlling that it deserves attention as an exemplar of the ways that communicative contexts affect behavior.

We will presently turn to analyses of communicative norms prevailing within these institutions and attempt to uncover their impact on individuals and their role in maintaining hierarchical organizations of society. Social relations are enacted on both the societal ("macro") level and the interpersonal ("micro") level. Human behavior in even the most personalized encounters is affected by wider social meanings. Although people may not be consciously aware of hidden constraints, they nonetheless act in accordance with unstated rules of behavior and communication. Encounters within institutional frameworks are influenced by the overall authority of institutions themselves, expressed interpersonally by specific participants through specific ways of speaking. Following discussion of these structured settings, we end the chapter by considering the role of mass media in constructing, reflecting, and reinforcing social beliefs.

The field of critical discourse analysis is particularly relevant in the analysis of communicative behavior in institutional contexts, although it adds significant perspectives to the study of informal interactions as well (Fairclough 2001). Critical discourse analysis emphasizes examination of power and dominance as they are produced and reproduced in the daily talk that occurs in many public and private settings. In addition, analyzing power uncovers unstated assumptions and presuppositions that are encoded covertly in institutional and media language. Presuppositions that have been thoroughly naturalized convey messages that are taken for granted and therefore unquestioned. They form dominant and dominating ideologies that most people do not challenge. Of course, it is possible to challenge these ideologies, but to do so may have negative consequences.

EDUCATION

Educational settings provide excellent demonstration of the role of hierarchy in allocating rights to direct encounters. The authority of teachers in the classroom is not only based on their institutional position, it is also based on the status of age (adult versus child) and often as well by that of class (middle class versus working class). Parents, too, are constrained in their interactions with school professionals because of institutionally derived rights of the latter to make decisions and to dispense or withhold rewards.

Communicative behavior in classrooms in the United States is typified by question-and-answer sequences. Either individual children are chosen to respond or they compete with each other through calling out or raising their hands for the right to respond. Such insistence on individualized answers, which seems so "natural" to those of us socialized in this system, creates difficulties for some groups of children. For instance, many Native American children are social-ized to refrain from behavior that isolates their performance in a competitive manner in front of peers. In a comparison of the classroom behavior of Native American children from the Warm Springs Reservation in Oregon with that of nearby non–Native American students, Susan Philips found that Native Americans were extremely reluctant to answer teachers' questions or to speak out in class. In contrast, in situations where they could have individual access to teachers, they were more likely than non–Native Americans to seek help, initiate questions, and engage in dia-logue (1978:397). Thus, it was the structure of settings, not inherent interest, that affected their responses.

People in other Native American cultures think of instruction as a process of discovery through observation by learners who arrive at conclusions based on information given to them and from which they deduce generalizations or applications. For instance, consider the following episode of a Cree elder speaking with a class of elementary schoolchildren in Alberta, Canada:

> An old man discussing number words in Cree and English first established with the children that one cannot say "one *moswa*" or "*peyak* moose." The students were left to make the general observation that both words have to be in the same language. The old man then showed them the symbol 1 and asked them which language that was in. The unanimous response was "English." The old man appeared startled but recovered quickly and began to make his point in a different way. He asked the chil-dren if the Ukrainians had a word for one and, after a moment of silence, was told that they did. He then asked about the Chinese and the children agreed that they too had a word for one. One boy then said, "I guess everybody has a word for one." The old man acknowledged that statement by saying, "Oh, I see." (Darnell 1985:69)

In contrast to this kind of interaction, in most US classrooms, questions are used explicitly to measure pupils' attentiveness and absorption of knowledge. Contextual examination of these speech events reveals that questions also function as control mechanisms. According to Elliot Mishler, "Through the act of questioning, one speaker defines the way in which the other is to continue with the conversation and thus defines their relationship to each other along a dimen-sion of power and authority" (1975:105).

In his study of adult–child interactions in first-grade classrooms, Mishler identified two types of "interrogative units," each composed of a sequence of three utterances including a ques-tion, a response from the addressee, and a confirmation from the initiator (ibid.:100–101):

I. Chaining
  1. Initial question
  2. Response/answer
  3. Confirmation/question (i.e., confirmation contains a further question)

Q: s1:	Did you really finish all your work before everybody else?
R/A: s2:	Yeah.
C/Q: s1:	What kind of work was it?
R/A: s2:	Well. We just had a piece of paper and it had all the names on it. And we had to see if it was odd or even.
C/Q: s1:	Do you know all the odd numbers and all the even numbers?
R/A: s2:	Uh huh.
C/Q: s1:	How far up can you count?

II. Arching

    1. Initial question

    2. Response/question

    3. Confirmation/response (i.e., response contains a question and confirmation is a response)

Q:	**s1:**	Whaddya mean? He is (S) He's
R/Q:	**s2:**	(S) Is he under water?
C/R:	**s1:**	He is. See now here's a scuba suit on him.
C:	**s2:**	I think he's dead.

Chaining was the predominant mechanism in all interrogative units in classrooms, but rates of chaining and arching differed, depending on the status of initiators. Adults employed **chaining**, asking another question after the child's response, in 84 percent of discourse series that they initiated, whereas **arching**, child responding to the adult's question with a question, occurred in only 30 percent of these interactions. In contrast, although chaining occurred in 69 percent of child-initiated sequences, arching had a higher frequency rate, at 78 percent (ibid.:107).

In sum, adults employ two methods of control: When initiating a discourse series, they use chaining (asking further questions) to regain control after a child's response; when children initiate a series, adults use arching (responding to questions with their own questions) to make a countermove, taking control from the child. Children do employ chaining at a substantial rate (69 percent) when initiating sequences with adults, but they seldom use arching (30 percent) to counter an adult's claim of control. Thus, status gives rights to determine the content and direction of talk, as well as rights to assert control over or take control away from interlocutors. Children learn these covert social lessons through the structure of their formal schooling.

Children also learn lessons about gender through classroom interactions. Although they are exposed to gender roles and associated conversational strategies in their homes (see Chapters 7 and 10), they become direct participants in the classroom when they engage in discussions and question-and-answer sequences. Boys tend to dominate class time with more frequent responses and lengthier turns. But teachers are the primary controllers and facilitators of talk in class, and they are responsible for constructing and reinforcing gender roles. In a study of classroom sequences, teachers (in this case, female teachers) helped boys dominate talk by more often turning toward them, gazing at them, and selecting boys to answer questions (Swann 1998).

Language plays a critical role in the micropolitics of interactions within educational institutions. Context, as always, provides the key to understanding the meaning of any utterance or series of utterances. Analyses of the taped transcripts of school meetings having the purported goal of making decisions about placing a child in special education programs reveal some ways that authority and order are managed (Mehan 1986). Participants included a school psychologist, principal, special education teacher, classroom teacher, and parent (usually the mother). Despite the overt goal of group involvement, decisions had actually been made by authorities (psychologist, principal, and special education teacher) prior to meetings. The meetings' real purpose, then, was to publicly ratify those decisions.

Numerous linguistic mechanisms were used by authorities in the process of "routinely inducing" others (teacher, parent) to agree (ibid.:141). Committee meetings began with lengthy presentations of information about the child, followed by brief segments of decision making (or decision affirming). In the first phase, high-status professionals spoke first. They presented data in "objective" terms, giving results of batteries of tests, filled with statistical percentages and technical terminology. The words chosen were dispassionate, global, and categorical. Authorities used professional terms and jargon without clarification. The effect is one of mystification, surrounding presentations in a linguistic mode of science, or, repeating Habermas's phrase, a "technocratic consciousness." And, as Habermas predicts, this mode is not questioned or challenged by others, particularly not by lower-status participants (1970).

In addition, psychologists often spoke in platitudes, for example, "He has difficulty applying himself" or "She does possibly have some fears and anxieties" (ibid.:149). Again, no one questioned the standards by which a child's "applying" him- or herself was measured, nor the relevance of "fears and anxieties" to the issue at hand.

The tapes further demonstrate that high-status participants often interrupted teachers' and parents' speaking turns by asking questions or commenting on prior statements. According to Mehan, the contributions of parents and teachers focused on "contingent" explanations of children's performance, providing background and contextual information (ibid.:155–156). These were dismissed by professionals as irrelevant because they are not measurable and comparable.

Authorities used specific linguistic devices to create a (false) impression of solidarity and reciprocity. Consider the following excerpt from the opening of a session (analysis based on data from Mehan 1986:147–149):

PSYCHOLOGIST: Um. What we're going to do is, I'm going to have a brief, an overview of the testing because the rest of, of the, the committee has not, uh, has not an, uh, been aware of that yet. And uh, then each of us will share whatever, whatever we feel we need to share.

PRINCIPAL: Right.

PSYCHOLOGIST: And then we will make a decision on what we feel is a good, oh placement for an, Shane.

Note especially the use of *we* in the very first sentence, setting the scene of a communal effort. *We* and *us* occur in nearly all of the psychologist's utterances. A similar effect is achieved with repetitive uses of the word *share*. The principal's contribution, *right,* serves to ratify the proceedings, affirm their legitimacy, and express consensus.

The decision-making phase of meetings tended to be short and succinct. Two examples follow.

PSYCHOLOGIST: Does the uh, committee agree that the, uh learning disability placement is one that might benefit him?

PRINCIPAL: I think we agree.

PSYCHOLOGIST: We're not considering then a special day class at all for him?

SPECIAL-EDUCATION TEACHER: I wouldn't at this point.

MANY: No.

PSYCHOLOGIST: Okay. Now, okay, now then, let's, why don't we take a vote. Um, for the Learning Disabilities Group pullout program. Um, is there anyone, anyone who does not agree? Okay. I think that was unanimous. (soft laughter) All right.

Decisions clearly are not being negotiated; rather, they are presented. There is little room for disagreement, particularly given overall institutional contexts and status imbalances among participants. Those with authority present conclusions and request (in fact, assume) compliance of subordinates. The latter, recognizing institutional rules, accept and thereby maintain their subordination. Their collusion may appear to be voluntary, but they are actually constrained by the hierarchical order of context.

The decision-making process in the school is not inconsequential; in fact, it may have lifelong implications for a student. In a later work, Mehan (1996) shows in detail the discourse processes that result in a child, a complex human being, receiving a label of *learning disabled*. At the end of a lengthy process of abstracting particulars from the density and ambiguity of experience, the child becomes an object in an official version of his or her life experiences and coping strategies. The institutional processes of "referral," "educational testing," and "placement" each generate a different sequence of discourse that is decontextualized and subsequently recontextualized in another setting. The complexity of experience is distilled into technical jargon that is then used to justify submitting the child to the next step in the procedure, eventually leading to a label and a consequent placement. A teacher makes a decision based on interactional and pedagogical facts that a particular student may need assistance of some kind, the teacher's report is discussed at a meeting of a "school appraisal team," the meeting generates a summary recommendation, and the school psychologist conducts educational testing and writes a report that is part of the discussion at a placement committee meeting that makes the final placement decision. The forms and reports generated at each stage "are decentered and indeed de-voiced" because, as they move through the system, they become "institutionally isolated from the interactional practices that generated them in the preceding events" (ibid.:259).

In a final placement meeting analyzed by Mehan, the "expert" (i.e., school psychologist) presented supposedly objective data using professional, technical jargon, while the child's teacher and mother spoke in ordinary, plain language. Despite, or rather because of, the fact that the psychologist's report was difficult to understand, she was never questioned for clarification, whereas the mother and teacher were frequently interrupted and asked to clarify their statements. As Mehan notes,

> The psychologist's report gains its authority by the very nature of its construction. The psychologist's discourse obtains its privileged status *because* it is ambiguous, *because* it is shot full of technical terms, *because* it is difficult to understand. When technical register is used and embedded in the institutional trappings of the formal proceeding of a meeting, the grounds for negotiating meaning are removed from under the conversation. To request a clarification from the psychologist, then, is to challenge the authority of a clinically certified expert. (ibid.:269–270; emphasis in original)

At the end of this process, the ambiguities and inconsistencies in a child's behavior, some indicating problems and others indicating great strengths, are all equally submerged under a label that contributes to constituting the child's educational and social identity. Labeling has far-reaching consequences for children's future educational experiences and for their life choices. The process of sorting students into categories that are then assigned specific meanings of "handicapped" or "normal" (Mehan 1991) is accomplished through specific discourse practices. These practices are generated and maintained outside the educational institution, but they are enacted within each setting and each interaction.

A study of teacher–pupil interactions in schools in South Africa prior to the end of apartheid demonstrates the effects of teacher demeanor on classroom interactions and on learning

(Muller 1989). Analysis of discourse practices in the schools revealed that the difference in teacher training and preparedness significantly affected children's perceptions of their teacher's competence. Well-trained and well-paid teachers in schools serving white children spoke with confidence and authority as they displayed their knowledge, while poorly trained and under-paid teachers in schools for Black children employed discourse styles that conveyed hesitation, uncertainty, and ambiguity. Because of these different discourse strategies, the teachers responded in contrasting ways to their pupils' contributions to class. Teachers in the white schools were authoritative in their responses to children's answers, categorically accepting or rejecting children's statements. Teachers in the Black schools were less definite in their responses, often mitigating or hedging and allowing for ambiguity in the search for accuracy. Children correctly evaluated their experience in the classroom, revealing their keen awareness of underlying messages of the teacher's authoritativeness. For example, one Black child commented, "I can say it's right…but what makes me not sure about the answer is that…the teacher was not sure…and so I didn't know the reason which made her not to be sure about it" (ibid.:325). However, there are some benefits to learning in the contexts of a less authoritative teacher. Students in these classes are more comfortable asking questions and seeking explanations for their own errors. In contrast, students whose teachers present themselves as the final word on truth are often intimidated and refrain from asking follow-up questions that could help them understand the material (ibid.:329).

MEDICAL ENCOUNTERS

In medical encounters, doctors routinely exert authority and control, and patients acquiesce to their authority. Medical encounters are speech events in which the legitimacy of technocratic consciousness is taken for granted. In this context especially, Habermas's assertion that the "dominant, rather glassy background ideology, which makes a fetish of science, is…irresistible and far-reaching" (1970:111) is pertinent.

Analyses of transcripts of medical interviews reveal several important recurrent themes. First, doctors direct encounters through use of questioning, establishing relevant topics and their development. Second, their reactions to patient contributions validate or invalidate responses and thereby reassert control. Third, they dismiss, by ignoring or redirecting, patients' talk if it is not consistent with the scientific medical model upheld by the doctor. By controlling and interpreting information dispensed to patients, doctors influence decisions that patients ostensibly have a right to make for themselves.

An intriguing issue that underlies an analysis of medical encounters is the creation of asymmetry between doctor and patient despite the fact that it is the patient who is the ultimate initiator. That is, it is the patient who decides to come to the doctor, but once he or she enters the medical establishment, it is the doctor who decides when to see the patient, thus effectively asserting interactional primacy. Thereafter, the doctor takes the active role as questioner and evaluator, while the patient's role is generally as a responder. In addition, doctors set up sequences consisting of three turns, occupying two of them. The first turn consists of a question posed by the doctor, the second turn is the patient's response, and the third turn is the doctor's assessment of the patient's answer (Ten Have 1991:150). These assessments may contain acknowledgments, ratifications, corrections, or summaries, but they function interactionally to maintain control of the topic and conversational flow.

These do not function as supportive backchannel cues to indicate active listenership but are used instead to limit the patient's contributions:

D: What's the problem?

P: (…) had since last Monday evening so it's a week of sore throat

D: hm hm

P: which turned into a cold…uhm…and then a cough.

D: A cold you mean what? Stuffy nose?

P: uh Stuffy nose yeah not a chest cold.

D: hm hm

P: uhm

D: And a cough.

P: And a cough…which is the most irritating aspect.

D: Okay. (hh) uh Any fever?

P: Not that I know of. I took it a couple of times in the beginning but haven't felt like—

D: hm. How bout your ears?

The following excerpt reveals strategies used by a doctor to direct the patient's talk into the "scientific" mode:

D: Hm hm. Now what do you mean by a lung infection?

P: What's a lung infection? Bronchitis or something.

D: Are you coughing anything up?

P: Yeah. Lots of stuff.

D: Hm hm hm hm

P: Mostly green stuff.

D: Hm hm. And how long has this been going on?

P: Its been getting worse for the last few months. Ever since I started smoking again.

D: Hm hm How much do you smoke?

P: I don't know. Enough to calm my nerves at night. Mostly at night when I'm trying to go to sleep.

D: What type of smoking are you talking about?

P: I've been smoking pot.

D: How long have you been smoking marijuana?

P: Since I've been married.

D: How long is that?

P: (giggle) Two years. (giggle) Well, I did quit for a while, but then I had more things on my mind and ya know since I got married I been in and out of work so I—I have to have something to go to sleep.

D: Hmm.

P: I mean I'm not gonna—It's either gonna be alcohol or pot, but pot satisfies me more than alcohol does. I don't like getting sick in the morning. I did have some Valium but they're only two milligrams and that's supposed to quiet me down during the day but it doesn't.

D: How often do you take them?

Of particular significance in this encounter is the doctor's reaction to the patient's insertion of personal content in her responses about her smoking. The doctor does not ask for clarification of implied connections between the patient's marriage and her drug abuse problem. Rather, he refers to the objectivity of numbers: "How long is that?" The doctor does allow the patient to elaborate on her personal message, but he does not comment on it. Instead, at the end, he returns again to scientific inquiry: "How often do you take them?" All of the patient's attempts to individualize her problem are diverted into and subsumed by a medical perspective. We do not know her motives, but if she were seeking support or help with her life situation, this goal was unfulfilled.

Moral messages are frequently uttered by doctors in the guise of scientific objectivity. For instance, in an interview recorded by Howard Waitzkin (1983), a doctor responded to a patient's anxiety about returning to work after a heart attack by moralizing about the benefits of working. Even assuming that the patient was well enough to return to work, the point is that doctors can influence patients' behavior through implied communicative messages as well as through overt medical explanations:

I would think that maybe we would plan on getting you back, say mid-June, to work, which I think is the best thing in the world for you, to get back to work...there's no reason why we can't get you back in the middle of things. (ibid.:152)

Doctors also exert their influence by providing or withholding information requested by patients who are in the process of making medical decisions. For example, a study of doctors' advice about contraceptive methods shows that medical professionals use their expert authority to steer patients toward decisions that they themselves endorse (Fisher and Todd 1986). In transcripts of medical interviews, the doctors, who all advocated use of birth control pills, stressed the efficiency and reliability of pills and the inconvenience and uncertainty of other methods. Conversely, negative consequences of the pills and the advantages of barrier devices were downplayed.

Many linguistic techniques employed by doctors had subtle rather than obvious effects and contributed to supporting their preferences. The following analysis is based on an interview between a doctor and a patient who requested advice about all contraceptive methods in order to choose the one best for her (ibid.). The doctor began with a long discourse on options, starting with the pill (his favorite), then proceeding to intrauterine devices (IUDs), diaphragms, and over-the-counter aids. The order of listing itself is significant, beginning with his preference and continuing through less and less desired choices. Not only did he selectively present scientific information about each option, he also used specific wordings to convey his message subtly. He made the following comments about pills (emphasis added):

"If you take them right, *you are going to be in* pretty good shape...*and of course,* everybody uses birth control pills."

He described some "short-term side effects," including the occurrence of blood clots, and further claimed:

"All side effects [are] short term*...but there are a lot of* little nuisance *problems"*
(e.g., headaches, skin rashes, and bad moods)

Throughout his discourse, the doctor made several switches of personal pronoun reference that had the effect of confounding the distinction between himself and the patient. While talking about birth control pills and the risks of cancer, he said:

"Now if you *told me* your *mama had cancer of the womb and* my *aunt had breast cancer and* my *grandmother died of female cancer, then maybe* we *should talk a little bit more."*

Because the patient had no such medical history, he continued,

"I think we *can feel safe on birth control pills."*

And, finally,

"When you decide, I want a child, I think it's good to get off them six months before you wanna start trying because there's such a thing called post-pill amenorrhea."

This use of language is undoubtedly not conscious, but it nonetheless contributes to the appearance of a jointly negotiated decision. By switching reference, the doctor adopts the patient's perspective, making her feel that their interests are identical.

In another interview, when a patient taking birth control pills wanted to change methods and asked about alternatives, the doctor responded in an extended monologue about the dangers of IUDs and ended by asserting, "So it sounds like maybe the pill really is the right thing" (ibid.:14). The surface form of this sentence implies input from both interlocutors, but in fact, only the doctor has contributed and therefore actually directs the decision-making process.

In all these medical encounters, it is true that patients have a role to play, contributing to and colluding with doctors' authority. Neither patient nor doctor acts independently of one another. However, a critical difference between the two is that the behavior of the former is primarily reactive, whereas that of the latter is largely determining. Professionals and clients in this institutional setting accept and adopt cultural models of rights that individuals have in their diverse roles. People with structural authority exert their influence through communicative strategies, whereas subordinates accede to institutional constraints.

Despite the constraints on patients to accede to doctors' agendas, patients are not totally powerless. Nancy Ainsworth-Vaughn's examination of interactions between 30 patients and six physicians in hematology–oncology practices in two Midwestern communities revealed several strategies patients used to claim power. Patients introduced or shifted to topics of concern to themselves through statements and questions posed to doctors. They also suggested diagnoses for their own conditions or challenged diagnoses offered by physicians, citing evidence from their own experiences. In addition, patients sometimes proposed treatments through declarative statements or questions. Through these and other mechanisms, patients were able to use narratives, personal interpretations, and suggestions to work with their physicians in co-constructing diagnoses and treatments (Ainsworth-Vaughn 1998:180–182). In general, patients attempted to make sense of their illnesses and cope with their changed way of life by grounding their experience in narratives of their world. Physicians sometimes attempted to avoid engaging in too much conversational talk with patients, possibly to save time, to avoid questions of their competence, or to avoid emotional involvement and identification with patients. But patients were often successful in adopting strategies that claimed power for themselves.

A study of medical narratives can uncover patients' moves to protect and embody their sense of self in a context characterized by depersonalization, detachment, and intrusion into the self. In an interview between an elderly male patient and his physician, the patient repeatedly incorporated material from his centrally self-defining life story, that of his experiences in a Nazi concentration camp during World War II. Although the doctor clearly attempted to interfere with the patient's tellings by interrupting, the patient insisted on their relevance. He intruded details in the midst of the doctor's history taking. For example, he told a detailed story about having contracted tuberculosis during the war. After a long narrative sequence, the doctor responded with a direct command returning to the medical interview, "Back to your heart" (Young 1999:433). The patient inserted a second story by saying, "I was not sick except this finger." This turn compels the doctor to ask, "What happened to that finger?" supplying the patient with the needed warrant to continue. And finally, the patient inserted a third narrative with the introductory statement, "I have to tell you how I got that bump [on his head]" (ibid.:436). Following rules of conversational patterning, the doctor is obliged to respond with "How?"

While this analysis examines only a single interview, it demonstrates the strategies that patients can employ to assert rights to their own stories and to claim personhood for themselves in a context framed by a discourse of depersonalization and authority.

Patients who do not speak the same language as the doctor face additional problems in having their concerns addressed. A study of the role of hospital-based medical interpreters in a public hospital in northern California demonstrated the complex ways in which the interpreters contributed to silencing the patients and enabled the doctors to ignore patients' concerns (Davidson 2001). In this study, Brad Davidson compared the interactions of patients and doctors who both spoke English with those of Spanish-speaking patients requiring interpreters. Rather than playing a neutral role in "translating" the patients' words, interpreters essentially functioned as "pre-diagnosticians" by failing to convey some of the patients' questions and comments to the doctors, presumably because the interpreter was complying with a hospital mandate to "be quick" as well as to "be accurate" (ibid.:171). All the questions asked by English-speaking patients received either immediate or eventual responses from the doctors, whereas for Spanish-speaking patients, more than half of the questions asked were answered by the interpreters and the doctors were not even aware that a question had been posed (ibid.:175). This pattern has two significant results. First, patients' concerns were not addressed by a medical practitioner licensed to deliver medical services. Second, doctors developed attitudes about immigrant patients' passivity and lack of interest in their own care, which could have consequences for the kind of care patients received.

The kinds of problems uncovered in Davidson's research will undoubtedly become even more significant nationally as the number of immigrant patients who lack skills in English increases. For instance, in the research setting, in 1993, approximately 40 percent of the total patient population requested the assistance of interpreters (ibid.:171).

LEGAL SETTINGS

Legal proceedings are among the most highly structured interactional events in our culture. As outlined in Chapter 4, many aspects of behavior in legal settings, especially in courtrooms, are formalized: The physical environment and spatial positioning of participants are predetermined, rights and obligations to speak are given according to role, and relevance of topics is narrowly defined. Each type of participant—judges, lawyers, and witnesses—has different speaking styles.

Language used in legal proceedings, in both written and oral form, maintains its prestige because of its dissimilarities with colloquial English. The fact that legal language (or "legalese") is not well understood by laypeople enhances the authority of attorneys and judges because they are familiar with the code of encounters. Lawyers frequently become interpreters or translators of legal proceedings for their clients, a role that both adds to their status and renders clients dependent.

Some characteristics of legal language include the following (Mellinkoff 1963:11–29):

1. Common words used with specialized meanings:
   instrument "legal document"; *serve* "deliver legal papers"
2. Rare words from Old and Middle English:
   aforesaid, forthwith, hereafter
3. Latin words and phrases:
   corpus delicti, nolo contendere, res judicata
4. French words not in the general lexicon:
   fee simple, voir dire, tort
5. Legalistic jargon:
   order to show cause, pursuant to stipulation

As an example of the mystifying effect of special terminology and complex syntactic constructions, consider the following formulation of instructions to a jury in a personal injury case. Most Americans, including well-educated speakers of English, would have difficulty understanding that the judge is telling the jury that if the plaintiff's injury was partly caused by his own negligence, he cannot recover damages. The wordiness and complexity of legal phrasings create a density that is hard to decipher. This density produces an aura of distance and secrecy, further contributing to the prestige of its speakers.

> You are instructed that contributory negligence in its legal significance is such an act or omission on the part of the plaintiff amounting to a want of ordinary care and prudence as occurring or co-operating with some negligent act of the defendant, was the proximate cause of the collision which resulted in the injuries or damages complained of. It may be described as negligence on the part of the plaintiff, if found to exist, as helped to produce the injury or the damages complained of, and if you find from a preponderance of all the evidence in either of these cases that plaintiff in such case was guilty of any negligence that helped proximately to bring about or produce the injuries of which plaintiff complains, then and in such place the plaintiff cannot recover. (ibid.:26)

The construction of lawyers and of the speech of law as privileged begins in law schools, where the education of future lawyers is highly regimented. Law school classrooms are characterized by the professor's rigid control over the students. Law professors typically call on students without their volunteering. The students must be ready to perform to the specifications of a formalized mode of interaction. They are trained in the strategic use of technical jargon and the citation of case law and legal precedents that function as authoritative sources. Through tight control of turn taking, encouragement of the use of technical legal terms, and the insistence that students perform when called upon, "a highly regimented discourse style contributes to an authoritative approach to language, as law students are trained to read and speak about the texts that they will call upon for authority in the practice of their profession" (Mertz 1996:245).

Authority and control are paramount recurring themes in legal settings. These social principles are not enacted covertly, as is often the case in educational and medical contexts. Rather, they are made explicit in the functioning of courts. The overt purpose of court proceedings is establishment of innocence or guilt and determination of fines or punishments. Interactions are typically based on adversarial principles: Attorneys representing inherently conflictual positions (for the "defense" or the "prosecution") "argue their cases" before a neutral "judge" in order to persuade members of a jury to render a "verdict" favoring their side. Attorneys' styles of speaking are critical influences on a jury's decisions. Witnesses, too, are assessed by both what they say and how they say it.

Researchers in the study of courtroom behavior have discovered stylistic attributes of witnesses and lawyers that influence the ways that their statements are assessed. Bonnie Erickson and her colleagues identified two styles of speaking, referred to as powerless and powerful. *Powerless* speech, used by low-status witnesses, is characterized by frequent use of intensifiers (*so, very*), hedges (*kinda, I think, I guess*), hesitation forms (*uh, well, you know*), questioning forms (rising intonation in declarative contexts), and polite forms (*please, thank you*). *Powerful* speech, used by high-status witnesses (e.g., parole officers, doctors, and other expert professionals), tends to be free of these markers and to result in a "more straightforward manner" (Erickson et al. 1978:267–268).

The following dialogue exemplifies the relevant linguistic contrasts (ibid.:270):

Q: Then you went next door?

A: (**POWERLESS**)   And then I went immediately next door, yes.

  (**POWERFUL**)   Yes.

Q: Approximately how long did you stay there before the ambulance arrived?

A: (**POWERLESS**)   Oh, it seems like it was about uh, twenty minutes. Just long enough to help my friend Mrs. Davis, you know, get straightened out.

  (**POWERFUL**)   Twenty minutes. Long enough to help get Mrs. Davis straightened out.

Q: Now how long have you lived in Durham?

A: (**POWERLESS**)   All my life, really.

  (**POWERFUL**)   All my life.

Q: You're familiar with the streets?

A: (**POWERLESS**)   Oh yes.

  (**POWERFUL**)   Yes.

Q: You know your way around?

A: **(POWERLESS)** Yes, I guess I do.

(POWERFUL) Yes.

Erickson and her colleagues presented testimony in the two styles to evaluators who rated witnesses on various scales. Witnesses who used powerful speech were perceived to be more credible (believable, convincing, trustworthy, and competent) and attractive (strong, active, likable, intelligent, and powerful) than those speaking in a powerless style (ibid.:274–275). Credibility of witnesses is obviously crucial when juries deliberate and arrive at verdicts. Hearers attribute positive characteristics to speakers of powerful speech for several interrelated reasons. First, such speech is generally associated with high-status people, who, by social position, receive deference and respect. The fact that powerful witnesses are often professionals with scientific or other technocratic expertise adds to their credibility. Second, the comparative lower social status of most members of juries makes them vulnerable to the influence of authorities. Third, powerful speech, with its use of technical terminology and direct formulations, implies the speaker's certainty and self-assurance. In contrast, powerless speakers, who use qualifiers, hesitations, and hedges, unconsciously transmit messages of uncertainty about their own assertions. They are less likely to be believed, partly because they themselves seem unsure of their beliefs.

The overall structure of witnesses' discourse also has an impact on how they are perceived (Lind and O'Barr 1979). When witnesses give "fragmented" testimony, that is, are asked frequent, direct, and limiting questions, they are evaluated as less competent than when giving "narrative" testimony, that is, allowed to give longer responses (ibid.:76–77). When witnesses are permitted long, self-directed turns, listeners (juries) understand that the lawyer respects them. In contrast, when lawyers interrupt and repeatedly question a witness, the witness is seen to be held in low esteem.

The primary mode of linguistic interaction in courts is the question-and-answer sequence. In a study of British courts, Sandra Harris (1984) found that magistrates and clerks used various types of questions to control the contributions of defendants and make subtle accusations against defendants. Magistrates' proceedings involve defendants, usually of low socioeconomic status, who are in court because they failed to pay previously imposed fines. The goal of magistrates is to question defendants, ascertain reasons for noncompliance, and impose a court-ordered schedule of payments. Questions are not isolated linguistic utterances; rather, they function within specific contexts of the court and its purposes. Therefore,

> it is difficult for the person with higher status in a clearly defined authority role (magistrate, clerk, lawyer) to ask a question which is perceived by the defendant or witness as simply an information question and not about fixing responsibility or ascribing blame. The securing of information often becomes secondary in this context to the maintenance of status relationships, where the questioner has the power to reject both topics and answers as inappropriate and to structure the course the discourse will take. (ibid.:7)

Magistrates' and clerks' questions fall into several categories based on syntactic form (ibid.:10–11):

1. Interrogatives:

    a. Polar interrogatives:
        Do you work?
        Are you fit again now?
    b. Disjunctive interrogatives:
        Are you married or single?
        Did you say five pounds or nine pounds?
    c. Declaratives + interrogative frame:
        Is it true that…
        Are you asking the Court to…
    d. Declaratives + interrogative tag:
        That means you've got to pay thirteen pounds, doesn't it?
        You'd better not argue with any foreman in the future, had you?
    e. Interrogative request:
        Will you stand up, Mr. B., please?

2. wh-interrogatives:
    How much do they earn per week?
    Where are your children now?
    When were you taken sick?
    What are you going to do about it?
    How are you going to pay it then?
    Why is it you're suddenly flush with money?

3. Declaratives calling for confirmation:
    You're unemployed. (Yeah.)
    And then you did two weeks' work. (During May sir—yes.)
    You mean a total of five pounds. (A total of five—that's two pounds off my arrears.)

Types of questions were not randomly distributed but occurred with different frequencies, as displayed in the following table (ibid.:13):

Classification of Questions by Type

Type	Number	Percentage
Interrogatives	130	69.1
a. Polar, tag, disjunctive	59	
	(45.4% of interrogatives; 31.4% of all questions)	
b. wh-interrogatives	71	
	(54.6% of interrogatives; 37.8% of all questions)	
Declaratives for confirmation	58	30.9
Total	188	100.0

The syntactic form of questions triggers particular kinds of responses. Polar interrogatives require a yes or no answer, tag questions ask for yes or no confirmations, and disjunctives provide two alternatives, constraining the addressee to choose one. Many wh-questions are also highly conducive and lead to narrow response alternatives. For instance, questions of "how much" or "what" require minimal responses, as do those of "where," "when," and "who." Only "why" and "how" questions allow some latitude and elaboration of replies. In Harris's transcripts, of all questions asked, 62.2 percent were either yes or no or disjunctive interrogatives. The following table presents a classification by response (ibid.:14):

Classification of Questions by Response Required

Response	Number	Percentage
Answered by yes or no or disjunctive	117	62.2
Answered by naming set amounts	39	20.7
Answered by restrictive responses	21	11.2
"Why" and "how" questions	11	5.9
Total	188	100.0

The data reveal that, taken together, 94 percent of the questions call for limited or restricted replies. When defendants attempted to give more than minimal responses to questions, they were interrupted with subsequent questions (i.e., chaining), which meant that their explanations were ignored and dismissed, as demonstrated in the following example. Whenever the defendant tried to explain his circumstances, the magistrate routinely interrupted, cutting off his attempts. By this technique, the magistrate exerted his authority to validate or invalidate the scope of responses (ibid.:15–16):

M: Um—and what is you—what are your three—your children living on—and your wife?

D: Well I do know they uh receive supplementary benefits sir—I realize entirely that it's up to me to counterbalance that by paying you know I know—.

M: Are you paying anything at all?

D: No. I haven't been able to—at all sir—no I get—.

M: Are you supporting anyone else?

D: Not at all—no—I live on my own sir.

M: And how much do you receive then?

D: Fourteen pounds thirty-five.

M: Well, can't you spare something of that—for your children?

D: Yes—I would do—.

M: When did you last pay—anything?

Questions in courts are understood within their institutional context, one that assigns rights of control to certain participants and denies those rights to others. Harris noted that magistrates and defendants come to these interactions with different views of reality. Magistrates assume defendants to be unwilling to pay, whereas defendants must try to convince the court that they are unable to pay. Due to the institutional framework, it is the magistrates' perspective that dominates and thereby leads to the underlying accusatory semantics of many questions. For example (ibid.:20):

M: Are you supporting anyone else? (= You don't support your ex-wife but you choose to support someone else when your wife should have priority.)

M: How many jobs have you applied for in the last two weeks, Mr. B.? (= You've not been trying to get a job because you don't want to work.)

M: How much did the carpet cost? (= You spend money on carpets which should be used to pay your fine.)

Form, content, and context are clearly relevant to the ways that addressees respond. The institutional context has a determining effect on interpretations of linguistic structure. Defendants comply with the directive nature of questions not only because of their conducive form, but also because of power relationships emanating from the structural authority of court officials.

When witnesses or others testifying in court attempt to elaborate on their responses or evaluate the questions posed to them, they are typically interrupted or reprimanded by either an attorney or a judge. For example, data from US criminal court proceedings included the following (Atkinson 1992:205–206):

Counsel: …didn't you tell the police that the defendant had been drinking?

Witness: No, I told them there was a cooler in the car and I never opened it.

Counsel: The answer, ah, may the balance be stricken your honor and the answer is no?

Judge: The answer is "No."

Although judges and magistrates exert institutional power and privilege, the social and economic class of a defendant or witness may significantly influence the way the judge treats her or him. The following two excerpts are taken from transcripts of an Austrian magistrate's court. Both defendants were accused of causing traffic accidents that led to serious injuries. Both defendants were found guilty. But notice the contrasts in the interactions between the defendant and the magistrate (Wodak-Engel 1984:98–100). Note that all participants are male:

(Middle-Class Speaker)

J: = Judge

D: = Defendant

J: G. F.?

D: Yes. Good morning.

J: You are a Ph.D.?

D: Yes.

J: In what field?

D: Philosophy.

J: Philosophy? How does that relate to your athletic activities?

D: I have been a member of the Austrian Alpine Club for several years. I have led expeditions and have undertaken difficult climbs.

J: You are single? You live at…

D: Yes.

J: Average income?

D: 6000 shillings.

J: 6000 shillings? No capital? No maintenance obligations?

D: No.

J: No previous convictions. Do you plead guilty or not guilty?

D: Yes, I plead guilty to not having seen the woman, even though I was paying full attention....

J: Now, what happened?

D: [Defendant describes in long detail how the accident occurred, how he was changing lanes, looking in his rearview mirror to make sure no one was in the lane beside him, then looked ahead and saw a woman in front of his car. He gives details about his thought processes and emotions. His turn occupies several minutes.]

J: [Judge accepts the defendant's version and his guilty plea and passes sentence.]

D: I wish to thank you for the conduct of the trial, and especially, for the mild sentence; and I accept the sentence.

J: I hope it will go all right in June. Then you will become a professor? Will you earn more then?

D: Professorship. Yes, one can live on that quite well.

J: Okay. Thank you.

(Working-Class Speaker)

D: Religion?

D: Catholic.

J: Married?

J: Yes.

J: Education?

D: Primary and secondary school.

J: Yes, and what else?

D: Yes, I was near the crossing, suddenly the car came from the right. I saw it, but I couldn't manage to brake, so....

J: You couldn't brake? Couldn't you try to swerve somehow?

D: No.

J: Do you know what that is?

D: No.

J: You can't answer that question either?

D: Yes, to steer somewhere else did you mean? Or...?

J: Yes. Every vehicle has a steering wheel. If one turns it around, the direction changes, doesn't it? If it's not broken. If one turns this thing, it is called "swerving," to put it briefly. Understood? Yes?

There are several significant features of contrast between these two interactions. While the judge takes an interest in the personal and professional life of the middle-class defendant, he asks the working-class defendant a series of short, terse questions, expecting only one-word answers. In addition, the judge allows the middle-class defendant to elaborate on the details of the accident, including his thought processes and feelings. But he interrupts the narrative of the working-class defendant, refusing to allow him to tell his own story. Indeed, the judge's interruption consists of a turn filled with sarcasm and disdain, giving the defendant a vocabulary lesson. In contrast, the judge's tone with the middle-class defendant is friendly and respectful, even ending the interaction with a "Thank you."

The messages transmitted in these two interactions distinguish the overt assertion of institutional power when dealing with working-class speakers, reminding them of their powerlessness not only in this context, but also in society at large, while middle-class speakers are treated as societal equals.

Styles of speech used by litigants can affect the way that judges evaluate their cases. For example, in studies of cases brought to small claims courts in several cities in the United States, John Conley and William O'Barr identified two different styles of presentation that they call "rule-oriented" and "relational-oriented" (2005:67–74). Rule-oriented accounts base their claims on "violations of specific rules, duties, and obligations, such as those inscribed in contracts" (ibid.:67). In such accounts, litigants state the relevant facts in chronological order and explicate specific cause-and-effect sequences. In contrast, relational-oriented accounts "base their entitlement to relief on general rules of social conduct" (ibid.:68). These narratives stress people's social obligations and rights to fair treatment. Speakers elaborate on issues of their lives and their circumstances.

In legal settings in the United States, rule-oriented accounts are taken more seriously and are thought to be more relevant to legal practice than are relational accounts. Therefore, people who have been exposed to and learned the privileged style are more likely to be taken seriously themselves. Lawyers, of course, are well schooled in the rule-oriented style. Other people with advanced education who appear in courts as witnesses or litigants on their own behalf are also able to communicate in this style.

Despite the strong pressures exerted by officials and lawyers in courts, ordinary people can assert their rights to be heard if they feel that they have legitimate knowledge and expertise. Data from a study of interactions between lawyers and "expert witnesses" in a land claims case involving Native Americans in the Southwest showed that some Native American witnesses did not accommodate the demands of lawyers but responded in ways consistent with their own cultural norms (Bunte and Franklin 1992). For example, in the encounter transcribed below, between a Paiute elder and an Anglo lawyer, the Paiute (speaking through a translator) gave testimony appropriate to his knowledge and position in the Paiute community. That is, among the Paiute, elders are respected for their experience and wisdom. According to Bunte and Franklin, "the elders have the dominant role. They decide the topic, as well as when and how long they will talk. The listeners/learners listen" (ibid.:21). Such a style of imparting knowledge differs considerably from courtroom encounters where the witness "is treated as a passive source of knowledge, rather than as a partner in the local management of talk. The goal is to get at the 'facts'—objectified, decontextualized knowledge" (ibid.:20). In the question-and-answer sequences, the Paiute elder, Joe Norman, voiced his annoyance at the attorney, whose demeanor contradicted Paiute norms of respectful listenership by directing, interrupting, and repeating questions (ibid.:22):

ATTORNEY:	In the year that Na'aintsitsi was born, did you see him [a Navajo] grazing his sheep?
NORMAN:	I just see him.
ATTORNEY:	Did you see him grazing his sheep?
NORMAN:	Yes, I used to see him. What's wrong with that [answer]?
ATTORNEY:	Do you know the year you were born?
NORMAN:	What's he going to do with that? (said to interpreter)
ATTORNEY:	I just want to know what year you were born.
NORMAN:	I'm 72 years old.

In this interaction, the witness refuses to acquiesce completely to the demands of the attorney. He adheres to Paiute, rather than Anglo, norms of behavior. Although the attorney is no doubt annoyed with Norman's responses, he must try to modify his own questioning because Norman is an "expert witness" whose knowledge is relevant and necessary to the case being heard. Had Norman's expertise not been so highly valued, or had he been a defendant rather than a witness, the attorney's style would probably not have been at all accommodating.

THE MEDIA

The importance of the media in contemporary society is undeniable. Print and electronic sources provide us with nearly continual news, information, and entertainment. Their ubiquity and our reliance on them help produce and disseminate particular constructions of reality. Because the mass media often promulgate views consistent with prevailing beliefs, they participate in the maintenance of the social system.

All media have the potential for expanding people's awareness of how local, national, and international events affect individual lives, but in actual practice they usually fall short of fulfilling this function. News articles and programs are selective in scope and perspective. They choose some topics as "newsworthy" and highlight certain aspects of events; other topics and viewpoints are ignored. This process derives from and expresses bias, providing receivers with only partial understandings. Without our conscious awareness, the media influence our opinions and our social knowledge. Of course, no account, whether on a mass scale or in personal narrative, is all-inclusive; unlike face-to-face conversations, however, the media's portrayal of events cannot be immediately questioned, challenged, or countered by recipients. People in our society tend to accept what they read, see, or hear through the media. The formats themselves contribute to this tendency because reports come to us in a highly technologic fashion from supposedly dispassionate and objective sources.

The media (and other instruments of public knowledge) operate on the basis of shared cultural myths, central among them the myth of neutrality (Schiller 1973:11). (Mis)perceptions of the neutrality of news reports are furthered by the manner in which they are offered. Two seemingly contradictory but, in fact, complementary approaches predominate. Television newscasts are often given by people who are familiar to, and therefore trusted by, their audiences. This familiarity is obviously false, but it nonetheless leads audiences to accept speakers' accounts. In contrast, print media create an aura of impartiality by the anonymity of most sources and writers.

In all media, specific linguistic devices are used to create and sustain points of view. The fact that certain forms of language are employed repeatedly indicates that the process is systematic, although not necessarily consciously manipulated. Linguistic analyses uncover recurring features of vocabulary and grammar. Of obvious importance are the words chosen to name (nouns) and describe (adjectives) participants and to depict actions (verbs and adverbs). Equally critical, but much less obvious, are syntactic constructions that relate participants to events. For example, sentence constructions can be changed to focus on different words. English sentences typically express agents of actions as grammatical subjects, but they can be made passive by transposing words and placing recipients of actions in subject positions. Agents then are expressed instrumentally:

> The child broke the toy.
>
> The toy was broken by the child.

This technique places focus on recipients rather than agents. A further grammatical step optionally omits agents entirely, resulting in even stronger emphasis on recipients:

> The toy was broken.
>
> The toy was broken when the child stepped on it.

Comparison of two newspaper articles describing the same event can reveal differences in focus and contrasting emphases in discussion of similar facts. For example, the following lead paragraphs report the acquittal of four New York City police officers accused of killing Amadou Diallo (an immigrant from Guinea, West Africa) in the Bronx in 1999. The trial was moved at the defense request to the upstate New York City of Albany. It ended with a verdict of not guilty in 2000. The excerpts are taken from the *New York Times* and the *Associated Press* article that ran in many newspapers across the country.

The New York Times, February 26, 2000:

> Four New York City police officers were acquitted today of all charges in the death of Amadou Diallo, the immigrant from Guinea who was fired on 41 times as he stood, unarmed, in the vestibule of his apartment building in the Bronx.
>
>   The verdict came in a tense and racially charged case that led to anti-police demonstrations, arrests, and a reorganization of the department's Street Crime Unit, to which the officers belonged.

Tom Hays, Associated Press, February 26, 2000:

> Four white New York City police officers were acquitted of all charges yesterday in the killing of unarmed African immigrant Amadou Diallo, whose death in a barrage of 41 bullets touched off weeks of civil disobedience over police treatment of minorities.

Several points of significant contrast emerge by comparing these two excerpts. The accounts given in the Associated Press report repeatedly remark on racial issues. In the very first sentence, the article notes the race of the officers and by implication referred to the race of the victim, describing him as "African." While not all Africans are black, in the American mind, the word "African" has come to transmit that meaning. The Associated Press article goes on to mention the racial composition in the second paragraph. In contrast, the first paragraph of the *New York Times* article omits reference to race. In fact, the *Times* does not mention the race of the officers or the racial composition of the jury until later in the article. And although the *Times* identifies the victim's homeland as "Guinea," a country in West Africa, the implications of his race are less direct. Their second paragraph does refer to a "racially charged case," but again the implications are not clearly spelled out.

Word choice in the two articles similarly distinguishes the emotional tone of the *Associated Press* from the *Times* reporting. The *Associated Press* uses the word "killing" to label the action of the police while the *Times* refers to Diallo's "death," a less impassioned term. The *Associated Press* also describes the police action as consisting of a "barrage of 41 bullets" while the *Times* says that Diallo was "fired on 41 times," similarly using a less vivid word. Finally, the papers differ in how quickly they mention that Mr. Diallo was "unarmed." In the *Associated Press* article, that attributive is the first descriptor of the victim, while in the *Times,* it comes toward the end of the sentence.

Taken together, the Associated Press reporting stresses issues of race and violence while the *Times*'s accounts are more dispassionate. In reporting the same events, discourse strategies employed create contrasting images and elicit different emotional responses.

Television news employs linguistic devices similar to those in print media. Visual images, though, supplement and reinforce messages. Citing an example from Peter Dahlgren (1987:38), "If birds-eye shots of 'demonstrators' in the street are followed by medium close-ups of 'officials' in their offices, presented with names and titles, the relative legitimacy of the two groups has been signified by the codes at work in the television news discourse." Dahlgren also stated, "We know the codes so well—they are so familiar—that we rarely notice them. Yet they prestructure our signification process as viewers." These communicative codes rely on and transmit cultural meanings that are taken for granted, but are all the more influential in both their systematic and localized effects.

Mainstream media are produced and constrained by dominant ideologies that support particular social and political agendas. They employ authoritative voices to give credibility to these ideologies framed around unstated assumptions. While discourse practices in the media include the use of quoted or reported speech, not all relevant voices are heard. Typically, the media quote "official" sources or report the words of prominent people. This practice privileges authoritative points of view and marginalizes opposition. There is an important contrast between quoting or reporting another's words. When a person is quoted directly, a boundary is maintained between the original speaker and the person quoting, but reported speech blurs the boundaries and allows the reporter to recast the original speech, either maintaining or distorting core meanings (Fairclough 1995:81). Although media consumers expect neutrality from reporters, events can be described to convey and elicit positive or negative attitudes. Even in reported speech, the way that words are framed produces varied inferences about the truthfulness of the person whose speech is reported. For instance, the neutral word *said* can be replaced by a word such as *claimed,* which implies a lack of trust in the speaker. Hedges can be used to mitigate or question truthfulness as well.

Media texts rely on and take from discourse practices derived from other genres that are familiar to consumers. For example, a British newspaper, the *Daily Telegraph,* printed the following report in 1993, two years after the end of the first Persian Gulf War (ibid.:95):

Saddam's UN Envoy Promises Good Behavior After Raid by US, British and French Aircraft
Gulf Allies Attack Iraqi Missiles
More than 100 aircraft blasted Iraqi missile sites last night after the Allies' patience with Saddam Hussein's defiance finally snapped.

This excerpt borrows from the discourse of parental authority in which disobedient children are properly chastised. It also personalizes an international crisis while demeaning and trivializing one of the antagonists.

The treatment of race and racial issues in both print and broadcast media transmits complex and subtle messages about social groups and social ideologies. In extensive research on discourse and racism in the Western European and US press, Teun van Dijk (1988, 1989, 1999) analyzes the strategies employed that marginalize members of ethnic and racial minorities. In studies of newspaper headlines and articles about ethnic and racial issues in the Netherlands, Great Britain, Germany, and the United States, van Dijk found that several themes dominate press coverage. For instance, stories about members of outgroups (immigrants and racial minorities) emphasize the "problems" that they cause, especially crime, violence, and drug use. They also cause problems by creating civil unrest, such as rioting or demonstrating. The fact that demonstrations or riots are responses to injustices of police or governmental action that discriminates against them is largely either ignored or downplayed. The structural racism of the dominant society remains invisible.

In addition, in press reports about ethnic and racial minorities, the voices of government officials, police representatives, and other leaders or experts from the dominant community are featured, while the voices of outgroup members are less frequently heard. And when they are included, their points of view tend to be overshadowed by the commentary of officials and experts.

When their lives are described, members of minority groups are portrayed as deviating from the norms of the dominant society. They have unusual customs, habits, and beliefs. They are criticized for speaking a nonstandard variety of language or, if they are immigrants, for not learning the language of their new country. Taken together, articles about minorities show them as deviant and disruptive.

Press reports that discuss government action dealing with minority groups emphasize the special legislation or programs directed at helping minority people improve their lives. For example, accounts of affirmative action programs in the United States in education, hiring, and housing center on special privileges available. These articles often quote people who suggest that the interests of minorities negatively affect the interests of the majority by granting them concessions not given to others.

According to van Dijk, the particular thematic content of media coverage influences the production and transmission of ideologies of race and ethnicity held by the public. Van Dijk asks a fundamental question: "How [do] the hostile cognitions and actions that structurally define the racism of the White dominant ingroup become shared so widely and effectively in the first place?" As he points out, most members of the ingroup have little if any direct extended experience with minority members. He suggests, therefore, that much of their knowledge and opinions derive from media sources. Additional sources of information and attitudes come from other types of elite discourse, including textbooks, cinema, public governmental debates, institutional decision making, scholarly articles, and courtroom dialogues (1989:201).

However, at the same time that media and other public discourses express and legitimate negative stereotypes and attitudes about minority groups, they also structure stories to conceal or actually deny the existence of racism (van Dijk 1999:541). For instance, even when news articles discuss instances of discrimination against minorities, they do not analyze underlying institutional and societal racism. When racism is described or attributed to anyone, it is portrayed as an attitude of extreme white supremacists, not as a factor that minority people confront daily. The press defends social norms as moderate and tolerant, and describes government programs as benevolent. The following excerpts from British press reports are illustrative (ibid.:549):

> Contrary to much doctrine, and acknowledging a small malevolent fascist fringe, this is a remarkably tolerant society. But tolerance would be stretched were it to be seen that enforcement of law adopted the principle of reverse discrimination.
>
> If the ordinary British taste for decency and tolerance is to come through, it will need positive and unmistakable action.
>
> Our traditions of fairness and tolerance are being exploited by every terrorist, crook, screwball and scrounger who wants a free ride at our expense.

The media's portrayal of society as tolerant provides the context to criticize people who point out racism and other forms of discrimination against minorities. With this reasoning, it is the antiracist positions that can be described as extreme.

Although the media in Western Europe and North America have diverse political orientations and do not all subscribe to one monolithic viewpoint, the majority of press and broadcast outlets concur with dominant social ideologies. These ideologies then become widely available and widely disseminated, influencing the construction of reality of media consumers.

Analysis of news interviews reveals many of the techniques inherent in media discourse. News interviews are characterized by speaker turns consisting of questions and answers. Typically, the interviewer (IR) asks questions and the interviewee (IE) answers them. Although IRs take a formal position of neutrality, they can frame their questions to incorporate implicit assumptions and attitudes. Indeed, questions, like any other form of speech, encode points of view. The IR's work balances the "journalistic norms of impartiality and adversarialness" (Heritage 2003:59).

Several distinctive discourse resources can be manipulated in various ways in order to navigate between these norms. First, IRs can ask questions that are open, allowing IEs to elaborate and control topic direction. In contrast, questions can be framed narrowly, giving the IE limited options. These may be yes or no questions or others that demand an answer from among a small set of offered possibilities. Second, questions may be prefaced with introductory statements that lay a background framework favorable to a particular position. If the IR is in general agreement with the IE, these prefaces may be supportive; if she or he disagrees with the IE, background statements may allude to negative aspects of the IE's positions. Modes of IR responses to the IE's answers also indicate point of view. IRs may respond to IEs' answers with agreement markers such as yes or even hmm, which essentially ratify previous speech. Allowing the IE to elaborate can also be interpreted as legitimating IE's contributions. In contrast, the IR may respond by pointing out contradictions in the IE's positions, areas of disagreement with other newsmakers, and opposition from the public. IRs may interrupt or in other ways question the IE's credibility or sincerity. For example, in the following interview that took place in 1993 between a British Broadcasting Corporation (BBC) reporter and Dragoslav Bokan, a Serbian commander suspected of war crimes in Bosnia, the reporter employs a number of discourse practices that question the credibility and indeed competence of the IE (ibid.:65–66):

IR: Mr. Bokan, are you prepared to make yourself available to UN investigators?

IE: hhhh ah, first of all, I…just want to say that it's you know, very strange you know, to hear all those accuses, ah, it's very strange to be in the (passive) role of hearing and ah ah not to have an opportunity you know to say anything…about yourself or your ah goals. In war…and—

IR: I'm not interested in your goals, Mr. Bokan. The question was, Are you prepared to make yourself available to UN investigators?

IE: You know uh, you know the answer, you know maybe better than myself. Because of you know from the beginning of war I have just one goal and that's to defend you know my people from the—

IR: Is that a yes or no?

IE: Is it a court or an interview?

IR: So you are prepared to make yourself available to UN investigators or not?

IE: Of course.

In this interview, the reporter challenges the credibility of the IE by interrupting and repeating his central question. His turn "Is that a yes or no?" challenges the IE's responses, implicitly accusing him of evading the question. We see here that the IR takes a strong position that is antagonistic to the IE, but he does this without explicitly abandoning his stance of neutrality. However, IEs have options in how they respond as well. They may acquiesce or they may assert their own interpretations. In this excerpt, the IE challenges the appropriateness of the IR's questioning by asking whether "Is it a court or an interview?" effectively pointing out the lack of expected neutrality on the part of the IR.

In the following example, taken from an American Public Broadcasting program, *NewsHour,* in 1992, the IR treats the IE (General John Vessey) in a quite different manner. The general has just returned from a trip to Vietnam as head of a team negotiating an agreement with the Vietnamese government concerning US soldiers missing in action (MIAs) from the Vietnam War (ibid.: 68–69):

IR: With us now for a newsmaker interview is the delegation chairman, former chairman of the Joint Chiefs of Staff retired Army General John Vessey. General, welcome.

IE: Thank you

IR: Sir, how would you describe the significance of this agreement?

In this excerpt, the IR treats the IE cordially, providing his full title and background. His opening question allows the general to control the topic, to elaborate as he chooses, and to frame the discussion in his own terms.

In addition to manipulating modes of questioning, IRs can covertly intrude their own points of view while claiming neutrality by prefacing assertions in the passive voice ("It is said…") or by making statements of general beliefs ("It is thought that…"; It is believed that…"). In addition, IRs can attribute opinions to a third-party ("But isn't this what critics say about…"; "Public opinion polls show that…"). These choices relate to issues of "footing" in media discourse through which IRs "can actively shape the course of the debate without entering it as a participant" (Clayman 1992:177). IRs can thus convey a particular stance while preserving overt neutrality, at the same time avoiding responsibility for their communicative actions.

In contrast to the neutrality expected in journalism, the genre of talk radio is an arena for confrontation. Discourse practices manipulated by hosts demonstrate methods for controlling topics and creating or exacerbating arguments. These practices violate general conversational norms that seek to minimize or mitigate disagreement. The topics of talk radio consist primarily of personal opinions about public issues. Although a caller might not initially frame his or her contribution around an argument, hosts often aggravate conflict by either focusing on points of disagreement or by encouraging callers to take extreme positions.

Talk radio episodes are constructed around a number of distinct phases. In the first phase, an introductory exchange of personal identification and greeting takes place. In the second phase, callers present their initial topic. In doing so, they are "oriented to their role of 'opinion-producers' [while situating] the host in their corresponding role of 'respondent and potential challenger' to caller's opinion" (Hutchby 1996:15). The third phase consists of the host's response to the caller and the caller's subsequent turn. Turn taking in this phase is relatively rapid, with frequent exchanges of opinions. The episode is terminated in the fourth phase by unilateral and often abrupt actions by the host. Rarely are these endings negotiated as they would be in informal conversations and rarely are they punctuated with exchanges of goodbyes, again violating typical conversational discourse practice.

Features of talk radio sequences demonstrate the ways that hosts control the flow of the topic and turn taking. Although the caller performs the initial action by making the call, the host takes up the dominant position by having the caller reveal his or her opinion first. The host then can be in the position of challenger. And, of course, it is up to the host to decide when to end the conversation.

Talk radio hosts vary in the degree to which they express their own opinions. Some do not claim neutrality but instead highlight disagreement with callers. Others use strategies to express opposition to the caller's opinions while at the same time positioning themselves as neutral. For example, they may attribute contrary opinions to third parties or to general community attitudes. Hosts endeavor to put callers on the defensive, again aggravating conflict.

Summary

Status and authority are not impersonal forces of nature. They are created and valued by people. To be valuable, they must be exercised, and to be exercised, they must be expressed. Talk and writing are major means of communicating status and influencing ideas and systems of belief.

Institutional settings provide contexts for repeated exposure to and maintenance of societal inequalities. Authority is manifested not in obvious displays of force, which themselves would be disruptive, but in the much more efficient means of seemingly benign interactions. Through influence over what is said, what is not said, and by whom and to whom it was said, privileged people are able to perpetuate their status. It is certainly true that ordinary people can challenge the talk of authorities, but they are usually so thoroughly socialized about the legitimacy of the social system that they collude with it in maintaining their own subordinate position.

Authorities within the institutions of education, medicine, and law foster compliance through various strategies, such as making supposedly dispassionate assertions, directing topics by interrupting or ignoring unwanted contributions, and generally usurping the rights of others to interact equally. The media also contribute to social meanings by the way they select "newsworthy" events and describe participants. These processes are not tangential to society but form its very essence. All the while, language is used to construct and reconstruct the system.

References

AINSWORTH-VAUGHN, NANCY. 1998. *Claiming Power in Doctor-Patient Talk.* New York: Oxford University Press.

ATKINSON, J. MAXWELL. 1992. Displaying neutrality: Formal aspects of informal court proceedings. In *Talk at Work: Language Use in Institutional and workplace Settings,* ed. P. Drew and J. Heritage. New York: Cambridge University Press, pp. 199–211.

BAKHTIN, MIKHAIL M. 1981. *The Dialogic Imagination, Four Essays.* Austin: University of Texas Press.

BONES, JAH. 1986. Language of the Rastafaris. In *Language & the Black Experience,* ed. D. Sutcliffe and A. Wong. London: Blackwell.

BOURDIEU, PIERRE. 1991. *Language and Symbolic Power.* Cambridge, MA: Harvard University Press.

BUNTE, PAMELA, AND ROBERT FRANKLIN. 1992. You can't get there from here: Southern Paiute testimony as intercultural communication. *Anthropological Linguistics* 34:19–44.

BURHAN, JAZIR. 1989. "National language politics and language instruction." In Politik bahasa nasional. (ed. Amran Halim). Jakarta: Balai Pustaka, pp. 65–83.

CLAYMAN, STEVEN. 1992. Footing in the achievement of neutrality: The case of news-interview discourse. In *Talk at Work: Language Use in Institutional and Workplace Settings,* ed. P. Drew and J. Heritage. New York: Cambridge University Press, pp. 163–198.

CONLEY, JOHN, AND WILLIAM O'BARR. 2005. *Just Words: Law, Language, and Power,* 2nd ed. Chicago, IL: University of Chicago Press.

DAHLGREN, PETER. 1987. Ideology and information in the public sphere. In *The Ideology of the Information Age,* ed. J. Slack and F. Fejes. Norwood, NJ: Ablex, pp. 24–45.

DARNELL, REGNA. 1985. The language of power in Cree interethnic communication. In *Language of Inequality,* ed. N. Wolfson and J. Manes. The Hague: Mouton, pp. 61–72.

DAVIDSON, BRAD. 2001. Questions in cross-linguistic medical encounters: The role the hospital interpreter. *Anthropological Quarterly* 74, no. 4:170–178.

ERICKSON, BONNIE, E. ALLEN LIND, BRUCE JOHNSON, AND WILLIAM O'BARR. 1978. Speech style and impression formation in a court setting: The effects of "powerful" and "powerless" speech. *Journal of Experimental Social Psychology* 14:266–279.

ERRINGTON, JOSEPH. 2000. Indonesian(s') authority. In *Regimes of Language: Ideologies, Polities, and Identities,* ed. P. Kroskrity. Santa Fe, NM: School of American Research Press, pp. 205–228.

FAIRCLOUGH, NORMAN. 1995. *Media Discourse.* London: Edward Arnold.

FAIRCLOUGH, NORMAN. 2001. *Language and Power,* 2nd ed. London: Longman.

FISHER, SUE, AND ALEXANDRA TODD. 1986. Friendly persuasion: Negotiating decisions to use oral contraceptives. In *Discourse and Institutional Authority: Medicine, Education and Law,* ed. S. Fisher and A. Todd. Norwood, NJ: Ablex, pp. 3–25.

GAL, SUSAN. 1989. Language and political economy. *Annual Review of Anthropology* 18:345–367.

GREENBERG, JEFF, S. L. KIRKLAND, AND TOM PYSZCZYNSKI. 1988. Some theoretical notions and preliminary research concerning derogatory ethnic labels. In *Discourse and Discrimination,* ed. G. Smitherman Donaldson and T. van Dijk. Detroit, MI: Wayne State University Press, pp. 74–92.

HABERMAS, JURGEN. 1970. *Toward a Rational Society.* Boston, MA: Beacon Press.

HARRIS, SANDAR. 1984. Questions as a mode of control in magistrates' courts. *International Journal of the Sociology of Language* 49:5–27.

HERITAGE, JOHN. 2003. Designing questions and setting agendas in the news interview. In *Studies in Language and Social Interaction,* ed. P. Glenn, C. LeBaron, and J. Mandelbaum. Mahwah, NJ: Lawrence Erlbaum, pp. 57–96.

HUTCHBY, IAN. 1996. *Confrontation Talk: Arguments, Asymmetries, and Power on Talk Radio.* Mahwah, NJ: Lawrence Erlbaum.

HYMES, DELL. 1996. *Ethnography, Linguistics, Narrative Inequality: Toward an Understanding of Voice.* London: Taylor & Francis.

KEENAN, ELINOR OCHS. 1974. Normmakers and normbreakers: Uses of speech by men and women in a Malagasy community. In *Explorations in the Ethnography of Speaking,* ed. R. Bauman and J. Sherzer. New York: Cambridge University Press, pp. 125–143.

LIND, E. ALLAN, AND WILLIAM O'BARR. 1979. The social significance of speech in the courtroom. In *Language and Social Psychology,* ed. H. Giles and R. St. Clair. London: Blackwell, pp. 66–87.

MEHAN, HUGH. 1986. The role of language and the language of role in institutional decision making. In *Discourse and Institutional Authority: Medicine, Education and Law,* ed. S. Fisher and A. Todd. Norwood, NJ: Ablex, pp. 140–163.

MEHAN, HUGH. 1991. The school's work of sorting students. In *Talk and Social Structure: Studies in Ethno Methodology and Conversation Analysis,* ed. D. Boden and D. Zimmerman. Berkeley: University of California Press, pp. 71–90.

MEHAN, HUGH. 1996. The construction of an LD student: A case study in the politics of representation. In *Natural Histories of Discourse,* ed. M. Silverstein and G. Urban. Chicago, IL: University of Chicago Press, pp. 253–276.

MELLINKOFF, DAVID. 1963. *The Language of the Law.* Boston, MA: Little, Brown.

MERTZ, ELIZABETH. 1996. Recontextualization as socialization: Text and pragmatics in the law school classroom. In *Natural Histories of Discourse,* ed. M. Silverstein and G. Urban. Chicago, IL: University of Chicago Press, pp. 229–249.

MILROY, LESLY. 2000. Britain and the United States: Two nations divided by the same language (and different language ideologies). *Journal of Linguistic Anthropology* 10, no. 1:56–89.

MISHLER, ELLIOT. 1975. Studies in dialogue and discourse. II. Types of discourse initiated and sustained through questioning. *Journal of Psycholinguistic Research* 4:99–121.

MISHLER, ELLIOT. 1984. *The Discourse of Medicine: Dialectics of Medical Interviews.* Norwood, NJ: Ablex.

MULLER, JOHAN. 1989. "Out of their minds": An analysis of discourse in two South African science classrooms. In *Conversation: An Interdisciplinary Approach,* ed. D. Roger and P. Bull. London: Multilingual Matters, pp. 313–337.

PARMENTIER, RICHARD. 1993. The political function of reported speech: Of Belauan example. In *Reflexive Language: Reported Speech and Metapragmatics,* ed. J. A. Lucy. New York: Cambridge University Press, pp. 261–286.

PHILIPS, SUSAN. 1978. Participant structures and communicative competence: Warm Springs children in community and classroom. In *A Pluralistic Nation,* ed. M. Lourie and N. Conklin. Rowley, MA: Newbury, pp. 390–407.

POUSSAINT, ALVIN. 1967. A Negro psychiatrist explains the Negro psyche. *The New York Times Magazine,* August 20.

SCHIEFFELIN, BAMBI. 2000. Introducing Kaulali literacy: Of chronology of influences. In *Regimes of Language: Ideologies, Polities, and Identities.* Santa Fe, NM: School of American Research Press, pp. 293–328.

SCHILLER, HERBERT. 1973. *The Mind Managers.* Boston, MA: Beacon Press.

SILVERSTEIN, MICHAEL. 2000. Whorfianism and the linguistic imagination of nationality. In *Regimes of Language: Ideologies, Polities, and Identities,* ed. P. Kroskrity. Santa Fe, NM: School of American Research Press, pp. 85–138.

SWANN, JOAN. 1998. Talk control: An illustration from the classroom of problems in analyzing male dominance of conversation. In *Language and Gender,* ed. J. Coates. Malden, MA: Blackwell, pp. 185–196.

TEN HAVE, PAUL. 1991. Talk and institution: A reconsideration of the "asymmetry" of doctor–patient interaction. In *Talk and Social Structure: Studies in Ethno Methodology and Conversation Analysis,* ed. D. Boden and D. Zimmerman. Berkeley: University of California Press, pp. 138–163.

TRUDGILL, PETER. 1972. Sex, covert prestige and linguistic change in the urban British English of Norwich. *Language in Society* 1:179–195.

VAN DIJK, TEUN. 1988. How "they" hit the headlines. In *Discourse and Discrimination,* ed. G. Smitherman- Donaldson and T. van Dijk. Detroit, MI: Wayne State University Press, pp. 221–262.

VAN DIJK, TEUN. 1989. Mediating racism: The role of the media in the reproduction of racism. In *Language, Power and Ideology: Studies in Political Discourse,* ed. R. Wodak. London: John Benjamins, pp. 199–226.

VAN DIJK, TEUN. 1999. Discourse and the denial of racism. In *The Discourse Reader,* ed. A. Jaworski and N. Coupland. London: Routledge, pp. 541–558.

VOLOSINOV, V. N. 1973 (1929). *Marxism and the Philosophy of Language.* Cambridge, MA: Harvard University Press.

WAITZKIN, HOWARD. 1983. *The Second Sickness: Contradictions of Capitalist Health Care.* New York: Free Press.

WETZEL, PATRICIA. 1988. Are "powerless" communication strategies the Japanese norm? *Language in Society* 17:555–564.

WODAK-ENGEL, RUTH. 1984. Determination of guilt: Discourse in the courtroom. In *Language and Power,* ed. C. Kramarae, M. Schulz, and W. O'Barr. Beverly Hills, CA: Sage, pp. 81–100.

WOLF, ERIC. 1982. *Europe and the People Without History.* Berkeley: University of California Press.

WONG, ANSEL. 1986. Creole as a language of power and solidarity. In *Language & the Black Experience,* ed. D. Sutcliffe and A. Wong. London: Blackwell, pp. 109–122.

WOOLARD, KATHRYN. 1985. Language variation and cultural hegemony: Toward an integration of social linguistic and social theory. *American Ethnologist* 12, no. 4:738–748.

YOUNG, KATHERINE. 1999. Narrative embodiments: Enclaves of the self in the realm of medicine. In *The Discourse Reader,* ed. A. Jaworski and N. Coupland. London: Routledge, pp. 428–441.

GLOSSARY

accusative case. Grammatical case indicating the direct object of a transitive verb; for example, Amy wrote *a letter.*

action/process verb. A verb denoting an action performed by an agent that also entails a process affecting a patient; for example, Amy *wrote* a letter.

action verb. A verb denoting an action performed by an agent; for example, The dog *ran.*

adjacency pair. A set of two linked turns in conversation. The first, said by one interlocutor, automatically triggers the second, said by another interlocutor; for example, greeting/greeting; offer/acceptance or refusal.

affix. A bound morpheme that attaches to a root, stem, or free morpheme; for example, English plural noun markers: root*s*; negative markers on adjectives: *im*possible.

affricate. A consonant beginning with complete blockage of air, followed by release of air as the sound continues; for example, in English, /c/, /j/, /s/, /z/.

agency. Ability of referent to initiate, control, direct, or affect actions or events.

agglutinating language. A language characterized by complex word formation in which many morphemes can combine within a word. Examples are Turkish and Tamil.

allomorph. A variant of a morpheme. Allomorphs of the same morpheme have identical meanings but differ in phonological form. Allomorphs occur in predictable environments, selected by allomorphic rules, for example, plural noun markers in English: -*z* follows sibilants (/kl sz/ classes); -*s* follows voiceless consonants (/ruwts/ roots); -*z* follows voiced consonants (/dOgz/ dogs) and vowels (/biyz/ bees).

allophone. A variant of a phoneme. Allophones of the same phoneme have different sounds. They occur in predictable environments, selected by allophonic rules. In English, voiceless liquids follow voiceless stops, and voiced liquids follow voiced stops, for example, truy/druy (true/drew); plat/blat (plot/blot).

American Sign Language. *See* ASL.

anglophone. A monolingual speaker of English or a bilingual with English dominance.

arching. Conversational strategy in which a person who is questioned responds by asking the first speaker another question rather than answering the initial question.

articulatory phonetics. The formation, or articulation, of sounds by speakers, including places of articulation of sounds in the vocal apparatus and manners of modifying or affecting the airstream as it passes through the vocal system.

ASL. American Sign Language, a system of communication using hand configurations and their placement and movement in order to convey meaning. ASL is employed primarily by deaf people in the United States.

aspect. A grammatical category of verbs that distinguishes the ways that an action or event occurs in time, for example, punctual, repetitive, continuous.

aspirated sound. A sound produced with a strong release or puff of air.

backchannel cue. A verbal or nonverbal signal given by interlocutors to register their continued attention to each other's talk. Verbalized signals include such utterances as "yeah," "right," and "hmmm"; nonverbal signals include head-nods, smiles, and eye contact.

bilingualism. Knowledge and use of two languages. The term applies both to individual speakers who know two languages and to communities in which two languages are employed by many, most, or all members.

case. A grammatical category of nouns and pronouns indicating their grammatical relations with other nouns or verbs within a clause. Cases may express such relations as subject (nominative), direct object (accusative), indirect object (dative), possessor (genitive), and instrument (instrumental).

caste. A system of social stratification that assigns people to a grouping (caste) by birth. Castes are hierarchically ordered. Members of a given caste are usually not able to alter their status and generally marry within their group.

chaining. A conversational strategy in which a speaker first asks the interlocutor a question, is given an answer, and then proceeds to ask another question.

code mixing. Incorporation of linguistic material from a second language into a base or matrix language. Morphological markers and/or grammatical rules of the matrix language are applied to the incorporated material.

code switching. A process employing linguistic material from two (or more) languages within a conversational segment. Switched material retains its own phonological and grammatical patterns and constraints.

cognitive control functions. *See* executive functions.

communicative competence. Knowledge of rules of language and language use. Communicative competence entails the ability to speak a particular language and knowledge of cultural and social norms of appropriate language use in given interactional contexts.

componential analysis. A method of analyzing words within a semantic domain in order to isolate underlying semantic features or components. This method has been applied to domains such as kinship—for example, analyzing words for relatives in terms of components such as sex of relative, generation, and lineal or collateral descent.

covert prestige. Implicit, but not overtly stated, prestige accruing to a particular speech style. Covert prestige may be demonstrated, for example, by some men's claims to employ more nonstandard speech than they actually do. Thus, standard speech has overtly recognized prestige, but for these speakers, nonstandard speech has covert prestige.

creole. A language historically derived from two or more languages in a context of cultural and linguistic contact. Creoles develop when speakers need a code to enable them to communicate with each other.

crossover pattern. A statistical pattern in which lower-middle-class speakers employ standard or prestige forms at higher rates than do upper-middle-class speakers.

cultural model. An implicit, often nonconscious, construction of reality that is created, shared, and transmitted by members of a group.

dative case. A grammatical case expressing the indirect object of a verb; for example, They gave the book to *the student.*

deep structure. The underlying order of words as they are generated by basic phrase structure rules.

denominal verb. A verb that is derived from a noun; for example, They *summered* in Canada.

diglossia. A pattern of language use in a bilingual community in which two languages (or two dialects of the same language) are systematically employed in different social contexts.

dipthong. A vowel whose articulation begins with the tongue in one place in the mouth and then shifts or glides during its production; for example, b*iy*t ("beet"), b*ow*t ("boat").

directive. An utterance used to direct an addressee to perform some action; for example, commands.

elaborated code. A style of speaking that expresses "universalistic" meanings by use of nouns, adjectives, and verbs with explicit meanings.

ellipsis. A process of linguistic cohesion that reduces output by omitting material that the speaker assumes the hearer can understand from the linguistic or interactional context.

embedding. A complex sentence construction in which one sentence is incorporated (embedded) inside another or matrix sentence; for example, The movie that I saw yesterday was quite tedious (The movie was quite tedious + I saw a movie yesterday).

emblem. An act of nonverbal communication that conveys a particular standardized meaning in a given culture; for example, a head-nod to mean assent or agreement.

endangered language. Language of a bilingual (or multilingual) community that is no longer spoken by as many people and/or in as many situations as it once was. The language is in danger of losing speakers and may eventually die out.

ethnography of communication. The study of communication in its widest cultural and social context, including rules of language, norms of appropriate language use in particular settings, and evaluations given by members of a culture to various speech styles.

ethnolinguistics. The study of interrelationships between language and other aspects of culture, including lexical specialization; the extent to which words in a language influence speakers' perceptions of their world; and the ways that words encode and transmit cultural, emotional, and symbolic meanings and values.

ethnoscience. A classification system in a given domain that organizes people's knowledge of aspects of their universe, for example, botanical or zoological terminologies. Ethnoscientific systems are based on taxonomic hierarchies of similarity and contrast.

ethnosemantics. Indigenous systems of meanings of a culture and its members as expressed in semantic features encoded in their language.

executive functions. Cognitive mechanisms involved in planning, attentional control, and the inhibition of habitual responses. Also known as *cognitive control functions.*

face. An individual's self-esteem or the public image that the person claims for her- or himself and wants respected by interlocutors.

face-threatening act (FTA). A linguistic (or nonlinguistic) act that threatens an interlocutor's maintenance of "face"; for example, receiving a command, making an apology.

focal meaning. The central sense or meaning of a word within the range of its possible uses; the "best" or "most typical" example of a word's possible meanings.

francophone. A monolingual speaker of French or a bilingual with dominance in French.

fricative. A type of consonant whose articulation entails a narrowing of the vocal chamber in order to produce turbulence or friction in the airstream as it passes through.

genitive case. A grammatical case expressing the possessor of a noun; for example, The student*'s* paper was excellent.

glide. A vowel whose articulation begins with the tongue in one place in the mouth and then shifts or glides to another during its production. *See* dipthong.

Gullah. A creole language derived from English and several African languages. Gullah is spoken by people residing along the coast of South Carolina and Georgia and on the Sea Islands off the coast.

habitual aspect. A verbal category referring to an event that occurs and is expected to recur.

hedge. An utterance that overtly or covertly indicates the speaker's uncertainty or desire to avoid a direct commitment to a statement; for example, "sort of," "perhaps," "I'm not sure but... ."

high language. A language or dialect used in a diglossic situation that carries prestige. It is generally employed in formal speech situations, such as those occurring at schools, government agencies, and religious institutions. *See* diglossia.

holophrastic utterance. A single-word utterance used by young children to convey broad semantic and contextual meanings, equivalent to a phrase or sentence in adult speech.

honorific. A linguistic form denoting the speaker's respect for the addressee or referent.

hypercorrection. Extension of linguistic rules in an overly generalized or regularized fashion to the point where an utterance is incorrect; for example, "They think I really likes going to school."

illocutionary act. A speech act that expresses the speaker's goal, purpose, or attitude in saying something; for example, asking a question, giving a warning.

imperative. A verbal construction used by the speaker in order to request an addressee to perform an action; for example, a command.

infix. An affix inserted into a root or stem.

inflecting language. A language that employs morphological markers on nouns in order to express case relations. Examples are Latin and Russian.

instrumental case. A grammatical case indicating an instrument used in the performance of an action; for example, Ruth cut the cake *with a knife.*

International Phonetic Alphabet. A standardized system of phonetic notation applicable to represent sounds in all languages.

intonation. A component of linguistic production entailing a constellation of prosodic features, such as velocity, volume, rhythm, and pitch contours.

isolating language. A language characterized by rules of word formation allowing relatively few morphemes per word. Examples are Chinese and English.

kinesics. The study of nonverbal gestures, facial expressions, eye contact, and body posture.

kinesogram. A device in the notation of nonverbal acts detailing and segmenting the internal structure of each type of act.

language death. The end result of a process in which a language is no longer spoken; the language dies as an active means of communication. Also known as *language obsolescence.*

language obsolescence. *See* language death.

length. A suprasegmental or prosodic feature indicating the temporal length of a sound's production.

lexicon. Vocabulary of a language.

lingua franca. A language used by people in a multilingual setting as a means of enabling native speakers of disparate languages to communicate with each other; for example, Swahili in Africa, English throughout the world.

liquid. A type of consonant whose articulation involves relatively little constriction of the vocal chamber and relatively little disturbance of the airstream; for example, *l, r.*

loanword. A word borrowed by one language from another.

locative. A grammatical case indicating the place or location of a noun or the direction of movement; for example, Put the book *on the table*!

locutionary act. A speech act of "saying something" containing the speaker's verbalized meaning.

low language. A language or dialect used in a diglossic situation that carries relatively low social prestige. Low languages are typically used in informal or familiar social contexts, as with friends or family. *See* diglossia.

maintenance model. A bilingual education program that fosters both learning a second language and retaining knowledge and use of one's native language.

manner of articulation. Component in the production of sounds referring to the ways that the airstream is affected or modified as it passes through the vocal apparatus.

manual language. A system of communication that employs hand movements to convey meanings. An example is American Sign Language (ASL) used by deaf people in the United States.

matched-guise technique. A research strategy used to uncover people's underlying attitudes toward particular languages by recording and playing samples of speech by the same speaker using two different languages (or dialects) and asking respondents to rate the speaker on various social, psychological, and/or intellectual scales.

metaphor. An implied comparison between one entity or event and another based on their sharing certain referential attributes. Metaphors highlight features of similarity between different entities.

metonymy. Substitution of one entity by another based on their shared occurrence in context.

minimal pair. Two words whose sounds are identical except for one contrasting phoneme; for example, *p*It/ *b*It (pit/bit).

mode. A grammatical category of verbs expressing the likelihood of an event's occurrence or a speaker's attitude toward the event's occurrence.

morpheme. The smallest linguistic unit having sound and meaning. A morpheme can be an independent word ("free morpheme") or it can be part of a word ("bound morpheme").

morphology. The study of the internal structure of words, analyzing the shapes and meanings of morphemes and their co-occurrence and order within words.

multilingualism. Use of three or more languages within a speech community.

national language. A language designated by a federal government as an acceptable language for use in public contexts.

negative politeness. A politeness strategy oriented to the hearer's desire not to be imposed upon, for example, making an implied request such as "I'm looking for a comb."

network. A group of people who interact frequently; they may be related, live in the same neighborhood, work together, or belong to the same clubs or organizations.

nominative case. A grammatical case indicating the subject of a verb; for example, *The dog* ran away.

official language. A language formally designated by a state or federal government as the language to be used in governmental and educational contexts.

perfective aspect. A verbal category indicating that an action or event is completed.

performance constraint. The inability of a language learner to produce sequences that require several transformations even though the learner is able to produce grammatical sequences containing each transformation separately.

perlocutionary act. A speech act that produces sequential effects upon the feelings, thoughts, or actions of hearers; for example, "He brought me to my senses; He annoyed me."

personification. A figurative use of language that attributes animate or human qualities to nonliving entities or events; for example, The window looks out over the mountains.

phoneme. A minimal unit of sound that serves to differentiate the meanings of words.

phonemics. Analysis of how sounds are used to differentiate meanings of words; for example, in English the words pit and bit are differentiated by the occurrence of the phonemes /p/ and /b/, respectively.

phonetics. The study of the articulation of sounds in a language and of their distribution in words.

phonology. The study of the distinctive, contrastive sounds (phonemes) of a language.

phrase structure rules. A set of rules that describes the possible units internal to sentences. The most basic phrase structure rule states that a Sentence is composed of a Noun Phrase and a Verb Phrase.

pidgin. A simplified language derived from two or more languages but having a rudimentary grammatical structure and a limited lexicon. Pidgins are not spoken as native languages but as codes for people who interact in a limited way, as in trade.

pitch. A prosodic feature of voice pitch accompanying a syllable's articulation. Variation in pitch results from changes in relative tension of the vocal cords.

place of articulation. Point or place in the vocal apparatus where a sound is formed; for example, bilabial, alveolar, velar.

positive politeness. A politeness strategy that recognizes the hearer's desire to be respected, such as making a criticism in a hedged manner. An example is "You really should sort of try harder."

prefix. A bound morpheme, or affix, that precedes a root or stem; for example, *un*familiar, *re*state.

presupposition. Implicit understandings that interlocutors have as part of their shared cultural and linguistic knowledge and assumptions.

process verb. A type of verb in which the subject is a semantic patient. The subject does not "do" anything; rather, something happens to it. An example is "The wood dried."

progressive aspect. A verbal category indicating that an action or event occurs within a given time frame; for example, "I was reading all morning."

prosodic feature. A feature of the production of sounds that alters the emphasis, timing, or rhythms of speech; for example, stress, length, pitch.

prototype. An idealized conceptualization of an object, quality, or activity against which real-life objects and activities are measured and assessed.

proxemics. The study of the use of space, touch, and distance as features of nonverbal communication.

restricted code. A style of speaking expressing "particularistic" meanings by use of words that are context-bound rather than an explicit, context-free statement of meanings.

roots/stems. Morphemes that represent basic lexical or referential meanings, referring to or naming objects, events, qualities, and ideas; for example, *cat, sing, good, happy.*

semantic domain. A set of words in a lexicon that share a topical feature of meaning; for example, color words, kinship terms.

semantic feature. A component of meaning internal to a word; for example, the word *cow* contains semantic features of animate, nonhuman, feminine, adult, and count.

semantic role. The role that the referent of a noun has in the event described by a sentence; for example, agent, patient, experiencer.

semantics. The study of meaning in language, including the analysis of meanings of words and sentences.

signing space. The physical space used in articulating hand signs in manual language. In American Sign Language, signing space encompasses the area from the top of the head to the waist and from side to side with arms extended and elbows bent.

sociolinguistics. The study of language use, including variation among members in a speech community motivated by criteria such as gender, class, and ethnicity and including variation motivated by different interactional contexts.

speech accommodation theory. A theory of language use that claims that speakers attempt to use speech styles similar to those of interlocutors who they assess positively.

speech community. A group of people who speak the same language, share norms about appropriate uses of language, and share social attitudes toward language and its use.

standardization. A process of superimposing phonological or grammatical rules derived from a language or variety with high prestige on local varieties of a language.

state. A type of verb that depicts inherent conditions or states of being. Subjects of states are semantic patients; for example, "The wood is dry."

stop. A consonant whose articulation involves complete blockage of the airstream; for example, *p, b.*

stress. A prosodic feature indicating the most prominent syllable in a word. Variation in stress may be produced by changes in loudness, length, or pitch.

suffix. A bound morpheme or affix that follows a root or stem; for example, root*s,* talk*ing.*

surface structure. The surface realization of a sentence as it appears in actual speech.

syntax. The study of the structure of sentences, including construction of phrases, clauses, and the order of words.

synthetic (polysynthetic) language. A type of language characterized by words having complex internal structures, allowing many morphemes to co-occur within a word. Synthetic languages tend to alter the sounds of morphemes when they are combined within words.

tag question. An utterance beginning with a statement and ending with a question about the truth of that statement; for example, "They won the game, didn't they?"

tense. A grammatical category of verbs indicating the time at which an event occurs; for example, past, present, future.

tone. *See* pitch.

transformation. A syntactic rule that acts on underlying components of deep structure and, by stages, results in actual speech.

transitional model. A bilingual education program aimed at students' acquisition of a second language with no effort made to help them retain knowledge of their native language.

tree diagram. A type of notation in syntactic analysis to depict constituents of phrases and their syntactic relations. Also known as *phrase marker.*

voiced sound. A sound whose articulation involves vibration of membranes in the vocal cords while air passes through them; for example, *b, z.*

voiceless sound. A sound whose articulation involves stillness of membranes in the vocal cords while air passes through them; for example, *p, s.*

INDEX

Note: The locators followed by 'f' and 't' refers to figures and tables cited in the text.